D1830523

A HISTORY OF ENGLISH EDUCATION IN INDIA

A HISTORY OF ENGLISH EDUCATION IN INDIA

By

SYED MAHMOOD

GYAN

©Author

All rights reserved. No part of this work may be reproduced, stored, adapted, or transmitted in any form or by any means, electronic, mechanical, photocopying, micro-filming recording or otherwise, or translated in any language, without the prior written permission of the copyright owner and the publisher. The book is sold subject to the condition that it shall not, by way of trade or otherwise, be lent, resold, hired out, or otherwise circulated without the prior publisher's written consent in any form of binding or cover other than that in which it is published.

The views and opinions expressed in this book are author(s) own and the facts reported by them have been verified to the extent possible, and the publishers are not in any way liable for the same.

ISBN : 978-81-212-1784-2(HB)

First Published, 1895

Published, 2018

Published by

Gyan Publishing House
5, Ansari Road
Daryaganj, New Delhi-110002
Phone: 011-47034999, 9811692060
www.gyanbooks.com
E-mail: books@gyanbooks.com

Printed at: G. Print Process, Delhi.

TO

SIR JOHN STRACHEY, G.C.S.I.

The illustrious statesman who, during his long and brilliantly successful career in India as a member of the Supreme Government and as Lieutenant-Governor of the North-West Provinces, appreciated the social and political drawbacks and difficulties which thwarted the progress of English education among Muhammadans, and who, with his timely sympathy and good will, generous support and liberal encouragement, helped them in their endeavours to spread knowledge of the English language, literature and sciences among their countrymen,

THIS WORK IS DEDICATED

.as a token of esteem, admiration and gratitude.

PREFACE.

Towards the end of 1893, I was invited by some of the leading members of the Muhammadan Educational Conference to deliver a Lecture in Hindustani on the rise, development, progress, and present condition of English Education in India with special reference to the Muhammadans. I accordingly delivered a somewhat elaborate Lecture which occupied two entire sittings of the Eighth Session of the Conference on the 28th December 1893, in the Central Hall of the Muhammadan Anglo-Oriental College, Aligarh, where more than 600 of the Members from all parts of India had assembled. Nearly 2,000 copies of that lecture have been distributed among the members and circulated during the last year. I was again requested by them to deliver, in continuation of my lecture, another discourse dealing with the present *rate* of progress of English education among the Muhammadans and their future prospects in this respect. I accordingly delivered my second lecture during the Ninth Session of that Conference, which assembled at Aligarh in December last. These two lectures form the substratum of this work, but their substance has undergone much alteration and amplification, and many important Statistical Tables, and extracts from the original sources and authorities relied on, have been added to render this work a useful book of information and reference for those interested in the cause of English education in India.

This work has no claims to originality, as my object has not been to write a book of my own, in the shape of an essay or dissertation, but to furnish a full history of the early origin, gradual growth, internal development, and present condition of English education among the Natives of India, together with the various phases of policy which it has undergone, and the various measures which have been adopted, from time to time, in this behalf, by the Government. The importance of the subject may be said to be universally recognized, and it frequently forms the theme of essays or articles in the periodical literature of the day. But, I think, it may, without exaggeration, be said, that the means of obtaining accurate information as to the facts and figures connected with the subject are very inaccessible, and so scattered among Parliamentary Blue-books and Official Reports, that no ordinary reader can be expected to afford the time, tion the and expense of collecting such a vast mass of materials to enable him to master the subject and fo. such opinion of his own in regard to a matter of such acknowledged importance to the moral, social, and political progress of India in the future.

In 1838, Sir Charles E. Trevelyan, then a young member of the Bengal Civil Service, published an essay on the Education of the People of India, not long after the controversy, between the supporters of Oriental Learning on the one hand and the advocates of English Education on the other, had been decided in favour ot the latter by Lord Macaulay's celebrated Minute of 2nd February 1835, which was adopted by Lord William Bentinck's Government in its Resolution of the 7th March 1835. The essay is very interesting and instructive, as setting forth the contending arguments of the two parties, and as describing the earliest phases of the history of English education. But the work has long been out of date and out of print. There is also another essay on Education in India, in the form of a letter to the Marquis of Ripon, when Viceroy and Governor-General of India, written by Dr. John Murdoch, LL. D., Indian Agent of The Christian Vernacular Education Society for India, and published at Madras in 1881. More recent is the *Le Bas Prize Essay* for 1890, on the history and prospects of British Education in India, written by Mr. F. W. Thomas, Scholar of Trinity College, Cambridge, printed and published at that place in 1891. I became acquainted with it only when nearly the whole manuscript of this work had gone to the Press. The Essay is very interesting, and an able exposition of views entertained by the essayist. Pamphlets and articles on the subject of English education in India have also been written at different times, dealing with isolated points or Sectarian subjects; but such compositions are only transitory and are not intended to supply the requirements of a permanent source of historical and statistical information upon the important subject of English education in India, taken as a whole and in its various aspects.

The present work has a different object for its aim. It seeks to avoid all controversial discussion or polemical arguments. Its aim is to narrate as fully, clearly, and simply as possible all the various facts, opinions, and measures which any person, interested in the cause of English education in India, would like to know in order to form his own opinion or adopt measures for promoting that education in the future. For this reason no facts or Statistics have been stated in this work without reference to Parliamentary Blue-books or Official Reports, and wherever reference to Government Resolutions, or Minutes recorded by Statesmen, has been found necessary, I have preferred to give ample extracts rather than only the substance and purport of their opinions. The figures and statistics have invariably been taken from University Calendars, or other authoritative official publications, though, for the sake of the reader's convenience and exposition of the subject, the figures thus obtained have been considerably manipulated in presenting Tabular Statements adapted to the purposes of this work.

The subject of primary and secondary English education has been only indirectly touched upon in this work. Such education though important in itself is so completely blended with Vernacular education that any attempt to do justice to it would unduly enlarge the size of this work, and would render it more in the nature of a Departmental publication than a book for the general reader interested in the broad subject of English education, its past, present, and future, with reference to its moral, social, and political bearings upon the welfare of the people of India. High English education is, therefore, the main theme of this work, and it is only as subsidiary thereto that English secondary education and its statistics have also been mentioned where reference to them has been considered necessary.

The subject of English education among the European, Eurasian, and Native Christian population of India rests for its discussion upon considerations so materially different from those affecting the advance of European enlightenment among the Natives of India, whether Hindus or Muhammadans, that it was excluded expressly from the consideration of the Indian Education Commission of 1882, of which I had the honour of being a Member. For similar reasons I have limited the scope of this work to the subject of English education, as affecting the main bulk of the native population which consists of Hindus and Muhammadans, though in the former term, Sikhs, Jains and other similar sects, denominating themselves Hindus, have also been included. The Buddhists, who are almost entirely limited to Burma, and the smaller sections of the population play no important part in high English education, but statistics relating to them are included in the general official returns wherever these have been quoted.

Again, English education, especially of the higher type, has made no perceptible progress among the Native female population of India. In Presidency towns a few Native young ladies have pursued the University course, but their number is so infinitesimally small that it is intangible in any general calculation of the statistics of high English education, whilst this work is not concerned with Vernacular education. Female education therefore has not been included among the subjects of this work.

According to the census of 1891, the Hindu population of India amounted to 207,731,727, and the Muhammadan to 57,321,164. The two Communities thus form the main bulk of the Indian population which, including all sects, has been stated in the *General Report* of the Census (page 171), to amount to 287,223,431 bearing a ratio to the population of the world, as at present computed, of about *one-fifth*, and being the largest appertaining to any single country with the exception of China. The Hindus therefore form the vast majority of the Indian population, but among others, by far the largest minority consists of Muhammadans though their proportion varies in different Provinces. As predecessors of the British in the supremacy of India, as also in point of their numerical strength, as well as social and political conditions, the educational interests of this community, which numbers more than the German-speaking population of Europe, cannot be considered insignificant. To quote the words of Lord Macaulay in his celebrated speech* in the House of Commons: "Her Majesty is the ruler of a larger heathen population than the world ever saw collected under the sceptre of a Christian sovereign since the days of the Emperor Theodosius. What the conduct of rulers in such circumstances ought to be is one of the most important moral questions, one of the most important political questions, that it is possible to conceive. There are subject to the British rule in Asia a hundred millions of people who do not profess the Christian faith. The Muhammadans are a minority: but their importance is much more than proportioned to their number: for they are an united, a zealous, an ambitious, a warlike class."

These words were spoken so long ago as the 9th of March, 1843, since which time the British Christian in India has greatly expanded, Her Majesty has become the ruler of many more scores of millions and

* On the Gates of Somnauth.

fills the unique position of being the Sovereign of a larger Muhammadan population than any other monarch in the world including even the Sultan of Turkey. According to the General Report of the Census of 1891 (at p. 174), "the Musalman population of the world has been roughly estimated at various amounts from 70 to 90 millions, so that whatever the real figure may be between those limits, the Indian Empire contains a large majority of the followers of the Prophet." This circumstance should never be lost sight of in considering any measures affecting the general welfare and prosperity of India, and attention has been invited to it here to explain the reason why a considerable portion of this work has been devoted to giving an accurate delineation of the state of English education among Muhammadans and the great and urgent need which still exists for promoting it by special efforts in that community. Upon the question, whether the present condition of English education among Muhammadans and the rates at which it has recently been progressing are satisfactory, much misapprehension exists, although, since the Education Commission of 1882, the Official Reports of the Educational Department are required to devote a separate section to this subject every year. As an illustration of such misapprehension the following passage may be quoted from Mr. F. W. Thomas' Essay, to which reference has already been made. He says (at page 143) :—

"The education of the Muhammadans can now scarcely be said to need special encouragement. In 1881-82, the scholars of this religion were in number less than a fourth of the Hindus. In 1887-88, they number over a third, and the proportion of Muhammadan scholars is greater than the proportion of Muhammadan population. How far the sentiments of Musalmans towards their rulers have changed, is perhaps uncertain. Sir Syed Ahmad Khan, who was one of the chief promoters of the education movement among his co-religionists, has always been very favourably inclined towards the English and towards English education. His great services have long been recognized by the Government; but the effect on the general body of Muhammadans is undetermined."

Such views are so plausible that they frequently find currency not only among the European officers of Government and other educationists, but also among the Muhammadans themselves, leading to a feeling of self-sufficiency and satisfaction at the prospects of English education in that community. But such opinions, though they cannot be denounced as misrepresentations, are so vague and general that they become delusive for want of precision. The incessant efforts of Sir Syed Ahmad Khan and his fellow-workers for spreading English education among Muhammadans, during more than a quarter of a century, have no doubt had beneficial effects on the Muhammadan population of that part of Upper India of which Aligarh, where the Muhammadan Anglo-Oriental College is situate, may be said to be the geographical centre, namely, the North-Western Provinces, Rohilkhand, Oudh, Behar, Punjab, and such portions of the Rajputana territories as are easily accessible by railways. But though the general effects of the educational movement, as represented by the Muhammadan Anglo-Oriental College and the Muhammadan Educational Conference, may have been felt far and wide, the Provinces included in the Presidencies of Madras and Bombay, as well as Bengal, Assam, and Burma, are so remote from the centre of the movement that its effects cannot fail to be very faint.

Again, in considering educational questions with reference to the Muhammadan population, it is supremely important to bear in mind the distinction between the various classes and grades of education included within the scope of the Department of Public Instruction. It has never been the crying complaint of the Muhammadans that they have been backward either in vernacular or primary education or even in the higher kind of education of the Oriental type. A knowledge of the Muhammadan Vernaculars has always been prevalent among that community, and the *Maktabs* or Primary schools teaching the *Koran* and elements of Persian and Arabic, are scattered all over the country, and the higher grades of Muhammadan learning are still taught and cultivated by eminent *Maulvis*, here and there, who charge no fees and devote their lives to advancing Muhammadan learning from motives of piety and religion. In respect of the elementary stages of English education, also, the Muhammadans have during recent years made a satisfactory advance; but such education is not sufficiently pursued further by them up to the higher grades of English standards, and falls far short of meeting the social, economical, and political needs of their population under the exigencies of the British Rule. For any tangible social economical and political effects on a community, the spread of higher English education is necessary in India, whilst it is obvious that for all the higher walks of life under the British Rule a competent knowledge of the English language is now indispensable.

The general advance of the Muhammadans in India is therefore dependent upon the progress of high English education among them, and in the Chapters of this work, specially devoted to the subject, the question of the spread of English education among them has been extricated from the confusion which arises from taking the statistics of all classes of education *en masse*, and deducing general conclusions from such jumbled statistics. For the purpose of precisely showing the facts, many Tabular Satements have been prepared from official figures, and coloured Diagrams have been inserted to illustrate the great backwardness of the Muhammadans in high English education. It will be seen, for instance, from the abstract Tabular Statement, at page 194 of this work, that during the 36 years of University education, from 1858 to 1893, inclusive, the aggregate number of Hindu and Muhammadan graduates in the various Faculties of the Indian Universities amounted to 15,627, of which only 546 were Muhammadans, yielding a percentage of only 3·5 instead of 23·75, which is the percentage of Muhammadans in the total Hindu and Muhammadan population. Again, from the calculations shown in the Tabular Statement at page 198, it will be observed that in the matter of University Degrees, the Muhammadans are still so backward that even according to the highest *rate* of progress yet achieved by them, more than half a century is still necessary for raising the percentage of Muhammadan graduates up to the level of the percentage of their co-religionists in the total Hindu and Muhammadan population of India.

Again, a general impression prevails even in high quarters, and among educationists in general, that, although in the past the Muhammadans were backward in English education, they have during recent years been making very satisfactory progress, leaving no further room for anxiety, or need of any exceptional effort or special encouragement. To expose the great fallacy of such views, is the main object of the latter part of Chapter XXX (pages 196 to 198), and of the whole of Chapter XXXI, which shows the present *rate* of the progress of English education among Muhammadans in Colleges and Secondary Schools, and their future prospects in this respect (*vide* pp. 201 to 205). From the calculations contained in the Tabular Statements, at pages 198, 203 and 205, it will appear: *first*, that the approximate number of years still required to raise the percentage of Muhammadan graduates in the Indian Universities to the level of the proportion of Muhammadans in the total Hindu and Muhammadan population varies in different Faculties of learning; but taking all the University Faculties together, the Muhammadans are no less than 53 years, or more than half a century, behind their fellow-countrymen; *secondly*, that they are no less than 45 years behind their compatriots in the matter of English education in Arts Colleges; and *thirdly*, that even in English Secondary Schools their backwardness is prominent, and the deficiency cannot be expected to be made up in less than 10 years, even according to the most favourable calculations based upon the highest *rate* of progress yet achieved by Muhammadans during any period. Thus the higher the standard of education the more prominent becomes the backwardness of Muhammadans,—a matter which seriously affects their economical, social, and political welfare and prospects as subjects of the British Empire in India.

Another matter of supreme importance, in connection with the subject of the spread of English education among Muhammadans, deserves to be mentioned here. In estimating the proportionate progress of the Muhammadans in English education, the usual method adopted in Official Reports is to compare the percentage of Muhammadans in the total general population with the percentage of Muhammadan students reading in English Colleges and Schools, and the backwardness of the Muhammadans is estimated according to the deficiency in their percentage among the total number of students in such educational institutions. This method of calculation which has passed into fashion, has also been adopted in this work in Chapter XXXI which deals with the present rate of the progess of English education among Muhammadans, and their future prospects. But, in truth, much fallacy lurks in this method of calculation, when the past political history of the Muhammadans and their present social and economical condition and position in the population of India is duly borne in mind. Mr. J. A. Baines of the Indian Civil Service, in his very interesting, able, and lucid *General Report* on the Census of India in 1891, after noticing (at page 8), "the very high proportion in all parts of the country of the population living by agriculture," goes on to say: "Taking it as a whole, about *two-thirds*, and indirectly perhaps nearly *three-fourths*, of the community are wholly or partially dedicated to Mother Earth, and in this case the uniformity is real, not merely nominal."

This significant fact should never be lost sight of in considering the import of any great political, social, or educational measure adopted for the prosperity of India. India is essentially an agricultural country, and discussions relating to the spread of English education in general, and high English education in particular, do not apply to agriculturists, but to the Urban population to whom English Colleges and Secondary Schools, established in cities and towns, are naturally most accessible. This fact is all the more important in connection with forming an estimate of the progress of English education among Muhammadans, owing to their past history and politico-economical position in the Indian Empire. From a practical point of view also, the significance of the distinction between the percentage of the Muhammadans in the total population of India (including agriculturists), and their percentage in the *Urban* population is prominent, and worthy of serious consideration. Mr. Baines, in his *General Report* on the Census of India in 1891, (at page 175), goes the length of suggesting that "so far as regards the large and heterogeneous class of urban Musalmans found all over the country, it is possible that that growth may have been actually impeded by the difficulty found in getting a living under the new conditions of British rule. For the minimum of literary instruction required now as a passport to even the lower grades of middle-class public employ is decidedly higher than it used to be, whilst the progress of learning amongst this class of Musalmans has not proportionately advanced, and with the comparatively small number of recruits for the army, police, and menial offices, that is now found sufficient, few outlets remain available."

It seems, therefore, clear, both in view of the past history of the Muhammadans and their present social, political, and economical condition, that the proportion of the Muhammadans in the *Urban* population, rather than their percentage in the total population of India, is the best standard for testing their progress in English education. Attention to this important matter has been invited at pages 181 and 206 and 207 of this work, and the calculations have been illustrated by Diagram VI, inserted opposite to page 206; whilst the general backwardness of Muhammadans in the University Examinations, with reference to their percentage in the general total population in 1891, is illustrated by Diagram VII, inserted opposite to page 207. It will, however, not be out of place here to give a succinct view of the condition of English education among Muhammadans in 1891-92, which is the latest period of which statistics are available, and to draw attention to the significant difference between the percentage of the Muhammadans in the general *total* population, and their percentage in the *Urban* population according to the Census of 1891. For this purpose the following Table has been prepared from the Tabular Statements at page 177 and 181, as well as 201 and 203 of this work—the figures in all those Tables having been taken from Official Reports:—

PROVINCE.	PERCENTAGE OF MUHAMMADANS IN—				DEFICIENCY IN THE PERCENTAGE OF MUHAMMADANS IN—			
					ENGLISH ARTS COLLEGES.		ENGLISH SECONDARY SCHOOLS.	
	Total population.	Urban population.	English Arts Colleges.	English Secondary Schools.	According to percent. in total population.	According to percent. in Urban population.	According to percent. in total population.	According to percent. in Urban population.
Madras	6·3	14·2	1·5	5·3	4·8	12·7	1·0	8·9
Bombay...	16·3	17·8	2·6	4·9	13·7	15·2	11·4	12·9
Bengal	32·9	27·5	5·7	13·5	27·2	21·8	19·4	14·0
N.-W. Provinces and Oudh ...	13·5	33·9	19·0	21·9	−5·5	14·9	−8·4	12·0
Punjab	55·8	50·8	18·2	33·1	37·6	32·6	22·7	17·7
Central Provinces	2·4	16·0	5·6	9·3	−3·2	10·4	−6·9	6·7
Burma { Upper	1·4	10·3 (Upper and Lower)	...	3·6	...	...	−2·2	6·7
Burma { Lower	4·5		...	5·3	...	...	−0·8	5·0
Assam	27·1	28·8	...	15·0	...	...	12·1	13·8
Coorg	7·3	23·3	...	1·0	...	...	6·3	22·3
Berar	7·2	20·7	...	8·3	...	...	−1·1	12·4

It will thus appear from the preceding Table that, backward as the condition of the Muhammadans is in English education with reference to their proportion in the general total population of India, their decadence is even much more deplorable when the agricultural population of India (to whom English education does not apply) is excluded, and the percentage of Muhammadans in the *Urban* population is taken into consideration. It is obvious, therefore, that if a forecast of the prospects of the Muhammadans in the matter of English education, especially of the higher type, were to be prepared by calculating the approximate number of years required to raise the percentage of Muhammadan students in English Colleges and schools to the level of the percentage of the Muhammadans in the *Urban* population, the results of the calculation would be even more lamentable than the calculations, in Chapter XXXI, which have been made with reference to the percentage of the Muhammadans in the total population.

Closely connected with the spread of English education in India, and almost its sequence and outcome, are the subjects of the Liberty of the Press, the employment of the Natives in the higher ranks of the Public Service, and the growth of Representative Institutions, such as Municipalities, District and Local Boards, and Legislative Councils. A historical narrative of the facts and statistics connected with these subjects, would no doubt be interesting, and, it would afford a fit opportunity for discussing, with reference to facts and figures, how far the English systems of suffrage by representation, and selection of candidates for Public Service by open competition, are applicable to the social, religious and political conditions of India, where, in addition to the multifarious diversities of race and creed, considerable difficulties are liable to arise in consequence of the vast disparity which exists in the matter of high English education among various sections of the population, especially between the Hindus and the Muhammadans. It is for the statesmen and politicians to consider how far the principles of representative Government are applicable, to a country like India, where diversities of race and religion are complicated with the further difficulties arising from vast disparity not only in point of numbers of the population but also in point of the standards of education achieved by the various nationalities of the people. Even the modern demi-god of democracy, republicanism and representative Government, *Joseph Mazzini*, in his celebrated work, "*On the Duties of Man*" does not lose sight of the conditions requisite for the application of representative principles of Government; and whilst dwelling upon the national demand: "*We seek a common education,*" he does not forget in addressing his readers, in language which he calls "words of conviction, matured by long years of study, of experience, and of sorrow," to caution them in the following terms:—

"Doubtless universal suffrage is an excellent thing. It is the only legal means by which a people may govern itself without risk of continual violent crises. Universal suffrage in a country governed by a common faith is the expression of the national will; but in a country deprived of a common belief, what can it be but the mere expression of the interests of those numerically the stronger, to the oppression of all the rest?"

The comparative spread of higher English education among the two most important sections of the population of India is therefore, even more important than purely educational discussions, and Chapter XXX of this work has therefore been devoted to a general survey of the comparative statistics of high English education among Hindus and Muhammadans from the earliest time of the establishment of the Indian Universities, in 1857, to the end of the year 1893, covering a period of 36 years. Calculations have been made in that Chapter with reference to the Census of 1881, because the statistics of that Census are better adapted for testing results of high English education, (which ordinarily requires a course of study extending over ten or twelve years), than the statistics of the Census of 1891. The proportion between the two populations, however, has undergone no change during the interval, and there can be no fallacy in drawing conclusions for purposes of comparison as to the spread of high English education in the two communities, whichever Census be taken as the basis of calculation. In the next Chapter, XXXI, relating to the present *rate* of the progress of English education among Muhammadans, and its future prospects, the statistics of the Census of 1891, have been taken into account, with reference to the figures contained in the Official Education Reports. Among these, the most important are Sir Alfred Croft's *Review of Education in India in* 1886, and Mr. A. M. Nash's *Second Quinquennial Review* of the Progress of Education in India from 1887 to 1892.

In Chapter XXXII (at pp. 208–13) of this work the latest available statistics of the general spread of English education in India, have been extracted from the *General Report* of the Census of India in 1891 by Mr. J. A. Baines, and the Tabular Statements given there show in detail the statistics of the extent of the English language among various classes of the population. From that Table it will appear that the entire number of literates in India, at the time of the Census, was 120,71,249, of whom only 5,37,811 were returned as knowing English (including Europeans, Americans, and Eurasians), and in regard to these figures, the following remarks of Mr. Baines (at page 224 of his Report) must be kept in view:—"The return of those who know English shows a ratio of 4·4 per cent. on the total literates. We must subtract, however, the Europeans and Eurasians from the account, which then amounts to 3·2 only, or 1·4 in every thousand of the community. . . . . The entire number returned as knowing English, including Europeans and Eurasians, was 537,811, or 386,032, if the foreign element be excluded. This, too, includes a certain proportion of those who are not yet emancipated from their studies." Of this aggregate amount, *viz.*, 386,032, which is the number of the English-knowing Natives of India, only 15,627 have taken degrees during the last 36 years of the Indian Universities, and out of this last number, the number of Muhammadan graduates was only 546. From these figures it may be judged how far English education, even in its widest sense, has spread in India, notwithstanding nearly a century of more or less energetic efforts in its behalf; how far the small English-knowing section can be said to be capable of representing the thoughts, feelings, and aspirations of the vast mass of nearly 287 millions which inhabit India (according to the Census of 1891), and also how far modern democratic institutions, which rely for their success in India upon the progress of English ideas of enlightenment and social and political advancement, are suited to the present conditions of the Indian population. Attention has been invited here to these broad facts of English education in India as they will be interesting alike to the statesman, the politician, the educationist and the philanthropist who may be concerned in the present welfare and future destinies of the Indian Empire.

In conclusion, I gladly acknowledge my obligations to the eminent statesmen and authors from whose works I have borrowed ample extracts, to make their views upon the important subject of English education in India easily accessible to the reader. I have also much pleasure in expressing my best thanks to my worthy friend Babu Jadav Chandra Chakravarti, M. A., Professor of Mathematics in the Muhammadan Anglo-Oriental College at Aligarh, to whose mathematical talent and labour I am indebted for the elaborate calculations contained in the Tabular Statements in Chapter XXX of this work, and also for the ready assistance which he has kindly given me in connection with other statistics whenever I have had occasion to consult him.

ALIGARH,
March, 1895.

SYED MAHMOOD.

TABLE OF CONTENTS.

CHAPTER I.

INTRODUCTORY.

CHAPTER II.

EARLY POLICY OPPOSED TO THE INTRODUCTION OF ENGLISH EDUCATION IN INDIA.—MR. CHARLES GRANT'S TREATISE WRITTEN IN 1792–97, A.D., ON THE MORAL AND INTELLECTUAL CONDITION OF INDIA.

CHAPTER III.

MR. CHARLES GRANT'S SCHEME FOR THE INTELLECTUAL, MORAL, AND SOCIAL REGENERATION OF THE PEOPLE OF INDIA, AS PROPOUNDED IN HIS TREATISE, 1792–97, A.D.—INTRODUCTION OF ENGLISH EDUCATION A MORAL DUTY OF THE STATE, AND NOT FRAUGHT WITH POLITICAL DANGER.

CHAPTER IV.

EARLY EFFORTS FOR THE EDUCATION OF THE NATIVES OF INDIA.—THE CALCUTTA MADRASSA FOUNDED IN 1781, AND THE SANSKRIT COLLEGE AT BENARES IN 1791.—LORD MINTO'S MINUTE ON EDUCATION, 1811.

CHAPTER V.

FIRST LEGISLATIVE PROVISION FOR PUBLIC INSTRUCTION IN INDIA.—ACT OF PARLIAMENT, 53 GEO. III., C. 155.—DESPATCH OF THE COURT OF DIRECTORS, DATED 3RD JUNE, 1814, ON EDUCATION.—EARLY EDUCATIONAL EFFORTS OF THE MISSIONARIES.—LORD MOIRA'S EDUCATIONAL MINUTE OF 2ND OCTOBER, 1815.

CHAPTER VI.

ORIGIN OF ENGLISH EDUCATION.—THE "*Vidyalaya*" OR ANGLO-INDIAN COLLEGE FOUNDED BY HINDUS OF CALCUTTA IN 1816.—RAJA RAM MOHUN ROY'S ADVOCACY OF ENGLISH EDUCATION.—COMMITTEE OF PUBLIC INSTRUCTION ESTABLISHED IN CALCUTTA IN 1823.—ITS PROCEEDINGS UP TO THE END OF 1831.

CHAPTER VII.

EARLY MEASURES FOR EDUCATION IN THE MADRAS PRESIDENCY.—SIR THOMAS MUNRO'S MINUTES ON EDUCATION, IN 1822 AND 1826 — COMMITTEE OF PUBLIC INSTRUCTION APPOINTED IN MADRAS, IN 1826.

CHAPTER VIII.

EARLY MEASURES FOR EDUCATION IN THE BOMBAY PRESIDENCY DURING 1815-23.—MINUTES BY THE HON'BLE MOUNTSTUART ELPHINSTONE AND THE HON'BLE F. WARDEN, ON EDUCATION, IN 1823 AND 1828.—SIR JOHN MALCOLM'S VIEWS AGAINST GENERAL EDUCATION IN ENGLISH, IN HIS MINUTE OF 1828.—DESPATCH OF THE COURT OF DIRECTORS TO THE BOMBAY GOVERNMENT, DATED 21ST SEPTEMBER, 1829, FAVOURING STUDY OF ENGLISH.—SIR JOHN MALCOLM'S MODIFIED VIEWS, IN HIS MINUTE, DATED 10TH OCTOBER, 1829.—DESPATCH OF THE COURT OF DIRECTORS TO THE BOMBAY GOVERNMENT, DATED 29TH SEPTEMBER, 1830, IN FAVOUR OF ENGLISH EDUCATION.—THE ELPHINSTONE INSTITUTION FOR ENGLISH EDUCATION IN BOMBAY.

CHAPTER IX.

Summary of the various stages of the measures for education of the Natives of India, and expenditure incurred by the East India Company under the Act of Parliament, Statute 53, Geo. III., Chapter 155,—from 1813 to 1830.

CHAPTER X.

Renewal of the East India Company's Charter in 1833.—Arrival of Lord Macaulay in India as a Member of the Governor-General's Council, in 1834.—Controversy as to the comparative merits of Oriental learning and English literature for education.—Lord William Bentinck's educational Resolution of 1835.—Protest of Muhammadans against the Resolution.

CHAPTER XI.

CONTENDING ARGUMENTS OF THE ADVOCATES OF ENGLISH EDUCATION, AND THE SUPPORTERS OF ORIENTAL LEARNING IN ARABIC AND SANSKRIT.

CHAPTER XII.

RELIGIOUS INSTRUCTION NO PART OF GOVERNMENT EDUCATIONAL POLICY.—MARQUIS OF TWEEDDALE'S MINUTE OF 1846, IN FAVOUR OF RELIGIOUS INSTRUCTION, DISAPPROVED BY COURT OF DIRECTORS.—PETITION OF THE NATIVES OF MADRAS TO PARLIAMENT, IN 1852, ON THE SUBJECT.—RESULT OF THE CONTROVERSY.

CHAPTER XIII.

EFFECTS OF PURELY SECULAR ENGLISH EDUCATION ON THE NATIVE MIND.—VIEWS OF MR. MARSHMAN AND SIR CHARLES TREVELYAN AS TO THE CHRISTIANIZING INFLUENCE OF ENGLISH EDUCATION.—MR. HOWELL'S VIEWS AS TO THE FIRST EFFECTS OF ENGLISH AND MISSIONARY TEACHING.—THE "BRAHMO SAMAJ" MOVEMENT.

CHAPTER XIV.

CHAPTER XV.

CHAPTER XVI.

CHAPTER XVII.

COMPREHENSIVE DESPATCH OF THE COURT OF DIRECTORS TO THE GOVERNMENT OF INDIA, DATED 19TH JULY, 1854, ON THE SUBJECT OF EDUCATION, KNOWN AS SIR CHARLES WOOD'S EDUCATIONAL DESPATCH OF 1854.—FORMATION OF THE EDUCATION DEPARTMENT.

CHAPTER XVIII.

ESTABLISHMENT OF THE INDIAN UNIVERSITIES, AND THE SCOPE AND CHARACTER OF THE EDUCATION RECOGNIZED AND CONTROLLED BY THEM.—STATISTICS OF UNIVERSITY COLLEGIATE EDUCATION, 1857 TO 1882.

CHAPTER XIX.

THE INDIAN EDUCATION COMMISSION OF 1882, AND SOME IMPORTANT FACTS AND STATISTICS COLLECTED BY IT IN REGARD TO ENGLISH COLLEGIATE EDUCATION.

CHAPTER XX.

THE GRANT-IN-AID SYSTEM INAUGURATED BY THE EDUCATIONAL DESPATCH OF 1854, AND CONSIDERED BY THE INDIAN EDUCATION COMMISSION OF 1882.

CHAPTER XXI.

VIEWS OF THE INDIAN EDUCATION COMMISSION IN REGARD TO THE WITHDRAWAL OF THE STATE FROM HIGHER ENGLISH EDUCATION.

CHAPTER XXII.

MORAL TRAINING AND RELIGIOUS TEACHING IN COLLEGES.—VIEWS OF THE INDIAN EDUCATION COMMISSION.—MR. KASHINATH TRIMBUK TELANG'S DISSENTIENT MINUTE.—VIEWS OF THE LOCAL GOVERNMENTS AND THE DECISION OF THE GOVERNMENT OF INDIA UPON THE SUBJECT.

CHAPTER XXIII.

Sir Alfred Croft's Review of Education in India in 1886, and its Statistics.

CHAPTER XXIV.

Mr. Nash's Quinquennial Review of the Progress of Education in India, 1887–88 to 1891–92, and its Satistics.—Financial position of the Indian Universities.—Resolution of the Government of India on the same, dated 7th September, 1894.—Some important matters dealt with in the Resolution.

CHAPTER XXV.

ENGLISH PROFESSIONAL EDUCATION IN COLLEGES IN 1881-82 to 1885-86, AND IN 1886-87 TO 1891-92.

CHAPTER XXVI.

BACKWARDNESS OF MUHAMMADANS IN ENGLISH EDUCATION.—MEASURES ADOPTED BY GOVERNMENT TO ENCOURAGE EDUCATION AMONG MUHAMMADANS IN 1871–73.—REFORMS IN THE CALCUTTA MADRASSA IN 1873.—IMPROVED APPLICATION OF THE MOHSIN ENDOWMENT AT HOOGHLY TO MUHAMMADAN EDUCATION IN BENGAL.

CHAPTER XXVII.

MEASURES ADOPTED BY THE VARIOUS LOCAL GOVERNMENTS AS TO MUHAMMADAN EDUCATION UNDER THE GOVERNMENT OF INDIA'S RESOLUTION OF 1871, AS STATED IN THE REPORT OF THE EDUCATION COMMISSION OF 1882.

CHAPTER XXVIII.

CONCLUSIONS AND RECOMMENDATIONS OF THE EDUCATION COMMISSION OF 1882, ON THE SUBJECT OF MUHAMMADAN EDUCATION.—REPORTS OF THE LOCAL GOVERNMENTS THEREON.—VIEWS OF THE GOVERNMENT OF INDIA UPON THE SUBJECT.

CHAPTER XXIX.

PROGRESS OF ENGLISH EDUCATION AMONG MUHAMMADANS, 1881-82 to 1891-92.—RESOLUTIONS OF THE GOVERNMENT OF INDIA ON THE SUBJECT, IN 1888 AND 1894.—DEFICIENCY OF HIGH ENGLISH EDUCATION AMONG MUHAMMADANS, 1882-92.

CHAPTER XXX.

GENERAL SURVEY OF THE STATISTICS OF HIGH ENGLISH EDUCATION AMONG MUHAMMADANS AS COMPARED WITH HINDUS, FROM THE ESTABLISHMENT OF THE INDIAN UNIVERSITIES TO THE PRESENT PERIOD—36 YEARS—1858 TO 1893.

CHAPTER XXXI.

POSITION OF MUHAMMADANS IN THE GENERAL POPULATION OF INDIA.—THE PRESENT *rate* OF THE PROGRESS OF ENGLISH EDUCATION AMONG MUHAMMADANS IN COLLEGES AND SECONDARY SCHOOLS, AND ITS FUTURE PROSPECTS.

CHAPTER XXXII.

GENERAL SPREAD OF ENGLISH EDUCATION IN INDIA, ACCORDING TO THE CENSUS OF 1891.

CHAPTER XXXIV.

Recapitulation and prospects of English education in India.

HISTORY

OF

ENGLISH EDUCATION IN INDIA.

CHAPTER I.

INTRODUCTORY.

The subject proposed.

The origin, rise and progress of English education in India, and its gradual development into an important branch of the administration of the State, constitute one of the most significant episodes, not only in the annals of India, but in the history of the civilized world. "The British rule in India is the most wonderful phenomenon the world has ever seen. That a race living in a distant region, differing from us in language, in manners, in religion,—in short, in all that distinguishes the inhabitants of one country from those of another, should triumph over the barriers which nature has placed in its way, and unite under one sceptre the various peoples of this vast continent, is in itself wonderful enough. But that they, who have thus become the masters of this soil, should rule its inhabitants, not with those feelings and motives which inspired the conquerors of the ancient world, but should make it the first principle of their government to advance the happiness of the millions of a subject race, by establishing peace, by administering justice, by spreading education, by introducing the comforts of life which modern civilization has bestowed upon mankind, is to us a manifestation of the hand of Providence, and an assurance of long life to the union of India with England."

Its importance.

Such were the words employed in an Address presented to Lord Lytton, when Viceroy of India, on the 8th January, 1877, on the occasion of his laying the foundation stone of the Mahomedan Anglo-Oriental College at Aligarh, a few days after the Imperial Assemblage at Delhi, held in honour of Her Majesty's assumption of the title of "*Empress of India.*" The words of the Address, when seriously considered, have greater significance than the figurative language of Oriental rhetoric. Of all the measures which the British rule has adopted for the material and moral progress and prosperity of India, none is more important or more enduring in its moral, social, and political effects than the inauguration of the policy of imparting knowledge of the English language, literature, and sciences to the people of India. The policy is unique in its nature; it has never been tried on such a grand scale by any other nation, within the range of ancient or modern history, and, indeed, though more than half a century old, has not yet passed the stage of experiment. That the spread of English education among the people of India has already produced a vast effect upon their religious, moral, social, and political ideas and aspirations, cannot be denied by any one acquainted with the country. Nor can it be denied, that, in all these respects, the spread of English education will produce even greater consequences, and more potent effects, upon the moral and material, social and political, condition of India in the approximate future. But so far as the present writer is aware, no attempt has yet been made by any author to describe, with requisite accuracy of detail, in what manner the policy of spreading education in India originated; what were the objects with which it was inaugurated; what were the principles upon which it proceeded in its gradual development; how it has steadily made progress, and what its general outcome has been, with reference to such statistical results as are within the reach of an historical account. Writers upon the general history of British India are naturally more concerned with battles and treaties, conquests and annexations, legislative measures and fiscal administrations, than with a subject such as the spread of

English education among the people of India. They could not be expected to spare time, or find space, for a subject which, however important and enduring its effects may be, presents so slow and gradual a growth as to escape the notice of the writers of political history, and, not unfrequently, the attention even of the statesmen who are naturally more concerned with the urgent work of present administration than with the past history of any special branch of the administrative policy. Thus, whilst even the best histories of India are entirely, or almost entirely, silent upon the subject of the rise and progress of English education in India, the official and other information upon the subject is so scattered among Departmental Blue-books and Parliamentary Papers, that no ordinary reader, however deeply interested, can be expected to find easy access to those records, or to spare time to arrange the main facts, and leading features and statistics of the subject of his interest. The need for a book which would furnish ready information upon such an important subject seems to be growing with the advance of English education, and the growth of intellectual and political thought among the people of India; and the present work is an attempt to supply such a need.

Its Arrangement.

It will be readily observed, that in accomplishing the task thus set before me, a considerable portion of this work must be devoted to describing the early history of the origin and objects of English education in India; the motives with which it was undertaken, and the principles upon which it has proceeded in its gradual advancement; the establishment of colleges and schools, as individual efforts in behalf of English education; the development of a system of education, and the organization of the Department of Public Instruction, as a branch of the State administration in India. It will then be necessary to pursue the subject further, by giving an account of the Indian Universities, and ascertaining the actual statistical results of the progress of high English education, under the system adopted by those Universities during the last thirty-six years, that is, from their establishment since 1857, down to the present period, ending with the year 1893. And in dealing with this part of the subject, it will be my duty to introduce, not an invidious, but a friendly, comparison between the progress of high English education among the Hindus and the Mahomedans, respectively, giving prominence to such facts and figures as may enable those interested in the intellectual and moral growth, and the social and political welfare of the Mahomedans of India, to form some approximate estimate of the future prospects of that community, and the means which may be adopted for their amelioration and prosperity, as contented and loyal subjects of the British rule in India.

CHAPTER II.

EARLY POLICY OPPOSED TO THE INTRODUCTION OF ENGLISH EDUCATION IN INDIA. MR. CHARLES GRANT'S TREATISE, WRITTEN IN 1792–97, A.D., ON THE MORAL AND INTELLECTUAL CONDITION OF INDIA.

Education no part of the early Administrative Policy.

During the early period of its administration, the East India Company did not recognize the promotion of education among the natives of India as part of its duty or concern. Like all commercial companies, its main object was pecuniary gain by trade, and if territorial acquisitions were made, it was more in the nature of investments of capital than laying the foundations of Imperial dominion, having for its object the progress, prosperity, and enlightenment of its subjects. In his statement before a Select Committee of the House of Lords, on the 15th June, 1853, the well-known historian of India, Mr. John Clarke Marshman, gave the following sketch of the early policy of English education in India:—

"For a considerable time after the British Government had been established in India, there was great opposition to any system of instruction for the Natives. The feelings of the public authorities in this country were first tested upon the subject in the year 1792, when Mr. Wilberforce proposed to add two clauses to the Charter Act of that year, for sending out school masters to India; this encountered the greatest opposition in the Court of Proprietors, and it was found necessary to withdraw the clauses. That proposal gave rise to a very memorable debate, in which, for the first time, the views of the Court of Directors upon the subject of education, after we had obtained possession of the country, were developed. On that occasion one of the Directors stated that we had just lost America from our folly, in having allowed the establishment of schools and colleges, and that it would not do for us to repeat the same act of folly in regard to India; and that if the Natives required anything in the way of education, they must come to England for it. For 20 years after that period, down to the year 1813, the same feeling of opposition to the education of the Natives continued to prevail among the ruling authorities in this country. In the year 1813, Parliament, for the first time, ordered that the sum of £10,000 should be appropriated to the education of the Natives, at all the three Presidencies. In 1817, Lord Hastings, after he had broken the power of the Mahrattas, for the first time, announced that the Government of India did not consider it necessary to keep the Natives in a state of ignorance, in order to retain its own power: consequent on this announcement, the Calcutta School-book Society and the Hindu College were immediately founded. Lord Hastings also gave the largest encouragement to Vernacular Education, and even to the establishment of Native newspapers; but those who at that time, and for a considerable time after, enjoyed the confidence of the Government in India, were entirely in favor of confining the assistance given to education to the encouragement of Sanscrit and Arabic Literature. This state of things continued down to the year 1835, when Lord William Bentinck, acting under the advice of Mr. Macaulay and Sir Charles Trevelyan, determined to withdraw the Government support from the Sanscrit and Arabic Institutions, and to appropriate all the funds which were at its disposal exclusively to English education."*

For the purposes of this work, however, it is necessary to trace, in fuller detail, and as far back as possible, the historical origin of the idea of spreading a knowledge of the English language, literature, and sciences among the people of India, and the various shades of political opinions which were, from time to time, entertained upon the subject.

The Right Honourable Mr. Charles Grant, an eminent Director of the East India Company.

Among the most notable philanthropic British statesmen, of the latter part of the last century, was the Right Honourable Charles Grant, descended from a noble Highland family of Scotland, the Grants of Schewglie. "He went early to India, became one of the most distinguished Directors of the East India Company, represented for many years the County of Inverness in Parliament, and was, along with Wilberforce, Thornton, Zachary Macaulay, and others, a leading member of the Clapham sect, described by Sir James Stephen in his *Ecclesiastical Essays*. He died in 1823, aged 77."† During his long, useful and distinguished career, the condition of the people of India and their future prosperity, were matters of great concern to him, and his position as a Member of Parliament, and, at the same time, one of the members of the Court of Directors of the East India Company, enabled him to take particularly active interest in the affairs of this country. In 1792, he wrote a considerable treatise: "*Observations on the state of Society among the Asiatic Subjects of Great Britain, particularly with respect to Morals; and on the means of Improving it.*"‡ This treatise, which appears to have been kept by its author for some years for improvement and revision, was at last submitted by him to his colleagues, the Court of Directors for the affairs of the East India Company, with a letter, dated 16th August, 1797, asking them (to use his own words): "That you may be pleased to receive this tract on the footing of one of those many *Papers of business*, with which the records of your Governments have been furnished, by the observation and experience of men whose time and thoughts have been chiefly employed in the concerns of active life." The treatise is a most valuable essay upon the moral, intellectual, and political condition of India at that time, and abounds in philosophical suggestions, philanthropic sentiments, and sound principles of administrative policy. It appears, however, to have remained buried in Parliamentary Blue-books as an appendix to the Parliamentary Papers of 1832, and I shall therefore quote considerable passages from it to throw light upon the early origin, reasons, and principles of the policy of the British rule, in introducing a knowledge of the English literature and sciences among the people of India.

The treatise begins with the following:—

His Philanthropic Treatise on the moral and intellectual condition of the Natives of India, written during 1792–97, A.D.

"Whatever diversity of opinion may have prevailed respecting the past conduct of the English in the East, all parties will concur in one sentiment, that we ought to study the happiness of the vast body of subjects which we have acquired there. Upon this proposition, taken as a truth of the highest certainty and importance, the following observations, now submitted with great deference, are founded.................... .... Although in theory it never can have been denied, that the welfare of our Asiatic subjects ought to be the object of our solicitude, yet, in practice, this acknowledged truth has been but slowly followed up, and some of the inferences which are deducible from it, remain, as it should seem, still to be discovered. Of late, undoubtedly much has been done, and excellently done,

* Printed Parliamentary Papers—*Second* Report of the Select Committee of the House of Lords (1852-53) on Indian Territories, p. 113.

† Chambers's Encyclopædia, Sup. Vol. X., p. 548.

‡ Printed Parliamentary Papers relating to the affairs of India: *General*, Appendix I; *Public* (1832), pp. 3 to 89.

to improve the condition of our subjects in the East; yet upon an attentive examination it may, perhaps, be found, that much still remains to the performed." *

After giving a short historical sketch of the territorial acquisitions of the East India Company, and a brief review of the British administration of those territories, the treatise devotes Chapter II. to a "*View of the State of Society among the Hindoo Subjects of Great Britain, particularly with respect to Morals*," and the following extract, taken from the earlier part of the chapter, represents Mr. Charles Grant's opinions upon the subject. It is quoted here, at the risk of prolixity, as deserving interesting consideration, being the views of an important statesman connected with the administration of India, expressed a century ago. He says:—

"In prosecuting the proposed inquiry, the State of Society and Manners among the people of Hindoostan, and more particularly among those who inhabit our territories, becomes, in the first place, a special object of attention. It is an object which, perhaps, has never yet received that distinct and particular consideration, to which, from its importance in a political and moral view, it is entitled.

His views as to Indian Society.

"It has suited the views of some philosophers to represent that people as amiable and respectable; and a few late travellers have chosen rather to place some softer traits of their characters in an engaging light, than to give a just delineation of the whole. The generality, however, of those who have written concerning Hindoostan, appear to have concurred in affirming what foreign residents there have as generally thought, nay, what the natives themselves freely acknowledge of each other, that they are a people exceedingly depraved.

"In proportion as we have become better acquainted with them, we have found this description applicable, in a sense, beyond the conception even of former travellers. The writer of this paper, after spending many years in India, and a considerable portion of them in the interior of our provinces, inhabited almost entirely by natives, towards whom, whilst acknowledging his views of their general character, he always lived in habits of good-will, is obliged to add his testimony to all preceding evidence, and to avow that they exhibit human nature in a very degraded, humiliating state, and are at once objects of dis-esteem and of commiseration. Discriminations in so vast a body as the whole Hindoo people, there must be, though the general features are very similar.

As to the character of the Bengalis.

"Among that people, the natives of Bengal rank low; and these, as best known and forming the largest division of our Asiatic subjects, are held more particularly in view in this essay. The Mahomedans who are mixed with them, may, in regard to manners and morals, often be comprehended under the same observations; but something distinct shall afterwards be subjoined concerning them.

"Of the Bengalese, then, it is true, most generally, that they are destitute, to a wonderful degree, of those qualities which are requisite to the security and comfort of Society. They want truth, honesty, and good faith, in an extreme, of which European Society furnishes no example. In Europe, those principles are the standard of character and credit; men who have them not are still solicitous to maintain the reputation of them, and those who are known to be devoid of them sink into contempt. It is not so in Bengal. The qualities themselves are so generally gone, that men do not found their pretensions in Society upon them; they take no pains to acquire or to keep up the credit of possessing them. Those virtues are not the tests by which connections and associations are regulated; nor does the absence of them, however plain and notorious, greatly lower any one in public estimation, nor strip him of his acquaintance. Want of veracity, especially, is so habitual, that if a man has truth to defend, he will hardly fail to recur to falsehood for its support. In matters of interest, the use of lying seems so natural, that it gives no provocation, it is treated as an excusable indulgence, a mode of proceeding from which general toleration has taken away offence, and the practice of cheating, pilfering, tricking, and imposing, in the ordinary transactions of life, are so common, that the Hindoos seem to regard them as they do natural evils, against which they will defend themselves as well as they can, but at which it would be idle to be angry. Very flagrant breaches of truth and honesty pass without any deep or lasting stain. The scandalous conduct of Tippoo, in recently denying to Lord Cornwallis, in the face of the world, the existence of that capitulation which he had shamefully broken, was merely an example of the manners of the country, where such things occur in common life every day.

Want of veracity.

"In the worst parts of Europe, there are no doubt great numbers of men who are sincere, upright, and conscientious. In Bengal, a man of real veracity and integrity is a great phenomenon; *one conscientious in the whole of his conduct*, it is to be feared, is an unknown character. Everywhere in this quarter of the globe, there is still much generous trust and confidence, and men are surprised when they find themselves deceived. In Bengal, distrust is awake in all transactions;

* Printed Parliamentary Papers relating to the affairs of India: *General*, Appendix I; *Public* (1832), p. 4.

bargains and agreements are made with mutual apprehensions of breach of faith, conditions and securities are multiplied, and failure in them excites little or no surprise.

"A serious proposal made to a Native, that he should be guided in all his intercourses and dealings by the principles of truth and justice, would be regarded as weak and impracticable. 'Do you know,' he would reply, 'the character of all those with whom I have to act? How can I subsist if I take advantage of nobody, while every person takes advantage of me?' Frauds, deceptions, evasions, and procrastinations, in every line of life, in all professions, perpetually occur, and forgeries also are often resorted to with little scruple.

Betrayal of confidence.

"If confidence is from necessity or credulity at any time reposed, it is considered by the other party as the season of harvest. Few will omit to seize such an opportunity of profit. The chief agent or steward of a landholder or of a merchant, will commonly endeavour to transfer to himself what he can gradually purloin of the property and the influence of his principal; this agent is in the meantime preyed upon in a similar way, though on a smaller scale, by his dependents, especially if prosperity has rendered him less vigilant. But suppose him, by a slow, silent, and systematic pursuit, to have accumulated a large fortune, and to leave it on his death to his son, the son, rich and indolent, is in turn imperceptibly fleeced by his domestics.

"Menial servants who have been long in place, and have even evinced a real attachment to their masters, are nevertheless in the habitual practice of pilfering from them. If a nephew is entrusted by an uncle, or a son by his father, with the management of his concerns, there is no certainty that he will not set up a separate interest of his own. Wardships and executorships, trusts of the most necessary and sacred kind, which all men leaving property and infant children must repose in surviving friends, are in too many instances grossly abused. The confidence to which the Bengalese are most true, is in the case of illicit practices, on which occasions they act upon a point of honour.

"Even the Europeans, though in general possessed of power and of comparative strength of character, which makes them to be particularly feared, yet as often as they are careless or credulous in their transactions with the Bengalese, find that they have fallen into the hands of harpies.

Venality of the Natives of India in the distribution of Justice.

"Through the influence of similar principles, power entrusted to a native of Hindoostan seldom fails of being exercised tyrannically, or perverted to the purposes of injustice. Official or ministerial employments of all sorts, and in all gradations, are generally used as means of peculation.

Their Corruption, and Perjury.

"It has already appeared that the distribution of justice, whenever it has been committed to natives, whether Hindoos or Mahomedans, has commonly become a traffic in venality; the best cause being obliged to pay for success, and the worst having the opportunity of purchasing it. Money has procured acquittance even for murder. Such is the power of money, that no crime is more frequent, hardly any less thought of, than perjury. It is no extraordinary thing to see two sets of witnesses swearing directly contrary to each other, and to find, upon a minute investigation, that few, probably, of the witnesses on either side have a competent knowledge of the matter in question. Now, as these corruptions begin, not in the practice of the Courts of Law, but have their origin in the character of the people, it is just to state them, in illustration of that character; for although the legal reforms introduced by Lord Cornwallis will purify, it may be hoped, the fountains of justice, yet the best administration of law will not eradicate the internal principles of depravity.

Selfishness and Avarice.

"Selfishness, in a word, unrestrained by principle, operates universally; and money, the grand instrument of selfish gratifications, may be called the supreme idol of the Hindoos. Deprived for the most part of political power, and destitute of boldness of spirit, but formed for business, artful, frugal, and persevering, they are absorbed in schemes for the gratification of avarice.

Cunning and hypocritical obsequiousness, mutual discord, malice, calumnies, &c.

"The tendency of that abandoned selfishness is to set 'every man's hand against every man,' either in projects, or in acts of open force. From violence, however, fear interposes to restrain them. The people of the Lower Provinces in particular, with an exception of the military caste, are as dastardly as they are unprincipled. They seek their ends by mean artifices, low cunning, intrigue, falsehood, servility, and hypocritical obsequiousness. To superiors they appear full of reverence, of humble and willing submission, and readiness to do every thing that may be required of them; and as long as they discern something either to expect or to fear, they are wonderfully patient of slights, neglects, and injuries. But under all this apparent passiveness and meanness of temper, they are immovably persisting in their secret views. With inferiors, they indemnify themselves by an indulgence of the feelings which were controlled before; and towards dependents, especially towards those whom an official situation subjects to their authority, they carry themselves with the mean pride of low minds. In the inferior, and by far the most numerous class of the community, where each man is nearly on a level with his neighbour, the native character appears with less disguise. The passions have a freer range, and new consequences are seen to result from the absence of the primary virtues of society. Discord, hatred, abuse, slanders, injuries, complaints, and litigations, all the effects of selfishness unrestrained by principle, prevail to a surprising degree. They overspread the land; they come perpetually before all men in authority. The deliberate malice, the falsehood, the calumnies, and the avowed enmity with which the people pursue each other, and sometimes from father to son, offer a very mortifying view of the human character. No stranger can sit down among them without being struck with this temper of malevolent contention and animosity, as a prominent feature in the character of the society. It is seen in every village; the inhabitants live among each other in a sort of repulsive state; nay, it enters into almost every family. Seldom is there a household without its internal divisions and lasting enmities, most commonly, too, on the score of interest. The women partake of this spirit of discord. Held in slavish subjection by the men, they rise in curious passions against each other, which vent themselves in such loud, virulent, and indecent railings, as are hardly to be heard in any other part of the world.

Robberies, thefts, and other secret crimes in Bengal.

"Though the Bengalese, in general, have not sufficient resolution to vent their resentments against each other in open combat, yet robberies, thefts, burglaries, river piracies, and all sorts of depredations, where darkness, secrecy, or surprise can give advantage, are exceedingly common, and have been so in every past period of which any account is extant. There are castes of robbers and thieves, who consider themselves acting in their proper profession, and having united their families, train their children to it. Nowhere in the world are ruffians more adroit or more hardened. Troops of these banditti, it is well known, are generally employed or harboured by the Zemindars of the districts, who are sharers in their booty. They frequently make attacks in bodies, and on those occasions murder is very common. But besides these regular corps, multitudes of individuals employ themselves in despoiling their neighbours. Nor is it only in large and populous places, and their vicinity, that such violences are practised; no part of the country, no village, is safe from them. Complaints of depredations in every quarter, on the highways, on the water as well as the land, are perpetual. Though these are the crimes more immediately within the reach of justice, and though numbers of criminals have been, and are, executed, the evils still subsist. Doubtless, the corrupt administration of criminal justice in Bengal, for many years under the authority of the Nabob, has greatly aggravated disorders of this nature; but they have their origin from the remoter springs. Robbers among the Hindoos, and frequently thieves also, are educated from their infancy in the belief that their profession is a right one. No ray of instruction reaches them to convince them of the contrary, and the feeble stirrings of natural conscience are soon overborne by example and practice. Besides this, they hold, in common with other Hindoos, the principle of fatalism, which in their case has most pernicious effects. They believe that they are destined by an inevitable necessity to their profession, and to all that shall befall them in it; they therefore go on without compunction, and are prepared to resign life, whenever the appointed period shall come, with astonishing indifference; considering the law that condemns them, not as the instrument of Justice, but as the power of a stronger party. And here, again, it is evident, that a radical change in principle must be produced, before a spirit of rapine thus nourished can be cured.

Hindoos not really benevolent, but cruel.

"Benevolence has been represented as a leading principle in the minds of the Hindoos; but those who make this assertion know little of their character. How is it possible that benevolence should be vigorous, where justice, truth and good faith are so greatly wanting? Certain modes, indeed, of distributing victuals to mendicants, and a scrupulous abstinence from some sorts of animal food, are prescribed by the religion of the Hindoos. But the ostentatious distribution is frequently commutative; an offering from the gain of iniquity bestowed on idle and sturdy priests. And though a Hindoo would shrink with horror from the idea of directly slaying a cow, which is a sacred animal among them, yet he who drives one in his cart, galled and excoriated as she often is by the yoke, beats her unmercifully from hour to hour, without any care or consideration of the consequence. Though, therefore, the institution of the two practices in question may be urged as an argument for the originally benevolent turn of the religion which enjoined them, it will not at all follow that individuals, who in future ages perform them, in obedience to that religion, must also be benevolent; and he who is cruel even to that creature for which he is taught by his religion to entertain the highest reverence, gives the strongest proof of an unfeeling disposition. It is true, that in many cases they are strict in observing forms. These are, indeed, their religion, and the foundation of their hopes; their castes are implicated in them, and in their castes their civil state and comfort. But of the sentiments which the forms would seem to indicate, they are totally regardless. Though from the physical structure of their bodies they are easily susceptible of impressions, yet that they have little real tenderness of mind, seems very evident from several circumstances. The first that shall be mentioned is the shocking barbarity of their punishments. The cutting off legs, hands, noses, and ears, putting out of eyes, and other penal inflictions of a similar kind, all performed in the coarsest manner, abundantly justify our argument.

Absence of Patriotism.

"A similar disposition to cruelty is likewise shown in their treatment of vanquished enemies. And in general a want of sensibility for others is a very eminent characteristic of this people. The apathy with which a Hindoo views all persons and interests unconnected with himself, is such as excites the indignation of Europeans. At any rate, his regards extend but to a very narrow circle. Patriotism is absolutely unknown in Hindoostan."*

Great moral and intellectual advance in Bengal.

It is not within the province of this work to discuss how far the above-quoted views of Mr. Charles Grant, in regard to the condition of Hindoo society, especially in Bengal, may be justifiable. His views were recorded just a century ago, and if his estimate of the moral condition of the Hindoo population of India, especially of Bengal, be taken to be even approximately correct, no one acquainted with the present condition of the Bengalis can help admiring the vast strides towards intellectual, moral, social, and political progress which they have made during a century of British rule, and nearly half a century of education in the languages, literature, and sciences of Great Britian.

Mr. Grant's views as to the character of Mahomedans.

I will now quote Mr. Charles Grant's views, written in the same treatise, in regard to the moral and social condition of the Mahomedans of India a century ago. He says :—

Proud, fierce, lawless, perfidious, licentious and cruel.

"Of the Mahomedans, who mix in considerable numbers with the former inhabitants of all the countries subdued by their arms in Hindoostan, it is necessary also to say a few words. Originally of the Tartar race, proud, fierce, and lawless ; attached also to their superstition, which cherished their native propensities, they were rendered by success yet more proud, sanguinary, sensual, and bigotted. Their government, though meliorated under the House of Timour, was undoubtedly a violent despotism, and the delegated administration of it, too often a severe oppression. Breaking through all the restraints of morals which obstructed their way to power, they afterwards abandoned themselves to the most vicious indulgences, and the most atrocious cruelties. Perfidy in them, was more signal than in the Hindoos. Successive treacheries, assassinations, and usurpations, mark their history more, perhaps, than that of any other people. The profession of arms was studied by them, and they cultivated the Persian learning. They introduced Arabic laws, formed for rude and ignorant tribes, and in the administration of them, as may be judged from the specimen above exhibited, were most corrupt.

Regard secular business irreconcilable with strict Virtue and Religion.

"Every worldly profession, indeed every course of secular business, was in their avowed opinion (an opinion which they still hold), irreconcilable with strict virtue. Commerce, and the details of the finances, they left chiefly to the Hindoos, whom they despised and insulted. Where their government still prevails, the character resulting from their original temper and superstition, aggravated by the enjoyment of power, remains in force. In our provinces, where their authority is subverted, and where many of them fall into the lower lines of life, that character becomes less obvious ; but with more knowledge, and more pretensions to integrity, they are as unprincipled as the Hindoos. Their perfidy, however, and licentiousness, are the perfidy and licentiousness of a bolder people.

Vices of Hindoos and Mahomedans, on the whole, similar, owing to their intermixture.

"From the government and intermixture of the Mahomedans, the Hindoos have certainly derived no improvement of character. The invaders may fairly be supposed to have contributed their share to the general evils, and even to have increased them. But they did not produce those evils, nor could they have perpetuated them, in opposition to the genius and spirit of the Hindoos, who are in number, probably, as eight to one. They may, therefore, be considered rather as constituting an accession, than as giving a character to the mass. The vices, however, of the Mahomedans and Hindoos are so homogenous, that in stating their effects, it is not inaccurate to speak of both classes under the description of the one collective body into which they are now formed.

Degeneracy of the Natives of India.

"Upon the whole, then, we cannot avoid recognizing in the people of Hindoostan, a race of men lamentably degenerate and base, retaining but a feeble sense of moral obligation, yet obstinate in their disregard of what they know to be right, governed by malevolent and licentious passions, strongly exemplifying the effects produced on society by great and general corruption of manners, and sunk in misery by their vices, in a country peculiarly calculated, y its natural advantages, to promote the happiness of its inhabitants. The delineation from which this conclusion formed, has been a task so painful, that nothing except the consciousness of meaning to do good could have

* Printed Parliamentary Papers relating to the affairs of India : *General*, Appendix I ; *Public* (1832), pp. 20–23.

induced the author to proceed in it. He trusts he has an affecting sense of the general imperfection of human nature, and would abhor the idea of needlessly or contemptuously exposing the defects of any man or set of men. If he has given an unfavourable description, his wish is not to excite detestation, but to engage compassion, and to make it apparent, that what speculation may have ascribed to physical and unchangeable causes, springs from moral sources capable of correction."*

Remarks on Mr. Grant's estimate of the character of Mahomedans.

This estimate of the character of the Mahomedan population presents, no doubt, a painful picture, but the author himself has expressed his views in an apologetic manner, and we have no reason to doubt the sincerity of philanthropic motives with which he appears to have recorded them. Nor must we forget that his opinions were formed and written about a century ago, between the years 1792 and 1797—a period when the fall of the Mahomedan Empire had produced warfare and anarchy, devastating the country and breaking up the entire fabric of Mahomedan Society and political organization. Constant rapine and bloodshed had for some time been raging in the land, creating a state of insecurity and convulsion which is destructive not only of social order but also of all the arts of peace and the progress of literature and sciences, which can thrive only in peace and under good government. Indeed, even a cursory view of the history of India of that period will show that, with the downfall of the Mahomedan system of government, the pursuits and character of the Mahomedans had also decayed. One incident alone seems sufficient to illustrate the extreme anarchy and wreck of the social system of the Mahomedans during that period, even in the centre of the Mahomedan Empire at Delhi, and its neighbouring provinces. It must be remembered that it was in the year 1788 that the Mahomedan system of government had so completely broken up, that the Rohilla chief, Ghulam Kadir Khan, forcing an entrance into the imperial palace at Delhi, put out the eyes of the then monarch, Shah Alam, and that it was not till the year 1803, when Lord Lake, after a very successful campaign against the Mahrattas, captured Delhi on behalf of the East India Company, that peace and order were restored in the capital, and suitable provision was made for the blinded emperor, his family and dependents. It must never be forgotten that the decay and downfall of any political system creates anarchy, anarchy produces disrupture of social ties, and manners, feelings, and motives of action; and it can never be doubted that the political downfall of any race brings with it moral, intellectual, and social degradation: such, indeed, had become the condition of the Mahomedan Society of India upon the downfall of the Mughal Empire, and if we carefully study the historical events of that period, in sober earnestness, we shall probably find that much of Mr. Charles Grant's condemnatory estimate of the moral and social condition of the Mahomedans had ample excuse at the time when he wrote.

Elegy, in the form of a *Ghazal*, composed by Shah Alam after being deprived of his eye-sight in 1788,—on the downfall of the Mughal Empire.

Perhaps, nothing throws a more vivid and picturesque light upon the political and social decadence of the Mughal Empire, about the time when Mr. Charles Grant wrote his Treatise, than an Elegy composed in Persian, in the form of a *Ghazal*, by the Emperor Shah Alam himself, soon after he had been deprived of his eye-sight in 1788. The poem has been printed in an Appendix to "*The History of the Reign of Shah-Aulum*," by Captain W. Francklin, published, so long ago as 1798, with a free translation in English verse. The historical importance and interest of the poem justify its being quoted here in the original, together with Captain Francklin's translation and Notes:—

صرصر حادثه برخاست پی خواری ما * داد برباد سر و برگ جهانداری ما
آفتاب فلک رفعت شاهی بودیم * برد در شام زوال آه سیه کاری ما
چشم ما کنده شد از جور فلک بهتر شد * که نه بینم که کند غیر جهانداری ما
داد افغان بچه شوکت شاهی برباد * کیست جز ذات منزه که کند یاری ما
کرده بودیم گناهی که سزایش این بود * هست امید که بخشند گنه کاری ما
کرد سی سال نظارت که مرا داد بباد * زود تر یافت تلافی ستمگاری ما
نازنینان پریچهره که همدم بودند * نیست جز محل مبارک به پرستاری ما
حق طفلان که ز سی سال فراهم کردند * کرده تاراج نمودند سبکساری ما
مهه و پیمان بمیان داده نمودند دغا * مغلیان خوب نمودند وفاداری ما
شیر دادیم به افعی بچه و پروردیم * عاقبت گشت مجوز پی خونخواری ما
قوم افغان و مغلیه همه بازی دادند * بسکه گشتند مجوز بگرفتاری ما
آن گدا زادهٔ همدانی که بدوزخ برود * بانی جور و ستم شد بدل افکاری ما

* Printed Parliamentary Papers relating to the affairs of India: *General*, Appendix I; *Public* (1832), pp. 30-1.

گل محمد که زمروان بشارت کم نیست * چه قدر کرد وکالت بگرفتاري ما
هم اله یاز و سلیمان و بدل بیگ لعین * هرسه بستند کمر بهر دل ازاري ما
شاه تیمور که دارد سر نسبت با من * زود باشد که بیاید بمددکاري ما
مادهوجي سیندهیه فرزند جگربند من است * هست مصروف تلافي ستمگاري ما
راجه و راؤ زمیندار امیر و چه فقیر * حیف باشد که نسازند بغمخواري ما
حال ما گشته بتر همچو اماماں ز یزید * کرد تقدیر ازل روزي ما خواري ما
بود جانکاه زر و مال جهان همچو مرض * دفع از فضل الهي شده بیماري ما
اصف الدوله و انگریز که دلسوز من اند * چه عجب گر بنمایند مددگاري ما
آفتاب از فلک امروز تباهي دیدي * باز فردا دهد ایزد سرو سرداري ما

"Where* with bright pomp the stately domes arise,
In yon dark tower an aged monarch lies,
Forlorn, dejected, blind, replete with woes,
In tears his venerable aspect shews;
As through the lonely courts I bent my way,
Sounds struck my ear, which said, or seemed to say:—
'Lo, the dire tempest gathering from afar,
In dreadful clouds has dimm'd the imperial star;
Has to the winds, and broad expanse of heaven,
My state, my royalty, and kingdom given!
Time was, O king! when clothed in power supreme,
Thy voice was heard, and nations hail'd the theme;
Now sad reverse—for sordid lust of gold,
By traitorous wiles, thy throne and Empire sold.
See yon fierce Afghan,† with intemperate haste,
Gleams like a meteor through the palace waste,
Frowning, terrific, threatens with a grave
Thy progeny, O Timoor, good and brave;
Yet, not the treatment from the inhuman foe,
Not all my kingly state in dust laid low,
Can to this breast such torturing pain impart,
As does, O Nazir,‡ thy detested art:
But tho' too late, the day of reckoning come,
The tyrant whom thou serv'dst has seal'd thy doom,
Has hurled thee, rebel, headlong from the height
Of power abused, and done thy sovereign right:
Chaste partners of my bed, and joys serene,
Once my delight, but now how changed the scene!
Condemned with me in plaintive strains to mourn,
The scanty pittance from our offspring torn!
The viper, whom with fostering care I nurst,
Deep in my bosom plants his sting accurst;
Riots in blood, and heedless of his word,
Pants for the ruin of his sovereign lord.
Nobles ingrate,§ upheld by power and pride,
To whom our favours never were denied;
See to what misery and dire disgrace,
Your perfidy accursed, has brought a royal race:
Bright northern star from Cabul's realms advance,
Imperial Timoor || poize the avenging lance.
On these vile traitors quick destruction pour,
Redress my wrongs, and kingly rights restore;
Thee, too, O Sindiah, illustrious chief,
Who once didst promise to afford relief;
Thee I invoke, exert thy generous aid,
And o'er their heads high wave the avenging blade.
And ye, O faithful pillars of my State,
By friendship bound, and by my power elate,
Hasten, O Asuf,¶ and ye English chiefs,**
Nor blush to sooth an injured monarch's griefs;
But stay! my soul, unworthy rage disown;
Learn to sustain the loss of sight and throne;
Learn that imperial pride, and star-clad power,
Are but the fleeting pageants of an hour;
In the true crucible of dire distress,
Purged of alloy, thy sorrows soon shall cease;
What though the sun of empire and command,
Shorn of its beams, enlightens not the land!
Some happier day, a providential care
Again may renovate the falling star;
Again, O King, raise up thy illustrious race,
Cheer thy sad mind, and close thy days in peace!'"††

* I have thought the first six lines, which are merely introductory and cannot be accounted any part of [illegible]iginal, to be better calculated to give satisfaction to the reader, than an abrupt commencement of the elegy, as in the King's o[illegible]rds.

† Gholaum Caudir Khan.

‡ Munsoor Ali Khan, Superintendent of the Household.

§ The Mogul nobility, who abandoned the King on the approach of the rebels.

|| Timoor Shah, King of Cabul, on his father, the Abdallee's, last visit to Delhi, was married to a princess of the royal family, which gives his son, Zimaun Shah, a claim to the throne of Hindoostan.

¶ Asuf Al Dawla, Vizier of the Empire.

** It is much to be lamented, that the state of politics at Calcutta could not, at that time, admit of Government interfering on the occasion—for such was the influence of the British name, that had the detachment stationed at Anopshire, only marched out of their cantonments, the brutal tyrant would have desisted, and the King's misfortunes been averted.

†† It may not be amiss to remark that several MS copies of the above Elegy having been circulated throughout India, various readings may have occurred. The one here presented, was obtained by the author whilst at Delhi, and therefore, appeared to him the most authentic; but he thinks himself bound to acknowledge he has read a poetic version of the same Elegy, which appeared in the *European Magazine* for May 1797, said to be written by Captain Symes, from whose researches into the history and antiquities of the interesting Kingdom of Ava, the public may expect to derive much useful and instructive information.

CHAPTER III.

MR. CHARLES GRANT'S SCHEME FOR THE INTELLECTUAL, MORAL AND SOCIAL REGENERATION OF THE PEOPLE OF INDIA, AS PROPOUNDED IN HIS TREATISE, 1792–97. A. D. INTRODUCTION OF ENGLISH EDUCATION A MORAL DUTY OF THE STATE, AND NOT FRAUGHT WITH POLITICAL DANGER.

Mr. Grant's Scheme for the improvement of the Natives of India represents typical notions of early English philanthropists.

Even more interesting than the passages quoted in the preceding chapter, is Chapter IV., of Mr. Charles Grant's Treatise, under the heading : "*Inquiry into the Measures which might be adopted by Great Britain, for the Improvement of the condition of her Asiatic Subjects ; and Answers to Objections.*" I may quote the following passages from it as descriptive of the earliest ideas of British philanthropic statesmen regarding the introduction of English education in India. They are all the more valuable, as after the lapse of a century of British rule, they enable us to compare the past with the present state of the policy of English education in India, and they are deeply interesting, as furnishing the means of judging how far the anticipations of statesmen, in regard to the progress and effect of English education among the people of India, have been realized. Mr. Charles Grant begins the chapter with the following observations :—

"We now proceed to the main object of this work,—for the sake of which all the preceding topics and discussions have been brought forward,—an inquiry into the means of remedying disorders, which have become thus inveterate in the state of society among our Asiatic subjects, which destroy their happiness, and obstruct every species of improvement among them.

Healing principle.

"That it is in the highest degree desirable, that a healing principle should be introduced, no man, surely, will deny. Supposing it to be in our power to convince them of the criminality of the annual sacrifice of so many human victims on the funeral pile ; of the profession of robbery, comprehending murder ; of the indulgence of one class of people in the whole catalogue of flagitious crimes, without any adequate punishment ; of the forfeiture of the lives of others, according to their institutes, for the merest trifles ; of the arbitrary imposition of burthensome rites, devoid of all moral worth ; of the pursuit of revenge, by offerings to vindictive deities ; of the establishment of lying, false evidence, gaming, and other immoralities, by law ; of the pardon of capital offences for money ; of trying to purchase the expiation of wilful and habitual iniquity, by ceremonial observances ; and of the worship of stocks, stones, impure and malevolent deities ; no man living, surely, would affirm that we ought, that we are at liberty, to withhold from them this conviction.

Great Britain not bound to preserve the enormities in the Hindoo system.

"Are we bound for ever to preserve all the enormities in the Hindoo system ? Have we become the guardians of every monstrous principle and practice which it contains ? Are we pledged to support, for all generations, by the authority of our government and the power of our arms, the miseries which ignorance and knavery have so long entailed upon a large portion of the human race ? Is this the part which a free, a humane, and an enlightened nation, a nation itself professing principles diametrically opposite to those in question, has engaged to act towards its own subjects ? It would be too absurd and extravagant to maintain, that any engagement of this kind exists ; that Great Britain is under any obligation, direct or implied, to uphold errors and usages, gross and fundamental, subversive of the first principles of reason, morality, and religion.

Example of Mexico.

"If we had conquered such a Kingdom as Mexico, where a number of human victims were regularly offered every year upon the altar of the Sun, should we have calmly acquiesced in this horrid mode of butchery ? Yet, for near thirty years, we have, with perfect unconcern, seen rites in reality more cruel and atrocious, practised in our Indian territories. If human life must be sacrificed to superstition, at least the more useless, worthless, or unconnected members of the society might be devoted. But in Hindoostan, mothers of families are taken from the midst of their children, who have just lost their father also, and by a most diabolical complication of force and fraud, are driven into the flames.

No attempt made to recall the Hindoos to the dictates of Truth and Morality.

"Shall we be in all time to come, as we hitherto have been, passive spectators of this unnatural wickedness ? It may, indeed, well appear surprising that in the long period during which we have held those territories, we have made no serious attempt to recall the Hindoos to the dictates of Truth and Morality. This is a mortifying proof how little it has been considered, that the ends of government, and the good of society, have an inseparable connection with right principles. We have been satisfied with the apparent submissiveness of these people, and have attended chiefly to the maintenance of our authority over the country, and the augmentation of our commerce and revenues; but have never, with a view to the promotion of their happiness, looked thoroughly into their internal state.

No force but Reason to be employed.

"If, then, we ought to wish for the correction of those criminal habits and practices which prevail among them, it cannot reasonably be questioned, that we ought also to make allowable attempts for this end; and it remains, therefore, only to consider in what manner this design may be best pursued.

"Shall we resort to the power we possess, to destroy their distinctions of castes, and to demolish their idols? Assuredly, not. Force, instead of convincing them of their error, would fortify them in the persuasion of being right; and the use of it, even if it promised happier consequences, would still be altogether unjust.

"To the use of reason and argument, however, in exposing their errors, there can be no objection. There is, indeed, the strongest obligation to make those errors manifest, since they generate and tend to perpetuate all the miseries which have been set forth, and which our duty, as rulers, instead of permitting us to view with silent indifference, calls upon us by every proper method to prevent.

Knowledge should be communicated to Natives of India.

"The true cure of darkness, is the introduction of light. The Hindoos err, because they are ignorant; and their errors have never fairly been laid before them. The communication of our light and knowledge to them, would prove the best remedy for their disorders; and this remedy is proposed, from a full conviction, that if judiciously and patiently applied, it would have great and happy effects upon them: effects honourable and advantageous for us.

Whether through their own Languages, or through English?

"There are two ways of making this communication: the one is, by the medium of the languages of those countries; the other is, by the medium of our own. In general, when foreign teachers have proposed to instruct the inhabitants of any country, they have used the Vernacular tongue of that people, for a natural and necessary reason, that they could not hope to make any other means of communication intelligible to them. This is not our case in respect of our Eastern dependencies. They are our own, we have possessed them long; many Englishmen reside among the Natives, our language is not unknown there, and it is practicable to diffuse it more widely. The choice, therefore, of either mode, lies open to us; and we are at liberty to consider which is entitled to preference. Upon this subject, it is not intended to pass an exclusive decision here; the points absolutely to be contended for are, that we ought to impart our superior lights, and that this is practicable: that it is practicable by two ways, can never be an argument why neither should be attempted. Indeed, no great reason appears why either should be systematically interdicted, since particular cases may recommend, even that which is, in general, least eligible.

English Language the superior medium of instruction.

"The acquisition of a foreign language is, to men of cultivated minds, a matter of no great difficulty. English teachers could, therefore, be sooner qualified to offer instruction in the native languages, than the Indians would be prepared to receive it in ours. This method would hence come into operation more speedily than the other; and it would also be attended with the advantage of a more careful selection of the matter of instruction. But it would be far more confined and less effectual; it may be termed a species of deciphering. The decipherer is required to unfold, in intelligible words, what was before hidden. Upon every new occasion, he has a similar labour to perform, and the information obtained from him is limited to the single communication then made. All other writings, in the same character, still remain, to those who are ignorant of it, unknown; but if they are taught the character itself, they can at once read every writing in which it is used. Thus, superior in point of ultimate advantage does the employment of the English language appear; and upon this ground, we give a preference to that mode, proposing here, that the communication of our knowledge shall be made by the medium of our own language. This proposition will bring at once to trial, both the principle of such communication, and that mode of conveyance which can alone be questioned; for the admission of the principle must, at least, include in it the admission of the narrowest means suited to the end, which we conceive to be the native languages. The principle, however, and the mode, are still distinct questions, and any opinion which may be entertained of the latter cannot affect the former; but it is hoped, that what shall be offered here concerning them, will be found sufficient to justify both.

English Language should be taught to the Natives.

"We proceed, then, to observe, that it is perfectly in the power of this country, by degrees, to impart to the Hindoos our language; afterwards, through that medium, to make them acquainted with our easy literary compositions, upon a variety of subjects; and, let not the idea hastily excite derision, *progressively* with the simple elements of our arts, our philosophy, and religion. These acquisitions would silently undermine, and at length subvert, the fabrick of error; and all the objections that may be apprehended against such a change, are, it is confidently believed, capable of a solid answer.

"The first communication, and the instrument of introducing the rest, must be the English language; this is a key which will open to them a world of new ideas, and policy alone might have impelled us, long since, to put it into their hands.

"To introduce the language of the Conquerors, seems to be an obvious means of assimilating a conquered people to them. The Mahomedans from the beginning of their power, employed the Persian language in the affairs of government, and in the public departments. This practice aided them in maintaining their superiority, and enabled them, instead of depending blindly on native agents, to look into the conduct and details of public business, as well as to keep intelligible registers of the income and expenditure of the State. Natives readily learnt the language of Government, finding that it was necessary in every concern of Revenue and of Justice; they next became teachers of it; and in all the provinces over which the Mogul Empire extended, it is still understood and taught by numbers of Hindoos.

Example of Mahomedan Conquerors introducing Persian.

It would have been our interest to have followed their example; and had we done so, on the assumption of the *Dewannee*, or some years afterwards, the English language would now have been spoken and studied by multitudes of Hindoos throughout our provinces. The details of the revenue would, from the beginning, have been open to our inspection; and by facility of examination on our part, and difficulty of fabrication on that of the natives, manifold impositions of a gross nature, which have been practiced upon us, would have been precluded. An easy channel of communication also, would always have been open between the rulers and the subjects, and numberless grievances would have been represented, redressed, or prevented, which the ignorance of the former in the country languages, and the hinderances experienced by the latter in making their approaches, have sometimes suffered to pass with impunity, to the encouragement of new abuses. We were long held in the dark, both in India and in Europe, by the use of a technical Revenue language; and a man of considerable judgment, who was a member of the Bengal Administration near twenty years since, publicly animadverted on the absurdity of our submitting to employ the unknown jargon of a conquered people. It is certain, that the Hindoos would easily have conformed to the use of English; and they would still be glad to possess the language of their masters, the language which always gives weight and consequence to the Natives who have any acquaintance with it, and which would enable every Native to make his own representation directly to the Governor-General himself, who, it may be presumed, will not commonly, henceforth, be chosen from the line of the Company's servants; and therefore, may not speak the dialects of the country. Of what importance it might be to the public interest, that a man in that station should not be obliged to depend on a medium with which he is unacquainted, may readily be conceived.

Should have been followed by the British, with much benefit to Administration.

"It would be extremely easy for Government to establish, at a moderate expense, in various parts of the provinces, places of gratuitous instruction in reading and writing English; multitudes, especially of the young, would flock to them; and the easy books used in teaching, might at the same time convey obvious truths on different subjects. The teachers should be persons of knowledge, morals, and discretion; and men of this character could impart to their pupils much useful information in discourse: and to facilitate the attainment of that object, they might, at first, make some use of the Bengalese tongue. The Hindoos would, in time, become teachers of English themselves; and the employment of our language in public business, for which every political reason remains in full force, would, in the course of another generation, make it very general throughout the country. There is nothing wanting to the success of this plan, but the hearty patronage of Government. If they wish it to succeed, it can and must succeed. The introduction of English in the Administration of the Revenue, in Judicial proceedings, and in other business of Government, wherein Persian is now used; and the establishment of free schools, for instruction in this language, would insure its diffusion over the country, for the reason already suggested, that the interest of the Natives would induce them to acquire it. Neither would much confusion arise, even at first, upon such a change; for there are now a great number of Portuguese and Bengalese clerks in the provinces, who understand both the Hindoostanny and English languages. To employ them in drawing up petitions to Government, or its officers, would be no additional hardship upon the poorer people, who are now assisted in that way by Persian clerks; and the opportunity afforded to others who have sufficient leisure, of learning the language of the Government gratuitously, would be an advantage never enjoyed under Mahomedan Rulers.

Facility of imparting English Education gratuitously, to supplant Persian in Administration.

"With our language, much of our useful literature might, and would, in time, be communicated. The art of printing would enable us to disseminate our writings in a way the Persians never could have done, though their compositions had been as numerous as ours. Hence the Hindoos would see the great use we make of reason on all subjects, and in all affairs; they also would learn to reason, they would become acquainted with the history

Art of Printing great help to dissemination of English ideas.

of their own species, the past and present state of the world; their affections would gradually become interested by various engaging works, composed to recommend virtue, and to deter from vice; the general mass of their opinions would be rectified; and above all, they would see a better system of principles and morals. New views of duty, as rational creatures, would open upon them; and that mental bondage in which they have long been holden would gradually dissolve.

A true knowledge of Nature would break the fabrick of the Hindu Religion.

"To this change, the true knowledge of Nature would contribute; and some of our easy explanations of natural philosophy might undoubtedly, by proper means, be made intelligible to them. Except a few Brahmins, who consider the concealment of their learning as part of their religion, the people are totally misled as to the system and phenomena of Nature: and their errors in this branch of science, upon which divers important conclusions rest, may be more easily demonstrated to them, than the absurdity and falsehood of their mythological legends. From the demonstration of the true cause of eclipses, the story of *Ragoo* and *Ketoo*, the dragons, who when the sun and the moon are obscured, are supposed to be assaulting them, a story which has hitherto been an article of religious faith, productive of religious services among the Hindoos, would fall to the ground; the removal of one pillar, would weaken the fabrick of falsehood; the discovery of one palpable error, would open the mind to farther conviction; and the progessive discovery of truths hitherto unknown, would dissipate as many superstitious chimeras, the parents of false fears, and false hopes. Every branch of natural philosophy might in time be introduced and diffused among the Hindoos. Their understandings would thence be strengthened, as well as their minds informed, and error be dispelled in proportion.

And enlighten the Hindus by promoting mechanical inventions.

"But, perhaps, no acquisition in natural philosophy would so effectually enlighten the mass of the people, as the introduction of the principles of Mechanics, and their application to agriculture and the useful arts. Not that the Hindoos are wholly destitute of simple mechanical contrivances. Some manufactures, which depend upon patient attention and delicacy of hand, are carried to a considerable degree of perfection among them; but for a series of ages, perhaps for two thousand years, they do not appear to have made any considerable addition to the arts of life. Invention seems wholly torpid among them; in a few things, they have improved by their intercourse with Europeans, of whose immense superiority they are at length convinced; but this effect is partial, and not discernible in the bulk of the people. The scope for improvement, in this respect, is prodigious.

Improvement in Agriculture, &c., would ensue by introduction of machinery.

"What great accessions of wealth would Bengal derive from a people intelligent in the principles of agriculture, skilled to make the most of soils and seasons, to improve the existing modes of culture, of pasturage, of rearing cattle, of defence against excesses of drought, and of rain; and thus to meliorate the quality of all the produce of the country. All these arts are still in infancy. The husbandman of Bengal just turns up the soil with a diminutive plough, drawn by a couple of miserable cattle; and if drought parches, or the rain inundate the crop, he has no resource; he thinks he is destined to this suffering, and is far more likely to die from want, than to relieve himself by any new or extraordinary effort. Horticulture is also in its first stage: the various fruits and esculent herbs, with which Hindoostan abounds, are nearly in a state of nature; though they are planted in inclosed gardens, little skill is employed to reclaim them. In this respect, likewise, we might communicate information of material use to the comfort of life, and to the prevention of famine. In silk, indigo, sugar, and in many other articles, what vast improvements might be effected by the introduction of machinery. The skilful application of fire, of water, and of steam, improvements which would thus immediately concern the interest of the common people, would awaken them from their torpor, and give activity to their minds. At present, it is wonderful to see how entirely they resign themselves to precedent: *custom* is the strongest law to them. *Following implicitly*, seems to be instinctive with them, in small things as well as great. The path which the first passenger has marked over the soft soil, is trodden so undeviatingly in all its curves, by every succeeding traveller, that when it is perfectly beaten, it has still only the width of a single track.

Most important communication to the Hindus, through English, would be Christianity, supplanting Idolatory and Superstition.

"But, undoubtedly, the most important communication which the Hindoos could receive, through the medium of our language, would be the knowledge of our religion, the principles of which are explained in a clear, easy way, in various tracts circulating among us, and are completely contained in the inestimable volume of Scripture. Thence they would be instructed in the nature and perfections of the One True God, and in the real history of man: his creation, lapsed state, and the means of his recovery, on all which points they hold false and extravagant opinions; they would see a pure, complete, and perfect system of morals and of duty, enforced by the most awful sanctions, and recommended by the most interesting motives; they would learn the accountableness of man, the final judgment he is to undergo, and the Eternal state which is to follow. Wherever this knowledge should be recieved, Idolatry, with all the rabble of its impure deities, its monsters of wood and stone, its false principles and corrupt practices, its delusive hopes and vain fears, its ridiculous ceremonies and degrading superstitions, its lying legends and fraudulent impositions, would fall. The reasonable service of the only, and the infinitely perfect God, would be established: love to Him, peace and good-will towards men, would be felt as obligatory principles.

Though such effects would be gradual.

"It is not asserted, that such effects would be immediate or universal; but admitting them to be progressive, and partial only, yet how great would the change be, and how happy at length for the outward prosperity, and internal peace of society among the Hindoos! Men would be restored to the use of their reason; all the advantages of happy soil, climate, and situation, would be observed and improved; the comforts and conveniences of life would be increased; the cultivation of the mind, and rational intercourse, valued; the people would rise in the scale of human beings; and as they found their character, their state, and their comforts improved, they would prize more highly the security and the happiness of a well-ordered Society. Such a change would correct those sad disorders which have been described, and for which no other remedy has been proposed, nor is, in the nature of things, to be found."*

Objections to Mr. Grant's Scheme: the main objection being Political Danger.

Having thus propounded his scheme for regenerating India and ameliorating the intellectual, social, and moral condition of the inhabitants, Mr. Charles Grant has devoted a considerable portion of his treatise to the discussion and refutation of eight principal objections, urged on the opposite side by those who held different views as to the aims, objects, and principles of the British Rule in India. Of those objections, there is one which deserves especial mention here, as it is closely connected with the progress of English education in India, and has a direct bearing upon its effects, so far as shey have shown themselves in the propaganda of the political agitation in India, which has during recent years been carried on by the "*Indian National Congress.*" Put in its strongest and amplest terms, the objection was thus expressed: "If the English language, if English opinions, and improvements, are introduced in our Asiatic possessions, into Bengal, for instance; if Christianity, especially, is established in that quarter; and if, together with these changes, many Englishmen colonize there, will not the people learn to desire English liberty and the English form of Government, a share in the legislation of their own country, and commissions in the army maintained in that country? Will not the army thence become, in time, wholly provincial, officered by natives of India, without attachment to the Sovereign State? Will not the people at length come to think it a hardship to be subject, and to pay tribute, to a foreign country? And finally, will they not cast off that subjection, and assert their independence?"†

This question is discussed at considerable length by the author,‡ and he ends his discussion upon the subject with the following observations, in regard to the introduction of the English language as the medium of instruction to the people of India:—

English Language should be introduced, and failing that, Indian Languages may be adopted as the medium of instruction.

"In coming, as we now do, to the close of the answer to the last and most material of the objections which are foreseen against the proposed scheme, that objection which questions the expediency of using the English language, it will be proper to call to recollection what was stated in the first opening of it,—that the *principle* of communicating our light and knowledge, and the *channel* or *mode* of communication, were two distinct things; that the admission of the former did not depend on the choice which might be made of the latter, and was alone absolutely contended for. The channel of the English language, however, has been preferred, in the present plan, as being deemed the most ample and effectual; and though new, also safe and highly advantageous. Against this channel, however, the writer thinks it possible, that reluctancies may remain when arguments are obviated. Strongly as he is himself persuaded, that great and peculiar advantages would flow from it, he nevertheless would do injustice to the cause for which he pleads, if he were to suspend its success entirely upon the adoption of this mode. The channel of the country languages, though less spacious, less clear, less calculated to transmit the general light of our opinions, our arts and sciences, attempt, also for the conveyance of the light of religion itself, is nevertheless so far capable of rendering this last and most important service, in which are essentially involved all the other proposed meliorations, that if the question were between making no attempt, or making it in this way, undoubtedly, there could be no hesitation. This mode ought by no means to be declined or neglected, if there were no other. Through the medium of the country languages, though more contracted, more

* Printed Parliamentary Papers relating to the Affairs of India: *General*, Appendix 1; *Public* (1832), pp. 59-62.

† *Ib.*, p. 72.

‡ The remarks of Mr. Charles Grant are so interesting and instructive, that they have been extracted *verbatim*, and printed in a later part of this work.

dim and distant, still something may be done, and that in a concern which is of the last importance to present and to future happiness. But in choosing this method, more instruments ought necessarily to be employed; and then the meliorations which are so much wanted, may in time be partly effected; and the apprehensions which some may entertain from the diffusion of the English language, will have no place. But still it must be maintained, that for every great purpose of the proposed scheme, the introduction and use of that language would be most effectual; and the exclusion of it, the loss of unspeakable benefits, and a just subject of extreme regret."*

Mr. Grant's Summary of his Thesis, and conclusions in regard to introduction of English Education in India.

In summing up his treatise, as to the means of improving the intellectual, moral, and social condition of the people of India, Mr. Charles Grant has made certain observations as the concluding portion of his thesis. Those observations are highly interesting, as showing the early policy of the scheme for spreading English education in India, and what was at that time expected from it. The passages may be quoted here, as they are not easily accessible, being in an old Parliamentary Blue-book, printed so long ago as 1832. They deserve perusal, both owing to their intrinsic worth and historical importance, in narrating the early phases of the policy of English education in India. After stating his reasons, the author observes :—

Improvement of India can be effected by the introduction of the English Language, and Christianity,

"Thus, we trust, it has been evinced, that although many excellent improvements have of late years been made in the Government of our Indian territories, the moral character and condition of the Natives of them is extremely depraved, and that the state of society among that people is, in consequence, wretched. These evils have been shown to lie beyond the reach of our regulations, merely, political, however good; they have been traced to their civil and religious institutions; they have been proved to inhere in the general spirit and many positive enactments of their laws; and more powerfully still in the false, corrupt, impure, extravagant, and ridiculous principles and tenets of their religion. Upon any of these points, it is conceived, that persons who either form their opinion, from actual observation, or from the current of testimony, will not greatly differ; shades of distinction there may be between them, but no substantial, radical contrariety. A remedy has been proposed for these evils;—the introduction of our light and knowledge among that benighted people, especially the pure, salutary, wise principles of our divine religion. That remedy has appeared to be, in its nature, suitable and adequate; the practicability also of applying it, has been sufficiently established; our obligation to impart it has been argued, we would hope, convincingly, from the past effects of our administration in those countries, from the more imperious consideration of the duties we owe to the people of them as our subjects, and from our own evident interest, as involved and consulted in their welfare. Our obligation has been, likewise, urged from another argument, the authority and command of that true religion which we have ourselves the happiness to enjoy and profess.† As the leading subject of this Essay has been intentionally treated, chiefly upon political grounds, the argument now mentioned has not been insisted upon at great length; but all its just rights are claimed for it, and it is transcendent and conclusive.

From which no political danger should be anticipated.

"Nothing, it would seem, besides these intrinsic properties of the proposed measure, and these powerful extraneous motives, can be necessary to recommend the adoption of it. Yet since some persons have appeared to think, that the improvement which they allow to be likely from the prosecution of the suggested scheme, might, by producing a course of increasing prosperity, at length, open the way to consequences unfavourable to the stability of our Indian possessions; these conceived consequences have also been largely examined; and if the whole of the reasoning used by the writer has not been erroneous, they have been found to resolve themselves, at last, into mere apprehensions, conjectures, and general surmises, which the causes assigned for them seem so little to warrant, that in proportion to the degree in which those causes may actually exist, effects propitious to the permanence, as well as prosperity of our Eastern Dominion, effects more propitious than our present system can generate, may rather be expected from them; as indeed, it would not be less a phenomenon in the political than in the natural world, that from a root the most excellent, the worst fruit should be produced. The principle also upon which such consequences are objected, and the improvement of our Heathen subjects opposed; the principle of keeping them for ever in darkness and error, lest our interest should suffer by a change, has been shown to be utterly inadmissible in a moral view, as it is likewise contrary to all just policy.

* Printed Parliamentary Papers relating to the Affairs of India: *General*, Appendix I; *Public* (1832), pp. 85, 6.

† To disallow either the fitness of our religion as a remedy, or our obligation to promote the knowledge of it, would be to differ from the reasoning of this Essay, in first principles; and such a difference, if any mind were influenced by it to resist the projected communication, ought, in candour, to be avowed.

And no reasons to the contrary have been shown.

"In reasoning about things future and contingent, the writer would wish to stand remote from whatever should have the appearance of dogmatical decision, which, indeed, is not the right of even superior penetration, and to speak with that diffidence of himself, and deference for others, which so well become him; he would wish to speak for no cause further than the truth will bear him out; but the views he entertains of the present subject, afford him no other conclusions than those he has advanced, and in them he thinks he is well supported. That a great remedy is wanted; that we have an excellent one in our hands; that it is our duty, on general and special grounds, to apply it; all these are, in his apprehension, positions nearly self-evident: from these alone a strong presumption, he conceives, arises, that it must be our interest to make the application; and if cogent, specific reasons are further adduced, to prove that our interest would, in fact, thus be promoted: opposition to this scheme ought, in his opinion, to be justified by arguments very clear and very powerful; and such, he must honestly say, he has not been able to discover.

It would be odious and immoral to keep India ignorant, owing to apprehended risks to British Rule.

"This subject has not hitherto received a formal consideration; but the objection which would resist all improvement, lest future inconvenience should arise from it, necessarily brings on this decisive question, whether we shall, in all time to come, passively leave our subjects in the darkness, error, and moral turpitude in which they now grovel, or shall communicate to them the light of Truth, and the means of melioration, and of happiness, personal and social? The question may more properly be,—Whether we should *keep* our subjects in their present state? For if improvement ought not to be communicated to them, we should not be merely passive, but be careful to exclude it; as, on the other hand, if it ought to be communicated; or if it is possible that any rays of light may fortuitously break in upon them, we should not leave the task to others, or to chance, but be ourselves the dispensers of the new principles they receive, and regulate the administration of them. This question then is to determine the grand moral and political principle, by which we shall henceforth, and in all future generations, govern and deal with our Asiatic subjects. Whether we shall make it our study to impart to them knowledge, light, and happiness; or, under the notion of holding them more quietly in subjection, shall seek to keep them ignorant, corrupt, and mutually injurious, as they are now? The question is not, whether we shall resort to any persecution, to any compulsion, to any sinister means. No; the idea has been frequently disclaimed; it is an odious idea, abhorrent from the spirit of true religion; but whether, knowing as we do the falsehood and impiety of idolatrous polytheistic superstitions; knowing the cruelties, the immoralities, the degrading extravagancies and impositions of the Hindoo system, we shall silently and calmly leave them in all the fulness of their operation, without telling our subjects, who ought to be our children, that they are wrong, that they are deluded, and hence plunged into many miseries? Whether, instead of rationally, mildly explaining to them the divine principles of moral and religious truth, which have raised us in the scale of being, and are the foundation of all real goodness and happiness, we shall wink at the stupidity which we deem profitable to us; and as governors, be in effect, the conservators of that system which deceives the people? Whether, in a word, we shall do all this merely from fear, lest in emerging from ignorance and error, they should be less easy to rule, and our dominion over them be exposed to any risk.

"The wisdom, as well as the fairness of such a proceeding, must also be determined; whether, on the whole, it would be the best policy for our own interest, even if we look only to the natural operation of things: and here, at least, we should be careful and clear; for if we mistake our interest, we lose our all, the very thing to which we sacrifice other considerations: especially, it should be pondered, whether, believing the moral government of the world, we can expect the approbation and continued support of the Supreme Ruler of it, by willingly acquiescing in so much error, so much moral and political evil, when so many just means for the alleviation of them are in our power.

Imparting Knowledge and Moral Instruction a strict duty of the British to India.

"These are the inquiries which this subject presents; the inquiries which fidelity to it, and to all the interests involved in it, would not permit the writer to suppress when be originally considered it; and the same motives, to which he may add, the duty of the station wherein he has since had the honour to be placed, forbid him to keep them back now. But does he, in stating them, mean to point them offensively to any individual or body of men? No,—far from it; they were, at first, penned, as they are now delivered, in good will and with a general aim; in this great question he strives rather to abstract his mind from personal recollections; and if it glances involuntarily at the idea of any one who he fears may not accord with his sentiments, if he should especially dread to find among such any whom he particularly respects and loves, it is a painful wound to his feelings. He cannot wish to offend or to dispute,—he has no objects to serve by such means; and is sufficiently aware of the situation in which a work of this nature may place him, both in Europe and in India, never to have brought it forward, but from some serious sense of duty. This question is a general one; if it seem to carry in it any retrospective censure, that censure applies to the country and to the age. Circumstances have now called for a more particular consideration of it, and of the result of that consideration he entertains encouraging hopes. He will not allow himself to believe, that when so many noble and beneficial ends may be served by our possession of an Empire in the East, we shall content ourselves with the meanest and the least, and for the sake of this, frustrate all the rest. He trusts we shall dare to do justice, liberal justice, and be persuaded, that this principle will carry us to greater heights of prosperity, than the precautions of a selfish policy. Future events are inscrutable to the keenest speculation, but the path of duty is open, the time present is ours. By planting our language, our knowledge, our opinions, and our religion, in our Asiatic territories, we shall put a great work beyond the reach of contingencies; we shall probably have wedded the inhabitants of those territories to this country; but, at any rate, we shall have done an act of strict duty to them, and a lasting service to mankind.

"In considering the affairs of the world, as under the control of the Supreme Disposer, and those distant territories, as by strange events, providentially put into our hands, is it not reasonable, is it not necessary, to conclude that they were given to us, not merely that we might draw an annual profit from them, but that we might diffuse among their inhabitants, long sunk in darkness, vice and misery, the light and the benign influences of Truth, the blessings of well-regulated society, the improvements and the comforts of active industry? And that, in prudently and sincerely endeavouring to answer these ends, we may not only humbly hope for some measure of the same success, which has usually attended serious and rational attempts for the propagation of that pure and sublime religion which comes from God, but best secure the protection of his providential government, of which we now see such awful marks in the events of the world.

Extension of British Commerce will ensue from the enlightenment of India.

"In every progressive step of this work, we shall also serve the original design with which we visited India, that design still so important to this country—the extension of our commerce. Why is it that so few of our manufactures and commodities are vended there? Not merely because the taste of the people is not generally formed to the use of them, but because they have not the means of purchasing them. The proposed improvements would introduce both. As it is, our woollens, our manufactures in iron, copper, and steel; our clocks, watches, and toys of different kinds; our glass-ware, and various other articles are admired there, and would sell in great quantities if the people were rich enough to buy them. Let invention be once awakened among them, let them be roused to improvements at home, let them be led by industry to multiply, as they may exceedingly, the exchangeable productions of their country; let them acquire a relish for the ingenious exertions of the human mind in Europe, for the beauties and refinements, endlessly diversified, of European art and science, and we shall hence obtain for ourselves the supply of four-and-twenty millions of distant subjects. How greatly will our country be thus aided in rising still superior to all her difficulties; and how stable, as well as unrivalled, may we hope our commerce will be, when we thus rear it on right principles, and make it the means of their extension! It might be too sanguine to form into a wish, an idea most pleasing and desirable in itself, that our religion and our knowledge might be diffused over other dark portions of the globe, where Nature has been more kind than human institutions. This is the noblest species of conquest, and wherever, we may venture to say, our principles and language are introduced, our commerce will follow.

"To rest in the present state of things, or to determine that the situation of our Asiatic subjects, and our connection with them, are such as they ought to be for all time to come, seems too daring a conclusion; and if a change, a great change, be necessary, no reason can be assigned for its commencement, at any future period, which will not equally, nay, more strongly, recommend its commencement now. To say, that things may be left to their own course, or that our European Settlements may prove a sufficient nursery of moral and religious instruction for the Natives, will be, in effect, to declare, that there shall be no alteration: at least no effectual and safe one.

Mahomedans, though for centuries intermixed with the Hindus, produced no radical change in their character.

"The Mahomedans, living for centuries intermixed in great numbers with the Hindoos, produced no radical change in their character; not merely because they rendered themselves disagreeable to their subjects, but because they left those subjects, during that whole period, as uninstructed in essential points as they found them. We are called rather to imitate the Roman Conquerors, who civilized and improved the nations whom they subdued; and we are called to this, not only by the obvious wisdom which directed their policy, but by local circumstances, as well as by sounder principles and higher motives than they possessed.

For similar reasons, the Portuguese, the Dutch, and the French failed to produce a permanent effect upon India.

"The examples also of modern European Nations pass in review before us. We are the fourth of those who have possessed an Indian Empire. That of the Portuguese, though acquired by romantic bravery, was unsystematic and rapacious; the short one of the French was the meteor of a vain ambition; the Dutch acted upon the principles of a selfish commercial policy; and these, under which they apparently flourished for a time, have been the cause of their decline and fall. None of these nations sought to establish themselves in the affections of their acquired subjects, or to assimilate them to their manners; and those subjects, far from supporting them, rejoiced in their defeat; some attempts they made to instruct the Natives, which had their use, but sordid views overwhelmed their effects. It remains for us to show how we shall be distinguished from these nations in the history of mankind; whether conquest shall have been in our hands the means, not merely of displaying a Government unequalled in India for administrative justice, kindness, and moderation; not merely of increasing the security of the subject and prosperity of the country, but of advancing social happiness, of meliorating the moral state of men, and of extending a superior light, further than the Roman Eagle ever flew.

Novelty of the Educational Scheme no valid objection against its introduction.

"If the novelty, the impracticability, the danger of the proposed scheme, be urged against it, these objections cannot all be consistent; and the last, which is the only one that could have weight, pre-supposes success. In success would lie our safety, not our danger. Our danger must lie in pursuing, from ungenerous ends, a course contracted and illiberal; but in following an opposite course, in communicating light, knowledge, and improvement, we shall obey the dictates of duty, of philanthropy, and of policy; we shall take the most rational means to remove inherent, great disorders, to attach the Hindoo people to ourselves, to ensure the safety of our possessions, to enhance continually their value to us, to raise a fair and durable monument to the glory of this country, and to increase the happiness of the human race." *

CHAPTER IV.

EARLY EFFORTS FOR THE EDUCATION OF THE NATIVES OF INDIA. THE CALCUTTA MADRASSA FOUNDED IN 1781, AND THE SANSKRIT COLLEGE AT BENARES, IN 1791. LORD MINTO'S MINUTE ON EDUCATION, 1811.

Mr. Fisher's Memoir on Education in India: written in 1827–32.

Whilst opinions and sentiments, such as those of Mr. Charles Grant, quoted in the preceding chapter, were being entertained and discussed by philanthropic British Statesmen of the more advanced type, in their deliberations respecting the future moral and intellectual progress of the Natives of India, it is important to consider what had actually been done by the Government of the East India Company in regard to the spread of Education in India. Upon this part of the subject full and valuable information is contained in an elaborate *Memoir*, dated, 7th February, 1827, with a Supplement, dated 23rd February, 1832, prepared under official orders, by Mr. Thomas Fisher, who then held the office of "*Searcher of the Records*," at the East India House, in London. This Memoir has been printed † as an Appendix to the Parliamentary Papers of 1832, and I will borrow extracts from it for the present purposes, as it is the most authoritative source of information available.

Calcutta Madrassa founded in 1781.

"*The Calcutta Madrissa, or Mahomedan College*, was founded at the request of several Mahomedans of distinction, in the year 1781, by the Governor-General, Warren Hastings, Esquire, who provided a building for it, at his own expense, amounting to Rs. 57,745, but which was afterwards charged to the Company. The Bengal Government, also, at the recommendation of Mr. Hastings, assigned lands of the estimated value of Rs. 29,000 per annum, for the support of the Institution. The original intention of the Founder appears to have been, to promote the study of the Arabic and Persian languages, and of the Mahomedan Law, with a view, more especially, to the production of well-qualified officers for the Courts of Justice. In 1785, the lands which had been granted for its support were regularly assigned by *Sunnud*, to be held during the pleasure of Government, to Mahomed Maiz-oo-deen, who had been appointed Superior, or Guardian of the Institution, and to his successors. In this officer was vested the immediate management of all the affairs of the Madrissa, and the administration of its revenues. He was directed to deliver in to the Committee of Revenue, monthly statements of the number of students actually maintained on the establishment, with their names and salaries. A Member of the Committee of Revenue was authorized and enjoined, once in every three months or oftener, to visit the Madrissa, in order to see that the building was kept in

* Printed Parliamentary Papers relating to the Affairs of India: *General*, Appendix I; *Public* (1832), pp. 86–89.

† *Ib.*, pp. 395–483.

proper repair, and that, in all other respects, the efficiency of the Institution was maintained. The *Naib Nasim*, or principal officer of the Native Courts of Law, was also instructed that, whenever vacancies should arise in the *Foujdarry* courts, they should be filled from the students of the Madrissa, upon the production of certificates from the Superior, that the individuals nominated by him were duly qualified for their respective appointments."*

Reforms in 1788–91, and subjects of study prescribed.

In 1788 and 1791 certain reforms were introduced, as to the management and working of the College, and the control of the Institution was placed in the hands of a Committee, and the following were the principal subjects prescribed for study:—Natural Philosophy, Theology, Law, Astronomy, Geometry, Arithmetic, Logic, Rhetoric, Oratory and Grammar. Subsequently, reforms and changes in the management of the Institution continued, but it is needless to enter into the details, beyond saying that the English language was not introduced as one of the subjects of study, although considerable sums of money were spent upon the Madrissa,—the amount appropriated for its expenses, from its foundation in 1781 to the end of the year 1824, being no less than Rs. 12,20,479.†

Benares Sanskrit College founded in 1791, and the subjects of study prescribed.

The Hindoo Sanskrit College at Benares was projected by Mr. Jonathan Duncan, the Resident at Benares, in 1791, as a means of employing, beneficially for the country, some part of a surplus which the public revenues yielded over their estimated amount. The expense for the first year was limited to Rs. 14,000—but in the following year it was augmented to Rs. 20,000. The object of this Institution was the preservation and cultivation of the Laws, Literature, and Religion of the Hindoos (and more particularly of their laws) in their sacred city; a measure which it was conceived would be equally advantageous to the Natives, and honourable to the British Government among them. The internal discipline was to be in all respects conformable to the *Dharma Shastra*, in the Chapter on Education, and the prescribed course of studies in the College comprehended Theology and Ritual, Medicine, including Botany, &c., Music, Mechanics, Arts, Grammar, Prosody, and Sacred Lexicography, Mathematics, Metaphysics, Logic, Law, History, Ethics, Philosophy and Poetry.

Changes and reforms were made from time to time in this Institution, and a considerable amount of money was spent upon it, the pecuniary aid given by Government, from its foundation in the year 1791 to the end of the year 1824, being no less than Rs. 6,74,000.‡

Lord Minto's Minute on Education, dated 6th March, 1811.

On the 6th of March, 1811, Lord Minto, the then Governor-General, wrote a Minute § on the subject of Education in India, and, as it forms an important document connected with the early policy of the British Rule in regard to Education, some significant passages may be quoted from it, as showing the beneficent spirit which then prevailed in the Counsels of Government. The Governor-General observed:—

Decay of Learning in India.

"It is a common remark, that science and literature are in a progressive state of decay among the Natives of India. From every inquiry which I have been enabled to make on this interesting subject, that remark appears to me but too well founded. The number of the learned is not only diminished, but the circle of learning, even among those who still devote themselves to it, appears to be considerably contracted. The abstract sciences are abandoned, polite literature neglected, and no branch of learning cultivated but what is connected with the peculiar religious doctrines of the people. The immediate consequence of this state of things is, the disuse, and even actual loss, of many valuable books; and it is to be apprehended, that unless Government interpose with a fostering hand, the rivival of Letters may shortly become hopeless, from a want of books, or of persons capable of explaining them.

And its Causes,—Want of Patronage.

"The principle cause of the present neglected state of Literature in India is to be traced to the want of that encouragement which was formerly afforded to it by Princes, Chieftains, and opulent individuals under the Native Government. Such encouragement must always operate as a strong incentive to study and literary exertions, but especially in India, where the learned professions have little, if any, other support. The justness of these observations might be illustrated by a detailed consideration of the former and present state of Science and Literature at the three principal seats of Hindoo learning, *viz.*, Benares, Tirhoot, and Nuddea. Such a review would bring before us the liberal patronage which was formerly bestowed, not only by Princes, and others in power and authority, but also by the Zemindars, on persons who had distinguished themselves by the successful cultivation of Letters at those places. It would equally bring to our view the present neglected state of learning at those once-celebrated places; and we should have to remark with regret that the cultivation of letters was now confined to the few surviving persons who had been patronized by the Native Princes and others, under the former Govern-

* Printed Parliamentary Papers relating to the Affairs of India: *General*, Appendix I; *Public* (1832), pp. 396, 397.

† *Ib.*, pp. 398, 399. ‡ *Ib.*, pp. 399–401. § *Ib.*, p. 484.

ments, or to such of the immediate descendants of those persons as had imbibed a love of science from their parents.

"It is seriously to be lamented that a nation particularly distinguished for its love, and successful cultivation of Letters in other parts of the Empire, should have failed to extend its fostering care to the Literature of the Hindoos, and to aid in opening to the learned in Europe the repositories of that literature.

Ignorance of the Natives of India obstructs good Government, and is conducive to crime.

"It is not, however, the credit alone of the national character which is affected by the present neglected state of learning in the East. The ignorance of the Natives in the different classes of society, arising from the want of proper education, is generally acknowledged. This defect not only excludes them as individuals from the enjoyment of all those comforts and benefits which the cultivation of letters is naturally calculated to afford, but operating, as it does, throughout almost the whole mass of the population, tends materially to obstruct the measures adopted for their better Government. Little doubt can be entertained that the prevalence of the crimes of perjury and forgery, so frequently noticed in the Official Reports, is in a great measure ascribable, both in the Mahomedans and Hindus, to the want of due instruction in the moral and religious tenets of their respective faiths. It has been even suggested, and apparently not without foundation, that to this uncultivated state of the minds of the Natives is in a great degree to be ascribed the prevalence of those crimes which were recently so great a scourge to the country.

Which can be remedied by Education.

"The latter offences against the peace and happiness of Society have, indeed, for the present, been materially checked by the vigilance and energy of the police, but it is probably only by the more general diffusion of knowledge among the great body of the people, that the seeds of these evils can be effectually destroyed." *

Observations as to Revival of Learning among the Mahomedans, in Lord Minto's Minute of 1811.

The Goveronr-General's Minute, after suggesting the principles of a scheme for promoting and maintaining learning among the Hindus, contains the following observations in regard to Mahomedans in particular :—

"It will be observed that, in the foregoing remarks, I have confined myself almost exclusively to the plan necessary to be adopted for the restoration of Hindu science and literature. Considerations similar to those which have weighed with me in recommending that plan, would naturally induce me to propose similar arrangements for the revival of Letters among our Mahomedan subjects, and the more general diffusion of knowledge among that part of the community. With the difference only in the population of Hindus and Mahomedans, all the arguments which have been above stated in support of the arrangements proposed to be adopted for the propagation of knowledge among the former, would equally apply to similar institutions for the benefit of the Mahomedans. A sentiment of deference, however, for the Honourable Court of Directors restrains me from recommending any extension of the plan until their orders shall have been received on the subject generally of this Minute. I deem it, therefore, sufficient to add, on the present occasion, that Mahomedan Colleges might be beneficially established at Bhaugulpore, Jounpore (where Persian and Arabic literature formerly flourished), and at some place in the Ceded and Conquered Provinces; and that it might be advisable to reform the Madrissa, or Mahomedan Collegiate Institution at Calcutta, on the principles recommended with respect to the Hindu Colleges." †

* Printed Parliamentary Papers relating to the Affairs of India: *General*, Appendix I; *Public* (1832), p. 484.

† *Ib.*, p. 485.

CHAPTER V.

FIRST LEGISLATIVE PROVISION FOR PUBLIC INSTRUCTION IN INDIA. ACT OF PARLIAMENT, 53 GEO. III., C. 155. DESPATCH OF THE COURT OF DIRECTORS, DATED 3RD JUNE, 1814, ON EDUCATION. EARLY EDUCATIONAL EFFORTS OF THE MISSIONARIES. LORD MOIRA'S EDUCATIONAL MINUTE OF 2ND OCTOBER, 1815.

Public instruction not yet recognized as part of a settled State Policy.

It will be observed, from the narrative contained in the preceding chapter, that, whilst during the thirty years from the foundation of the Calcutta Madrassa, in 1781, down to the time when Lord Minto recorded his Minute of 6th March, 1811, individuals of high official rank in the Administration of India were not altogether oblivious of the moral duty and administrative necessity of spreading knowledge among the people of India, no systematic effort was made to place the education of the Natives upon a firm and organized footing, as a part of the State Policy. There was indeed, a vast and powerful section of Anglo-Indian Administrators, who were far from conceding that Public Instruction should either be undertaken by the State, or, was free from serious political dangers to the security of British dominion in India. The only effect yet given to the policy of educating the Natives of India consisted in the foundation of the Calcutta Madrassa by Warren Hastings, in 1781, and of the Sanskrit College at Benares, by Mr. Jonathan Duncan, in 1791. But both these Institutions were, on the one hand, purely Oriental in their course of studies (as has been described in the preceding chapter), and on the other hand, their main object was to provide a regular supply of qualified Hindu and Mahomedan law-officers for the judicial administration. The proposals contained in Lord Minto's Minute of 6th March, 1811, in regard to the establishment of Hindu Colleges, in Nuddea and Tirhoot, proceed upon principles similar to those of the Sanskrit College at Benares; but those proposals seem to have remained in abeyance for some years, as will be shown hereafter, and finally, they took the form of the establishment of a Hindu Sanskrit College at Calcutta.

Inquiry by Parliament into Indian affairs, and renewal of the E. I. Company's Charter, by Act 53, Geo. III, c.155, in 1813.

Meanwhile, important events were taking place in England in regard to the renewal of the East India Company's Charter by the British Parliament, and since they have an important bearing upon the general advancement of India, and mark an epoch in the history of the educational policy of the British rule in India, a short account of the transactions of that period will not be out of place here. As early as the year 1808, while the House of Commons appointed a Select Committee to enquire into the state of affairs of the East India Company, Mr. Dundas, on the part of the Board of Control and the Crown, suggested to the Directors the propriety of endeavouring, without delay, to come to an understanding on the subject of a new Charter, in order that it might be submitted to the early consideration of Parliament. Negotiations between the Government and the Directors of the Company ended in failure, and "on the 22nd of March, 1813, Lord Castlereagh submitted to the House of Commons a series of thirteen resolutions, containing the leading provisions, which it was proposed to embody in an Act renewing the Company's Charter. Most of the questions discussed were then novel, and both the dangers apprehended by the one party, and the expectations entertained by the other, made it necessary for the Legislature to proceed with the utmost caution. Information was sought from all quarters, and whole volumes of evidence were taken from those who were supposed most competent to give it. In the debates which afterwards ensued, there were few speakers of eminence in either house who did not deliver their sentiments, and deem them of so much importance as to justify the subsequent revisal and publication of their speeches. So great, however, has been the progress of Political Economy as a science, and so strong the light which has been thrown upon it by experience, since this famous debate, that many of the propositions most elaborately argued, are now regarded as truisms, and much of the alarm sounded is felt to be mere exaggeration. The result is, therefore, the only thing which now possesses much historical interest, and nothing more is necessary here than to give a very brief analysis of the most important sections of the Act, 53 Geo. III, c. 155, which, while essentially modifying and curtailing the privileges formerly possessed by the Company, renewed their Charter for another period of twenty years, to be computed from the 10th day of April 1814." *

* Beveridge's *History of India* Vol. III., pp. 3, 4.

Statutory recognition of the Policy of Education in India.

It is not necessary for the present purposes to give an account of the various provisions of the Act relating to the administration and trade of India, but it is desirable to describe the provisions of the Act, so far as they related to the education of India, as they mark the first definite step taken by the State in this direction, in the shape of legislative affirmation of the educational policy of the British Rule in India—a policy which till then was far from being founded on a sound and stable basis. A passage from Mr. Beveridge's History of India (vol. III, p. 5) may be quoted here as containing the requisite information. Speaking of the provisions of the Act 53, Geo. III, c. 155, which was passed in 1813, he goes on to say:—

Lord Castlereagh's Resolution recognizing the duty of Great Britain to educate the Natives of India, passed by Parliament in 1813.

"The above provisions for opening and regulating the trade with India constitute the main features in the Act, but there were others not of a commercial nature which met with strenuous opposition, and were denounced by many as dangerous in the extreme, if not absolutely incompatible with the existence of the British power in India. After reading the earnest and virulent declamation directed against the 13th Resolution proposed by Lord Castlereagh, one is surprised, and at the same time relieved, on finding that, both as it was originally expressed and as it now stands embodied in the 43rd Section of the Act, it pledged the Legislature to nothing more than the following simple proposition: That 'it is the duty of this country to promote the interest and happiness of the native inhabitants of the British dominions in India, and such measures ought to be adopted as may tend to the introduction among them of useful knowledge, and of religious and moral improvement; and in furtherance of the above objects, sufficient facilities ought to be afforded by law to persons desirous of going to and remaining in India, for the purpose of accomplishing those benevolent designs, so as the authority of the Local Governments, respecting the intercourse of Europeans with the interior of the country, be preserved, and the principles of the British Government, on which the natives of India have hitherto relied for the free exercise of their religion, be inviolably maintained.' In order to give effect to this declaration, the Section proceeds to enact, that 'persons desirous of going to and remaining in India for the above purposes,' or 'for other lawful purposes,' should apply for permission to the Court of Directors, who should either grant it, or, in the event of refusal, transmit the application, within one month of the receipt of it, to the Board of Control, who were empowered finally to dispose of it. All persons obtaining permission, whether from the Court or from the Board, were to be furnished by the Directors with certificates, entitling them, 'so long as they shall properly conduct themselves, to the countenance and protection of the several Governments of the said Company in the East Indies, and parts aforesaid, in their respective pursuits, subject to all such provisions and restrictions as are now in force, or may hereafter be judged necessary with regard to persons residing in India.' The only pecuniary provision made in connection with this Section, was the allotment of a sum of not less than £10,000 annually, for the 'revival and improvement of literature, and the encouragement of the learned natives of India, and for the introduction and promotion of a knowledge of the sciences among the inhabitants of the British territories in India.' Such a sum, paltry as it was, was not permitted to do the good which might have been expected from it, and instead of being employed in instructing the Natives generally, continued for many years to be partly paid away to learned Mahomedans and Hindus, for explaining and inculcating their respective dogmas, and partly allowed to accumulate, as if expenditure for native education were impracticable or useless.*"

Section 43, Statute 53, Geo. III., C. 155, quoted as marking a new epoch.

The abovementioned Section, 43, of the Act of Parliament, St. 53 Geo. III., Chap. 155, may be said to represent the beginning of a new epoch in the history of public education in India, and, being the first legislative enactment in that behalf, possesses historical value and interest, as indicating, in formal language, the early policy of public instruction as part of the administration of the British Rule. The Section runs in the following words:—

"And be it further enacted, that it shall be lawful for the Governor-General in Council to direct that out of any surplus which may remain of the rents, revenues, and profits arising from the said territorial acquisitions, after defraying the expenses of the military, civil, and commercial establishments, and paying the interest of the debt, in manner hereinafter provided, a sum of not less than one *lac* of rupees in each year shall be set apart and applied to the revival and improvement of Literature, and the encouragement of the learned natives of India, and for the introduction and promotion of a knowledge of the sciences among the inhabitants of the British territories in India; and that any schools, public lectures, or other institutions, for the purposes aforesaid, which shall be founded at the Presidencies of Fort William, Fort St. George, or Bombay, or in any other parts of the British territories in India, in virtue of this Act, shall be governed by such Regulations as may from time to time be made by the said

* Beveridge's History of India, Vol. III., pp. 4, 5.

Governor-General in Council; subject, nevertheless, to such powers as are herein vested in the said Board of Commissioners for the Affairs of India, respecting colleges and seminaries; provided always, that all appointments to offices in such schools, lectureships, and other institutions, shall be made by or under the authority of the Governments within which the same shall be situated."

The first Despatch of the Court of Directors to the Governor-General, dated 3rd June, 1814, conveying directions on the subject of education.

In a letter dated the 6th September, 1813, the Court of Directors called the attention of the Governor-General in Council to the above Section of the new Act of Parliament, and promised to take an early opportunity of communicating their instructions as to the mode in which "the wise and liberal intention of the Legislature in this respect should be accomplished." Accordingly, on the 3rd June, 1814, they despatched a letter to the Governor-General in Council upon the subject. That letter appears to be the *first* Official Despatch addressed by the Court of Directors to the authorities in India, on the subject of education, and possesses much historical interest, as showing the earliest beginning of the State policy in regard to the nature of the measures which might be adopted for the education of the people of India. Some passages from the letter may be quoted here with advantage:—

Directions as to the mode of giving effect to Sec. 43, of Statute 53, Geo. III., C. 155.

"In our letter of the 6th September last, in the Public Department, we directed your attention generally to the 43rd Clause in the Act of the 53rd of the King, by which our Governor-General in Council is empowered to direct that a sum of not less than one *lac* of rupees, out of any surplus revenues that may remain, shall be annually applied to the revival and improvement of Literature, and the encouragement of the learned natives of India. We purpose in this Despatch to convey to you our sentiments as to the mode in which it will be advisable you should proceed, and the measures it may be proper you should adopt with reference to that subject. In the consideration of it, we have kept in view those peculiar circumstances of our political relation with India which, having necessarily transferred all power and preëminence from Native to European Agency, have rendered it incumbent upon us, from motives of policy as well as from a principle of justice, to consult the feelings, and even to yield to the prejudices, of the Natives, whenever it can be done with safety to our dominions.

Two objects of the Clause in the Act of Parliament,—cannot be gained by establishing Colleges.

"The clause presents two distinct propositions for consideration: *First*, the encouragement of the learned Natives of India, and the revival and improvement of Literature; *secondly*, the promotion of a knowledge of the sciences amongst the inhabitants of that country. Neither of these objects, is, we apprehend, to be obtained through the medium of public Colleges, if established under the rules, and upon a plan similar to those that have been founded at our Universities, because the Natives of caste and of reputation will not submit to the subordination and discipline of a College; and we doubt whether it would be practicable to devise any specific plan which would promise the successful accomplishment of the objects under consideration. We are inclined to think that the mode by which the learned Hindoos might be disposed to concur with us in prosecuting those objects, would be by our leaving them to the practice of an usage, long established amongst them, of giving instruction at their own houses, and by our encouraging them in the exercise and cultivation of their talents, by the stimulus of honorary marks of distinction, and in some instances by grants of pecuniary assistance.

Political aspect of Education with respect to the feelings of the Natives as to the sanctity of Benares.

"In a political point of view, considerable advantages might, we conceive, be made to flow from the measure proposed, if it should be conducted with due attention to the usages and habits of the Natives. They are known to attach a notion of sanctity to the soil, the buildings, and other objects of devout resort, and particularly to that at Benares, which is regarded as the central point of their religious worship, and as the great repository of their learning. The possession of this venerated city, to which every class and rank of the Hindoos is occasionally attracted, has placed in the hands of the British Government a powerful instrument of connexion and conciliation, especially with the Mahrattas, who are more strongly attached than any other to the supposed sanctity of Benares. Deeply impressed with these sentiments, we desire that your attention may be directed in an especial manner to Benares, and that you call upon your public representatives there to report to you what ancient establishments are still existing for the diffusion of knowledge in that city; what branches of science and literature are taught there; by what means the professors and teachers are supported; and in what way their present establishments might be improved to most advantage. In the pursuit of this information they will have opportunities of obtaining a knowledge of individual characters, which may enable them to point out to your notice those natives with whom it might be desirable you should consult, and through whose instrumentality the liberal intentions of the Legislature might most advantageously be advanced..

Sanskrit Learning to be encouraged.

"We are informed that there are in the Sanscrit language many excellent systems of ethics, with Codes of Laws and compendiums of the duties relating to every class of the people, the study of which might be useful to those natives who may be destined for the Judicial Department of Government. There are also many tracts of merit, we are told, on the virtues of plants and drugs, and on the application of them in medicine, the knowledge of which might prove desirable to the European practitioner; and there are treatises on Astronomy and Mathematics, including Geometry and Algebra, which, though they may not add new lights to European science, might be made to form links of communication between the natives and the gentlemen in our service, who are attached to the Observatory and to the Department of Engineers, and by such intercourse the Natives might gradually be led to adopt the modern improvements in those and other sciences. With a view to these several objects, we have determined that due encouragement should be given to such of our servants, in any of those departments, as may be disposed to apply themselves to the study of the Sanskrit language, and we desire that the teachers, who may be employed under your authority for this purpose, may be selected from those amongst the Natives who may have made some proficiency in the sciences in question, and that their recompense should be liberal.

"We encourage ourselves to hope, that a foundation may in this way be laid for giving full effect in the course of time to the liberal intentions of the Legislature, and we shall consider the money that may be allotted to this service as beneficially employed, if it should prove the means, by an improved intercourse of the Europeans with the Natives, to produce those reciprocal feelings of regard and respect which are essential to the permanent interests of the British Empire in India." *

Three noticeable points in the Despatch of the Court of Directors, dated 3rd June, 1814.

Such were the earliest instructions issued by the Court of Directors to the authorities in India on the subject of education. They represent the embryonic or infantile stage of the policy of spreading Education and enlightenment among the people of India. Three important points are, however, noticeable in them: *First*, that they are confined to the promotion of Sanskrit learning among the Hindus; *secondly*, that they entirely ignore the interests of the Mahomedan Community, and of their learning and sciences, contained in Arabic and Persian works; and, *thirdly*, that they do not afford the least indication of any intention to introduce a knowledge of the English language, literature, and sciences among the people of India.

Omission to act upon the Charter of 1813.

At the time when the Despatch arrived, the Government of India was engaged in the war with Nepal, and subsequently in tranquilising Central India, and the expense and financial embarrassments entailed by these measures, prevented immediate attention being paid to the views of the Court of Directors in regard to education, and the Indian Government, during this period, seems to have had no settled policy or even intention on the subject of education.

Missionary movement in behalf of education.

"About this time a new stimulus began to be applied to the cause of education in India, of a nature which has been steadily increasing in power from that day to this; which is growing, and of which it is impossible to foresee the result. It would unreasonably prolong this Note to attempt to give any history of Missionary enterprise in this country, except in so far as it bears upon educational progress, but the alliance of the two had been celebrated in 1813, and the fruits of the alliance were now to appear. Towards the end of 1799, two Baptist Missionaries, Marshman and Ward, of small means and humble origin, landed in Calcutta, with the intention of joining Mr. Carey, who had been deputed thither by the same Society about six years previously. Being provided with no license from the East India Company, and fearful of being sent back to England, they settled themselves in the small Danish Settlement of Serampur. Their professed object was conversion, and if, ridicule † in England or discouragement in India could have thwarted them, their efforts would have been short-lived. Not that the Governor-General personally was inclined to treat them with rigour. On the contrary, Lord Wellesley appointed Mr. Carey Sanscrit Professor in the newly-established College of Fort William, and generally seems to have held an even balance between the section represented by Mr. Charles Grant and Sir John Shore on the one hand, and the anti-educational party on the other. In 1807, however, the little colony had a narrow escape. Certain addresses to the Hindus and Mussalmans, published at Serampore, and marked by more fervour than discretion, attracted the attention of Lord Minto's Government, and an order was passed that the Press, and those who maintained it, should be removed to surveillance at Calcutta. The order was withdrawn at the instance of the Danish Government, and on the receipt of a temperate and respectful memorial from the missionaries, who regretted the publications complained

* Printed Parliamentary Papers relating to the Affairs of India: *General*, Appendix I; *Public* (1832), pp. 486, 487.

† See *Edinburgh Review*—"*Indian Missions*," 1808.

of, and promised to issue no more of a similar character. But the warning was unmistakeable, and the proceedings of the Government were approved by the Court of Directors, in a despatch (dated 7th September, 1808) which contains their first declaration of strict religious neutrality, and of the refusal to add the influence of authority to any attempt made to propagate the Christian religion. From that date until the renewal of the Charter in 1813, the Mission was contemptuously tolerated by the local authorities; but its labours were incessant, it continued the Printing Press, and edited a series of Vernacular works for educational purposes, and by 1815, it had established no less than 20 schools in the neighbourhood of Calcutta, containing about 800 native children. The Calcutta Benevolent Institution, founded in 1809, for the instruction of poor Christian and other children, still remains as a monument of the Mission's exertions.

Lord Moira's Educational Minute of 2nd October, 1815.

"On his return from the North-Western Provinces, Lord Moira issued, on the 2nd October, 1815, a Minute declaring his solicitude for the moral and intellectual condition of the Natives, and his anxiety to see established and maintained some system of public education. He thought that the humble but valuable class of village schoolmasters claimed the first place in the discussion, and that the efforts of Government should be directed to the improvement of existing tuition, and to the diffusion of it to places and persons now out of its reach. The Minute was followed by a direct application to the Court of Directors for permission to encourage schools formed on principles altogether different from the Oriental Institutions, which alone, up to that date, had enjoyed the regular support of Government. In November, 1815, Lord Moira visited the little colony at Serampore, a step worth recording, as the first kind of direct encouragement, which Missionary effort in behalf of education had received from a Governor-General of India."*

CHAPTER VI.

ORIGIN OF ENGLISH EDUCATION.—THE "*VIDYALAYA*" OR ANGLO-INDIAN COLLEGE FOUNDED BY HINDUS OF CALCUTTA IN 1816.—RAJA RAM MOHUN ROY'S ADVOCACY OF ENGLISH EDUCATION.—COMMITTEE OF PUBLIC INSTRUCTION ESTABLISHED IN CALCUTTA IN 1823.—ITS PROCEEDINGS UP TO THE END OF 1831.

Apathy of the Indian Government towards English Education, and zeal of the advanced Hindus who founded the "*Vidyalaya*," or Anglo-Indian College at Calcutta in 1816.

The subject of Education seems to have been regarded with much apathy by the authorities in India at the time when the Court of Directors sent their first Eductional Despatch of 1814, and no significant measures seem to have been adopted for some years to fulfil the intentions of the Act of Parliament abovementioned. The more advanced section of the Hindu community, however, seem to have been alive to the expediency and benefit of introducing a knowledge of the English literature and sciences among their countrymen, and in the year 1816 some of the native gentlemen of Calcutta, possessing wealth, intelligence, and public spirit, associated together and subscribed a capital sum of Rs. 113,179, to found a Seminary for the instruction of the sons of Hindus in the European and Asiatic languages and sciences. The institution was called the *Vidyalaya* or Anglo-Indian College, and represents the first effort made by the natives of India themselves, for the education of their children in the English language and literature. The origin of the institution is extremely interesting, and may be described in the words of Rev. A. Duff, D.D., in his evidence before a Select Committee of the House of Lords, on the 3rd June, 1853. He said:—

Origin of English Education in India. Mr. David Hare and Raja Ram Mohun Roy.

"English Education was in a manner forced upon the British Government; it did not itself spontaneously originate it. The system of English Education commenced in the following very simple way in Bengal. There were two persons who had to do with it, one was Mr. David Hare, and the other was a Native, Ram Mohun Roy. In the year

* *Education in British India, prior to* 1854. By Arther Howell, Esquire, pp. 8, 9.

1815, they were in consultation one evening with a few friends, as to what should be done with a view to the elevation of the native mind and character. Ram Mohun Roy's proposition was that they should establish an Assembly, or Convocation, in which, what are called the higher or purer dogmas of Vedantism or ancient Hinduism, might be taught; in short, the Pantheism of the *Vedas*, or their *Upanishads*, but what Ram Mohun Roy delighted to call by the more genial title of Monotheism. Mr. David Hare was a watch-maker in Calcutta, an ordinary illiterate man himself; but being a man of great energy and strong practical sense, he said the plan should be to institute an English School, or College, for the instruction of native youth. Accordingly, he soon drew up, and issued a circular on the subject, which gradually attracted the attention of the leading Europeans, and among others, of the Chief Justice, Sir Hyde East. Being led to consider the proposed measure, he entered heartily into it, and got a meeting of European gentlemen assembled in May 1816. He invited also some of the influential Natives to attend. Then it was unanimously agreed that they should commence an institution for the teaching of English to the children of the higher classes, to be designated 'The Hindu College of Calcutta.' A large Joint Committee of Europeans and Natives was appointed to carry the design into effect. In the beginning of 1817 the College, or rather school, was opened; and it was the very first English Seminary in Bengal, or even in India, as far as I know. In the Joint Committee there was a preponderance of Natives; and partly from their inexperience and inaptitude, and partly from their absurd prejudices, and jealousies, it was not very well managed nor very successful. Indeed, had it not been for the untiring perseverance of Mr. Hare, it would have soon come to an end. The number of pupils enrolled at its first opening was but small, not exceeding 20; and even, all along, for the subsequent five or six years, the number did not rise above 60 or 70. Then it was, when they were well nigh in a state of total wreck, and most of the Europeans had retired from the management in disgust, that Mr. Hare and a few others resolved to apply to the Government for help, as the only means of saving the sinking Institution from irretrievable ruin. The Government, when thus appealed to, did come forward and proffer its aid, upon certain reasonable terms and conditions; and it was in this way that the British Government was first brought into active participation in the cause of English Education."*

Popularity and success of the "*Vidyalaya*," or Indian College.

The Institution grew in popularity, and soon claimed superiority over any other Seminary (such as Missionary Schools, &c.) affording instruction to the Natives in the English language. The Report of 1825 gives a still more favourable view of the general character of the Institution, the benefits of which the most respectable classes of the native community of Calcutta had evinced a disposition to secure to their children, by sending them to pay for their education,—a state of things ascribed principally to "the diffusion of liberal ideas, and to the confidence felt by the parents of the pupils to the present system of management." The number of scholars was stated at 200, and it was added that, so long as such a number, all respectably connected, "can be trained in useful knowledge and the English language, a great improvement may be confidently anticipated in the intellectual character of the principal inhabitants of Calcutta."† The reports of 1827 and 1828 state that "The studies in this Institution were natural and experimental philosophy, chemistry, mathematics, algebra, Tytler's Elements of General History, Russell's Modern Europe, with Milton and Shakespeare; that the progress of the students had been satisfactory; that it had increased gradually, and was in the year 1828, greater than in any preceding year"—the number of students having gradually risen to 436.‡

An advanced Hindu, Joynarain Ghossal, founds an English School at Benares, in 1818.

Nor was Calcutta the only place where the Hindus evinced their desire to advance English Education among their countrymen. "When the Governor-General visited the Upper Provinces in 1814, Joynarain Ghossal, an inhabitant of Benares, presented a petition to his Lordship, with proposals for establishing a school in the neighbourhood of that city, and requesting that Government would receive in deposit the sum of Rs. 20,000, the legal interest of which, together with the revenue arising from certain lands, he wished to be appropriated to the expense of the Institution. The design meeting with the approbation of Government, Joynarain Ghossal was acquainted therewith. Accordingly, in July 1818, he founded his school, appointing to the management thereof, the Rev. D. Corrie, Corresponding Member of the Calcutta Church Missionary Society, and a member of their Committee, and at the same time constituting the members of that Committee trustees."§ In this school the English, Persian, Hindustani and Bengali languages were taught, and in April 1825, the son of the founder enhanced the endowment by a donation of Rs. 20,000.

* Printed Parliamentary Papers (1852-53): *Second* Report of the Select Committee of the House of Lords on Indian Territories, pp. 48, 49.

† Printed Parliamentary Papers relating to the Affairs of India: *General*, Appendix 1; *Public* (1832), p. 410.

‡ *Ib.*, p. 437. § *Ib.*, p. 404.

Inactivity of the Mahomedans as to English Education. The Calcutta School-book Society formed in 1817.

Thus whilst the Hindus were showing readiness, zeal, and generosity towards the spread of English Education among their countrymen, even at such an early period, the Mahomedans seem to have remained completely dormant, and indeed, took up a hostile attitude towards the progress of English education among them, as will be shown later on. Among other efforts which were made on behalf of education was the foundation of the *Calcutta School-book Society.* "This institution had its origin in the year 1817, and was formed with a view to the promotion of the moral and intellectual improvement of the Natives, by the diffusion among them of useful elementary knowledge. The plan of the Society carefully excludes all means calculated to excite religious controversy; and its affairs are conducted by a Committee composed of English gentlemen, Mahomedans, and Hindus, in about equal proportions. In May, 1821, the Society, having at that time put into circulation 126,446 copies of various useful works, found its finances in so low a state as to render it necessary to seek assistance from the Government, which assistance was immediately granted, to the extent of Rs. 7,000. An annual grant of Rs. 6,000, in aid of the Institution, was also ordered, accompanied by the most unreserved expression of the Government's satisfaction with the plan and object of the Society, and with the mode in which its affairs appeared to have been conducted." *

The Calcutta Sanskrit College founded by Government at the suggestion of Mr. H. H. Wilson, in 1821.

The most significant measure adopted by Government at that period was the foundation of the Calcutta Hindu Sanskrit College, in lieu of the two Colleges in Nuddea and Tirhoot, which had been projected in Lord Minto's Minute of 1811, from which passages have already been quoted in this work. "On the 21st of August, 1821, the Governor-General in Council having taken into consideration the state of the projected Institutions for the advancement of Hindu Literature in Nuddea and Tirhoot, the failure of which appearing to admit of no doubt, it was considered that the Government was relieved from the pledge given in 1811, for the establishment of those institutions. A communication from Mr. H. H. Wilson, a member of the Benares Committee, was at the same time brought upon record, containing several reasons for abandoning the design of forming Colleges in Nuddea and Tirhoot, and suggesting instead thereof, the foundation at the Presidency of a similar Institution to that of Benares, but upon a larger scale. The necessity for European Superintendence, the facility with which it might be obtained in Calcutta, the accessibility of that city to all parts of India, together with several other reasons suggested by Mr. Wilson, determined the Governor-General in Council to adopt the measure proposed by that gentleman, and establish in Calcutta a Hindu College similar to that at Benares, under a Committee of Superintendence." †

Committee of Public Instruction appointed at Calcutta in 1823.

During this period the subject of education appears to have engaged special attention of the Government, and active measures were adopted to place public instruction upon an organized footing as a part of the state administration. "On the 17th July 1823, the Governor-General in Council took into consideration a Note or Memorandum, on the subject of Education and of the improvement of the morals of the Natives of India, which had been prepared and submitted to them by Mr. Holt Mackenzie, their Secretary in the Territorial Department, and which is recorded on the proceedings of that date. In pursuance of suggestions contained in the paper abovementioned, the Bengal Government resolved to form a General Committee of Public Instruction at the Presidency, for the purpose of ascertaining the state of education in the territories under the Bengal Presidency, and of the public institutions, designed for its promotion, and of 'considering, and from time to time submitting to Government the suggestion of such measures as it might appear expedient to adopt with a view to the better instruction of the people, to the introduction among them of useful knowledge, and to the improvement of their moral character.'" ‡ The annual sum of one *lac* of rupees, which by the Act of Parliament, 53, Geo. III, C. 155, was appropriated to the purposes of education, was placed at the disposal of the Committee, which from this period must be regarded as the sole organ of the Government in everything that concerns public instruction.

Most significant Protest by enlightened Hindus, through Raja Ram Mohun Roy, in 1823, against expenditure of Money on Sanskrit Learning instead of English Education.

Soon after the Committee had entered upon its deliberations, a most significant event occurred, which, on the one hand, throws light upon the condition of advancement and enlightenment at which some of the more prominent Hindus of Bengal had arrived, in regard to their desire to acquire a knowledge of English literature and sciences, and, on the other hand, shows the comparative apathy of the Government towards the introduction of the English language and literature among the people of India. Just as the Hindus of Calcutta were foremost in founding

* Printed Parliamentary Papers relating to the Affairs of India: *General*, Appendix 1; *Public* (1832), p. 405.

† *Ib.*, p. 406. ‡ *Ib.*, p. 408.

the *Vidyalaya*, or Anglo-Indian College, in 1816, for educating their sons in the English language, literature and sciences, so they were now foremost in protesting against the measures which the Government was then adopting to devote further funds to the promotion of Sanskrit learning in the Sanskrit College at Calcutta. "In December 1823, (Raja) Ram Mohun Roy addressed the Governor-General, in the name of his countrymen, expressing an opinion adverse to the supposed object of the British Government, in the foundation of this College in Calcutta, which he considered as calculated only to perpetuate a species of literature, which was, in his judgment, and that of those whom he represented, utterly worthless, and recommending, instead thereof, the employment of Europeans of character to instruct the Natives of India in mathematics, natural philosophy, chemistry, anatomy, and those other useful sciences, which the nations of Europe had carried to a pitch of perfection, that had raised them above the inhabitants of other parts of the world. (Raja) Ram Mohun Roy particularly adverted to that period in the history of Great Britain, when Lord Bacon is considered, as having by his writings, set aside the legendary lore of the dark ages, and introduced true science in its stead."*

Bishop Heber's opinion of Raja Ram Mohun Roy.

Raja Ram Mohun Roy was a distinguished patriot, having the improvement of his countrymen sincerely at heart, and was sufficiently well acquainted, both with Oriental and European literature, to be able to form a correct opinion of their relative value. Speaking of him, and of his address to Lord Amherst, against Oriental studies, Bishop Heber, in a letter to Sir Wilmot Harton, dated March, 1824, published in the Appendix, to his *Journal*, said: "Ram Mohun Roy, a learned Native, who has sometimes been called, though, I fear, without reason, a Christian, remonstrated against this system last year, in a paper which he sent me to be put into Lord Amherst's hands, and which, for its good English, good sense, and forcible arguments, is a real curiosity, as coming from an Asiatic." The Memorial fully deserves the eulogium bestowed on it by Bishop Heber, and, as it is an important document, throwing light upon the mode of thought and educational aims, it may be quoted here with advantage, *in extenso*.

The Memorial runs thus:—

"To His Excellency the Right Honourable Lord Amherst, Governor-General in Council.

"MY LORD,

Raja Ram Mohun Roy's Memorial, in favour of English Education, presented to Lord Amherst in 1823.

Humbly reluctant as the natives of India are to obtrude upon the notice of Government the sentiments they entertain on any public measure, there are circumstances when silence would be carrying this respectful feeling to culpable excess. The present rulers of India, coming from a distance of many thousand miles, to govern a people whose language, literature, manners, customs, and ideas, are almost entirely new and strange to them, cannot easily become so intimately acquainted with their real circumstances as the natives of the country are themselves. We should, therefore, be guilty of a gross dereliction of duty to ourselves, and afford our rulers just ground of complaint at our apathy, did we omit, on occasions of importance like the present, to supply them with such accurate information as might enable them to devise and adopt measures calculated to be beneficial to the country, and thus second, by our local knowledge and experience, their declared benevolent intentions for its improvements.

"The establishment of a new Sanskrit School in Calcutta evinces the laudable desire of Government to improve the natives of India by education,—a blessing for which they must ever be grateful; and every well-wisher of the human race must be desirous that the efforts made to promote it should be guided by the most enlightened principles, so that the stream of intelligence may flow in the most useful channels.

"When this seminary of learning was proposed, we understood that the Government in England had ordered a considerable sum of money to be annually devoted to the instruction of its Indian subjects. We were filled with sanguine hopes that this sum would be laid out in employing European gentlemen of talents and education to instruct the natives of India in mathematics, natural philosophy, chemistry, anatomy, and other useful sciences, which the nations of Europe have carried to a degree of perfection that has raised them above the inhabitants of other parts of the world.

"While we looked forward with pleasing hope to the dawn of knowledge thus promised to the rising generation, our hearts were filled with mingled feelings of delight and gratitude; we already offered up thanks to Providence for inspiring the most generous and enlightened nations of the West with the glorious ambition of planting in Asia the arts and sciences of modern Europe.

"We find that the Government are establishing a Sanskrit School under Hindu Pundits, to impart such knowledge as is already current in India. This seminary (similar in character to those which existed in Europe

* Printed Parliamentary Papers relating to the Affairs of India: *General*, Appedix 1; *Public* (1832), p. 436.

before the time of Lord Bacon) can only be expected to load the minds of youth with grammatical niceties and metaphysical distinctions, of little or no practical use to the possessors or to Society. The pupils will there acquire what was known two thousand years ago, with the addition of vain and empty subtilties since produced by speculative men, such as is already commonly taught in all parts of India.

"The Sanskrit language, so difficult that almost a lifetime is necessary for its acquisition, is well-known to have been for ages a lamentable check on the diffusion of knowledge; and the learning concealed under this almost impervious veil, is far from sufficient to reward the labour of acquiring it. But if it were thought necessary to perpetuate this language for the sake of the portion of valuable information it contains, this might be much more easily accomplished by other means than the establishment of a new Sanskrit College; for there have been always, and are now, numerous professors of Sanskrit in the different parts of the country, engaged in teaching this language as well as the other branches of literature which are to be the object of the new Seminary. Therefore, their more diligent cultivation, if desirable, would be effectually promoted by holding out premiums, and granting certain allowances to their most eminent professors, who have already undertaken, on their own account, to teach them, and would by such rewards be stimulated to still greater exertions.

"From these considerations, as the sum set apart for the instruction of the natives of India was intended by the Government in England for the improvement of its Indian subjects, I beg leave to state, with due deference to your Lordship's exalted situation, that if the plan now adopted be followed, it will completely defeat the object proposed; since no improvement can be expected from inducing young men to consume a dozen of years of the most valuable period of their lives in acquiring the niceties of *Byakaran*, or Sanskrit grammar. For instance, in learning to discuss such points as the following: *khad*, signifying to eat, *khaduti*, he, or she, or it eats; query, whether does *khaduti*, taken as a whole, convey the meaning he, she, or it eats, or are separate parts of this meaning conveyed by distinctions of the words? As if, in the English language, it were asked, how much meaning is there in the *eat*, how much in the *s*? and is the whole meaning of the word conveyed by these two portions of it distinctly, or by them taken jointly?

"Neither can much improvement arise from such speculations as the following, which are the themes suggested by the *Vedant*:—In what manner is the soul absorbed into the Deity? What relation does it bear to the divine essence? Nor will youths be fitted to be better members of Society by the Vedantic doctrines, which teach them to believe that all visible things have no real existence; that as father, brother, &c., have no actual entity, they consequently deserve no real affection, and, therefore, the sooner we escape from them, and leave the world, the better. Again, no essential benefit can be derived by the student of the *Mimangsa*, from knowing what it is that makes the killer of a goat sinless on pronouncing certain passages of the *Vedant*, and what is the real nature and operative influence of passages of the *Vedas*, &c.

"The student of the *Nyayushastra* cannot be said to have improved his mind after he has learned from it into how many ideal classes the objects in the Universe are divided, and what speculative relation the soul bears to the body, the body to the soul, the eye to the ear, &c.

"In order to enable your Lordship to appreciate the utility of encouraging such imaginary learning as above characterized, I beg your Lordship will be pleased to compare the state of science and literature in Europe before the time of Lord Bacan with the progress of knowledge made since he wrote.

"If it had been intended to keep the British nation in ignorance of real knowledge, the Baconian philosophy would not have been allowed to displace the system of the school-men, which was the best calculated to perpetuate ignorance. In the same manner the Sanskrit system of education would be the best calculated to keep this country in darkness, if such had been the policy of the British Legislature. But as the improvement of the native population is the object of the Government, it will consequently promote a more liberal and enlightened system of instruction; embracing mathematics, natural philosophy, chemistry, anatomy, with other useful sciences, which may be accomplished with the sum proposed, by employing a few gentlemen of talents and learning, educated in Europe, and providing a College furnished with the necessary books, instruments, and other apparatus.

"In representing this subject to your Lordship, I conceive myself discharging a solemn duty which I owe to my countrymen, and also to that enlightened sovereign and legislature which have extended their benevolent care to this distant land, actuated by a desire to improve its inhabitants, and, therefore, humbly trust you will excuse the liberty I have taken in thus expressing my sentiments to your Lordship.

"I have the honour, &c.,

(Signed) RAM MOHUN ROY."*

* Trevelyan, on the Education of the People of India, pp. 65–71.

The Memorial disregarded by Government.

The Government of Bengal regarded this letter as having been penned under a somewhat erroneous impression respecting the views of Government in the establishment of the Sanskrit College, but forwarded the letter to the Committee of Public Instruction for their information. The fate it met with may be conjectured from the spirit which then animated that body. The Memorial remained unanswered, and the design of founding a new Sanskrit College was carried into execution.

Views of the Court of Directors as to the nature of the studies, in their Despatch of 18th February, 1824.

The question as to the nature of the studies to be encouraged in India, appears to have been the subject of consideration by the Court of Directors, on an occasion when the Bengal Government had reported certain measures adopted by it for the reform of the existing Oriental Colleges, and the establishment of the new Sanskrit College, at Calcutta. The Despatch* of the Court of Directors to the Bengal Government, dated the 18th February, 1824, contains observations, as follows :—

Useful knowledge to be encouraged.

"The ends proposed in the institution of the Hindoo College, and the same may be affirmed of the Mahomedan, were two: the first, to make a favourable impression, by our encouragement of their literature, upon the minds of the Natives; and the second, to promote useful learning. You acknowledge that if the plan has had any effect of the former kind, it has had none of the latter; and you add, that 'it must be feared that the discredit attaching to such a failure has gone far to destroy the influence which the liberality of the endowment would otherwise have had.'

"We have from time to time been assured that these Colleges, though they had not till then been useful, were, in consequence of proposed arrangements, just about to become so; and we have received from you a similar prediction on the present occasion.

"We are by no means sanguine in our expectation that the slight reforms which you have proposed to introduce will be followed by much improvement; and we agree with you in certain doubts, whether a greater degree of activity, even if it were produced, on the part of the masters, would, in present circumstances, be attended with the most desirable results.

Oriental sciences useless.

"With respect to the sciences, it is worse than a waste of time to employ persons either to teach or to learn them, in the state in which they are found in the Oriental books. As far as any historical documents may be found in the Oriental languages, what is desirable is, that they should be translated, and this, it is evident, will best be accomplished by Europeans, who have acquired the requisite knowledge. Beyond these branches, what remains in Oriental literature is poetry, but it has never been thought necessary to establish Colleges for the cultivation of poetry; nor is it certain that this would be the most effectual expedient for the attainment of the end. In the meantime, we wish you to be fully apprized of our zeal for the progress and improvement of education among the Natives of India, and of our willingness to make considerable sacrifices to that important end, if proper means for the attainment of it could be pointed out to us. But we apprehend that the plan of the institutions, to the improvement of which our attention is now directed, was originally and fundamentally erroneous. The great end should not have been to teach Hindoo learning, or Mahomedan learning, but useful learning. No doubt, in teaching useful learning to the Hindoos or Mahomedans, Hindoo *media* or Mahomedan *media*, as far as they were found most effectual, would have been proper to be employed, and Hindoo and Mahomedan prejudices would have needed to be consulted, while every thing which was useful in Hindoo or Mahomedan literature, it would have been proper to retain; nor would there have been any insuperable difficulty in introducing, under these reservations, a system of instruction, from which great advantage might have been derived. In professing, on the other hand, to establish seminaries for the purpose of teaching mere Hindoo, or mere Mahomedan literature, you bound yourselves to teach a great deal of what was frivolous, not a little of what was purely mischievous, and a small remainder, indeed, in which utility was in any way concerned. We think that you have taken, upon the whole, a rational view of what is best to be done. In the institutions which exist on a particular footing, alterations should not be introduced more rapidly than a due regard to existing interests and feelings will dictate, at the same time, that incessant endeavours should be used to supersede what is useless or worse, in the present course of study, by what your better knowledge will recommend."†

The letter of the Court of Directors, from which these extracts have been taken, was communicated by the Bengal Government to the Committee of Public Instruction, who in reply, submitted some observations, which may be quoted here, as showing the views then entertained by them in regard to the principles and nature

* The Despatch is said to have been drafted by Mr. James Mill, the philosophical historian of British India, who was then employed in the India Office.

† Printed Parliamentary Papers relating to the Affairs of India: *General*, Appendix 1; *Public* (1832), p 436, also at p. 488.

of the education entrusted to their supervision and control. They defend their views in a letter,* dated the 18th August, 1824, addressed to Lord Amherst, Governor-General in Council. They observe :—

Observations on the above Despatch by the Committee of Public Instruction, in their letter to Government, dated 18th August, 1824.

"In the first place, without denying that the object of introducing European literature and science may have been somewhat too long overlooked, it may be questioned whether the Government could originally have founded any other seminaries than those which it actually established, *viz.*, the Madressa, to teach Mahomedan literature and law, and the Benares College, to teach Sanscrit literature and Hindoo law. Those Colleges were founded for Mahomedans and Hindoos, respectively, and would have been of little value to either, if they had proposed to teach what neither were disposed to learn. It may be added—What else had the Government to offer on any extensive scale? What means existed of communicating anything but Mahomedan and Hindoo literature, either by teachers or books? It was, therefore, a case of necessity; and almost all that the Government, in instituting a seminary for the higher classes, could give, or the people would accept, through such a channel, was Oriental literature, Mahomedan or Hindoo. Instruction in the English language and literature could have been attempted only on the most limited scale, and as they could not, we apprehand, have been at all introduced into seminaries designed for the general instruction of the educated and influential classes of the Natives, the success of the attempt may well be doubted. * * * * * * * * * *

"In proposing the improvement of men's minds, it is first necessary to secure their conviction that such improvement is desirable. Now, however satisfied we may feel that the Native subjects of this Government stand in need of improved instruction, yet every one in the habit of communicating with both the learned and unlearned classes, must be well aware that they continue to hold European literature and science in very slight estimation. A knowledge of English, for the purpose of gaining a livelihood is, to a certain extent, a popular attainment; and a few of the Natives employed by Europeans, accustomed to an intimate intercourse with their masters, may perceive that their countrymen have something in the way of practical science to learn. These impressions, however, are still very partial, and the Maulavi and Pundit, satisfied with his own learning, is little inquisitive as to anything beyond it, and is not disposed to regard the literature and science of the West as worth the labour of attainment. As long as this is the case, and we cannot anticipate the very near extinction of such prejudice, any attempt to enforce an acknowledgment of the superiority of intellectual produce amongst the Natives of the West, could only create dissatisfaction, and would deter those whose improvement it is most important to promote, as the best means of securing a more general amelioration, the members of the literary classes, from availing themselves of the beneficence of the Government, by placing themselves within the reach of instruction.

* * * * * * * * * * *

"Without wishing to enhance the value of Oriental studies beyond a fair and just standard, we must beg further permission to state, that in our judgment the Honourable Court has been led to form an estimate of their extent and merits not strictly accurate. The Honourable Court are pleased to observe, that 'it is worse than a waste of time' to employ persons either to teach or learn the sciences, in the state in which they are found in Oriental books. This position is of so comprehensive a nature, that it obviously requires a considerable modification, and the different branches of science intended to be included in it, must be particularised, before a correct appreciation can be formed of their absolute and comparative value. The metaphysical sciences, as found in Sanskrit and Arabic writings, are, we believe, fully as worthy of being studied in those languages as in any other. The Arithmetic and Algebra of the Hindoos lead to the same results, and are grounded on the same principles as those of Europe; and in the Madressa, the elements of mathametical sciences which are taught, are those of Euclid; law, a principal object of study in all the institutions, is one of vital importance to the good government of the country, and language is the ground-work upon which all future improvements must materially depend. To diffuse a knowledge of these things, language and law especially, cannot therefore be considered a waste of time; and, with unfeigned deference to the Honourable Court, we most respectfully bring to their more deliberate attention, that in the stated estimate of the value of the Oriental sciences, several important branches appear to have escaped their consideration." †

Measures adopted by Committee of Public Instruction. Agra College founded in 1823, and a College at Delhi in 1829.

Whilst holding these views, the first measures of the Committee of Public Instruction were to complete the organization of the Sanskrit College, then lately established by the Government at Calcutta, to take under their patronage and greatly to improve the *Vidyalaya* or Anglo-Indian College, which, as has already been stated, had been

* Printed Parliamentary Papers: *Sixth* Report of the Select Committee of the House of Commons on Indian Territories (1853), pp. 18–20.

† *Ib.*, pp. 18–20.

founded so far back as 1816, by the voluntary contributions of the Hindoo gentry for the education of their youth in English literature and science. The Committee also founded two entirely new Colleges, one at Agra in 1823, and another about the same time at Delhi, for the cultivation of Oriental literature. Its further measures were "to commence the printing of Sanskrit and Arabic books on a great scale, besides liberally encouraging such undertakings by others; and to employ an accomplished Oriental scholar in translating European scientific works into Arabic, upon which undertaking large sums were subsequently expended. English classes were afterwards established in connection with the Mahomedan and Sanskrit Colleges at Calcutta, the Sanskrit College at Benares, and the Agra College; and a separate institution was founded at Delhi, in 1829, for the cultivation of Western learning, in compliance with the urgent solicitation of the authorities at that place."*

First indications of the Policy of English Education in the Court of Directors' Despatch, dated 29th September, 1830.

At this stage it is important to consider the exact nature of the educational policy which the Court of Directors had in view. It has already been shown, that in their earlier Despatches no stress was laid upon the promulgation of English education among the natives of India. Almost the first indication of their change of policy in favour of English education is to be found in a letter addressed by them to the Governor-General in Council of Bengal, dated the 29th September 1830, from which the following extracts are sufficiently important to be quoted. After a review of the state of the several Colleges which had been placed under the supervision and control of the Committee of Public Instruction, the letter goes on to say:—

"Such having been the success of the seminaries for native education already established, and the proficiency as well as the number of the students at each, receiving every year a considerable increase, those institutions must now annually send forth a number of students, who have learned all which the Colleges where they were educated are adequate, on their present footing, to teach; and it is therefore of the greatest importance, that to these and to others of the native youth, the means should be afforded of cultivating the English language and literature, and acquiring a knowledge of European science, and a familiarity with European ideas, in a higher degree than has yet been within their power. The documents now under review afford most gratifying proofs that a scheme of this extended nature would now be warmly welcomed by the higher ranks of the Natives under your Government. Of the spirit which prevails in the Lower Provinces, the establishment and success of the Anglo-Indian College is sufficient evidence. And we learn with extreme pleasure the opinion of the General Committee of Public Instruction, partly founded on the personal observation and inquiries of several of their members, that 'the time has arrived when English tuition will be widely acceptable to the Natives in the Upper Provinces.'

"Your attention has been anxiously directed to the means of accomplishing this object, and, in particular, to the comparative expediency of establishing separate English colleges, or of enlarging the plan of the existing institutions, so as to render them adequate to that more extensive purpose. You have transmitted to us several most interesting communications from the General Committee of Public Instruction, and from the Local Committee of the Delhi College, on this question.

Separate Colleges for the Study of English.

"Both the Committees give a decided preference to the plan of establishing separate Colleges for the study of English, and for the cultivation of European knowledge, through the medium of the English language. They urge, that a thorough knowledge of English can only be acquired by Natives through a course of study, beginning early in life and continued for many years; that the knowledge of our language and of European science, which could be acquired in a course of education mainly directed to other objects, would not contribute in any high degree to the improvement of the native character and intellect, while the native languages and literature may be adequately pursued, as a subordinate branch of education, in an English college; and that anything beyond the mere elements of European knowledge is most advantageously taught through the European languages, with the additional recommendation, that, when so taught, it comes into less direct collision with the sacred books of the Mahomedans and Hindoos.

"By these arguments you have been convinced, and you have accordingly authorised the establishment of an English college at Delhi, and another at Benares. The project of establishing one at Calcutta seems to have been tacitly abandoned; the Anglo-Indian College, under its present superintendence, being found capable of answering the purpose.

"While we attach much more importance than is attached by the two Committees, to the amount of useful instruction which can be communicated to the Natives, through their own languages, we fully concur with them in thinking it highly advisable to enable and encourage a large number of the Natives to acquire a thorough knowledge of English; being convinced that the higher tone and better spirit of European literature, can produce their

* Trevelyan, on the Education of the People of India, pp. 3, 4.

full effect only on those who become familiar with them in the original languages. While, too, we agree with the Committee that the higher branches of science may be more advantageously studied in the languages of Europe, than in translations into the Oriental tongues, it is also to be considered that the fittest persons for translating English scientific books, or for putting their substance into a shape adapted to Asiatic students, are Natives who have studied profoundly the original works.

"On these grounds we concur with you in thinking it desirable that the English course of education should be kept separate from the course of Oriental study at the native Colleges, and should be attended for the most part by a different set of students. This, however, does not necessarily imply that the two courses of study should be prosecuted in two separate institutions. At the Agra College the Persian and the Hindoo branches are perfectly distinct, and though some of the students are attached to both departments, the greater number confine themselves to one or the other. If an English department were similarly attached to that College, or to the College at Delhi, the English language and literature might be taught classically, and the sciences might be taught in English, notwithstanding that studies of another character were pursued within the same walls. * * * * * *

English Science may be encouraged by translations.

"While we thus approve and sanction the measures which you propose for diffusing a knowledge of the English language, and the study of European science through its medium, we must at the same time put you on your guard against a disposition of which we perceive some traces in the General Committee, and still more in the local Committee of Delhi, to underrate the importance of what may be done to spread useful knowledge among the Natives through the medium of books and oral instruction in their own languages. That more complete education which is to commence by a thorough study of the English language, can be placed within the reach of a very small proportion of the Natives of India; but intelligent Natives who have been thus educated, may, as teachers in colleges and schools, or as the writers or translators of useful books, contribute in an eminent degree to the more general extension among their countrymen of a portion of the acquirements which they have themselves gained, and may communicate in some degree to the native literature, and to the minds of the native community, that improved spirit which it is to be hoped they will themselves have imbibed from the influence of European ideas and sentiments. You should cause it to be generally known that every qualified Native who will zealously devote himself to this task, will be held in high honour by you; that every assistance and encouragement, pecuniary or otherwise, which the case may require, will be liberally afforded; and that no service which it is in the power of a Native to render to the British Government, will be more highly acceptable."† * * * *

* * * * * * * * * * * *

Natives to be educated for Public Service.

"In the meantime we wish you to be fully assured, not only of our anxiety that the judicial offices to which Natives are at present eligible should be properly filled, but of our earnest wish and hope to see them qualified for situations of higher importance and trust. There is no point of view in which we look with greater interest at th exertions you are now making for the instruction of the Natives, than as being calculated to raise up a class of persons qualified, by their intelligence and morality, for high employments in the Civil Administration of India. As the means of bringing about this most desirable object, we rely chiefly on their becoming, through a familiarity with European literature and science, imbued with the ideas and feelings of civilized Europe, on the general cultivation of their understandings, and specifically on their instruction on the principles of morals and general jurisprudence. We wish you to consider this as our deliberate view of the scope and end to which all our endeavours with respect to the education of the Natives should refer. And the active spirit of benevolence, guided by judgment, which has hitherto characterized your exertions, assures us of your ready and zealous co-operation towards an end which we have so deeply at heart.

English to be gradually adopted in official business.

"With a view to give the Natives an additional motive to the acquisition of the English language, you have it in contemplation gradually to introduce English as the language of public business in all its departments; and you have determined to begin at once by adopting the practice of corresponding in English with all Native Princes or persons of rank who are known to understand that language, or to have persons about them who understand it. From the meditated change in the language of public business, including judicial proceedings, you anticipate several collateral advantages, the principal of which is, that the judge, or other European officer, being thoroughly acquainted with the language in which the proceedings are held, will be, and appear to be, less dependent upon the Natives by whom he is surrounded, and those Natives will, in consequence, enjoy fewer opportunities of bribery or other undue emolument.

† Printed Parliamentary Papers relating to the Affairs of India: *General*, Appendix I; *Public* (1832), pp. 494, 495.

"If the question were solely between retaining the Persian as the language of public business and replacing it by the English, the change would not be *primâ facie* decidedly objectionable, and we should willingly rely upon your judgment and superior local knowledge as a security that its advantages and inconveniences would be duly weighed. But if any change be made in the existing practice, it is deserving of great consideration, whether that change ought not rather to be the adoption of the Vernacular language than of our own, as the language at least of judicial proceedings.

Justice to be administered in the language of the people.

"It is highly important that justice should be administered in a language familiar to the judge, but it is of no less importance that it should be administered in a language familiar to the litigant parties, to their *Vakeels*, and to the people at large; and it is easier for the judge to acquire the language of the people than for the people to acquire the language of the judge. You are indeed partly influenced by a desire to render this last acquirement more common; but the poorer classes, who are the parties concerned in the great majority of the cases which come before our courts, cannot be expected to learn a foreign language, and we, therefore, are of opinion, that at least the proceedings of the Courts of Justice should be excepted from the practice which you propose gradually to introduce, and be conducted in the Vernacular language of the particular *zillah*, or district, unless, upon consideration, you should see good reasons for adhering to the present practice."*

Principles of their proceedings explained by the Committee of Public Instruction in their report in December, 1831.

While such was the policy in regard to education laid down by the Court of Directors in their Despatch of the 29th September, 1830, from which the above extracts have been quoted, it is important to consider the principles which guided the proceedings of the Committee of Public Instruction since its establishment under the Governor-General's Resolution of 17th July, 1823. Those principles were explained by the Committee in their printed report dated in December, 1831, and the following extracts from it may be quoted as throwing light upon one important stage of the progress of education in India. The Report of the Committee runs thus :—

"The introduction of useful knowledge is the great object which they have proposed as the end of the measures adopted or recommended by them, keeping in view the necessity of consulting the feelings and conciliating the confidence of those for whose advantage their measures are designed.

"The Committee has, therefore, continued to encourage the acquirement of the native literature of both Mahomedans and Hindoos, in the institutions which they found established for these purposes, as the Madrissa of Calcutta and Sanskrit College of Benares. They have also endeavoured to promote the activity of similar establishments, of which local considerations dictated the formation, as the Sanskrit College of Calcutta and the Colleges of Agra and Delhi, as it is to such alone, even in the present day, that the influential and learned classes, those who are by birthright or profession teachers and expounders of literature, law, and religion, Maulavis and Pundits, willingly resort.

"In the absence of their natural patrons, the rich and powerful of their own creeds, the Committee have felt it incumbent upon them to contribute to the support of the learned classes of India, by literary endowments, which provide, not only directly for a certain number, but indirectly for many more, who derive from collegiate acquirements, a consideration and subsistence amongst their countrymen. As far also, as Mahomedan and Hindoo law are concerned, an avenue is thus opened for them to public employment, and the State is provided with a supply of able servants and valuable subjects; for there is no doubt that, imperfect as Oriental learning may be in many respects, yet the higher the degree of the attainments even in it, possessed by any Native, the more intelligent and liberal he will prove, and the better qualified to appreciate the acts and designs of the Government.

"But whilst every reasonable encouragement is given to indigenous native education, no opportunity has been omitted by the Committee of improving its quality and adding to its value. In all the Colleges the superintendence is European, and this circumstance is of itself an evidence and a cause of very important amelioration. In the Madrissa of Calcutta, and the Hindoo College of Benares, institutions of earlier days, European superintendence was for many years strenuously and successfully resisted. This opposition has long ceased. The consequences are a systematic course of study, diligent and regular habits, and an impartial appreciation of merits, which no institution left to Native superintendence alone has ever been known to maintain.

"The plan of study adopted in the Colleges is, in general, an improvement upon the Native mode, and is intended to convey a well-founded knowledge of the languages studied, with a wider range of acquirement than is common, and to effect this in the least possible time. Agreeably to the Native mode of instruction,—for instance, a Hindoo or Mahomedan lawyer devotes the best years of his life to the acquirement of law alone, and is very

* Printed Parliamentary Papers relating to the Affairs of India: *General*, Appendix I; *Public* (1832), p. 497.

imperfectly acquainted with the language which treats of the subject of his studies. In the Madrissa and Sanskrit College the first part of the course is now calculated to form a really good Arabic and Sanskrit scholar, and a competent knowledge of law is then acquired, with comparative facility, and contemporaneously with other branches of Hindoo or Mahomedan learning.

"Again, the improvements effected have not been limited to a reformation in the course and scope of native study; but whenever opportunity has favoured, new and better instruction has been grafted upon the original plan. Thus in the Madrissa, Euclid has been long studied, and with considerable advantage: European anatomy has also been introduced. In the Sanskrit College of Calcutta, European anatomy and medicine have nearly supplanted the native systems. At Agra and at Delhi the elements of geography and astronomy, and mathematics, are also part of the College course. To the Madrissa, the Sanskrit College of Calcutta, and the Agra College, also, English classes are attached, whilst at Delhi and Benares distinct schools have been formed for the dissemination of the English language. Without offering therefore any violence to native prejudices, and whilst giving liberal encouragement to purely native education, the principle of connecting it with the introduction of real knowledge has never been lost sight of, and the foundation has been laid of great and beneficial change in the minds of those who, by their character and profession, direct and influence the intellect of Hindustan.

Spread of English ideas.

"In addition to the measures adopted for the diffusion of English in the provinces, and which are yet only in their infancy, the encouragement of the *Vidyalaya*, or Hindoo College of Calcutta, has always been one of the chief objects of the Committee's attention. The consequence has surpassed expectation. A command of the English language, and a familiarity with its literature and science have been acquired to an extent rarely equalled by any schools in Europe. A taste for English has been widely disseminated, and independent schools, conducted by young men reared in the *Vidyalaya*, are springing up in every direction. The moral effect has been equally remarkable, and an impatience of the restrictions of Hinduism, and a disregard of its ceremonies are openly avowed by many young men of respectable birth and talents, and entertained by many more who outwardly conform to the practices of their countrymen. Another generation will probably witness a very material alteration in the notions and feelings of the educated classes of the Hindoo community of Calcutta." *

CHAPTER VII.

EARLY MEASURES FOR EDUCATION IN THE MADRAS PRESIDENCY.—SIR THOMAS MUNRO'S MINUTES ON EDUCATION, IN 1822 AND 1826.—COMMITTEE OF PUBLIC INSTRUCTION APPOINTED IN MADRAS IN 1826.

It will not be out of place here to take a brief survey of what had in the meantime been done in the Presidencies of Madras and Bombay, in regard to the education of the Natives of those territories.

Early Educational Measures in Madras.

In the Presidency of Madras it appears that from a very early period, "the Protestant Mission, under the patronage of the Society for Promoting Christian Knowledge, had schools at their several stations, of Madras, Cuddalore, Tanjore and Trichinopoli, in which they instructed the Natives, and in aid of which they obtained occasional grants from the Local Governments, and permission from the Court of Directors to receive from the Society in England various supplies free of freight. In 1787 the Court of Directors authorized a permanent annual grant towards the support of three schools, which had been established with the sanction of the respective Rajas, at Tanjore, Ramenedaporam and Shevagunga, of 250 pagodas each. These schools were under the direction of Mr. Swartz. The Court further directed that a similar allowance should be granted to any other schools which might be opened for the same purpose." † Accordingly, a Protestant School was opened at Combaconum, and in January 1812, a Sunday School was established at St. Thomas' Mount, at the suggestion and under the direction of the Military Chaplain at that cantonment, and by the voluntary contributions of several Europeans of the Presidency. The object of this school was to afford elementary instruction to the half-caste and native children of the military and others resident there. In 1817 and 1818, the Reverend Mr. Hough, Chaplain at Palamcottah, established a Free

* Quoted in Trevelyan, *On the Education of the People of India*, pp. 4–9.

† Printed Parliamentary Papers relating to the Affairs of India: *General*, Appendix I; *Public* (1832), p. 412.

School there, and another at Tinnevelly, under the auspices of the Madras Corresponding Committee of the Church Missionary Society, for the instruction of native youth in reading, writing, arithmetic, and the elements of English grammar, but these were not supported by the Government.

Sir Thomas Munro's Minutes on Education, dated 25th June 1822, and 10th March 1826.

No systematic effort, however, appears to have been made in Madras by the Government till Sir Thomas Munro, Governor of the Presidency, wrote a Minute * on the subject, on the 25th June 1822, recommending, as an object of interest and importance, that the best information should be obtained of the actual state of education in its various branches among the native inhabitants of the provinces under the Madras Government. A Circular Letter was accordingly addressed to the several Collectors, requiring them to furnish information upon certain specified points, and on the 10th March, 1826, Sir Thomas Munro recorded another Minute † reviewing the information which had thus been collected, and some passages may be quoted from it, as showing the educational condition of the people at that time, and the nature of the measures which that eminent statesman proposed for the progress of education. He observed :—

Low state of Education in Madras.

"The state of education here exhibited, low as it is compared with that of our own country, is higher than it was in most European countries at no very distant period. It has no doubt been better in earlier times; but for the last century it does not appear to have undergone any other change than what arose from the number of schools diminishing in one place and increasing in another in consequence of the shifting of the population, from war, and other causes. The great number of schools has been supposed to contribute to the keeping of education in a low state, because it does not give a sufficient number of scholars to secure the service of able teachers. The monthly rate paid by each scholar is from four, to six or eight annas. Teachers, in general, do not earn more than six or seven rupees monthly, which is not an allowance sufficient to induce men properly qualified to follow the profession. It may also be said that the general ignorance of the teachers themselves is one cause why none of them draw a large body of scholars together; but the main causes of the low state of education are the little encouragement which it receives, from there being but little demand for it, and the poverty of the people.

Endowment of Schools by Government.

"These difficulties may be gradually surmounted: the hindrance which is given to education by the poverty of the people, may in a great degree, be removed by the endowment of schools throughout the country by Government, and the want of encouragement will be remedied by good education being rendered more easy and general, and by the preference which will naturally be given to well-educated men in all public offices. No progress, however, can be made without a body of better-instructed teachers than we have at present; but such a body cannot be had without an income sufficient to afford a comfortable livelihood to each individual belonging to it; a moderate allowance should, therefore, be secured to them by Government, sufficient to place them above want; the rest should be derived from their own industry. If they are superior, both in knowledge and diligence, to the common village schoolmasters, scholars will flock to them and augment their income. * * * * * * *
Whatever expense Government may incur in the education of the people, will be amply repaid by the improvement of the country; for the general diffusion of knowledge is inseparably followed by more orderly habits, by increasing industry, by a taste for the comforts of life, by exertion to acquire them, and by the growing prosperity of the people. It will be advisable to appoint a Committee of Public Instruction, in order to superintend the establishing of the public schools; to fix on the places most proper for them, and the books to be used in them; to ascertain in what manner the instruction of the Natives may be best promoted, and to report to Government the result of their inquiries on this important subject."‡

Committee of Public Instruction, appointed in Madras, 1826.

Sir Thomas Munro's views were accepted by the Madras Council, with very slight modifications, and a Committee of Public Instruction was appointed at Madras, and the members were informed that the object of their appointment was the general improvement of the education of the people in the territories subject to Fort St. George. They were directed to acquaint themselves fully with its actual state, and to consider and to report to Government, from time to time, the results of their enquiries and deliberations respecting the best means of improving it. They were also informed that it was intended to commit to them the duty of directing and superintending the conduct of such measures as might be deemed proper to adopt with reference to that great object. Detailed instructions were given to them, founded on the suggestions contained in the Minute by Sir Thomas Munro, and nearly in the terms of that Minute, and the Committee submitted its preliminary report on the 16th May 1826. *A School-Book Society* was also established in Madras, the constitution of which was similar to that at Calcutta. §

* Printed Parliamentary Papers relating to the Affairs of India: *General*, Appendix I; *Public* (1832), p. 500.

† *Ib.*, pp. 506, 507. ‡ *Ib.*, pp. 506, 507. § *Ib.*, p. 417.

Approval by the Court of Directors: their Despatch of the 29th September, 1830, as to English Education.

The measures adopted by the Government of Madras, and especially the appointment of the Committee of Public Instruction, were approved by the Court of Directors, but the Committee limited its efforts to primary or elementary education. The Court of Directors, however, in a Despatch, dated the 29th September, 1830, communicated important instructions to the Government of Madras, and the following passages may be quoted from it, as showing the improvement which the Educational Policy had undergone in favour of higher education of the English type :—

Higher branches of Knowledge to be encouraged for Public Service.

"By the measures originally contemplated by your Government, no provision was made for the instruction of any portion of the Natives in the higher branches of knowledge. A further extension of the elementary education which already existed, and an improvement of its quality, by the multiplication and diffusion of useful books in the native languages, was all that was then aimed at. It was, indeed, proposed to establish at the Presidency, a central school for the education of teachers; but the teachers were to be instructed only in those elementary acquirements, which they were afterwards to teach in the Tehsildary and Collectorate Schools. The improvements in education, however, which most effectually contribute to elevate the moral and intellectual condition of a people, are those which concern the education of the higher classes: of the persons possessing leisure and natural influence over the minds of their countrymen. By raising the standard of instruction among these classes, you would eventually produce a much greater and more beneficial change in the ideas and feelings of the community than you can hope to produce by acting directly on the more numerous class. You are, moreover, acquainted with our anxious desire to have at our disposal a body of Natives, qualified, by their habits and acquirements, to take a larger share, and occupy higher situations in the Civil Administration of their country, than has hitherto been the practice under our Indian Governments. The measures for native education, which have as yet been adopted or planned at your Presidency, have had no tendency to produce such persons.

English Education to be encouraged on same Principles as in Bengal.

"Measures have been adopted by the Supreme Government for placing within the reach of the higher classes of Natives, under the Presidency of Bengal, instruction in the English language and in European literature and science. These measures have been attended with a degree of success, which, considering the short time during which they have been in operation, is in the highest degree satisfactory, and justifies the most sanguine hopes with respect to the practicability of spreading useful knowledge among the natives of India, and diffusing among them the ideas and sentiments prevalent in civilized Europe. We are desirous that similar measures should be adopted at your Presidency.

"We have directed the Supreme Government to put you in possession of such part of their proceedings, and of the information which they have collected, as is calculated to aid you in giving effect to our wishes; and in order to place you generally in possession of our views on the course which ought to be pursued, we enclose (as numbers in the packet) two Despatches, which we have addressed to the Supreme Government, under date, the 5th September, 1827, and 29th September, No. 39, of 1830. We wish you to take into consideration the expediency of enlarging the plan of the Central School for the education of teachers, and rendering it a seminary for the instruction of the Natives generally, in the higher branches of knowledge. We wish that there should be an English teacher at the Institution, who should not only give instruction in the English language to such students as may be desirous of acquiring it, but who may, likewise, be capable of assisting them in the study of European science."*

* Printed Parliamentary Papers relating to the Affairs of India: *General*, Appendix I, *Public* (1832), pp. 510, 511.

CHAPTER VIII.

EARLY MEASURES FOR EDUCATION IN THE BOMBAY PRESIDENCY DURING 1815-23.—MINUTES BY THE HON'BLE MOUNTSTUART ELPHINSTONE AND THE HON'BLE F. WARDEN, ON EDUCATION, IN 1823 AND 1828.—SIR JOHN MALCOLM'S VIEWS AGAINST GENERAL EDUCATION IN ENGLISH, IN HIS MINUTE OF 1828.—DESPATCH OF THE COURT OF DIRECTORS TO THE BOMBAY GOVERNMENT, DATED 21ST SEPTEMBER 1829, FAVOURING STUDY OF ENGLISH.—SIR JOHN MALCOLM'S MODIFIED VIEWS, IN HIS MINUTE, DATED 10TH OCTOBER, 1829.—DESPATCH OF THE COURT OF DIRECTORS TO THE BOMBAY GOVERNMENT, DATED 29TH SEPTEMBER, 1830, IN FAVOUR OF ENGLISH EDUCATION.—THE ELPHINSTONE INSTITUTION FOR ENGLISH EDUCATION IN BOMBAY.

Early educational measures in Bombay.

In the Presidency of Bombay also, as in Madras, the cause of education had a small and unorganized beginning. The maintenance of Charity Schools for general education appears to have been a part of the duty of the East India Company's Chaplains, for which they occasionally received special allowances or gratuities. In March, 1752, two additional Chaplains were appointed for Tellicherry and Anjengo, "that the rising generation might be instructed in the Protestant religion." The Court of Directors, in 1756, also recommended to the Bombay Government "the setting up and establishing Charity Schools, wherein the children of soldiers, mariners, topasses, and others, might be educated, as well at the Subordinates, as at Bombay," and promised the Company's assistance in the execution of any plan which might be found practicable. By a subsequent order, bastards, and the children of slaves, on one side, were to be admitted to the schools, if the children would mix with them.*

Society for Promotion of Education in Bombay, founded in 1815.

Nothing of importance, however, appears to have occurred till the 29th January, 1815, when a voluntary assembly of the inhabitants of Bombay took place in the Vestry-room, at which a Society was formed, under the designation of "*Society for Promoting the Education of the Poor within the Government of Bombay.*" The plan of tuition adopted by the Society was that which had been ascribed to Dr. Bell, and under its auspices a Central School was established at Bombay, and in 1818 and 1819, four native schools were also established in that city; whilst in 1817, it had established schools at Surat, Tannah, and Broach. Certain Regimental Schools were also placed under the management of the Society, which received from the Bombay Government, grants of ground for the sites of its several schools.†

Hindoo College founded at Poona, in 1821.

By far the most important educational measure adopted at that time was the foundation of the Hindoo College, at Poona, which was projected by Mr. Chaplin, the Commissioner in the Deccan, and established by authority of the Bombay Government, on the 7th October, 1821, at an annual charge to the East India Company of about Rs. 15,250, which was confirmed by the Court of Directors. The College was designed to contain 100 students, divided into 10 classes: three of divinity, one of medicine, one of metaphysics, one of mathematics and astronomy, one of law, one of logic, one of *belles lettres* and rhetoric, and one of grammar. At the instance of Mr. Warden, a reference was made to this College in 1825, desiring to know whether they were willing to have a branch of English education added to the institution, and holding out the prospect of being supplied with a library of the most useful works,—elementary and practical,—in all departments of literature, arts, and sciences. The proposal was acceded to with readiness.‡

Bombay Native School-book Society, founded in 1823.

The *Bombay Native School-book and School Society*, was formed at Bombay, in the year 1823, for the purpose of promoting education among the Natives, by the establishment of schools, and by patronizing and encouraging the compilation of elementary books in the native languages, as well as by purchasing and disseminating such as might be judged worthy of the countenance of the Society. It was one of the fundamental principles of the Society to

* Printed Parliamentary Papers relating to the Affairs of India: *General*, Appendix I; *Public* (1832), p. 417.
† *Ib.*, p. 418. ‡ *Ib.*, p. 431.

adhere to the principles and rules on which education is conducted by the Natives themselves. In October, 1823, the Society applied to the Governor in Council for pecuniary aid in furtherance of their plans, and obtained a grant of Rs. 12,720 per annum. The Bombay Government also supplied the Society, gratuitously, with a lithographic press, and recommended the publication of several useful works, particularly elementary books in geometry and in ethics, so written as to discountenance the marriage of infants, expensive feasts, and other erroneous practices of the Hindoos.* In 1824-25 a liberal contribution was made by certain native gentlemen towards erecting buildings for the use of the Society, and elementary works were printed and published, comprehending grammars, dictionaries, and spelling books of the Mahrattee, Goojratee, and Hindoostanee languages, with some elementary books of Arithmetic, Geometry and Geography and a few books of fables and tales.

Hon'ble Mr. Elphinstone's Minute on Education, dated 13th December, 1823.

The first measure of any importance, however, in behalf of education in the Bombay Presidency, appears to have originated in a Minute, dated the 13th December, 1823, recorded by the Honourable Mountstuart Elphinstone, then Governor of Bombay. The views expressed by that eminent statesman may be quoted here, as throwing light upon the then state of education in Bombay, and also as indicating the sketch of the plan which he proposed for its improvement. He observes:—

"I have attended, as far as was in my power, since I have been in Bombay, to the means of promoting education among the Natives, and from all that I have observed, and learned by correspondence, I am perfectly convinced that, without great assistance from Government, no progress can be made in that important undertaking. A great deal appears to have been performed by the Education Society in Bengal, and it may be expected that the same effects should be produced by the same means at this Presidency. But the number of Europeans here is so small, and our connection with the Natives so recent, that much greater exertions are requisite on this side of India than on the other.

"The circumstance of our having lately succeeded to a Brahmin Government, likewise, by making it dangerous to encourage the labours of the missionaries, deprives the cause of Education of the services of a body of men who have more zeal and more time to devote to the object, than any other class of Europeans can be expected to possess.

The Bombay Education Society to be helped by Government.

"If it be admitted that the assistance of Government is necessary, the next question is, how it can best be afforded, and there are two ways which present themselves for consideration. The Government may take the education of the Natives entirely on itself, or it may increase the means and stimulate the exertions of the Society already formed for that purpose. The best result will probably be produced by a combination of these two modes of proceeding. Many of the measures necessary for the diffusion of education must depend on the spontaneous zeal of individuals, and could not be effected by any resolutions of the Government. The promotion of those measures, therefore, should be committed to the Society; but there are others which require an organized system, and a greater degree of regularity and permanence than can be expected from any plan, the success of which is to depend upon personal character. This last branch, therefore, must be undertaken by the Government.

"It would, however, be requisite, when so much was entrusted by Government to the Society, that all the material proceedings of that body should be made known to Government, and that it should be clearly understood that neither religion nor any topic likely to excite discontent among the Natives should ever be touched on in its schools or publications.

Educational measures suggested.

"The following are the principal measures required for the diffusion of knowledge among the Natives: *First*, To *improve* the mode of teaching at the native schools, and to *increase* the number of schools. *Second*, To supply them with school-books. *Third*, To hold out some encouragement to the lower orders of natives to avail themselves of the means of instruction thus afforded them. *Fourth*, To establish schools for teaching the European sciences and improvements in the higher branches of education. *Fifth*, To provide for the preparation and publication of books of moral and physical science in native languages. *Sixth*, To establish schools for the purpose of teaching English to those disposed to pursue it as a classical language, and as a means of acquiring a knowledge of the European discoveries. *Seventh*, To hold forth encouragement to the Natives in the pursuit of those last branches of knowledge." †

Education, as a Duty of the State, and its benefits.

After discussing these various heads of enquiry, the Minute ends in the following declaration of educational policy, and religious neutrality in such matters:—

* Printed Parliamentary Papers relating to the Affairs of India: *General*, Appendix I; *Public* (1832), p. 419. † *Ib.*, pp. 511, 512.

"I can conceive no objection that can be urged to these proposals, except the greatness of the expense, to which I would oppose the magnitude of the object. It is difficult to imagine an undertaking in which our duty, our interest, and our honour are more immediately concerned. It is now well understood, that in all countries the happiness of the poor depends in a great measure on their education. It is by means of it alone that they can acquire those habits of prudence and self-respect from which all other good qualities spring, and if ever there was a country where such habits are required, it is this. We have all often heard of the ills of early marriages and overflowing population; of the savings of a life squandered on some one occasion of festivity; of the helplessness of the ryots, which renders them a prey to money-lenders; of their indifference to good clothes or houses, which has been urged on some occasions as an argument against lowering the public demands on them; and, finally, of the vanity of all laws to protect them, when no individual can be found who has spirit enough to take advantage of those enacted in their favour: there is but one remedy for all this, which is education.

"If there be a wish to contribute to the abolition of the horrors of self-immolation and of infanticide, and ultimately to the destruction of superstition in India, it is scarcely necessary now to prove, that the only means of success lie in the diffusion of knowledge.

Religious sensitiveness of the Natives.

"In the meantime the dangers to which we are exposed from the sensitive character of the religion of the Natives, and the slippery foundation of our Government, owing to the total separation between us and our subjects, require the adoption of some measures to counteract them; and the only one is, to remove their prejudices, and to communicate our own principles and opinions by the diffusion of a rational education.

Neglect of Education, a reproach to the British Rule.

"It has been urged against our Indian Government, that we have subverted the States of the East and shut up all the sources from which the magnificence of the country was derived, and that we have not ourselves constructed a single work, either of utility or splendor. It may be alleged, with more justice, that we have dried up the fountain of native talent, and that, from the nature of our conquest, not only all encouragement to the advancement of knowledge is withdrawn, but even the actual learning of the nation is likely to be lost, and the productions of former genius to be forgotten. Something should surely be done to remove this reproach.

* * * * * * * * * * * * * *

Religious neutrality in Education.

"To the mixture of religion, even in the slightest degree, with our plans of education, I must strongly object. I cannot agree to clog with any additional difficulty a plan which has already so many obstructions to surmount. I am convinced that the conversion of the Natives must infallibly result from the diffusion of knowledge among them Evidently they are not aware of the connection, or all attacks on their ignorance would be as vigorously resisted as if they were on their religion. The only effect of introducing Christianity into our schools would be to sound the alarm, and to warn the Brahmins of the approaching danger; even that warning might perhaps be neglected as long as no converts were made; but it is a sufficient argument against the plan, that it can only be safe as long as it is ineffectual; and in this instance, the danger involves not only failure of our plans of education, but the dissolution of our Empire."*

Dissentient Minute of Hon'ble F. Warden, dated 29th December, 1823.

Somewhat different views were entertained by Mr. Francis Warden, Member of the Governor's Council at Bombay, and on the 29th December, 1823, he recorded a dissentient Minute from which the following passages† may be quoted as throwing light upon the nature of the controversy. Mr. Warden observed:—

Government should not undertake too great responsibility in Education.

"I mean to contend that India is not without the means of supplying agents, not only for the affairs of the Government, but also for the advancement of individual interests. I question whether the intellect of the mass of the population is in a more degraded state in India than that of the United Kingdom. But it is the furthest from my intention to contend that a higher order of education, and in particular a better, a purer, and more perfect system of morality is not indispensably necessary. But the means by which that improvement is to be attained, is a delicate and difficult question. I must repeat my opinion that the Government should not be too forward in taking the education of the Natives on itself, nor interfere too much in the institutions that exist in the country, imperfect as they may be.

"Though aware of the impolicy of the former measure, the Governor's propositions yet appear to infringe on both those positions in too great a degree. From an over anxiety to complete so good a work, we run the

* Printed Parliamentary Papers relating to the Affairs of India: *General*, Appendix I; *Public* (1832), pp. 517–519.

† *Ib.*, pp. 520–522.

danger of attempting too much at once, and defeating our object. I would leave the native village schools untouched and unnoticed, without attempting to institute examinations, or to distribute prizes, on the part of the Government. I question whether this interference, even if practicable through so extensive a range of country, would not be prejudicial. The schools to be established on a better model, in addition to these, should be few in number, but efficient in the means of instruction, and of producing schoolmasters.

Missionaries should be indirectly encouraged and helped by Government.

"I would not ostensibly, but indirectly, give every encouragement to the Missionaries; for although I entirely concur with the Governor in the expediency of abstaining from all attempts at religious improvement, yet so long as the Natives do not complain of the interference of the Missionaries with their prejudices, and so long as they prosecute their labours with the caution and judgment they have hitherto manifested, their exertions cannot fail of being profitable; even if they combine religious with moral instruction, no danger will arise out of their agency. The beneficial result may not be immediately conspicuous, yet it must ultimately appear, even if limited to the education of the lower classes of the Natives. If education should not produce a rapid change in their opinions on the fallacy of their own religion, it will at least render them more honest and industrious subjects.

* * * * * * * * * * * * * *

Dangers of introducing printing in India.

"If types are to be bought and distributed throughout the country, boys ought to be attached to the different Presses at Bombay to learn the duty of compositors. Whatever may be my own views on the subject, a most important question, which has been much discussed under the Presidency of Bengal, presents itself, what would be the effects of the power and influence of the Press in the present state of the country, if the Natives are to be taught the art of printing? The dissemination of whatever they choose to publish, would, of course, immediately follow. If we could control the Press, which a distribution of types would necessarily establish and multiply, by publishing only what the local authorities might approve, it would be well; but such a precaution would manifest to the discrimination of the Natives, so great a dread of the effect of our own policy in facilitating the means of diffusing knowledge, that we should excite a spirit of enquiry and of agitation under a controlled system, which would not be very favourable to our character for consistency, or to any confidence in the stability of our supremacy. The distribution of types throughout the country demands the gravest consideration.

English Language the best means of Education.

"No doubt the progress of knowledge can be most effectually and economically promoted by a study of the English language, wherein, in every branch of science, we have, ready compiled, the most useful words, which cannot be compressed in tracts and translated in the native languages, without great expense and the labour of years. A classical knowledge of English ought to constitute the chief object of the Bombay Seminary. As far as I have conversed with the Natives, they are anxious that their children should be thoroughly grounded in the English language; some of the wealthiest would be glad to send their children to England for education, were it not for the clamorous objection of their mothers; nothing can be more favourable for commencing, or for the establishment of a good system of education, than such a disposition." *

Natives of Bombay aid and encourage study of English, by founding English Professorships in honour of Mr. Elphinstone,—1827.

The desire for English education appears to have rapidly increased in the Bombay Presidency among the native population. "In November, 1827, when Mr. Elphinstone was about to resign his office of President of the Bombay Council, the principal native princes, chieftains, and gentlemen connected with the West of India, assembled, and resolved to subscribe a sum of money to be invested as an endowment for three Professors of the English language and European arts and sciences, and to request that the Government would permit a part of the Town Hall to be appropriated for the several establishments for native education, and solicit the Court of Directors to allow properly qualified persons to proceed to Bombay, there to reside in the capacity of teachers. The subscription and proposed Institution were declared to be in honour of the Governor, then about to return to Europe, after whom they were to be designated, '*The Elphinstone Professorships.*' The Bombay Government acquiesced in the suggestion, and committed to the Native Education Society the measures which might be considered proper for carrying the proposal into effect. That Society immediately took charge of the subscription, which then amounted to Rs. 120,000, composed of sums of money of which the largest single subscription was Rs. 17,800 and the smallest Rs. 300, and which had been collected within the space of three months. The Education Society also proposed that the persons to be selected should be truly eminent men, selected from other candidates 'by public examination as to their fitness, and on no account to be

* Printed Parliamentary Papers relating to the Affairs of India: *General*, Appendix I; *Public* (1832), pp. 520–522.

nominated by private choice or patronage. The sphere of one Professor to be languages and general literature; of another, mathematics and natural philosophy, including astronomy, elementary and physical; of the third, chemistry, including geology and botany; the knowledge of the two last Professors to be particularly imparted with relation to the useful arts and the future profitable employment of it by the Natives in life.'"*

These proposals led to a discussion by the Government of Bombay on the subject of native education generally, and ended in a difference of opinion among the members of the Government, Mr. Francis Warden, one of the Members of the Council, taking a view entirely in favour of English Education, whilst Sir John Malcolm, the Governor of Bombay, and Mr. Goodwin, another member of Council taking a different view. They recorded separate Minutes on the subject, and since they relate to some of the radical principles of educational policy at that time, some passages may with advantage be quoted from them. Mr. Warden's Minute, dated the 24th March, 1828, has the following:—

Dissentient opinions in regard to promotion of English Education in Bombay.

Mr. Warden's Minute of 24th March, 1828, in favour of encouraging English.

"Yielding to no individual in a conviction of the advantages of education to every country, I have yet differed widely in respect to the best means of successfully prosecuting that object. I am so far from abandoning the grounds of that opinion, that every year's experience rather confirms me in its soundness. I have urged the policy of directing our chief effort to one object, to a diffusion of a knowledge of the English language, as best calculated to facilitate the intellectual and moral improvement of India. We have as yet made that only a secondary object.

"I must confess that I did not expect to receive so unqualified a corroboration of the popularity at least of that opinion among the Natives, as is afforded by the letter from the leading members of the native community of Bombay, bringing forward a proposition for establishing professorships to be denominated '*The Elphinstone Professorships*,' for the purpose of teaching the Natives, the English language, and the arts, sciences and literature of Europe, to be held, in the first instance, by learned men to be invited from Great Britain, until natives of the country shall be found perfectly competent to undertake the office.

"Nor did I expect to find so decisive a proof of the facility with which the English language could be diffused, as is evidenced by the report recently published in the papers, of an examination at Calcutta, of the Natives educated at that Presidency, which exhibits a display of proficiency in that tongue almost incredible. Under these impressions, I subscribe entirely to the opinion expressed by the author of the 'Political History of India,' that it is better and safer to commence by giving a good deal of knowledge to a few, than a little to many; to be satisfied with laying the foundation stone of a good edifice, and not desire to accomplish in a day what must be the work of a century.

English Study, primary object of Native Education.

"But the object of giving a good deal of knowledge to a few can only be promoted by a better system of education; and the surest mode of diffusing a better system is by making the study of the English language the primary, and not the merely secondary object of attention in the education of the Natives. The reviewer of the work above alluded to remarks, in which I still more cordially concur, that a more familiar and extended acquaintance with the English language would, to the Natives, be the surest source of intellectual improvement, and might become the most durable tie between Britain and India. In any plan, therefore, for the public education of the Natives, the complete knowledge of our language ought to form so prominent an object as to lay ground for its gradually becoming at least the established vehicle of legal and official business. The English tongue would in India, as in America, be the lasting monument of our dominion; and it is not too much to hope that it might also be the medium through which the inhabitants of those vast regions might hereafter rival the rest of the civilized world, in the expression of all that most exercises and distinguishes human intellect.

"If it be desirable to diffuse a better system of education, we ought at once to encourage the study of the English tongue, as the leading object with the Native Education Society. I attended its last Annual Meeting, and had only to regret that a sufficient progress had not been made by the Natives to enable them to benefit by the higher instruction to be derived from the Professors on their arrival in India, instruction which must be given in the English language; its study then should be strongly recommended to the Native Education Society. No one, I imagine, contemplates the education of a hundred million or of seven million of Natives in the English language; but I perceive nothing chimerical in laying the foundation-stone of a good edifice for teaching what the higher classes of Natives are eager to acquire: a knowledge of English. The example will be followed, and its effects in diffusing a better system than in sending forth, as at present, school-masters, and in circulating translations which not one in a hundred can read or understand, with a smattering of knowledge, will very soon be seen and felt."†

* Printed Parliamentary Papers relating to the Affairs of India: *General*, Appendix I; *Public* (1832), p. 469.

† *Ib.*, pp. 523, 524.

Sir John Malcolm's views against general Education in English.

On the other hand, Sir John Malcolm's opinion was opposed to any general introduction of English education among the people of India, and since his views are still shared by some thinkers on the problems of Indian Education, the following passages from his Minute, written in 1828, may be quoted here with advantage. The earlier part of his Minute has the following :—

His Minute, written in 1828, in favour of Vernacular Education.

"I concur with Mr. Warden as to the desirable object of diffusing education, but differ as to the mode. I am of opinion the method adopted at this Presidency is of all others the best that can be pursued. The chief ground on which I anticipate advantages from the establishment of the Elphinstone Professorships, is, that a certain proportion of the Natives will be instructed by them not only in the English language, but in every branch of useful science. To Natives so educated, I look for aid, in the diffusion of knowledge among their countrymen, through the medium of their Vernacular dialects; and I certainly think it is only by knowledge being accessible through the latter medium, that it ever can be propagated to any general or beneficial purpose.

Example of English History.

"This question may be decided by reference to the History of England. Before the Reformation, our best books on religion, morality, philosophy, and science were veiled in the classical languages of Greece and Rome; and it is a remarkable fact, that since all those works have been translated into the Vernacular language of our native country, though gentlemen, men of learned professions, and those who are to instruct youth, still study the classical languages, as the fountains of our knowledge, these are unknown to the great bulk of our countrymen, to whom improved education has been so useful. The reason is plain; the latter have neither that time nor money to spare which is necessary for such studies. There is a still greater necessity that the natives of India, whom it is our object to instruct, should have the path of knowledge rendered as short and as smooth as possible; all that we are now doing tends to that object, the complete accomplishment of which will be effected by the establishment of the Elphinstone Professors, whose duty it will be to teach the few who are to teach the many, and from whom, as a source, the Natives of this quarter of India will be able to obtain that information and knowledge which is best suited to their wishes, their talents, and their various occupations in life.

"I have on political grounds a consolation, derived from my conviction of the impossibility of our ever disseminating that half-knowledge of our language, which is all, any considerable number of the Natives could attain. It would decrease that positive necessity which now exists for the servants of Government making themselves masters of the languages of the countries in which they are employed, and without which they never can become in any respect competent to their public duties.

Further employment of Natives in Administration.

"One of the chief objects, I expect, from diffusing education among the natives of India, is our increased power of associating them in every part of our administration. This I deem essential on grounds of economy, of improvement, and of security. I cannot look for reduction of expense in the different branches of our Government from any diminution of the salaries now enjoyed by European public servants, but I do look to it from many of the duties they now have to perform being executed by Natives on diminished salaries. I further look to the employment of the latter in such duties of trust and responsibility, as the only mode in which we can promote their improvement; and I must deem the instruction we are giving them dangerous, instead of useful, unless the road is opened wide to those who receive it, to every prospect of honest ambition and honourable distinction.

Knowledge of English not necessary for Natives beyond the Presidency.

"To render men who are employed beyond the immediate limits of the Presidency fit for such duties, I contemplate, no knowledge of the English language is necessary. The acquisition of that would occupy a period for other studies and pursuits, but it is quite essential to aspiring Natives that they should have the advantage of translations from our language of the works which are best calculated to improve their minds, and increase their knowledge, not only of general science, but to enable them to understand the grounds which led us to introduce into the system of the administration we have adopted for India the more liberal views and sounder maxims of our policy and legislation in England. It is to the labours of the Elphinstone Professors that we must look for that instruction which is to form the native instruments that must become the medium of diffusing such knowledge; and as no duty can be more important than that of men who are placed at the very head of this course of instruction, and as the power of selecting those qualified for the important task will much depend upon the liberality of the salaries assigned them, I trust, with Mr. Warden, that the Honourable Court will make a grant, to promote this Institution, of a sum at least equal to that subscribed by the Natives of this Presidency."*

* Printed Parliamentary Papers relating to the Affairs of India: *General*, Appendix I; *Public* (1832), p. 525.

Despatch of the Court of Directors of 21st September, 1826, to the Government of Bombay, favouring the study of English.

The views of Sir John Malcolm were generally concurred in by Mr. Goodwin, his colleague in Council, but when the matter went up to the Court of Directors, they, without laying down any definite decision between the conflicting views, as to the exceptional claims of English Education advocated by Mr. Warden, and the kind of education proposed by Sir John Malcolm, recorded a Despatch, dated the 21st September 1829, to the Bombay Government, in which, referring to the subject of Education they made the following significant observations :—

"The measures which you have as yet adopted for the furtherance of this important object, are inconsiderable, compared with those which you have in comtemplation. There is one of them, however, to which we are disposed to attach very considerable importance, the establishment of an English School at the Presidency (under the superintendence of the Committee of the Native School-Book Society), where English may be taught grammatically, and where instruction may be given in that language, on history, geography, and the popular branches of science; and we are happy to find that Mr. Warden bears testimony to the anxious desire of many among the Natives to obtain the benefit of an English Education for their children." *

Sir John Malcolm's views modified in favour of English Education, in his Minute, dated 10th October, 1829.

In the meantime, Sir John Malcolm appears to have modified his views in regard to English Education, as is shown from the following passage in a Minute recorded by him on the 10th October, 1829 :—

English Schools may be established.

"I have given my sentiments most fully upon the inexpediency, as well as impracticability, of conveying general instruction to our native subjects in India, through the medium of the English language, but I by no means desire to express an opinion that schools for that purpose should not be extended. While records of offices, a part of the judicial proceedings, and all correspondence and accounts, are written in English, there will be profitable employment for all who learn to read and write this language, and a familiarity with it will open to those who possess it, new sources of knowledge, and qualify them to promote improvement. From English schools being established at no place, but Bombay, the pay of writers and accountants is immoderately high; and when these move from the Presidency, they require still higher wages; and when well qualified, they can, from their limited numbers, command almost any pay they demand. This introduces a tone of extravagance of demand from this class of persons in all our departments. Of some remedies for this evil I shall speak hereafter; but the real mode to decrease price is to multiply the article. English Schools should be established or encouraged at Surat and Poona, and I look to the small colony of East Indians about to be established at Phoolsheher, with great hope of aid in this as in other branches of improvement." †

Despatch of the Court of Directors to the Bombay Government, dated 29th September, 1830, in favour of English Education.

In their Despatch, dated the 29th September, 1830, to the Government of Bombay, the Court of Directors however, gave clear expression to their views in regard to English Education, as is shown by the following extract from that Despatch :—

"It is our anxious desire to afford to the higher classes of the natives of India, the means of instruction in European science, and of access to the literature of civilized Europe. The character which may be given to the classes possessed of leisure and natural influence, ultimately determines that of the whole people. We are sensible, moreover, that it is our duty to afford the best equivalent in our power to these classes, for the advantages of which, the introduction of our Government has deprived them; and for this and other reasons, of which you are well aware, we are extremely desirous that their education should be such as to qualify them for higher situations in the Civil Government of India, than any to which Natives have hitherto been eligible.

"That the time has arrived when efforts may be made for this purpose, with a reasonable probability of success, is evidenced by various facts, one of the most striking of which is, the liberal subscription which has recently been raised among the Natives under your Presidency for the foundation of an institution, at which instruction is to be given in the English language and literature, and in European science, through the medium of the English language. To this projected institution we have already, at your recommendation, expressed our willingness to afford liberal support, but we delayed authorizing any specific subscription, in consequence of our not having received, either from yourselves or from the native subscribers, any mature and well-digested plan.

"We have since received from the Supreme Government a further report of the progress of the seminaries for the education of the Natives, which have been established under the Presidency of Bengal. The success of those institutions has heen in the highest degree satisfactory; and the various experiments which have been made

* Printed Parliamentary Papers relating to the Affairs of India: *General*, Appendix I; *Public* (1832), p 522. † *Ib.*, p. 539.

in that part of India, have afforded so much valuable experience, that we now no longer feel that uncertainty which we expressed in our Despatch last referred to, with respect to the choice of means, for an end we have so deeply at heart.

Example of successful English Education in Bengal.

"Among the Native Colleges which now exist and flourish in Bengal, none has had so great success as the Anglo-Indian College, which originated, like the proposed Elphinstone Institution, in a subscription among the Natives, and is directed to the same objects. This College is partly supported by Government, and is under the inspection of the General Committee which has been appointed by the Supreme Government for the Superintendence of Public Instruction.

The Elphinstone Institution may be helped, like the Anglo-Indian College at Calcutta.

"In forming a plan for the Elphinstone Institution, it is of course proper that the wishes of the subscribers should be consulted. They, however, like the Natives who established the Anglo-Indian College, would, we have little doubt, be willing that the institution should be under your general superintendence, and a Committee of their own body might be associated in the management, with some officer, or officers, of Government, in such manner as you might judge most advisable.

"If the subscribers are willing to acquiesce in such an arrangement, we authorize you to concert with them a plan for the formation of the projected institution, taking the Anglo-Indian College at Calcutta, generally, for your model; and if the plan when completed should not differ very materially from that of the college last mentioned, we authorize you to make such donation, or such annual subscription, to the Elphinstone Institution, as may appear to you advisable, with reference to the importance of the object in view." *

Subscriptions for the Elphinstone Institution. The Court of Director's Despatch to the Bombay Government, dated 12th December, 1832, regarding Aid and Superintendence of the Institution.

In November 1830, the total amount of subscriptions for the Elphinstone Institution at Bombay reached Rs. 2,15,000, and the Court of Directors were requested to subscribe a similar amount on the part of the Company, and to receive the total sum so subscribed by the natives of Bombay and the Government, on interest at 6 per cent., into the Public Treasury at Bombay—the interest of this Capital Fund to go towards defraying the expenses of the Institution. Relative to this subject, the following extract from the Despatch of the Court of Directors to the Government of Bombay, dated the 12th December, 1832, may be quoted, as showing how far the policy of imparting English education to the natives of India had advanced in that Presidency. The passage runs as follows:—

"We have already, in our letter of 19th September, 1830, empowered you to grant such sum as you may deem advisable, in aid of the proposed Elphinstone Institution; your suggestions as to the mode of constituting that institution appear judicious. You think that the teachers to be furnished from this country should be,—'one superior Professor of mathematics, astronomy, and all branches of natural philosophy, together with an under Professor or teacher, who ought to possess a complete knowledge of the practical application of the sciences of architecture, hydraulics, mechanics, &c., to the useful purposes of life.' To the latter person you propose allotting Rs. 600 per mensem; to the former, Rs. 800, with use of the house built for the astronomer, and the charge of the Observatory and instruments. As the study of the English language and literature was one of the main objects for which the institution was founded, it is, of course, intended that either the head Professor, or his assistant should be competent to give instruction on those subjects as well as on science." †

* Printed Parliamentary Papers relating to the Affairs of India: *General*, Appendix I; *Public* (1832), p. 542. † *Ib.*, p. 548.

CHAPTER IX.

SUMMARY OF THE VARIOUS STAGES OF THE MEASURES FOR EDUCATION OF THE NATIVES OF INDIA, AND EXPENDITURE INCURRED BY THE EAST INDIA COMPANY, UNDER THE ACT OF PARLIAMENT, STATUTE 53, GEO. III., CHAPTER 155,—FROM 1813 TO 1830.

Stages of the policy of Education in India. The earliest stage—Inactivity.

The narrative contained in the preceding chapters may be summarized as indicating certain marked stages of the progress and development of the policy of education in India. The earliest stage was the period when education of the natives of India was not regarded as a part of the administrative policy of the East India Company, which, indeed, did not at that time possess any territorial dominion or recognized political authority. Such authority had its legal beginning in the grant of the *Diwani* of Bengal, Behar and Orissa, by the Emperor Shah Alam, to the East India Company, in 1765, and the political circumstances of that period left no time or inclination for the promotion of learning, or formulation of any educational policy.

The 2nd Stage—Encouragement of Oriental Studies, 1781 to 1791.

The *second* stage was the foundation, by Warren Hastings, of the Calcutta Madrissa, in 1781, and the Benares College in 1791, for the purpose of training Mahomedan and Hindu officers for ranks in the Judicial and other Administrative offices of the Company.

The 3rd Stage—Unorganized Individual Efforts.

The *third* stage was, whilst in various places, some individual efforts were made for promoting education, no organized system existed, nor had the principles of a definite educational policy been declared. This stage, however, was an important one, as discussions, as to the expediency and policy of educating the natives of India, engaged attention, as shown by the elaborate treatise of Mr. Charles Grant, which was written during 1792, and submitted to the Court of Directors in 1797, and also by Lord Minto's Minute on Education, written in 1817.

The 4th Stage—Legislative recognition of Education, as a duty of the State, in 1813.

The *fourth* stage is represented by the Resolution passed by the House of Commons declaring it to be the duty of England to promote the interests and happiness of the native inhabitants of the British dominions in India, and to adopt such measures as may tend to the introduction among them of useful knowledge and moral improvement—a declaration to which effect was given in section 43 of the Act of Parliament, 53, Geo. III., Chapter 155, which was passed in 1813.

The 5th Stage—Apathy of the Indian Government towards Education.

The *fifth* stage is one of comparative apathy, on the part of the authorities in India, because, notwithstanding the fact that the Court of Directors, in their Despatch of the 3rd June, 1814, invited the special attention of the Governor-General to the provisions of the new Act regarding Education, no measures of any significant kind were taken for some years, to give effect to the benevolent intentions of the Act of Parliament.

The 6th Stage—Appointment of Committees of Public Instruction, 1823 to 1826.

The *sixth* stage is remarkable for the activity of the authorities in India, in adopting systematic measures for promoting education among the people. It was during this period that the Committees of Public Instruction were appointed: One at Calcutta in 1823, another in Madras in 1826, and the Education Society at Bombay, in 1823.

The question of English Education remains unsettled.

The operation of these Societies, and the policy of Government on the subject of education, have been described in the preceding chapters, and it is apparent that up to the year 1830 the educational policy in regard to the conflicting claims of Oriental learning on the one hand, and of English education on the other, had not been settled either by the Governments of the three Presidencies in India, or by the Court of Directors in England. Nor does it appear that the spread of education was regarded, during this period, as having higher aims than a desire to procure a supply of trained native officials to fill subordinate ranks in the administration.

Expenditure on Education in India, under Section 43 of Act of Parliament, 53, Geo. III., C. 155, 1813 to 1830.

It will be the object of the following chapter to describe how a great and radical change came upon the Educational policy of Government, immediately after this period, decisively in favour of English Education, as distinguished from Oriental studies in Arabic and Sanskrit. In the meantime, however, it will be interesting to see how far the Government in India had carried out the intentions of Parliament expressed in Section 43, of the Act, 53 Geo. III., chapter 155, which laid down that "a sum of not less than one *lac* of rupees in each year shall be set apart and applied to the revival and improvement of literature, and the encouragement of the learned natives of India, and for the introduction and promotion of a knowledge of the sciences among the inhabitants of the British territories in India." It will be remembered that the Act was passed in the year 1813, and the following table, taken from the printed Parliamentary Papers * of 1832, gives an account of all sums that had been applied to the purpose of educating the natives of India, from the year 1813 to the year 1830, both inclusive, covering a period of 18 years:—

Years.	Bengal.	Madras.	Bombay.	Total.
	£	£	£	£
1813	4,207	480	442	5,129
1814	11,606	480	499	12,585
1815	4,405	480	537	5,422
1816	5,146	480	578	6,204
1817	5,177	480	795	6,452
1818	5,211	480	630	6,321
1819	7,191	480	1,270	8,941
1820	5,807	480	1,401	7,688
1821	6,882	480	594	7,956
1822	9,081	480	594	10,155
1823	6,134	480	594	7,208
1824	19,970	480	1,434	21,884
1825	57,122	480	8,961	66,563
1826	21,623	480	5,309	27,412
1827	30,077	2,140	13,096	45,313
1828	22,797	2,980	10,064	35,841
1829	24,663	3,614	9,799	38,076
1830	28,748	2,946	12,636	44,330
Grand Total, 1813 to 1830 ...	2,75,847	18,400	69,233	3,63,480

Actual Expenditure double the minimum amount required by the Act of Parliament.

This account yields an average expenditure of £20,193 a year, which, even according to the higher value of the rupee in those days, may be roundly stated to be more than two *lacs* of rupees, that is, more than double the amount required by the abovementioned Act of Parliament to be spent on education in India. Whatever, therefore, may be said as to the Educational Policy of the East India Company during this period, and apart from the question whether the sum of one *lac* of rupees, named as the minimum annual expenditure on Education by the Act of Parliament was sufficient, neither the Court of Directors nor the authorities in India can be accused either of having endeavoured to evade the intentions of Parliament, or to have exercised undue parsimony in giving effect to those intentions.

* Printed Parliamentary Papers relating to the Affairs of India: *General*. Appendix I; *Public* (1832), p. 483.

CHAPTER X.

RENEWAL OF THE EAST INDIA COMPANY'S CHARTER IN 1833.—ARRIVAL OF LORD MACAULAY IN INDIA AS A MEMBER OF THE GOVERNOR-GENERAL'S COUNCIL, IN 1834.—CONTROVERSY AS TO THE COMPARATIVE MERITS OF ORIENTAL LEARNING AND ENGLISH LITERATURE FOR EDUCATION.—LORD WILLIAM BENTINCK'S EDUCATIONAL RESOLUTION OF 1835.—PROTEST OF MAHOMEDANS AGAINST THE RESOLUTION.

Most important period in the History of Education in India—1830 to 1835.

This Chapter opens with perhaps the most important period in the annals of Education in India, under the British rule. The term of the Charter of the East India Company, which had been renewed for twenty years by the Act of Parliament, 53, Geo. III., Chapter 155, was to expire on the 10th of April, 1834, and grave discussions arose in England as to whether it ought to be renewed at all, and if renewed, under what conditions. "As early as 1829, the leading towns of the United Kingdom had begun to agitate the subject, and to load the tables of both Houses of Parliament with petitions against the renewal of the Charter; and in February, 1830, Select Committees were appointed, on the recommendation of ministers themselves,—Lord Ellenborough making the motion in the Lords, and Sir Robert Peel in the Commons. Both movers carefully abstained from giving any indication of the views entertained by the Cabinet, and the Committees were simply appointed 'to inquire into the present state of the affairs of the East India Company, and into the trade between Great Britain and China, and to report their observations thereupon to the House.'" * It is from the reports of the Parliamentary Committees so appointed, and the enormous mass of oral and documentary evidence which they collected, printed in bulky Parliamentary Blue-books, in 1832, that a considerable portion of the information and quotations given in the preceding chapters have been collected.

Renewal of the East India Company's Charter by Parliament, in 1833.

It falls beyond the scope of this work to discuss the various political and commercial affairs with which Parliament was then concerned, but it is necessary to mention such matters as have a bearing upon the subject of education in India. It is enough to say that on the 13th of June 1833, the subject of the renewal of the Company's Charter was introduced to the House of Commons by Mr. Charles Grant † (afterwards Lord Glenelg) the President of the Board of Control, who concluded a long explanatory speech, by moving three resolutions, of which the third, having a bearing upon the subject of education in India, may be quoted here. The resolution ran as follows:—

Parliamentary Resolution in favour of educating India.

"That it is expedient that the Government of the British Possessions in India be intrusted to the said Company, under such conditions and regulations as Parliament shall enact, for the purpose of extending the commerce of this country, and of securing the good government, and promoting the religious and moral improvement of the people of India."

Promotion of Education recognized as duty of the Company's Government. Absence of interest in Indian affairs in Parliament.

The resolution is important, as showing, that among the objects for which the Company was to be intrusted with the Government of the British Possessions in India, was "*promoting the religious and moral improvement of the people of India.*" Vague and general as these expressions were, they may furnish a pretext to those who cavil against the *bonâ fide* motives of the British rule in India, in regard to its policy of English education; for saying that its real object was to promote conversion to Christianity. As throwing light upon the small amount of interest then taken by Parliament in Indian affairs, the historian ‡ calls attention to the fact that the Resolutions, though involving the future Government of India, and the consequent condition of its myriads of inhabitants, were passed almost without discussion, and awakened so little interest that a very large majority of the members of the House of Commons did not even deign to be present. Adverting to the fact a few weeks afterwards, Lord Macaulay thus expressed himself:—"The House

* Beveridge's *History of India*, Vol. III., p. 230.

† Son of the Right Honourable Charles Grant, from whose treatise on the "*Condition of the Natives of India*," quotations have been given in the preceding chapters of this work.

‡ Beveridge's *History of India*, Vol. III., p. 234.

has neither the time, nor the knowledge, nor the inclination to attend to an Indian Budget, or to the statement of Indian extravagance, or to the discussion of Indian local grievances. A broken head in Coldbath Fields excites greater interest in this House than three pitched battles in India ever would excite. This is not a figure of speech, but a literal description of fact, and were I called upon for proof of it, I would refer to a circumstance which must be still in the recollection of the house. When my right honourable friend, Mr. Charles Grant, brought forward his important propositions for the future Government of India, there were not as many members present as generally attend upon an ordinary turnpike bill."

The Act of Parliament for the better Government of India, 3 and 4 Wm. IV., c. 85, received Royal assent on 28th August, 1833. Rights of Educated Natives to State offices affirmed.

The Bill which gave effect to the abovementioned Resolutions, was passed by Parliament and received the Royal assent on the 28th of August, 1833. It ranks in the Statute-book as 3 and 4 Wm. IV., C. 85, and is entitled, "*An Act for effecting an arrangement with the East India Company, and for the better Government of His Majesty's Indian Territories, till the 30th day of April*, 1854." As bearing upon the prospects of the educated natives of India, the 87th Section of the Act is important, which enacts, "That no native of the said territories, nor any natural-born subject of His Majesty, resident therein, shall, by reason only of his religion, place of birth, descent, colour, or any of them, be disabled from holding any place, office, or employment under the said Company." The Act introduced considerable changes in the administrative machinery of the Government of India, and under one of its provisions, Lord Macaulay was appointed the first Law Member of the Council of the Governor-General, and arrived in India on the 10th June, 1834, and soon joined Lord William Bentinck, then Governor-General of India.

Lord Macaulay's arrival in India, in 1834, an important event in Educational Policy.

Lord Macaulay's arrival in India to hold such a high office in the administration of the country, was an important event in the history of education in India, as it was principally due to his personality and opinions, which were adopted by the Governor-General, that the advancement of English education found a decisive and emphatic declaration of policy, and a firm basis, upon which the present system still rests. As to the state of things which then prevailed in regard to education in India, I borrow the following observations from a contemporary witness, Sir Charles Trevelyan. In his treatise on the "*Education of the People of India*," he says :—

Taste for English Literature widely disseminated, as contrasted with Oriental learning.

"Meanwhile, the progress of events was leading to the necessity of adopting a more decided course. The taste for English became more and more 'widely disseminated.' A loud call arose for the means of instruction in it, and the subject was pressed on the Committee from various quarters. English books only were in any demand: upwards of thirty-one thousand English books were sold by the School-book Society in the course of two years, while the Education Committee did not dispose of Arabic and Sanskrit volumes enough, in three years to pay the expense of keeping them for two months, to say nothing of the printing expenses. Among other signs of the times, a petition was presented to the Committee by a number of young men who had been brought up at the Sanskrit College, pathetically representing that, notwithstanding the long and elaborate course of study which they had gone through, they had little prospect of bettering their condition ; that the indifference with which they were generally regarded by their countrymen left them no hope of assistance from them, and that they, therefore, trusted that the Goverment, which had made them what they were, would not abandon them to destitution and neglect. The English Classes which had been tacked on to this and other Oriental Colleges, had entirely failed in their object. The boys had not time to go through an English, in addition to an Oriental course, and the study which was secondary was naturally neglected. The translations into Arabic, also, appeared to have made as little impression upon the few who knew that language, as upon the mass of the people who were entirely unacquainted with it.

Difference of opinion among Members of the Education Committee as to comparative claims of English and Oriental learning.

"Under these circumstances, a difference of opinion arose in the Committee. One section of it was for following out the existing system,—for continuing the Arabic translations,—the profuse patronage of Arabic and Sanskrit works, and the printing operations ; by all which means fresh masses would have been added to an already unsaleable and useless hoard. An edition of Avicenna was also projected, at an expense of 2,000*l* ; and as it was found that, after hiring students to attend the Arabic College, and having translations made for their use at an expense of thirty-two shillings a page, neither students nor teachers could understand them, it was proposed to employ the translator as the interpreter of his own writings, at a further expense of 300 rupees a month. The other section of the Committee wished to dispense with this cumbrous and expensive machinery for teaching English science through the medium of the Arabic language ; to give no bounties in the shape of stipends to students, for the encouragement of any particular kind of learning ; to purchase or print only such Arabic and Sanskrit books as might actually be required for the use of the different colleges; and to employ that portion of their annual income, which would by these means be set free, in the establishment of new seminaries for giving instruction in English and the Vernacular languages, at the places where such institutions were most in demand.

Obstruction caused in consequence.

"This fundamental difference of opinion long obstructed the business of the Committee. Almost everything which came before them was more or less involved in it. The two parties were so equally balanced as to be unable to make a forward movement in any direction. A particular point might occasionally be decided by an accidental majority of one or two, but as the decision was likely to be reversed the next time the subject came under consideration, this only added inconsistency to inefficiency. This state of things lasted for about three years, until both parties became convinced that the usefulness and respectability of their body would be utterly compromised by its longer continuance. The Committee had come to a dead stop, and the Government alone could set it in motion again, by giving a preponderance to one or the other of the two opposite sections. The members, therefore, took the only course which remained open to them, and laid before the Government a statement of their existing position, and of the grounds of the conflicting opinions held by them.

Government called upon to decide the issue between English and Oriental learning.

"The question was now fairly brought to issue, and the Government was forced to make its election between two opposite principles. So much, perhaps, never depended upon the determination of any Government. Happily, there was then at the head of affairs one of the few who pursue the welfare of the public, independently of every personal consideration: happily, also, he was supported by one who, after having embellished the literature of Europe, came to its aid when it was trembling in the scale with the literature of Asia."*

Lord Macaulay's celebrated Minute in favour of English Education, dated 2nd February, 1835.

The first allusion in the preceding passage is to Lord William Bentinck, then Governor-General of India, and, the second to Lord Macaulay, who had recently arrived from England, as a Member of the new Supreme Council in India. "On his arrival, Macaulay was appointed President of the Committee; but he declined to take any active part in its proceedings until the Government had finally pronounced on the question at issue. Later, in January 1835, the advocates of the two systems, than whom ten abler men could not be found in the Service, laid their opinions before the Supreme Council; and, on the 2nd of February, Macaulay, as a Member of that Council, produced a Minute in which he adopted and defended the views of the English section in the Committee."† The Minute contains some passages which are interesting and instructive, as throwing light upon the spirit and nature of the new educational policy, and they may be quoted here:—

English Literature pre-eminent, and best suited for Education in India.

"How stands the case? We have to educate a people who cannot at present be educated by means of their mother-tongue. We must teach them some foreign language. The claims of our own language it is hardly necessary to recapitulate. It stands pre-eminent even among the languages of the West. It abounds with works of imagination not inferior to the noblest which Greece has bequeathed to us; with models of every species of eloquence; with historical compositions, which, considered merely as narratives, have seldom been surpassed, and which, considered as vehicles of ethical and political instruction, have never been equalled; with just and lively representations of human life and human nature; with the most profound speculations on metaphysics, morals, government, jurisprudence, and trade; with full and correct information respecting every experimental science which tends to preserve the health, to increase the comfort, or to expand the intellect of man. Whoever knows that language has ready access to all the vast intellectual wealth which all the wisest nations of the earth have created and hoarded in the course of ninety generations. It may safely be said that the literature now extant in that language is of far greater value than all the literature which three hundred years ago was extant in all the languages of the world together. Nor is this all. In India, English is the language spoken by the ruling class. It is spoken by the higher class of Natives at the seats of Government. It is likely to become the language of commerce throughout the seas of the East. It is the language of two great European communities which are rising, the one in the south of Africa, the other in Australasia; communities which are every year becoming more important, and more closely connected with our Indian Empire. Whether we look at the intrinsic value of our literature or at the particular situation of this country, we shall see the strongest reason to think that, of all foreign tongues, the English tongue is that which would be the most useful to our Native subjects.

"The question now is simply whether, when it is in our power to teach this language, we shall teach languages in which, b of India, Vol. III.ession, there are no books on any subject, which deserve to be compared to

ght Honourable Charles G.

eceding chapters of this wan— *On the Education of the people of India*, pp. 9–13.

Yistory of India, Vol. III., an's *Life of Macaulay*, Ed. 1881; p. 290

our own; whether, when we can teach European science, we shall teach systems which, by universal confession, whenever they differ from those of Europe, differ for the worse; and whether, when we can patronise sound philosophy and true history, we shall countenance, at the public expense, medical doctrines, which would disgrace an English farrier—astronomy, which would move laughter in the girls at an English boarding-school—history, abounding with kings thirty feet high, and reigns thirty thousand years long—and geography made up of seas of treacle and seas of butter.

Analogous cases of educational effort.

"We are not without experience to guide us. History furnishes several analogous cases, and they all teach the same lesson. There are in modern times, to go no further, two memorable instances of a great impulse given to the mind of a whole society—of prejudice overthrown—of knowledge diffused—of taste purified—of arts and sciences planted in countries which had recently been ignorant and barbarous.

Revival of letters in Europe at the close of the 15th and the beginning of the 16th century.

"The first instance to which I refer is the great revival of letters among the Western nations at the close of the fifteenth and the beginning of the sixteenth century. At that time almost every thing that was worth reading was contained in the writings of the ancient Greeks and Romans. Had our ancestors acted as the Committee of Public Instruction has hitherto acted; had they neglected the language of Cicero and Tacitus; had they confined their attention to the old dialects of our own island; had they printed nothing, and taught nothing at the universities, but chronicles in Anglo-Saxon, and romances in Norman-French, would England have been what she now is? What the Greek and Latin were to the contemporaries of More and Ascham, our tongue is to the people of India. The literature of England is now more valuable than that of classical antiquity. I doubt whether the Sanscrit literature be as valuable as that of our Saxon and Norman progenitors. In some departments in history, for example, I am certain that it is much less so.

Example of intellectual progress in Russia.

"Another instance may be said to be still before our eyes. Within the last hundred and twenty years, a nation which had previously been in a state as barbarous as that in which our ancestors were before the Crusades, has gradually emerged from the ignorance in which it was sunk, and has taken its place among civilised communities. I speak of Russia. There is now in that country a large educated class, abounding with persons fit to serve the State in the highest functions, and in no wise inferior to the most accomplished men who adorn the best circles of Paris and London. There is reason to hope that this vast Empire, which in the time of our grandfathers was probably behind the Punjab, may, in the time of our grandchildren, be pressing close on France and Britain in the career of improvement. And how was this change effected? Not by flattering national prejudices; not by feeding the mind of the young Muscovite with the old woman's stories which his rude fathers had believed; not by filling his head with lying legends about St. Nicholas; not by encouraging him to study the great question, whether the world was or was not created on the 13th of September; not by calling him 'a learned native,' when he has mastered all these points of knowledge; but by teaching him those foreign languages in which the greatest mass of information had been laid up, and thus putting all that information within his reach. The languages of western Europe civilised Russia. I cannot doubt that they will do for the Hindoo what they have done for the Tartar."*

Lord William Bentinck adopts Lord Macaulay's views: Government Resolution, dated 7th March, 1835, in favour of English Education.

This Minute was concurred in by Lord William Bentinck and his Council, and on the 7th March, 1835, they passed the following Resolution, which set the question at rest once and for ever, and which is one of the most memorable records in the history of Education in India. It was thus worded:—

"The Governor-General of India in Council has attentively considered the two letters from the Secretary to the Committee, dated the 21st and 22nd January last, and the papers referred to in them.

"*2nd.*—His Lordship in Council is of opinion that the great object of the British Government ought to be the promotion of European literature and science amongst the natives of India, and that all the funds appropriated for the purposes of education would be best employed on English education alone.

"*3rd.*—But it is not the intention of his Lordship in Council to abolish any college or school of native learning, while the native population shall appear to be inclined to avail themselves of the advantages which it affords; and his Lordship in Council directs that all the existing professors and students at all the institutions under the superintendence of the Committee shall continue to receive their stipends. But his Lordship in Council decidedly objects to the practice which has hitherto prevailed, of supporting the students during the period of their education. He conceives that the only effect of such a system can be to give artificial encouragement to branches of learning which, in the natural course of things, would be superseded by more useful studies; and he directs that

* Trevelyan's *Life of Macaulay*, Ed. 1881; pp. 290–292.

no stipend shall be given to any student who may hereafter enter any of these institutions, and that when any professor of Oriental learning shall vacate his situation, the Committee shall report to the Government the number and state of the class, in order that the Government may be able to decide upon the expediency of appointing a successor.

"*4th.*—It has come to the knowledge of the Governor-General in Council that a large sum has been expended by the Committee, in the printing of Oriental works. His Lordship in Council directs that no portion of the funds shall hereafter be so employed.

"*5th.*—His Lordship in Council directs, that all the funds which these reforms will leave at the disposal of the Committee be henceforth employed in imparting to the native population a knowledge of English literature and science, through the medium of the English language; and His Lordship in Council requests the Committee to submit to Government, with all expedition, a plan for the accomplishment of this purpose."*

Feelings of the Hindus entirely in favour of English Education.

While such was the nature of the future educational policy declared by Government, it is important to consider the feelings with which it was regarded by the Native population. It has already been shown that the Hindus in Bengal had already been foremost in their desire to learn the English language, literature, and sciences, and had for this purpose founded the *Vidyalaya* or Anglo-Indian College, from their own voluntary contributions, so far back as 1816, and that Raja Ram Mohun Roy, the recognised leader of their advanced and enlightened party, had submitted his able and eloquent Memorial, in 1823, protesting against the expenditure of money on Sanskrit learning, and praying that all available funds and endeavours should be devoted to the promotion of education in the English language, literature, and sciences, among the people of India. It has also been stated that, in 1827, the Hindus of Bombay raised a vast subscription exceeding two *lacs* of rupees as an endowment for Professors of the English language, and European arts and sciences, in honor of Mr. Elphinstone, the late Governor of the Presidency, and that their efforts resulted in the foundation of the Elphinstone Institution, or College, in Bombay. There can, therefore, be no doubt that the Governor-General's Resolution of the 7th March, 1835, was greeted with joy by the Hindus, and contemporary evidence is not wanting to show that such was the case. Sir Charles Trevelyan, who at that time held important office in the Indian Civil Service, bears his testimony to the then state of things, in the following words:—

Sir Charles Trevelyan's testimony as to the popularity of English Education among the Hindus.

"This brings us to the second point which we had to consider, namely, whether, supposing English literature to be best adapted for the improvement of the people of India, they are themselves ready to profit by the advantages which it holds out. If it can be proved that tuition in European science has become one of the sensible wants of the people, and that, so far from being satisfied with their own learning, they display an eager avidity to avail themselves of every opportunity of acquiring the knowledge of the West, it must be admitted that the case put by the Committee of 1824 has occurred, and that, according to their own rule, the time has arrived when instruction in Western literature and science may be given on an extensive scale, without any fear of producing a re-action.

Excessive sale of English School-books during 1834-35.

"The proofs that such is the actual state of things have been already touched upon. As the principle of the School-book Society is, to print only such books as are in demand, and to dispose of them only to those who pay for them, its operations furnish, perhaps, the best test of the existing condition of public feeling in regard to the different systems of learning which are simultaneously cultivated in India. It appears, from their last printed Report, that from January 1834 to December 1835, the following sales were effected by them:—

"English books	31,649
Anglo-Asiatic, or books partly in English and partly in some Eastern language	4,525
Bengalee	5,754
Hinduee	4,171
Hindusthanee	3,384
Persian	1,454
Uriya	834
Arabic	36
Sanskrit	16

"Indeed, books in the learned native languages are such a complete drug in the market, that the School-book Society has for some time past ceased to print them; and that Society, as well as the Education Committee,

* Trevelyan—*On the Education of the people of India*, pp. 13–15.

the a considerable part of its capital locked up in Sanskrit and Arabic lore, which was accumulated during the period when the Oriental mania carried everything before it. Twenty-three thousand such volumes, most of them folios and quartos, filled the library, or rather the lumber-room, of the Education Committee at the time when the printing was put a stop to, and during the preceding three years, their sale had not yielded quite one thousand rupees.

Small sale of Oriental Books.

"At all the Oriental Colleges, besides being instructed gratuitously, the students had monthly stipends allowed them, which were periodically augmented till they quitted the institution. At the English seminaries, not only was this expedient for obtaining pupils quite superfluous, but the native youth were ready themselves to pay for the privilege of being admitted. The average monthly collection on this account from the pupils of the Hindoo College, for February and March, 1836, was, sicca rupees, 1,325. Can there be more conclusive evidence of the real state of the demand than this? The Hindoo College is held under the same roof as the new Sanskrit College, at which thirty pupils were hired at 8 rupees each, and seventy at five rupees, or 590 rupees a month in all.

Hindu Scholars educated in the *Vidyalaya*, propagate taste for English language and literature.

"The Hindoo College was founded by the voluntary contributions of the Natives themselves, as early as 1816. In 1831, the Committee reported, that 'a taste for English had been widely disseminated, and independent schools, conducted by young men reared in the *Vidyalaya* (the Hindoo College), are springing up in every direction.' This spirit, gathering strength from time, and from many favourable circumstances, had gained a great height in 1835; several rich Natives had established English schools at their own expense; Associations had been formed for the same purpose at different places in the interior, similar to the one to which the Hindoo College owed its origin. The young men who had finished their education propagated a taste for our literature, and, partly as teachers of benevolent or proprietary schools, partly as tutors in private families, aided all classes in its acquirement. The tide had set in strongly in favour of English education, and when the Committee declared itself on the same side, the public support they received rather went beyond, than fell short of what was required. More applications were received for the establishment of schools than could be complied with; there were more candidates for admission to many of those which were established than could be accommodated. On the opening of the Hooghly College, in August, 1836, students of English flocked to it in such numbers as to render the organization and classification of them a matter of difficulty. Twelve hundred names were entered on the books of this department of the College within three days, and at the end of the year there were upwards of one thousand in regular attendance. The Arabic and Persian classes of the institution at the same time mustered less than two hundred. There appears to be no limit to the number of scholars, except that of the number of teachers whom the Committee is able to provide. Notwithstanding the extraordinary concourse of English students at Hooghly, the demand was so little exhausted, that when an auxiliary school was lately opened within two miles of the College, the English department of it was instantly filled, and numerous applicants were sent away unsatisfied. In the same way, when additional means of instruction were provided at Dacca, the number of pupils rose at once from 150 to upwards of 300, and more teachers were still called for. The same thing also took place at Agra. These are not symptoms of a forced and premature effort, which, as the Committee of 1824 justly observed, would have recoiled upon themselves, and have retarded our ultimate success."*

Mahomedans oppose English Education and memorialize against the Government Resolution of 7th March, 1835. Testimony of Mr. H. H. Wilson.

This state of things was, however, limited to the Hindus. Far different were the feelings of the Mahomedans, whose attitude towards English education was anything but friendly. Contemporaneous evidence of this circumstance is furnished by the evidence of the celebrated Sanskrit scholar, Mr. H. H. Wilson, who at that period, and since 1823, had been a member and Secretary of the Committee of Public Instruction at Calcutta, and was otherwise deeply interested and concerned in the spread of Education in India. He was examined upon the subject of the measures taken by Government in 1835, as a witness before a Select Committee of the House of Commons, on the 18th July 1853. The question put to him was: "From your intimate acquaintance with literary men, when you were in India, what is your impression of the opinion that they formed of that neglect of the languages of India, which you say has been manifested?" His answer was that, "Upon the determination to abolish the stipends, and the proposal to appropriate all the funds to English education, there was a petition from the Mahomedans of Calcutta, signed by about 8,000 people, including all the most respectable Maulavis and native gentlemen of that city. After objecting to it upon general principles, they said that the evident object of the Government was the conversion of the Natives; that they encouraged English exclusively, and discouraged Mahomedan and Hindu studies, because they wanted

* Trevelyan—*On the Education of the people of India*, pp. 78–83.

to induce the people to become Christians; they looked upon their exclusive encouragement of English as a step towards conversion."*

Such feelings of aversion towards English education entertained by the Mahomedans, and evinced so early as 1835, stand in strong contrast to the attitude of the Hindu community, who, as has been shown, had zealously proved their desire to acquire a knowledge of the English language, literature, and sciences, by founding the Anglo-Indian College, so far back as 1816, and by the Memorial which had been presented on their behalf by Raja Ram Mohun Roy to Lord Amherst, then Governor-General of India. This difference between the sentiments of the two communities towards English education, is the real key to the reasons of the vast disparity of progress in English education which the two nationalities have respectively made. The effects of this disparity have been most baneful to the interests of British India in general, and to the Mahomedan community in particular, and those effects have not yet disappeared, as will be shown in a later part of this work.

CHAPTER XI.

CONTENDING ARGUMENTS OF THE ADVOCATES OF ENGLISH EDUCATION, AND THE SUPPORTERS OF ORIENTAL LEARNING IN ARABIC AND SANSKRIT.

The Controversy—English Education *versus* Oriental learning.

In a historical review of the progress of education in India, it would scarcely be fair that the account of the controversy which raged between the advocates of the Oriental classical education, and the advocates of education in the English language, literature, and sciences, should be limited to what has been stated in the preceding chapter as to Lord Macaulay's Minute of 2nd February 1835, and the decision of the controversy by the Government Resolution of 7th March 1835. Whatever the merits of the controversy may be, it is one of so much importance that it can never lose its historical interest. The views and arguments of the advocates of English education have been summed up by Sir Charles Trevelyan in the following words :—

Arguments of the Advocates of English Education.

"The Hindu system of learning contains so much truth, as to have raised the nation to its present point of civilization, and to have kept it there for ages without retrograding, and so much error, as to have prevented it from making any sensible advance during the same long period. Under this system, history is made up of fables, in which the learned in vain endeavour to trace the thread of authentic narrative; its medicine is quackery; its geography and astronomy are a monstrous absurdity; its law is composed of loose contradictory maxims, and barbarous and ridiculous penal provisions; its religion is idolatry; its morality is such as might be expected from the example of the gods and the precepts of the religion. *Suttee*, *Thuggee*, human sacrifices, *Ghaut* murder, religious suicides, and other such excrescences of Hinduism, are either expressly enjoined by it, or are directly deduced from the principles inculcated by it. This whole system of sacred and profane learning is knitted and bound together by the sanction of religion; every part of it is an article of faith, and its science is as unchangeable as its divinity. Learning is confined by it to the Brahmins, the high priests of the system, by whom and for whom it was devised. All the other classes are condemned to perpetual ignorance and dependence; their appropriate occupations are assigned by the laws of caste, and limits are fixed, beyond which no personal merit or personal good fortune can raise them. The peculiar wonder of the Hindu system is, not that it contains so much or so little true knowledge, but that it has been so skilfully contrived for arresting the progres of the human mind, as to exhibit it at the end of two thousand years fixed at nearly the precise point at which it was first moulded. The Mahomedan system of learning is many degrees better, and 'resembles that which existed among the nations of Europe before the invention of printing;' so far does even this fall short of the knowledge with which Europe is now blessed. These are the systems under the influence of which the people of India have become what they are. They have been weighed in the balance, and have been found wanting. To perpetuate them, is to perpetuate the degradation and misery of the people. Our duty is not to teach, but to unteach them,—not to rivet the shackles which have for ages bound down the minds of our subjects, but to allow them to drop off by the lapse of time and the progress of events.

* Printed Parliamentary Papers (1853): *Sixth* Report of the Select Committee of the House of Commons on Indian Territories, p. 12.

"If we turn from Sanskrit and Arabic learning, and the state of Society which has been formed by it, to Western learning, and the improved and still rapidly improving condition of the Western nations, what a different spectacle presents itself! Through the medium of English, India has been brought into the most intimate connection with this favoured quarter of the globe, and the particular claims of the English language as an instrument of Indian improvement have thus become a point of paramount importance.† * * * *

Importance of the English language.

"As of all existing languages and literatures the English is the most replete with benefit to the human race, so it is overspreading the earth with a rapidity far exceeding any other. With a partial exception in Canada, English is the language of the Continent of America, north of Mexico; and at the existing rate of increase there will be a hundred millions of people speaking English in the United States alone at the end of this century. In the West India Islands we have given our language to a population collected from various parts of Africa, and by this circumstance alone they have been brought many centuries nearer to civilization than their countrymen in Africa, who may for ages grope about in the dark, destitute of any means of acquiring true religion and science. Their dialect is an uncouth perversion of English, suited to the present crude state of their ideas, but their literature will be the literature of England, and their language will gradually be conformed to the same standard. More recently the English language has taken root in the Continent of Africa itself, and a nation is being formed by means of it in the extensive territory belonging to the Cape, out of a most curious mixture of different races. But the scene of its greatest triumphs will be in Asia. To the South a new Continent is being peopled with the English race; to the north, an ancient people, who have always taken the lead in the progress of religion and science in the East, have adopted the English language as their language of education, by means of which they are becoming animated by a new spirit, and are entering at once upon the improved knowledge of Europe, the fruit of the labour and invention of successive ages. The English language, not many generations hence, will be spoken by millions in all the four quarters of the globe; and our learning, our morals, our principles of constitutional liberty, and our religion, embodied in the established literature, and diffused through the genius of the Vernacular languages, will spread far and wide among the nations.

Objections to the early proceedings of the Education Committee.

"The objection, therefore, to the early proceedings of the Education Committee is, that they were calculated to produce a revival, not of sound learning, but of antiquated and pernicious errors. The pupils in the Oriental Seminaries were trained in a complete course of Arabic and Sanskrit learning, including the theology of the *Vedas* and the *Koran*, and were turned out accomplished *Maulavies* and *Pundits*,—the very class whom the same Committee described as 'satisfied with their own learning; little inquisitive as to anything beyond it, and not disposed to regard the literature and science of the West as worth the labour of attainment.' And, having been thus educated, they were sent to every part of the country to fill the most important situations which were open to the Natives, the few who could not be provided for in this way, taking service as private tutors or family priests. Every literary attempt connected with the old learning, at the same time, received the most liberal patronage, and the country was deluged with Arabic and Sanskrit books. By acting thus, the Committee created the very evil which they professed to fear. They established great corporations, with ramifications in every District, the feelings and interest of whose members were deeply engaged on the side of the prevailing errors. All the murmuring which has been heard has come from this quarter; all the opposition which has been experienced has been headed by persons supported by our stipends, and trained in our Colleges. The money spent on the Arabic and Sanskrit Colleges was, therefore, not merely a dead loss to the cause of truth; it was bounty money paid to raise up champions of error, and to call into being an Oriental interest which was bound by the condition of its existence to stand in the front of the battle against the progress of European literature." ‡

Professor H. H. Wilson's views in favour of Oriental learning, and criticism of the Government Resolution of 7th March 1835.

The views entertained by the opposite section of the educationists may be explained in the words of Professor Wilson who, referring to the change of educational policy under the Resolution of Government, dated, the 7th March 1835, makes the following observations :—

"The efforts made in the territories more favourably circumstanced, to promote the advance of useful knowledge, received from the Governor-General the most solicitous encouragement; and considerable progress was made under his auspices, in the multiplication of educational establishments, and the cultivation of the English language and literature. English classes or seminaries were instituted at several of the principal stations in the Upper Provinces, as well as in Bengal; while at the same time the system of native study pursued at the Colleges, exclusively appropriated to the education of Hindus and Mahomedans, was diligently superintended and improved,

† Trevelyan.—*On the Education of the People of India*, pp. 83–86.

‡ *Ib.*, pp. 87–91.

and was in the course of being rendered co-operative in the dissemination of sound knowledge, by providing instructors qualified to enrich their own literature through the medium of translations from the English language. Influenced, however, by the examples of extraordinary progress in English made, at Calcutta, under peculiarly favourable circumstances, and misled by advisers, who had no knowledge of India or its people, beyond a limited intercourse with the anglicised portion of the inhabitants of the metropolis, Lord W. Bentinck, shortly before his departure, adopted the notion that English might be made the sole channel of instruction; and resolved, that all the funds appropriated to the purposes of education should be employed in imparting to the native population a knowledge of English literature and science, through the medium of the English language alone. In order to carry this resolution into effect, the endowments heretofore granted to the students of the native colleges were to be resumed, and the colleges themselves were to be abolished upon the diminution of the number of the students, which was effectually provided for by depriving them of their principal, and often, only means of prosecuting their studies. In this exclusive encouragement of the study of English, the circumstances of the great body of the people were wholly disregarded. In Calcutta, where a considerable portion of the more respectable inhabitants were in constant and intimate association with Englishmen of every degree, and where numbers found employment in public or private offices, there were both an extensive want of the language, and abundant facilities, and ample leisure for its acquirement. Beyond Calcutta, the accomplishment was of no practical usefulness, and no inducement existed to engage in a necessarily long and arduous course of study. It was, therefore, evidently impossible that it should be cultivated to any extent; and all attempts to introduce it universally, could be attended with but imperfect success. The great truth was also overlooked, that a national literature can only co-exist with a national language; and that as long as knowledge is restricted to a foreign garb, it can be the property only of the few who can command leisure and opportunity for its attainment. It was obvious that a language so difficult as English, and so utterly discordant with every Indian dialect, could never become the universal medium of instruction; and that, even if it should be extensively studied, which, beyond certain narrow limits, was highly improbable, it would constitute the literature of a class—never that of the people. The means of improving the spoken dialects, and fitting them to become the vehicles of sound instruction, were at hand in the languages considered classical by Hindus and Mahomedans, the Sanskrit and Arabic, and through them an easy passage might be found for the infusion of European thought into Vernacular expression; but whether they were to be employed, as had previously been done in accomplishing the object, or whether it might be more expedient to attempt the literary use of the spoken languages at once, it was undeniable that the exclusive encouragement of English was unjust to the native literary classes, and was of no benefit to the bulk of the population." *

The promotion of Vernacular Education not excluded by the Government Resolution of 7th March, 1835.

This can scarcely be said to be a fair criticism of the proceedings of the Committee of Public Instruction, after the Government Resolution of the 7th of March, 1835, and the matter has been explained by Sir Charles Trevelyan: "In the long discussion which preceded the change in the plan of the Committee, there was one point on which all parties were agreed: this was, that the vernacular languages contained neither the literary nor scientific information necessary for a liberal education. It was admitted on all sides that while the instruction of the mass of the people, through the medium of their own language was the ultimate object to be kept in view, yet, meanwhile, teachers had to be trained, a literature had to be created, and the co-operation of the upper and middle classes of Native Society had to be secured. The question which divided the Committee was—What language was the best instrument for the accomplishment of these great objects? Half the members contended that it was English, the other half that it was Sanskrit and Arabic. As there was no dispute about the Vernacular language, no mention was made of it in the Resolution of the 7th March, 1835, which contained the decision of the Government. This omission led many, who were not acquainted with the course the discussion had taken, to fear that the point had been altogether overlooked; and in order to obviate this misapprehension, the Committee made the following remarks, in the first Annual Report submitted by them to the Government after the promulgation of the resolution referred to:—

First Annual Report of the Education Committee recognizes importance of Vernacular Education.

"'We are deeply sensible of the importance of encouraging the cultivation of the Vernacular languages. We do not conceive that the order of the 7th of March precludes us from doing this, and we have constantly acted on this construction. In the discussions which preceded that order, the claims of the Vernacular languages were broadly and prominently admitted by all parties, and the question submitted for the decision of Government, only concerned the relative advantage of teaching English on the one side, and the learned Eastern languages on the other. We therefore conceive that the phrases 'European literature and sciences,'

* Wilson's *History of British India*, Vol. III. (Ed. 1848), pp. 305–307.

English Education alone,' and 'imparting to the native population a knowledge of English literature and science, through the medium of the English language,' are intended merely to secure the preference to European learning, taught through the medium of the English language, over Oriental learning, taught through the medium of the Sanskrit and Arabic languages, as regards the instruction of those Natives who receive a learned education at our seminaries. These expressions have, as we understand them, no reference to the question, through what ulterior medium such instruction, as the mass of the people is capable of receiving, is to be conveyed. If English had been rejected, and the learned Eastern tongues adopted, the people must equally have received their knowledge through the Vernacular dialects. It was therefore quite unnecessary for the Government, in deciding the question between the rival languages, to take any notice of the Vernacular tongues, and consequently we have thought that nothing could reasonably be inferred from its omission to take such notice.

"We conceive the formatiom of a Vernacular literature to be the ultimate object to which all our efforts must be directed. At present, the extensive cultivation of some foreign language, which is always very improving to the mind, is rendered indispensable by the almost total absence of a Vernacular literature, and the consequent impossibility of obtaining a tolerable education from that source only. The study of English, to which many circumstances induce the Natives to give the preference, and with it the knowledge of the learning of the West, is therefore daily spreading. This, as it appears to us, is the first stage in the process by which India is to be enlightened. The Natives must learn before they can teach. The best educated among them must be placed in possession of our knowledge, before they can transfer it into their own language. We trust that the number of such translations will now multiply every year. As the superiority of European learning becomes more generally appreciated, the demand for them will no doubt increase, and we shall be able to encourage any good books which may be brought out in the native languages, by adopting them extensively in our seminaries.

"A teacher of the Vernacular language of the Province is already attached to several of our institutions, and we look to this plan soon becoming general. We have also endeavoured to secure the means of judging for ourselves of the degree of attention which is paid to this important branch of instruction, by requiring that the best translations from English into the Vernacular language, and *vice versâ*, should be sent to us after each Annual Examination, and if they seem to deserve it, a pecuniary prize is awarded by us to the authors of them." *

CHAPTER XII.

RELIGIOUS INSTRUCTION NO PART OF GOVERNMENT EDUCATIONAL POLICY.—MARQUIS OF TWEEDDALE'S MINUTE OF 1846, IN FAVOUR OF RELIGIOUS INSTRUCTION, DISAPPROVED BY COURT OF DIRECTORS.—PETITION OF THE NATIVES OF MADRAS TO PARLIAMENT, IN 1852, ON THE SUBJECT.—RESULT OF THE CONTROVERSY.

Controversy as to Religious Neutrality in Education.

Somewhat akin to the controversy as to the comparative claims of the English language, literature, and sciences on the one hand, and of the Oriental learning on the other, was another discussion of almost equal importance. The question was whether the education provided by the State should be entirely secular, or should also include religious and moral instruction. It is important to deal with this subject at some length, not only because the British rule in India has not unfrequently been accused of having adopted its educational policy with the real object of propagating Christianity, but also because the subject in itself is one which even now, in some form or other, becomes matter of consideration by educationists in India. Another reason why this matter is sufficiently important to be historically investigated, is that, as a matter of fact, unfounded suspicions, on the part of the Mahomedan community in particular, as to the motives of the Government, have in a large measure operated to keep them aloof from English education, with the lamentable result, as will hereafter be shown, that they have been

* Trevelyan, *On the Education of the people of India*, pp. 20–24. See also Printed Parliamentary Papers: *Second* Report of the Select Committee of the House of Lords (1852-53), Appendix I, p. 481.

left far behind their Hindu fellow-countrymen in the knowledge of the English language, literature, and sciences, and have consequently suffered great loss of prosperity in all the various branches of worldly occupations. It has been seen that upon the passing of the Government Resolution of the 7th March, 1835, in favour of English education, they were the first to raise the cry that the change in the educational policy inaugurated by that Resolution was due to a clandestine motive of propagating Christianity among the people of India, and they seem to have more or less adhered to this suspicion till very recent years.

Religious Neutrality in Education adopted as State Policy.

The facts of history, however, show that such suspicions were entirely unfounded. Whatever the views of individual philanthropists, like Mr. Charles Grant, who originally devoted their attention to the intellectual, moral, and social welfare of the people of India, may have been, it is certain that the State, in its relations with India, never adopted a proselytizing policy. The language of section 43 of the Act of Parliament, 53, Geo. III., Chap. 155, whilst requiring that "A sum of not less than one *lac* of rupees in each year shall be set apart and applied to the revival and improvement of literature, and the encouragement of the learned Natives of India, and for the introduction and promotion of the sciences among the inhabitants of the British territories in India," makes absolutely no mention of any religious instruction, and the Despatch of the Court of Directors, dated the 3rd June, 1814, explaining the effect of that legislative provision, and containing directions to the Government of India, is equally careful in avoiding any reference to religious instruction. Indeed, the words of the Statute are so far from bearing any interpretation of a proselytizing tendency that, when in 1835, the controversy raged as to the expediency of introducing English education, the party who advocated Oriental learning, seriously contended that, "It was not the intention of Parliament, in making this assignment, to encourage the cultivation of sound learning and true principles of science, but to bring about a revival of the antiquated and false learning of the *shastars*, which had fallen into neglect in consequence of the cessation of the patronage which had in ancient times been extended to it by the Native Hindu Princes." Nor in the various Minutes recorded by eminent Anglo-Indian Statesmen and other State papers, such as Despatches from the Court of Directors on the subject of education, which have been amply quoted in the preceding chapters of this work, is there the least trace of any tendency to make the educational policy of the British Rule a means of proselytizing the natives of India to Christianity. Indeed, in the various schools and colleges which the Missionaries had founded at their own expense, the Bible was openly recognized as a class-book, and instruction in the doctrines of Christianity formed part of the course of studies. But these institutions owed their origin to private subscriptions of religious people in Great Britain or America, and had no connection with the Government, which then, as now, has uniformly adhered to the wise principle of religious neutrality and toleration in matters of public instruction.

Proposal in Madras to introduce the Bible as a class-book.

That such was the case is borne out by the evidence of official documents. It appears that the Council of Education in Madras, which had been formed on the lines of the Committee of Public Instruction of Bengal, addressed a letter to the Governor of Madras, proposing the establishment of several provincial schools, and suggesting that the Bible may be introduced as a subject of study in the classes receiving English education. The letter was dated the 4th July, 1846, and the Marquis of Tweeddale, then Governor of the Presidency, recorded a Minute, dated the 24th August, 1846, from which the following passages may be quoted, as bearing both upon the subject of English Education, and the proposition to introduce the study of the Bible in the Government educational institutions:—

Minute of the Marquis of Tweeddale, dated 24th August 1846, in favour of the proposal.

"From the number of native languages spoken in this Presidency, it is clearly of importance, independent of other considerations, that one universal language—English—should form a prominent object of study at the Government Schools. It will also be found the best, if not the sole, means of extending scientific knowledge and the literature of Europe, as well as facilitating mercantile transactions between the native community and captains of vessels trading to the ports of this Presidency. I fully approve, therefore, of the prominence given to the study of English, as proposed.

"I think the standard fixed by the Council, under present circumstances, judicious; but I would add a provision for special cases, that whenever the Council are satisfied that the master of a provincial school is fully equal to the task, and can form a class of students of superior intelligence, he should be required to instruct this class in algebra, mathematics, and trigonometry, and in something more than the elements of geography and history.

"I observe that there is a proposition of the Council to introduce the Bible into the English classes, as a class-book, and from the mixed character of that body, I conclude that the Council are fully satisfied, from their knowledge of Native Society at this Presidency, that this measure will not interfere with the general usefulness of the schools to the native community at large; and I understand that experience has shown this to be the case.

"I consider that a very important proviso has been added by the Council, *viz.*, 'That attendance on the Bible-class be left entirely optional.'

Attendance on the Bible-class to be optional.

"In carrying out their proposition, it appears to me necessary that there should be two classes for English reading, the one with, and the other without, the Bible as a class-book; otherwise the rule might virtually negative the advantages to be derived from the English Class generally.

"To avoid all difficulties on this head, I would propose that there should be invariably two classes for English reading, the one with, and the other without the Bible, the latter class to precede the former in their hour of instruction, and those inclined should have the advantage of attending both classes, and in a very short time I have no doubt all would belong to the Bible-class.

Moral Instruction necessary.

"In considering the important question of imparting education to the inhabitants of a country, the great object with a Government must always be to improve the moral character of the subjects over whom it rules; whilst, at the same time, it affords facilities for the cultivation of their minds; and those who have been engaged in the spread of education on these principles, must have witnessed the elevation of mind and character which attends such a combination of instruction.

Religious Instruction advisable.

"The value of a religious and practical education, to fit our own countrymen for the various duties of life, has been established beyond all doubt; and the increasing exertion which is now making, to rescue those living in the dark recesses of our great cities at home, from the state of degradation consequent on their vicious and depraved habits, the offspring of ignorance and sensual indulgence, is the most convincing evidence of the importance attached to the moral character of all classes. I should infer, that the ignorance and degradation of a great bulk of the inhabitants of this country requires a remedy as active, to be applied by a process as simple, in order to elevate them in the scale of human beings, as that needed by our unfortunate countrymen.

More solid foundation of morality required for Public Service, than that to be found in the Hindu or Mahomedan faith.

"Even amongst the more respectable classes employed in the service of Government, we have constant proofs that, in this country, it requires a more solid foundation than is to be found in the Hindoo or Mahomedan faith, to bear the change which learning operates on the mind of those who emerge out of a state of ignorance, and attain those mental acquirements which enlarged education gives, or who are placed by their superior ability in responsible situations in the employ of Government."*

Despatch of the Court of Directors to the Government of Madras, dated 23rd March, 1847, prohibiting the introduction of the Bible in Government Seminaries.

These views having been communicated to the Court of Directors, they conveyed their orders in a Despatch, dated the 23rd March, 1847, to the Governor of Madras, approving of the policy of founding schools, but prohibiting the introduction of the Bible as the subject of study in the Government educational institutions. The words of the Despatch on this subject are as follows:—

"The Council of Education propose that the Bible be included in the studies of the English classes, attendance on the Bible-class being left optional. You have suggested, in qualification of this proposal, that there shall be two separate English classes, from one of which the Bible shall be excluded, and that it shall be left optional to the students to attend either class. You have thought it right, however, before sanctioning either of them, to solicit our instructions as to the desirableness of the measure, not only in regard to the provincial institutions, but as to its application to the University.

"The Provincial Schools at the Madras University are intended for the especial instruction of Hindoos and Mahomedans in the English language and the sciences of Europe; we cannot consider it either expedient or prudent to introduce any branch of study which can in any way interfere with the religious feelings and opinions of the people. All such tendency has been carefully avoided at both the other Presidencies, where native education has been successfully prosecuted. We direct you, therefore, to refrain from any departure from the practice hitherto pursued."†

Petition to Parliament from the natives of Madras, dated 10th December, 1852, protesting against religious interference in Education.

Notwithstanding such clear directions, the authorities in Madras appear to have given some cause of complaint to the native inhabitants of that Presidency, who, in a petition to Parliament, dated the 10th December, 1852, represented their grievances on the subject of religious partiality in education, as follows:—

"That with reference to the subject of National Education, your petitioners are anxious to bring to the notice of your Honourable House certain proceedings which are now in train, in order to appropriate part of the

* Printed Parliamentary Papers (1853): *Sixth* Report of the Select Committee of the House of Commons on Indian Territories; 189, 190.

† *Ib.*, p. 191.

Educational Grant towards the assistance of Missionary, or convertising operations, as they exist at various stations throughout this Presidency, under the name of a 'Grant-in-aid System,' by which it is proposed to extend the pecuniary assistance of Government 'to other institutions, which are now, or can be made, the instruments of imparting a sound and liberal education, whether conducted by Missionary bodies or others;' with which view the Government has issued a Circular, in the Public Department, to the different Collectors, in which each is directed to 'furnish the Government with the best and fullest information in your power regarding the educational institutions within your district, whether conducted by private parties, or missionary or other public bodies;' and has further recorded in Minutes of Consultation, dated 1st November, 1852, 'The Governor in Council is not of opinion that any Government Schools should be set up at stations in the provinces where private Missionary, or other public seminaries have already been established, and have been found adequate to the instruction of the people. To that opinion he will now add, that he considers it very desirable to extend moderate pecuniary assistance to such schools, as a means of diffusing education, on sound and unexceptionable principles, and he proposes that the Honourable Court be solicited to entrust the Government with a discretionary power on this point.'

Protest against appropriation of Educational Funds to Christian Institutions.

"That your petetioners would point out for the consideration of your Honourable House, that this proposed appropriation of the Education Funds to the support of Christian Institutions was rejected by the Court of Directors, in a Despatch to this Government, dated 24th August, 1844, in reply to an official application in behalf of an institution at the Presidency, called 'Bishop Corrie's Grammar School,' on the ground that it did not come 'within the object of the funds set apart for the promotion of native education.' There is also on record a letter of the Court of Directors with reference to the introduction of the Bible as a class-book into the schools to be established from those funds; which says, 'The provincial schools and the Madras University are intended for the especial instruction of the Hindoos and Mahomedans in the English language and the sciences of Europe; we cannot consider it either expedient or prudent to introduce any branch of study which can in any way interfere with the religious feelings and opinions of the people. All such tendency has been carefully avoided at both the other Presidencies, where native education has been successfully prosecuted. We direct you, therefore, to refrain from any departure from the practice hitherto pursued.'

Educational Grant should not be devoted to Proselytism.

"That your petitioners hereupon represent to your Honourable House, if it be contrary to the intentions for which the Educational Grant was bestowed, to devote any portion of it in aid of an institution where convertism is neither professed nor practised, as at Bishop Corrie's Grammar School, or to permit the establishment of a Bible-class in any of the Government Schools, although the attendance at such class was to be left entirely optional with the pupils, it would be a much wider divergence from the object, and a much greater 'interference with the religious feelings and opinions of the people,' to apply the funds especially at the discretion of the Madras Government, at all times notorious for its proselyting propensities, in support of Missionary Institutions, wherein the study of the Bible is not optional, but compulsory, and which are avowedly set on foot and maintained for the single object of convertising the pupils, to whom on that account education is imparted free of charge; and your petitioners conceive that the support of such institutions by the Government would be productive of the worst consequences, as it would distinctly identify the ruling authorities with the one grand object of such schools,—the proselytism of the Natives, the only difference between which and the undisguised practice of convertism in the schools supported solely by the State would amount to this:—Government would pay twice the price for a convert of its own direct making, which it would have to pay under the 'Grant-in-aid,' to the seminaries of the Missionaries; at the same time it would place itself at the head of all the Missionary Societies in the Presidency, doubling their pecuniary resources, enabling them to increase the number of their agents, and to extend their convertising operations, exactly in proportion to the 'discretionary power' with which this Government, in the Minutes above quoted, desires to be entrusted.

Complaint against the Marquis of Tweeddale's Minute of 24th August, 1846.

"That your petitioners cannot avoid remarking, that the desire of the Madras Government, with regard to rendering the educational funds committed to its trust subservient to the purposes of proselytism, is of some standing. The Marquis of Tweeddale, while entertaining the proposition of the Council of Education, to adopt the Bible as a class-book, recorded his approbation of the measure, observing, in a Minute, dated the 24th August, 1846, 'The value of a religious and practical education to fit our countrymen for the various duties of life has been established beyond all doubt;' and again, 'The reports and complaints so constantly made to Government against the integrity of the native servants, are sufficient evidence that something is wanting to ensure a faithful service from them;' and again, 'It requires a more solid foundation than is to be found in the Hindu or Mahomedan faiths to bear the change which learning operates on the mind of those who are placed by their superior ability in responsible situations in the employ of Government.' And the present Governor in Council, in his Minute, approving of the 'Grant-in-aid' to the Missionaries, has deemed it expedient to record, 'Although it is, perhaps, not immediately relevant to the subject of these proceedings, yet as it is a momentous point in looking at the general question of education to the Natives, the Governor in Council is compelled to state, both from observation and sedulous inquiry, that he has arrived at the conclusion, that the people of this part of India, at least, have neither, by any means, had their minds expanded and enlarged to the degree that might have been anticipated through the instruction and care that has been bestowed upon them, nor has he seen any sufficient reason to indulge a belief that their innate prejudices have been removed or even lessened, or their moral character and sense of veracity, integrity, and proper principle, improved. He does not deny, but that there may be occasional bright exceptions; but he is of opinion that, whatever system of education may be enforced hereafter, its chief aim ought to be directed to moral improvement, combined with extirpating the foul vices of untruthfulness and dishonesty, which are hardly now held by the great masses to be a reflection, unless discovered.'

Complaint against the Marquis of Tweeddale's insulting language towards the Native Community.

"That your petitioners do not consider this the proper place to remark upon the gratuitous insult offered to their whole community by the Government, in recording such an opinion for the sole purpose of transmission to the Governors of the Madras University, one-half of whom, to the number of seven, are Natives, under its Constitution; but they beg to observe that it ill becomes the Government to taunt the Natives with 'the instruction and care that has been bestowed on them,' whilst it has for so many years declined disbursing one-half of the educational grant, and contented itself with keeping up a school of 160 pupils, established so far from the town of Madras as to make it inconvenient for persons to send their children, besides charging a school fee beyond the means of payment by the masses: and when, besides this ill-located and over-charging institution, there is not a Government School over all the 140,000 square miles comprising the Madras territories.

Study of the Bible, no *panacea* for immorality.

"That the sweeping condemnation, if it be justly founded, which your petitioners are rather loth to believe, seeing that Sir Henry Pottinger has never been known to mix with the Natives, except now and then, when he may have presided at the Annual University Examinations, and other such meetings, and with the servants of his household, exhibit the fallacy of both the past and present Governments, in imagining the study of the Bible to be a *panacea* for the 'vices of untruthfulness and dishonesty;' for, as the whole of the instruction and care bestowed on the Natives, beyond that bestowed upon the 160 pupils of the University, has been Missionary care and instruction, devoted to the study of the Bible, and that in the proportion of thousands to tens, it must be apparent that the 'sound and unexceptionable principles' adverted to in the Minute, have done literally nothing for the 'moral improvement' of the pupils into whose minds they have been so sedulously instilled; and therefore, there can be no valid reason for extending a 'Grant-in-aid' to institutions which have thus essentially failed; but there is a very strong reason against such aid being given, in order to assist in the conversion of the people, with whose religious feelings and opinions the Court of Directors has so frequently pledged itself not to interfere; and with regard to which the present Charter Act, passed by the Imperial Parliament, enacts and requires, that the Governor-General in Council shall, by laws and regulations, provide for the protection of the Natives within the British territories from insult and outrage, in their persons, religions, or opinions."*

Attempt to introduce the Bible in Government Seminaries not made in any other part of India.

No cause for any such complaint appears to have arisen in any other part of British India, nor does the Government ever appear to have departed from its wise and tolerant principle of religious neutrality in adopting measures to promote education among the natives of India. It is indeed true that the Missionaries and other fervent Christians among the English officers of the Government, from time to time, expressed the view that the study of the Bible, together with elementary doctrines of Christianity, might be made part of an optional course of study in Government Schools and Colleges, but such views were invariably rejected by the Government, which has, therefore, been unduly slandered by those who have attributed to it a proselytizing tendency in its educational policy. The sober opinions of the more prominent and important English officers of Government are exemplified by the views expressed by Sir Frederick Halliday,† in his evidence before a Select Committee of the House of Commons, on the 25th July, 1853. His opinion was asked as to the propriety of introducing the Bible as a class-book in the Government Schools, and his answer was as follows:—

* Printed Parliamentary Papers (1853): *First* Report of the Select Committee of the House of Commons on Indian Territories; pp. 464, 465; App.

† An eminent Bengal Civilian, who was Secretary to the Government of India, and afterwards became Lieutenant-Governor of Bengal.

Sir Frederick Halliday's evidence before the House of Commons, on 25th July, 1853, against the introduction of the Bible in Government Seminaries.

"There are two ways of introducing the Bible into schools. One is as a class-book; by which I understand a horn-book for teaching the language merely; that they should read out of that in preference to reading out of any other English book. Another way is, that they should read out of it intelligently, so as to inquire, and be informed, of the full meaning of it, which involves, of course, the whole teaching of Christianity. I cannot understand that there is any third way of introducing it. Either the Bible is to be read simply as a book for the teaching of English, or it is to be read as a means of acquiring a knowledge of Christianity. If it be the first which is meant, so far as it can be considered entirely distinct and capable of being separated from the actual teaching of Christianity, I should object to it anywhere as a desecration. I do not think it is advisable that you should teach little boys to thumb the Bible in that way; they learn to look upon it, in all after life, as an abomination, for which they were flogged and cuffed through their early years; and I think that that objection applies quite as much to Christian countries as to heathen countries. But if it be intended to introduce the Bible as a class-book, which shall be read with a view to instruction in its doctrines, and that, in fact, it shall be the means of giving a knowledge of Christianity, I object to it as being, in my judgment, a wrong means to a most desirable end; I being most seriously and entirely satisfied that it is by the careful and systematic keeping out of the Government Schools, and out of the Government practice, all forcible and influential attempts at conversion, that we stand where we stand, and that the Natives are willing to receive Missionary teaching and to hear Missionaries; and that they do, in fact, evince that very tolerance, which is now brought forward by zealous persons on that side of the question, as a reason for altering the system hitherto pursued by the Government. I believe the persons who talk in that way, are utterly unaware of the hand which has put them where they are, and holds them where they are; I believe the very tolerance, or as they sometimes call it, indifference of the Natives to Missionary teaching; and the very reason why the Missionaries go in perfect security and teach and preach all over the country, without stint or limit; without the slightest interference, or even exciting the anger of the Natives in any great degree, is that the Natives are thoroughly persuaded, by a long course of observation of the conduct of the Government, that the whole thing is a matter of private exhortation and private influence; and that the force and influence of the Government, whether in the schools or out of the schools, is never intended to be applied to that purpose. But I have a very strong conviction, that if any other course were pursued; if the Government, in the schools or out of the schools, were, by reason of the present quiet and apparent tolerance of the Natives, to attempt to convert either by influence or by force, it might produce a very serious convulsion, which would throw the Missionaries back a great number of years." *

The Bible not to be introduced even as an optional subject in Government Schools.

Again; being asked whether he thought it objectionable that the Government should give permission to any class in the Government Schools, which wished it, to use the Bible, he said :—

"The meaning of that always is, for I have seen it attempted to be introduced in a private school, about which there was a great deal of discussion, that if little boys from 6 to 12 years old, under the influence of the master, can be got to say they were willing to be taught Christianity, they ought to be taught it, without reference to the will of their parents. I look upon that to be the grossest bad faith. If you are to teach Christianity, let it be done, not only with the knowledge of the children, who are beside the question altogether, but also of their parents and the people of the country; but do not entice people into the school under the pretence of saying you will only teach them Christianity if those little boys wish it, which is nothing but saying that it shall be taught at the option and discretion of the master for the time being. If, however, it be added, 'and with the permission of their parents,' which is never added on this speculation, then I answer that the permission of only one set of parents, or even the majority of the parents belonging to one school, would not suffice. I do not think the permission of even the whole set of parents of one school ought to suffice, in a political view of the question, to induce the Government to alter its system. But if, which is a thing not to be looked forward to, the parents all over India were of that opinion, then the whole aspect of the question would be changed."...... †

"The Bible is very extensively read by the Natives; if anybody says, as I see has been said in a paper which has been put into my hands by a gentleman in this room, that the Bible is 'systematically proscribed,' or 'authoritatively proscribed,' I cannot understand the meaning of it; persons who write in that way must mean something which I am unable to fathom; or they are not acquainted with the facts. It is not true that the Bible is proscribed in the Government Schools; it is put into the Government School libraries universally,

* Printed Parliamentary Papers (1853): *Sixth* Report of the Select Committee of the House of Commons on Indian Territories, p. 55.

† *Ib.*, pp. 55, 56.

and the students are allowed, to the top of their bent, to read it from beginning to end. I will not say that they are encouraged to do so; but when you consider that they have to read and be examined in Milton, in Johnson, in Addison, in Abercromby's Moral Philosophy, and in a variety of books of that class, and looking also to the sort of examination which is required of them, and the full, complete, and comprehensive knowledge of all the subjects of which those books treat, which is expected from those young men, it is perfectly clear that they can do nothing without knowing that which appears sprouting upon the surface of every one of those books at all times. It has been truly said by Sir Charles Trevelyan, in the Committee of the House of Lords, that we are not conscious ourselves to the full extent of the amount of Christian teaching involved in a thoroughly classical English education, independently of all direct efforts at conversion. It renders necessary a knowledge of the Bible, and I may say a knowledge of the great doctrines of Christianity, which those young men who have that peculiar desire to improve themselves, which is the characteristic of the Natives of Bengal, are perfectly able to perceive, and perfectly desirous of following out; the consequence is, that they do read and study the Bible, no body objecting to, or standing in the way of their so doing. I believe there is more knowledge of the Bible in the Hindu College of Calcutta, than there is in any public school in England."*

Testimony of Mr. John Clarke Marshman as to Religious Neutrality in Government Schools.

To the evidence of Sir Frederick Halliday may be added the statement of another important witness, the well-known Mr. John Clarke Marshman, whose unusually long residence in India was devoted principally to matters relating to education and enlightenment among the people of India. He was examined by the Select Committee of the House of Commons on the 8th of July, 1853, and being asked what the rule was in the Government Schools respecting religious instruction, said:—

His Deposition given before the House of Commons, on 8th July, 1853.

"The Government considers itself pledged to the principle of perfect neutrality on the subject of religion, and religious instruction is therefore entirely excluded from the Government Schools; the education is completely confined to mere secular branches of instruction. The Bible is altogether excluded, and great care is taken to avoid any instruction which might be interpreted into a wish to use education as a means of proselytism, or to tamper with the religious faith of the students. I have always thought that the union of religious and secular instruction was absolutely indispensable to a good and complete education, and that the exclusion of all reference to religious truth in the Government institutions was a matter of very great regret. The Natives themselves also have always been accustomed to give a very high religious tone to secular education. In fact, among the Natives themselves, religion is completely identified with education; they go so far as to represent even the very alphabet as having been communicated to men by the gods; and all the knowledge which the Natives possess, relative to history, geography, astronomy, or any other kind of secular instruction, is given to them under a religious sanction. * * * * * * The introduction of the Bible, or the doctrines of Christianity, into those seminaries would create the greatest possible agitation in Native Society; in fact, such a degree of excitement as we have never seen before, far more intense than any thing which was raised upon the question of *Suttees*, or even upon the recent occasion of the passing of the Liberty of Conscience Act. The orthodox party would be joined by the liberal party, and they would immediately meet, and probably form a kind of Committee of religious safety; they would, throughout the newspapers, both English and Native, spread the report that the Government, after having for so long a period acted upon the principle of neutrality, had now entered upon a crusade against their religion, and that it was endeavouring to make the education of the Natives the means of proselytism. This powerful body in Calcutta would very probably determine, and the determination would be supported by all the Hindoos in Calcutta, to exclude from the pale of Native Society every individual who dared to send his children to those schools, till the obnoxious rule was repealed. The introduction therefore of Christian instruction would be a source of very great embarrassment to the Government. I think the immediate effect of it would be to close the schools, and that it would be found in some measure to shake the cofidence of the community in the maintenance of that principle of religious neutrality, which is at present so great a source of political security.

English Professors indifferent to Christianity.

"I think that another reason, which should not be overlooked, may be found, although it is a subject of great delicacy to touch on, in the views of some of those who have superintended the public institutions connected with the State. I think there has been a very strong impression upon the minds of many, that the exclusion of Christianity from the public institutions was with them a source of no regret; and that they have voluntarily placed in

* Printed Parliamentary Papers (1853): *Sixth* Report of the Select Committee of the House of Commons on Indian Territories p. 56.

very influential situations, in those institutions, men who were avowedly indifferent to Christianity; and some who openly professed the principles of infidelity. I think that the character of the present Members of the Committee of Public Instruction affords a sufficient guarantee against the recurrence of any such unpleasant and objectionable proceedings; but still there are, doubtless, some among the Europeans employed as tutors in the English Colleges, who regard the truths of Christianity with perfect indifference, and who, if an appeal were made to them by any of the students, regarding the principles of Christianity, would very likely give such an answer as would impair the value of those truths in the minds of the Natives. We must also remember, that a very large proportion of the teachers in the Government Institutions are Natives, very respectable and well-educated Natives, but still Hindus, who do not consider Christianity to be a Divine revelation; and I cannot imagine that there would be much advantage in the inculcation of Christian truth by those who did not appreciate its importance; and that it would be better altogether to avoid any attempt to disseminate Christian truth in the institutions of the Government, when there was any danger of its being accompanied with remarks calculated to throw discredit upon the doctrines of the Bible. I think those circumstances tend rather to mitigate the regret that every sincere Christian would otherwise feel at the exclusion of religious instruction, that is, of instruction in the truths and doctrines of Christianity, from the public institutions of the Government."*

Mr. Arthur Howell's views on Religious Neutrality in Education.

The most suitable way to close this Chapter is to quote the following passages from an official publication† on the subject of education in British India prior to 1854, by Mr. Arthur Howell (Under-Secretary to the Government of India), whose views upon the subject deserve consideration:—

Religious Neutrality declared by Lord William Bentinck.

"Before leaving India, Lord William Bentinck had an opportunity of declaring, on two memorable occasions the strict policy of religious neutrality, which is still observed in the matter of education. Alarmed by the views of the Anglicists, and by the rumour of the probable result of the controversy of the day, the Mussalman inhabitants of Calcutta petitioned the Government to spare the Madrassa, and to abstain from measures 'systematically directed towards the destruction of the literature and religious system of Islam,' or dictated by the desire to forward the views of those 'who wish the conversion of all to their own faith.' The Governor-General replied,‡ that 'such motives never have influenced, never can influence, the Counsels of the Government,' and that he would feel 'uneasiness if he thought that the Government authorities had in any part of their conduct afforded ground or occasion of any kind for such an apprehension to be entertained by any class of the subjects of the State.'

Religious Neutrality re-affirmed.

"In the same spirit, in reply to a parting address from the Missionaries, the Governor-General declared that 'the fundamental principle of British rule, the compact to which the Government stands solemnly pledged, is strict neutrality. To this important maxim, policy as well as good faith have enjoined upon me the most scrupulous observance. The same maxim is peculiarly applicable to general education. In all schools and colleges supported by Government this principle cannot be too strongly enforced, all interference and injudicious tampering with the religious belief of the students, all mingling direct or indirect teaching of Christianity with the system of instruction, ought to be positively forbidden.'

Despatch of the Court of Directors, dated 13th April, 1858, as to strict Religious Neutrality.

"It may not be out of place to record here how these sentiments of Lord William Bentinck's were confirmed twenty-three years afterwards, in one of the last Despatches§ issued from the Court of Directors.

"'The Government will adhere, with good faith, to its ancient policy of perfect neutrality in matters affecting the religion of the people of India, and we most earnestly caution all those in authority under it, not to afford, by their conduct, the least color to the suspicion that that policy has undergone or will undergo any change.

"'It is perilous for men in authority to do as individuals that which they officially condemn. The intention of the Government will be inferred from their acts, and they may unwillingly expose it to the greatest of all dangers, —that of being regarded with general distrust by the people.

"'We rely upon the honorable feelings which have ever distinguished our Service for the furtherance of the views which we express. When the Government of India makes a promise to the people, there must not be afforded to them grounds for a doubt as to its fidelity to its word.'

* Printed Parliamentary Papers (1853): *Sixth* Report of the Select Committee of the House of Commons on Indian Territories, pp. 26. 27.

† *Education in British India* prior to 1854. By Arthur Howell, Esq., 1872; pp. 33–35.

‡ Dated 9th March, 1835.

§ No. 52, dated 13th April, 1858.

"I have quoted this Despatch which, as is well known, was strongly re-affirmed on the transfer of the sovereignty to the Crown, in order to show how firm is the basis of that most remarkable feature in Indian education, the Religious Neutrality of the Government. This feature is no doubt a relic of the extreme apprehension which prevailed in 1793, and whether its original declaration was a wise one or not is far too deep and many-sided a question to be discussed here. We must accept the fact as we find it. But it is, I believe, absolutely without precedent or parallel elsewhere, besides being entirely opposed to the traditional idea of education current in the East. In Europe, it is almost an axiom that the connection of any State system of education with religion is not the mere result of tradition;* 'it is an indissoluble union, the bonds of which are principles inseparable from the nature of education.' This is admitted almost universally. Even the French system is religious, not in the sense in which all European systems profess to be more or less so, in inculcating the precepts of a certain universal and indisputable morality; but in inculcating morality in the only way in which the masses of mankind will ever admit it, in its connection with the doctrines of religion. In Holland, primary instruction was decided in a much debated law to be designed to train 'to the exercise of all Christian and social virtues,' while respecting the convictions of Dissenters. In Switzerland, religion stands on the same footing as reading, writing, grammar and arithmetic, as a fundamental part of the scheme. In Germany, generally, religion still forms, as it has always done, the first and staple subject of the elementary school, and the religion of the master must be in conformity with that of the majority of his pupils. The American system, while repudiating all doctrinal or dogmatic teaching, provides everywhere for the regular daily reading of the Bible and for prayer. And, lastly, the framers of the English Education Act, 1870, have been able to assume as a matter of course that every elementary school would be connected with a recognised religious denomination, and that Government aid might, therefore, be offered to all alike for secular education only.†

Religious Neutrality considered.

"In India, not only is there no religious teaching of any kind in Government Schools, but even the aided schools under native managers, are generally adopting the same principle. I believe this result was never anticipated, and I am sure it requires attention. Looking to the rapid growth of our educational system, and to the enormous influence for good or evil that a single able and well-educated man may exercise in this country; and looking to the dense but inflammable ignorance of the millions around us, it seems a tremendous experiment for the State to undertake, and in some Provinces almost monopolise, the direct training of whole generations above their own creed, and above that sense of relation to another world upon which they base all their moral obligations; and the possible evil is obviously growing with the system. It is true that things go smoothly and quietly, but this is attained by ignoring not only the inevitable results of early training on the character, and the great needs of human nature, especially in the East, but by also ignoring the responsibility which devolves on the Government that assumes the entire control of direct education at all. If, therefore, while fanaticism is raging around, there is a calm in our schools and colleges, it is an ominous and unnatural calm, of impossible continuance, the calm of the centre of the Cyclone.

No religious teaching in Government Schools.

"The subject is one of extreme difficulty, that grows with the consideration devoted to it. Of course, it is out of the question to recede in any degree from the pledges of the past; and it is probable that the evil is less serious in primary schools where the instruction given does not necessarily destroy religious belief, whereas our higher instruction does. Therefore, although the State may establish and maintain Primary Schools, where no local effort is forthcoming, it would still seem very desirable that it should retire as rapidly and as completely as practicable from the entire control of all direct instruction, and especially higher instruction, and leave it to local management, to be encouraged by the State, and aided in conformity with the English principle, which, without any interference in the religious instruction imparted, practically ensures, by the constitution of the Local Boards, that some religious instruction is regularly given."‡

Question of Religious Instruction difficult.

* *Public Education.* By Sir J. K. Shuttleworth, p. 290.
† Mr. Gladstone's speech. *Hansard*, Vol. cciı, p. 267.
‡ *Education in British India prior to 1854.* By Arthur Howell, Esq., 1872; pp. 33–35.

CHAPTER XIII.

EFFECTS OF PURELY SECULAR ENGLISH EDUCATION ON THE NATIVE MIND.—VIEWS OF MR. MARSHMAN AND SIR CHARLES TREVELYAN AS TO THE CHRISTIANIZING INFLUENCE OF ENGLISH EDUCATION.—MR. HOWELL'S VIEWS AS TO THE FIRST EFFECTS OF ENGLISH AND MISSIONARY TEACHING.—THE "BRAHMO SAMAJ" MOVEMENT.

Mr Marshman's views as to the effect of purely secular English Education.

The effect which a purely secular English instruction had upon the minds of the native students, was also the subject of a question in reply to which Mr. Marshman said :—

"I think, although Christianity is entirely excluded from the Government Institutions, yet the instruction which is given in them has had the effect of raising the Natives infinitely above their own creed. There are few of those who have received a complete education at the Government Institutions, who do not hold the doctrines and principles of Hindooism in the most thorough contempt. And this is easily accounted for; for all those geographical, and astronomical, and historical absurdities which are believed by the Hindoos, are derived entirely from the *Shastras*. The Native obtains his religious creed from the same source as his scientific knowledge, and from the same books which, as Mr. Macaulay mentioned in his Minute on Education, teach him the existence of seas of treacle and seas of clarified butter. Now, when the Native finds that the existence of those two seas, and, indeed, all the facts regarding geography and history given in the *Shastras* are entirely fabulous; when his faith is shaken in one portion of the system, it is scarcely possible that it should not also be shaken in others. Such has been my experience, that the study of English literature, and the knowledge of European science which is obtained by the Natives, although unaccompanied with religious instruction, or instruction in the truths of Christianity, has produced the great effect of shaking the fabric of Hindooism to its very foundation; and that the indirect result which has thus followed the exertions of the Government in the cause of education is highly satisfactory. At the same time, I ought to mention that those Natives who have received a superior education, and through that education have been raised above the absurdities of their creed, are still found to be, perhaps, the most strenuous opponents of Christianity; and the Missionaries have remarked that they do not encounter more strenuous opposition from any class than that of educated native youths. And it is to this circumstance, that is, to the Natives having been raised above their own superstitious creed, without embracing Christianity, that we are to attribute the great success which has attended the attempt to establish that sect of Vedantists, originally founded by Ram Mohun Roy: This sect at the present time includes 300 or 400 of the very best educated Natives in Calcutta, and no Christian can regard the popular idolatry of the country with feelings of greater contempt than this body of Vedantists, who profess to derive the doctrine of 'One God' from the Vedas. They have established a Chapel in Calcutta, where they hold weekly meetings, and where monotheistic hymns from the Vedas are chanted, and some eminent Brahmin connected with their Society stands up and repeats some moral sentence from the Vedas, and explains it to the assembled audience, and endeavours to enforce its doctrine upon their consciences." *

Sir Charles Trevelyan's views as to religious instruction in Government Seminaries for teaching English.

Upon the subject of religious instruction in the Government Institutions, and the extent to which a knowledge of Christianity is acquired by the students of English literature, without the Bible being regarded as a class-book, and also upon the merits of the policy of Government in this matter, the facts and opinions stated by so eminent a statesman as Sir Charles Trevelyan, in his deposition before a Select Committee of the House of Lords, on the 28th June, 1853, deserve special attention, and may be quoted here as throwing considerable light upon the subject, as it was then considered and discussed. He said :—

"The Bible is not admitted as a class-book into the Government Seminaries. This rule has been objected to, as implying hostility to the progress of Christian truth; but no opinion was ever more mistaken. When we formed English libraries in connexion with the different Government institutions, on the re-organization of the system of instruction, after the Resolution of 1835, the Bible was placed in all the libraries; and, I understand that it is now desired that Mant's, and other Commentaries on the Bible, should also be placed there, to which I see no objection; nor

* Printed Parliamentary Papers (1853): *Sixth* Report of the Select Committee of the House of Commons on Indian Territories, p. 28.

is there any objection to the best religious books being placed there. As has been already stated, the books of English literature which are ordinarily studied in the Government Seminaries, such as Milton, Bacon, Locke, Addison, and Johnson, are replete with allusions to the Bible, and frequent reference to the Bible is indispensably necessary in order to their being properly understood. The Bible is, accordingly, constantly referred to by the teachers and students, in the course of their instruction, and it is often found at the examinations that the young men have in this way, and by reading the Bible out of school, acquired a considerable amount of Christian knowledge. There is no restriction whatever to prevent it. In reference to this part of the subject, I beg to read the following extract from Mr. Kerr's '*History of Native Education in Bengal and Agra*': 'In none of the rules recently published is there any such prohibition; and, in practice, the teacher is left at liberty to speak to his pupils on religion, on Christianity, on the distinct evidences of Christianity, with nearly the same freedom as he might do in a theological seminary. In institutions where Milton and Addison and Johnson are class-books, it is impossible to abstain from all reference to religion. Bacon's works, too, which form one of our text-books; the Essays, the Advancement of Learning, and even the *Novum Organum*, are full of Scriptural illustrations, for the proper understanding of which the student must be referred to the Bible. It may be added, that our text-books on Moral Philosophy are wholly Christian in their spirit and tendency. In Abercrombie's Intellectual Powers, which is carefully studied without curtailment, there is a distinct chapter on the Evidences of Christianity. In the same author's work, on the moral feelings, which is also studied without omitting any part of it, the existence and attributes of God, the relation of man to God, the probability of a Divine Revelation, the nature and province of Faith—all viewed in a Christian light—are some of the subjects which come under review, and which our students are expected to master. Even Adam Smith's work, which does not directly touch on religion, is full of noble, and what may truly be called, Christian sentiments. I do not presume to say that religion forms as prominent a branch of study in the Government Colleges as in the Missionary Institutions. But neither is it excluded with that jealous care that is sometimes supposed. The primary design of the Government scheme of education is to advance the progress of civilization in India by the diffusion of useful knowledge, as the phrase is generally understood The design of the Missionary Institutions is to convert the Natives to Christianity. The two objects are distinct, but they are by no means opposed to one another.' It is added as a note here, 'Addison closes the Essay No. 7 of 'The Spectator,' in a strain of serious piety. 'I know but one way' says he, 'of fortifying my soul against these gloomy presages and terrors of mind, and that is by securing to myself the friendship and protection of that Being who disposes of events and governs futurity. When I lay me down to sleep, I recommend myself to his care; when I awake, I give myself up to his direction.' Can any one doubt that it must be improving to Hindoo students, in a religious and moral point of view, to read such passages? When the Essay was read, not long ago, in one of the Colleges, the teacher told his students that, though Hindoos, they might well imitate the example of Addison, 'when they lay themselves down to sleep, recommending themselves to God's care; and when they awake, giving themselves up to His direction.' To this, as they always do when the conversation turns upon religious subjects, they listened with serious attention. It is sometimes said that the education we give makes our students sceptical. It does make them sceptical—sceptical of all those degrading ideas with which the notion of a Deity is associated in Hindoo minds.' * * * 'In the first place, the efforts of the educational authorities, and of those immediately engaged in the business of instruction, are systematically directed towards the object of communicating truth in historical, philosophical, and scientific subjects. Are the opponents of the Government system prepared to say that the communication of true knowledge on these subjects has a tendency unfavourable to belief in true religion? It would be unreasonable to suppose that it has any such tendency. Secondly, it is stated, that we take from the Hindoos their own belief, and give them nothing in its place. It is true, that the knowledge we communicate clears the Hindoo mind of much that is frivolous and false in their own religious system. But it cannot be admitted that it shakes in the least their belief in those principles which form the foundation of all religion, such as the existence of God, the greatness and goodness of God, the providence of God, the probability of a future state of rewards and punishments. So far from these invaluable principles being shaken by our system of education, they are brought into clearer light by it, and belief in them is confirmed. If our system had, indeed, the effect of depriving the Hindoos of their belief in these principles, and of the hopes built upon them, it might fairly be denounced as most pernicious. Thirdly, if we look at actual results, it will be found that of the well-educated converts to Christianity, nearly as many have come from the Hindoo College and other Government Institutions, as from the Missionary Seminaries. The fact is generally admitted; and perhaps it is not so strange as may at first appear. In the Missionary Seminaries religious instruction is commenced at an early age, before the understanding is ripe for its reception. The youths are systematically drilled in Catechisms and in the Evidences of Christianity. They acquire a habit of listening with apparent attention, of admitting every thing that the teacher requires; of answering questions on religion by rote, without any exercise of the understanding. In some cases a habit of dissimulation is formed, unknown to the Missionary, who, unconsciously, and from the best motives, has been cultivating one of the prominent vices of the native character. It is surely needless to point out that the youth in whom this habit of dissimulation is formed, is most unlikely ever to act with manliness, or to do anything that demands a sacrifice, such as conversion to Christianity very often demands. From all these dangers the Government institutions are free. The principles of a foreign religion are not pressed prematurely upon unripe minds. The pupils are expected on no occasion to express what they do not believe. When they begin, of their own accord, to turn their attention to the Christian religion, to enter into conversation, and to read books upon the subject, it is with a keen relish, and with minds untainted by habits unfavourable to a sincere reception of Truth. The consequence is, that some of the most intelligent among them, voluntarily, and from the purest motives, embrace Christianity.' I conceive that it would not be for the advantage of Christian truth that the Bible should be treated as a lesson-book for learning to read. The system of teaching the Bible as an ordinary class-book is now generally rejected by persons who take an interest in education. We would not teach it to our own children in that manner. In order that the Bible may be successfully taught, teachers should be selected who have not only a satisfactory knowledge of the doctrines of the Bible, but who have their heart in the object, and sincerely desire its success. In other words, if the Bible were to be taught in the Government Seminaries, it would be necessary to organize them for theological instruction, in the manner in which Dr. Duff's and other Mssionary schools are organized. If the Bible were taught in a rantive, perfunctory and irreverent manner by a common master, as a common class-book, it would have an injurious effect upon the young Natives, by producing a deadness and indifference of feeling; and if, beyond that, the persons employed to teach the Bible were not themselves good Christians, and their life and conduct were not conformable to what they taught, it would have a most pernicious effect upon the young man, for the Native children are extremely acute, and are very good judges of character. I therefore think it would be far better that there should be a division of labour in this as well as in other subjects; that the Government should continue to go, as far as they safely can, in the instruction given by them; that is, that they should give the best possible practical general education, with a friendly feeling towards Christian truth, in common with all other truth; and that the Missionaries, and others, more immediately interested in the progress of Christianity, should take any means they think proper for instructing and influencing the young men so brought up. They might, if they thought proper, establish a lecture-room opposite every one of the Government Institutions, as Dr. Duff did, opposite the Hindu College. They might distribute Bibles and religious books, and books on the Evidences of Christianity, to any extent they think proper; and I am satisfied that, in this manner, if Christianity has a 'fair field and no favour,' it must ultimately prevail. As long as the old system, according to which it was held to be the duty of the magistrate to 'maintain truth,' as well as to 'execute justice,' prevailed, the matter was extremely simple, and the resources of the State were employed in teaching the particular opinions held by those who happened to be in the possession of the Government. But since the principle of toleration has been established, from the Reformation downwards, very considerable modifications have been made in this principle. The Scotch and Irish Colleges are one modification, and it is precisely on that model that the Government Seminaries are established; that is, that the young men attend them daily, living at their own homes, or in places provided by their relations or friends, and receive such religious instruction as their relations, and others interested in their welfare, think proper. The Privy Council system, in its dealing with the Dissenters, is another modification of the original principle. That also I propose to take as the model of an advanced measure for assisting and extending education in India. The extracts from the Bible in the schools in Ireland form another instance; but I do not think it will be proposed to extend that system to India. Now, if it has been necessary that there should be a compromise of this kind in England, and in the United Kingdom, where the religious differences are only minor differences on the non-essential points of Christianity, how much more necessary is it in India, where the difference is between Christianity and its opposites,—Hindooism and Mahomedanism. A very plausible *primâ facie* argument might be adduced of this kind. It might be said, suppose that in any particular district of British India, Dacca for instance, two-thirds of the Natives of the place were willing that the Bible should be introduced into the Government College, what solid objection can there be in that case to its introduction? My answer is, that if the Dacca District comprehended the whole of British India, certainly the point ought to be yielded, because it is clearly our duty to give the Natives the best instruction which, on a large and sound view of their prevailing disposition, they are willing to receive. But the Dacca District is not the whole of British India. There are hundreds of other districts which are in very unequal stages of advancement. In most of them the Natives are still, religiously considered, in a very unreformed, unadvanced, and sensitive state; and if the British Government should depart in any one instance from the great principle of religious neutrality, upon which it has constantly acted up to the present time, they would become seriously alarmed. And if, besides that, conversions took place in the Dacca District, in consequence of the system contended for being adopted, which is the object aimed at by those who advocate the plan, the alarm would be still more increased. I mentioned in my former evidence, that one very important feature of the present state of India is, that zealous, and vital religion has made great progress among the Europeans, at which I greatly rejoice. But if this element is not properly dealt with, it may be productive of very dangerous and evil consequences. So long as the zealously religious English people have no official footing in the Government Seminaries, no harm can ensue, and their efforts find plenty of scope elsewhere. They may promote Missionary efforts in any part of the country. They may instruct at other hours the young men who are brought up at the Government Seminaries; but, if we once, by allowing the Bible to be studied in the Government Seminaries as a class-book, give to zealous Christians an official footing in those seminaries, it is impossible to say what the consequences might be. All barriers would then be broken down, and the principle of neutrality, which has hitherto been our great security, and the great cause of our success in enlightening the Natives, both in secular and divine knowledge, would be at an end. In the Madras Presidency, a different course has been followed, and the consequence has been that while the Europeans have been disputing whether religion should be taught by the Government, the Natives have, with certain limited exceptions, remained without any instruction; which is the more to be regretted, because there is no intermediate language in the Madras Presidency like Persian, which so long baffled our efforts in Bengal; and English is already in extensive use as a common medium of communication between persons speaking different languages. Lastly, even supposing that every other objection to the employment of the Government Seminaries, for giving instruction to the Natives in Christianity, were got over, the question would immediately arise. What form of Christianity ?—and then the unhappy and damaging fact of the existence of considerable differences of opinion among Christians would be made apparent; and the spirit of religious controversy, which is happily nearly dormant in India, because Christians of every persuasion are on an equality, and they all pursue their respective objects on the voluntary principle without interfering with each other, would be evoked." *

Sir Charles Trevelyan's opinions and expectations as to the Christianizing influence of English Education.

Sir Charles Trevelyan, from whose evidence the preceding extract has been taken, belonged to that class of Anglo-Indian Statesmen of the first-half of the present century, who whilst upholding the principle of religious neutrality in Government Educational Institutions, on the ground of good policy, maintained the opinion that the natural effect of the general advance of the English language, literature, and science, will be the propagation of Christianity among the natives of India. The views of such an eminent statesman upon such a delicate subject, are sufficiently important to be quoted in his own words. Before a Select Committee of the House of Lords, on the 28th June, 1853, he said :—

"I conceive that we have reached an advanced stage in the progress of education in India, namely, that all schools in which a good general education is given, may be assisted, whatever may be the religion taught; and I believe that that plan may now safely be adopted; but far be it from me to say that the time may not come when direct Christian instruction may be given even in the Government Seminaries. I conceive that our ruling principle ought to be, to give the best education which, on a sound general view, our fellow-subjects are willing to receive. There can be no doubt that all education is imperfect, which is not based on Christian instruction; and it follows, that when the greater part of India has been brought to a level with those parts which are most advanced, it will be our duty to give Christian instruction. But I am of opinion that the time has not yet arrived to attempt this very forward and advanced step, which at this stage of our progress would only lead to a violent reaction. We ought never to lose sight of the possible effect upon our Native Army, of any measures that may be urged upon us which would be likely to excite the religious feelings of the Mahomedans and Hindoos. The Rajpoots were to our predecessors the Moguls, what the sepoys are to us; and the alienation of the Rajpoots by religious intolerance, was the first step to the downfall of the Empire * * * * * Before I left Calcutta, I had a list made of all the converts to Christianity from the educated class, and I found that at that time the majority of this class of converts, whose character and cultivation, and strength of mind, offer the best assistance to Christianity, were from the Hindoo College. I think many persons mistake the way in which the conversion of India will be brought about. I believe it will take place at last wholesale, just as our own ancestors were converted. The country will have Christian instruction infused into it in every way by direct missionary instruction, and indirectly through books of various kinds, through the public papers, through conversation with Europeans, and in all the conceivable ways in which knowledge is communicated; and then, at last, when Society is completely saturated with Christian knowledge, and public opinion has taken a decided turn that way, they will come over by thousands." †

* Printed Parliamentary Papers. *Second* Report of the Select Committee of the House of Lords on Indian Territories (1852-53), pp. 193-196

† *Ib.*, pp. 203, 204.

Christianising influence of English education a fallacy.

That such expectations of the wholesale conversion of the natives of India to Christianity through the agency of English education, were entirely fallacious, is shown by the facts of the progress of English education during the last fifty years. High education in the English language, literature, and sciences, has undoubtedly the effect of sapping the foundations of idolatry and superstition, and improving the perception of the well-recognized principles of morality and independent thought, which the educated native of India is prone to share with the more advanced social and political thinkers of Europe. But so far as religious tendencies of English education are concerned, the Christian doctrine has far less prospects of acceptance than Free Thought, Scepticism, and Agnosticism. Doctrines somewhat akin to what is known as the Philosophy of Positivism usually take the place of religion, in the case of the Indian youth educated in the English literature and science, and the worldly concerns of this life seldom leave time for consideration of any such prospects of a future life as Christianity may have to offer. How the matter was regarded by the Missionaries is discussed in the following chapter. Meanwhile the following passages from an official publication* on the subject of education may be quoted here, as representing the first effects of English education and missionary teaching on the Native mind :—

First effects of English, and Missionary teaching.

"In one of his striking orations at the convocation of the Calcutta University, a late Vice-Chancellor (Sir Henry S. Maine, 1864-65) observed that if the founders of false systems of religion or philosophy had confined themselves to disclosing moral errors only, or false propositions, about the unknown and unseen world, their empire, would, in most societies, and certainly in Oriental societies, have been perpetual. But happily for the human race, some fragment of physical speculation has been built into every false system. Here is its weak point,—here it is that the study of physical science forms the inevitable breach that finally leads to the overthrow of the whole fabric. The remark received a powerful illustration on the first introduction of European knowledge into India. It is well known that religion is not among the Hindoos, or indeed the Mahomedans, as it is with us, a separate study, but it pervades almost every science, and almost every social relation. The learned Native obtains his creed and science from the same source, and it is impossible to give even a tolerable Sanskrit or Arabic education without a great deal of direct instruction in religion. You cannot teach the European system of geography, astronomy, or medicine without exploding the Hindoo system ; you cannot teach political economy, or social science, without coming into collision with the theory and practice of caste. In this respect the Koran, the Hidayah, and other Mahomedan books, are of the same character as the Shashtras. The result, therefore, of introducing the wide range of European literature and science into the native community at Calcutta, was to open a new, strange world to students. As Greek literature was in the Augustan age at Rome, or as Latin and Greek were at the mediæval revival of letters in the Western World, so English became to the young collegians. Every day opened to them, for the first time, a succession of new and strange phenomena in the unsealed realm of history, science, and philosophy ; they were suddenly thrown adrift from the moorings and anchorages of old creeds, and tossed upon the wide sea of speculation and extravagance. It was no wonder that moral and social obligations began to share the fate of religious beliefs, and that the whole community was in alarm at the spread of the new views. This was precisely the state of things which Mr. Charles Marsh had eloquently anticipated during the discussion of the Charter of 1813 :—'It is one thing,' he said, 'to dispel the charm that binds mankind to established habits and ancient obligations, and another to turn them over to the discipline of new institutions and the authority of new doctrines. In that dreadful interval,—that dreary void where the mind is left to wander and grope its way without the props that have hitherto supported it, or the lights that have guided it,—what are the chances that they will discern the beauties or submit to the restraints of the religion you propose to give them.'

The Brahmo Samaj movement.

"The 'dreadful interval' and 'the dreary void' had arrived, and it is impossible to say how far Native Society might not have been disorganised had not the Missionaries stepped in and supplied a new direction to the awakening scepticism, and a fresh subject to attract the newly-aroused spirit of speculation. It was not that the immediate result was conversion to Christianity, except in the case of a very few. The immediate result was the establishment of a new creed, which united the pure Theism of the Vedas to the morality of the Gospel, with which it was essentially kindred, and from which it drew all its best practical precepts. The new sect was subsequently called the Brahmo Samaj ; and so far from it being the case, as was anticipated, that missionary teaching would form an additional element to danger and alarm, it is certain that when popular Hinduism at Calcutta was crumbling into ruins before European science, Missionary teaching pointed to a foundation upon which a purer system might be built, though the superstructure might differ from that which the Missionary had hoped for. From this time no account of the state of education in India would be at all adequate unless it included the results of Missionary effort." †

* *Education in British India prior to* 1854. By Arthur Howell, Esq., pp. 10–12.

† *Ib.*, pp. 10–12.

CHAPTER XIV.

VIEWS OF THE MISSIONARIES OPPOSED TO RELIGIOUS NEUTRALITY IN EDUCATION.—THE OBJECTS OF THE MISSIONARY EDUCATIONAL INSTITUTIONS.—REV. A. DUFF'S STATEMENT BEFORE THE HOUSE OF LORDS, IN 1853, AS TO MISSIONARY ENDEAVOURS FOR EDUCATION.—HIS VIEWS AS TO EFFECTS OF PURELY SECULAR EDUCATION.—OPINIONS OF THE CELEBRATED PHILOSOPHIC THINKER, REV. SYDNEY SMITH, AS TO THE EFFORTS OF THE MISSIONARIES IN INDIA.

Religious neutrality in Education disapproved by Missionaries.

There can be no doubt that whilst the Government scrupulously adhered to the policy of religious neutrality in matters of public instruction, the Missionaries regarded such neutrality with disapproval. As a specimen of their views upon the subject, some passages may be quoted from the observations recorded by the well-known Rev. Alexander Duff, D.D., on Lord William Bentinck's Resolution of the 7th March, 1835, regarding English education. Dr. Duff was examined as a witness by a Select Committee of the House of Lords, on Indian Territories, on the 3rd of June, 1853, and in answer to the question—'What change in the system of education was effected by that Resolution,' he presented to the Committee some written remarks, from which the following extract may be quoted as throwing light upon the attitude of the Missionaries and other enthusiastic Christians, on the subject of the absence of religious instruction from the Government educational institutions :—

Rev. Alexander Duff's opinion adverse to Religious Neutrality in education.

"Even since the passing of Lord W. Bentinck's Act, *four new institutions* have been organized in large towns along the Ganges, after the model of the Calcutta College; and every year fresh additions will be made to the number. What, then, will be the *ultimate* effect of these yearly augmenting educationary forces? We say *ultimate*, with emphasis, because we are no visionaries; we do not expect miracles; we do not anticipate sudden and instantaneous changes; but we do not look forward with confidence to a *great ultimate revolution*. We do regard Lord W. Bentinck's Act as laying the foundation of a train of causes which may for a while operate so insensibly as to pass unnoticed by careless or casual observers, but not the less surely as concerns the great and momentous issue: like the laws which silently, but with resistless power, regulate the movements of the material universe, these educationary operations, which are of the nature and force of moral laws, will proceed onwards till they terminate in effecting a universal change in the national mind of India. The sluices of a superior and quickening knowledge have already been thrown open, and who shall dare to shut them up? The streams of enlivening information have begun to flow in upon the dry and parched land, and who will venture to arrest their progess? As well might we ask with the poet :—

> Shall burning Ætna, if a sage requires,
> Forget her thunders, and recall her fires?
> When the loose mountain trembles from on high,
> Shall gravitation cease, while you go by?

"But highly as we approve of Lord W. Bentinck's enactment, *so far as its goes*, we must, ere we conclude, in justice to our own views, and to the highest and noblest cause on earth, take the liberty of strongly expressing our own honest conviction that *it does not go far enough*. Truth is better than error in any department of knowledge, the humblest as well as the most exalted; hence it is that we admire the moral intrepidity of the man who decreed that, in the Government Institutions of India, true literature and true science should henceforth be substituted in place of false literature, false science, and false religion. But while we rejoice that true literature and science is to be substituted in place of what is demonstrably false, we cannot but lament that no provision whatever has been made for substituting the only true religion—Christianity—in place of the false religion which our literature and science will inevitably demolish.

Typical views of the Missionaries as to Religious Neutrality in education.

"We are aware that plausible views of political expediency, and certain admitted peculiarities in our position in India, *seem* to forbid the interference of Government in *directly* communicating a knowledge of Christianity to its native subjects. Into such views *we* could never enter. Our firm belief has always been, that if there were the *will*, means *might* be devised that would obviate all *reasonable* objections; but be this as it may, we cannot help regarding the absence of all provision for the inculcation of Christian truth as a grand omission—a capital deficiency. If man had been destined merely to 'strut his little hour' on the stage of Time, and then drop into a state of non-existence, it would be enough to provide for the interests of Time; but the case is widely different, when reason and revelation constrain us to view him as destined to be an inhabitant of Eternity—an inheritor of never-ending bliss or never-ending woe. Surely, in this view of man's destiny, it is, in the scale of divine magnitude, but a pitiable and anomalous philanthropy after all, that can expend all its energy in bedecking and garnishing him to play his part well on the stage of Time, and then cast him adrift, desolate and forlorn, without shelter and without refuge, on the shoreless ocean of Eternity.

Christianity should not be sacrificed to worldly expediency.

"But we are persuaded that even time can never be *rightly* provided for by any measure that shuts eternity wholly out of view. So inseparably and unchangeably connected, in the wise ordination of Providence, are the best interests of Time and the best interests of Eternity, that one of the surest ways of providing aright for the former, is to provide thoroughly and well for the latter. Our maxim, accordingly, has been, is now, and ever will be, this:—*Wherever, whenever, and by whomsoever, Christianity is sacrificed on the altar of worldly expediency, there and then must the supreme good of man lie bleeding at its base.*

Neglect of Government to propagate the Gospel should encourage the Christian Churches to undertake the task.

"But because a Christian Government has chosen to neglect its duty towards the religion which it is sacredly bound to uphold, is that any reason why the Churches of Britain should neglect their duty, too? Let us be aroused, then, from our lethargy, and strive to accomplish our part. If we are *wise in time*, we may convert the Act of the Indian Government into an ally and a friend. The extensive erection of a machinery for the destruction of ancient superstition we may regard as opening up new facilities, in the good providence of God, for the spread of the everlasting Gospel; as serving the part of a humble pioneer in clearing away a huge mass of rubbish that would otherwise have tended to impede the free dissemination of Divine Truth. Wherever a Government Seminary is founded, which shall have the effect of battering down idolatry and superstition, there let us be prepared to plant a Christian institution that shall, through the blessing of Heaven, be the instrument of rearing the beauteous superstructure of Christianity on the ruins of both."*

Proselytizing views limited to Missionaries and exceptionally enthusiastic Europeans.

Views such as these were held only by the Missionaries and some enthusiastic Christians among the European officers, who thought that English education might be safely and properly rendered the vehicle of Christian knowledge, and a means of propagating Christianity among the natives of India. But such views were uniformly repudiated by the Government in India and the higher authorities in England.

Educational policy of the Missionaries.

But whilst the Government firmly took up a position of religious neutrality in English education, the Missionaries, whose great help and energetic efforts must always be recognized as a prominent factor in the intellectual progress of India, adopted a policy which can best be described in the words of the Rev. Alexander Duff, D.D., in his evidence before a Select Committee of the House of Lords, on 3rd June, 1853:—

Statement of Rev. A. Duff before the House of Lords, on 3rd June, 1853.

"Acting, not officially, nor authoritatively in any way, nor in connexion with the Government, but simply upon our own responsibility as individuals, we very plainly and simply tell the Natives what we mean to teach. We avow to them what our general and special objects are. No Native need come to us but with his eyes open, and of his own free accord; but everybody who does come spontaneously, will be taught such and such subjects, the doctrines of Christianity being an essential part of the instruction. With regard to the immediate objects of such an institution as that which I was sent out to establish, they may be thus briefly stated: One great object was to convey, as largely as possible, a knowledge of our ordinary improved literature and science to those young persons; but another and a more vital object was, simultaneously with that, as already indicated, to convey a thorough knowledge of Christianity, with its evidences and doctrines. Our purpose, therefore, was twofold, to combine as it were together, in close, inseparable and harmonious union, what has been called a useful secular, with a decidedly religious education. The ample teaching of our improved European literature, philosophy, and science, we knew would shelter the huge fabric of popular Hindooism, and crumble it into fragments. But as it is certainly not good simply to destroy, and then leave men idly to gaze over the ruins; nor wise to continue building on the walls of a tottering edifice; it has ever formed the grand and distinguishing glory of our institution, through the introduction and zealous pursuit of Christian evidence and doctrine, to strive to supply the noblest substitute in place of that which has been demolished, in the form

* Printed Parliamentary Papers (1852-53): *Second Report of the Select Committee of the House of Lords on Indian Territories*, pp. 414, 415. App. E.

of sound general knowledge and pure evangelical truth. In this way we anticipated that, under the ordinary blessing of Divine Providence on the use of appointed means, many of the young men would become Christian in understanding, and a fair proportion of them Christian in heart. We then reckoned that if, of either or both of these classes, one and another were added in continued succession, the collective mind would at length be freely set lose from its ancient fixed and frozen state, and awakened into light, and life, and liberty. And as life is self-propagating, and light communicative in its nature, we entertained the humble but confident hope that we might ultimately and happily succeed in combining the three inestimable blessings—individual good, the ever-renovating principle of self-preservation, and the power of indefinite extension : of these, our immediate and ultimate objects, no concealment was ever made ; on the contrary, they were at all times, and in every imaginable form, openly avowed and proclaimed. And lest any Native should lie under any delusive impression on the subject, it was a standing rule in our institution, from its very commencement, that no young person should be admitted unless his father, if he was alive, or his guardian, came along with him, and saw what was doing, and, therefore, personally could judge for himself whether he would allow his son or ward to remain there or not.

Hindu Students in Missionary Schools become gradually christianized.

"They all come to us at first as Hindoos in point of religious faith; and as long as they are attending a Christian course of instruction, they are merely learners or scholars; they are learning to know what the truth is; they are mastering the subject of Christianity as far as the human intellect, apart from Divine influence, can master it, much in the same way as they may come there to master the true system of geography, or the true system of astronomy; or any other true system whatever: they begin with the first elements or principles, and they are initiated into the rest, step by step, so that at last they peruse every part of the Bible, and are systematically instructed in the evidences, doctrines, and precepts of Christianity. Christian books of every description are read by them, and they are examined upon these; and if, in the end, any of them should have their minds impressed with the truth of those things, and their hearts changed and turned to God, then they openly embrace Christianity, as several have already done. Many others do become intellectually Christians, and are brought therefore into a condition very much the same as that of the great bulk of intelligent professing Christians in this country, who are Christians in head or intellect, but not in heart;—in the case of all such there is intellectual conviction, but not heart conversion: the former may come from man, the latter only from God."*

Missionary views as to the effects of purely secular English Education.

The views of the Rev. Alexander Duff, D.D., as to the political results of a purely secular English education, may also be quoted here with advantage, as they are typical, as representing the opinions of the Missionaries and others seeking the propagation of Christianity in India. In reply to the question, what he contemplated would be the ultimate result to the British Government, if it succeeded in effecting a great improvement in the education of the Hindus, he said :—

"My own impression is, that if we go on giving them a thorough English secular education, without any mollifying and counteracting influences of sufficient potency—disturbing them out of all their old ways and habits of thinking and feeling, and creating the very materials out of which spring restlessness and discontent, envy and jealousy, selfish and exorbitant ambition for power and place, irrespective of the needful moral and mental qualifications—there will not, there cannot be, generally speaking, that sentiment of devotedness or loyalty to the British Government, which, for their own sakes and for the sake of their country, we should desire them to possess. And the ultimate result of such unfriendly or disloyal sentiments becoming widespread in the case of men of quickened intelligence, and having unlimited command of a Free Press, with the English as a common medium of communication, it is not certainly difficult to foresee. I have a distinct impression, on the other hand, and I speak in this respect from experience, that any education, however highly advanced, which may be given to the natives of India, if accompanied by those mollifying and counteracting influences which are connected with the sober yet zealous inculcation of the Christian faith, so far from producing any feeling of hostility or disloyalty towards the British Government, will produce an effect entirely the other way. I should say, without any hesitation, that, at this moment, there are not in all India more devoted and loyal subjects of the British Crown than those Natives who have openly embraced Christianity; and, next to these, with the feeling of loyalty in varying degrees of strength, those Natives who have acquired this higher English education, in immediate and inseparable connexion with Christian knowledge and Christian influence. On this vitally important subject, alike as regards the honour and welfare of India and of Britain, I could well expatiate, equally in the way of argument and fact; and shall be ready at any time to do so, if required. Meanwhile, I have in answer to the question, briefly given expression to the conviction which has been

* Printed Parliamentary Papers (1852–53) *Second Report of the Select Committee of the House of Lords on Indian Territories*, pp. 57, 58.

growing in my own mind ever since I began to get practically acquainted with the real state and tendencies of things in India, 23 years ago. In the face of all plausible theories and apparent analogies, whether deduced from the conduct and policy of ancient Rome or any other State—plainly involving conditions and relations wholly incompatible with any that can exist between ours, as a Christian Government, and its non-Christian subjects in India—I have never ceased to pronounce the system of giving a high English education, without religion, as a blind, short-sighted, suicidal policy. On the other hand, for weighty reasons, I have never ceased to declare that, if our object be, not merely for our own aggrandisement, but very specially for the welfare of the Natives, to retain our dominion in India, no wiser or more effective plan can be conceived than that of bestowing this Higher English education in close and inseparable alliance with the illumining, quickening, beautifying influences of the Christian faith; indeed, I have never scrupled to avow and proclaim my sincere conviction, that the extension of such higher education, so combined, would only be the means of consolidating and perpetuating the British Empire in India for years, or even ages to come—vastly, yea, almost immeasurably, to the real and enduring benefit of both." *

Opinions of the celebrated philosophic thinker, Rev. Sydney Smith, as to the efforts of the Missionaries in India.

Whilst such were the views entertained by the Missionaries as to the policy of English education, it may be interesting to consider what opinions were entertained by independent philosophic thinkers upon the subject. As a specimen of their views, the following passages from the writings of the celebrated Rev. Sydney Smith may be quoted. Referring to the Missionaries, and their efforts in India, his writings contain the following passages:—

"The plan, it seems, is this. We are to educate India in Christianity, as a parent does his child; and, when it is perfect in its catechism, then to pack up, quit it entirely, and leave it to its own management. This is the evangelical project for separating a colony from the parent country. They see nothing of the bloodshed, and massacres, and devastations, nor of the speeches in Parliament, squandered millions, fruitless expeditions, jobs, and pensions, with which the loss of our Indian possessions would necessarily be accompanied; nor will they see that these consequences could arise from the *attempt*, and not from the completion, of their scheme of conversion. We should be swept from the peninsula by Pagan zealots; and should lose, among other things, all chance of ever really converting them.

"It may be our duty to make the Hindoos Christians—that is another argument; but, that we shall by so doing strengthen our empire, we utterly deny. What signifies identity of religion to a question of this kind? Diversity of bodily colour and of language would soon overpower this consideration. Make the Hindoos enterprising, active, and reasonable as yourselves—destroy the eternal track in which they have moved for ages—and, in a moment, they would sweep you off the face of the earth.

"When the tenacity of the Hindoos on the subject of their religion is adduced as a reason against the success of the Missions, the friends of this undertaking are always fond of reminding us how patiently the Hindoos submitted to the religious persecution and butchery of Tippo. The inference from such citations is truly alarming. It is the imperious duty of Government to watch some of these men most narrowly. There is nothing of which they are not capable. And what, after all, did Tippo effect in the way of conversion? How many Mahomedans did he make? There was all the carnage of Medea's Kettle, and none of the transformation.

"Upon the whole, it appears to us hardly possible to push the business of proselytism in India to any length, without incurring the utmost risk of losing our empire. The danger is more tremendous, because it may be so sudden; religious fears are a very probable cause of disaffection in the troops; if the troops are generally disaffected, our Indian Empire may be lost to us as suddenly as a frigate or a fort.

"No man (not an Anabaptist) will, we presume, contend that it is our duty to preach the Natives into an insurrection, or to lay before them, so fully and emphatically, the scheme of the Gospel, as to make them rise up in the dead of the night and shoot their instructors through the head. Even for Missionary purposes, therefore, the utmost discretion is necessary; and if we wish to teach the Natives a better religion, we must take care to do it in a manner which will not inspire them with a passion for political change, or we shall inevitably lose our disciples altogether. To us it appears quite clear, that neither Hindoos nor Mahomedans are at all indifferent to the attacks made upon their religion; the arrogance and irritability of the Mahometan are universally acknowledged; nor do the Brahmans show the smallest disposition to behold the encroachments upon their religion with passiveness and unconcern.

"How is it in human nature that a Brahman should be indifferent to encroachments upon his religion? His reputation, his dignity, and in great measure his wealth, depend upon the preservation of the present superstitions; and why is it to be supposed that motives which are so powerful with all other human beings, are

* Printed Parliamentary Papers (1852-53): *Second* Report of the Select Committee of the House of Lords on Indian Territories, pp. 88, 89.

inoperative with him alone? If the Brahmans, however, are disposed to excite a rebellion in support of their own influence, no man, who knows anything of India, can doubt that they have it in their power to effect it.

"Our object, therefore, is not only not to do anything violent and unjust upon subjects of religion, but not to give any strong colour to jealous and disaffected Natives for misrepresenting your intentions.

"All these observations have tenfold force, when applied to an empire which rests so entirely upon opinion. If physical force could be called in to stop the progress of error, we could afford to be misrepresented for a season; but 30,000 white men living in the mist of 70 millions of sable subjects, must be always in the right, or, at least, never represented as grossly in the wrong. Attention to the prejudices of the subject is wise in all Governments, but quite indispensable in a Government constituted as our Empire is India is constituted; where an uninterrupted series of dexterous conduct is not only necessary to our prosperity, but to our existence.

"You have 30,000 Europeans in India, and 60 millions of other subjects. If proselytism were to go on as rapidly as the most visionary Anabaptists could dream or desire, in what manner are these people to be taught the genuine truths and practices of Christianity? Where are the clergy to come from? Who is to defray the expenses of the establishment?—and who can foresee the immense and perilous difficulties of bending the laws, manners, and institutions of a country, to the dictates of a new religion? If it were easy to persuade the Hindoos that their own religion was folly, it would be infinitely difficult effectually to teach them any other. They would tumble their own idols into the river, and you would build them no churches: you would destroy all their present motives for doing right and avoiding wrong, without being able to fix upon their minds the more sublime motives by which you profess to be actuated.

"If there were a fair prospect of carrying the Gospel into regions where it was before unknown,—if such a project did not expose the best possessions of the country to extreme danger, and if it was in the hands of men who were discreet as well as devout, we should consider it to be a scheme of true piety, benevolence, and wisdom: but the baseness and malignity of fanaticism shall never prevent us from attacking its arrogance, its ignorance, and its activity. For what vice can be more tremendous than that which, while it wears the outward appearance of religion, destroys the happiness of man, and dishonours the name of God?"*

Discussions as to English Education take no special notice of Mahomedans, as they refrained from such education.

It will be observed, that throughout the discussion of the question, whether English education should be purely secular, and what effect it was likely to have upon the religious convictions of the Natives of India, views have been expressed only in regard to the Hindus, and no special reference has been made to the Mahomedans or their religion, either by the witnesses examined by the Select Committees of the Houses of Parliament, or by those who wrote upon the subject. The reason for this circumstance is not far to seek. The opposition of the Mahomedans to English education, founded as it was upon a misapprehension of the motives of the educational policy of the Government, as laid down in Lord William Bentinck's Resolution of the 7th of March, 1835, was evinced by them so far back as that year, and continued almost unabated, with the lamentable result that extremely few Mahomedan youths pursued the study of English, and consequently no special attention appears to have been given to their special, social and political condition. Their backward condition seems, indeed, to have remained almost unnoticed, till very recent years, as will be shown in another part of this work.

* *The Wit and Wisdom of the Rev. Sydney Smith.* Longmans, Green and Co., London (1886), pp. 68–74.

CHAPTER XV.

PROGRESS OF ENGLISH EDUCATION UNDER THE POLICY OF LORD WILLIAM BENTINCK'S EDUCATIONAL RESOLUTION OF 7TH MARCH, 1835.—LORD AUCKLAND'S EDUCATIONAL MINUTE OF 1839.—LORD HARDINGE'S EDUCATIONAL RESOLUTION OF 1844.—POLICY OF MAKING ENGLISH THE LANGUAGE OF OFFICIAL BUSINESS.—PROGRESS OF ENGLISH EDUCATION IN BENGAL.—VIEWS OF SIR FREDERICK HALLIDAY.

Lord Auckland's Educational Minute of 24th November, 1839, slightly modifying the policy of exclusive English Education.

It is now necessary to pursue the history of the progress of English education under the policy inaugurated by Lord William Bentinck's Educational Resolution of 7th March, 1835. After the passing of that Resolution, the supporters of Oriental Education were naturally dissatisfied at the prospect of the ultimate abolition of their favourite Colleges, and they tried, again and again, to get that Resolution abrogated. A new controversy, in consequence, arose, reviving something of the old acrimony, so that at last Lord Auckland, then Governor-General, came forward apparently as a mediator in the matter, and recorded a Minute, dated November 24th, 1839, which was designed to effect something like a compromise between the parties. One object of his Minute was to uphold to the utmost all that Lord William Bentinck had done with the view of promoting English literature and science through the medium of the English language; but, on the other hand, his purpose was to abrogate so much of Lord William Bentinck's Resolution as went to the ultimate abolition of the Sanskrit and Mahomedan Colleges.* Professor H. H. Wilson, in his History of India (Vol. III., pp. 307–8), referring to the Minute, says that, " it gave the most liberal encouragement to the extension of English study, rescued the Native Colleges from the misappropriation of the funds specially assigned to them; and by a liberal distribution of Scholarships to all the seminaries alike, remedied, in some degree, the discontinuance of the Subsistence Allowances, on which most of the students, like the poor scholars of the middle ages in Europe, had been accustomed, under all previous rule, Hindoo, Mahomedan, or Christian, to depend."

Lord Hardinge's Educational Resolution of 10th October, 1844, in favour of the employment of successful Native Students.

Lord Auckland's Educational Minute of the 24th November, 1839, cannot be regarded as any departure from the principle of promoting English education, and the policy upon which Lord William Bentinck's Educational Resolution of the 7th March, 1835, was based. English education continued to be the order of the day, but " there was a considerable prejudice in the minds of some members of the Civil Service, and of the officers of Government generally, against the employment in the Public Service of those who had received this English education. The plausible excuse which they gave for that objection was, that men who were crammed, as they said, with mathematics, and were able to repeat Shakespeare, and to quote Johnson and Addison, were unfitted for the duties of the Public Service, which required a great deal of official knowledge and experience; but in proportion as the men who had adopted those prejudices left the Service, the feeling gradually died out, and in the course of time a conviction arose in the minds of the most influential members of the Service, that those seminaries ought to be made the nursery of the Public Service, and that the Government, which was at so large an expense for the purposes of Education, ought to obtain some benefit from it, by being enabled to place the most advanced students in situations of public trust. It was this growing feeling which gave rise to the celebrated Notification of Lord Hardinge, at the close of 1844."† That Notification, known as " Lord Hardinge's Educational Resolution," of the 10th October, 1844, aimed at giving indirect encouragement to English education, by holding out prospects of Government employment to successful and meritorious students. The Principal part of the Resolution runs as follows :—

" The Governor-General having taken into his consideration the existing state of education in Bengal, and being of opinion that it is highly desirable to afford it every reasonable encouragement, by holding out to those who have taken advantage of the opportunity of instruction afforded to them, a fair prospect of employment in the Public Service, and thereby not only to reward individual merit, but to enable the State to profit as largely,

* Dr. Alexander Duff's evidence—Printed Parliamentary Papers: *Second* Report of the Select Committee of the House of Lords (1852-53) on Indian Territories, p. 54.

† Mr. J. C. Marshman's evidence—Printed Parliamentary Papers: *Sixth* Report of the Select Committee of the House of Commons (1853) on Indian Territories, p. 31.

and as early as possible, by the result of the measures adopted of late years for the instruction of the people, as well by the Government as by private individuals and Societies, has resolved that, in every possible case, a preference shall be given, in the selection of candidates for public employment, to those who have been educated in the institutions thus established, and especially to those who have distinguished themselves therein by a more than ordinary degree of merit and attainment."*

Policy of making English the language of official business, was indicated so early as 1829.

This Resolution, no doubt, gave considerable stimulus to English education, though some complaints were made against its operation, and it had only a gradual and partial effect. The Resolution, however, is significant, as marking an important step of the policy of employing in the Government service, persons who had satisfied the tests of the Government English educational institutions—a policy which had lain dormant for many years. "A very general opinion had prevailed for some years past, that Persian ought to be discarded; but there was not the same concurrence of sentiment as to what language ought to be substituted for it. One party advocated the use of English, on the ground, that it was of more importance that the judges, who had to decide a case, should thoroughly understand it, than the persons themselves who were interested in it: that if the European officers used their own language in official proceedings, they would be much more independent of the pernicious influence of their administrative officers; and that the general encouragement which would be given to the study of English, by its adoption as the official language, would give a powerful impulse to the progress of native enlightenment. Some years ago this opinion was the prevailing one among those who were favourable to the plan of giving the Natives a liberal European education, and it was even adopted by the Bengal Government."† This appears from a letter from the Secretary to the Bengal Government (in the Persian Department) to the Committee of Public Instruction, dated the 26th June, 1829, from which the following extract may be quoted, as throwing light upon the policy of introducing the English language as the language of business in public offices, even at that early period. The letter ran as follows :—

Letter of the Government of Bengal, dated 26th June, 1829, announcing the future adoption of English in Public Offices.

"One of the most important questions connected with the present discussion is, that of the nature and degree of encouragement to the study of the English language, which it is necessary and desirable for the Government to that, out, independently of providing books, teachers, and the ordinary means of tuition. Your Committee has observed, that unless English be made the language of business, political negotiation, and jurisprudence, it will not be universally or extensively studied by our native subjects.—Mr. Mackenzie, in the Note annexed to your Report, dated the 3rd instant, urges strongly the expediency of a declaration by Government, that the English will be eventually used as the language of business; otherwise, with the majority of our scholars, he thinks, that all we 'do to encourage the acquisition must be nugatory;' and recommends that it be immediately notified, that, after the expiration of three years, a decided preference will be given to candidates for office, who may add a knowledge of English to other qualifications. The Delhi Committee have also advocated, with great force and earnestness, the expediency of rendering the English the language of our public tribunals and Correspondence, and the necessity of making known that such is our eventual purpose, if we wish the study to be successfully and extensively prosecuted.

"Impressed with a deep conviction of the importance of the subject,—and cordially disposed to promote the great object of improving India, by spreading abroad the lights of European knowledge, morals, and civilisation,—his Lordship in Council, has no hesitation in stating to your Committee, and in authorising you to announce to all concerned in the superintendence of your Native Seminaries, that it is the wish, and admitted policy of the British Government to render its own language gradually and eventually the language of public business, throughout the country; and that it will omit no opportunity of giving every reasonable and practicable degree of encouragement to the execution of this project. At the same time, his Lordship in Council, is not prepared to come forward with any distinct and specific pledge as to the period and manner of effecting so great a change in the system of our internal economy; nor is such a pledge considered to be at all indispensable to the gradual and cautious fulfilment of our views. It is conceived that, assuming the existence of that disposition to acquire a knowledge of English, which is declared in the correspondence now before Government, and forms the groundwork of our present proceedings, a general assurance to the above effect, combined with the arrangements in train for providing the means of instruction, will ensure our obtaining, at no distant period, a certain, though limited, number of respectable native English scholars; and more effectual and decisive measures may be adopted hereafter, when a body of competent teachers shall have been provided in the Upper Provinces, and the superiority of an English education is more generally recognised and appreciated.

* Mr. J. C. Marshman's evidence—Printed Parliamentary Papers: *Sixth* Report of the Select Committee of the House of Commons (1853) on Indian Territories, p. 415, App. F.

† Trevelyan—*On the Education of the People of India*, p. 145.

"As intimated, however, by the Delhi Committee, the use of the English in our public correspondence with Natives of distinction, more especially in that which is of a complementary nature, would in itself be an important demonstration in favour of the new course of study, as serving to indicate pretty clearly the future intentions of Government; and there appears to be no objection to the immediate application of this incentive to a certain extent, and under the requisite limitations. The expediency, indeed, of revising the Governor-General's correspondence with the higher classes of Natives on the above principles, has before, more than once, undergone discussion and consideration; and the Governor-General in Council, deems the present a suitable occasion for resolving to address the Native Chiefs and nobility of India in the English language, (especially those residing in our own Provinces,) whenever there is reason to believe, either that they have themselves acquired a knowledge of it, or have about them persons possessing that knowledge, and, generally, in all instances where the adoption of the new medium of correspondence would be acceptable and agreeable."*

Policy of adopting English as the language of official business announced so early as 1829, and followed in Lord Hardinge's Resolution of 10th October, 1844.

The policy of ultimately adopting English as the language of official business, though announced so far back as 1829, as is apparent from the preceding extract, could not be put into operation for many years to come, and, indeed, when that policy was more practically recognized by Lord Hardinge's Educational Resolution of the 10th October, 1844, much difficulty arose in putting it into operation. Upon the Resolution being communicated to the Committee of Public Instruction, that body framed certain rules for holding examinations for those who were to receive certificates of qualification for Government service. The scheme of examination thus established gave prominence to those subjects of study which were recognized in the Government Colleges, to the exclusion of subjects of a religious character, which formed the distinguishing feature of the educational institutions established by the Missionaries. Referring to this matter, Mr. J. C. Marshman, in his evidence before a Select Committee of the House of Commons, on the 21st July, 1853, said:—

Dissatisfaction caused by the proceedings of the Education Committee under that Resolution.

"A feeling of the greatest possible dissatisfaction was thus created among the Missionaries, as may well be supposed, and it became a subject of remonstrance with the Council of Education; and this led to a long discussion, which was carried on with feelings not of mutual concession, and only ended in exasperating both parties. The education given in the Missionary Schools is not altogether, but very considerably, of a religious character; consequently the books which are used differ greatly from those which are employed in the Government Institutions, and the discussion which arose had reference to the books which should be made the subject of examination. The Missionaries had manifested an objection to the study of Shakespeare and of the English dramatists. On the other hand, the Committee of Public Instruction had an equally strong objection to examine the students of the Missionary Institutions in Paley's Evidences of Christianity, and other books of the same character. The consequence has been very deplorable, because it has sown discord among those who have the same object in view, namely, the enlightenment of the Natives. It has also produced a very unfavourable effect on the minds of the students of the Missionary Colleges; whether right or wrong, they have been led to suppose that there were two castes in education, the Brahmin and the Soodra caste, and that those who were trained up in the regular Orthodox Colleges of the Government were of the Brahmin caste, and those who had been educated in the Missionary Institutions belonged to a lower and an inferior class. Now, as the object of this examination was not to test the acquirements of the students in any particular book, but rather to ascertain their progress in general literature, it is very possible that a spirit of conciliation might have removed every difference; but there was no spirit of conciliation, I am sorry to say, manifested on either part; and the consequence has been, that both parties are now exasperated against each other, and I do not see any prospect whatever of having this discord healed under existing circumstances."†

Progress made by English Education, especially in Bengal.

Lord Hardinge's Resolution of 1844, though intended to encourage English education by offering prospects of Government patronage to those who had successfully learnt the English language, could not be put into operation as much as might be expected, partly on account of political and administrative reasons upon which it is unnecessary to dwell here. It is more to the purpose to describe how far English education had made progress at that period and for some years afterwards. Speaking of the state of English education, Mr. J. C. Marshman gave the following description in his deposition before a Select Committee of the House of Commons, on the 18th July, 1853.

* Trevelyan — *On the Education of the People of India*, pp. 145–147, *note*.

† Evidence of Mr. J. C. Marshman—Printed Parliamentary Papers: *Sixth* Report of the Select Committee of the House of Commons (1853) on Indian Territories, pp. 31, 32.

"Within the Bengal Presidency, we have three descriptions of English schools and seminaries. The first consists of those which are paid by the State, and are under the immediate direction of the Government. In Bengal and Behar there are 31 such schools and colleges, embracing 4,241 scholars. The various Missionary Societies in the same provinces, have also established various schools and colleges, for the education of the Natives in the English language and in European science, and I find, according to the latest return, that the number of schools and colleges connected with them amounted to 22, and that the number of students was about 6,000. As the study of English is exceedingly popular among the Natives of Bengal, and they are anxious to give their children as large a knowledge of it as possible, many of those Natives who have received an English education, either in the Missionary or in the Government Schools, have established proprietary schools for English tuition, where all those who are able to pay either a smaller or a larger sum receive instruction. I have never been able to obtain any return, either of the number of schools or of the number of scholars in those proprietary institutions; but I should think that, in and about Calcutta, the number of scholars does not fall much short of 1,500. The number, however, may be considerably greater. I find, according to the last Report, in the Agra Presidency, that the number of Government Schools and Colleges amounts to eight, and the number of scholars in them to 1,548. In the same Presidency, the Missionaries have 22 English schools, in which 1,754 students are receiving education; but as English is not so popular in the North-Western Provinces as it is in Bengal, I am not aware that there are any proprietary schools in any of the great cities in those Provinces. The education has been carried to a very high pitch in the Government Institutions. The students receive the same kind of instruction which is comprised in the compass of a liberal education in this country, and go through the whole circle of literature, of philosophy, and of science. Many of the Missionary Schools also embrace the same large range of instruction, and the education given in them is equally comprehensive. In some of the inferior Missionary Schools, and more particularly in the lower class of proprietary schools, where they have not the same command of resources for obtaining superior tutors, the education is of rather an inferior character, and more elementary than in the higher institutions. The Natives exhibit great sharpness and great precocity of intellect. They have also very great powers of application. In many of those institutions, the youths, who have reached the head of them, have obtained an amount of knowledge, which would not do discredit to some of the best institutions in this country."*

General statistics as to English Education in 1852.

Similar progress, upon a more or less extended scale, was made by English education in the Presidencies of Madras and Bombay, and the following Abstract Statement† respecting education under each Presidency in British India, dated East India House, 4th May, 1852, presented to the House of Lords, throws light upon the general educational statistics of that period:—

Nature of Instruction.		No. of Institutions.	Expense.	Teachers.	Pupils.	Scholarships. Number.	Scholarships. Value per annum.
Bengal, L. P. ...	English, and mixed ...	37	3,87,110	283	5,465	291	Rs. 49,524
	Vernacular ...	104		104	4,685	...	...
Ditto, N.-W. P. ...	English, and mixed ...	7	1,33,521	112	1,582	232	22,932
	Vernacular ...	8		48	...	...	...
Madras ...	English, and mixed ...	1	43,558	13	180	...	...
	Vernacular ...	...		Cannot be given.		...	...
Bombay ...	English, and mixed ...	14	1,50,408	62	2, 066	84	5,880
	Vernacular ...	233		233	11,394	...	...
	Total ...	......	Rs. 7,14,597 or £66,993	855	25,372	607	78,336

* Evidence of Mr. J. C. Marshman—Printed Parliamentary Papers: *Sixth* Report of the Select Committee of the House of Commons (1853) on Indian Territories, pp. 25, 26.

† *Returns* and *Papers* presented to the House of Lords, relative to the affairs of the East India Company (1852-53), p. 37.

As a general view of the condition and progress of English education during the period to which this chapter relates, the following statement of Sir Frederick Halliday before a Select Committee of the House of Commons, on the 25th July, 1853, may be quoted:—

Sir Frederick Halliday's general view as to the condition of English Education in 1853.

"I think the progress of education since 1833 has been satisfactory; it has been continuous, and, on the whole, in the right direction; the results, as far as we can judge of them by observing the conduct and character of those who have been educated at the institutions, and have gone forth into the world, of whom a great many have been employed in Government situations, and a good many in private situations, are that they are improved very much in morals, and in conduct, by the education which they have received; I think they are a superior class, altogether to those who preceded them, who were either less educated according to our views, or not educated at all. There is yet, however, a good deal to be done; it is not the opinion of those who are interested in education in India, that enough money is spent upon it, the reason being, of course, that there has not been hitherto, generally, money to spend; the desire is, that as fast as means can be found, as fast as the Government is in possession of means for that purpose, those means should be applied to the extension of education; it being a matter, in the opinion of persons in authority in India, of the very last importance, superior perhaps to all others, towards the improvement of our administration. There is an opinion, also, that education has not been extended sufficiently in the way of Vernacular teaching, and in that respect I see room for improvement; but on the whole, as I began by saying, the results are satisfactory and promising." *

CHAPTER XVI.

PROPOSALS TO ESTABLISH UNIVERSITIES IN INDIA IN 1845.—PARLIAMENTARY ENQUIRY INTO INDIAN AFFAIRS IN 1853.—PETITION TO PARLIAMENT BY MR. C. H. CAMERON, FOR ESTABLISHING UNIVERSITIES IN INDIA.—VIEWS OF SIR CHARLES TREVELYAN, MR. MARSHMAN, PROFESSOR H. H. WILSON, AND SIR FREDERICK HALLIDAY, ON THE SUBJECT.

From the account which has been given in the preceding chapters, it is apparent that the earliest and greatest activity in the cause of Public Instruction was evinced in Bengal, not only by the Government, but also by the people themselves; who indeed, had been foremost in seeking English education. It was, therefore, in that Presidency, that the first proposal to found a University in India was made. So far back as the 25th of October, 1845, the Council of Education at Calcutta, under the Presidency of Mr. Charles Hay Cameron, prepared a plan for a University at Calcutta, from which the following extract may be quoted, as throwing light upon the early history of University Education in India. The proposed plan began with the following:—

Scheme of a University at Calcutta, proposed in 1845.

"The present advanced state of education in the Bengal Presidency, with the large and annually increasing number of highly-educated pupils, both in public and private institutions, renders it not only expedient and advisable, but a matter of strict justice and necessity, to confer upon them some mark of distinction, by which they may be recognized as persons of liberal education and enlightened minds, capable, from the literary and scientific training they have undergone, of entering at once upon the active duties of life; of commencing the practical pursuit of the learned professions, including in this description the business of instructing the rising generation; of holding the higher offices under Government open to natives, after due official qualification; or of taking the rank in society accorded in Europe to all members and graduates of the Universities.—The only means of accomplishing this great object is by the establishment of a Central University, armed with the power of granting degrees in Arts, Science, Law, Medicine and Civil Engineering, incorporated by a Special Act of the Legislative Council of India, and endowed with the privileges enjoyed by all Chartered Universities in Great Britain and Ireland. After carefully studying the laws and constitution of the Universities of Oxford

* Printed Parliamentary Papers: *Sixth* Report of the Select Committee of the House of Commons, on Indian Territories (1853), p. 53

and Cambridge, with those of the recently established University of London, the latter alone appears adapted to the wants of the native community."*

The University was to consist of a Chancellor, a Vice-chancellor and Fellows, constituting a Senate divided into the Faculties of Law, Science and Civil Engineering, Medicine and Surgery, and a Faculty of Arts for general control and superintendence. An examination of candidates, for Degrees in all the Departments was to be held at least once a year, and conducted either by Examiners appointed from among the Senate, or by any other persons specially nominated by that body, and the benefits of those examinations were to be extended to all institutions, whether Government or private, approved of by the Senate, provided the candidates from such institutions conform to such Regulations as may be enacted respecting the course, extent and duration of study, with the certificates that will be required, authority being granted for the issue of the same. After giving an outline of the proposed Regulations, the scheme ended with the following observations :—

Constitution of the proposed University at Calcutta.

"The above is a rough outline of a plan, the carrying out of which would form one of the most important eras in the history of education in India. It would open the paths of honour and distinction alike to every class and every institution; would encourage a high standard of qualification throughout the Presidency, by bestowing justly-earned rewards upon those who had spent years in the acquisition of knowledge, and rendering their literary honours a source of emolument as well as of social distinction. It would remove most of the objections urged against the existing system of examination of candidates for public employment, without lowering the standard of information required; and would in a very few years produce a body of native public servants, superior in character, attainments, and efficiency, to any of their predecessors. It would encourage the cultivation of the arts and sciences, and call into existence a class of native architects, engineers, surveyors and educated landholders, whose influence would rapidly and certainly diffuse a taste for the more refined and intellectual pleasures and pursuits of the West, to the gradual extinction of the enervating and degrading superstitions of the East. Increased facilities of intercourse, by means of Railroads, with the interior of the country, the North-West Provinces, and with Europe, would cause these influences to radiate from the centre of civilization, with a velocity and effect heretofore unknown in India, and, in fact, would be attended with all the advantages that have been recorded in history to have followed a judicious, enlightened, extended and sound system of education, encouraged by suitable rewards and distinctions. The adoption of the plan would only be attended with a very trifling expense to Government in the commencement; for in the course of a few years the proceeds of the *Fee Fund* would be more than sufficient to defray every expense attended upon the University. It would raise the character and importance of the whole Education Department in public estimation, and ultimately place the educated natives of this great empire upon a level with those of the western world. That the time for such a measure has arrived, is fully proved by the standard of excellence attained in the senior scholarship examinations of the Council of Education, and the creditable skill and proficiency exhibited by the graduates of the Medical College, whose examinations, in extent and difficulty, are much greater than those of any of the Colleges of *Surgeons* in Great Britain, and in a purely professional point of view, nearly on a par with those required from the Medical graduates of most British Universities."†

Benefits expected from the proposed University at Calcutta.

These proposals made so far back as 1845 for the establishment of a University at Calcutta were discountenanced by the authorities in England, and appear to have lain in abeyance for many years. It was not till Parliament took up the subject of the renewal of the East India Company's Charter in 1852-53, that the proposals received any tangible attention. Under the Act of Parliament 3 and 4, Wm. IV., C. 85, the term of the Company's Government in India was to expire on the 30th of April, 1854, and it was deemed necessary to hold a Parliamentary enquiry into the Indian affairs as had been the custom before renewing the Charter. For this purpose Select Committees of the House of Lords, and of the House of Commons were appointed, and they collected a mass of evidence, from which much information can be gathered as to the progress and policy of English education in India. The enquiry resulted in the Act of Parliament, 16 and 17 Vic., C. 95, which was passed on the 20th of August, 1853, and by which, until Parliament should otherwise provide, all the territories then in the possession and under the Government of the East India Company, were to continue under such Government, in trust for Her Majesty. The Act was avowedly temporary, and remained in force only for a very short period, but as having a bearing upon English

The proposal for establishing a University at Calcutta remains in abeyance till Parliamentary inquiry in 1853, preceding St. 3 and 4, Wm. IV., C. 85.

* Printed Parliamentary Papers: *Second* Report of the Select Committee of the House of Lords on Indian Territories (1852–53), p. 618, App. O.

† *Ib.*, p. 620.

education, it contained a provision by which the appointments to the Civil Service and the Medical Service in India were withdrawn from the Directors of the Company and thrown open to public competition.

Petition to Parliament by Mr. Charles Hay Cameron for establishing Universities in India, dated 30th November, 1852.

In the course of the Parliamentary enquiry abovementioned, many petitions were presented to Parliament, and among others, there was one which deserves historical importance, in connection with High English Education in India, and may be quoted here *in extenso* as it is full of important matter expressed in very brief language. It runs as follows :—

"*The humble Petition of Charles Hay Cameron, late Fourth Member of the Council of India, President of the Indian Law Commission, and of the Council of Education for Bengal.*

"HUMBLY SHEWETH—

"That, as President of the Council of Education for Bengal, your petitioner had opportunities of observing the desire and the capacity of large numbers of the native youth of India, for the acquisition of European literature and science, as well as the capacity of the most distinguished among them, for fitting themselves to enter the Civil and Medical Covenanted Services of the East India Company, and to practise in the learned professions.

"That the said native youth are hindered from making all the progress they are capable of in the acquisition of the said literature and science:

"*First.* Because there is not in British India any University, with power to grant Degrees, as is done by Universities in Europe.

"*Secondly.* Because the European instructors of the said native youth do not belong to any of the Covenanted Services of the East India Company, and do not, therefore, whatever may be their learning and talents, occupy a position in Society which commands the respect of their pupils.

"*Thirdly.* Because no provision has been made for the education of any of the said native youth in England, without prejudice to their caste or religious feelings.

"Your petitioner, therefore, prays,—

"That one or more Universities may be established in British India.

"That a Covenanted Education Service may be created, analogous to the Covenanted Civil and Medical Services.

"That one or more Establishments may be created, at which the native youth of India may receive, in England, without prejudice to their caste or religious feelings, such a secular education as may qualify them for admission into the Civil and Medical Services of the East India Company,—

"And your petitioner will ever pray.

"30*th November* 1852. "C. H. CAMERON."*

Views of eminent witnesses before the House of Lords, as to establishing Universities in India.

Upon the proposal contained in this petition, much evidence was taken by the Select Committees, and the views of some of the important witnesses, on the proposal to establish Universities in India may be quoted here. Mr. C. H. Cameron, upon being asked as to the proposal contained in his petition regarding the establishment of Universities in India, explained his views before a Select Committee of the House of Lords, on the 7th July, 1853, in the following words :—

Mr. Cameron's explanation of his proposals.

"My suggestion would amount to this, that there should be in each of the great Capital Cities in India a University; that is to say, at Calcutta, at Madras, at Bombay, and at Agra; those four cities being the centres of four distinct languages; Calcutta being the focus of the Bengalee language, Madras of the Tamul, Bombay of the Mahrattee, and Agra of the Hindee. In those four Universities would be taught, according to my notions, the English language, and all the literature that it contains; and science also in the same language; and at the same time, the four languages that I have mentioned would also be cultivated. Native students would be practised in translations from English into each of those languages and from each of those languages into English. Every encouragement which the Government can give, would be given to the production of original works in those native languages. That system already exists to a considerable extent; but there is no University; there is no body which has the power of granting degrees; and that sort of encouragement appears to be one which the Natives are fully desirous of. They have arrived at a point at which they are quite ripe for it, and they themselves are extremely desirous of it: that is to say, those who have already benefited by this system of English education

* Printed Parliamentary Papers: *First* Report of the Select Committee of the House of Commons on Indian Territories (1853), pp. 510, 511, App. No. 7.

are extremely desirous of those distinctions, and are extremely desirous of having that sort of recognition of their position as subjects of the Queen of Great Britain."*

Upon the same subject, Sir Charles Trevelyan's views were expressed in the following words :—

Sir Charles Trevelyan's views.

"I think an University should be established at each of the Presidencies, consisting of two departments: one department should be for the purpose of an examination for all-comers, wherever educated, in all the superior and advanced branches of secular knowledge, and for giving diplomas and degrees in them. One important subject of examination will be English literature: the young men from the Government Colleges will bring up their Shakespeare, their Milton, their Spectator, their Johnson,—while the young men from the Missionary Schools will bring up their Paley, their Butler, their Burnet's History of the Reformation, their Daubigne's Life of Luther, and so forth. In Sanscrit and Arabic literature, the young men educated at the Government Colleges will vie with those who have received their instruction from private teachers, according to the original native fashion. Another subject of examination will be medicine and surgery; another will be law; another will be civil engineering, surveying, and architecture; another will be natural philosophy, chemistry, metallurgy, &c.; another will be the fine arts. And I consider that a distinct relation and channel of communication should be established, for the purpose of transferring young men who pass the best examinations in law to the public service."†

The views of another important witness, Mr. J. C. Marshman, may also be quoted :—

Mr. Marshman's views.

"The great object of desire in India, as a remedy for this state of things, is the establishment of Universities; one University at each of the four Presidencies, at Agra, Calcutta, Madras and Bombay. It is a matter of great importance to the progress of education in India, that this University should be established upon the exact model of the London University here; that its functions should not be to teach any branch of knowledge, but to examine and to classify, and to give degrees to those who had been taught in other institutions. The Government Colleges would then stand in precisely the same relationship to the University as the Missionary Colleges, or any other institutions throughout the country. * * * * * * * * * The Universities would, of course, grant degrees in law, and all those who were anxious to obtain them, as a passport to celebrity, would make themselves as perfect masters of the science as possible. The advantage to be derived from such Universities would be great; they would create a spirit of laudable emulation among the various educational institutions in the country, and give a very great stimulus, generally, to the cause of education, and at the same time enable the Government to ascertain who were the most qualified students for public employment, connected with all the institutions throughout the country."‡

Professor H. H. Wilson's views opposed to the proposal.

There were also other important witnesses who favoured the proposal to establish Universities in India; but among those who were opposed to the scheme, the name of Professor H. H. Wilson, the distinguished Orientalist, cannot pass unnoticed. Referring to the proposal, he said :—

"I confess I cannot imagine that any good would arise from it; but without knowing the exact plan of the Universities, it would perhaps be difficult to form a conclusive opinion. I do not know what is meant by a University in India; if it is to consist in wearing caps and gowns, and being called Bachelors of Arts, and Masters of Arts, I do not see what advantage is likely to accrue from it. The Natives certainly could not appreciate the value of such titles; it would be of no advantage to a young man to be called a Bachelor of Arts amongst the Natives of India, who could attach no positive idea to it; it would be inconvenient if it gave him place and precedence amongst Europeans; in fact, I cannot consider that any advantages at all would be derived from such an institution. Certificates and diplomas given to the young men who acquire scholarships, and those who have merit, are sufficient proofs of their eligibility for office."§

Sir Frederick Halliday's apprehension as to failure of proposed Universities.

Another class of opposition to the scheme of establishing Universities in India, is represented by the views expressed by Sir Frederick Halliday, in his evidence before a Select Committee of the House of Commons, on the 25th July, 1853, and which may be quoted here as completing the account of the various phases of opinion entertained upon the subject at that time. He said :—

"I am not very sanguine about Universities in India; certainly I would not have them established on the footing proposed by Mr. Cameron in his evidence before the Committee of the House of Lords. He wishes that they should be established upon a great scale, with a Chancellor and Vice-Chancellor, and Faculties, and things of

* Printed Parliamentary Papers—*Second* Report of the Select Committee of the House of Lords on Indian Territories (1852–53), p. 275. † *Ib.*, p. 163. ‡ *Ib.*, p. 124. § *Ib.*, p. 269.

that sort, which appear to me to involve more than we require, and to be running ahead of the necessities of the times in India; besides which, there are some difficulties, which Mr. Cameron has in some respects himself proved, arising out of that very Resolution of Lord Hardinge. Lord Hardinge's Resolution was to the effect, that all distinguished students in public or private seminaries should be preferred, other things being equal, for appointments in the public service; and he remitted this Resolution to the Council of Education, with directions to frame the details of a system to carry it into effect. The Council of Education very naturally thought that the only way to do this was to establish general examinations, to which all persons might come, and which should test their acquirements; and that then, at those examinations, certificates should be given, and those certificates should carry in them the effect of Lord Hardinge's Resolution. Now, as far as that went, if it did not form a University, it was the germ of a University; at all events it was intended to be so. I believe Mr. Cameron, who was the framer of the plan, had that in his head when he framed it. It was also entirely in accordance with what must be done if a University were established, that the standard should be so fixed as to correspond in its highest degree with the highest instruction given at any affiliated institution. I suppose that under any conceivable University system that must be done, and that was done. What was the consequence?—A storm of reprobation which has assailed this plan ever since, and prevented its fair operation. It was immediately said, 'this standard is an unattainable standard; it is the standard of the highest and best students of the Government Institutions; it is one to which our students can never attain.' This was said by persons having an interest in private seminaries. It was also said, 'this is a standard of literature and mathematics, and a very high one; whereas many of our students are kept from attaining any eminence in those branches of knowledge by having their attention chiefly directed to the doctrines of Christianity. Unless, therefore, you put the whole thing into our hands, and enable us to say what is distinction as regards the students in our institutions, we repudiate your plan, and will have nothing to do with it.' They acted in that way, and have ever since done so; and they have vilified the scheme, and the framers of it to the utmost of their power. It appears to me, that if that were the consequence of establishing a system of examination, to give certificates which should carry a man into the public service, it must be the consequence of establishing a University to give degrees to pass a man into the public service. You must always have a highest standard, and that standard must be always in accordance with the highest standard of instruction in any of the affiliated institutions. The same results would follow, if a system of Universities were carried out. We have to deal at present with a number of Government Institutions, some of them carrying education to a very high pitch; and we have to deal with a great number of missionary and some private institutions, which are, generally speaking, very far inferior to the Government Colleges in point of literary and mathematical attainments. Here and there one or two of them come near the Government Colleges; but still they are below them. The Government Institutions stand forth in the eyes of the Natives, and ought to stand forth in such a manner that distinctions in them must be more coveted and sought for than distinctions in private institutions." *

CHAPTER XVII.

COMPREHENSIVE DESPATCH OF THE COURT OF DIRECTORS TO THE GOVERNMENT OF INDIA, DATED 19TH JULY, 1854, ON THE SUBJECT OF EDUCATION, KNOWN AS SIR CHARLES WOOD'S EDUCATIONAL DESPATCH OF 1854.—FORMATION OF THE EDUCATION DEPARTMENT.

The Educational Despatch of the Court of Directors, dated 19th July, 1854.

It has been stated in the preceding chapter, that by the Act of Parliament, 16 and 17 Vic., chapter 95, which was passed on the 20th of August, 1853, the British Territories in India were to continue under the Government of the East India Company until Parliament should otherwise provide. The Parliamentary enquiry into Indian affairs, which preceded that enactment, appears to have borne good fruit, so far as the subject of education in

* Printed Parliamentary Papers—*Sixth* Report of the Select Committee of the House of Commons on Indian Territories (1853), p. 64.

India is concerned. In 1854, the education of the whole population of India was definitely accepted as a State duty, and the Despatch from the Court of Directors of the East India Company, No. 49, of the 19th July, 1854, laid down in clear, though general, terms the principles which should govern the educational policy of the Government of India. It set forth "a scheme of education for all India, far wider and more comprehensive than the Supreme, or any Local Government, could ever have ventured to suggest." Up to the time of its issue the efforts of the Government in the cause of education had been marked neither by consistency of direction, nor by any breadth of aim. The annual expenditure upon Public Instruction had been insignificant and uncertain; and the control of its operations had not been deemed worthy the attention of any special department of the State. The educational system elaborated in the Despatch was indeed, both in its character and scope, far in advance of anything existing at the time of its inception. It furnished, in fact, a masterly and comprehensive outline, the filling up of which was necessarily to be the work of many years.*

Its purport.

The Educational Despatch of 1854 still forms the charter of education in India, and its purport was thus summarized in the Report of the Indian Education Commission of 1882:—

"The Despatch of 1854 commends to the special attention of the Government of India, the improvement and far wider extension of education, both English and Vernacular, and prescribes as the means for the attainment of these objects:—

(1) The constitution of a separate department of the administration for education.
(2) The institution of Universities at the Presidency towns.
(3) The establishment of institutions for training teachers for all classes of schools.
(4) The maintenance of the existing Government Colleges and High Schools, and the increase of their number when necessary.
(5) The establishment of new Middle Schools.
(6) Increased attention to Vernacular Schools, indigenous or other, for elementary education; and
(7) The introduction of a system of Grants-in-aid.

Directions as to educational policy.

"The attention of Government is specially directed to the importance of placing the means of acquiring useful and practical knowledge within reach of the great mass of the people. The English language is to be the medium of instruction in the higher branches, and the Vernacular in the lower; English is to be taught wherever there is a demand for it, but it is not to be substituted for the Vernacular languages of the country. The system of Grants-in-aid is to be based on the principle of perfect religious neutrality. Aid is to be given (so far as the requirements of each particular District as compared with other Districts, and the funds at the disposal of Government may render it possible) to all schools imparting a good secular education, provided they are under adequate local management, and are subject to Government inspection, and provided that fees, however small, are charged in them. Grants are to be for specific objects, and their amount and continuance are to depend on the periodical reports of Government Inspectors. No Government Colleges or Schools are to be founded, where a sufficient number of institutions exist, capable, with the aid of Government, of meeting the local demand for education; but new Schools and Colleges are to be established and temporarily maintained where there is little or no prospect of adequate local effort being made to meet local requirements. The discontinuance of any general system of education entirely provided by Government, is anticipated with the gradual advance of the system of grants-in-aid; but the progress of education is not to be checked in the slightest degree by the abandonment of a single school to probable decay. A comprehensive system of scholarships is to be instituted, so as to connect Lower Schools with Higher, and Higher Schools with Colleges. Female education is to receive the frank and cordial support of Government. The principal officials in every District are required to aid in the extension of education; and in making appointments to posts in the service of Government, a person who has received a good education is to be preferred to one who has not. Even in lower situations, a man who can read and write is, if equally eligible in other respects, to be preferred to one who cannot."†

Policy of the Educational Despatch of 1854.

The main feature of the despatch, and the Policy of Education laid down by it, is contained in the following extract from it, so far as English instruction is concerned:—

"It is well that every opportunity should have been given to those (the higher) classes for the acquisition of a liberal European education, the effects of which may be expected slowly to pervade the rest of their fellow-countrymen, and to raise, in the

* Resolution of the Government of India, appointing the Indian Education Commission, No. $\frac{1}{60}$, dated 3rd February, 1882, printed as Appendix A to the Commission's Report, p. 623.

† Report of the Indian Education Commission (1882), pp. 22, 23.

end, the educational tone of the whole country. We are, therefore, far from under-rating the importance, or the success, of the efforts which have been made in this direction; but the higher classes are both able and willing, in many cases, to bear a considerable part, at least, of the cost of their education; and it is abundantly evident that in some parts of India no artificial stimulus is any longer required in order to create a demand for such an education as is conveyed in the Government Anglo-Vernacular Colleges. We have, by the establishment and support of these Colleges, pointed out the manner in which a liberal education is to be obtained, and assisted them to a very considerable extent from the public funds. In addition to this, we are now prepared to give, by sanctioning the establishment of Universities, full development to the highest course of education to which the natives of India, or of any other country, can aspire; and besides, by the division of University degrees and distinctions into different branches, the exertions of highly educated men will be directed to the studies which are necessary to success in the various active professions of life. We shall, therefore, have done as much as a Government can do to place the benefits of education plainly and practically before the higher classes in India."*

Formation of the Education Department, 1855-67.

The principles of the Despatch of 1854 were confirmed by the Secretary of State, in the Despatch of 7th April, 1859, which laid further stress upon the necessity of promoting Vernacular instruction, suggesting the expediency of imposing a special rate on the land for the provision of elementary education. Meanwhile, in pursuance of the Despatch of 1854, "steps were taken to form an Education Department in each of the great territorial divisions of India as then constituted; and before the end of 1856, the new system was fairly at work. The formation of the separate departments continued over a period of about 12 years, from 1854-55 in the larger Provinces, to 1866-67 in the Haidarabad Assigned Districts. A Director of Public Instruction was appointed for each Province, with a staff of Inspectors and Deputy, or Assistant Inspectors under him. This organization of control and inspection remains substantially unchanged to the present day, with such modifications and additions as were required by the creation of new territorial divisions, or by the amalgamation of old ones. The Education Department in each Province acts directly under the orders of the Provincial Government, and has developed a system of working more or less distinctively its own. Everywhere it took over the Government or the Board Institutions which had grown up under the earlier efforts of the East India Company."†

Estimated extent of Collegiate Education at formation of the Education Department in various Provinces.

The Education Department was formed in various Provinces at different periods, and the following tabular statement, which has been prepared from the tabular statements given in the Report of the Indian Education Commission of 1882 (pages 33, 36, 40 and 43) will show, in one glance, the estimated extent of Collegiate Education in the various Provinces at the time of the formation of the Education Department:—

Estimate of the extent of Collegiate Education in the First Departmental Year, in the various Provinces of British India.

Province.	First Departmental Year.	Nature of the Maintaining Agency.	Arts Colleges, English and Oriental.	
			Number.	Pupils.
Madras	1855-56	Departmental	1	302
		Aided and Inspected	...	...
		Extra Departmental	...	...
		Total ...	1	302
Bombay	1855-56	Departmental	2	103
		Aided and Inspected	...	...
		Extra Departmental	...	...
		Total ...	2	103

* Report of the Indian Education Commission (1882), p. 24.

† *Ib.*, p. 25.

PROVINCE.	First Departmental Year.	Nature of the Maintaining Agency.	ARTS COLLEGES, ENGLISH AND ORIENTAL.	
			Number.	Pupils.
Bengal and Assam ...	1854-55 ...	Departmental	8	921
		Aided and Inspected	...	...
		Extra Departmental	6	?
		Total ...	14	921
N.-W. P. and Oudh ...	1854-55 ...	Departmental	4	1,920
		Aided and Inspected	...	...
		Extra Departmental	...	...
		Total ...	4	1,920

The figures given in the above Table in regard to Collegiate education in the North-West Provinces and Oudh, are much greater than they should be, as they include the College with its attached High Schools at Delhi, which at that time was included in the North-Western Provinces. The College ceased to exist during the Mutiny of 1857, so that, at the commencement of the Education Department in the Punjab, in 1856-57, no institution for Collegiate instruction existed in that Province. In the Central Provinces, the Education Department was formed in 1862, and in the Hyderabad Assigned Districts of the Berars in 1866, but no institutions for Collegiate instruction were founded there, or in any Provinces not mentioned in the preceding Table, and, therefore, no further reference to those Provinces is necessary, so far as the condition of Collegiate education is concerned at the period of the commencement of the Education Department.

CHAPTER XVIII.

ESTABLISHMENT OF THE INDIAN UNIVERSITIES, AND THE SCOPE AND CHARACTER OF THE EDUCATION RECOGNIZED AND CONTROLLED BY THEM.—STATISTICS OF UNIVERSITY COLLEGIATE EDUCATION, 1857 TO 1882.

Establishment of the Indian Universities.

With the foundation of Universities in India begins the most important epoch in the history of English education in India. In Chapter XVI of this work an account has been given of how the subject was proposed by the Council of Education at Calcutta, so far back as 1845, and how the matter was discussed by some eminent witnesses in their evidence before the Select Committees of the Houses of Parliament during the inquiry into the Indian affairs, in 1852-53. It has also been shown how, during the discussions which then took place, the concensus of opinion was that the University of London, on account of the non-sectarian character of its system, should be recommended as a model for Indian Universities, in preference to the Universities of Oxford and Cambridge, where the system of residence within the University precincts, and religious instruction and discipline, formed an essential part of the system of education.

Guiding principles for Indian Universities.

It was, no doubt, in view of such recommendations that the Court of Directors, in their Educational Despatch of 1854, issued the following instructions as the guiding principles upon which the Universities in India were to be founded :—

"Some years ago, we declined to accede to a proposal made by the Council of Education, and transmitted to e recommendation of your Government, for the institution of an University in Calcutta. The rapid ı liberal education among the natives of India since that time; the high attainments shown by the native candidates for Government scholarships, and by native students in private institutions; the success of the Medical Colleges, and the requirements of an increasing European and Anglo-Indian population, have led us to the conclusion that the time is now arrived for the establishment of Universities in India, which may encourage a regular and liberal course of education, by conferring academical degrees, as evidences of attainments in the different branches of art and science, and by adding marks of honour for those who may desire to compete for honorary distinction.

"The Council of Education, in the proposal to which we have alluded, took the London University as their model; and we agree with them that the form, government, and functions of that University (copies of whose charters and regulations we enclose for your reference) are the best adapted to the wants of India, and may be followed with advantage, although some variation will be necessary in points of detail.

London University to be taken as model.

"The Universities in India, will, accordingly, consist of a Chancellor, Vice-Chancellor, and Fellows, who will constitute a Senate. The Senates will have the management of the funds of the Universities, and frame regulations for your approval, under which periodical examinations may be held in the different branches of Art and Science by examiners selected from their own body, or nominated by them.

Constitution of Indian Universities.

"The function of the Universities will be to confer degrees upon such persons as, having been entered as candidates according to the rules which may be fixed in this respect, and having produced from any of the 'affiliated institutions' which will be enumerated on the foundation of the Universities, or be from time to time added to them by Government, certificates of conduct, and of having pursued a regular course of study for a given time, shall have also passed at the Universities such an examination as may be required of them. It may be advisable to dispense with the attendance required at the London University for the Matriculation Examination, and to substitute some mode of Entrance Examination which may secure a certain amount of knowlege in the candidates for degrees, without making their attendance at the Universities necessary, previous to the final examination.

Functions of Indian Universities.

"The examinations for degrees will not include any subjects connected with religious belief; and affiliated institutions will be under the management of persons of every variety of religious persusions.

Religious subjects to be excluded.

"The detailed regulations for the examination for degrees should be framed with a due regard for all classes of the affiliated institutions; and we will only observe upon this subject that the standard for common degrees will require to be fixed with very great judgment. There are many persons who well deserve the distinction of an academical degree, as the recognition of a liberal education, who could not hope to obtain it if the examination was as difficult as that for the senior Government Scholarships; and the standard required should be such as to command respect without discouraging the efforts of deserving students, which would be a great obstacle to the success of the Universities. In the competitions for honors, which, as in the London University, will follow the examinations for degrees, care should be taken to maintain such a standard as will afford a guarantee for high ability and valuable attainments,—the subjects for examination being so selected as to include the best portions of the different schemes of study pursued at the affiliated institutions.

Regulations for the examination for degrees.

"It will be advisable to institute, in connection with the Universities, professorships for the purpose of the delivery of lectures in various branches of learning, for the acquisition of which, at any rate in an advanced degree, facilities do not now exist in other institutions in India. Law is the most important of these subjects; and it will be for you to consider whether, as was proposed in the plan of the Council of Education to which we have before referred, the attendance upon certain lectures, and the attainment of a degree in law, may not, for the future, be made a qualification for Vakeels and Moonsiffs, instead of, or in addition to, the present system of examination, which must, however, be continued in places not within easy reach of an University.

Professorships in connection with Universities, especially in Law.

"Civil Engineering is another subject of importance, the advantages of which, as a profession, are gradually becoming known to the natives of India; and while we are inclined to believe that instructions of a practical nature, such as is given at the Thomason College of Civil Engineering at Roorkee, is far more useful than any lectures could possibly be, professorships of Civil Engineering might, perhaps, be attached to the Universities, and degrees in Civil Engineering be included in their general scheme.

Civil Engineering may be a subject for degrees.

"Other branches of useful learning may suggest themselves to you in which it might be advisable that lectures should be read, and special degrees given; and it would greatly encourage the cultivation of the Vernacular languages of India, that professorships should be founded for those languages, and perhaps, also, for Sanskrit, Arabic, and Persian. A knowledge of the Sanskrit language, the root of the Vernaculars of the greater part of India, is more especially necessary to those who are engaged in the work of composition in those languages; while Arabic, through Persian, is one of the component parts of the Urdu language, which extends over so large a part of Hindustan, and is, we are informed, capable of considerable development. The grammar of these languages, and their application to the improvement of the spoken languages of the country, are the points to which the attention of these professors should be mainly directed; and there will be an ample field for their labors unconnected with any instruction in the tenets of the Hindoo or Mahomedan religions. We should refuse to sanction any such teaching as is directly opposed to the principles of religious neutrality to which we have always adhered.

Sanskrit, Arabic, and Persian may be included among the subjects consistently with religious neutrality.

"We desire that you take into your consideration the institution of Universities at Calcutta and Bombay upon the general principles which we have now explained to you, and report to us upon the best method of procedure, with a view to their incorporation by Acts of the Legislative Council of India. The offices of Chancellor and Vice-Chancellor will naturally be filled by persons of high station, who have shown an interest in the cause of education; and it is in connexion with the Universities that we propose to avail ourselves of the services of the existing Council of Education at Calcutta, and Board of Education at Bombay. We wish to place these gentlemen in a position which will not only mark our sense of the exertions which they have made in furtherance of education, but will give it the benefit of their past experience of the subject. We propose, therefore, that the Council of Education at Calcutta and the Board of Education at Bombay, with some additional members to be named by the Government, shall constitute the Senate of the University at each of those Presidencies.

Councils of Education at Calcutta and Bombay to constitute the Senates of the Universities, respectively.

"The additional members should be so selected as to give to all those who represent the different systems of education which will be carried on in the affiliated institutions—including natives of India of all religious persuasions, who possess the confidence of the native communities—a fair voice in the Senates. We are led to make these remarks, as we observe that the plan of the Council of Education, in 1845, for the constitution of the Senate of the proposed Calcutta University, was not sufficiently comprehensive.

Additional Members of the Senate, including Natives of India.

"We shall be ready to sanction the creation of an university at Madras, or in any other part of India, where a sufficient number of institutions exist, from which properly qualified candidates for degrees could be supplied; it being in our opinion advisable that the great centres of European Government and civilization in India, should possess Universities similar in character to those which will now be founded, as soon as the extension of a liberal education shows that their establishment would be of advantage to the native communities.

University to be founded at Madras also, if circumstances permit.

"Having provided for the general superintendence of education, and for the institution of Universities, not so much to be in themselves places of instruction, as to test the value of the education obtained elsewhere, we proceed to consider, *first*, the different classes of colleges, and schools, which should be maintained in simultaneous operation, in order to place within the reach of all classes of the natives of India the means of obtaining improved knowledge suited to their several conditions of life; and, *secondly*, the manner in which the most effectual aid may be rendered by Government to each class of educational institutions."*

Colleges and Schools subsidiary to the Universities.

It was under these instructions that the Universities of Calcutta, Madras, and Bombay, were incorporated, on the model of the University of London, in 1857, notwithstanding the tumult and anarchy of the Indian Mutiny which then prevailed.

The Universities founded in 1857.

The University of Calcutta was incorporated by Act II of 1857, passed on the 24th January, 1857, and the preamble of the Act may be quoted here as throwing light upon the objects of the institution :—

The Calcutta University incorporated in January, 1857.

"Whereas, for the better encouragement of Her Majesty's subjects of all classes and denominations within the Presidency of Fort William in Bengal and other parts of India in the pursuit of a regular and liberal course of education, it has been determined to establish a University at Calcutta for the purpose of ascertaining, by means of examination, the persons who have acquired proficiency in different branches of Literature, Science,

* *Education in British India prior to* 1854. By Arthur Howell, Esq., pp. 198, 199.

and Art, and of rewarding them by Academical Degrees as evidence of their respective attainments, and marks of honour proportioned thereunto; and whereas, for effectuating the purposes aforesaid, it is expedient that such University should be incorporated: It is enacted as follows."

The Bombay University incorporated in July, 1857, and the Madras University in September, 1857.

With a similar preamble and similar objects, Act XII of 1857 was passed on the 18th July, 1857, incorporating the University of Bombay, and by Act XXVII of 1857, which was passed on the 5th September, 1857, the University of Madras was incorporated.

Constitution of the three Universities.

The constitutions of the three Universities are as similar as their objects. They are merely examining bodies with the privilege of conferring degrees in Arts, Law, Medicine and Civil Engineering. Their constitution is composed of a Chancellor, Vice-Chancellor and the Senate, divided into Faculties of the various branches of learning recognized by the Universities. The governing body or Syndicate consists of the Vice-Chancellor and certain members of the Senate. The Universities control the whole course of higher education by means of prescribing subjects and holding examinations. The Entrance Examination for matriculation is open to all; but when that is passed, candidates for higher stages must enrol themselves in one or other of the affiliated Colleges.

The Punjab University, its history and objects.

The Punjab University has a peculiar history. The Delhi College which had been closed during the Mutiny was revived by the Punjab Government in 1864, when a second College was established at Lahore. For sometime there had been a de re among the community in the Punjab, both Native and European, for the establishment of a local institution which should have for its object the development of learning, and that such institution should take the form of a University. The history of the early movement in this behalf has been fully stated in the *Gazetteer of the Punjab* (Provincial Volume, 1888-89) from which the following information may be incorporated here with advantage:—

Movement for a University in the Punjab, 1865-69.

The Anjuman-i-Panjab Society was formed in January, 1865, with the two-fold object of reviving the study of ancient Oriental learning, and of diffusing useful knowledge through the medium of the Vernacular.

"While the advantages of an English education were fully recognized on all hands, it was felt that the system of State education altogether ignored the historical, traditional, and religious aspects of the educational question in India. It attempted to impose the European system without sufficient modification to bring it into harmony with national feeling and the requirements of the country; and it had been so rigidly enforced on a standard pattern throughout the country that indigenous educational institutions had well nigh perished. English, as a language and as a medium for education, had already acquired the support of a strong official organization, the *Anjuman-i-Panjab* in no way objected to this, but pleaded the cause of those important features of the educational requirements of the country which had, it thought, been neglected or forgotten.

Sir Donald McLeod, at that time Lieutenant-Governor, extended his hearty sympathy to the movement which had thus been originated, and the deliberations of the two hundred members who had by this time joined the Society resulted in the conclusion that the best and surest remedy for the defects of the existing system and for combining in one the efforts of the Government and of the people in educational matters, was the establishment of an Oriental University. This institution was to support the existing educational work, but was to add to it the proper encouragement of the study of the Oriental classical languages, and the general diffusion of useful knowledge in the 'Vulgar tongue.' The classical languages of India were the sources not only of the languages spoken at the present day, but also the traditions, religions and ancient history of the Indian nation. No system which ignored Arabic or Sanskrit could hope to meet with respect, popularity, or support from the people of India, while any errors in scientific teaching, which the ancient literature might contain, could easily be eliminated or corrected by the light of modern European knowledge. The idea of an Oriental University for Northern India, or for the Punjab, was enthusiastically received. A European Committee of support was formed, and a scheme drawn up in some detail.

Nature of the University demanded by the promoters.

The nature of the demands of the promoters of the movement for an University may be gathered from the outlines of the proposals published in 1865. In this the promoters asked for an Oriental University. The word *Oriental* was not used to represent that the English language and Western science were not to be encouraged and supported; but that the University was to bear the impress of an Oriental nation; that the Oriental classics and Vernacular languages of the country were to be encouraged and developed; that the masses of the people should have the boon of the civilizing influences of education extended to them in their own language; and that the institution should not be a mere body for holding examinations in the European Curriculum only, but should also teach and examine in the languages used by, and dear to the people. Sir Donald McLeod had himself advocated the revival of ancient learning and the perfection of the Vernaculars of the country, not at the expense of an English education, but side by side with it, and supplying the deficiencies of the latter. This line was excepted by the promoters.

Sympathy of Sir Donald McLeod with the movement.

The proposals having been revised and matured by the Society and the European Committee, Messrs. Brandreth and Aitchison were deputed to lay them before His Honour the Lieutenant-Governor. This was done on the 13th October, 1865, and His Honour promised his support to the movement, but intimated that the portions of the scheme which related to Academic Degrees required the sanction of the Government of India. In February, 1866, the leading gentlemen of Lahore and Amritsar presented an address to Sir Donald McLeod, whose reply expressed great satisfaction at the development of a movement in which the people of the Province had displayed so much interest; the views of the Government were given at considerable length, and in conclusion, His Honour assured those who had taken part in the address that, 'for the encouragement of educational efforts so entirely in accordance with the Educational Despatch of 1854,' Government aid, to such extent as might be deemed advisable, would not be refused.

Desire for a University in the North-Western Provinces in 1867.

The Society continued to advocate its views with wavering success, but unswerving persistency until 1867, when their action aroused the rivalry of the British Indian Association in the North-Western Provinces. In August of that year, the Association petitioned the Viceroy, pointing out objections to the educational system, and recommending the establishment in the North-Western Provinces of a University in which the Eastern Classics and the Vernaculars would be duly encouraged, side by side with English education. This rivalry was the fortunate cause of again drawing public attention to the popular feeling on the subject of education, and established the fact that the agitation which had arisen was a genuine one. In replying to the Association, the Government of India expressed itself ready and willing to support the principles laid down in the Despatch of 1854, and to encourage the study of Western science, through the medium of the Vernacular; but while promising every assistance to societies or individuals like those in the Punjab and North-West, it was unable to establish at once a University; money, assistance, careful consideration and official recognition were promised, but not the immediate incorporation of a University.

A University proposed for Lahore in 1868, but incorporation refused by Government of India in 1868.

His Honour the Lieutenant-Governor of the Punjab at this time expressed an opinion that owing to the difficulty of forming a proper governing body, in the Upper Provinces for a University, it would perhaps be better to induce the Calcutta University to modify or enlarge its existing rules. The Senate of the Calcutta University, however, declined to modify their schemes and recommended a separate University for Upper India. On the 12th March, 1868, a general meeting of those interested in the promotion of the University scheme was held under the presidency of Sir Donald McLeod, and resolutions were passed in favour of a University, specially for the Punjab, to be situated at Lahore. The people of Delhi had in the meantime, taken measures to advocate the claims of that time-honoured capital as the seat of the proposed University, but when the agitation arose in the North-Western Provinces, they agreed to sink all differences rather than lose the chance of a University for the Punjab. The principles already set forth were reiterated, and the Punjab Government accepted these proposals and caused a letter to be drafted to the Government of India in terms of these resolutions. It contained a complete scheme for the constitution of the propsod University, and a request for a sufficient grant-in-aid. The movement had received the support of the Chiefs, Nobles, and influential classes of the Punjab, and already a sum of Rs. 1,00,000 had been raised from private sources while much more was expected. But the reply received from the Government of India was unfavourable to the immediate incorporation of a University.

This decision caused great disappointment in the Punjab, but was not received as a final settlement of the question; Sir Donald McLeod replied, thanking the Government of India for the concessions made, but he feared that these concessions would not be of much practical value unless the scheme submitted were also sanctioned, and that the withholding of this sanction was likely to discourage and bring to an end the educational movement which had sprung up amongst the leading members of the aristocracy and gentry of the Punjab. In subsequent correspondence the Punjab Government met all the objections which had been raised and expressed their own willingness and that of the promoters of the movement for a University to accept, in the first instance, a status lower than that of a full University, until the Government of India were satisfied that the complete powers of a University might with credit and safety be entrusted to the governing body which should be created.

On the 23rd of May, 1869, the Government of India wrote as follows:—

The Government of India give sanction to the Punjab University College.

"The Governor-General in Council was fully sensible of the value of the spontaneous efforts which had been made by the Community of the Punjab, both Native and European, for the establishment of a local institution which should have for its object the development of learning, especially in connection with the Vernacular languages.

"His Excellency was glad to find that the chief objections which had until then prevented him from giving a cordial sanction to the measure had been removed. The principal of these had been that if the proposed institution were at once established as a University it would probably, at first, confer a lower class of degrees than those given by other Universities in India, and this would tend to degrade the character and lessen the value of an Indian University degree.

"It was, however, understood that the Punjab Government was willing that the proposed institution should not at once assume the full character of a University; but that until the number of students and the power of teaching in any branch of study or in any faculty, could be shown to be sufficient to warrant the conferring of a University degree, it should not have the power of granting degrees, but of certificates only.

"It was also understood that the study of English would not only form one of the most prominent features of the teaching in all the Schools or Colleges connected with the institution, but that both teaching and examination in subjects which cannot, with advantage, be carried on in the Vernacular would be conducted in English.

"It was accepted as a principle that the examinations should be entrusted to other persons than those who were engaged in teaching the students; and the Lieutenant-Governor had expressed his willingness to accept any rules which should be laid down with a view to secure this object.

"Lastly it was understood that although certain subjects should be taught in the Vernacular, the teaching in mental and physical science would be free from the patent errors which prevail in ancient and even in modern Vernacular literary and scientific works."

On these conditions the establishment of the proposed institution was sanctioned. The governing body was to have power to teach, confer fellowships and scholarships and certificates of proficiency. It was to be, with the educational officers of Government, the consulting body in all matters of public instruction, including primary education.

Approved by the Secretary of State.

Meanwhile the papers went to the Secretary of State for India who accepted the conclusions of the Government of India, remarking that—

'The institution will be competent to grant certificates but not degrees, and may hereafter, if attended with due success, be expanded into a University.'

"The Government of India, in forwarding the final authority, required—

"That the institution should be called by some such title as *University College* which would mark the fact that the present arrangement was only temporary, and was intended only as preliminary to the possible establishment, at some future time, of a University in the Punjab."*

Notification of Government of India, dated 8th December, 1869, establishing Lahore University College.

In pursuance of these views the Government of India by a Notification, No. 470, dated 8th December, 1869, (Educational Department), sanctioned the establishment of an institution at Lahore to be styled "*Lahore University College*," the Notification mentions that the establishment of the institution was sanctioned "in accordance with the recommendations of His Honor the Lieutenant-Governor, and in part fulfilment of the wishes of a large number of the chiefs, nobles, and influential classes of the Punjab," and the special objects of the College were specified to be—

(1) To promote the diffusion of European science, as far as possible, through the medium of the vernacular languages of the Punjab, and the improvement and extension of vernacular literature generally;

(2) To afford encouragement to the enlightened study of Eastern classical languages and literature; and

(3) To associate the learned and influential classes of the province with the officers of Government in the promotion and supervision of popular education.

Whilst these were the special objects of the institution, it was at the same time declared that every encouragement would be afforded to the study of the English language and literature; and in all subjects which cannot be completely taught in the Vernacular, the English language would be regarded as the medium of instruction and examination. A constitution of the governing body somewhat upon the lines of the older Universities, was also prescribed, but the institution was not to have the status of a University having the power of conferring Degrees.

* *Gazetteer of the Punjab* (Prov. Vol., 1888–89), pp. 166–170.

Working of the Punjab University College from 1870 to 1876.

Under this incomplete constitution the Punjab University College entered upon its existence. The arrangement effected resulted in the Schools and Colleges having either to prepare candidates for two separate systems of examinations, *viz.*, those of the Calcutta University, and those of the new institution—the tests being altogether different in their character though of equivalent standards—or else to disregard the Punjab University College tests altogether. By liberal scholarships and considerable efforts, the latter catastrophe was avoided; but the difficulty of the dual system of studies caused considerable inconvenience to both pupils and teachers throughout the Province. The candidates were anxious to obtain the proper academic distinctions which the Calcutta University could alone confer, while the Punjab University College desired to assert its own position as the proper source of academic distinction in this Province.

The history of this institution divides itself into two nearly equal periods, one extending from January, 1870, to December, 1876, and the other from the last-named date to the passing of the Act of Incorporation of the Punjab University, on the 5th of October, 1882. The first six years were devoted to the growth and developement of the Punjab University College, and the work done during this period was of so substantial a character that at the time of the Imperial Assemblage the Viceroy and Governor-General, Lord Lytton, pledged himself 'to introduce a Bill as soon as possible into the Legislative Council for the purpose of giving to this institution the status of a University with the power of conferring degrees.' He promised that this pledge would be fulfilled as soon as the necessary formalities could be completed. Up to this time the Government of India had more than once refused to convert the University College into a full University, but in six years the institution had acquired strength and completeness and had been attended with such a 'measure of success' that the Government of India had promised to accede to the request at once.

Between 1870 and the end of 1876, the Endowment Fund rose from Rs. 1,05,660 to Rs. 3,55,300. The annual income reached Rs. 45,000, the whole of which was expended. The Senate Hall building commenced in 1874, was completed and brought into use at a cost of Rs. 35,283, of which sum His Highness the Nawab of Bhawalpur munificiently contributed Rs. 27,331. The founders of the University were made its first governing body by the name of the Senate; the first meeting was held on the 11th of January, 1870; the first six months were devoted to organization and to the making of rules and regulations for the conduct of business and examinations; an Executive Committee was appointed, and faculties were organized; and regular work commenced about July.

The Calcutta University held the control of the Schools and Colleges which taught in English, and it was not possible for a body with the defective constitution of the University College to replace it at once. Its first and great object was therefore to encourage and develop those places of educational work which had hitherto been neglected, namely: the revival of the study of Sanskrit and Arabic; and the diffusion of knowledge through the medium of the Vernacular. The first examinations were accordingly held in Arabic, Sanskrit and Persian in July, 1870; and sixty-seven candidates presented themselves, of whom forty-three passed successively as Moulvies, Pandits, or Munshis, respectively.

In 1871, an Entrance and First Arts Examination were added to the examinations held. The Medical School Examinations were taken over, and were conducted under the auspices of the University, diplomas as Licentiates being conferred upon those who passed at the final examination. In 1873, the Arts schemes were revised by a Committee, which represented both the University College and the Department of Public Instruction, and in 1874 the Entrance, Proficiency and High Proficiency Examinations were held in addition to the Oriental series in Sanskrit, Arabic, Persian, general knowledge, and native medicine. Arrangements were made in this year for examinations in the Faculties of Law and Engineering, which were held in 1874 and 1875, respectively, for the first time. Up to 1876, about 1,800 candidates appeared at the various examinations, of whom over 1,000 passed.

The first Calendar was brought out in 1874. In that year the University College had completed the work of its own organization, rules and regulations having been framed in every department. The years 1875 and 1876, were therefore, the first years of full work. Between 1870 and 1876 great advances had been made in the work of translation of books required in the curricula of the Schools and Colleges, and the Vernacular Department had made great strides.

Study of Oriental Languages.

In order to teach the Oriental languages upon modern principles, and to impart a knowledge of modern sciences through the medium of the Vernacular, an Oriental School was opened in August, 1870. This school had been originally founded in 1865 by the *Anjuman-i-Punjab* and it had then been the object of large donations from native chiefs. When, for certain reasons the Oriental School was closed, the subscriptions and donations ceased. After its re-opening, under improved auspices, very liberal subscriptions and donations again poured in. And when some of the students matriculated and passed higher examinations on the Oriental side, a College department was added, and the name Oriental College

was given to this, the chief teaching institution of the University College. Its position in 1877 is thus described in the reports :—

" To recapitulate briefly, the objects of the College are two-fold : (1) to give a high classical Oriental education, together with instruction, in branches of general knowledge ; and (2) to give a practical direction to every study. Men who intend to devote themselves entirely to literature or science have scholarships and fellowships to look forward to with their incumbent duties of teaching and translating, or they may return to their homes as thoroughly trained *Moulvies* or *Pundits* who have also received a liberal education. Those who aspire to the dignity and function of *Qazis* are trained in their own Law. Persons who wish to take up the practical work of teaching in Army Schools or in the Educational Department, will, it has been promised, be admitted to a course in the Normal School."

Thus it was the object of the Oriental College to embody as a teaching institution, those principles which the Punjab University College in another capacity enunciated in its examinations. It emphasized the Oriental as the Government College did the English side of the educational system.

Studies in Law.

The Law School was first established by the *Anjuman-i-Panjab* in 1868. Down to 1874 no University Examinations in Law were held, but the students were sent up to the Pleaders' Examinations held under the Legal Practitioners' Act, and the rules framed thereunder by the Judges of the Chief Court. These examinations were, however, handed over to the University College in that year, thus recognizing and assuring the position of the Law School in the most practical and efficient manner possible.

Working of the Punjab University College, from 1877 to 1882.

A very brief record will suffice to give an account of this the last period of the existence of the Punjab University College. In December 1876, the Senate presented a last memorial to the Viceroy, which resulted in the promise of a University which was made public at the Imperial Assembly in January, 1877. Each year had seen the University College attain greater success and solidity, and a few statistics will best explain what had been effected. The Endowment Fund did not increase with much rapidity owing, no doubt, to the 'hope deferred' of past years, and the delay in fulfilling the pledges given, Rs. 3,84,495, stood in Government Securities to the credit of the new University in 1882. The Senate Hall building is now estimated at Rs. 40,000. The income rose to Rs. 75,000, and the expenditure expanded accordingly as the following figures show :—

DETAILS.	1877.	1878.	1879.	1880.	1881.	1882.
	Rs.	Rs.	Rs.	Rs.	Rs.	Rs.
Income	44,914	53,230	55,991	63,115	64,953	75,495
Expenditure	53,014	56,495	57,573	59,598	63,881	70,419

The Government grant still stood at Rs. 21,000. In the year 1879, the Punjab Government promised to reconsider the grant when the University was established.

Large number of Institutions affiliated.

A large number of institutions were affiliated to the University College in the sense that they taught up to its standards and upon its principles, and received in return grants-in-aid or Scholarships. The University Act emphasizes the liberal principles of the University by making no provision for affiliation in the sense in which that term is used in other Universities. The Punjab University throws open its examinations to all institutions alike, as well as to private students. It demands a definite course of reading and standards based upon its own principles, it also offers its aid and Scholarships upon the results attained and upon nothing else. In this sense all competent institutions are affiliated to it. Its teaching institutions, the Oriental College and Law School, continued to develop and flourish from 1876 to 1882. Much was achieved in the direction of supplying a Vernacular literature. The Fellowship holders have translated many important works, especially those required for the various curricula of instruction in Medicine, Natural Science, Mathematics, History, and other branches of knowledge. Indeed, in several branches, instruction and examination is now successfully carried on through the medium of the Vernacular up to the Master of Arts standard. In Law and Engineering also much progress was made in the translation of works of importance.

The examination work was from the first conducted by examiners appointed by the Senate, who have been altogether unconnected with the teaching of the candidates in the various subjects. Indeed, most of the examiners have been entirely unconnected with the University and the Province. This principle was prescribed by the original Statutes of 1869, and has had the effect of silencing criticism and of giving confidence in the genuineness of the work done. The lower examinations have been conducted at several centres, besides Lahore; Delhi and Lucknow being the most important. The number of candidates during this period was 3,600, the number who passed was 1,911.

Examiners.

Apart from the purely Oriental Examinations, the Vernacular candidates for the various Arts Examinations of the Punjab University, from 1871 to 1882 (inclusive), numbered 652. The total number of candidates in the various Oriental Examinations, from 1870 to 1882 (inclusive), was 2,351.

Final Constitution of a University demanded.

On the 13th November, 1880, the pledges given had not been fulfilled, but the Secretary of State had in the meanwhile sanctioned the proposal of the Government of India, and the necessary legislation alone remained for consideration. Accordingly a very large and influential deputation of the Senate, headed by the Honourable Sir Robert Egerton and His Highness the Maharaja of Kashmir, G.C.S.I., waited upon the Viceroy, on the occasion of his visit to Lahore, and presented an address to the following effect, namely, they felt sure that the Marquis of Ripon would support the pledges given by Lord Lytton, and would repeat the promise to complete at once their great National Institution. They referred to Sir Robert Egerton's letters of the 7th July, 1877, and 12th July, 1879, for the arguments in favor of a Punjab University written by His Honour soon after succeeding to the Government of this Province. They, however, more specially brought to the notice of His Excellency that 729 students had already passed the Entrance Examination of the College, and that as many as 60 undergraduates were now prosecuting their studies for higher honours in English by the aid of scholarships from the University funds. They also pointed out that out of 1,747 students who had presented themselves for the various examinations in Arts 1,217 had come up for the English examinations, and that the number of candidates for the Entrance Examination in English had increased from 26 in 1873 to 193 in the examination for 1880. They trusted that this would be a sufficient reply to any objections that might be raised that the Punjab University College did not sufficiently encourage the study of English.

Lord Ripon's Government passes the Punjab University Act, XIX of 1882.

Lord Ripon's reply was most favourable. A Bill was presently introduced into Council and eventually passed as Act XIX of 1882, and on the 14th of October of that year a Notification by the Punjab Government formally constituted the Punjab University. The inaugural convocation was held at Lahore on the 18th November, 1882, in the presence of the Viceroy who is the patron of the University. The new constitution completely fulfilled the wishes of the donors, subscribers and promoters of the institution. An Oriental University has been combined with an English University, provision has been made for the due encouragement and development of the national Classical and Vernacular languages, as the teaching, examining and literary functions of the Senate have been emphasized, and, lastly, the governing body is largely representative in its character and possesses the right to represent its views to the Government and the privilege of being consulted by it. It is thus a National University in the truest sense. The Statutes of 1869, provided that the highest honors should only be conferred when proficiency in Arabic or Sanskrit or some other Oriental language was combined with a thorough acquaintance with English. The Act separates the two faculties and gives equal recognition and honor to each while the Regulations provide for the acquisition, by graduates, of the combined honors of both as being naturally the highest distinction. Each faculty possesses an equal series of degrees, while the Oriental Faculty possesses special powers for honoring proficiency in Oriental languages by the conferring of Oriental literary titles and marks of honor. This separation which still permits of interchange, leaves both sides free to develop, side by side, without conflict and will afford a healthy emulation between the two systems. Both English and Vernacular are recognised and honored to the full extent, and both are open to the people of the country. The new Degrees naturally took the names of Bachelor, Master and Doctor, respectively, of Oriental Learning.

Constitution of the governing body of the Punjab University.

The next point for consideration is the constitution of the governing body. His Excellency the Governor-General was unable, for various reasons, to accept the office of Chancellor, and it was decided to constitute the Lieutenant-Governor of the Punjab for the time being, Chancellor of the University, and thus the head of the University is in a position himself to supervise its working, while the original proposal of the promoters has been carried out. The Vice-Chancellor is appointed by the Chancellor. The Act makes a distinction between the original founders and donors by providing that the Fellows named in Part II of the Schedule to the Act, do not cease to be such when they quit India permanently, while those who may be appointed subsequently vacate office upon leaving India without the intention of returning or by remaining absent from India for more than four years. It was not deemed necessary or proper to make any distinctions amongst the Fellows themselves—all being equal. A great concession, from an Anglo-Indian stand point, was made by the Legislature in leaving the Senate to elect a number of Fellows equal to the number nominated, from time to time, by the Chancellor. This provision gives a representative character to the Senate which cannot fail to be a source of good, the principle of Self-Government has thus been liberally conceded in this particular.

The powers of the Senate over the affairs of the University are very complete and full, and the necessary supervision has been effected in such a way as not to interfere with the Senate's exercising all the authority which is required for the purposes for which it has been founded. The Senate possess the 'entire management of and superintendence over the affairs, concerns and property of the University.' The Local Government is empowered to enforce the Act, Statutes, Rules and Regulations where the Senate may fail to do so. The Statutes, Rules and Regulations which may be framed require the sanction of Government, and the Local Government can require such examination and audit of the accounts of the University as may appear necessary. Internal autonomy is thus secured, unless and until inefficiency or worse is displayed. In carrying out these principles the Senate have had to re-draft their Statutes, and this has been done with scrupulous regard to the wishes of the promoters, and subject to the altered condition of things at the time."*

The Allahabad University incorporated in September, 1887.

The Allahabad University was incorporated by Act XVIII of 1887, which was passed on the 23rd September, 1887. The constitution of the University closely resembles that of the University of Calcutta, consisting of a Chancellor a Vice-Chancellor and Fellows forming a Senate, divided into Faculties of various branches of learning which are regulated by the Boards of studies. The Syndicate of the University is the executive governing body as in the other Indian Universities, and the subjects of examination, with minor alterations, are the same as in the University of Calcutta, though hitherto the working of the University has been confined to the Faculties of Arts and Law.

Scope and character of Collegiate Education.

The general scope and character of education in the Colleges affiliated to the Indian Universities was thus described by the Indian Education Commission of 1882:—

"In scope and character, collegiate instruction is now almost uniform throughout India. Purely Oriental Colleges must, of course, be excepted. These, however, are so few in number that they scarcely enter into a consideration of collegiate education in its modern development. With the exception, indeed, of the Oriental College at Lahore, and of the Oriental Department of the Canning College, Lucknow, they are but relics of that order of things which existed previous to the publication of Lord William Bentinck's famous Resolution. The college of to-day aims at giving an education that shall fit its recipient to take an honourable share in the administration of the country, or to enter with good hope of success the various liberal professions now expanding in vigorous growth. It follows, therefore, that the advancement of learning in India is in a large measure through science, and altogether according to the scientific method. The English and Oriental classics, of course, occupy an important place in the college scheme; but, apart from the refinement of character and elevation of thought which are incidental to their study, their chief function is to discipline the intellect. In history, philosophy, mathematics, and physical science, English is the medium of instruction and the passport to academic honours. The dialectics of Hindoo philosophy and the subtleties of Muhammadan law have naturally disappeared from a course of studies intended to be of so practical a character; the profound scholarship and lifelong devotion to learning which India once boasted, are sacrifices made to the appreciation of an active career. Few regrets are felt on this score, though there are those who hold that the present exclusive use of English is neither beneficial nor necessary. Through the Vernaculars, to some extent already and largely in the near future, they believe that general knowledge of the higher kind might be imparted, and that an education of wider national profit would be the certain result."†

Duration of College courses and standards of examination in the Universities of Calcutta, Madras and Bombay.

The duration of the College courses and the standards of examination in the Universities of Calcutta, Madras and Bombay, were thus described in the Report of the Indian Education Commission of 1882:—

"In Bengal, the College course extends over five years from matriculation to the M. A. degree. In Madras, there is a course of four years up to the B. A. degree, and those who appear for the M. A. examination commonly spend at least two years more in study, though none of the Colleges have regular classes beyond the B. A. standard. In Bombay, three years is the period; but, on the other hand, the school course is one year longer, and the Entrance examination of a somewhat more difficult character. The usual age at which an Indian student seeks admission to the University is between sixteen and eighteen years. Having by that time completed the High School course, he is examined by means of printed papers (and, in the Bombay and Punjab Universities, orally) in English, a

* *Gazetteer of the Punjab* (Prov. Vol., 1888-89) pp. 170-175. † Report of the Indian Education Commission (1882), pp. 269, 270.

classical or vernacular language, history, geography, mathematics, and in Madras and Bombay, in elementary physical science, the exact standard in each of these subjects need not be stated here. But, roughly speaking, the knowledge required is about that which, at the age of sixteen, an English boy of average intelligence will be found to possess. Success in this examination admits a student to any of the affiliated colleges. There, after attendance for two years (for one year in Bombay), he is permitted to present himself for the First Examination in Arts, or the Previous Examination, as it is styled in Bombay. At the Calcutta University the subjects of examination are English, a classical language (Oriental or European), history, mathematics, logic, and either psychology or elementary chemistry. In Madras, human physiology holds the place of logic, psychology, or chemistry, in the Calcutta course. In Bombay the scheme is identical with that in Calcutta, except that natural science takes the place of the optional subjects. Two years later again (in Bombay there is an Intermediate examination) comes the examination for the B.A. degree." *

"The B.A. degree is followed by the M.A. degree. Here the examination is practically confined to one or other of the following branches of knowledge: (1) Languages; (2) History; (3) Mental and Moral Philosophy; (4) Mathematics, pure and mixed; (5) Natural and Physical Science. At Calcutta the candidate is allowed to take up one or more of these branches either in the same or in different years; in Madras and Bombay a classical language (Oriental or European) is coupled with English, and Philosophy with History and Political Economy. With the M.A. degree the College course comes to an end, though in the Calcutta University the Premchand Roychand Studentship is the final goal of academic distinction." †

Statistics of some important results of Collegiate education under the Universities of Calcutta, Madras and Bombay, 1857-82.

Such being the course of studies in the Universities of Calcutta, Madras and Bombay, which were founded in 1857, it is important to exhibit in a summary form some of the more important results of Collegiate education under those Universities for a quarter of a century from their establishment, the Punjab University and the Allahabad University having no existence during that period. The following table has been prepared from two tables given at page 269 of the Report of the Indian Education Commission of 1882.

COLLEGIATE EDUCATION, 1857 TO 1882.

Provinces.	In 1857—1870-71.				In 1871-72—1881-82.			
	Maximum number of English Arts Colleges.	Number of students who passed the F.A., B.A. and M.A. Examinations.			Maximum number of English Arts Colleges.	Number of students who passed the F.A., B.A. and M.A. Examinations.		
		F.A.	B.A.	M.A.		F.A.	B.A.	M.A.
Madras	12	784	152	6	25	2,032	890	22
Bombay	4	244	116	28	6	709	340	34
Bengal	17	1,495	548	112	22	2,666	1,037	284
N.-W. P. and Oudh	9	96	26	5	9	365	130	33
Punjab	4	47	8	...	2	107	37	11
Central Provinces	...	...	...	...	1	90	...	...
Total ...	46	2,666	850	151	65	5,969	2,434	385

Examinations conducted by the Punjab University.

The preceding table shows the progress which Collegiate English education had made under the auspices of the older three Universities during the first quarter of a century of their existence. The distinctive features of the course of education in the Punjab

* Report of the Indian Education Commission (1882), p. 270. † *Ib.*, p. 272.

University established in 1882, have already been described, and the following extract gives further information upon the subject :—

"There are two examinations leading to the degree in Arts—the Intermediate, corresponding to the First Arts Examination; the High Proficiency Examination, corresponding to that for B.A. Those who pass the High Proficiency standard through the medium of English, receive the degree of B.A.; while on those who pass it through the medium of the Vernacular is conferred the degree of B.O.L., or Bachelor of Oriental Learning. Graduates of either class are entitled to present themselves at a later date for examination by the Honours in Arts standard, and those who pass receive the degrees of M.A. and M.O.L. respectively. Similarly on the Oriental side, examinations are held in Arabic for the titles successively of Maulavi Alim and Maulavi Fazil, in Persian for the titles of Munshi Alim and Munshi Fazil, and for Visharad and Shastri in Sanskrit. Examinations are also held in Gurmukhi, or the literature of the Sikhs. The Senate of the University further acts as the constituted adviser of the Government on educational matters. Among many important subjects referred to that body for discussion and opinion may be mentioned—vacations in schools and dates of public examinations; systems of grants-in-aid; the award of scholarships; primary standards for boys' and girls' schools; the inspection of girls' schools; proposals for a new Punjabi Dictionary; the European Education Code; rules for Training Colleges; and tests for admission to the public service in various grades. The conduct of the Middle School Examination was also transferred to the University. Thus it is evident that the Punjab University occupies towards the Government of the Province a position which is not filled by any other University in India."*

CHAPTER XIX.

THE INDIAN EDUCATION COMMISSION OF 1882, AND SOME IMPORTANT FACTS AND STATISTICS COLLECTED BY IT IN REGARD TO ENGLISH COLLEGIATE EDUCATION.

Indian Education Commission of 1882.

In 1882, the Government of India passed a Resolution, No. $\frac{1}{60}$, dated the 3rd February, 1882, by which it appointed a Commission to report upon the subject of education, and the following extracts from the Resolution will show its nature and objects :—

Resolution appointing the Commission, dated 3rd February, 1882.

"In view of the facts that, since the measures set forth in the Despatch of 1854 came into active operation, a full quarter of a century has elapsed, and that it is now ten years since the responsible direction of the educational system was entrusted to the Local Governments, it appears to His Excellency the Governor-General in Council that the time has come for instituting a more careful examination into the results attained, and into the working of the present arrangements, than has hitherto been attempted. The experience of the past has shown that a mere critical review or analysis of the returns and reports of the different provinces fails to impart a thoroughly satisfactory knowledge of the actual state of things in the districts, and that there are many points which only an acquaintance with local circumstances can adequately estimate or explain. His Excellency in Council has therefore decided to appoint a Commission on behalf of Government to enquire into the present position of education in British India, and to nominate to this Commission a sufficient number of persons from the different provinces to secure the adequate and intelligent consideration of the facts that will be laid before it." †

Duties assigned to the Commission.

The Commission thus appointed consisted of European and Native members representing the various sections of the community interested in the subject of education. Sir W. W. Hunter was appointed President, and the general duties assigned to the Commission were thus prescribed :—

"It will be the duty of the Commission to enquire particularly (subject only to certain limitations to be noticed below) into the manner in which effect has been given to the principles of the Despatch of 1854; and to suggest such measures as it may think desirable in order to the further carrying out of the policy therein laid down. The Government of India is firmly convinced of the soundness of that policy, and has no wish to depart

* Review of Education in India in 1886; by Sir Alfred Croft, p. 30.

† Report of the Indian Education Commission (1882), p. 624; App. A.

from the principles upon which it is based. It is intended only at the present time, to examine into the general results of its operation, and to scrutinize the efficiency of the machinery that has been set on foot for bringing about those ends which the Government from the outset had especially in view."* "It will not be necessary for the Commission to enquire into the general working of the Indian Universities, which are controlled by corporations comprising representatives of all classes interested in collegiate education. Of the results of their operation a fair estimate can always be formed independently of a special enquiry such as is now proposed. Nor will it be necessary for the Commission to take up the subject of special or technical education, whether medical, legal, or engineering. To extend the enquiry to these subjects would expand unduly the task before the Commission. Again the Government of India has itself very recently dealt with the question of European and Eurasian education, and no further enquiry is necessary as regards that. But, with these exceptions, the Governor-General in Council is of opinion that the Commission may usefully consider the working of all branches of the Indian educational system. These branches are, it is believed, so closely connected one with another, that it is only by examining the system as a whole that any sound conclusions are likely to be come to."†

Policy of encouraging the grant-in-aid system to secure gradual withdrawal from high English education.

Another passage from the Resolution requires quotation here as it announces the policy of the Government to give further encouragement to the grant-in-aid system with the object of securing the gradual withdrawal of the State from high English education. After inviting the attention of the Commission to the great importance which the Government attaches to the subject of primary education, the Resolution (in paragraphs 9 and 10) goes on to say:—

"The resources at the disposal of Government, whether imperial, provincial or local, are, and must long remain, extremely limited in amount, and the result is, not only that progress must necessarily be gradual, but that if satisfactory progress is to be made at all, every available private agency must be called into action to relieve and assist the public funds in connection with every branch of Public Instruction. It was in view of 'the impossibility of Government alone doing all that must be done to provide adequate means for the education of the Natives of India,' that the grant-in-aid system was elaborated and developed by the Despatch of 1854; and it is to the wider extension of this system, especially in connection with high and middle education, that the Government looks to set free funds which may then be made applicable to the promotion of the education of the masses. 'The resources of the State ought,' as remarked by the Secretary of State in Despatch No. 13 of 25th April 1864, 'to be so applied as to assist those who cannot be expected to help themselves, and the richer classes of the people should gradually be induced to provide for their own education.'

"In pursuance of this policy it is the desire of Government to offer every encouragement to native gentlemen to come forward and aid, even more extensively than heretofore, in the establishment of schools upon the grant-in-aid system: and His Excellency in Council is the more anxious to see this brought about, because, apart altogether from the consequent pecuniary relief to Government, it is chiefly in this way that the native community will be able to secure that freedom and variety of education which is an essential condition in any sound and complete educational system. It is not, in the opinion of the Governor-General in Council, a healthy symptom that all the youth of the country should be cast, as it were, in the same Government educational mould. Rather is it desirable that each section of the people should be in a position to secure that description of education which is most consonant to its feelings and suited to its wants. The Government is ready, therefore, to do all that it can to foster such a spirit of independence and self-help. It is willing to hand over any of its own colleges or schools, in suitable cases, to bodies of native gentlemen who will undertake to manage them satisfactorily as aided institutions; all that the Government will insist upon, being that due provision is made for efficient management and extended usefulness. It will be for the Commission to consider in what mode effect can most fully be given to these views; and how the grant-in-aid system may best be shaped so to stimulate such independent effort, and make the largest use of the available Government funds."‡

Information as to Collegiate Education collected by the Commission.

Although the subject of the general working of the Indian Universities was excluded from the enquiry to be made by the Commission, yet much valuable information was collected by it in connection with collegiate education, and some passages from the Report may, therefore, be quoted here, as such instruction is carried on in Colleges which are affiliated to the Universities and pursue the course of instruction prescribed by them:—

"The affiliated Colleges are of two grades; those whose students go no further than the First Arts, or Previous

* Report of the Indian Education Commission (1883), p. 624; App. A.

† *Ib.*, p. 625; Appendix A.

‡ *Ib.*, pp. 625, 626; Appendix A.

Examina-tion, and those in which they proceed to the B.A. and M.A. degrees. The strength of the teaching staff varies with the wealth of the institution, the numbers of the students, and the class of examinations for which candidates are sent up. Thus the Presidency College in Calcutta, has a Principal, eleven Professors, and two teachers of Sanskrit and Arabic. This staff provides for lectures being given in all the various subjects of all the examinations. A smaller college will be content with a Principal, two Professors, a Pandit, and a Maulavi; but with no larger staff than this, restrictions are necessary as to the choice of subjects in the alternative courses, and but little help can be afforded to students reading for the M.A. degree." *

Views of the Commission as to Academic discipline.

In regard to academic discipline of the students prosecuting their studies in the Colleges affiliated to the Indian Universities, the Indian Education Commission expressed their views in the following words :—

"In their scheme of discipline, and in the academic life of their students, Indian Colleges have but little analogy with those of the older of the English Universities, their resemblance being closer to those of Scotland and Germany. Residence in college buildings is not only not generally compulsory, but the colleges are few in which any systematic provision is made for control over the students' pursuits out of college hours. Boarding-houses are, indeed, attached to certain institutions, and their number increases year by year. But, unless the student's home be at a distance from the collegiate city, and he have no relatives to receive him, it is seldom that he will incur the expense which residence involves. Two principal reasons account for this feature in our system. First, the initial outlay upon buildings is one from which Government and independent bodies alike shrink. For so poor is the Indian student that it would be impossible to demand of him any but the most moderate rent—a rent perhaps barely sufficient to cover the cost of the annual repairs. The second obstacle lies in the religious and social prejudices which fence class from class. Not only does the Hindu refuse to eat with the Musalman, but from close contact with whole sections of his own co-religionists he is shut off by the imperious ordinances of caste. Experience, however, has already proved that the barriers of custom are giving way. In the North-Western Provinces and the Punjab, where the residential system has been widely tried, the success has been considerable; and nothing but want of funds stands in the way of a fuller development. In the more important Bombay Colleges, also, a considerable number of the students are in residence; in Bengal and Madras the system has been less fully recognised. Yet it is the one thing which will give the departmental officer a hold upon the lives of those whose intellects he trains with such sedulous elaboration. From any attempt to touch the religious side of the student's character, the Government educational officer is debarred by the principle of religious neutrality. All the more important therefore, is it that he should be able to exercise the moral influence of a close and watchful discipline." †

Statistics of Collegiate instruction, 1881-82.

The following table ‡ shows the statistics of attendance in English Arts Colleges, for the official year 1881-82 :—

STATISTICS OF ATTENDANCE IN ENGLISH ARTS COLLEGES, FOR 1881-82.

Provinces.	Departmental.		Aided.		Unaided.		Total.	
	Colleges.	Students.	Colleges.	Students.	Colleges.	Students.	Colleges.	Students.
Madras	10	742	11	803	3	124	24	1,669
Bombay	3	311	2	139	1	25	6	475
Bengal	12	1,305	5	895	4	538	21	2,738
N.-W. Provinces and Oudh ...	3	172	2	157	1	20	6	349
Punjab	1	103	...	...	...	...	1	103
Central Provinces	1	65	...	...	...	...	1	65
Total ...	30	2,698	20	1,994	9	707	59	5,399

* Report of the Indian Education Commission (1882), p. 272.

† *Ib.*, pp. 272, 273.

‡ *Ib.*, p. 274 (extract from Table No. I).

Average cost of Collegiate Education per student, 1881-82.

Among the statistics collected by the Indian Education Commission of 1882 (*vide* page 279 of the Report), the following tabular statement is interesting, as showing the average annual cost (calculated on the average monthly number of the students enrolled) of educating each student in English Arts Colleges, for the official year 1881-82 :—

AVERAGE ANNUAL COST OF EDUCATING EACH STUDENT IN ENGLISH ARTS COLLEGES, IN 1881-82.

Provinces.	Departmental Colleges.		Aided Colleges.		Unaided Colleges.
	Total average annual cost.	Average annual cost to Provincial Funds.	Total average annual cost.	Average annual cost to Provincial Funds.	Total average annual cost.
	Rs. A. P.	Rs. A. P.	Rs. A. P.	Rs. A. P.	Rs. A. P.
Madras	257 13 8	210 1 2	125 2 8	29 9 8	93 1 2
Bombay	446 12 8	274 13 0	271 10 9	35 14 7	331 10 2
Bengal	320 9 5	217 5 8	185 5 6	28 0 7	48 7 8
N.-W. P. and Oudh... ...	758 4 2	534 8 6	312 9 8	111 14 0	125 14 0
Punjab	498 15 8	477 1 10	......	......	......
Central Provinces	186 3 1	165 8 5	......	......	......
Average for British India, excluding Ajmir and Burma ...	354 9 1	253 9 9	178 7 7	35 14 3	97 8 2

Tuition Fees in Arts Colleges in 1881-82.

The following table* gives an approximate idea of the tuition fees paid by students in Arts Colleges during the official year 1881-82, and the proportion which the income from such fees bears to total expenditure in the various classes of the Colleges, excluding the expenditure on buildings and scholarships :—

TUITION FEES IN ARTS COLLEGES IN THE OFFICIAL YEAR, 1881-82.

Provinces.	Departmental Colleges.		Aided Colleges.		Unaided Colleges.		Percentage of Income from fees to Total Expenditure in—		
	Highest Fee.	Lowest Fee.	Highest Fee.	Lowest Fee.	Highest Fee.	Lowest Fee.	Departmental Colleges.	Aided Colleges.	Unaided Colleges.
	Rs.	Rs.	Rs.	Rs.	Rs.	Rs.			
Madras	5	3	4	2	3	...	17·78	23·76	31·02
Bombay	10	3	8	4	5	3	18·28	21·72	14·56
Bengal	12	3	6	5	3	...	27·51	29·16	41·19
N.-W. P. and Oudh ...	5	2	5	1	4	1	5·65	5·29	16·63
Punjab	5	2	...	...	...	...	4·38	...	...
Central Provinces ...	2	2	...	...	...	...	11·09	...	...
Average for India ...	12	2	8	1	5	1	19·53	23·44	27·05

* Prepared from Table No. VIII, at page 280 of the Report of the Indian Education Commission (1882).

Approximate statistics of the after-career of Indian graduates, 1871-1882.

In regard to the results of higher English education, the following tabular statement (*vide* Indian Education Commission Report, 1882, page 281), showing an estimate of the number of graduates from collegiate institutions who, between 1871 and 1882, took up various professions, gives an approximate idea of the after-career of our Indian graduates :—

PROVINCES.	Number of graduates between 1871-82.	Having entered the public service, British or Native.	Legal profession.	Medical profession.	Civil Engineering profession.
Madras	808	296	126	18	...
Bombay	625	324	49	76	28
Bengal	1,696	534	471	131	19
N.-W. P. and Oudh	130	61	33	...	6
Punjab	38	21	5	...	...
Central Provinces	14	8	...	...	...
Total ...	3,311	1,244	684	225	53

CHAPTER XX.

THE GRANT-IN-AID SYSTEM INAUGURATED BY THE EDUCATIONAL DESPATCH OF 1854, AND CONSIDERED BY THE INDIAN EDUCATION COMMISSION OF 1882.

Objects of the Despatch of 1854, as to the Grant-in-aid system.

To use the language employed by the Indian Education Commission, " the Despatch of 1854 contains the first declaration of the policy of the Government in a matter which lies at the root of any national system of education, that is to say, the determination of the parts which can be most effectively taken in it by the State and by the people. The immediate aims of the Government of that time were the same as those to which the attention of every European state was first directed when organising its system of public instruction. The existing schools of all kinds were to be improved and their number increased, systematic inspection was to be established, and a supply of competent teachers was to be provided. But in India the attitude of the State to national education was effected by three conditions to which no European state could furnish a parallel. In the *first* place, the population was not only as large as that of all the European states together that had adopted an educational system, but it presented, in its different Provinces, at least, as many differences of creed, language, race and custom. *Secondly*, the ruling power was bound to hold itself aloof from all questions of religion. *Thirdly*, the scheme of instruction to be introduced was one which should culminate in the acquisition of a literature and science essentially foreign. While therefore, on the one hand, the magnitude of the task before the Indian Government was such as to make it almost impossible of achievement by any direct appropriation from the resources of the Empire, on the other, the popular demand for education, so important a factor in the success of the European systems — had in general to be created. The Government adopted the only course which circumstances permitted. It was admitted that 'to imbue a vast and ignorant population with a general desire for knowledge, and to take advantage of that desire when excited to improve the means for diffusing education amongst them, must be a work of many years' ; and this admission was followed by the announcement that 'as a Government, we can do no more than direct the efforts of the people, and aid them wherever they appear to require most assistance.' In pursuance of this resolution the earlier part of the Despatch is occupied with a review of all the agencies for education which were already in existence in India, whether maintained by Government or by private persons or bodies, native and foreign ; and it was declared that the extension and increased supply of schools and colleges should for the future be mainly effected by the grant-in-aid system. Notice was taken of the increasing desire on the part of the natives of India for the means of obtaining a better education, as shown by the liberal sums which had recently been contributed with that object; and attention was drawn to the zeal and munificence which Hindus and Muhammadans for ages had manifested in the cause of education. Cordial recognition was also given to the efforts of Christian Associations in diffusing knowledge among the natives of India, specially among uncivilized races. In such circumstances it was hoped that the grant-in-aid system could be introduced into India, as it had been into England, with every prospect of success. The introduction of that system was necessitated by a conviction of the impossibility of Government alone doing all that must be done in order to provide adequate means for the education of the natives of India; and it was expected that the plan of thus drawing support from local sources, in addition to contributions from the State, would result in a far more rapid progress of education than would follow a mere increase of expenditure by the Government, while it possessed the additional advantage of fostering a spirit of reliance upon local exertions, and combination for local purposes, which was, of itself, of no mean importance to the well-being of a nation." *

Scope and character of the Grant-in-aid system.

In regard to scope and character, " the system was to be based on an entire abstinence from interference with the religious instruction conveyed in the schools assisted, and aid was to be given within certain limits to all schools which imparted a good secular education, provided that they were under adequate local management, that is, under persons responsible for the general superintendence of the school and for its permanence for a given time. Such schools were to be open to Government inspection, and to be subjected to such other rules as Government might, from time to time, impose. It was further required that some fee, however small, should be levied in all aided schools; and that grants should be made for specific objects, such as the augmentation of the salaries of the head-teachers, the supply of junior teachers, the provision of scholarships, the supply of school-books, or the erection of buildings, and not for the general expenditure of the school. On these principles it was hoped that local management, under Government inspection and aided by grants, would be encouraged wherever it was possible to take advantage of it; and it was ruled that when such management so aided was capable of adequately meeting the local demand for education, Government institutions were not to be founded. The Despatch looked forward to the time when any general system of education entirely provided by the Government might be discontinued with the gradual advance of the system of grants-in-aid; and when many of the existing Government institutions, especially those of the higher order, might be safely closed or transferred to the management of local bodies, under the control of, and aided by, the State. But it was expressly provided that the spread of education was not to be checked in the slightest degree by the abandonment of a single school to probable decay; and while the desired object was to be kept steadily in view, the Government and the local authorities were enjoined to act with caution, and to be guided by special reference to the particular circumstances of the locality concerned. The higher classes would thus be gradually called upon to depend more upon themselves; while, for the education of the middle and lower classes, special attention was directed, both to the establishment of fitting schools for that purpose and also to the careful encouragement of the native schools which had existed from time immemorial, and none of which, perhaps, could not in some degree be made available to the end in view."†

Relations of the State to private effort.

" The relations of the State to private effort, as indicated in the Despatch of 1854, may therefore be summed up as follows. The state undertook —

(1) to give pecuniary assistance on the grant-in-aid system to efficient Schools and Colleges;

(2) to direct their efforts and afford them counsel and advice;

(3) to encourage and reward the desire for learning in various ways, but chiefly by the establishment of Universities;

(4) to take measures for providing a due supply of teachers, and for making the profession of teaching honourable and respected.

" Of all these provisions the most important and far-reaching was the introduction of the grant-in-aid system. It was found in the Despatch of 1859, that in the rules framed for the allotment of grants-in-aid careful attention had been paid to the foregoing principles. It was also stated in that Despatch that, while the system had been readily accepted by schools of higher education, it had been unsuccessful in its application to those of a lower class."‡

Necessity of encouraging private effort. Limitations of the policy of withdrawal.

" The Despatch also pointed out, in reference to the small number of scholars in the Government Colleges and Schools of higher education, that there was ample scope for the employment of every form of agency that could be brought into the field of educational labour; and urged that every agency likely to engage in the work with

* Report of the Indian Education Commission (1882), pp. 351, 352 † *Ib.* pp. 352, 353. ‡ *Ib.* p. 355.

earnestness and efficiency should be made use of and fostered. It laid stress on the great advantage of promoting in the native community a spirit of self-reliance, in opposition to the habit of depending on Government for the supply of local wants; and it accordingly declared that if Government should accept the duty of placing elementary education within reach of the general population, those persons or classes who required more than this might, as a general rule, be left to exert themselves to procure it, with or without the assistance of Government. But in summarising the objects of the Despatch of 1854, it made no further reference to the withdrawal of Government from any of its own institutions, or to their transfer to the management of local bodies. On the contrary, it stated, what had not before been stated so explicitly, that one of the objects of that Despatch was the increase, where necessary, of the number of Government Colleges and Schools,—a declaration which was repeated and enforced in the Despatch of the 23rd January, 1864. Moreover, while it has been often reiterated as a general principle that Government should withdraw, wherever possible, from the direct maintenance and management of institutions of the higher class, stress has always been laid upon the need of caution in the practical application of the principle. Thus, in the Despatch No. 6, of the Secretary of State, dated 14th May 1862, it is expressly said that in any such withdrawal 'attention must necessarily be given to local circumstances,' and that 'Her Majesty's Government are unwilling that a Government School should be given up in any place where the inhabitants show a marked desire that it should be maintained, or where there is a manifest disinclination, on the part of the people, to send their children to the private schools of the neighbourhood.' And again in Despatch No. 6 of the Secretary of State, dated the 26th May 1870, in reply to a proposal from the Government of India 'to reduce the Government expenditure on Colleges in Bengal to an equality with the sum total of the endowments and fees of the Colleges,' the fear is expressed lest the proposal would tend 'entirely to paralyse the action of high education in Bengal,' and that 'a large and sudden reduction in the Government grant will tend to the diminution, rather than the augmentation, of private liberality.' Thus, while the time has always been looked forward to when, in the words of the Despatch of 1854, 'many of the existing Government institutions, especially those of the higher order, may be safely closed or transferred to the management of local bodies under the control of, and aided by, the State,' more recent Despatches have laid particular emphasis on the further statement, 'it is far from our wish to check the spread of education in the slightest degree by the abandonment of a single school to probable decay.' *

Limitation of State expenditure on Higher Education.

"The necessity of requiring the wealthier classes to contribute to the cost of their education, and thus to make Government schools more self-supporting than before, was strongly insisted on in 1861 (Despatch No. 14, dated 8th April, 1861), in reference to the levy of fees in high schools, when it was declared to be impossible, even if desirable, that the State should bear the whole expense of education in so densely populated a country as India. A similar view was expressed in 1864 (Despatch No. 13, dated 25th April, 1864), when it was laid down that, in determining the distribution of expenditure between different classes of education, the resources of the State should, as far as possible, be so applied as to asist those who could not be expected to help themselves, and that the richer classes of the people should gradually be induced to provide for their own education,—for example, by the payment of substantial fees in higher schools. At the same time the interests of the upper classes and the importance of higher schools were in no way ignored or neglected; and in 1863 (Despatch No. 12, dated 24th December, 1863), when it was declared to have been one great object of the Despatch of 1854 to provide for the extension to the general population of those means of education which had theretofore been too exclusively confined to the upper classes, it was expressly added that while Her Majesty's Government desired that the means of obtaining an education calculated to fit them for their higher position and responsibilities should be afforded to the upper classes of society in India, they deemed it equally incumbent on them to take suitable measures for extending the benefits of education to those classes who were incapable of obtaining any education worthy of the name, by their own unaided efforts.

Ultimate objects of the Grant-in-aid System.

"The grant-in-aid system was, therefore, designed to be an auxiliary to the Government system, for the further extension of higher education by the creation of aided schools; and it was anticipated, not only that an exclusively Government system of education would by this means be discontinued with the development of a concurrent system of grants-in-aid, but that in course of time many of the existing Government institutions, especially of the higher order, might themselves be closed or transferred to local management. In short, the grant-in-aid system was intended to supplement, and in time partly to supersede, the Government system of higher education. It was, however, found to be unsuited, in its existing form, to the supply of education for the masses. At the same time the education of the masses was declared to be the primary object towards which the efforts of Government were to be directed, and to the promotion and encouragement of which State aid in some form or other was to be liberally devoted. Such a

* Report of the Indian Education Commission (1882), pp. 355, 356.

declaration does not, of course, involve the State in the responsibility of providing all the funds required for mass education, under any method of aid that may be adopted."*

General financial result of private effort.

The Indian Education Commission after giving an account of the growth of private enterprise in education in various provinces, recorded the following observations on the general financial result :—

"Perhaps nothing that has come to our notice in this historical review is more instructive than the varying extent to which the expenditure on education in the different provinces is supplied from public funds and from private sources, respectively. In public funds we include not only provincial grants derived from the whole tax-paying community, but also those local contributions which are paid from local rates or municipal revenues. In proportion as these local contributions are taken under the operation of law from local resources, they tend, as has been shown above, to diminish the means available for spontaneous effort. But as the application of local funds is mainly, and of municipal funds is partially, determined by departmental influence, we have throughout this Report treated both these funds as public. The comparison which we wish to institute will be evident from the following statement:—"†

PROVINCE.	Expenditure on education from public funds in 1881-82.	Expenditure on education from all sources in 1881-82.	Percentage of column 2 to column 3.
1	2	3	4
	Rs.	Rs.	
Madras	13,97,448	29,94,707	46·66
Bombay	17,71,860	23,69,916	74·76*
Bengal	22,97,917	55,59,295	41·33
North-Western Provinces and Oudh	15,06,882	18,55,572	81·20
Punjab	10,95,321	14,42,556	75·92
Central Provinces	5,16,517	6,35,824	81·23
Assam	1,94,203	3,01,548	64·40
Coorg	20,293	22,737	89·25
Hyderabad Assigned Districts	3,23,441	3,51,296	92·07

Summary of the views of the Education Commission as to private efforts.

The conclusions of the Indian Education Commission on the subject of the growth of private enterprise in education are thus summarized :—

"Our review appears to be sufficient to show that with free scope and cordial encouragement, private effort in education may everywhere produce beneficial and satisfactory results. In almost every Province it has done enough, in point of both quantity and quality, to prove its vitality and its capacity for constantly increasing usefulness. Even where least successful, the plan of aiding private effort to establish institutions for secondary and even higher instruction has by no means proved a failure. Still private effort has hitherto had important disadvantages almost everywhere to contend against. The departmental system was, in most cases, first in the field; and even where private enterprise has been most freely encouraged, departmental institutions, which were often originally established at head-quarter stations or other large and populous centres, have continued to occupy the most favourable ground and have left to private enterprise the task of cultivating a poorer soil. We do not overlook the obligation imposed on the Department by the Despatch of 1854, of opening schools and colleges of its own, whether as models or as the only means available, at first, of providing many localities with the facilities they required for advanced instruction; and we are sensible of the great advantages which the people of India have derived from such departmental institutions. Still it is plain that private effort has not yet been elicited

* Report of the Indian Education Commission (1882), pp. 356, 357. † *Ib.* pp. 378, 379.

on such a scale as to take the position in the general scheme of education which was contemplated in the Despatch of 1854. Nor in the circumstances is this surprising. Departmental institutions have absorbed a large part of admittedly insufficient funds, so that means have not been available for developing private enterprise to the full. Such enterprise has probably been checked in many cases by the mainfest impossibility of its competing successfully with institutions backed by the resources of the State; and in some Provinces the steady development of the departmental system has undoubtedly fostered in the native community a disposition to rely more and more on Governmant for the whole provision of the means of advanced instruction. In short, experience has shown that private effort cannot attain the development or produce the results anticipated in the Despatch of 1854, unless the action of Government is such as to lead the community at large to feel that most departmental institutions are chiefly intended to supply a temporary want, and that the people must themselves more largely provide the means of advanced instruction. This is no argument for the hasty or premature reduction of the departmental system, but only for cautious yet steadily progressive action in the direction of its withdrawal,—a subject, however, which is so important and yet so delicate that we propose to devote a section of the present chapter to its further consideration."*

CHAPTER XXI.

VIEWS OF THE INDIAN EDUCATION COMMISSION IN REGARD TO THE WITHDRAWAL OF THE STATE FROM HIGHER ENGLISH EDUCATION.

The Indian Education Commission dealt with this important subject in a separate section of their report, and some passages from it may be quoted here: They observe—

Withdrawal of the State from higher education.

"Perhaps none of the many subjects here discussed is encompassed with greater difficulty or has elicited more various shades of opinion, alike among the witnesses we have examined and within the Commission itself, than that of the withdrawal of Government from the direct support and management of educational institutions, especially those of the higher order. The difficulty of the subject arises from the great number of opposing considerations, each of which must have proper weight allowed it and be duly balanced against others. Complete agreement is not to be expected in a matter where so many weighty arguments on opposite sides have to be taken into account.

Opinions of witnesses before the Commission.

"The points to which we invited the attention of witnesses were mainly these: We asked them to explain the admitted fact that the policy of withdrawal indicated in the Despatch of 1854, had as yet been hardly initiated. We asked them also their view as to the propriety of further and more decisive action in this direction. For the fact in question many reasons were assigned, the chief of which were the success and popularity of the Government institutions, which naturally made the Department anxious to retain them, and the difficulty of finding suitable agencies able and willing to accept the transfer, without detriment to education in the locality concerned. With regard to future action two strongly opposed lines of argument are followed. On the one hand, it was urged that the very success of the advanced institutions supported directly by the State is a reason for maintaining them; that the people regard the maintenance of such institutions as an important part of the duty of the State as representing the community, which cannot justifiably be neglected or shifted to other shoulders; that the example of many civilised communities is in favour of the management of advanced education by the State; that this duty is now carried out in India at a cost which bears an insignificant proportion to the whole expenditure upon education and still more insignificant when compared with the whole resources of the State; that as a rule there are no agencies to whom such institutions can be safely transferred; that the order of withdrawal must be from below upward, and that, even admitting that the time is come or is approaching when Government may withdraw from secondary schools, the time for its withdrawal from colleges is still distant, or may never arrive; that no resources but those of the State are adequate to procure a steady supply of men fit to teach in the highest institutions; and that any withdrawal of the State from higher education would necessarily throw it into the hands of Missionary bodies, the chief advocates of a change which would cause distrust and apprehension in the great mass of the native community. On the other hand, it was urged that if ever education is to be adequate, it must be national in a wider

* Report of the Indian Education Commission (1882), pp 279, 280.

sense than is implied in mere State management, and must be managed in a great measure by the people themselves; that the very success of Government institutions is itself a bar and a discouragement to that local combination and self-reliance which it is the primary object of the grant-in-aid system to encourage; that as a matter of course the people will not exert themselves to supply their educational wants so long as it is understood that Government is ready to undertake the task, that, therefore, the greatest stimulus which Government can give to private effort is to put an end to arrangements which make it needless; that there is some analogy between the action of Government in the matter of education and in the matter of trade, because though Government can do more than any one trader it cannot do so much as all, and yet it discourages all, for none can compete with Government; that Government action thus represses free competition and creates a monopoly injurious to the public interest; that the absence of bodies willing to manage higher institutions is rather the effect than the cause of the unwillingness of the Department to withdraw from the direct provision of the means of education; that closing or transferring Government institutions of the higher order would not result in any diminution of the means of higher education, but would provide fresh funds for its extension in backward Districts, so that education would soon be far more widely diffused than at present; and lastly, that if the policy of withdrawal be accepted, it can be readily guarded by provisions that will bar its application to any Missionary agency, and that this policy will, on the contrary, so devolope native effort as to make it in the long run vastly superior to all Missionary agencies combined.

Bearing of the policy of withdrawal on Missionary Education.

"The question how far the withdrawal of the State from the direct provision of means for higher education would throw such education into the hands of Missionary bodies, held the foremost place in all the evidence bearing on the topic of withdrawal. Prominent officers of the Department and many native gentlemen argued strongly against any withdrawal, on the ground that it must practically hand over higher education to Missionaries. As a rule the missionary witnesses themselves, while generally advocating the policy of withdrawal, expressed quite the contrary opinion, stating that they neither expected nor desired that any power over education given up by the Department should pass into their hands. In a country with such varied needs as India, we should deprecate any measure which would throw excessive influence over higher education into the hands of any single agency, and particularly into the hands of an agency which, however benevolent and earnest, cannot on all points be in sympathy with the mass of the community. But the fear which some departmental officers and some native gentlemen in all provinces have expressed so strongly, appears to most of us to attach too little weight to the following considerations. No doubt if all Government Colleges and high schools were to be suddenly closed, few, except missionary bodies, and in all probability extremely few of them, would be strongly enough to step at once into the gap. But any such revolutionary measure would be wholly opposed to the cautious policy prescribed in all the Despatches. There is no reason why a wise and cautious policy of withdrawal on behalf of local managers should favour missionary more than other forms of private effort. It might, on the contrary, have the effect of encouraging and stimulating native effort in its competition with missionary agency." *

Withdrawal in favour of Missionaries to be avoided.

"At the same time we think it well to put on record our unanimous opinion that withdrawal of direct departmental agency should not take place in favour of missionary bodies, and that departmental institutions of the higher order should not be transferred to missionary management. In expressing this view, we are merely re-echoing what is implied in the Resolution appointing the Commission; since it is 'to bodies of native gentlemen who will undertake to manage them satisfactorily as aided institutions,' that Government in that Resolution expresses its willingness 'to hand over any of its own colleges or schools in suitable cases.' It is not impossible that the restriction thus imposed upon the policy of transfer or withdrawal, may be represented as opposed to strict neutrality, which should altogether set aside the question whether a school or a body of managers inculcates any religious tenets or not. But it is so manifestly desirable to keep the whole of the future developments of private effort in education free from difficulties connected with religion, that the course which we advise seems to us to be agreeable to the spirit, if not to the letter, of the strictest doctrine of neutrality.

Position of Missionary enterprise in education.

"In the point of view in which we are at present considering the question, missionary institutions hold an intermediate position between those managed by the department and those managed by the people for themselves. On the one hand, they are the outcome of private effort, but on the other they are not strictly local; nor will encouragement to them directly foster those habits of self-reliance and combination for purposes of public utility which it is one of the objects of the grant-in-aid system to develope. Missionary institutions may serve

* Report of the Indian Education Commission (1882), pp. 451–453.

the great purpose of showing what private effort can accomplish, and thus of inducing other agencies to come forward. They should be allowed to follow their own independent course under the general supervision of the State; and so long as there are room and need for every variety of agency in the field of education, they should receive all the encouragement and aid that private effort can legitimately claim. But it must not be forgotten that the private effort which it is mainly intended to evoke is that of the people themselves. Natives of India must constitute the most important of all agencies if educational means are ever to be co-extensive with educational wants. Other agencies may hold a prominent place for a time, and may always find some place in a system in which great variety is on every ground desirable. But the higher education of the country will not be on a basis that can be regarded as permanent or safe, nor will it receive the wide extension that is needed, until the larger part of it at all events is provided and managed by the people of the country for themselves.

Limits of opposing views within the Commission.

"With such wide differences—differences amounting to a complete conflict of opinion—among witnesses, it could not be expected that entire agreement could be easily arrived at in a body so large and of such varied composition as the Commission. It is important, however, to indicate the limits within which the differences in our own views were all along confined. They are in effect the limits indicated in the Despatch of 1854. That Despatch, as we have already pointed out, looks forward to the time when 'many of the existing Government institutions, specially those of the higher order, may be safely closed or transferred to the management of local bodies under the control of, and aided by, the State.' This clearly implies that, though individual institutions might long require to be maintained directly by the State, the hope was entertained that a time would come when any general system of education entirely provided by Government should be no longer necessary—a result towards which some progress has been made in many Provinces. On the other hand, the same Despatch lays down as clearly that the progress of education is not to be checked by the withdrawal which it directs to be kept in view, and that not a single school is to be abandoned to probable decay. Subsequent Despatches, as we have shown in Section 1 of the present Chapter, have specially emphasised and in some respects extended this limitation of the policy of withdrawal. For instance, in paragraphs 45 and 46 of the Despatch of 1859, while it is remarked that the existing Government colleges are on the whole in a satisfactory state, and where defects exist are to be placed on a better footing, stress is laid on the substitution of private for Government agency in the management of secondary schools only—a substitution which it was hoped would eventually be universal. To all such limitations we felt bound to give great weight, not less because they have been laid down by the highest authority than because we regarded them ourselves as wise and right. The reasons in favour of action tending towards the withdrawal of the State from direct management appeared to us conclusive; while the need of the greatest caution if withdrawal is not to be altogether premature, and therefore widely injurious, appeared equally indisputable. Our difficulty lay in co-ordinating the two classes of opposing considerations so as to determine the proper path for present action. It may be well to point out what are the opposing considerations to which most importance should be attached in arriving at a decision on this matter." *

Considerations for and against the policy of withdrawal.

The Report of the Education Commission then proceeds to discuss the main considerations for and against the policy of the withdrawal of the State from higher education. The main heads of the considerations in favour of withdrawal are stated to be, (1) Saving to public funds; (2) Possibility of improvement in the results of private effort; (3) Need of variety in the type of education; and (4) Encouragement to religious instruction. The main considerations opposed to the withdrawal were enumerated to be, (1) The danger of a false impression being made on the public mind to the effect that Government no longer feels any interest in the spread of liberal education; (2) Difficulty of maintaining Colleges of the highest type by native effort; (3) Influence of Government Institutions in keeping up the standard of education; and (4) The state of popular feeling against the withdrawal of the State from higher education. Having discussed these various considerations, the general conclusions at which the Commission arrived are thus expressed :—

General conclusion as to the policy of withdrawal.

"Our discussions brought out clearly the fact that, while anxious to encourage any natural and unforced transfer of institutions from departmental to private management, we are not prepared as a body to adopt any form of expression that may be construed into a demand for the immediate or general withdrawal of the State from the provision of the means of high education. We are convinced that while transfer of management under the limitations stated is eminently desirable, it is only by slow and cautious steps that it can ever be really attained. We are convinced that the wisest policy is to consider each case on its own merits, and whenever a body of native

* Report of the Indian Education Commission (1882), pp. 453–455.

gentlemen are willing to undertake the management of a College or secondary school, to hold out to them every inducement and encouragement, provided there is a reasonable prospect that the cause of education will not suffer from the transfer of management. The Department should cordially welcome every offer of the kind, and should accept it if it can be accepted without real loss to the community; but while encouraging all such offers, its attitude should be not that of withdrawing from a charge found to be burdensome, and of transferring the burden to other shoulders, but of conferring a boon on those worthy of confidence and of inviting voluntary associations to co-operate with Government in the work and responsibilities of national education. We have certainly no desire to recommend any measures that will have the effect of checking the spread of continuous improvement of higher education. On the contrary, it is only in the confidence that the withdrawal of the Department from direct management may, in many instances, be found to serve the best interests of education, by connecting local bodies more closely with those institutions, and by inducing and enabling them, in course of time, to raise and expend more money from private sources for their maintenance and to establish other institutions of the same kind, that the following Recommendations are made. We therefore recommend, in the first place, *that in order to evoke and stimulate local co-operation in the transfer to private management of Government institutions for collegiate or secondary instruction, aid at specially liberal rates be offered for a term of years, whenever necessary, to any local body willing to undertake the management of any such institution under adequate guarantees of permanence and efficiency.*

Recommendation as to withdrawal explained.

"This Recommendation, which is of course subject to certain exceptions to be hereafter stated, secured our unanimous approval and may be understood to show the extent to which we are agreed in desiring to see steps taken towards the substitution of private for departmental management. It implies that we regard the form of management of any institution which the common good requires to be kept up, as a matter subordinate to the efficiency of such management. But it implies also that when permanence and efficiency are adequately secured, we regard an institution that is provided by the people for themselves as greatly preferable to one that is provided by official agency. We think it well that this preference should be marked by special encouragement being held out to those who are willing to take over the management of institutions now in the hands of the Department. In some cases perhaps, when once it is understood that the Department and the State are cordially favourable to the transfer being made, the ordinary rules for grants-in-aid may supply all the encouragement that is needed. In other cases the ordinary rate of aid may come to be sufficient in course of time, as local resources become greater. But it is more difficult to maintain in full efficiency an institution that has long had State resources to support it than one which has been gradually developed in the hands of managers, on whom their circumstances have always enforced economy. This difficulty should not be allowed to be a hindrance to the transfer. Even if the efficient maintenance of the institution should require the bestowal for a term of years of a grant as large as the present net outlay of the State and even if there be thus for a considerable period no actual saving to public funds, the transfer should still be made on other grounds.

Expected result of withdrawal.

"We hope that the result of thus encouraging rather than forcing the change desired by Government will be that in due time and without the smallest permanent injury to high education, departmental institutions will be mainly transferred to private management; that the function of the State will be largely confined to aid, supervision, and control; and that high education will become more widely extended, more varied in character, and more economical than it is at present. This end should be kept steadily in view, and the extent to which the Department is able to work towards it should be regarded as an important element in judging of its success. But the attempt to reach this end prematurely, that is, before at least the more thoughtful members of the native community are prepared cordially to approve it, would certainly do more to retard than to hasten its accomplishment." *

General principles as to transfer of State Colleges to private management.

As giving effect to these views, the Commission made certain recommendations as to the general principles which should regulate the transfer of colleges from the State to local private management. The recommendations are thus worded :—

"That in dealing with the question of the withdrawal of Government from the management of existing colleges, these colleges be regarded as divided into three classes, *viz* :—

(1) Those from which it is premature for Government to consider the propriety of withdrawal, on the ground that they are, and will long continue to be, the institutions on which the higher education of the country mainly depends.

(2) Those that might be transferred with advantage, as a measure promising useful political results to bodies of native gentlemen, provided the new managers give satisfactory guarantees that the college

* Report of the Indian Education Commission (1882), pp. 464–466.

will be maintained: (i) permanently, (ii) in full efficiency, (iii) in such a way as to make it adequate for all the wants of the locality.

(3) Those which have been shown to be unsuccessful or of which the cost is out of proportion to the utility, and from which Government might advantageously withdraw even with less stringent guarantees for permanent efficiency. Such colleges should be closed if, after due notice, no local body be formed to carry them on with such a grant-in-aid as the rules provide."*

While making these recommendations, the Education Commission took care to make the following important observations:—

Views of the Commission as to its recommendations regarding transfer of Colleges to private management.

"The maintenance of the chief Government colleges appeared to a large majority of us to be still indispensable. We do not think that a body of native managers is likely to arise for a considerable time, to whom such colleges can be entrusted without danger to their efficiency, and danger accordingly of lasting injury to the higher education of the whole Province. Private management, like all other agencies, must be trained by long and fairly successful discharge of lower duties, before it can be wisely entrusted with duties that are higher and more difficult. It is true that we have recommended that liberal aid be offered to any local body willing to undertake the management of any Government College, under adequate guarantees of permanence and efficiency; but in the case of the leading Government Colleges of the different Provinces, it is open to question whether any body of native gentlemen can furnish at present such guarantees as should be held sufficient. There is, however, another class of departmental colleges in some Provinces, which it is by no means improbable that local effort may adequately provide for, and which it is highly desirable to transfer to local management whenever this can be done without injury to education. In such cases our general Recommendation will at once apply, and any reasonable amount of aid should be offered that may be found necessary to induce native gentlemen to undertake the maintenance of such colleges as we are now considering. There is still a third class of colleges in the Provinces of Madras and Bengal. In some cases that come under this third class, the Department, when it established its college, seems to have lost sight of the principle that Government Institutions are not to be set up in places where aided local effort can supply all real educational wants. In other cases, circumstances have so changed since the college was established, that its continuance has ceased to have any other than a purely local importance. If private bodies are ready to undertake the management of any college included in this third class, aid should be offered at the rate that may be fixed for colleges generally in the grant-in-aid rules, after they have undergone the revision that has already been recommended. If such aid does not induce any local body to maintain any college belonging to this class, it may be held as sufficient proof that the college may be safely closed."†

With these principles in view, the Commission proceeded to make certain specific recommendations in regard to some colleges in Madras, Bombay, and Bengal, and concluded their observations on the general subject of withdrawal of the State from higher education in the following words:—

Expectations of the Commission as to transfer of Colleges to bodies of native gentlemen.

"We venture to hope that the line of action we have marked out in the above Recommendations will result, not all at once yet with no longer interval than is always required for changes fruitful of large results, in public sentiment, taking a direction which will lead to the gradual, and by and by to the rapid, transfer to bodies of native gentlemen of the institutions now maintained by Government. On condition that the transfer be thus effected with the approval and active co-operation of those who have the welfare of their country most at heart, we are convinced that the withdrawal, in large measure, of departmental management, though not of departmental supervision, will result in a wide extension of collegiate and secondary education, in placing it on a firm and satisfactory basis, and in making it more varied in character, and therefore more adapted to all the wants of the community."‡

These recommendations of the Commission were considered by the Government of India in a Resolution, No. $\frac{10}{309}$, dated 23rd October, 1884, in which the proposals of the Commission, so far as they concern advanced education, were summarized (in paragraph 30) in the following words:—

Recommendations of the Commission as to high education summarized.

"That for all kinds of such education private effort should in future be increasingly and mainly relied on, and that every form of private effort should be systematically encouraged in such ways as these:—

(*a*) By clearly showing that, whilst existing State institutions of the higher order should be maintained in complete efficiency, wherever they are necessary, the improvement and extension of institutions under private managers will be the principal care of the Department.

* Report of the Indian Education Commission (1882), p. 468 also p. 478.

† *Ib.*, pp. 468, 469.

‡ *Ib.*, p. 470.

(b) By leaving private managers free to develop their institutions in any way consistent with efficiency, and the protection of neighbouring institutions from unfair competition.

(c) By insisting on all institutions, maintained from public funds and under official management, refraining from undue competition with corresponding aided schools, by such means as charging lower fees.

(d) By liberal rates of aid, so long as aid is needed.

(e) By co-operation in the gradual raising of fees, so that less and less aid may be required ; and

(f) By favouring the transfer to bodies of native gentlemen of all advanced institutions maintained from public funds, which can be so transferred without injury to education generally."

Such being the summary of the recommendations of the Commission, the Government of India, in the abovementioned Resolution, recorded the following passage, which is important as indicating the final decision of Government in regard to the policy of the withdrawal of the State from advanced education :—

Decision of Government as to policy of withdrawal from high education.

" The Government of India accepts the cautious and well-considered proposals of the Commission on the subject of the gradual withdrawal of Government from the charge of institutions of a high order, and especially from colleges. These recommendations are quite in accordance with the policy of Government, as explained in paragraph 10 of the Resolution appointing the Commission. * * * * * * It is left to the Local Governments to give effect to the recommendations on this subject, gradually, and as local circumstances permit. It is, as has been repeatedly declared, in no degree the wish of the Government of India to discourage high education in any way whatever. On the contrary it believes it to be one of its most important duties to spread and foster it. What it specially, however, desires, is to secure assistance to the limited funds of the State by calling forth every available private agency in connection with every branch of public instruction. It is in connection with high education, and in view of the direct pecuniary advantages which it holds out to those who follow it, that the Government thinks it can most properly insist on the fullest development of the principle of self-help."

CHAPTER XXII.

MORAL TRAINING AND RELIGIOUS TEACHING IN COLLEGES.—VIEWS OF THE INDIAN EDUCATION COMMISSION.—MR. KASHINATH TRIMBUK TELANG'S DISSENTIENT MINUTE.—VIEWS OF THE LOCAL GOVERNMENTS AND THE DECISION OF THE GOVERNMENT OF INDIA UPON THE SUBJECT.

Views of the Commission as to moral and religious instruction.

Besides dealing with statistics and numerous details connected with Collegiate Education, the Education Commission also considered some important matters of principle relating to the nature of the education itself. Among these subjects their views as to moral training and religious teaching in colleges deserve special attention, as relating to points of permanent interest to the well-wishers of High English Education in India. The views of the Commission may be quoted in their own words :—

Moral training in Colleges.

" The subject of moral training in colleges is replete with difficulties—difficulties, however, that are mainly practical. For there is no difference of opinion as to moral training being as necessary as intellectual or physical training, and no dissent from the principle that a system in which moral training was wholly neglected would be unworthy of the name of education. Nor, again, is there any difference of opinion as to the moral value of the love of law and order, of the respect for superiors, of the obedience, regularity, and attention to duty which every well-conducted college is calculated to promote. All these have, by the nearly universal consent of the witnesses, done a great deal to elevate the moral tone and improve the daily practice of the great bulk of those who have been trained in the colleges of India. The degree in which different colleges have exerted a moral influence of this kind is probably as various as the degree of success that has attended the intellectual training given in them, and has doubtless been different in all colleges at different times, depending as it does so largely on the character and personal influence of the Principal and Professors, who may form the staff at any given period. So far, all the witnesses, and probably all intelligent men, are substantially agreed. Difficulties being when the question is raised whether good can be done by distinct moral teaching, over and above the moral supervision which all admit to be good and useful, and which all desire to see made more thorough than it is at present. In colleges supported by Missionary Societies, in the Anglo-Muhammadan College, Aligarh, and in at least one other college under native management, the attempt has been made to give such moral teaching on the basis of religion. In Government Colleges there has been no attempt at direct moral teaching. In them entire reliance has, as a rule, been placed on such moral supervision as can be exerted during college hours, and on such opportunities for indirect moral lessons as are afforded by the study of the ordinary test-books and by the occurrences of ordinary academic life. Religious education, and the possibility of connecting it with Government Colleges, we shall consider separately. The present point is the possibility or wisdom of introducing distinct moral teaching in places where there is no religious instruction. The question that was put to bring out the views of our witnesses on the point stood thus :—'Does definite instruction in duty and the principles of moral conduct occupy any place in the Course of Government Colleges and Schools ?—Have you any suggestions to make on this subject ?—None of the witnesses raised any objection in principle to such instruction being given. A considerable number held that there is no need for such instruction, and two of these, the Principals of Government Colleges in Bombay and Madras, held that no good result can flow from devoting a distinct portion of time to the teaching of duty and the principles of moral conduct. Some also held that the practical difficulties in the way of introducing moral instruction into Government Colleges, are so great, that it is expedient to leave matters as they are. The great majority, however, of the witnesses that dealt with the question at all, expressed a strong desire that definite moral instruction should form part of the College Course. If we may judge by the utterances of the witnesses, there is in the North-Western Provinces and the Punjab a deep-seated and widespread feeling that discipline and moral supervision require to be supplemented by definite instruction in the principles of morality. The feeling seems not to be so strong in the provinces where Western education has been longer and more firmly established, but some of the witnesses in every Province, and some of every class, Native and European equally, have asserted that there is urgent need that the principles of morality should be definitely expounded. A review of the evidence seems to show that moral instruction may be introduced into the Course of Government Colleges, without objection anywhere, and in some Provinces with strong popular approval. Those who wish definite moral instruction to be introduced, generally advocate the teaching of some moral text-book. No one however, has pointed to any text-book that he is prepared to recommend for immediate introduction. One witness has indicated a difficulty that requires consideration, *viz.*, that if morality be introduced as a definite subject of study, a demand will certainly arise for testing proficiency in it by means of examinations, and that while, on the one hand, acquaintance with theories of morality implies no moral improvement, on the other, examinations can never test actual growth in practical morality. The difficulty thus suggested is that students will not pay serious attention to the moral instruction given them unless it is made to tell in their favour at University or other public examinations. It is certainly undesirable to attempt to gauge morality by means of the University, but it seems too unfavourable an estimate of Indian students to hold that they care for nothing beyond passing or standing well at examinations ; or even if such a state of feeling be too prevalent at present, it seems premature to argue that no better state of feeling can be induced.

Religious Teaching in colleges.

"Government having deliberately adopted the policy of religious neutrality, there is no religious teaching in the colleges managed by the Department of Education. The Grant-in-aid System is based upon the same policy, and it might, therefore, seem that the subject of religious teaching in aided colleges has no place in the Report of this Commission. Nor would it if the question had not been raised by some of the witnesses, whether another policy than the present be not equally consistent with the religious neutrality of Government Colleges, the policy, namely, not of excluding all religions, but of giving equal facility for instruction in them all. This has been advocated by several native witnesses, especially in the Punjab. The argument adduced in favour of such a policy seems generally to be, that the minds of students are so filled with their secular studies, that religion drops out of view and ceases to influence them, and that home influence has been found in practice too weak to counteract the anti-religious or rather non-religious, influence which exclusive attention to the subjects studied at college is exerting: This is expressed, as follows, by one who pleads strongly for a change in this respect. 'Children are sent to school as soon as they are able to talk and move about freely, and they spend a number of years in school, until, in fact, they are passed out as full-blown B. A.'s, or some such thing..................Their whole time and attention being devoted to school-books, they fall very little under what is called the home influence..................The unfavourable impressions which the children receive in the school, for a series of years, at the early part of their age, sit deep in their hearts and exert a very demoralising influence upon them in after-life, to the prejudice of themselves and of those who come in their way. Will Government tolerate such a state of things ? Will it still persist in a policy which excludes religion from the State education, but encourages something which is anti-religious, though in the most indirect manner ?'

The remedy proposed is that Government should employ teachers of all prevalent forms of religion to give instruction in its colleges, or should, at least, give such teachers admission to its colleges if their services are provided by outside bodies. We are unable to recommend the adoption of any plan of this kind. However praiseworthy the feelings that underlie such a proposal, we are satisfied that no such scheme can be reduced to practice in the present state of Indian Society. The system of grants-in-aid was in part designed to meet the difficulty complained of, and those who regret the absence of religious teaching from Government Colleges are at liberty to set up colleges, giving full recognition to the religious principles they prefer. In doing this, they should be most liberally helped, and it may be worth while to point out that the successful establishment of a college in which any form of religion is inculcated, would not lose its effect even though the Government College in which religion is not taught should continue to be maintained beside it. Students cannot be kept apart, and cannot but affect one another. Any influence, whether good or bad, that is felt among the students in one college spreads rapidly to those of another that is near it. Thus, those who regard any particular form of religious teaching as a good thing, may be sure that by establishing a college in which such teaching is imparted, they are influencing not only the students their own college may attract, but the students in Government Colleges as well."*

In another part of their Report the Education Commission have made the following observations in regard to the possibilities of giving encouragement to religious instruction :—

Religious Instruction in Aided Institutions.

"Again, there is the important question of securing a religious element in Higher Education, or at all events of there being no practical hindrance to the presence of such an element when the people of the country wish for it. The evidence we have taken shows that in some Provinces there is a deeply-seated and widely-spread desire that culture and religion should not be divorced, and that this desire is shared by some representatives of native thought in every Province. In Government Institutions this desire cannot be gratified. The declared neutrality of the State forbids its connecting the institutions directly maintained by it with any one form of faith; and the other alternative of giving equal facilities in such institutions for the inculcation of all forms of faith involves practical difficulties which we believe to be insuperable. In Chapter VI. we have shown that we are not insensible to the high value of the moral discipline and example which Government Institutions are able to afford; but we have also shown that we regard something beyond this as desirable for the formation of character and the awakening of thought. To encourage the establishment of institutions of widely different types, in which may be inculcated such forms of faith as various sections of the community may accept, whether side by side with, or in succession to, Government Institutions, is one mode in which this difficulty can be practically solved, though it is a mode not free from objections and even dangers of its own. It is clear that whatever other efforts in this direction may be made, such encouragement would be afforded in a high degree by the withdrawal of Government Institutions. when the people professed their desire and manifested their ability to establish an institution in which special religious instruction could be given. It is true that a Government or other secular institution meets, however incompletely, the educational wants of all religious sects in any locality, and thus renders it easier for them to combine for educational purposes; while a denominational college runs some risk of confining its benefits to a particular section of the community, and thus, of deepening the lines of difference already existing. Still this is a solution of the difficulty suggested by the Despatch of 1854, which expresses the hope that 'Institutions conducted by all denominations of Christians, Hindus, Mahomedans, Parsis, Sikhs, Buddhists, Jains, or any other religious persuasions, may be affiliated to the Universities, if they are found to afford the requisite course of study, and can be depended upon for the certificates of conduct which will be required.' Apart from the strictly moral or religious aspect of this question, we may point out that the existence of institutions of the various classes thus referred to, will contribute to the intellectual development of the Indian Community, by arousing enquiry on the highest themes of human thought, and thus helping to meet what is probably the greatest danger of all higher education in India at present—the too exclusive attention to the mere passing of examinations and to the personal advantages to be derived therefrom."†

Holding such views as to religious instruction, the Commission, in paragraph 338 made, *inter alia*, the following recommendations upon the subject of moral teaching:—

Recommendation as to a Text-Book for moral instruction.

"(8). *That an attempt be made to prepare a moral text-book, based upon the fundamental principles of natural religion, such as may be taught in all Government and non-Government Colleges.*

"(9). *That the Principal or one of the Professors, in each Government and Aided College, deliver to each of the College Classes, in every Session, a series of lectures on the duties of a man and a citizen.*"‡

* Report of the Indian Education Commission (1882); pp. 294–296. † Ib., pp. 459, 460. ‡ Ib., p. 312.

Mr. Telang's dissentient Minute against the preparation of a Moral Text-Book and lectures.

These recommendations evoked a strong and able dissent from one of the most distinguished native members of the Commission, the late Mr. Kashinath Trimbuk Telang, C.I.E., whose untimely death has recently deprived the Bombay High Court of one of the ablest Native Judges. His views represent the opinions of the more advanced type of Indian educationists, and in view of the importance of the subject to which they relate and the ability with which they are expounded they may be quoted *in extenso*:—

"I next proceed to consider two Recommendations which deal with a point, certainly one of the most important in connection with education. I allude to the Recommendation regarding moral education in colleges. In stating the opinions which I have formed on this point, I know I run a certain risk of misinterpretation. But I am bound to say that, after the best consideration which I have been able to give to the Recommendations made by the Commission, and the arguments adduced in support of them, I am still strongly of opinion that the proposed measures will be impotent for good and may result in mischief. I will first take up the latter of the two Recommendations referred to. That prescribes that a series of lectures on the duties of a man and a citizen should be delivered in each college in each Session. Now, first, what is the object of this new departure—for it is a new departure—in our system of academical instruction? Many of those who recommend this new departure, admit that there is nothing in the character of the students of our State Colleges, taken as a class, which can be used in support of this recommendation. Others, however, of the same mode of thinking, have distinctly said that the effects of education in our State Colleges on the morals * of the students has certainly been mischievous, not to say disastrous. One gentleman, who has been particularly active in what I cannot help charactersing as the misguided and mischievous agitation which preceded the appointment of the Commission, has held up to the gaze of the British public a picture of the effects of State education in India (*See* Mr. Johnstone's 'Our Educational Policy in India,' pages XV, 8, 10, 26), which, if it is a faithful one, would certainly justify some new departure in the direction indicated. But is it a faithful picture? On that we have a statement submitted to the Commission by five gentlemen of the same party as the author of the pamphlet above alluded to. These gentlemen undertake to say that 'the result of Government so-called neutrality, has been, *by common consent*, decidedly injurious from a moral and religious point of view.' What these gentlemen mean by '*common consent*' it is not very easy to understand. The evidence before the Commission (which is summarised in the Report, Chapter VI), is absolutely overwhelming in favour of the reverse of that which these gentlemen describe as admitted by 'common consent.' And I owe it to the system under which I, myself, and many of my friends have been nurtured, to put it solemnly on record that, in my judgment, the charges made against that system are wholly and absolutely unsustainable; and are the results of imperfect or prejudiced observation, and hasty generalisation put into words by random, and often reckless, rhetoric. I do not deny that there may be individuals among men of the class to which I have the honour to belong, who have strayed away, more or less widely, from the path of honour and virtue. But if that fact affords sufficient ground for a condemnation of our system, what system, I would ask, is there under the sun which will not have to be similarly condemned? A considerable portion of the sensational talk that is going about on this subject is, I feel persuaded, due to a misapplication of that unhappy phrase—'Educated Native.' That misapplication is referred to upon another point in the Report (*see* Chapter VIII), but it is necessary to enter a caveat with regard to it in this connection also. On the one hand, it is confined, and of course quite erroneously, to those who have acquired some knowledge of the English language; and on the other, it is extended, equally erroneously, to those who, like Macaulay's Frenchman, have just learnt enough English to read Addison with a dictionary. The latter error is the one which must be specially guarded against in discussions like the present.

Lectures on the duties of a man inefficacious for Moral Training.

"But it may be said that the new departure, if not justified by the injurious effects of the system hitherto in vogue, may still be justified in the ground that it is calculated to strengthen the beneficial effects of that system. And here I am prepared to join issue with those who maintian that it will have any such operation. I cordially accept the dictum of Mr. Matthew Arnold, that 'conduct is three-fourths of life, and a man who works for conduct works for more than a man who works for intelligence.' And, therefore, I should be quite willing to join, as indeed I have joined, in any Recommendation encouraging such 'work for conduct' (see the Bombay Provincial Report, page 148). But I cannot perceive that 'Lectures on the duties of a Man and a Citizen' at a College, constitute such 'work' at all. In a primary school, lessons on the duties of a man would probably be useful; in a secondary school they would probably be innocuous; but in a collegiate institution they would probably be neither useful nor innocuous. At the earliest stage of a student's life, ignorance of what is right is probably an important force, and then to correct that ignorance, moral lessons are a perfectly appropriate agency; although, even here, I

* Bishop Meurin's statement (page 3) pronounces an unfavourable judgment on our system. His language is curiously like that used against the University of Paris in days gone by. *Cf. Schools and Universities on the Continent.* By Mr. M. Arnold; p. 23.

should be inclined to rely more upon 'lessons' like Miss Edgeworth's,* for instance, than on those like the extracts from 'The whole Duty of Man,' by D. A. Eisdale, which were published in Bombay at the American Mission Press, in 1841. When the student has advanced to a secondary school, much of the ignorance above referred to has presumably given place to knowledge. But still, the habit of analysis and criticism is in a very rudimentary condition, and such lessons will, in all probability, do little harm. But if collegiate education is to subserve one of its most important purposes, and is to cultivate the intelligence so as to enable it to weigh arguments and form independent judgments, then these moral lessons present an entirely different aspect. At that stage, it is almost entirely unnecessary to instruct the intelligence, while it is of great use to discipline the will and to cultivate the feelings. The proposed lectures will, I fear, have little or no effect in this latter direction; while, in some individual cases, their effect in the former direction, being meant to operate not on the intellect but on conduct, may be the reverse of that which is desired, something like that on the Cambridge scholar, about whom I read many years ago, whose first doubts about the divine character of Christianity were said to have been roused by a study of 'Paley's Evidences.' That sense of moral responsibility in man which impressed Kant with the same awe as the starry heavens, can receive no strengthening from lectures on the duties of a man, any more than the awe which the starry heavens inspire can be produced by lectures on the rings of Saturn or the phases of the moon. Such strengthening must come from the emotions and the will being worked upon by the histories of great movements, the lives of great men, and the songs of great poets. It must come from the training of the will and the emotions by the actual details of academic life, by the elevating contact † with good professors and fellow-students, by the constant engagement of the attention on the ennobling pursuits of literature, science, and philosophy; by the necessity, so often felt, 'to scorn delights and live laborious days;' and, even in our very modern State Colleges of this country, though on a very humble scale, by 'that mass of continuous traditions, always powerful and generally noble,' of which Mr. Gladstone ‡ spoke so eloquently in his inaugural address to the University of Edinburgh.

"That is the only course of moral education in which I have any faith. That is the course which alone, in my opinion, can be efficacious. Lectures on the duties of a man can at the best, only lead to the 'cold decrees of the brain.' They have little or no efficacy in cooling down the 'hot temper, which leaps over' those decrees. These views might be easily supported by a mass of authority, but I will only refer here to that of one who is at once a writer on Moral Philosophy, a University Professor of the same subject, and a Chairman of a School Board in Scotland. I allude to Professor Calderwood, who has said in his recent work on Teaching: its Ends and Means that 'moral training is gained, not so much by formal inculcation of duty, as by practice in well-doing throughout the common engagements of life' (page 73; and *see* also pages 25, 83, 123, &c.).

Lectures on the duties of a citizen inadvisable.

"So far I have dealt only with the first part of the Recommendation. The second part, dealing with the duties of a citizen, appears to me to stand on a somewhat different footing. It seems to be intended to point rather to what may be called political, as distinguished from social, morality. Lectures on this subject may be of use, as the subject is one on which there is some real ignorance, which may be dispelled by lectures addressed to the intellect. But I must own that I am afraid of the practical operation of this part of the Recommendation. In ordinary times, it may not be very material one way or the other, though even in ordinary times, one can conceive the inconvenient results which may flow from it. But in times of excitement, such as those through which we have scarcely yet emerged, I much fear that the result will be to drag the serene dignity of the academy into the heat and dust of platform warfare. If the Professor's lectures tend to teach the pupils the duty of submission to the views of Government, without a murmur of dissatisfaction, there is sure to come up a set of Liberal Irreconcileables, who will complain that Government is endeavouring to enslave the intellect of the nation. If the Professor's lectures are supposed to lead in the opposite direction, there will be some Tory Irreconcileables ready to spring up and say, even more loudly and quite as erroneously as they are saying it now, that the colleges supported from State revenues are hot-beds of sedition.§ This is almost certain to occur in times of excitement. It may not unlikely occur in quiet times also. And with this risk, I confess, it seems to me that the advantages of such lectures will have been dearly purchased. If it is argued that the Professors in our colleges are not now prevented from doing that which may afford a target for similar denunciation, my reply is that the Professors may well

* Notwithstanding Dr. Whately's protest, in a note in his edition of Bacon's Essays.

† *Cf.* Matthew Arnold in *Nineteenth Century* (November; 1882), p. 714.

‡ See *Gleanings of Past Years*, Vol. VII, p. 18.

§ *Cf. Gladstone's Gleanings*, Vol. VII, p. 13; and the evidence of Sir William Wedderburn and Mr. Wordsworth, and the Honourable Amir Ali. Mr. Johnstone, in the pamphlet above referred to, attacks us on this ground also, but his frame of mind may be judged of by his unhappy reference to the necessity of the Vernacular Press Act—a point on which one need not now waste a single syllable.

do what they deem proper in their private capacity as citizens. But it becomes a very different thing when they deliver lectures at college, in their capacity as Professors appointed by the State for the express purpose. The position on that point is exactly analogous to the position on the point of religious instruction, under the Despatch of 1859, Sections 59–61.

A Moral Text-book will be useless.

"I now come to the other Recommendation. The whole theory of moral education here adopted is one which I consider erroneous in principle, and likely to be bad in practical operation, as tending to withdraw attention from the necessity of making, not one or two hours of academic life, but the whole of it, a period of moral education. Holding that view, it follows, of course, that I cannot accept the suggestion about the Moral Text-book. But further objections to that suggestion are stated in the Bombay Provincial Report, to which I still adhere. I will only add that the view there enunciated receives support from the history of a similar experiment tried many years ago in Ireland. No less a person than Archbishop Whately endeavoured to do for the elements of Christianity what Bishop Meurin proposes, and the Commission recommends, should be done for the elements of morality based on Natural Religion. With what result? The text-book was written, approved, sanctioned for use, and used, in the Irish schools, both Protestant and Roman Catholic. Then the tide turned, and the book had to be abandoned, and Archbishop Whately himself, the Lord Justice Christian, and Mr. Baron Greene resigned their seats on the School Board, upon the ground that what was done was a breach of faith with the people.* It is not necessary to enquire which, if either, of the parties to the contest was in the wrong. The lesson to be derived from the occurrence is equally clear and equally entitled to 'give us pause' in the course on which we are recommended to enter, whether the fault in that particular matter lay with the Protestants or the Roman Catholics; with Archbishop Whately or with Archbishop Murray, or his successor.

Religious instruction impracticable.

"I will only add one word here, with respect to the question of religious instruction which was raised before the Commission. I deeply sympathise with the demand of some witnesses, whose evidence has come before us, that provision should be made in our educational system for that religious instruction, without which, as Lord Ripon declared before the University of Calcutta, all education is imperfect. I sympathise with this demand, but do not see my way to suggest any feasible means of satisfying it. There are only two possible modes, which can be adopted in justice and fairness, of practically imparting religious instruction. Either you must teach the principles common to all religions, under the name of Natural Religion, or you must teach the principles of each religious creed to the students whose parents adopt that creed. The difficulties of these alternatives have been indicated by no less an authority than Mr. Cobden (*see* his speeches, page 588, *et seq.*) Those difficulties are certainly not less great in this country than in England. They appear to me to be so great that we must be content to 'take refuge,' as it has been expressed, 'in the remote haven of refuge for the educationists—the secular system.' But I would also point out to all those who ask for this religious education, that the cultivation of those feelings of human nature to which religion appeals is not even now entirely neglected, and that the further direction to be given to those feelings, according to the principles of each religious creed, ought to be undertaken, as it is best carried out, not by a Government like the British Indian Government,† but by the Professors of the several creeds. 'Under the legislation of 1806,' says Mr. Matthew Arnold ‡ 'it was not permitted to public schools to be denominational. The law required that the instruction in them should be such as to train its recipients for the exercise of all social and Christian virtues, but no dogmatic religious instruction was to be given by the teacher, or was to be given in the school. Measures were to be taken, however, said the law, that the scholar should not go without the dogmatic teaching of the communion to which he belonged. Accordingly, the Minister of the Home Department exhorted by circular the Ministers of the different communions to co-operate with the Government in carrying the new law into execution, by taking upon themselves the religious instruction of the school children belonging to their persuasion. The religious authorities replied favourably to this appeal, and nowhere, perhaps, has the instruction of the people been more eminently religious than in Holland, while the public schools have, by law, remained unsectarian.'§ That seems to me to indicate, though only in a general way, the true procedure to be followed in this matter by those who are dissatisfied with the religious results of our educational system. Some agencies of this sort, more or less organised, more or less powerful, are at present working. Whether a more complete organisation will bring out results more satisfactory to those who are now asking for a

* *Life of Dr. Whately.* By Miss Whately, Vol. II, p. 264.

† *Cf. Gladstone's Gleanings*, Vol. VII, p. 109.

‡ Report of the Education Commission (1861), Vol. IV, page 189; and *see* page 151. Still the schools were called 'Godless' (*see* page 144) in Holland.

§ *Cf.* the quotation from Sir R. Peel, in the evidence of Mr. Wordsworth.

change, is a matter upon which I own I am somewhat sceptical. And some of the grounds of my scepticism have been already indicated in what I have said above, on the kindred question of moral education. But at all events, on this I am quite clear, that our institutions for secular instruction should not be embarrassed by any meddling with religious instruction; for such meddling, among other mischiefs, will yield results which, on the religious side will satisfy nobody, and on the secular side will be distinctly retrograde.*"†

Views of the Local Governments as to introduction of a Moral Text-book.

The proposals of the Indian Education Commission, in regard to the introduction of a Moral Text-book in Colleges, met with very scanty support from the Local Governments. In Madras, "no belief is reposed in the virtues of a suitable Moral Text-book, based upon the fundamental principles of Natural Religion, even were its preparation possible. Nor is any credit given to the efficacy of lectures on the duties of a man and a citizen. The proposal, would necessitate a scrutiny of the Professor's social and political views, to which this Government is in the strongest manner opposed." His Excellency the Governor of Bombay was not prepared to say that the proposal was impracticable, but thought it no easy matter to arrange a text-book which would be generally acceptable, or which could be pressed on both Government and non-Government Colleges. The Lieutenant-Governor of the North-Western Provinces was unable to support the project. He thought it no part of the functions of a Government in India to draw up a code of morality, and issue it officially for the instruction of students, since these could hardly be charged with ignorance of the commonly accepted code of civilised communities, or with an acceptance of principles contrary to that code. Nor could Sir Alfred Lyall approve of a course of lectures on the duty of a man and a citizen. Possibly, no two Professors would agree as to what this duty consisted in; and it was clearly undesirable to introduce into schools and colleges discussions on subjects that opened out such a very wide field of debate. The Chief Commissioner of the Central Provinces did not like the proposals. Without a religious basis, a moral text-book could be little better than a collection of copy-book maxims. The course of a student's reading and the influence of his Professors were far more potent factors in his moral education, and had produced results in the matters of honesty, truthfulness, and general good-conduct, such as no text-book of morality could achieve.‡

Decision of the Government of India as to the proposed Moral Text-book.

Upon this subject the Government of India, in its Resolution No. $\frac{10}{309}$, dated the 23rd October 1884, reviewing the Report of the Education Commission, made the following observations:—

"It is doubtful whether such a moral text-book as is proposed could be introduced without raising a variety of burning questions; and, strongly as it may be urged that a purely secular education is imperfect, it does not appear probable that a text-book of morality, sufficiently vague and colourless, to be accepted by Christians, Mahomedans and Hindus, would do much, especially in the stage of collegiate instruction, to remedy the defects or supply the shortcomings of such an education. The same objection appears to apply to the proposal that a series of lectures should be delivered in each College on the duties of a man; and as to the proposed lectures on the duties of a citizen, Mr. Tellang's objections at page 612, of the Report, appear to be unanswerable. The Secretary of State intimates his concurrence in the views of the Government of India on this matter, but adds that, possibly, hereafter some book in the nature of a Text-book of Moral Rules may be written of such merit as to render its use desirable. In that event the question can be reconsidered."

Orders of the Secretary of State (Lord Cross) as to preparation of a Moral Text-book. Summary of the views on the subject.

The matter, however, did not rest there, as Lord Cross, who succeeded Lord Kimberley as Secretary of State for India, took a somewhat different view, and "in a Despatch dated the 29th September, 1887, requested the Government of India to take steps for the preparation of a book suitable for use in schools in India. Before passing final orders on the subject, the Government of India requested the Local Governments and Administrations to state their views as to the best way of giving effect to the wishes of the Secretary of State, whether by the adoption of new text-books, or the revision of the existing books, in order to introduce into them extracts from the various great writers who have dealt with the question of personal conduct in its various aspects. The replies received show that the majority of the educational authorities in India are of opinion that a text-book containing moral precepts or rules of personal conduct would be either useless or injurious, at least in schools, though there is an equally strong consensus of opinion that good may be done by the indirect teaching of morality by means of illustrative stories in the readers used in schools. A few, however, think that even this is unnecessary, and that a good teacher will find means of giving moral instruction to his pupils without requiring any specially designed text-book or reader, while such helps will

* See *Morley's Struggle for National Education, passim.*

† Report of the Indian Education Commission (1882); pp. 610–614.

‡ Sir Alfred Croft's *Review of Education in India in 1886*; p. 331, 332.

be of no use in the hands of a bad teacher. The arguments against the introduction of a special text-book are so various that it is impossible to attempt a detailed analysis of them, but two or three extracts may be given. 'The only lessons in morality which are likely to have a practical effect on a boy's conduct in after-life are,' in the judgment of the Lieutenant-Governor of the North-Western Provinces, 'those which are taught him at home during his childhood, and which are received by him from observation of his daily surroundings, and the tone of the society in which he grows up. His Honour sees no sufficient ground for believing that their salutary influence will be strengthened by instruction in the principles of Natural Religion or natural morality, as laid bare in the fleshless skeletons of moral text-books, proficiency in which may enable boys to trace the articulations, but never to construct for themselves a living semblance of a higher moral existence. The difficulties of composing suitable moral text-books for the use of children of Eastern origin would be far greater than in the case of the children of English race, whose minds, dispositions, and sympathies are cast in a kindred mould to that of their teachers, and whose daily life is passed among scenes and societies where the value attached to the observance of morality, in its several forms, is brought home to them more impressively than in India. It is probable that the greater part of the Mahomedan community would still agree with the *dictum* attributed to the Caliph Omar, and would hold that moral text-books are 'either in conformity with the Word of God, or they are not. If they are, that Word is sufficient without them; if they are not, they ought to be destroyed.' Sir Alfred Croft says: 'Moral science is now taught in our Universities as a branch of psychology, or mental science, in general, and being taught and studied as a merely intellectual exercise, it does no harm. But bring down such discussions, in however elementary a form, to the school-room (and I hold that, if any didactic compendium of moral precepts be enjoined, such discussions cannot be altogether avoidable), and the moral atmosphere which the boys breathe is vitally changed. There is no longer that healthy, instinctive, spontaneous doing of the right, which marks the frank and honest school-boy: spontaneity is replaced by a baneful self-conciousness, and to use a homely phrase, the boy becomes a prig, or worse. At least, I believe, there is danger of this. It is not to direct moral instruction, but much more to the influence of teachers and the discipline of school-life, that I am inclined to look for aid in strengthening and developing the better impulses of school-boys.' The Lord Bishop of Bombay says: 'About the usefulness of lessons, and lesson-books on personal conduct, I am very sceptical. Their value, if they have any, will depend entirely on the tone of the teacher. In the hands of a man of the right stamp they may be of some use, as formulating for the memory what is enforced by discipline and example. But, as a rule, I should say that they would be useless in the hands of a bad master and superfluous in those of a good one.' In some cases the objection to lessons on morals is based upon the difficulty of expressing such lessons in language sufficiently simple to be understood by boys in Indian schools. Even in books specially compiled for use in Indian schools, teachers find these lessons too difficult for the scholars. Thus the Assam Director says: 'In High and Middle English schools, the moral class-books, Chambers' Educational Course and Lethbridge's Moral Reader are in general use; both these books contain good and useful lessons on moral subjects, especially the latter, where the lessons are supplemented by stories culled from eminent writers, illustrating the moral lessons. During my winter inspection, I made it a point at each inspection to call attention to this subject, but, strange to say, I almost invariably found that the moral lessons had been omitted, and the stories read . . . . . On enquiring why the moral lessons had been left out, the invariable answer was that the language was more difficult than in the stories, and passages were harder to explain.' A Madras writer goes further, and states that some of the extracts from eminent writers, given in the Middle School course are too difficult even for the teachers to understand.

Resolution of the Government of India on the subject, dated 17th August, 1889.

"The views of the majority were accepted by the Government of India, and the final orders on the subject are contained in the following extract from the Resolution :—'Having given this important question its fullest consideration, the Government of India, is satisfied that the end in view would not be attained by prescribing for use in colleges and schools a treatise on ethics, or a book of didactic instruction in the rules and principles of conduct. It believes that the careful selection and training of teachers provide the most effectual method of establishing a good moral tone in a school; but it also considers that the influence of the teacher may be greatly strengthened, and the interests of morality promoted, by the use in schools of text-books having a direct bearing on conduct either by means of precept or example.' After referring to the adoption of a book of this kind as a text-book for the Entrance Examination of the Calcutta University, the Resolution goes on to say: 'All that remains now to be done, in Bengal at all events, is to supplement this action of the University by providing for the lower grades of schools, and for each class in those grades, suitable text-books compiled on similar lines. Similar action in other Provinces is equally called for, and accordingly the Governor-General in Council desires that each Local Government and Administration should take this matter at once in hand, and either by the appointment of a

Committee, or by employing selected individuals, who need not necessarily be officials; or by the offer of suitable prizes, effect a revision of the existing readers, in the direction indicated above; or, where necessary, procure for use in schools an entirely new set of books compiled on these principles. His Excellency in Council will be glad to learn from time to time the progress made in each Province in this undertaking.'

" Regarding the action taken by the various Local Governments, complete information is not available."*

CHAPTER XXIII.

SIR ALFRED CROFT'S REVIEW OF EDUCATION IN INDIA IN 1886, AND ITS STATISTICS.

Resolution of the Government of India reviewing the Education Commission's Report.

In the Resolution No. $\frac{10}{309}$, dated 23rd October, 1884, recorded in the Home Department, the Governor-General in Council reviewed the Report of the Education Commission, and laid down for the future guidance of Local Governments and Administrations the broad lines of the Educational Policy which the Government of India desired to pursue. That Resolution met with the general concurrence of Her Majesty's Secretary of State, who, in expressing his approval, communicated the following instructions to the Government of India. "In order to stimulate the efforts of the various authorities in the promotion of education on the lines now laid down, it would, I think, be well if Your Excellency in Council would direct the preparation of a General Annual Report, embracing the important features of the several Provincial Reports (including Madras and Bombay), and transmit copies of the same to the Secretary of State, with a Resolution by the Government of India reviewing such General Report."†

Sir Alfred Croft's review of Education in 1886.

In pursuance of these directions, the task of preparing the first General Report was entrusted by the Government of India to Sir Alfred Croft, K.C.I.E., Director of Public Instruction in Bengal, and his Report, in the form of " A Review of Education in India in 1886," contains much valuable information and statistics, which, in a manner, supplement the information collected by the Indian Education Commission of 1882, and some important passages and statistics from it may therefore be conveniently quoted in this chapter, so far as they relate to Higher English Education of the collegiate type recognized by the Indian Universities.

Collegiate Education defined.

In regard to the exact meaning of collegiate education, the following observations in the Report have to be borne in mind:—

" The application of the term 'College' should strictly be confined to those institutions in which the students have passed the Matriculation Examination, and are reading one or other of the courses prescribed by the University for its higher examinations. This is in accordance with the definition accepted by the Government of India in the Resolution of the 29th October, 1883, in which colleges—that is, colleges affiliated to an Indian University—are divided into, (i) Arts Colleges, English, whose students have passed the matriculation examination, and are reading a course prescribed by the University for degrees in Arts; (ii) Oriental Colleges, whose students have passed an examination declared by the Local Government to be equal in difficulty to the Matriculation Examination, and are reading a course of Oriental subjects prescribed by the University; (iii) Professional Colleges, whose students have passed the Matriculation Examination, and are reading for degrees in law, medicine, or engineering. There is no uncertainty as to the first and third of these classes. With regard to Oriental Colleges, there is some diversity of practice, as the term is also applied to institutions like the Benares Sanskrit College, in which the students have passed no Matriculation Examination, and in which the subsequent examinations and titles for which they read are conducted and conferred by their own Professors."‡ With Oriental Education this work is not concerned.

* *Progress of Education in India*, 1887-88 *to* 1891-92. By A. M. Nash, Esquire, M. A., (1893); pp. 361–363.

† *Vide* Resolution of the Government of India in the Home Department (Education), No. 199, dated 18th June, 1888.

‡ *Review of Education in India in* 1886. By Sir Alfred Croft; p. 136

Comparative Statistics of Collegiate Education, 1881 to 1885.

Bearing in mind this definition, the following table * compares the number of institutions of different classes, and of students, during 1881-82, with those in 1884-85 :—

ARTS COLLEGES, ENGLISH, 1881-82 TO 1884-85.

PROVINCES.	1881-82.								1884-85.							
	UNDER PUBLIC MANAGEMENT.		AIDED.		UNAIDED.		TOTAL.		UNDER PUBLIC MANAGEMENT.		AIDED.		UNAIDED.		TOTAL.	
	Colleges.	Students.	Colleges.	Students.	Colleges.	Students.	Colleges.	Students.	Colleges.	Students.	Colleges.	Students.	Colleges.	Students.	Colleges.	Students.
Madras	10	742	12	828	3	124	25	1,694	10	895	18	1,488	2	132	30	2,515
Bombay	3	311	2	139	1	25	6	475	3	522	.2	233	1	47	6	802
Bengal	12	1,305	5	895	5	545	22	2,745	13	946	5	877	7	956	25	2,779
N.-W. Provinces ...	3	172	2	157	1	20	6	349	3	165	5	194	3	26	11	385
Punjab	1	103	...	...	...	...	1	103	1	186	1	39	...	...	2	225
Central Provinces ...	1	65	...	...	1	2	2	67	1	31	1	24	1	1	3	56
Burma	1	9	...	...	...	...	1	9	1	18	...	...	...	...	1	18
Total ...	31	2,707	21	2,019	11	716	63	5,442	32	2,763	32	2,855	14	1,162	78	6,780

Comparative expenditure on English Arts Colleges, 1881 to 1885.

The following Tabular Statement compares the expenditure on English Arts Colleges in the year 1881-82 with that in 1884-85. The Statement has been prepared from two Tables given in paragraph 38, at page 33, of Sir Alfred Croft's Review of Education in India in 1886 :—

EXPENDITURE ON ARTS COLLEGES, ENGLISH, 1881-82 TO 1884-85.

CLASS OF INSTITUTIONS.	1881-82.					1884-85.					REMARKS.
	EXPENDITURE FROM—					EXPENDITURE FROM—					
	Provincial Revenues.	Municipal Grants.	Fees.	Subscriptions, Endowments, &c.	Total.	Provincial Revenues.	Municipal Grants.	Fees.	Subscriptions, Endowments, &c.	Total.	
	Rs.	Rs.	Rs.	Rs.	Rs.	Rs.	Rs.	Rs.	Rs.	Rs.	
Government ...	6,23,516	3,000	1,68,321	73,967	8,68,804	6,75,610	6,114	1,91,129	48,827	9,21,680	* Includes Rs. 5,964 from the Revenues of Native States.
Aided ...	65,641	...	73,657	1,81,002	3,20,300	1,05,412	7,869	1,10,725	2,41,429	4,65,435	
Unaided ...	...	...	6,679	*19,004	*25,683	...	...	9,970	†46,845	†56,815	† Includes Rs. 5,727 from the Revenues of Native States.
Total ...	6,89,157	3,000	2,48,657	2,73,973	12,14,787	7,81,022	13,983	3,11,824	3,37,101	14,43,930	

* *Review of Education in India in 1886.* By Sir Alfred Croft; p. 31.

Average Fee of each pupil—1881 to 1885.

The Average Fee paid by each pupil in the various kinds of Arts Colleges during the year 1881-82, as compared with the year 1884-85 is shown in the following Table * :—

AVERAGE FEE PAID BY EACH PUPIL IN THE ARTS COLLEGES.

Province.	1881-82.			1884-85.		
	Departmental Colleges.	Aided Colleges.	Unaided Colleges.	Departmental Colleges.	Aided Colleges.	Unaided Colleges.
	Rs.	Rs.	Rs.	Rs.	Rs.	Rs.
Madras	45·5	30·7	28·9	62·2	47·7	45·3
Bombay	81·7	59·0	48·2	83·6	58·0	61·2
Bengal	88·2	54·1	...	80·9	45·2	...
N.-W. Provinces	42·9	16·5	20·9	45·3	27·4	25·3
Punjab	21·9	...	...	21·4	24·2	...
Central Provinces	20·7	...	...	24·5	22·7	...
Burma	42·7	...	...	44·9	...	...
Average for India	69·2	42·1	30·9	69·1	45·5	45·8

It will be interesting to compare the figures of this Table with those of one of the preceding Tabular Statements,† which shows the average annual cost of educating each student in English Arts Colleges, in 1881-82. The comparison will show that in India, as elsewhere, High Education is far from being self-supporting, and cannot entirely rely upon tuition fees for its maintenance.

Increasing success of Non-Departmental Colleges in 1881 to 1885.

With reference to the question of the proposed gradual withdrawal of the State from Higher English Education, the following table ‡ shows the increasing success of Non-Departmental Colleges by introducing a comparison between the Statistics of the year 1881-82 with those of the year 1884-85 so far as the First Arts, the B.A. and the M.A. examinations are concerned :—

Class of Institutions.	1881-82.				1884-85.			
	Number of students on the rolls.	Passed at—			Number of students on the rolls.	Passed at—		
		F.A.	B.A.	M.A.		F.A.	B.A.	M.A.
Departmental	2,707	421	166	29	2,763	589	288	50
Non-Departmental	2,735	466	121	12	4,017	473	285	37

The figures show that while there was an increase of 40 per cent., 73 per cent., and 72 per cent., respectively, in the number of successful candidates from departmental institutions at the First Arts, B.A. and M.A. examinations, the corresponding proportions of increase among candidates from institutions under private management were 2 per cent., 169 per cent., and 208 per cent., respectively.

Statistics of Collegiate Education in 1885-86.

The Statistics of English Collegiate Education for the year 1885-86 are of special importance as by that time the revised systems of classification consequent upon the Report of the Indian Education Commission, were in general use, and the technical terms of education were employed uniformly in the same sense.

* *Review of Education in India in 1886.* By Sir Alfred Croft; p. 34. ‡ *Ib*, p. 37. † *Vide* page 101 *ante.*

English Arts Colleges, 1885-86. The number of English Arts Colleges of different classes in each province in 1885-86, and the number of students reading in them are shown in the following table * :—

ARTS COLLEGES, ENGLISH, 1885-86.

Province.	Under Public Management.		Under Private Management, Aided.		Under Private Management, Unaided.		Total.	
	Colleges.	Students.	Colleges.	Students.	Colleges.	Students.	Colleges.	Students.
Madras ...	9	938	17	1,483	4	267	30	2,688
Bombay ...	5	608	3	433	...	...	8	1,041
Bengal ...	13	949	6	875	7	1,174	26	2,998
N.-W. Provinces ...	3	186	4	228	6	34	13	448
Punjab ...	1	248	1	59	...	...	2	307
Central Provinces...	1	39	2	39	1	1	4	79
Burma ...	1	20	...	...	...	...	1	20
Total ...	33	2,988	33	3,117	18	1,476	84	7,581
Total for 1884-85 ...	33	2,810	32	2,855	13	1,115	78	6,780

Expenditure in Arts Colleges, 1885-86. The Statistics of the expenditure on Arts Colleges in 1885-86 is shown in the following table†:—

EXPENDITURE ON ARTS COLLEGES, 1885-86.

Province.	From Provincial Revenues.			From District and Municipal Funds.	From fees.	From other sources.	Total.
	In Colleges under public management.	In Aided Colleges.	Total.				
	Rs.	Rs.	Rs.	Rs.	Rs.	Rs.	Rs.
Madras	1,36,564	42,216	1,78,780	M. 1,027	1,20,148	1,03,131	4,03,086
Bombay	88,514	9,400	97,914	M. 3,000	58,413	72,873	2,32,200
Bengal	2,90,493	24,217	3,14,710	......	1,25,296	1,07,216	5,47,222
N.-W. Provinces ...	68,343	29,186	97,529	{D. M.} 7,586	14,423	65,999	1,85,537
Punjab	45,797	5,400	51,197	M. 1,200	8,110	6,927	67,434
Central Provinces ...	9,199	2,376	11,575	M. 3,711	1,660	11,365	28,311
Burma	22,274	...	22,274	......	1,012	......	23,286
Total ...	6,61,184	1,12,795	7,73,979	1,6524	3,29,062	3,67,511	14,87,076
Total for 1884-85 ...	6,77,410	1,03,612	7,81,022	13,983	3,11,824	3,37,101	14,4 3,930

* *Review of Education in India in 1886.* By Sir Alfred Croft; p. 138.

† *Ib.*, p. 140.

Proportionate expenditure from public and from private funds on Collegiate Education, 1885-86.

The following tabular statement, extracted from the table given in paragraph 98 at page 110 of Sir Alfred Croft's *Review of Education in India in* 1886, shows the different proportions in which public and private funds, respectively, contributed to the support of Collegiate Education in the various Provinces where such education prevails :—

PROPORTIONATE EXPENDITURE ON COLLEGIATE EDUCATION, FROM PUBLIC AND FROM PRIVATE FUNDS, IN 1885-86.

PROVINCE.	EXPENDITURE.	
	From Public Funds.	From Private Funds.
	Rs.	Rs.
Madras	45·2	54·8
Bombay	47·7	52·3
Bengal	65·7	34·3
North-Western Provinces and Oudh	74·	26·
Punjab	77·7	22·3
Central Provinces	54·	46·
Burma	95·7	4·3
Average for India	60·	39·9

Expenditure from Fees in Colleges—1885-86.

The importance of requiring that students of colleges should pay fees proportionate in some degree to the cost of their education, was insisted on by the Education Commission. The following Table* shows the average yearly rate of fee paid by students—the yearly fee in each case being calculated on the average monthly roll-number :—

AVERAGE YEARLY RATE OF FEE PAID BY STUDENTS IN COLLEGES, IN 1885-86.

PROVINCE.	Departmental Colleges.	Aided Colleges.	Unaided Colleges.
	Rs.	Rs.	Rs.
Madras	57·9	48·0	43·9
Bombay	86·4	65·2	39·3
Bengal	71·5	49·2	...
North-Western Provinces	39·7	27·9	28·6
Punjab	27·4	37·2	...
Central Provinces	29·3	14·5	27·0
Burma	48·2	...	...
Average for India	65·4	47·6	41·3

* *Review of Education in India in* 1886. By Sir Alfred Croft; p. 141.

Proportion of Fee-receipts to total cost in Colleges—1885-86.

The proportion of Fee-receipts to total expenditure, in different classes of Colleges, in 1885-86, is shown in the following Statement* of Percentages.

PERCENTAGE OF FEE-RECEIPTS TO TOTAL COST IN COLLEGES, IN 1885-86.

Province.	Government Colleges.	Aided Colleges.
	Rs.	Rs.
Madras	26·3	32·5
Bombay	26·1	37·9
Bengal	20·2	29·3
North-Western Provinces	9·5	6·9
Punjab	12·0	12·2
Central Provinces	8·8	3·7
Burma	4·8	...
Average for India	20·6	25·5

Average cost of the education of each pupil in Colleges, 1885-86.

The following is a convenient Table† for reference and comparison, as showing the cost of educating each pupil in colleges:—

AVERAGE COST OF EDUCATING EACH PUPIL IN COLLEGES, IN 1885-86.

Class of Institutions.		Cost of each Pupil to—			
		Provincial Revenues.	Local and Municipal Funds.	Private Sources.	Total.
		Rs.	Rs.	Rs.	Rs.
Colleges.	Arts	104·4	2·2	92·4	199·0
	Professional ...	178·1	...	49·4	227·5

The statement of cost in this Table is an average derived from Institutions under every form of management—departmental, local or municipal, and private, whether aided or unaided.

Result of University Examinations in Arts, 1885-86.

As showing the progress of higher English collegiate education, the number of successful candidates at the different University Examinations of students in Arts Colleges, for the year 1885-86, is shown in the following table‡:—

UNIVERSITY EXAMINATIONS IN ARTS, IN 1885-86.

Province.	M. A.	B. A.	B. Sc.	First Arts, or equivalent Examinations.
Madras	8	163	...	456
Bombay	3	69	3	238
Bengal	31	410	...	636
North-Western Provinces	2	51	...	91
Punjab	2	15	...	58
Central Provinces	...	...	...	21
Burma	...	...	...	3
Total ...	46	708	3	1,503
Total for 1884-85	23	569	4	1,087

* *Review of Education in India in 1886.* By Sir Alfred Croft; p. 148.   † *Ib.*, p. 111.   ‡ *Ib.*, p. 144.

In reference to the growing share which Colleges under private management are taking in the higher education in the country, it is necessary to enquire how far these Colleges are successful, so far as success can be estimated by the ability of their students to pass the examinations of the University. The figures necessary for forming a judgment on this point are given in the following Tabular Statement*:—

Comparative success of Government and other Colleges in University Examinations, 1885-86.

COMPARATIVE SUCCESS OF GOVERNMENT AND OTHER COLLEGES IN UNIVERSITY EXAMINATIONS, 1885-86.

Province.	M.A.				B.A.				First Arts (or equivalent).			
	Government Colleges.	Aided Colleges.	Unaided Colleges and private students.	Total.	Government Colleges.	Aided Colleges.	Unaided Colleges and private students.	Total.	Government Colleges.	Aided Colleges.	Unaided Colleges and private students.	Total.
Madras	...	...	8	8	87	71	5	163	211	182	63	456
Bombay	2	1	...	3	62	10	...	72	135	84	19	238
Bengal	21	5	5	31	149	135	126	410	244	139	253	636
North-Western Provinces ...	1	1	...	2	23	23	5	51	33	44	14	91
Punjab	2	...	...	2	12	1	2	15	41	9	8	58
Central Provinces	...	...	...	...	...	...	...	...	14	6	1	21
Burma	...	...	...	...	...	...	...	...	3	...	...	3
Total ...	26	7	13	46	333	240	138	711	681	464	358	1,503

CHAPTER XXIV

MR. NASH'S QUINQUENNIAL REVIEW OF THE PROGRESS OF EDUCATION IN INDIA, 1887-88 TO 1891-92, AND ITS STATISTICS.—FINANCIAL POSITION OF THE INDIAN UNIVERSITIES.—RESOLUTION OF THE GOVERNMENT OF INDIA ON THE SAME, DATED 7TH SEPTEMBER 1894.—SOME IMPORTANT MATTERS DEALT WITH IN THE RESOLUTION.

Mr. Nash's Review of Education in India—1887 to 1892.

The preparation of the second Quinquennial Review of the progress of Education in India, during the years 1887-88 to 1891-92, was entrusted by the Government of India to Mr. A. M. Nash, a Professor of the Presidency College, Calcutta. The orders were that the Report should be a compendium, in continuation of Sir Alfred Croft's Report of 1886, of the information supplied by the different Local Governments, as regards the condition of education in each Province, the methods and organization by which it is imparted, and the extent to which effect is being given to the recommendations of the Education Commission. In accordance with these instructions, Mr. Nash has extracted from the Departmental Reports of each Province the most important facts connected

* *Review of Education in India in* 1886. By Sir Alfred Croft; p. 148— Prepared from the three Tables on that page.

with the history of education, and statistics to show the nature and extent of the progress made during the preceding five years. The report is thus merely a continuation of Sir Alfred Croft's report which was written in 1886, and it is therefore necessary to borrow the Statistics, which will throw light upon the progress and condition of English Collegiate Education down to the year 1892—these statistics being the latest available.

Increase of attendance in Arts Colleges, 1887 to 1892.

The following Table* shows the enormous increase in the number of students, reading in the Arts Colleges in the various provinces, during the five years, 1887 to 1892:—

ATTENDANCE IN ARTS COLLEGES, 1887 to 1892.

Province.	Number of Students in Arts Colleges on the 31st March.						Increase per cent.	Number of boys of school-going age, among whom one was reading in an Arts College in—	
	1887.	1888.	1889.	1890.	1891.	1892.		1887.	1892.
Lower Burma	14	30	27	23	25	44	214	21,332	8,794
North-Western Provinces ...	478	637	699	931	1,194	1,311	174·3	7,205	2,781
Central Provinces ...	100	134	153	152	212	232	132	8,741	4,207
Bengal	3,215	4,494	5,168	4,882	5,232	5,225	62·5	1,584	1,050
Punjab	319	305	322	358	389	462	44·8	4,801	3,654
Bombay	955	1,020	1,179	1,229	1,289	1,332	39·5	1,877	1,574
Madras	2,979	3,036	3,069	3,043	3,205	3,818	28·2	769	693
Total ...	8,060	9,656	10,617	10,618	11,546	12,424	54·14	1,975	1,432

The above Table shows that the increase in the number of students is very unequally distributed, and that in some Provinces the rate of increase varies very much from year to year. The last three columns are important, as indicating a comparison between the progress made during the five years and the previous extent of Collegiate Education in the different Provinces. As might be expected, the rate of increase is greatest in those Provinces in which University Education had made least progress before 1887, and the order of the figures indicating the rate of increase differs from the order of the figures in the succeeding column only with respect to the North-Western Provinces and Bengal, in both of which Provinces the increase is relatively greater than might have been expected. In the North-Western Provinces this is due to the establishment of the University of Allahabad, and the high rate of increase in Bengal can be accounted for by the fact that the standard of the Entrance Examination was lowered in the year 1887, resulting in an unusual increase of Collegiate Students.

Number of English Arts Colleges in 1887 and 1892.

The following table† shows for each Province the number of Colleges of each class, and the number of students in them on the 31st March, 1887, and the corresponding period in 1892:—

* *Progress of Education in India*, 1887-88 *to* 1891-92. By A. M. Nash, Esq., M.A. (1893); p. 61. † *Ib.*, p 59.

ARTS COLLEGES, ENGLISH, 1886-87 TO 1891-92.

Province.	1886-87.								1891-92.							
	Under Public Management.		Under Private Management, Aided.		Under Private Management, Unaided.		Total.		Under Public Management.		Under Private Management, Aided.		Under Private Management, Unaided.		Total.	
	Colleges.	Students.	Colleges.	Students.	Colleges.	Students.	Colleges.	Students.	Colleges.	Students.	Colleges.	Students.	Colleges.	Students.	Colleges.	Students.
Madras	8	955	19	1,753	4	271	31	2,979	7	1,029	24	2,569	4	220	35	3,818
Bombay	5	509	4	446	...	...	9	955	4	476	4	613	1	243	9	1,332
Bengal	13	1,085	7	795	7	1,335	27	3,215	12	1,668	7	1,097	15	2,460	34	5,225
N.-W. P. and Oudh ...	3	212	4	237	5	29	12	478	3	498	4	659	5	154	12	1,311
Punjab	1	248	1	55	1	16	3	319	2	162	3	211	1	89	6	462
Central Provinces ...	1	47	2	53	...	...	3	100	1	88	2	144	...	...	3	232
Lower Burma	1	14	...	...	...	...	1	14	1	44	...	...	...	...	1	44
Total ...	32	3,070	37	3,339	17	1,651	86	8,060	30	3,965	44	5,293	26	3,166	100	12,424

It will be observed that the total number of Colleges increased by 14, or 16·3 per cent. During the preceding five years the increase was 23 colleges, or 36·5 per cent. This diminution in the rate of increase was more than compensated by the increased size of the Colleges; for, while in 1887, the average number of students in each college was 94, in 1892 the number was 124. The total increase in the number of students during the last five years was 4,364, or 54·14 per cent., against an increase of 2,648, or 48·93 per cent., during the previous five years. The increase in the number of students is common to all the Provinces of India, but the number of colleges has increased in only three Provinces. In Bengal 7 Colleges have been added to the list, in Madras 4, and in the Punjab 3.

Classification of Arts Colleges, 1887 to 1892.

The classification of Arts Colleges, according to management and grade, is shown in the following Table.* Colleges affiliated to a University up to the B.A. standard being classed as first grade, and those affiliated to a lower standard, as second-grade colleges:—

Management.	1886-87.		1891-92.	
	First Grade.	Second Grade.	First Grade.	Second Grade.
Government	20	9	19	4
Native States	1	1	1	1
Municipal	...	1	...	5
Aided	19	18	25	19
Unaided	5	12	13	13
Total	45	41	58	42

* *Progress of Education in India*, 1887-88 *to* 1891-92. By A. M. Nash, Esq., M. A. (1893); p. 63.

Most important Colleges in India.

The following is a list* of some of the most important colleges in India with the number of students on the rolls on the 31st March 1892:—

Government Colleges—

Presidency College, Calcutta	428
Presidency College, Madras	371
Muir Central College, Allahabad	282
Elphinstone College, Bombay	265

Missionary Colleges—

Christian College, Madras	767
St. Joseph's College, Trichinopoly	389
General Assembly's Institution, Calcutta	381
Free Church Institution, Calcutta	319

Native Colleges—

Metropolitan Institution, Calcutta	508
City College, Calcutta	454
Ripon College, Calcutta	447
Fergusson College, Poona	243

Expenditure on Arts Colleges, in 1887 to 1892.

The following Table† shows the total expenditure from different sources on Arts Colleges in each Province, in 1886-87 and in 1891-92:—

EXPENDITURE IN ARTS COLLEGES, ENGLISH, 1886-87 TO 1891-92.

Province.	1886-87.							1891-92.						
	From Provincial Revenues			From District and Municipal Funds.	From Fees.	From other sources	Total.	From Provincial Revenues.			From District and Municipal Funds.	From Fees.	From other sources.	Total.
	In Colleges under Public Management.	In Aided Colleges.	Total.					In Colleges under Public Management.	In Aided Colleges.	Total.				
	Rs.	Rs	Rs.	Rs.	Rs.	Rs.	Rs.	Rs.	Rs.	Rs.	Rs.	Rs.	Rs.	Rs.
Madras	1,57,481	54,640	2,12,121	-1,286	1,46,978	1,14,713	4,72,526	1,61,562	79,547	2,41,109	...	1,90,527	1,22,618	5,54,254
Bombay	98,895	22,000	1,20,895	4,494	57,698	66,247	2,49,334	94,221	43,132	1,37,353	13,524	87,281	76,142	3,14,300
Bengal	2,83,116	26,855	3,09,971	...	1,33,896	1,01,104	5,44,971	2,67,845	24,841	2,92,686	78	2,75,505	1,38,836	7,07,105
N.-W. Provinces and Oudh ...	71,424	30,264	1,01,688	10,570	15,877	70,459	1,98,594	54,976	38,126	93,102	9,742	46,000	86,286	2,35,130
Punjab	38,187	5,400	43,587	1,200	12,014	12,581	69,412	38,349	9,000	47,349	5,759	25,052	25,826	1,03,986
Central Provinces	9,948	4,820	14,768	6,300	2,021	15,143	38,232	14,672	3,293	17,965	1,500	4,638	20,650	44,753
Lower Burma	33,193	...	33,193	...	460	...	33,653	40,291	...	40,291	...	2,490	...	42,781
Total ...	6,92,244	1,43,979	8,36,223	21,278	3,68,974	3,80,247	16,06,722	6,71,916	1,97,939	8,69,855	30,603	6,31,493	4,70,358	20,02,309

It will be observed in this Table, that in 1886-87 the total expenditure in Arts Colleges, from all sources, was Rs. 16,06,722, and that during the five years ending in 1891-92, it rose to Rs. 20,02,309, thus showing an increase of Rs. 3,95,587, or 24·6 per cent.

Proportionate expenditure on Arts Colleges from public and private funds, 1887 to 1892.

The following Tabular Statement,‡ extracted from the Table given in paragraph 17, at page 30, of Mr. Nash's *Quinquennial Review of Education in India in* 1887-88 *to* 1891-92, compares the different proportions in which public and private funds, respectively, contributed to the support of collegiate education during those years, in the various Provinces where such education prevails.

* *Progress of Education in India in* 1887-88 *to* 1891-92. By A. M. Nash, Esq., M. A.; p. 63. † *Ib.*, p. 64. ‡ *Ib.*, p. 30.

PROPORTIONATE EXPENDITURE ON COLLEGIATE EDUCATION FROM PUBLIC AND FROM PRIVATE FUNDS IN 1886-87 AND 1891-92.

Province.	1886-87.		1891-92.	
	From Public Funds.	From Private Funds.	From Public Funds.	From Private Funds.
Madras	44·9	55·1	48·7	51·3
Bombay	51·4	48·6	51·4	48·6
Bengal	67·2	32·8	54·9	45·1
North-Western Provinces and Oudh ...	73·0	27·0	62·4	37·6
Punjab	68·7	31·3	66·4	33·6
Central Provinces	55·1	44·9	44·4	55·6
Burma (Lower)	98·6	1·4	94·2	5·8
Total ...	60·7	39·3	54·9	45·1

Average Annual Fees per pupil in Arts Colleges, in 1887 and 1892.

Referring to the table of expenditure in Arts Colleges, given above, for the years 1886-87 and 1891-92, it will appear that, whilst in the former year the expenditure from fees amounted to Rs. 3,68,974, in the latter year it had risen to Rs. 6,31,493, thus showing an increase of Rs. 2,62,519, or 71·1 per cent. In 1886-87 the fees amounted to rather less than 23 per cent. of the entire expenditure, but in five years the proportion rose to 31½ per cent. The increase is in a great measure due to the rise in the number of pupils, and the following Table * gives the average fee paid per annum by each pupil in the different Classes of Colleges:—

AVERAGE YEARLY FEES PAID BY STUDENTS IN ARTS COLLEGES IN 1886-87 AND 1891-92.

Province.	1886-87.			1891-92.		
	Colleges under Public Management.	Aided Colleges.	Unaided Colleges.	Colleges under Public Management.	Aided Colleges.	Unaided Colleges.
	R.	R.	R.	R.	R.	R.
Madras	60·2	54·1	76·6	63·2	58·9	50·
Bombay	85·1	45·2	28·3	97·9	71·1	34·7
Bengal	77·7	51·0	17·3	82·4	48·	26·1
N.-W. P. and Oudh ...	39·2	27·1	24·1	43·0	30·4	30·7
Punjab	36·3	44·5	15·1	76·7	54·5	23·9
Central Provinces ...	24·8	17·9	...	29·8	14·8	...
Burma	27·1	...	...	55·3	...	...
Average for India ...	66·1†	49·2	30·4	72·6	52·6	28·2

* *Progress of Education in India* in 1887-88 to 1891-92 : By A. M. Nash, Esquire, M. A., p. 67.

† This figure is omitted, probably by a misprint, in the Official Report, and as the total amount of Fees paid by students in colleges under public management is not shown in any other Table, the same for each Province has been calculated by multiplying the average amount of fees with the number of Pupils for that Province, as shown in another Table in this Chapter — the total amount of fees for India thus calculated being Rs. 2,02,969, and the total number of pupils in such colleges being 3,070 in 1886-87.

Percentage of Expenditure in Arts Colleges from fees, in 1887 and 1892.

The following Table* shows what percentage of the total expenditure in different Classes of Colleges was met from the Fee-income in 1886-87 and 1891-92.

PERCENTAGE OF FEE-RECEIPTS TO TOTAL EXPENDITURE IN COLLEGES IN 1886-87 AND 1891-92.

PROVINCE.	1886-87.			1891-92.		
	Government Colleges.	Aided Colleges.	Unaided Colleges, including Native-States Colleges.	Government Colleges.	Aided Colleges.	Unaided Colleges, including Native-States Colleges.
Madras	24·4	34·9	45·0	22·6	41·3	31·0
Bombay	22·3	33·1	6·9	23·8	32·0	28·2
Bengal	22·5	28·0	41·5	34·9	36·0	57·7
N.-W. P. and Oudh ...	10·4	6·7	3·5	26·8	16 2	13·6
Punjab	19·5	14·9	5·1	21·5	24·3	55·9
Central Provinces ...	7·5	3·9	...	12·7	8·2	...
Burma	1·3	...	...	5·8	...	...
Average in India ...	20·7	26·4	23·3	27·6	32·8	42·6

Averege cost per pupil in Arts Colleges.

The following Table † gives a Summary regarding the cost of educating a pupil in institutions of different classes:—

AVERAGE COST OF THE COLLEGIATE EDUCATION OF EACH PUPIL IN 1886-87 AND 1891-92.

CLASS OF INSTITUTION.	1886-87.				1891-92.			
	Provincial Revenues.	Local and Municipal Funds.	Private Sources.	Total.	Provincial Revenues.	Local and Municipal Funds.	Private Sources.	Total.
Colleges { Arts	102·8	2·5	93·3	198·6	71·2	2·5	88·3	162·0
Colleges { Professional	185·4	...	41·4	226·8	196·8	2·2	56·3	255·3

The large decrease in the cost of educating a student in Arts Colleges is due to the large increase in the average number of students in each College; though the fees have increased more rapidly than the number of students, the subscriptions, etc., have not risen in proportion, and hence there is a small decrease in the average amount paid from private sources.

* *Progress of Education in India*, 1887-88 *to* 1891-92. By A. M. Nash, Esquire, M.A. (1893), p 69. † *Ib*, p. 34.

In regard to the subject of expenditure, the following detailed informatoin * is interesting. The annual cost to Government of educating a student in the principal College of each Province, in 1891-92, is shown below :—

Average annual cost to Government per pupil in Government Colleges.

		Rs.
Madras	Presidency College	276
Bombay	Elphinstone College	243
Bengal	Presidency College	223
North-Western Provinces	Muir Central College	99
Punjab	Lahore Government College	295
Central Provinces	Jubbulpore College	165
Burma	Rangoon College	895

The average cost to Government for each pupil in Aided Colleges varies considerably in different Provinces; the figures for 1886-87 and 1891-92, are given below, the nearest rupee being taken:—

Average annual cost to Government in Aided Colleges.

	1886-87.	1891-92.
Madras	36	37
Bombay	50	74
Bengal	35	21
North-Western Provinces	101	56
Punjab	95	75
Central Provinces	93	25
Average for India	47	42

Results of University Examinations in 1891-92.

In consequence of great variations in the standard of the examinations, which unfortunately are very common in the Indian Universities, the progress made during the last five years cannot be accurately estimated by comparing the number of candidates, who passed the examinations in 1891-92, with the corresponding figures for 1886-87. With reference, however, to the Tabular Statement of the results of University Examinations in Arts, in the year 1885-86, given towards the end of the preceding Chapter, it will be interesting to give here a similar Tabular Statement for the year 1891-92, as showing the latest information as to the extent of Collegiate Education in Arts. The following Table has been extracted from three Tabular Statements given in paragraph 60, at pages 70 and 71 of Mr. Nash's *Quinquennial Review of Education in India* :—

UNIVERSITY EXAMINATIONS IN ARTS, 1891-92.

PROVINCE.	M.A.	B.A.	B.Sc.	First Arts, or Equivalent Examinations.
Madras	6	316	...	970
Bombay	6	129	3	314
Bengal	46	273	...	1,011
North-Western Provinces	15	112	...	161
Punjab	2	45	...	164
Central Provinces	4	19	...	59
Burma	...	4	...	11
Total ...	79	898	3	2,690
Total † for 1885-86 ...	46	708	3	1,503

* *Progress of Education in India*, 1887-88 to 1891-92. By A. M. Nash, Esquire, M. A., p. 66.

† The figures for 1885-86 have been taken from Sir Alfred Croft's *Review of Education in India* in 1886, p. 148.

The figures in the above Table indicate a general advance in higher English education in Arts during the five years preceding the year 1893; the increase in the number of successful candidates in the M.A. Examination being most noticeable, and the progress in the B.A. Examination, also, since 1885-86 being satisfactory—the number of successful candidates having risen from 708 in 1886, to 898 in 1892, showing an increase of no less than 190. In regard to the spread of higher English education, however, Mr. Nash, speaking of the proportion of graduates to matriculated students, observes that, "in the Universities of Oxford and Cambridge, it is probable that at least 60 per cent. of the students, who matriculate, ultimately obtain the degree of B.A.; taking all the Indian Universities together, the proportion is probably below 20 per cent. It would be interesting to ascertain the proportion stopping short at each stage of the University course, but unfortunately, neither the departmental Returns nor the University Records furnish sufficient data for a complete investigation of the question. * * * * When the number of 'Passes' at the Matriculation increases or decreases very much, the number of students entering a College increases or decreases in a much smaller proportion, which appears to indicate that the boys who do not go any further than the Matriculation Examination belong chiefly to the class of weak students, who could not derive much profit from study in a College." *

General advance in Higher English Education during 1887–92.

With reference to the policy of the withdrawal of Government from the direct management of Colleges, it is interesting to observe how far Colleges, other than Government Institutions, are successful in passing the higher examinations of the Universities in Arts. The following Table, which has been prepared from two Tabular Statements given in paragraph 68, at page 74 of Mr. Nash's Report, gives a classification of the candidates who passed the M.A. and the B.A. (including the B.Sc.) Examinations in the years 1886-87 and 1891-92, according to the management of the Colleges:—

Comparative success of Government and other Colleges in University Examinations, in 1887 and 1892.

COMPARATIVE SUCCESS OF GOVERNMENT AND OTHER COLLEGES IN UNIVERSITY EXAMINATIONS IN ARTS, 1886-87 AND 1891-92.

PROVINCES.	1886-87.										1891-92.									
	Institutions under public management.		Aided Institutions.		Unaided Institutions.		Private.		Total.		Institutions under public management.		Aided Institutions.		Unaided Institutions.		Private.		Total.	
	M.A.	B.A.	M.A.	B.A.	M.A.	B.A.	M.A.	B.A.	M.A.	B.A.	M.A.	B.A	M.A.	B A.	M.A.	B.A.	M.A.	B-A.	M.A.	B.A.
Madras	...	82	...	74	...	1	3	1	3	158	...	66	...	105	...	12	6	133	6	316
Bombay	6	68	2	13	...	...	...	...	8	81	5	85	1	47	...	...	...	...	6	132
Bengal	40	118	13	114	6	108	4	29	63	369	24	123	3	67	4	73	15	10	46	273
N.-W. P. and Oudh	5	29	1	34	...	3	...	...	6	66	6	41	3	66	...	2	6	3	15	112
Punjab	...	14	...	6	...	...	...	4	...	24	2	22	...	16	...	...	...	7	2	45
Central Provinces	...	3	...	7	1	3	...	...	1	13	1	3	3	14	...	...	...	2	4	19
Burmah, Lower...	...	...	...	...	...	...	...	1	...	1	...	4	..	...	...	...	...	...	...	4
Total ...	51	314	16	248	7	115	7	35	81	712	38	344	10	315	4	87	27	155	79	901

The Statistics given in this Chapter may be closed with the following Table, which gives a summary of the general statistics of expenditure on high English education from various sources. The Table has been extracted from the Table given in paragraph 15, at page 23, of Mr. Nash's Report:—

Summary of expenditure on high English Education in 1887 and 1892.

EXPENDITURE ON HIGH ENGLISH EDUCATION, 1886-87 AND 1891-92.

SOURCES OF EXPENDITURE.	1886-87.			1891-92.		
	Colleges.	Universities.	Total.	Colleges.	Universities.	Total.
	Rs.	Rs.	Rs.	Rs.	Rs.	Rs.
Provincial Revenues ...	13,43,190	44,860	13,88,050	15,37,677	32,662	15,70,339
Local Funds ...	6,759	...	6,759	10,834	1,512	12,346
Municipal Funds ...	14,519	4,618	19,137	28,263	...	28,263
Fees	4,73,268	3,19,965	7,93,233	7,96,572	3,98,959	11,95,531
Other Sources ...	4,10,807	— 468	4,10,339	4,99,487	40,009	5,39,496
Total ...	22,48,543	3,68,975	26,17,518	28,72,833	4,73,142	33,45,975

* *Progress of Education in India*, 1887-88 to 1891-92. By A. M. Nash, Esquire, M.A., p. 72.

Rise of Fees in Colleges satisfactory.

The most satisfactory feature in this Table is the rise of Fees in Colleges, from Rs. 4,73,268 in 1886-87, to Rs. 7,96,572 in 1891-92, showing a large increase, amounting to Rs. 3,23,304, or 68 per cent., in the expenditure from fees in Colleges; whilst the rate of increase during the same period of the number of scholars has been much less. This goes to show that the people are gradually learning to appreciate the value of high English education, and to rely more upon their own recourses, and less on the State and the generosity of others.

Financial position of the Indian Universities.

In connection with the question, how far high English Education is gradually becoming self-supporting, it is interesting to consider the latest information in regard to the financial position of the Indian Universities, and with this object the following passage is quoted here from the latest Official Report:—

Madras University self-supporting.

"The University of Madras is a Self-supporting Institution. In the year 1891-92 the income amounted to Rs. 1,92,722, including Rs. 1,78,534 from Examination Fees, and the expenditure was Rs. 1,64,846; out of the general funds of the University, a sum of Rs. 1,85,000 has been invested as a Reserve Fund. The Fees for the Matriculation, First Arts, and B.A. Examinations, are 20 per cent. higher than in the other Indian Universities. The total amount of private benefactions, for the endowment of scholarships and prizes, is much smaller than in Bombay and Calcutta, amounting to only Rs. 64,300.

Bombay University is partly dependent on Government.

"The Bombay University is partly dependent upon Government, and receives an annual grant of Rs. 15,000. The total expenditure in 1891-92 was Rs. 1,17,572, and the income from Fees Rs. 85,217. The question of raising the Examination Fees, in order to render the University self-supporting, is now before the Senate. The University is very richly endowed with scholarships, prizes, &c., the total amount of the investments for this purpose being about 5¼ lakhs. A nearly equal amount has also been given by private individuals towards the cost of the University building and library; one gentleman, Mr. Premchand Roychand, contributing 4 lakhs of rupees for this purpose.

Calcutta University independent of Government Grant-in-aid.

"The University of Calcutta receives no aid from Government; the income in 1891-92 amounted to Rs. 1,79,302, and the Examination Fees alone, to Rs. 1,54, 795; the annual accounts show an expenditure of Rs. 1,05,710 during the year, but the expenditure for the year was nearly Rs. 1,50,000. The annual accounts are very misleading, as the fees for the Arts Examinations are received in December and January, while only a portion of the cost of the examinations, and this a variable one, is paid before the end of the official year. In order to render the accounts a better test of the financial position of the University, it has recently been decided to count the financial year from the 1st July. On the 31st March, 1892, the Reserve Fund amounted to Rs. 1,25,000. On the same date, the total amount of the endowments for scholarships, &c., was rather more than 6¼ *lakhs*, including 3 *lakhs* for the Tagore Law Professorship, and Rs. 2,38,000 for the Premchand Roychand Studentships, established by the gentlemen whose donation to the Bombay University has just been mentioned.

Expenditure on the Punjab University.

"The total expenditure of the Punjab University, exclusive of the cost of the Oriental College and the other teaching institutions connected with the University, was Rs. 65,375; this amount included Rs. 17,662 from Provincial Revenues, Rs. 1,512 from Local Funds, and Rs. 37,735 from fees. The endowments include Rs. 1,89,600 for the general purposes of the University and Rs. 2,23,900 in special Trusts.

Finances of the Allahabad University.

"For the Allahabad University the Director's Report shows an expenditure of Rs. 30,132, all of which was met from fees. As yet, the endowments are small, amounting to less than Rs. 15,000." *

Resolution of the Government of India, dated 7th September, 1894, reviewing Mr. Nash's Quinquennial Report on Education, 1887–92.

Mr. Nash's Quinquennial Review of Education in India, from the official year 1887-88 to 1891-92, was considered by the Government of India, in a Resolution, No. $\frac{2\text{—Education}}{224\text{—}235}$, dated the 7th September, 1894, and the following extracts may be quoted from it, as it deals with the subject of High English Education in India, and gives the latest information as to the views of the Government on the subject.

University Collegiate Education, and its progress,—1882 to 1893.

"The highest division of the Indian System of Public Instruction comprises those students who are reading, in a College affiliated to the University, one or other of the courses prescribed by the University for its higher examinations. The following figures indicate the progress of Collegiate Education:—

* *Progress of Education in India*, 1887-88 *to* 1891-92. By A. M. Nash, Esquire, M.A., pp. 57-58.

Official Year.	Arts.		Law.		Medical.		Engineering.		Total.	
	Colleges, English and Oriental.	Students.	Colleges.	Students.	Colleges.	Students.	Colleges.	Students.	Colleges.	Students.
1881-82	67	6,037	12	739	3	476	3	330	85	7,582
1886-87	89	8,764	16	1,602	4	654	4	474	113	11,494
1891-92	104	12,985	27	1,925	4	778	4	484	139	16,172
1892-93	108	13,387	28	1,915	4	811	4	519	144	16,632

Statistics of Collegiate Education in 1893, as compared with previous years.

"The figures given for 1881-82 and 1886-87, are those shown in the Resolution of the Government of India, of June, 1888; the number of Law Colleges in 1886-87 is given in the present Report as 17. There were in 1892-93 two colleges also for students of professional teaching, containing 57 students. In 1886-87, the only institution of this nature was in the Madras Presidency, and was attended by 7 students. An Agriculture College, containing 45 students, completes the list of Colleges in general, Table III of Mr. Nash's Report. English Arts Colleges under public management have decreased from 32 to 30. Aided Colleges of this description have risen in number from 37 to 46, and Unaided ones from 17 to 27. Colleges of these latter descriptions are, generally speaking, taking the place of Government Institutions. Fifty-eight of the Colleges were affiliated up to the B. A. Standard in 1891-92, against 45 in 1886-87. It is the policy of the Government to maintain at the head-quarters of each Local Government, a College, teaching up to the highest standard; and, consequently the most important Government Colleges are those at Calcutta, Madras, Bombay, and Allahabad. It is satisfactory to observe that, under the heads of expenditure on English Arts Colleges, the largest increase is in that met from fees (Rs. 3,68,974, to Rs. 6,31,493). The average numerical strength of the Colleges has increased, and the cost of educating a student has fallen from Rs. 211 to Rs. 166 per annum. The cost to Government of educating a student in the Rangoon College, where there are but a small number of pupils, is extraordinarily high (Rs. 895 per annum). In Aided (English Arts) Colleges, the average cost to Government per pupil, annually, is Rs. 42. The number of M.A. Degrees taken annually has remained almost stationary during the five years (81, in 1886-87, and 79, in 1891-92); that of B.A. Degrees rose from 710 to 898; while at examinations, intermediate between these examinations and the Matriculation, 2,690 students passed in 1891-92, against 2,105 in 1886-87. The figures do not, on the whole, show a rapid increase in the number of persons passing the University Examinations. Of the Masters of Arts who took their degrees during the quinquennium, 70 per cent. belonged to Lower Bengal. Mr. Nash comments on the low percentage of success among candidates at the B.A. Examination in Bengal, which he is disposed to attribute, in part, to the lowering of the Entrance Standard. The scientific course for the B.A. Degree has been chosen by a fair proportion of the successful candidates during the five years. In Madras nearly one-half, in Bombay one-third, at the Calcutta University 22 per cent., and about the same proportion at the Punjab University, selected this course. At Allahabad the propotion was smaller. Pursuant to recommendations of the Education Commission, a College, affiliated to the Bombay University, up to the B.A. and B.Sc. Examinations, has been established, under the name of "The Daya Ram Jethmal Sind College," at Karachi, by means of subscriptions, supplemented by a Grant from Government. In 1892, there were 66 students on the rolls of this Institution. Indian graduates now form the majority of the Professors at most Colleges, and at some, they compose the whole teaching staff, with the exception of the Principal. Colleges of inferior standing have in many cases been transferred to private management, as was recommended by the Education Commission; and, where superfluous, they have been closed. In 1888, the Oriental College, at Lahore, was re-formed, the abuses of the system of stipends to pupils being remedied, and the method of teaching Oriental languages being changed. The number of students, however, has greatly diminished. At the Benares Sanskrit College, which has been rendered a separate institution from the Arts College, the number of students has somewhat fallen, but the number of candidates appearing for the examinations has largely increased. No fees are paid by the students at this Institution.

"An Act of the Legislature was passed in 1887 for the establishment of a University at Allahabad, and the University was inaugurated in November of that year. Two thousand nine hundred and nine candidates have since passed the Entrance Examination of the University, and a number of Colleges have been affiliated.

Establishment of the Allahabad University in 1887. Degrees granted by Indian Universities, and their condition.

All the Indian Universities grant the degrees of Bachelor, and Master of Arts: the Bombay University grants the degree of Bachelor of Science: in the Punjab University the degrees of Bachelor, Master, and Doctor of Oriental Learning are also bestowed In the Universities of Calcutta, Bombay, and Madras a system has been introduced, under which the privilege of electing, subject to the approval of the Chancellor, a proportion of the Fellows has been conferred on the Masters of Arts and holders of equivalent degrees. Generally speaking, the proportion of graduates who take the degree of M.A. is very small. By far the largest number of such degrees are taken at the Calcutta University, where, in the five years under review, the number reached 299. The Punjab University is a teaching as well as an examining body. The greater part of the expenditure in the Universities is met from fees, together with income from endowments; only the Bombay and Punjab Universities receiving aid from public funds."*

Some important educational topics in the Government of India's Resolution, dated 7th September, 1894.

There are also some other important matters of general application to educational topics, in the Resolution of the Government of India (Home Department), dated the 7th September, 1894, which may, with advantage, be quoted here, as expressive of the present policy of Government on those subjects. The necessary abstracts are the following:—*

Policy of withdrawal, as affecting the Educational Service.

"In reviewing the recommendations of the Education Commission, the Government of India laid down the proposition that, in proportion as the Department withdraws from pushing its own institutions, its machinery for inspection would require strengthening, as a Grant-in-aid System postulates a thorough inspection of all institutions brought under it. In Bengal the number of State-aided Schools, and the staff employed on inspection duties are far stronger than in any other Province. Besides the Inspectors and Assistant and Deputy Inspectors, there are upwards of 900 Inspecting School-masters, *pandits* and *gurus*. The numbers of the Inspecting Staff do not, in general, show an increase, but most Local Governments and Administrations have revised the inspection circles, and satisfied themselves of the adequacy of the staff. Female Inspectors have also been appointed in several Provinces. The reports do not appear to the Governor-General in Council to be sufficiently precise in showing whether the work of inspection is thoroughly carried out, and His Excellency in Council trusts that this important subject may be commented on more fully in future. The question of the re-organization of the Education Department has recently been under the consideration of the Government of India, in connection with the Report of the Public Service Commission. The views of the Secretary of State were communicated to the Government of India in His Lordship's Despatch, No. 9 (Public), dated 28th January, 1892. In this Despatch, Viscount Cross held that, though it was ultimately desirable, the proposed abolition of the graded superior service could not be carried out forthwith, and approved the principle of a five year's probationary term for officers appointed from England. As regards Professors, the suggestion was commended to the Government of India, that all Professors might be allowed to rise in ten year's service, to a salary of Rs. 1,000 per mensem. Of Inspectors, one-half (it was said) might be recruited in India. These proposals as to the superior service were referred to Local Governments and Administrations. Several of the Governments consulted, in replying, sent up schemes for the re-organization of the whole Education Department in their respective Provinces: and it has been necessary to call for further reports and opinions prior to the preparation of a matured scheme for submission to the Home Government. These are now under the consideration of the Government of India. It is contemplated that the Educational Service shall, in future, be divided into, (1) the European Educational Service, for which recruitment will be made in England; (2) the Provincial Educational Service; and (3) the Subordinate Educational Service.

Moral Training in Colleges and Schools.

"The views which the Government of India provisionally endorsed, in the matter of discipline and Moral Training in Schools and Colleges, were summarized in paragraph 26 of the Home Department Resolution, No. 199, dated 18th June, 1888. The Government of India then added that, while they would gladly see an increase in the number of Aided Colleges and Schools in which religious instruction was given, they at the same time, did not admit that it had been shown to be impossible to impart moral instruction in State Colleges, although the tenets of any particular religious belief could not be taught in them. Attention was again invited to the proposal of the Education Commission that a Moral Text-book should be prepared for general use, based upon the fundamental principles of Natural Religion. Orders were issued on these subjects by a Resolution from the Home Department, No. $\frac{6}{371\text{-}383}$, dated 17th August, 1889. The action that has been taken in ensuing years is noticed in Chapter XIV of Mr. Nash's Review. The

* *Supplement to the Gazette of India*, 8th September, 1894; pp. 1269, 1270.

Resolution had noticed, with approval, the promotion of physical education in the various Provinces; and advised that a system of marks and prizes for proficiency in gymnastics and athletic sports should be everywhere introduced. The suitable forms of punishment were enumerated, and it was said that the Provincial Authorities should prescribe rules for the guidance of masters in employing them. The use of good-conduct registers was recommended, and the extension of the system of boarding-houses attached to the higher schools and colleges was approved. The Government of India observed that time would show whether the monitorial system—notwithstanding the fact that Indian schools are mostly day-schools—was suited for Indian boys, but expressed the belief that probably the adoption of such rules as were in force at the Elphinstone High School on this subject, would be productive of advantage. In the matter of inter-school rules—designed to prevent a boy from obtaining advancement in class, or avoiding the consequences of misconduct by changing his school—the rules in force in Bengal, and the North-Western Provinces and Oudh, were recommended for general adoption in other Provinces: it was added that the Universities should be invited to co-operate in securing their adoption in Unaided Institutions. With reference to the proposed preparation of a Moral Text-book, the Governor-General in Council expressed the conclusion that it would not be advantageous to prescribe for use in schools a treatise, or didactic discourse, on the subject, but that books of extracts selected from standard authors, and bearing on individual conduct, should be prepared, such as Mr. Tawney, the Principal of the Presidency College at Calcutta, had already been desired to prepare, by the Syndicate of the Calcutta University. Local Governments were requested to take measures for the purpose described, either by the appointment of Committees or the employment of individuals, to revise the existing readers, or to compile new ones.

Physical Education in Colleges and Schools.

"The Government of India are pleased to observe that the question of physical education has received attention throughout India. In Madras, in all schools and colleges under public management, gymnastic apparatus is provided. Gymnastic and drill instructors are entertained, trained for the most part by the Madras Physical Training and Field Games Association, where examinations are held and certificates granted. In Bombay, simple gymnastic apparatus is said to be possessed even by many Primary Schools. Apparatus and instructors have been provided for most of the Zilla Schools in Bengal, but it appears from the Review that nothing has been done yet in Middle and Primary Schools. In the Punjab distinct physical courses are prescribed for Primary, Middle, and High Schools: physical training has been made compulsory in schools under public management, and provision has been made for the supply of competent teachers; these rules are in course of being carried out. In the Central Provinces all the Secondary Schools and most of the Primary Schools have been provided with gymnasia. In Assam (as appears from the Provincial Report for 1892-93) the masters in the High Schools at Shillong, Cachar, and Dibrugarh are instructed in physical exercise, and the pupils are regularly practised therein: the adoption of similar arrangements in the other Government High Schools is under consideration. Rules have been laid down regarding punishments in schools under public management, in the Codes of Madras, the Punjab, and Burma. Fines are not mentioned in these Codes. In the Central Provinces corporal punishment for boys under 15 years of age has been regulated. The offences punishable with corporal punishment in schools are dealt with by fines in Colleges. In Assam instructions have been issued in a Circular to all headmasters of schools. The Review does not show whether any other Governments have issued instructions on the subject of punishments in the manner requested. The competition of rival High Schools and Colleges in Bengal is described as a fruitful source of misconduct, and as offering impunity for it. Conduct Registers have been generally introduced, though their use is only partial in the Punjab and in Berar, while the Bombay and Burma Reports do not show what has been done. Financial difficulties have restricted the extension of boarding-houses. They are, it would seem from the Review, not attached to Government Schools for Natives in Madras. In Bombay there are no hostels attached to Government High Schools. They are attached to nearly all Government Colleges and Zilla Schools in Bengal. In the North-Western Provinces nearly all Zilla Schools have boarding-houses. About 12 per. cent. of the students reside in them, and they are described as very successful. In the Punjab, it is a standing regulation that, as far as possible, a boarding-house should be attached to every Secondary School: the cost, it is stated, falls almost exclusively on Municipalities. In Burma the system has been partially introduced. Mr. Nash has suggested that columns should be added in general Tables III and IV, to show the attendance and expenditure in boarding-establishments and this suggestion will be referred to Local Governments. The information available as to the introduction of the Monitorial System and its results is very imperfect. Apparently, in the Punjab and the Central Provinces it has been tried with success in boarding-houses. The Inter-school Rules have been revised in most Provinces. In Madras they are in force in all colleges and schools recognized by the University. In Bombay, a Leaving Certificate is substituted, but admission to another school is not restricted by definite rules. The rules in Lower Bengal are stated to have been made, by the University's action, practically compulsory in Unaided Schools, though they have not yet been formally accepted by the University. In the North-Western Provinces inter-college rules have been accepted by the University, and similar rules have been made for Anglo-Vernacular Schools. The Punjab Rules debar from re-admission for six months only. The Bengal Rules have been adopted for most grades of schools in Assam. The rules are said to have proved very salutary in Bengal, though some supervision of the masters, in the matter of the refusal of transfer certificates, is now required. In Bengal certain readers or books of selections have been chosen by the Central Text-Book Committee, as being of the ethical tendency desired by the Government of India. These are specially recommended to the notice of managers in the approved list of books; but text-books are not prescribed by the Department for any class of schools. English readers have been revised in the North-Western Provinces; but information is not given as to Vernacular readers. The English and Vernacular books have been adopted in Assam, from the North-Western Provinces and Bengal, respectively. In the Punjab a special moral text-book is used in Anglo-Vernacular High Schools; and in all schools the class readers are framed so as to convey moral instruction. In Burma a new set of Burmese readers is being prepared. In Berar the text-books in use in Primary and Middle-Schools are stated to have been, since some years past, prepared or selected with the view of conveying moral lessons. In colleges in India, insubordination and grave breaches of college discipline are rare; but instances occur of personation at examinations, the use of forged certificates, and similar offences. The suggestions of the Government of India on the subject of college discipline have been generally accepted by Local Governments.

Educational Conferences.

"The fifteenth and sixteenth chapters of the Review deal with recommendations of the Education Commission relating to Educational Conferences, and the preparation of text-books. The recommendations on the first subject, pointed to assemblages of Educational Officers, together with managers of Aided and Unaided Schools, and to local meetings of schoolmasters under the superintendence of Deputy Inspectors. In Madras, Conferences have been held on three occasions, a moiety (*i. e.*, generally about six) of those attending being representatives of institutions under private management, and such important matters as the alternative final examination for High Schools and the tests for admission to the public service have been discussed by them. In the Punjab the Senate of the University advises the Government on all grades of education. A Departmental and a General Conference are held annually at Lahore, and the latter has discussed nearly all the important matters in which action has been taken of late years. In Lower Burma the Educational Syndicate is a permanent consultative board. A conference in 1889, which revised the grant-in-aid rules, was composed to the extent of three-fourths of representatives of schools under private management. In Bombay and Assam no conferences appear to have been held of late years; and only local assemblages have been held in Bengal. There is little information available as to other Provinces; but conferences have been held in the North-Western Provinces, and apparently Annual District Assemblies are held in the Central Provinces. In Berar an Annual Conference and circle gatherings take place.'

Committees for selection of School-books.

"'After obtaining reports from Local Governments on the subject of the school-books in use, the Government of India, in the year 1877, convened a small General Committee, comprising representatives of the different Provinces, to formulate recommendations for action. The Committee deprecated the attempt to issue an Imperial Series of text-books, but advised that a Standing Committee should be constituted in each Province to report yearly, and approve all books to be used in Government or Aided Institutions, and that a corresponding English Text-Book Committee should also be appointed. In a Resolution, dated 10th January 1881, the Government of India accepted the view that an Imperial Series of text-books should not be prepared, and decided that Local Governments should supervise the preparation of text-books, assisted, if necessary, by Standing Committtees containing a fair number of independent members, and should communicate with the Standing Committees of other Provinces. The subject was to be noticed in a separate section of the annual Provincial Educational Reports. The Government of India declined to restrict Aided Schools to the use of the Government school-books. The Education Commission, in 1883, recommended that the Provincial Text-book Committees should continue their operations, and that the function of Government depôts should be confined to the supply and distribution of Vernacular text-books. Passing to the period now under review, it appears that in Madras there was no permanent Text-book Committee until 1892. The Committee then appointed consists mostly of specialists in the various lines, and 8 out of 26 members are non-officials. In 1889, the Madras Government withdrew from the publication of school-books, and private presses are now allowed to produce works of which Government has the copyright, after approval of the proofs. In Bombay, English text-books are not apparently submitted to a Committee, but several Committees exist, dealing with Vernacular Text-books. In Bengal, the duty of selecting suitable books has, since 1875, been performed by the Central Text-book Committee, the members of which are divided into six Sub-Committees, according to the subject-matter of the text-books submitted to them.

"The Director annually revises the list of books according to the Committee's recommendations. The Committee, which is composed of the best scholars available, undertook in 1891-92, at the request of the Director, to prepare lists of authorized text-books for High and Primary Schools also. There are branch Committees for Behar and Orissa. The Calcutta School Book Society, which has numerous Agencies, is the chief medium for the distribution of school-books. In the North-Western Provinces and Oudh, there are four Committees for selecting Zila School Text-books, and four for selecting books for Vernacular Schools in different quarters of the Provinces. The lists are subject to the Director's revision. The request of the Government of India that a separate section of the Annual Report should deal with text-books, is no longer complied with in the North-Western Provinces and Oudh, and this omission should be rectified in future. The Punjab Text-book Committee, which was established in 1877, undertakes the preparation as well as the examination of books: there are eight Sub-Committees. Text-book Committees have been appointed also in the Central Provinces and in Burma. In Burma there is an officer, called the Editor of Vernacular School Text-books, who examines Vernacular works, in the first instance, and also makes translations and selections.

Prominent educational results during 1887 to 1892.

"The more prominent results brought out from the history of education in India during the five years covered by Mr. Nash's Report may be briefly enumerated. The number of institutions public and private, coming within the purview of the Education Department has risen from 127,116 to 141,793, or by 11·5 per cent., and the number of pupils from 3,343,544 to 3,856,821, or by 15·3 per cent. The increase in pupils is to the extent of 63,340 accounted for by the inclusion, for the first time, of returns from Upper Burma. Though the advance has occurred in a slightly higher ratio in Colleges and Secondary Schools than in Primary Schools, the difference has not been sufficiently marked to cause any substantial change in the proportions of students in these three stages of education. A satisfactory indication of the change of attitude of the Mahomedan Community towards the educational system adopted by the Government, is to be found in the increase in the number of Mahomedan students by nearly 18 per cent. The number of Hindus attending School or College has also increased by 12·8 per cent. Female education has made a substantial advance, the number of girls at school at the end of 1891-92 having been 27·3 per cent., in excess of the number at the end of 1886-87. Something has been done to cultivate a taste for technical education, by the general introduction of drawing into the School Course. In many Provinces even this is still in the experimental stage, and the further development of technical education has not yet been generally systematized. A defect in the educational system which demands serious attention is the inadequacy of the course of training given in many of the Training Schools for teachers.

Efficient inspection of aided institutions necessary.

"As Government recedes from directly managing its own schools, and confines itself more and more to aiding schools not maintained by the Educational Department, the duty of securing an efficient inspection of schools receiving grants-in-aid becomes greater. This question merits the close and continued attention of Local Governments and Administrations. One of the most satisfactory features in connection with the progress of education during the five years under review is to be found in the increase of expenditure by over 20 per cent., and in the change in the sources from which that expenditure has been met. The expenditure from Municipal and Local funds has materially increased, while the share of the total expenditure borne by public funds (in which are included Local and Municipal, as well as State revenues) has slightly declined. It is most encouraging to find that the payments of the public have, during five years, increased from 117½ to 149 *lakhs*, and particularly, that the receipts from fees have increased by over 35 per cent." *

CHAPTER XXV.

ENGLISH PROFESSIONAL EDUCATION IN COLLEGES, IN 1881-82 TO 1885-86, AND IN 1886-87 TO 1891-92.

Professional subjects in the Indian Universities.

The subject of professional and technical education was not included within the scope of the enquiry made by the Indian Education Commission of 1882; but the various Indian Universities recognize in their curriculum of studies the subjects of Law, Medicine, and Engineering, and Sir Alfred Croft, in his *Review of Education in India in 1886*, has collected valuable statistical and other information, which may be borrowed here.

* *Supplement to the Gazette of India*; 8th September 1894; pp. 1278–1282.

Law Departments in Colleges.

Law Departments are in all cases attached to Arts Colleges, since the Universities require that candidates for the degrees of Bachelor of Law should have taken the B.A. Degree, or passed some other examination in Arts, which the University concerned may consider sufficient as the preliminary to the study of law. In Madras, a course of two years, and in Bombay a course of three years is required, subsequent to graduation. In the Calcutta University, the course is for three years, of which two must be subsequent to the degree, and the two courses are sometimes read, in part at any rate, simultaneously. Similar courses, with minor modifications required by local circumstances, are prescribed by the Punjab University and the Allahabad University—the former requiring that the candidate for the degree of Bachelor of Laws should either have passed an intermediate law examination, or should have graduated in Arts, and the latter prescribing that "any Undergraduate of the University may be admitted to the Examination, provided he has prosecuted a regular course of study in a school of Law affiliated to the University, for not less than two academical years, after having fully passed the Intermediate Examination in Arts." The subjects of legal studies, with some local modifications, are similar in all the Universities.

Medical Colleges.

The institutions which exist in India for the training of students for the License in Medicine and Surgery, or for the degree of Bachelor of Medicine, as well as for the higher degree of Doctor of Medicine, are the Medical Colleges of Madras and Calcutta, the Grant Medical College of Bombay, and the Lahore Medical School. "The qualification for the License in Medicine and Surgery differs from that required for the Bachelor of Medicine Degree, both in the preliminary educational test and in the final standard of examination. In Madras, the initial qualification for the license is the University Entrance Examination; and the course extends over four years, divided into two parts, by the first and second Licentiate Examination. For the degree, candidates must have passed the First Arts Examination, and have subsequently studied medicine for five years; during the course, of which they have to pass one preliminary scientific and two professional examinations. To those students who have graduated in Arts, taking physical science, before entering on their medical course, the preliminary scientific examination and one year of study are remitted. In Bombay the only examination below that for the Doctor's degree is that for the license. A candidate must have passed the Matriculation Examination and have studied medicine for four years, during which he has to undergo three examinations. In Calcutta, candidates, whether for the degree or for the license, must have passed the First Arts Examination; and in either case the course, extends over five years. The only difference is the requirement of comparative anatomy and physiology for the degree; a similar distinction being made in Madras. The Lahore Medical School exists for the benefit of students from the North-Western Provinces, as well of those from the Punjab, and both alike are eligible for the Government Scholarships tenable in the institution."*

Engineering Colleges.

There are four Engineering Colleges in India maintained by Government: at Madras, Poona in the Bombay Presidency, Seebpore in Bengal, and Roorkee in the North-Western Provinces.

The Madras Engineering Colleges.

"The requirements of the Madras University for the degree of Bachelor of Civil Engineering, are that a candidate shall have passd the First Examination in Arts, and shall have subsequently read for two years in an Engineering College. All candidates for the degree are examined in mathematics, natural philosophy, mensuration, and the framing of estimates; those for the Civil branch are also examined in surveying and levelling, constructive engineering, and architectural and topographical drawing; those for the Mechanical branch, in mechanical engineering and machine drawing."† The Madras College of Engineering has been recently re-organized, and is the recognized institution for imparting instruction in that subject in that Presidency.

Engineering College at Poona.

"In Bombay, the University requires of candidates for the License in Civil Engineering, (1) the matriculation certificate, (2) a course of three years' study, which may be reduced in the case of candidates, with higher initial qualifications to two years, or to one and a-half. The examination comprises, (1) mathematics and natural philosophy, (2) experimental and natural science; (3) civil engineering, (4) one out of the following list:—(*a*) analytical geometry, and the differential and integral calculus, (*b*) optics and astronomy, (*c*) mining and metallurgy, (*d*) architecture, (*e*) mechanical engineering, (*f*) chemical analysis, (*g*) botany, and meteorology. Candidates must also pass a practical test in experimental science and mechanica engineering. Instruction in the University Course, both theoretical and practical, is given in the Poona College of Science with its attached workshops."‡

Civil Engineering College at Seebpore near Calcutta.

"For the License in Engineering of the Calcutta University, a candidate must have passed the Entrance Examination, and have subsequently studied for four years in an affiliated institution. If he has passed the First Arts Examination, he will be entitled to the degree of B. E. The course comprises the following subjects: mathe-

* Sir Alfred Croft's *Review of Education in India in* 1886; p. 251. † *Ib.*, p. 252. ‡ *Ib.*, pp. 252, 253.

matics, engineering, construction, geodesy, drawing, and either natural science or machinery, according as the candidate selects the Civil or the Mechanical branch of the course. The course in mathematics is exceptionally high, and includes, besides other subjects, analytical geometry, the differential and integral calculus, and hydrostatics. Proposals are under consideration for reducing the extent of this compulsory course. The Government Civil Engineering College at Seebpore, near Calcutta, is the institution in which candidates are prepared for the University Degrees during a course of five years." *

Thomason Civil Engineering College at Roorkee.

"The Thomason Civil Engineering College at Roorkee is maintained by the Public Works Department of Government for the requirements of the public service; and it has no connexion with any University. It is, however, noticed in this place, since it discharges the same functions as those that are so connected. The College contains three departments. Candidates for the Engineering Class have to pass an Examination in English and Hindustani (and also in a third language, if their Vernacular is English); in elementary science, in drawing, and in mathematics to a somewhat high standard. The course of study extends over two years, at the end of which time an examination is held in mathematics, applied mechanics, experimental science, civil engineering, drawing, and surveying. Students of this class are educated for the engineer branch of the Public Works Department, in which four or five appointments, in alternate years, are guaranteed to the best of those who pass. (For comparison, it may here be repeated, that the number of guaranteed appointments for the students of the Poona College is two a year; of the Seebpore College, two and one in alternate years; of the Madras College, one a year). The upper subordinate class at Roorkee is intended to provide men for overseerships, and the lower subordinate for sub-overseerships, in the Public Works Department. The course for the former extends over three years, of which the last is devoted to practical training on works in progress. The course for lower subordinates is limited to a year and a-half. The final examination for upper and for lower subordinates, includes mathematics, engineering, drawing, and surveying, to different standards for the two classes." †

Professional Colleges, 1881-82 to 1884-85.

The following Tabular Statement ‡ gives the comparative statistics of Professional Colleges during the year 1881-82 to 1884-85.

PROFESSIONAL COLLEGES, 1881-82 TO 1884-85.

Province.	1881-82.						1884-85.					
	Law.		Medicine.		Engineering.		Law.		Medicine.		Engineering.	
	Institutions.	Students.	Institutions.	Students.	Institutions.	Students.	Institutions.	Students.	Institutions.	Students.	Institutions.	Students.
Madras Government ...	1	112	1	76	1	9	1	127	1	116	1	19
Bombay ditto ...	1	136	1	283	1	151	1	180	1	370	1	184
Bengal ditto ...	7	270	1	117	1	170	6	125	1	132	1	149
Ditto, Unaided ...	1	190	...	...	...	...	2	524	...	...	...	...
N.-W. P., Government ...	...	...	...	...	...	...	...	...	...	...	1	155
Ditto, Aided ...	2	31	...	...	...	...	2	94	...	...	...	...
Ditto, Unaided ...	...	...	...	...	...	...	1	17	...	...	...	...
Punjab, Government ...	...	...	...	...	...	...	...	...	1	188	...	...
Total ... Government ...	9	518	3	476	3	330	8	432	4	806	4	507
Total ... Aided ...	2	31	...	...	...	...	2	94	...	...	...	...
Total ... Unaided ...	1	190	...	...	...	...	3	541	...	...	...	...
Grand Total ...	12	739	3	476	3	330	13	1,067	4	806	4	507

* Sir Alfred Croft's *Review of Education in India in* 1886; p. 253. † *Ib.*, p. 254. ‡ *Ib.*, p. 41.

Cost of Professional Colleges in 1884-1885.

The total cost of professional education connected with the University in 1881-82, as compared with 1884-85, is shown in the following Table*:—

COST OF PROFESSIONAL COLLEGES.

HEAD OF CHARGE.	1881-82.				1884-85.			
	Provincial Revenues.	Fees.	Other sources.	Total.	Provincial Revenues.	Fees.	Other sources.	Total.
	Rs.	Rs.	Rs.	Rs.	Rs.	Rs.	Rs.	Rs.
Law	527	39,496	7,433	47,456	406	32,186	4,886	36,666
Medicine ...	1,78,157	35,607	...	2,13,764	2,13,889	53,366	2,411	2,69,666
Engineering ...	1,03,886	9,921	...	1,13,807	2,70,560	13,256	5,749	2,89,565
Total ...	2,82,570	85,024	7,433	3,75,027	4,84,043	98,808	13,046	5,95,897

Law classes almost self-supporting. Results of the University Examinations in professional subjects, in 1881-1885.

It will be observed in this table that the Law classes practically pay for themselves, whilst considerable expense is incurred by Government on education in Medicine and Engineering. The results of the University examinations in these various branches in 1881-82 and 1884-85 is shown in the following table † which includes only those who passed the final examination in each case, whether for the License or the Degree:—

RESULTS OF UNIVERSITY EXAMINATIONS (PROFESSIONAL), 1881-82 AND 1884-85.

PROVINCE.	LAW.		MEDICINE.		ENGINEERING.	
	1881-82.	1884-85.	1881-82.	1884-85.	1881-82.	1884-85.
Madras	12	25	4	10	1	7
Bombay	5	13	14	24	16	7
Bengal	67	77	20	14	6	...
N.-W. Provinces	2	...	...	...	...	3
Punjab	...	...	...	11	...	...
Total ...	86	115	38	59	23	17

* Sir Alfred Croft's *Review of Education in India*, 1886; p. 42.

† *Ib.*, p. 43.

Professional Colleges, 1885-86.

The subjoined Table * shows the number of Colleges, or departments of Colleges, in Law, Medicine, and Engineering, and the number of students reading in them on the 31st March 1886:—

PROFESSIONAL COLLEGES, 1885-86.

Province.	Law.		Medicine.		Engineering.	
	Institutions.	Students.	Institutions.	Students.	Institutions.	Students.
Madras, Government ...	1	141	1	136	1	18
Bombay, do. ...	2	221	1	296	1	116
Bengal, do. ...	6	110	1	152	1	156
Ditto., Unaided ...	4	772	...	...	...	...
N.-W. P., Government ...	1	61	...	...	1	154
Ditto., Aided ...	1	48	...	...	...	...
Ditto., Unaided ...	1	18	...	...	...	...
Punjab, Government ...	...	...	1	183	...	...
Total { Government ...	10	533	4	767	4	444
Total { Aided ...	1	48	...	...	...	...
Total { Unaided ...	5	790	...	...	...	...
Grand Total ...	16	1,371	4	767	4	444
Total in 1884-85. ...	13	1,067	4	806	4	507

Cost of Professional Colleges, 1885-86.

The following Table † shows the cost of professional Collegiate Education in 1885-86:—

COST OF PROFESSIONAL COLLEGES, 1885-86.

Profession.	Provincial Revenues.	Fees.	Other sources.	Total.
	Rs.	Rs.	Rs.	Rs.
Law	1,082	42,415	5,339	48,836
Medicine	2,11,672	54,678	3,863	2,70,213
Engineering	2,60,032	15,548	189	2,75,769
Total ...	4,72,786	1,12,641	9,391	5,94,818
Total for 1884-85 ...	4,84,043	98,808	13,046	5,95,897

* Sir Alfred Croft's *Review of Education in India in 1886*; p. 250.

† *Ib.*, p. 255.

The flourishing and almost self-supporting condition of the Law classes is noticeable in the above Table in contrast to the figures relating to the subjects of Medicine and Engineering in both of which the income from fees falls enormously short of the expenditure.

Results of University Professional Examinations, 1885-86.

The following statement * shows the number of those who graduated in the Universities in the various professional branches in 1885-86: or passed the final examination of the Roorkee Engineering College in the North-Western Provinces:—

RESULTS OF UNIVERSITY EXAMINATIONS (PROFESSIONAL) 1885-86.

PROVINCE.	Law.	Medicine.	Engineering.
Madras	38	26	3
Bombay	17	39	13
Bengal	120	32	3
North-Western Provinces	...	...	4
Punjab	...	7	...
Total ...	175	104	23
Total for 1884-85 ...	115	59	17

Present condition of English Professional Education.

Information in regard to English Professional Education in Colleges during the five years succeeding the year 1886 is given in Mr. Nash's Quinquennial Review of the Progress of Education in India, and since such information is the latest available, certain Statistics may be borrowed from it here as showing the present condition of Professional Education in Indian Colleges.

Law Colleges, 1887 and 1892.

The following Table† shows the number of Law Colleges and Schools in 1887 and 1892, and the number of students in them:—

ATTENDANCE IN LAW COLLEGES AND SCHOOLS.

PROVINCE.	1886-87.				1891-92.			
	Colleges.	Pupils.	Schools.	Pupils.	Colleges.	Pupils.	Schools.	Pupils.
Madras	1	182	...	...	1	360	...	...
Bombay	2	249	...	...	4	230	...	...
Bengal	10	1,078	...	...	12	563	...	...
North-Western Provinces ...	3	117	...	...	7	612	...	...
Punjab	1	71	...	...	1	85	...	...
Central Provinces	...	...	...	...	2	82	...	...
Assam	...	...	1	19	...	...	2	39
Total ...	17	1,697	1	19	27	1,932	2	39

* Sir Alfred Croft's *Review of Education in India*, 1886, p. 254.

† *Progress of Education in India*, 1887-88 *to* 1891-92, by A. M. Nash, Esquire, M.A. (1893); p. 220.

Noticeable increase in Law Colleges.

In this Table the increase in the number of Law Colleges from 17 to 27 in five years is very noticeable, taken in conjunction with the fact that the increase in the number of students has been in much less proportion. "The Calcutta University has reduced the course of study from three years to two, and withdrawn the privilege of attending lectures before passing the B.A. Examination, the changes being exactly the opposite of those made by the Madras University. A similar change was also made by the High Court in the rules for the Pleadership Examination, for which many of the students of the Law Colleges are preparing, and these changes have caused the reduction of the number of students from 1,078 to 563 in spite of an increase of two in the number of Colleges.

"In the North-Western Provinces the number of Law Classes and of students has increased very rapidly since the establishment of the local University, but it is doubtful to what extent this is the cause of the increase, for the Principal of one of the Government Colleges says: 'The very great majority of our Law Students have no intention or desire of appearing at the University Examination or at the High Court Examinations, and it is not clear to me with what precise object they pay the fees and attend the law lectures for two years.' Allahabad is the only University in India that confers degrees in Law upon persons who have not graduated in Arts; candidates are required to attend lectures for two years after passing the Intermediate Examination, but in order to prevent the wholesale immigration from other Provinces of candidates who have failed at the B.A. Examination, no examination of any other University lower than the B.A. is recognized as qualifying for admission to a Law College."*

Legal studies almost self-supporting.

Legal studies seem to continue to be almost self-supporting. "The aggregate cost of all the Law Classes during the year 1891-92 amounted to Rs. 99,596 of which the students themselves paid Rs. 93,543 in the shape of fees. Local funds contributed only Rs. 34, and Municipal funds Rs. 659, while the expenditure from Provincial Revenues was more than balanced by the receipts from fees in Government Institutions, the net profit to Government amounting to Rs. 3,303."†

Advance of legal studies in 1887 to 1892.

As showing the advance of legal studies during the period of five years ending in 1892, the total number of persons who obtained the degree of Bachelor of Law, or the License in Law of the Punjab University, during that period is shown below:—‡

Madras	210
Bombay	139
Bengal	855
North-Western Provinces	50
Punjab	28
Central Provinces	11
Total	1,293

"In Madras one candidate obtained the degree of Master of Laws; in Bombay there is no degree beyond the LL.B., but merely an examination for Honours, which no candidate has attempted; in the Calcutta University the degree of D.L. is given, but none of the candidates were successful; in the Punjab University the degrees of LL.B. and LL.D., were not instituted till 1891-92, and no examinations have been held. The number of graduates in Law appears to be increasing in every Province, except perhaps in Bengal; in this Province there has been a large decrease during the last two years, but this is mainly due to the fact that during this period the date of the examination was changed, and new rules were introduced."§

Progress of Medical studies, in 1887 to 1892.

The progress of Medical studies during the five years 1886-87 to 1891-92 appears from the following Table:—

* *Progress of Education in India*, 1887-88 *to* 1891-92, by A. M. Nash, Esquire, M.A. (1893); p. 221.

† *Ib.*, p. 222. ‡ *Ib.*, p. 223. § *Ib.*, p. 223.

MEDICAL COLLEGES AND SCHOOLS, 1886-87 AND 1891-92.

Province.	1886-87.				1891-92.			
	Colleges.		Schools.		Colleges.		Schools.	
	Institutions.	Pupils.	Institutions.	Pupils.	Institutions.	Pupils.	Institutions.	Pupils.
Madras	1	138	4	204	1	157	3	347
Bombay	1	276	3	123	1	222	4	216
Bengal	1	172	9	793	1	255	9	1,035
North-Western Provinces and Oudh ...	...	...	1	125	...	...	2	212
Punjab	1	68	1	143	1	144	1	178
Central Provinces	...	...	...	...	...	...	...	...
Upper Burma	...	...	...	...	...	...	...	...
Lower Burma	...	...	...	...	...	...	...	...
Assam	...	...	...	...	...	...	...	...
Coorg	...	...	...	...	...	...	...	...
Hyderabad Assigned Districts ...	...	...	...	...	...	...	...	...
Total ...	4	654	18	1,388	4	778	19	1,988

Expenditure on Medical Education in 1887 and 1892.

The following Table* gives the total expenditure from different sources in each province on institutions for Medical Education, comparing the figures for 1886-87 with those for 1891-92:—

EXPENDITURE IN MEDICAL COLLEGES AND SCHOOLS, 1886-87 AND 1891-92.

Province.	1886-87.				1891-92.			
	Provincial Revenues.	Local and Municipal Funds.	Fees.	Total.	Provincial Revenues.	Local and Municipal Funds.	Fees.	Total.
	Rs.	Rs.	Rs.	Rs.	Rs.	Rs.	Rs.	Rs.
Madras	31,000	35,550	18,244	94,011	1,11,254	10,184	22,175	1,49,060
Bombay	31,774	...	22,742	56,545	33,886	1,497	21,911	59,483
Bengal	2,30,826	...	27,996	2,59,439	2,69,468	...	33,006	3,04,903
N.-W. P. and Oudh ...	14,822	...	...	14,822	21,162	...	...	24,126
Punjab	67,097	...	...	67,097	64,762	6,552	2,512	74,084
Total Rs. ...	3,75,519	35,550	68,982	4,91,914	5,00,532	18,233	79,604	6,11,656

* *Progress of Education in India*, 1887-88 to 1891-92. By A. M. Nash, Esquire, M.A. (1893), p. 228.

Medical Degrees and Licences, in 1887 to 1892.

The number of candidates who have obtained University Degrees or Licences in Medicine, during the period of five years ending in 1892, is shown in the following Table* :—

TOTAL PASSES IN FINAL MEDICAL EXAMINATIONS FROM 1887-88 TO 1891-92.

Universities.	M. D.		M. B.		L. M. S.	
	Men.	Women.	Men.	Women.	Men.	Women.
Madras	...	...	8	1	61	2
Bombay	2	...	...	...	130	3
Bengal	3	...	33	2	69	1
Punjab	...	...	3	...	38	2
Total ...	5	...	44	3	298	8

"The total number of medical graduates in Bengal is less than the sum of the numbers in the different columns, for many candidates appear at both the L. M. S. and M. B. Examinations. Taking the figures for 1886-87 and 1891-92, there is a decrease in the number of medical graduates in every province, the decrease is most marked in Bombay, where there were only 44 in 1891-92, against 60 in 1886-87. The degree of M. B. is not conferred by the Bombay University; and in the Punjab the first examination for this degree was held 1891."*

Statistics of Engineering Colleges in 1887 and 1892.

The following Table has been extracted from the Table given in paragraph 194 at page 275 of Mr. Nash's Report, and gives the usual Statistics of attendance in Engineering Colleges and Schools for the years 1886-87 and 1891-92.

ENGINEERING COLLEGES AND SCHOOLS, 1886-87 and 1891-92.

Province.	1886-87.				1891-92.			
	Engineering Colleges.		Engineering and Surveying Schools.		Engineering Colleges.		Engineering and Surveying Schools.	
	Institutions.	Pupils.	Institutions.	Pupils.	Institutions.	Pupils.	Institutions.	Pupils.
Madras	1	17	1	164	1	10	1	185
Bombay	1	153	1	11	1	50	1	14
Bengal	1	146	3	210	1	244	3	417
N.-W. P. and Oudh	1	158	...	...	1	180	...	...
Punjab	...	...	...	...	...	...	...	...
Central Provinces	...	...	...	...	...	...	1	11
Upper Burma	...	...	...	...	...	...	5	116
Lower Burma	...	...	9	231	...	...	12	295
Assam	...	...	...	...	...	...	1	4
Coorg	...	...	...	...	...	...	...	...
Hyderabad Assigned Districts ...	...	...	...	...	...	...	...	...
Total ...	4	474	14	616	4	484	24	1,042

* *Progress of Education in India*, 1887-88 to 1891-92. By A. M. Nash, Esquire, M.A. (1893), p. 229.

The figures in this Table show that during the five years concerned, there has not been any marked increase in the number of pupils in the Engineering Colleges, whilst the increase in the Schools has been considerable, having risen from 616 in 1887 to 1,042 in 1892.

CHAPTER XXVI.

BACKWARDNESS OF MUHAMMADANS IN ENGLISH EDUCATION.—MEASURES ADOPTED BY GOVERNMENT TO ENCOURAGE EDUCATION AMONG MUHAMMADANS IN 1871-73.—REFORMS IN THE CALCUTTA *MADRASSA* IN 1873.—IMPROVED APPLICATION OF THE MOHSIN ENDOWMENT AT HOOGHLY TO MUHAMMADAN EDUCATION IN BENGAL.—

Early opposition of Muhammadans to English Education.

The attitude of opposition to English education at its very outset taken up by the Muhammadan Community has already been shown* to have been evinced as early as 1835, when the Council of Education at Calcutta first inaugurated the policy of English education under the auspices of Lord William Bentinck, who under the advice of Lord Macaulay passed the celebrated Educational Resolution of the Government of India, dated the 7th March 1835, in favour of English education. The Indian Education Commission of 1882, dealt with the question of Muhammadan education in a separate section of their Report which begins with the following summary of the early efforts in the cause of Muhammadan education :—

Persistent apathy of the Muhammadans towards English Education—1792 to 1832.

"When in 1782 the Calcutta *Madrassa* was founded by Warren Hastings, it was designed 'to qualify the Muhammadans of Bengal for the public service ...... and to enable them to compete, on more equal terms, with the Hindus for employment under Government.' Some fifty years later, after the introduction of English into the course of studies, the Council of Education had to confess that 'the endeavour to impart a high order of English education' to the Muhammadan Community had completely failed. Forty years later again, 'the condition of the Muhammadan population of India, as regards education, had of late been frequently pressed upon the attention of the Government of India.' The Muhammadans were not even then competing on equal terms with the Hindus for employment under Government, nor had the endeavour to impart to them a high order of education been attended by any adequate success. Matters were, no doubt, in a more promising condition than in 1832, and, as regards the general spread of education, in a much more promising condition than in 1792. A considerable proportion of Muhammadans were learning English, a large proportion were in schools of one kind or another. But the higher English education was not cultivated, in any appreciable degree, more extensively than it had been in 1832.

Alleged causes of the backwardness of Muhammadans in English Education summarized by the Education Commission.

"What the causes were which deterred the Muhammadans from such cultivation was debated even among themselves. While some held that the absence of instruction in the tenets of their faith, and still more the injurious effects of English education in creating a disbelief in religion, were the main obstacles, others, though a small minority, were of opinion that religion had little to do with the question. Some contended that the system of education prevailing in Government Schools and Colleges corrupted the morals and manners of the pupils, and that for this reason the better classes would not subject their sons to dangerous contact. The small proportion of Muhammadan teachers in Government institutions; the unwillingness of Government educational officers to accept the counsel and co-operation of Muhammadans; numerous minor faults in the Departmental system, the comparatively small progress in real learning made by the pupils in Government Schools; the practice among the well-to-do Muhammadans of educating their children at home; the indolence and improvidence too common among them; their hereditary love of the profession of arms; the absence of friendly intercourse between Muhammadans and Englishmen; the unwillingness felt by the better born to associate with those lower in the social scale; the poverty nearly general among Muhammadans; the coldness of Government towards the race; the use in Government Schools of books whose tone was hostile or scornful towards the Muhammadan religion;—these and a variety of other causes have been

* *Vide ante*, p 53.

put forward at different times by members of the Muhammadan community to account for the scant appreciation which an English education has received at their hands. All such causes may have combined towards a general result, but a candid Muhammadan would probably admit that the most powerful factors are to be found in pride of race, a memory of by-gone superiority, religious fears, and a not unnatural attachment to the learning of Islam. But whatever the causes, the fact remained; though the enquiries made in 1871-73 went to prove that, except in the matter of the higher education, there had been a tendency to exaggerate the backwardness of the Muhammadans.

General Statistics of Muhammadan Education in 1871-72.

"The following Table shows the percentage of Muhammadans to the total population in the six more important Provinces of India and the percentage of Muhammadans under instruction in schools of which the Department had cognizance to the total number of all classes in such schools. In the former case the percentage is 22·8, in the latter 14·7. It must also be borne in mind that in 1870-71 there were among the 16,77,11,037 inhabitants of the six Provinces about four millions who belonged to the aboriginal tribes, or semi-Hinduised aborigines, and to other non-Aryans hardly touched by our education. Deducting these, and excluding Native States, the Musalmans form about 25 per cent. of the total population:—

STATISTICS OF EDUCATION AMONG MUHAMMADANS IN 1871-72.

Provinces.	Total Population.	Muhammadans.	Percentage.	At School.		
				Total.	Muhammadans.	Percentage.
Madras	31,281,177	1,872,214	6	123,689	5,531	4·4
Bombay	16,349,206	2,528,344	15·4	190,153	15,684	8·2
Bengal and Assam ...	60,467,724	19,553,420	32·3	196,086	28,411	14·4
N.-W. Provinces ...	30,781,204	4,188,751	13·5	162,619	28,990	17·8
Oudh	11,220,232	1,111,290	9·9	48,926	12,417	25·3
Punjab	17,611,498	9,102,488	51·6	68,144	23,783	34·9
Total ...	167,711,041	38,356,507	22·8	789,617	114,816	14·5

"It will be observed that in the North-Western Provinces, and to a much larger extent in Oudh, the proportion of Muhammadan school boys to the total number is greater than the proportion of Muhammadans in the population. In the other Provinces it is much less; the population percentage of the Muhammadans in these Provinces taken together, being over 26 and the school percentage under 10."*

Resolution of the Government of India, No. 300, dated 7th August, 1871, on Muhammadan Education.

The backward condition of education among Muhammadans attracted the attention of the Government of India under the Earl of Mayo, and its Resolution No. 300, dated Simla the 7th August, 1871, invited the attention of the various Local Governments and Administrations to the subject. The Resolution is an important document being the first of a series of measures adopted by the Government for the encouragement of education among the Muhammadans, and may be quoted here *in extenso*:—

Backwardness of education among Muhammadans deplorable. Muhammadan literature may be encouraged.

"The condition of the Muhammadan population of India as regards education has of late been frequently pressed upon the attention of the Government of India. From statistics recently submitted to the Governor-General in Council, it is evident that in no part of the country, except perhaps the North-Western Provinces and the Punjab, do the Muhammadans adequately, or in proportion to the rest of the community, avail themselves of the educational advantages that the Government offers. It is much to be regretted that so large and important a class, possessing a classical literature replete with works of profound learning and great value, and counting among its members a section especially devoted to the acquisition and diffusion of knowledge, should stand aloof from active co-operation with our educational system and should lose the advantages both material and social, which others enjoy. His Excellency in Council believes that secondary and higher education

* Report of the Indian Education Commission (1882); pp 483, 484.

conveyed in the vernaculars and rendered more accessible than now, coupled with a more systematic encouragement and recognition of Arabic and Persian literature, would be not only acceptable to the Muhammadan community but would enlist the sympathies of the more earnest and enlightened of its members on the side of education.

Muhammadan teachers of English to be appointed and Muhammadans encouraged by grants-in-aid to create schools and their vernacular literature.

"2. The Governor-General in Council is desirous that further encouragement should be given to the classical and vernacular languages of the Muhammadans in all Government Schools and Colleges. This need not involve any alterations in the subjects, but only in the media of instruction. In avowedly English Schools established in Muhammadan Districts, the appointment of qualified Muhammadan English teachers might, with advantage, be encouraged. As in Vernacular Schools, so in this class also, assistance might justly be given to Muhammadans by grants-in-aid to create schools of their own. Greater encouragement should also be given to the creation of a vernacular literature for the Muhammadans—a measure the importance of which was specially urged upon the Government of India by Her Majesty's Secretary of State on more than one occasion.

Indian Universities to encourage Arabic and Persian literature.

"3. His Excellency in Council desires to call the attention of Local Governments and Administrations to this subject, and directs that this Resolution be communicated to them and to the three Universities in India, with a view of eliciting their opinions whether, without infringing the fundamental principles of our educational system, some general measures in regard to Muhammadan education might not be adopted, and whether more encouragement might not be given in the University course to Arabic and Persian literature. The authorities of the Lahore University College, who are believed to have paid much attention to the subject, should also be invited to offer their views on the important questions above referred to. This may be done through the Punjab Government." *

The Resolution approved by the Secretary of State in his Despatch, No. 12, dated 14th December, 1871.

This Resolution was duly communicated to the Secretary of State, who concurred generally in the policy therein indicated, on the understanding, however, that as regards the encouragement of the languages of Muhammadans in the schools of the country, the Government of India did not contemplate any change in the subjects taught, but only in the mode of instruction.

Suggestions by the Government of India as to Muhammadan Education in 1871, summarized.

The suggestions made by the Government of India to the Local Governments in the above Resolution have been summarized by the Education Commission† of 1882, as follows:—

(1) That further encouragement should be given to the classical and vernacular languages of the Muhammadans in all Government Schools and Colleges;

(2) That in avowedly English schools established in Muhammadan districts, the appointment of qualified Muhammadan English teachers might, with advantage, be encouraged;

(3) That as in vernacular schools, so in avowedly English schools, assistance might justly be given to Muhammadans by grants-in-aid to create schools of their own;

(4) That greater encouragement should also be given to the creation of a vernacular literature for the Muhammadans.

Resolution of the Government of India, dated 13th June, 1873, on the condition of education among Muhammadans.

The reports received from the Local Governments and Administrations, in reply to this Resolution were reviewed by the Government of India (under the Earl of Northbrook), in a Resolution, dated 13th June, 1873, and as it is one of the most important documents connected with the progress of English education among Muhammadans, it may be quoted here *in extenso* for facility of reference especially as it is not easily accessible to the general reader:—

Recital of the Government of India's Resolution of 7th August, 1871, on Muhammadan Education.

"On the 7th August, 1871, the Government of India issued a Resolution upon the condition of the Muhammadan population of India as regards education, in which, after regretting that so large and important a class should stand aloof from co-operation with our educational system, His Excellency the Earl of Mayo in Council desired that more systematic encouragement should be given to the classical and vernacular languages of the Muhammadans in all schools and colleges. The Resolution was circulated to all Local Governments and Administrations for their opinion as to what measures should be adopted toward promoting this object, by modifying the methods and means through which teaching should be given, so as to make the higher branches of it more accessible to Muhammadans without altering the essential principles of our public instruction. Whether the creation of a vernacular literature might not be added by the State, and whether more ample

* Selections from the Records of the Government of India (Home Department), No. CCV. (1886); p. 152.

† *Vide* Report, p. 484.

recognition should not be given in the University Courses to Arabic and Persian, were matters on which advice and propositions were particularly invited.

State of Muhammadan Education reported upon.

"2. The reports now collected from all the Provinces of British India present a fair survey of the actual state of Muhammadan education throughout the Empire; and they discuss largely how far, and in what direction, should the further steps be taken which are most consistent with the needs of the people and the duties of the Government. It may be useful to describe in broad outline, the place now allotted to Muhammadan instruction in the educational scheme of each Government, and then to touch briefly on the measures proposed for improvement and advance.

Primary Education in the Vernacular languages affects growth of Secondary and Higher Education among Muhammadans who are accustomed to Hindustani or Urdu characters.

"3. In the Resolution of 1871, there is no direct mention of primary education. Its importance was not overlooked, but the needs and defects to be remedied appeared to press more urgently in the higher than in the lower gradations of State instruction. From the reports, however, which are now under review, there appears some ground for doubting whether many of the disadvantages under which Muhammadans have been placed as to higher education may not be traced down to their sources in the earlier stages of our system. As a matter of fact, it may be inferred generally that, wherever the ordinary vernacular of the country is read and written in the Hindustani or Urdu character, there the Muhammadans have occupied their proper position in the Primary and Secondary Schools founded or added by the State. In the North-Western Provinces, in Oudh, and in the Punjab, the attendance of Muhammadans in the lower and middle schools is, on the whole, rather above than below the proportion which all Muhammadans bear to the total population; in Oudh the Muhammadans furnish a much larger comparative contingent than the Hindus to the schools, though in the Punjab, out of a Muhammadan element of 53 per cent. on the total population, not more than 35 per cent. of the scholars are Muhammadans. Then in all these provinces the indigenous Muhammadan schools are very numerous, and thrive up to a certain point; they are encouraged and assisted by the Government Officers; the grants-in-aid are offered on conditions which suit Muhammadan schooling as well as any other, and the whole course of primary education is so shaped as to favour the Muhammadan at least equally with the Hindu. On the other hand, in Provinces where the Muhammadans are scatttered, and are not numerous, where they mostly talk a different language from that of the majority, or where their teaching, at any rate, is in a different tongue and according to entirely separate traditions, there the special arrangements which these circumstances require for them have been not always organized, and their claims to it have been often inevitably disregarded. Where the Muhammadan uses a form of the country dialect, as in Eastern Bengal and in parts of Bombay, he goes with others to the Primary Government schools for the rudiments of education; but where his mother-tongue is different, in speech and in written character, he cannot attend them. And the peculiar obstacles which keep him apart from our school system grow stronger as he emerges beyond those elements which are common to all teaching. In Bengal the Bengali-speaking Eastern Muhammadans frequent the lower schools in good number, but they found themselves more or less excluded from following out their education into the upper classes by the absence, up to 1871, of any adequate provision for that distinctive course of instruction which the customs of their society require. All over Western India, in part of the Central Provinces, in Berar, and very generally in Madras, the same difficulty had arisen, and had not been satisfactorily surmounted. The Government expenditure on education is necessarily limited, and could not suffice for the support of two separate classes of schools; the money available was naturally bestowed entirely upon those classes of the people which are homogeneous for educational purposes, are by far the more numerous, the richer, and the more eager to make use of the grant.

Backwardness of Muhammadans in higher Collegiate and University Education most remarkable. Unsuitability of the courses of instruction a possible cause; if so, it must be remedied.

"4. It is, however, in the higher Schools, in the Colleges, and in the Universities, that the absence or backwardness of Muhammadans has been shown to exist remarkably. The reports all agree that our system has not attracted them to the higher ranges of our educational course, or to persevere up to the point at which studies impress real culture, and fit young men for success in the services and open professions. How far this state of things can be attributed to the want of a connected scheme of courses of instruction suitable for Muhammadans, leading up through the lower to the higher standards, and how far to the general disinclination of Muhammadans to exchange their earlier modes of study for others more consonant with modern habits of thought, is a question which need not here be closely examined. It may be conjectured that, at the present epoch, Muhammadans are discovering that the ancient paths are unprofitable to stand upon, while their traditions and natural predilections still hold them back from setting out energetically upon newly opened roads. For, while it is confessed that Muhammadans nowhere appear in satisfactory strength upon the lists of our higher Schools, Colleges, or Universities, on the other hand those institutions which have purposely preserved the ancient exclusively Muhammadan type, and which have been restricted to instruction in the languages and sciences which belong peculiarly to Muhammadanism, have also been found to be falling gradually but steadily into neglect. We may perhaps assume, therefore, that the Muhammadans are not so much averse to the subjects which the English Government has decided to teach, as to the modes or machinery through which teaching is offered. And if it thus appear that to the traditions and reasonable hesitation which keep aloof our Muhammadan fellow-subjects are added certain obstacles which our system itself interposes,—either by using a language that is unfamiliar, or machinery that is uncongenial,—it is plain that many of the drawbacks to the universality of our educational system are susceptible of removal.

Endeavours to remedy Muhammadan educational backwardness gratifying.

"5. His Excellency in Council, therefore, perceives with gratification from the reports now before him, that judicious endeavours are being made to diminish, so far as they can be remedied, these inequalities in the distribution of State aid, and to place the Muhammadans, wherever this may be possible, upon a more even footing with the general community throughout the whole course of our public instruction.

Steps taken in Madras and Bombay for Muhammadan Schools and encouragement of Persian and Arabic.

"6. In Madras the Government has now directed the Department of Public Instruction to take steps without delay for establishing elementary Muhammadan schools, and corresponding classes in other schools, at the principal centres of the Muhammadan population, where instruction may be given in the Urdu language by qualified teachers through appropriate text-books. In the Madras University special recognition is already given to Arabic and Persian, and the question of awarding special prizes for proved excellence in those languages is under deliberation. As the Syndicate observe, this is a project in which leading Muhammadan gentlemen might be invited themselves to co-operate. From Bombay, the Director of Public Instruction reported in 1871, that he was engaged in settling a course of Persian instruction for the Upper Standards in Vernacular Schools, for English Schools, and for High Schools, which will be arranged so as to prepare for the study of Persian at the University, where Arabic and Persian are already admitted as classical languages for graduates in the Arts. In 1870, a Professor of Persian and Arabic was appointed to the Elphinstone College; and the Government, and the University now join in recommending to the Government of India the endowment of a University Professorship of Arabic and Persian, founding their proposition upon the great importance to Muhammadans in that Presidency of familiarity with the tongues of Western Asia. His Excellency in Council agrees that it may be advisable to establish such professorships, and any scheme for doing so, would be favourably entertained, especially if there were any prospect of aid from private sources to the endowment.

Measures being adopted in Bengal to restore Muhammadan education by aid of the Mohsin Endowments.

"7. In Bengal, the Lieutenant-Governor now desires to restore Muhammadan education by a well-connected and substantial reforming of existing material. Orders were issued in 1871 to establish special classes for teaching Arabic and Persian to Muhammadans in the ordinary schools, wherever the demand should justify the supply, and wherever the Muhammadans should agree to conform, in addition, to the regular course of study in the upper school classes, so that both kinds of instruction must be taken. The collegiate instruction in the Calcutta *Madrassa* will be remodelled and reinforced, while the Mohsin Endowments, which now support the Hooghly College, will be employed, wherever in Bengal their employment seems most advantageous, for encouraging and extending education among Muhammadans. Moreover, the University of Calcutta has decided to examine in Persian as well as in Arabic for the degrees.

System of State Instruction in the N.-W. Provinces and Oudh and in the Punjab, as favourable to Muhammadans as to Hindus. Attention to Muhammadan education in the Central Provinces, Mysore, Coorg and Berar.

"8. In the North-Western Provinces, in the Punjab, and in Oudh, the existing system of State Instruction is already at least as favourable to Muhammadans as to Hindus. At Lahore there is a University College, and the Muhamadans themselves share the unanimous opinion that no special educational privileges to their community are needed. From the North-Western Provinces it was reported that nothing more was needed to consummate the entire course of Muhammadan classics than the admission of Persian as a subject for the higher University Examinations, which has been done for all examinations up to the degree. And an important committee of Muhammadans at Benares are contemplating the establishment of an Anglo-Oriental College for the better diffusion of learning among their co-religionists. In Oudh, the Canning College embraces an ample Muhammadan curriculum. In the Central Provinces, in Mysore, in Coorg, and in Berar, the administration has directed that wherever the number of Muhammadans is sufficient to form a class, or fill a school, there a class or a school shall be established. His Excellency in Council assumes that in these as in all other provinces where Muhammadans are few, and often exposed to all the disadvantages which affect a religious minority without wealth or superior influence, it will be the special care of Government to satisfy themselves that these endeavours to encourage the education of Muhammadans are persistently maintained. It is the paramount duty of an imperial department thus to fill up gaps in the ranks of elementary education, and to range the various divisions of this vast population in one advancing line of even progress.

Principles on which Muhammadan Education should be encouraged by the State.

"9. As to the principles upon which the education of Muhammadans should be encourged by the State, His Excellency in Council need say little here, for they appear to be understood by all Administrations, and with general consent accepted by the people—by none more openly than by the leading Muhamadans of India. The State has only to apply its educational apparatus and aid so as they may best adjust themselves to existing languages and habits of thought among all classes of the people; without diverging from its set mark and final purpose—the better diffusion and advancement of real knowledge in India. His Excellency in Council is anxious that the atainment of this object shall in no class of the population be hindered by differences of language or of custom; and with this view the Government of India is very willing that the entire body of Muhammadan [as of Hindu] classic literature shall be admitted and take rank among the higher subjects of secular study, and that the languages shall form an important part of the examinations for University degrees. In short, His Excellency is prepared to listen favourably to any well-considered proposal for modifying or extending in these directions the existing educational system. One measure to which the Resolution of 1871 particularly adverted was the development of a Vernacular literature for Muhammadans—His Excellency in Council would be slow to believe that such a literature still needed creation. To this suggestion Local Governments attach differing degrees of importance or practicability and, on the whole, His Excellency in Council sees reason to believe that we must be cautious in attempting to proceed in this direction much beyond the point we have reached already. It is most desirable to frame a series of high class text-books to encourage the printing and publication of valuable Muhammadan works and to offer prizes either for good translations of foreign works or for original studies. But in regard to the patronage of what may be properly called literature, the exercise of it must necessarily be restricted by the pressing demands of general education upon our finance, and by the difficulty of making a fair selection, or of distributing any money available with due discrimination and indubitable advantage.

Local Governments to encourage Muhammadan Education according to local circumstances.

"10. His Excellency in Council has now reviewed rapidly the general measures which have been taken or are being taken, for the encouragement of education among Muhammadans. The papers before him, received from all parts of British India, show that the Earl of Mayo's Resolution has succeeded in its main purpose of drawing the attention of all Administrations to needs and obligations which before had, perhaps, not everywhere been adequately realized. These needs and obligations may now be entrusted with confidence to the care of local Governments. The Supreme Government has satisfied itself that the principles upon which Muhammadan education should be supported or subsidised are clearly understood; while the conditions and rate of progress in this as in all branches of public instruction, the range of its operations, and all other practical details, depend chiefly in each Province upon local circumstances, adminstrative skill, and financial resources." *

This Resolution together with the earlier Resolution of the Government of India, No. 300, dated the 7th August, 1871, which has already been quoted † form the most important declaration of the policy of the Government towards the education of the Muhammadans.

Summary purport of the Government of India's Resolution on Muhammadan Education, dated 13th June, 1873.

The purport of the above Resolution which was issued by His Excellency the Earl of Northbrook in Council, may be stated to be, "that generally wherever the ordinary vernacular of the country was read and written in the Hindustani or Urdu character, there the Muhammadans occupied their proper position in the primary and secondary schools founded or aided by the State. In all provinces where this was the case, the indigenous Muhammadan schools were numerous, and up to a certain point in a thriving condition. They were encouraged and assisted by the Government officers; the grants-in-aid were offered on condition on the whole fairly suitable for Muhammadan requirements; and the course of primary education was so shaped as to favour the Muhammadan at least equally with the Hindu. On the other hand in provinces where the Muhammadans were scattered and not numerous, where they mostly spoke a different language from that of the majority of the population, or where their teaching was in a different tongue and according to entirely separate traditions, there the special arrangements requisite to meet these circumstances had not always been organised, and the claims of the Mussalman community had been often almost inevitably disregarded. Where the Muhammadan

* Selections from the Records of the Government of India (Home Department), No. CCV. (1886); pp. 226, 229.

† *Vide* p. *ante*.

used a form of the country dialect, he attended with others the primary Government schools for the rudiments of education; but where his mother-tongue was different in speech and in written character, he was naturally precluded from availing himself of this teaching. The peculiar obstacles which kept him apart from the ordinary school system naturally grew stronger as he emerged beyond those elements which are common to all teaching. The difficulties which had arisen from these causes had nowhere been satisfactorily surmounted. The Government expenditure on education being necessarily limited, and insufficient for the support of two separate classes of schools, the money available was naturally bestowed too exclusively upon those classes that not only formed the more numerous section of the people, but were both homogeneous for educational purposes and more eager to make use of the grant. It was however in the colleges, higher schools, and universities that the absence or backwardness of Muhammadans was most conspicuous. The reports all agreed that the existing system had not attracted them to the higher ranges of the educational course, or induced them to persevere up to the point at which studies impress real culture and fit young men for success in the services and open professions. * * * * * The Resolution then proceeded to notice in general terms the measures adopted in the several Provinces to give effect to the views of the Supreme Government. * * * * The Governor-General in Council assumed that in all Provinces where Muhammadans were few, and often exposed to all the disadvantages which affect a religious minority without wealth or superior influence, it would be the special care of Government to satisfy themselves that these endeavours to encourage the education of Muhammadans would be persistently maintained. It was recognised as the paramount duty of an Imperial Department thus to fill up the gaps in the ranks of elementary education, and to range the various divisions of the vast population in one advancing line of even progress." *

Reforms in the Calcutta *Madrassa* in 1871-73.

About this time a separate correspondence was being carried on with the Government of Bengal on the subject of the management of the Calcutta *Madrassa*, established by Warren Hastings in 1780, and with reference to the status and conditions of the *Madrassa* and College at Hooghly supported out of an endowment bequeathed in 1806 by Mahommed Mohsin in trust for "pious uses." In connection with these Mohsin funds, not only had large accumulations to the credit of the trust been permitted to accrue, but the funds had been in part appropriated to the benefit of a wholly different class from that for which the endowment was destined. The Government of India, accordingly desired that the whole subject of the application of the funds in promotion of Muhammadan education should be fully reconsidered and plans matured for their disbursement more in consonance with the intentions of Mahommed Mohsin. The Government of Bengal, in its letter dated the 17th August, 1872, in submitting to the Government of India the views of the Lieutenant-Governor in regard to the general measures to be taken for the promotion of Muhammadan education in Bengal, put forward certain suggestions as to the utilisation of these funds. It proposed to reform the Calcutta and the Hooghly *Madrassa*, and to take upon itself the cost of the non-Musalman side of the Hooghly College, hitherto entirely supported from the Mohsin funds, but at the same time to accept from the funds a fair contribution for the *Madrassa* attached to the College and for special benefits to Muhammadan students studying in the College. As, in the opinion of the Lieutenant-Governor (Sir George Campbell), it would be difficult to justify the devotion of provincial funds to special Muhammadan education in the province generally, while the Mohsin endowment supplied a legitimate means of effecting the purpose in view, the Government of Bengal further expressed its intention to devote the money thus saved from the Hooghly College to aid and extend Muhammadan education elsewhere. Proposals for the establishment of new *Madrassas* at Dacca and other local centres in Eastern and Northern Bengal were then explained in detail; but as the Mohsin funds would not be adequate to enable the Government to equip efficiently these new *Madrassas*, the Lieutenant-Governor trusted that the Government of India would contribute to make up the difference. The main questions left for the decision of the Government of India were (1) whether the Government of India approved of the proposed distribution of the Mohsin funds and of the establishment of *Madrassas*; and (2) whether the Government of India would give some special aid towards the establishment of *Madrassas* in Eastern and Northern Bengal.

In reply the Government of India, on 13th June, 1873, wrote to the Government of Bengal as follows:—

Views of the Government of India upon the subject—13th June, 1873.

"The general principles upon which the Lieutenant-Governor desires to see these institutions † administered and directed for the better promotion of high Muhammadan education appear to the Government of India to be sound, and the obstacles to working upon them are not practically insurmountable. * * * It is agreed, by common consent, that the intention of the British Government in supporting these institutions is to give to Muhammadans their full share of high-class intellectual training and of sound knowledge useful to them in life, combined but not

* Resolution of the Government of India in the Home Department (*Education*), No. $\frac{7}{215\text{-}25}$, dated 15th July, 1885.

† Calcutta and Hooghly *Madrassas*.

clashing with that Oriental erudition which belongs to their race and country. And it is also agreed that, in shaping our methods towards these ends, we are bound to avoid, so far as may be possible, any unwelcome abandonment of the old ways of Muhammadan study, or any slight upon the classic learning of Muhammadan Asia. On the contrary, the importance to Muhammadans of such studies is admitted, and their intrinsic value as instruments of literary training in this country is not under-rated.

"But the point of difficulty is also recognised by all to whom the subject is familiar. It lies in the problem of framing for Muhammadans a course of secular education, which is the only kind that can be given in Government institutions, upon the study of a literature which on so many sides of it is intimately connected with their religion and doctrinal tenets.

"His Excellency in Council, nevertheless, believes that the problem thus presented is capable of solution; that a course of study can be laid down which shall maintain and encourage the cultivation of Arabic and Persian, of the history, literature, and philosophy which these languages convey, of their logical system, and of such parts of Muhammadan law as deal with purely temporal interests, without compromising the Government to the support of any peculiar school of religious teaching.

"His Excellency in Council is willing to sanction the preliminaries of any plan for re-constituting the two *Madrassas*, which may fall within the limits of these principles." *

After referring with approval to the details of the proposals regarding the re-organisation of the *Madrassas*, the Government of India continued with reference to the Hooghly institution :—

Application of the Mohsin Funds towards Muhammadan Education in general in Bengal.

"The Lieutenant-Governor's proposition is to withdraw the greater part of the Mohsin Funds from the Hooghly College, which has no particular local claim, and to use the money for encouraging Muhammadan education elsewhere, apportioning it according to need. So much of the present cost of the Hooghly College as would be left unprovided for by this subtraction of the endowment funds might, His Honour suggests, be then defrayed by the State.

"His Excellency in Council approves the outlines of this proposal, and considers that some such arrangement would be consistent with the purposes of the Mohsin endowment, and generally advantageous to Muhammadan education. But, with regard to the employment of the Mohsin funds thus to be set free, His Excellency remarks that there are such valid objections to any separate system of denominational schools or colleges that the Government of India prefers not to move further in that direction, although there is no intention of disturbing what may already exist. His Excellency in Council thinks that the memorandum of Mr. Bernard, and the Lieutenant-Governor's observations upon it, suggest the alternative of strengthening certain selected Government institutions on their Muhammadan side, instead of setting up new ones. For instance, the high schools or colleges at Chittagong and Dacca, in the midst of a great Muhammadan population, might be thus re-inforced both in the way of teaching Arabic and Persian more thoroughly, and of generally cheapening education to Muhammadans by scholarships and the like. Or a portion of the Mohsin Funds might go toward increasing the public grants-in-aid of Muhammadan schools and colleges." †

The details of any scheme which might be worked out upon this design were left in the hands of the Bengal Government. As to the request for Imperial aid, the Government of India consented, chiefly in view of Sir George Campbell's scheme for encouraging Muhammadan education, to increase the regular provincial assignment by an annual additional grant of Rs. 50,000.

On the 29th July 1873, the Government of Bengal forwarded for the information of the Government of India, a copy of a Resolution recorded by the Lieutenant-Governor explaining the measures which Sir George Campbell had adopted consequent on the instructions of the Government of India set forth above and the additional assignment of Rs. 50,000. The measures proposed included a liberal scheme of scholarships for Muhammadan youths attending colleges and zilla schools, especially for those lads who should elect to pursue the ordinary English course of study and to read physical science.

Sir George Campbell's Resolution regarding measures adopted for Muhammadan Education, 29th July, 1873.

These proceedings were reported to the Secretary of State in the despatches marginally noted, ‡ and His Lordship on 13th November 1873, replied as follows :—

Approval by the Secretary of State of the abovementioned measures, 13th November, 1873.

"I fully concur in the views stated in the elaborate Resolutions recorded by Your Excellency in Council, under date of June the 30th, and observe with much gratification that throughout India efforts are being made with great

* Selections from the Records of the Government of India (Home Department), No. CCV. (1886); pp. 229, 230. † *Ib.*, p. 230.

‡ Despatch from Home Department, No. 5, dated the 30th June, 1873.
Despatch from Financial Department, No. 295, dated the 21st July, 1873.
Despatch from Home Department, No. 6, dated the 1st September, 1873.

judgment and earnestness to induce the Muhammadans to partake of the many benefits of our educational system.

"I approve of the proceedings of Your Excellency in Council in relation to Muhammadan education in Bengal.

"Your Lordship in Council is fully aware of the many and peculiar difficulties which surround the subject, and has issued some very judicious and discriminating instructions to the Government of Bengal. I approve of the additional assignment of Rs. 50,000 which you have granted to that Government.

"With your Despatch of the 1st of September, you have transmitted to me a letter from the Lieutenant-Governor of Bengal explanatory of the measures which he has adopted consequent on your instructions and the additional assignment. The arrangements of the Lieutenant-Governor indicate a very careful disposition of the means placed at his disposal, and an intelligent appreciation of the great importance of the whole subject.

"I cannot conclude without an expression of my cordial satisfaction with the careful and complete manner in which Your Excellency has dealt with a question surrounded with so many difficulties, and so intimately connected with the best interests of a very large and influential portion of Her Majesty's subjects in India."*

CHAPTER XXVII.

MEASURES ADOPTED BY THE VARIOUS LOCAL GOVERNMENTS AS TO MUHAMMADAN EDUCATION UNDER THE GOVERNMENT OF INDIA'S RESOLUTION OF 1871, AS STATED IN THE REPORT OF THE EDUCATION COMMISSION OF 1882.

The measures adopted by the various Local Governments in consequence of the abovementioned Resolution of the Earl of Mayo's Government in 1871, are very fully discussed in the Report of the Education Commission, with reference to the statistics of the year 1881-82. The facts of each of the principal provinces have been separately stated and their results have also been indicated; but since they are contained in a very bulky folio volume not accessible to the general reader, the following paragraphs may be extracted from it, one of the main objects of this work being to supply and preserve accurate and full information regarding the progress of English education among the Muhammadans, not only for the present but also for the purposes of facilitating reference in discussing measures for the future advancement of English education among that community.

Measures taken in Madras for Muhammadan Education under the Government of India's Resolution No. 300, dated 7th August 1871.

"Upon the receipt of the Resolution of the Government of India, the Government of Madras invited the Syndicate of the University to consider whether any steps could be taken by it which would be likely to attract a larger number of Muhammadan undergraduates. In its reply the Syndicate expressed an opinion that 'the regulation of the University should not be modified with the view of encouraging a particular section of the population, but that the Musalmans should be treated in precisely the same manner as all other inhabitants of the Madras Presidency,' .... and while deploring the undoubted fact of the Muhammadans being behind the Hindus as regards educational progress, they did not see that any steps could be taken by the University to modify this state of things. The view taken by the Director of Public Instruction was not more encouraging. He considered that the Department had done all that it could for Muhammadan education, and pointed out that a special concession had been made to Musalman students by exempting them from the new regulations regarding fees. The Government of Madras was, however, convinced that the existing scheme of instruction was framed with too exclusive reference to the requirements of Hindu students, and that Muhammadans were placed at so great a disadvantage that the wonder was, not that the Muhammadan element in the schools was so small, but that it existed at all. The Governor in Council, therefore, issued orders that the Director should, without delay, 'take steps with a view to the establishment of elementary schools at Arcot and Ellore, and corresponding classes in the existing schools at the principal centres of the Muhammadan population, such as Trichinopoly, Cuddapah, Kurnool, and perhaps Mangalore, in

* Selections from the Records of the Government of India (Home Department), No. CCV. (1886); pp. 235, 236.

which instruction will be given in the Hindustani language, and Muhammadan boys may thus acquire such a knowledge of the English language and of the elementary branches of instruction as will qualify them for admission into the higher classes of the Zillah and Provincial schools and other similar institutions.'......Arrangements were also, without loss of time, to be made for the training of Muhammadan teachers; and instruction in Persian was to be provided in any high school in which there was a sufficient number of Muhammadan students.

Results of measures for Muhammadan Education taken in Madras.

"Coming to the year 1880-81, we find that the measures taken during the interval and the results obtained were as follows: The special schools maintained by Government were 11 in number, 7 of them being Anglo-vernacular middle schools, and 4 Anglo-vernacular primary schools. Nine schools, Anglo-vernacular or vernacular, were maintained by Municipalities, and of aided schools with a special provision for Musalman pupils, there were 4 Anglo-vernacular, and 210 vernacular. Other inducements had also been held out to Musalman students. They were admitted in all schools upon payment of half the usual fees, seven scholarships were specially reserved for Musalman candidates at the University examinations; a special Deputy Inspector of Musalman schools had been appointed; an elementary Normal school had been established at Madras; and the University of Madras still continued to allot to the Arabic and Persian languages at its examinations a maximum of marks considerably larger than that carried by vernacular languages. The combined results of these measures were eminently satisfactory. In place of the 5,531 Musalmans at school in 1870-71; the returns for 1880-81 give 22,075, or 6·7 per cent. of the total number under instruction, while the percentage of Musalmans to the total population of the Presidency is only 6 per cent. The proportion of boys at school to those of a school-going age is for Muhammadans 15·1, for Hindus 13·7. But it is not in numbers only that progress has been made. Taking the results of the middle school examinations we find that the percentage of passed candidates to those examined was, for Brahmans 44, for Hindus not Brahmans, 35, for Muhammadans 41. In the lower University examinations, taking only the percentage of successful candidates to those examined, the results for 1880-81 are equally satisfactory, as the following Table will show:—

Race.	Entrance.			First Arts.		
	Examined.	Passed.	Percentage of passed to examined.	Examined.	Passed.	Percentage of passed to examined.
Brahmans	2,150	670	31·2	486	295	60·7
Hindus not Brahmans ...	1,066	290	27·2	173	86	49·7
Musalmans	71	19	26·8	10	6	60·0

In the Entrance examination, the percentage for Hindus other than Brahmans and for Musalmans is thus practically the same. It must be remembered, however, that the proportion of students to population is about three times as great for Hindus (including Brahmans) as for Musalmans. In the latter case, the percentage of passed candidates is even more favourable to the Musalmans; but the proportion of candidates to population is five times as great for Hindus (including Brahmans) as for Musalmans. Of college education, beyond the first examination in Arts, Muhammadans, speaking generally, do not avail themselves at all, though there is no reason to suppose that the general system of education beyond that standard is not as well suited to the Muhammadans as that below it. The attendance of Musalmans in the various institutions, Government aided, and unaided, as compared with the total attendance, was in 1881-82 as follows:—

Class of Institutions.	Total number of Students.	Musalmans.	Percentage.
Colleges, English	1,669	30	1·7
" Oriental	38	...	...
High Schools, English	4,836	117	2·4
Middle " "	18,553	723	3·8
" " Vernacular	511	2	·4
Primary " English	63,295	4,973	7·8
" " Vernacular	276,983	19,232	6·9
High " English, Girls'	2	...	...
Middle " " "	190	...	...
" " Vernacular, Girls'	197	1	·5
Primary " English "	1,897	...	...
" " Vernacular "	18,468	427	2·3
Normal Schools for Masters	799	42	5·2
" " Mistresses	157	...	...
Total ...	387,595	25,547	6·5

Measures for Muhammadan Education taken in Bombay.

"Though the Musalmans in the Bombay Presidency are reckoned in the census of 1872 at 2,528,344, or 15·4 per cent. of a total population of 16,349,206, no less than 1,354,781 belong to Sind alone. Excluding that Division the percentage falls to 7·1. Of the total number at school, 15,684, or 8·2 per cent., were Musalmans. As in Madras, therefore, the circumstances which called forth the Resolution of the Government of India existed only on a small scale. Sind, no doubt, was in a very backward state, and the feelings of the Musalman community there were strongly against the study of English. Out of a population of 1,354,781, only 10,115 were in schools known to the Department, and of that number, only 3,225, or 31·8 per cent. of the total number at school, were Musalmans, though their proportion to the rest of the inhabitants was as four to one. Looking at the Presidency as a whole, the indifference of the Musalmans was not so much to education generally as to education in its higher branches. This fact had already engaged the attention of the Department; and enquiries which were set on foot some two years before the issue of the Resolution of the Government of India showed that in the Government colleges and English schools of a total of 16,224, the Musalmans numbered 1,499 only. The distribution was as follows:—

In colleges	14
" high schools	59
" middle schools	1,426
Total ...	1,499

'Here,' the Director of Public Instruction remarks, 'is the weak point. The Muhammadans avail themselves of our lower schools, but do not rise to the higher schools and colleges. In the list of University graduates there are one Musalman M.A., and two B.A.'s. I think that the reason is to be found not in the poverty of the Muhammadan community (for beggar Brahmans abound in the high school), but in their poverty and depressed social status combined. In this matter the Brahman and Musalman are at opposite poles. Thus we have in Gujarat 10 Brahmans in the colleges and 20 in the high schools for every Musalman, but only 3 Brahmans for every Musalman in the middle class, and not 2 for every Musalman in the lower class schools.' In the Government institutions generally the disproportion of Musalmans to the total number at school was much less than in those aided and inspected. Thus out of 161,283 students in the former, 14,629, or 9·1 per cent., were Musalmans, while the latter had but 968, or 5·2 per cent., of a total of 16,443. The measures taken by the Director, Mr. Peile, to remedy the state of things which his enquiries revealed had reference alike to the higher and the lower grades of education. The University having placed Persian on the list of languages in which examination is held for its degrees, sanction was obtained to the appointment of a Professor of Persian and Arabic in the Elphinstone College, where up to that time it had been impossible, for want of a competent teacher, that those languages should be studied in a scholarly manner. Persian teachers were also appointed in the Elphinstone and Surat High Schools. By the provision of stipends and teachers for Musalmans in the vernacular training college, the foundation was laid of a supply of qualified teachers in vernacular and Musalman schools. In regard to lower education, Mr. Peile pressed upon the Government the necessity of imposing town school-rates for class wants, since the rates then administered by the Education Department belonged almost exclusively to the villages, and the share of the public grant for vernacular education which belonged to the towns was too small to admit of adequate provision for such wants. His representations, though the imposition of these rates was not conceded, at all events secured to Musalman schools a fair share of the vernacular grant. Mr. Peile also drew up a course of Persian instruction for the upper standards in vernacular schools, and for English and High schools. This course was graduated from the beginning up to the matriculation standard, and so arranged as to prepare for the study of Persian as a classic in the Arts Colleges. Later on the number of special Musalman schools was considerably increased, and Musalman Deputy Inspectors were appointed to inspect them. 'But the most promising feature in connection with the progress of Musalman education during the past decade' [1871 to 1881] 'has been the formation and recognition of a Society known as the Anjuman-i-Islam, which it is hoped will in time establish a net-work of secular schools in Bombay. This Society is so important that it was felt advisable to make special rules for its assistance. At present it receives a fixed subsidy of Rs. 500 a month from Government. By the end of the year 1880-81 the Society's first school was fairly started. Its Hindustani and Anglo-Hindustani Departments, together with a large class of children reading the Kuran, contained in all 102 pupils. Since then the operations of the Society have been extended.' *

Results of measures for Muhammadan Education in Bombay.

"In 1871-72 the number of Musalmans at school, according to Mr. Peile's estimate, was 15,577, or about 8·7 per cent. of the total number at school; in 1881-82 the number had risen to 41,548, or 11·7 per cent. of the total number at school. There were also in the latter year 22,284 Muhammadan children in indigenous schools, which would raise the percentage to 14·7. The distribution was as follows :—

Class of Institution.	Total number of Students.	Musalmans.	Percentage.
Colleges, English	475	7	1·4
High Schools, English	5,731	118	2·0
Middle " "	14,257	781	5·4
Primary " Vernacular	312,771	39,231	12·5
Middle " English Girls'	555	2	·3
Primary " Vernacular "	19,917	1,366	6·8
Normal Schools for Masters	480	42	8·7
" " Mistresses	73	1	1·3
Unaided Indigenous Schools	78,755	22,284	28·2
Total	433,014	63,832	14·7

* Bombay Provincial Report, page 55.

Measures for Muhammadan Education taken in Bengal.

"The following Table shows the proportion of Musalmans to Hindus and others in those colleges and schools of Bengal and Assam which in 1871 furnished returns to the Department:—

	Hindus.	Musalmans.	Others.	Total
Schools	149,717	28,096	15,489	193,302
Arts Colleges	1,199	52	36	1,287
TOTAL ...	150,916	28,148	15,525	194,589

"Thus, while the Musalmans of Bengal were 32·3 per cent. of the total population, their proportion to the total number in schools known to the Department was only 14·4 per cent. 'This result,' remarks the Director in his Report for 1871-72, 'shows that the education of Musalmans demands much careful attention. They have fallen behind the time, and require still the inducements held out forty years ago to the whole community, but of which the Hindus only availed themselves. Such, however, has been the progress of education and the influence of the grant-in-aid system in promoting self-help, that the encouragement which was then considered just and right would now be called downright bribery; still unless the strong inducements in general use forty years ago are held out to Musalmans now, I have little hope of seeing them drawn to our schools.' But if the number of Musalmans in the schools generally was greatly out of proportion to the total number in the Presidency, still more conspicuous was the disproportion in the colleges, where out of 1,287 students only 52, or 4·04 per cent., belonged to that race. In regard to University distinctions, the Director remarks:—'During the last five years, out of 3,499 candidates who passed the Entrance Examination from these Provinces, 132, or 3·8 per cent. only, were Musalmans. They ought to have been ten-fold more numerous. Out of 900 passed for the First Arts in the same period, Musalmans gained only 11, or 1·2 per cent., and out of 429 passes for the B.A., they gained only 5, or 1·1 per cent. Hence, not only the number of Musalmans who pass the Entrance is less than one-tenth what it ought to be, but this painful inferiority steadily increases in the Higher Examinations. Taking the candidates generally, out of every 100 who pass the Entrance, 26 go on and pass the First Arts, and 12 pass the B.A.; but of every 100 Musalmans who pass the Entrance, only 8 pass the First Arts and 3 the B.A.' Various causes, some general and some particular, were assigned by the officers consulted as the obstacles which had barred the progress of education, both higher and lower. Among the general causes assigned by them were the apathy of the Musalman race, their pride, their religious exclusiveness, the love of their own literature among those of them who cared for any education at all, the idea so persistently held that education ought to be a free gift. Among the particular causes, a want of sympathy between Hindu teachers and Musalman pupils, a want of consideration in the arrangements of the Education Department, and, perhaps above all, the depressed condition of the bulk of Bengali-Musalmans, Musalmans in the first instance by conversion only and not by descent. In different degrees of efficiency and with varying influence according to locality, these causes combined to account for the backwardness of the race. Many of them were of course beyond any immediate removal. Others were a matter of administration, and with these the Government of Bengal promptly endeavoured to deal.

The Mohsin Endowment at Hooghly applied to English Education among Muhammadans in Bengal.

"On the question of establishing special schools for Musalmans, the almost unanimous opinion of those consulted was that, with the schools already in existence, there was no sufficient justification for expending State funds in this direction. The vernacular of the mass of Musalmans in Bengal was known to be Bengali, and the ordinary *pathsalas* of the country were held to supply the proper means of elementary education. Schools of all classes might be made more attractive by increasing the number of Musalmans throughout the various grades of the Department in Musalman districts; and especially by encouraging Musalmans to qualify themselves for the profession of teaching by a course of training in the Normal schools. In all Zilla schools it was decided that Urdu and Arabic or Persian should be taught up to the standard of the Entrance Examination; and, as a special concession, wherever there was a sufficient demand to justify the supply, there was to be a special class to teach Arabic and Persian after the Musalman fashion. The Persian language had recently been included by the University among the subjects for the F.A. and B.A. Examinations, and this it was expected would have a powerful effect in increasing the number of college students. A new Code of grant-in-aid rules was about to be drawn up, and advantage would be taken of this to offer specially liberal terms to schools managed by Musalmans.

These measures for the most part had reference only to lower education. In respect to the higher, the Musalmans of Bengal had a special grievance in the appropriation to English education of a certain endowment originally assigned to the promotion of oriental (Arabic and Persian) learning. Of that endowment, known as the Mahomed Mohsin Trust, some account has already been given in Chapter VI.* To remove all cause for complaint, the Lieutenant-Governor at the instance of the Supreme Government, which added a sum of Rs. 50,000 for that purpose to the Provincial assignment for education, declared that the maintenance of the English side of that College should be a charge upon the Provincial funds. It was also decided to devote a portion of the endowment to the oriental side, or *Madrassa*, and the remainder to the foundation of three new *Madrassas*, to the establishment of scholarships, and towards the payment of the fee of Musalman students in English colleges and schools. The three *Madrassas* were established at Dacca, Rajshahye, and Chittagong; and each was placed under an Arabic scholar of repute, assisted by a competent staff of Maulavis. It was intended that in each of them the full course of the Calcutta *Madrassa* should in time be taught; English was to be added to the course wherever the pupils showed a desire to learn that language, and at Dacca a teacher of English was at once appointed. To the payment of scholarships tenable by Musalmans in *Madrassas* or in English colleges and schools, there was allotted the sum of Rs. 9,000, while Rs. 18,000 went to the payment of two-thirds of the fees of Muhammadan pupils in Government colleges and schools outside Calcutta, and also to the payment of Maulavis in these schools. At the same time the Calcutta *Madrassa* was thoroughly re-organised, arrangements were made for the more thorough teaching of the Arabic and Persian languages with a reasonable amount of Muhammadan law; and the salary of the European Principal was raised to Rs. 1,000 a month. A description of the character and status of this *Madrassa* has been given elsewhere, and it is therefore unnecessary to enter into particulars here. A few years later, a proposal was made to connect the *maktabs* throughout Bengal with the institutions for higher Muhammadan Education in Calcutta and the Mofussil. The attempt, however, was not successful, and it was abandoned in favour of an opposite policy, which was expressed in the hope that the *maktabs* might be 'gradually moulded into true primary schools.' Accepting the indigenous schools of the country in the form in which, under the special conditions of locality, they were most popular, the Bengal system endeavoured by the promise of Government support to introduce into the traditional course of study certain subjects of instruction which should bring the schools so aided into some relation, more or less close, with the general system of education in the Province. The object being to encourage natural and spontaneous movement, it followed that if in any locality the existing system had a religious basis, the religious character of the school should be no bar to its receiving aid, provided that it introduced a certain amount of secular instruction into the course. Many hundreds of *maktabs* have in this way been admitted into the primary system of Bengal.

* The following is a fuller account:—"In the year 1806, a Muhammadan gentleman of the *Shia* sect died, leaving an estate yielding Rs. 45,000 per annum and called Saidpur, in the Hugli district, in trust for 'pious uses.' The deed of trust appointed two trustees, to each of whom a share of the proceeds, amounting to one-ninth, was assigned. Three shares of the same proportion were assigned to certain specific objects, *viz.*, the performance of certain religious rites and ceremonies, the repair of an *Imambarah* or place of worship, &c., and the remaining four-ninths were dedicated to the maintenance of certain establishments and payment of pensions. Up to 1810 the estate remained in the hands of the trustees appointed under the deed; but in that year they were accused of malversation, and, after protracted litigation, were dismissed in 1816. The Government then constituted itself a trustee, and assumed the management of the estate and the superintendence of the disbursements in conjunction with another trustee appointed by itself. In 1817, the estate was farmed out in *putnee*, that is, settled in perpetuity at fixed rates with the tenants. The amounts received from these tenants as consideration for the *putnee* settlement, with the arrears which had accumulated during litigation and the one-ninth share drawn by Government as a trustee, were in 1835 devoted to the building and endowment of an institution at Hugli, comprising an English Department, costing Rs. 1,780 per mensem, and an Oriental Department costing Rs. 1,295 per mensem. This appropriation of the trust funds was at the time justified on the ground that the maintenance of an educational institution was a 'pious use,' and so within the testator's intentions.

"The college was opened on the 1st August, 1836, and within three days counted 1,200 pupils in the English, and 300 in the Oriental Department; the proportion of Muhammadans to Hindus being 31 to 948 in the former, and 138 to 81 in the latter. The reports for 1836, and the few following years, contain a full account of the progress of this institution, but nowhere does it appear to have been sufficiently borne in mind, that the interpretation placed on the declared intentions of the founder was only applicable to Muhammadan education. And in this spirit the College has been maintained as it was founded, the last report showing that of 664 students on the rolls only 167 are Muhammadans; the numbers in the Law Department, the Collegiate School, and the Branch School being 5 Muhammadans to a class of 65, 87 to 393, and no Muhammadans to a class of 246, respectively. This result, like that of the Delhi College, has long been a grievance to the Musalman community, and during the current year special enquiry has been made to remedy it. But it is only fair to remember that the Oriental Department, as constituted in 1836, was quite adequate for the number of students who came forward to avail themselves of it, and that the Committee of Public Instruction would certainly have enlarged this Department, had the demand for the kind of education it offered increased." (*Education in British India prior to 1854*, by Arthur Howell, Esq., 1872; p. 41.)

Results of measures for Muhammadan Education in Bengal.

"The results of the measures taken at this time are shown, to some extent, by the very considerable increase in the number of Musalmans under instruction in 1881-82. Including the *Madrassas*, in which there were about 1,000 students, the number then stood as follows:—

CLASS OF INSTITUTIONS.	Total number.	Number of Musalmans.	Percentage.
Colleges, English	2,738	106	3·8
Colleges, Oriental	1,089	1,088	99·90
High Schools, „	43,747	3,831	8·7
Middle „	37,959	5,032	13·2
Ditto „ Vernacular	56,441	7,735	13·7
Primary „ „ Boys'	880,937	217,216	24·6
High Schools, Girls', English	184	...	...
Middle „ „	340	4	1·1
Ditto „ Vernacular	527	6	1·1
Primary „ ditto	17,452	1,570	8·9
Normal Schools for Masters	1,007	55	5·5
„ „ Mistresses	41	...	...
Private Uninspected Schools	57,305	25,244	44·0
TOTAL ...	1,099,767	261,887	23·8

"The last column is important as showing how rapidly the proportion of Musalman students falls in schools of the higher classes. The proportion in colleges is, indeed, even smaller now than it was in 1871 when, as previously stated, 4·04 per cent. were Musalmans. Still, owing to the ready way in which Musalmans have accepted the primary system of instruction there is a very satisfactory increase in the total number of pupils of that race, which has risen from 28,148 in 1871 to 262,108 (including students in technical schools and colleges) in 1882; the proportion of Musalmans being now 23·8 per cent. against 14·4 in 1871. In each of the *Madrassas* of Hugli, Dacca, Rajshahye and Chittagong the full Arabic course of the Calcutta *Madrassa* is taught, and in each also instruction in English is given to all pupils who wish it. In the Dacca *Madrassa* the course in English is carried up to the Entrance standard. Of 1,089 pupils in the six *Madrassas*, as many as 322 learn English. The privilege of reading at one-third of the ordinary fees has also, by recent orders of the Government of Bengal, been extended to Muhammadan students of any college in Calcutta, whether Government or other. In the case of non-Government colleges, aided and unaided, the amount of the remissions is paid from the Provincial Revenues.

Measures for Muhammadan Education taken in the North-Western Provinces.

"According to the Director's Report for 1871-72, the proportion of Musalmans to the total number in schools recognised by the Department was 17·8 per cent., and as the proportion of Musalmans to the total population of the Provinces was only 13·5 per cent., it could not be asserted that in regard to education generally they were in a backward state. In the colleges and in the upper classes of the high schools, their numbers were not in the same high proportion, though in the Entrance examination of 1870, 21 out of 175, or 12 per cent., were Musalmans. In the reply made by the Government of the North-Western Provinces to the Resolution of the Government of India, it was maintained that the authorities were doing all that could be reasonably expected for Muhammadan literature and education; and since Persian was in 1871 included among the subjects of the higher University examinations, the Musalmans can hardly complain if they have not taken full advantage of the facilities offered them in respect to the higher as well as the lower education. On the four points of the Resolution, *viz.*, the encouragement of the classical and vernacular languages of the Musalmans in all Government schools and colleges, the appointment of Musalman teachers, the assistance of Musalman schools by grants-in-aid, and the encouragement to be given to the creation of a vernacular literature, Mr. Griffith, then officiating as Director, submitted a full and interesting Report. In this he showed that Persian and Arabic held a due place in the colleges and zilla schools, that the former was taught in the *tahsili* and in some of the *halkabandi* schools, that of 30 Deputy Inspectors, 15 were Musalmans, that of the *tahsili* teachers in the Meerut Circle, where there was the largest proportion of Musalman pupils, 76 were Musalmans against 65 Hindus, that prizes to the value of Rs. 5,000 were annually given to encourage the formation of a vernacular literature, that the better class of Musalman schools already received liberal grants-in-aid, and that the lower or indigenous schools failed to obtain the same assistance only because they resented the visits of Government officials and rejected advice when offered. The unpopularity of Government education with the Musalmans was accounted for on various grounds. Thus 'the Musalmans of India object to the study' [of geography] 'and think that their children are merely wasting time in acquiring information about countries which they will never see. They think, too, that Urdu, as a language, neither requires nor deserves study by a Musalman, and that Persian and Arabic are the only tongues which are worthy of their cultivation. *Halkabandi* and *tahsili* schools are now looked upon with more favour as Persian, and, in some cases, Arabic, has been admitted into the scheme of studies; but they will not be thoroughly popular with the people of Islam unless great preponderance is given to classical studies, and geography, and some other subjects are altogether excluded. So violent a change in the system of instruction is, of course, out of the question. It would be unfair to the great majority of the students, and would not advance the true interests of the minority.'

Results of measures for Muhammadan Education in the North-Western Provinces.

"The following Table shows the proportion of Musalmans in 1881-82 to the total number of students in the various institutions of the Province:—

Class of Institutions.	Total number of Students.	Musalmans.	Percentage.
Colleges, English	223	29	13·0
" Oriental	444	17	3·8
High and Middle Schools, English ... for Boys	4,273	697	16·3
" " " English ... " Girls	62	...	...
" " " Vernacular for Boys	3,267	662	20·2
" " " Vernacular " Girls	6	...	...
Primary Schools, English	9,852	2,022	20·5
" " Vernacular	144,373	19,339	13·3
" " English, for girls	664	...	...
" " Vernacular, "	5,990	1,616	26·9
Normal Schools for Masters	239	44	18·1
" " " Mistresses	83	...	...
Total	169,476	24,426	14·41

Independent efforts made by the Muhammadans of the North-Western Provinces for English Education.

"It appears, then, that neither in the proportion of Musalmans at school in 1871-72, nor in the endeavours since made to encourage a further advance, was there any great cause for reproach. On the other hand, there was great cause for hopeful anticipation in the movement set on foot, about this time, by certain of the Musalman gentry of the Provinces. If dissatisfied with the scanty progress made by their race in the higher education, their dissatisfaction was as much with themselves as with the education they neglected. But it was not of that kind which contents itself with querulous fault-finding. Recognising the evil, these Musalman gentlemen were determined to discover the remedy; and, led by Maulavi Sayyid Ahmad Khan,* whose life has been one long devotion to the cause of liberal education, they formed themselves into a society with the primary purpose of ascertaining the specific objections felt by the Musalman community towards the education offered by Government, and of ascertaining the kind of education which would be welcomed in its place. It was plain to them that a return to the old methods of Oriental instruction was impossible. Much as they might venerate the traditions of their forefathers and prize the treasures of a copious and elegant literature, the Society held that the only education which could bring their race into harmony with the civilisation around them, and so restore it to a position of influence, was an education frankly acknowledging the advance of science, catholic in its sympathies with all that was admirable in the literature, history, and philosophy of other countries, broad in its outlines and exact in its studies. At the first, as might be expected, this very liberality was the danger which threatened the undertaking. To appeal to the Musalman community at large upon principles so much at variance, not with the Muhammadan religion in its essential doctrines, but with the Muhammadan religion as interpreted by the majority of those who held it, was to stir up active antagonism. Well aware of this, the Society yet hoped for ultimate triumph. For some time the support they obtained was grudging. Slowly, however, the opposition slackened in the face of the persistent courage of the yet small band of reformers. Men of eminence, like the late Sir Salar Jung, came forward with support valuable not only in its material shape, but in its influence with those to whom a great name was a great security. The personal character of the leaders of the movement vouched for its disinterested aims. Unreasonable fears gave way before a closer view of the dreaded innovation. Some of the fiercest opponents of early days were converted into warm partisans. Princes and Nobles, Musalman and Hindu alike, enrolled themselves as patrons of the project, and offered munificent endowments to the contemplated college. Nor was liberality altogether wanting on the part of Englishmen. The handsome donation of Rs. 10,000 made by the Earl of Northbrook founded a system of scholarships called after his name; and among other benefactors were Lord Stanley of Alderley, the Earl of Lytton, Sir William Muir and Sir John Strachey. Thirteen years have now passed since the Society met to shape its scheme; and it may well be doubted whether the most sanguine of those who then devoted themselves to their task looked forward to the rapid success which they have lived to witness. The noble college now fast rising at Aligarh bids fair to be the rival of the Government colleges in their best characteristics; while in some of the most important principles of education its superiority is manifest. Of the progress already made we have given some account in Chapter VI.† But there

* Now, Sir Syed Ahmed Khan, Bahadur, K. C. S. I., Hon. LL.D. (Edin.).

† "The circumstances that gave rise to the foundation of the Muhammadan Anglo-Oriental College at Aligarh are thus described in a letter from the Honourable Sayyid Ahmed Khan, Bahádur, Honorary Secretary, Muhammadan Anglo-Oriental College Fund Committee, to the Director of Public Instruction, North-Western Provinces, dated June, 1881: 'It will be sufficient to say that a body of influential Muhammadan gentlemen, who interested themselves in education, being mournfully aware of the backwardness of the Muhammadan population in the matter of English Education, regarded the circumstances as a great evil, not only to the immediate moral, social, and political welfare of their own co-religionists, but to the country at large. Their enquiries roused the most serious apprehensions in regard to the future of their co-religionists under the British rule, and they formed themselves into a Committee to raise funds for establishing the present College. The original object of some of the supporters of the Committee was to confine the College to the Muhammadans for whose special benefit educational facilities were to be provided. But so much good-will, sympathy, and generosity were displayed by the Hindoo nobility and gentry, that the Committee in establishing the College declared it open to Hindoo students also, especially as the curriculum (beyond religious instruction) pursued in the College suited Hindus and Muhammadans alike, and the former showed a readiness to join the College. In the matter of scholarships, prizes, and other college rewards, the rules of the college show no partiality to either Hindus or Muhammadans, whilst the committee has provided separate boarding-houses for Hindu students. The college is conducted upon the most advanced principles of toleration, and whilst the immediate control of it is vested in a European Principal and a European Headmaster, the staff of Professors and Teachers consists of Hindus and Muhammadans. The committee can congratulate themselves upon the circumstance that they have never observed the smallest indication of any feeling other than friendly spirit between the Hindu and Muhammadan students, and they are sincerely convinced that the college (though naturally a place of exceptional attraction to Muhammadan students) may, as an educational agency, be regarded as suited alike to Hindoos and Muhammadans.' The committee formed for the collection of funds began its work in 1872, and up to the present time the amount realised is something over three lakhs of rupees, exclusive of the contributions to the building fund. The annual income of the college is Rs. 34,000, while the expenditure for the last year exceeded the income by Rs. 2,538. Fully to carry out the scheme of the college, it is calculated that the income must be raised to Rs. 60,000 per annum; but it may reasonably be expected that the Government will before long find it possible to increase the amount of its grant-in-aid (now only Rs. 6,000 out of Rs. 34,000), and a considerable addition will accrue from the fees as soon as a larger number of quarters is completed for the residence of boarders. For the college buildings, including 164 rooms for boarders, a sum of Rs. 5,31,000 will ultimately be required, and of this Rs. 1,62,963 has already been subscribed. At present the buildings completed consist of eleven class rooms, and one central hall; twenty-five rooms for first class boarders, and forty-nine for those of the second class; a house for the headmaster; a small dispensary and some temporary boarding-houses. Besides these, the foundations of the entire college have been sunk, a park has been laid out, and the wall on one side of the

are features in the constitution of the Aligarh College which deserve further notice. Among the reasons which are said to have deterred the Musalmans from accepting the Government system, we have mentioned the absence of all religious instruction and the scant attention paid to morality and manners. It is here that the Aligarh College asserts its special excellence. Religious instruction is a part of the daily exercise, and places of worship are to be among the college buildings. The pious Musalman, therefore, has no fear that his son will grow up careless of his ancestral faith or ignorant of religious truth. His mind is at rest, also, on the question of morality and good manners. For residence in college is compulsory upon all students coming from a distance, and a healthy discipline varied by healthy amusement preserves much of the influence of home life, while fostering a manliness of character which home life would fail to give. The importance of the college, however, is not confined to the special nature of the education it affords. Politically its influence is great and will be greater; for it is the first expression of independent Musalman effort which the country has witnessed since it came under British rule. The Aligarh Society has indeed set an example which, if followed to any large extent, will solve the problem of national education; and it is difficult to speak in words of too high praise of those whose labours have been so strenuous, or to overrate the value of the ally which the State has gained in the cause of education and advancement.

Measures for Muhammadan Education taken in the Punjab.

"On the receipt of the Resolution of the Government of India, enquiries were made as to the extent to which the Musalmans of the Province had availed themselves of the education offered them. These enquiries showed that 34·9 per cent. of the total number of pupils under instruction were Musalmans. Taking each class of School separately, the percentage in Government village schools was 38, in higher vernacular schools 30, in middle English schools from 24 to 29, in higher English schools 20, and in Colleges 5. In the Districts east of the river Jhelam the number of Musalman students was almost in exact proportion to the total Musalman population, while in many of the Districts of the Delhi, Hissar, Ambala and Amritsar Divisions the percentage in schools of all classes was considerably above the ratio which the Musalmans bore to the total population. On the other hand, in the Derajat and Peshawar Divisions, where the Musalmans formed more than 90 per cent. of the whole population, their proportion to the total number at schools was only 55 per cent.; and so completely in many parts had education been disregarded by them, that

college grounds has been finished. Beginning with about 20 students in June 1875, the school and college now contain nearly 300, of whom 29 are in the latter department. Since 1877, fifty-five candidates have gone up for the Entrance Examination, of whom 36 have passed; 10 out of 17 have succeeded in the F. A. during the three years the college has been affiliated up to that standard; and there are now 8 students reading for the B. A. degree. As originally constituted, the college had two departments, the English and the Oriental. In the former, all subjects were taught in English; Arabic, Persian or Sanskrit, being taken up as a 'second language;' in the latter, either Arabic or Persian was studied for its literature; while history, geography, mathematics, &c., were taught in Urdu, and English became the 'second language.' But this Department, which has never attracted many students, and now numbers 15 only, will probably be abolished before long. At the head of the college is a European Principal, with seven Native Professors, three of whom are Masters of Arts in the Calcutta University; the school has a European Headmaster, seven Native English Teachers, and six Arabic, Persian, and Hindi Teachers. In scholarships the college awarded Rs. 3,764 during the past year. Of these, some were from permanent endowments for special purposes, such as the Patiala and the Northbrook Scholarships, some from yearly donations by private gentlemen, and some from the college income. Religious instruction is given to *Sunnis* by a *Sunni* Teacher, to *Shias* by one of their own sect, in either Arabic or Persian, according as the one language or the other has been chosen by the student for his college course; and the managing committee is willing that similar instruction should be given to Hindu students in their own sacred books. The business of the college is managed by two committees; one, composed of Native and European gentlemen, dealing with matters of instruction only; the other, composed entirely of Native gentlemen, which regulates the general concerns of the institution. Much of the popularity of the college is due to the provision for the residence of students belonging to families of the upper classes. The rooms of the first class boarders are scarcely less comfortable than those of an under-graduate at Oxford or Cambridge, and the Musalmans take their meals together in a dining hall. To a first class boarder the cost of living at the college is about Rs. 300 a year, which includes rent, board, medical attendance, and tuition fees: a second class boarder pays about Rs. 190. Of the two classes there were, in 1881-82, 171 in residence, of whom 16 were Hindus. At the outset, the undertaking met with very great opposition from many Musalmans of the old school. All sorts of rumours were spread abroad as to the character of the institution and the heterodoxy of the supporters. Fortunately, however, the originator of the scheme, the Hon'ble Sayyid Ahmed Khan, was not to be daunted by opposition, or deterred by want of sympathy. In the esteem of the more liberal minded of his co-religionists he held the highest place; and his perseverance was before long rewarded by the hearty co-operation of powerful friends. Chief among those who came forward to his support was Sir Salar Jang, Prime Minister to the Nizam. His lead was followed by many influential Musalmans in all parts of the country; and though the college funds are at present insufficient for the complete working of the scheme, the number of students is now limited chiefly by the want of accommodation. If, then, the Musalmans are to be reproached for not having availed themselves at an earlier stage of the benefits of the education offered them by Government, they have certainly set an example to the generality of the population by founding and maintaining, almost without State aid, a college in some respects superior to any educational institution in India, and one which bids fair to be of the greatest importance from a political as well as from an educational point of view."—(Report of the Education Commission, 1882; pp. 266–268).

it would be a considerable time before the schools, whether Government or aided, could expect to attract any large number of pupils. Simultaneously with these enquiries, the Government of the Punjab consulted a large number of gentlemen as to the necessity of any special measures, other than those which had already been taken, for the furtherance of education among the Musalmans. Among those consulted were the Members of the Senate of the Punjab University College, and English and Native officers, both Musalman and Hindu. The replies received almost unanimously deprecated any such measures. The Musalman members of the Senate recommended, indeed, a system of special scholarships, and would be glad to see moral and religious instruction given in the Government schools; but they were unanimous in declaring that no religious prejudices existed among the more enlightened classes against the education afforded either in the Government or in the Mission schools, that no change was needed in the course of study, and especially that there should be no restriction upon the study of English. In regard to the establishment of aided schools, the Government of the Punjab pointed out that the matter was very much in the hands of the people themselves; but that if any exertion were made in that direction, it would meet with liberal encouragement from Government, and that in such schools it would be for the managers to provide whatever religious instruction they thought fit. So far as the Musalmans had shown an indifference, to the education offered them, that was ascribed by the Government to the disproportionate attention given by them to religious studies, to a preference, as more practical, for the course of study in indigenous schools, and to the impoverishment which was said to have affected most Muhammadan families of note. That, as a class, the Musalmans had been subject to any special disabilities, was emphatically denied; and the conclusion drawn from the general body of evidence went to show that the suggestions made by the Government of India had already been adopted in the Punjab. No special measures, therefore, have since been taken, but the percentage of Musalmans at school has risen since 1871-72 from 34·9 to 38·2, and the increase has been in the higher rather than in the lower class of schools. The following Table gives the statistics for 1881-82:—

Class of Institutions.	Total number of Students.	Musalmans.	Percentage.
Colleges, English	103	13	12·6
" Oriental	122	71	58·1
High Schools, English	453	91	20·0
" Vernacular	132	64	48·4
Middle Schools, English	2,671	703	26·3
" Vernacular	2,704	935	34·5
Primary Schools, English	23,019	7,176	31·1
" Vernacular	70,641	28,378	40·1
Middle Schools, Girls,' English	8	...	...
Primary " "	141	2	1·4
" " Vernacular	9,066	4,235	46·7
Normal Schools for Masters	220	101	45·9
" " Mistresses	138	59	42·7
Central Training College	58	16	27·5
Total ...	109,476	41,844	38·2

"The following Table shows the proportion of Musalmans to the total number at school in 1871-72:—

Measures for Muhammadan Education taken in Oudh.

Class of Institutions.		Total number of Students.	Musalmans.	Percentage.
Government ...	Higher Schools, English	2,340	630	27·0
	Middle ditto ditto and Vernacular ...	7,390	2,732	36·9
	Lower ditto Vernacular	31,525	6,235	19·7
	Female ditto	1,908	1,072	56·1
	Normal ditto	187	71	38·0
Aided ...	College	720	195	27·0
	Higher Schools, English	200	37	18·5
	Middle Class, English and Vernacular ...	3,983	993	24·9
	Lower Schools, Vernacular	1,222	200	16·3
	Female Schools	451	252	55·8
	Total ...	49,926	12,417	24·8

"This Table is, in itself, enough to show that the education of Musalmans in Oudh had not been neglected, and that the Musalmans were far from indifferent to the advantages held out to them. The course of studies, indeed, was Urdu-Persian rather than Hindi-Sanskrit. If any section of the community had cause for complaint, it was the Hindus. But, in reality, they had no grievance; for, Urdu being the language of the Courts, and Government service being to the vast majority alike of Hindus and Musalmans the great incentive to education, the requirements of all were best met by the adoption of Urdu as a medium of instruction. Persian was also taught in the schools, and was a study popular with the better class of Musalmans. For Arabic there seemed to be little or no demand. To know the Koran by heart was, indeed, as in other parts of India, the beginning of wisdom. In most cases it was also the end. Facilities for the study of Arabic as a language were abundantly offered in the Canning College, Lucknow, at which, however, though 'situated in a city containing 111,397 Muhammadans, or about 9,000 Muhammadan boys of a school-going age, there are but 144 Musalman students.' That number, the Director had no doubt, might be increased by hundreds, perhaps by thousands, by the offer of stipends, or even of daily rations of food. Such students, however, he confessed, would not be attracted by the love of Oriental literature, nor would they continue their studies if more advantageous occupation offered itself. Towards 'the creation of a vernacular literature,' or, as the Director more accurately puts it, 'the provision of a suitable literature' for Musalmans and Hindus, something might be done. But 'it seems to me,' wrote the Director, 'that special machinery for the production of school-books, and for the reward of native authors, is required. At present no such machinery exists. The Government of India, I believe, are afraid lest the works produced by translators should not be popular and remain unsold. So at present authors can only be encouraged by the purchase of their books, for prizes or special rewards. But there is no machinery even to estimate the value of the books submitted; the books are forwarded to the Director of Public Instruction, and he must, in addition to his other multifarious duties, go over each book presented, and accurately guage its merits, or he may call upon some of his subordinates as hard-worked as himself, to assist in the criticism of books submitted for publication. Moreover, many, nay most, of those who write and adapt books for school use are either not acquainted at all with Western science and art, or at best have but a superficial acquaintance with these subjects. Thus, the books that are printed follow a stereotyped Eastern groove, or are unidiomatic and bald versions of some trifling English work. If a special office for the examination and publication of works in Hindi, Urdu, Persian and Bengalee were established, and this office were connected with the Educational Departments of Bengal, the North-Western Provinces, and the Punjab, and were under the control of some one of these Departments, I cannot but think that a better class of literature would be produced than under the present system.' ... ...

"The following is the comparative Table for Oudh in 1881-82:—

CLASS OF INSTITUTIONS.	Total number of Students.	Musalmans.	Percentage.
Colleges, English	126	7	5·5
" Oriental	113	51	45·1
High and Middle Schools, English	1,081	195	18·0
" " " Vernacular	536	134	25·0
Primary Schools, English	4,388	1,317	30·0
" " Vernacular	45,899	9,449	20·5
" " Girls,' English	350	156	44·5
" " " Vernacular	1,722	1,080	62·7
Normal Schools for Masters	67	11	16·4
" " for Mistresses	6	...	...
TOTAL ...	54,288	12,400	22·8

Measures for Muhammadan Education taken in the Central Provinces, Mysore, Coorg, and the Berars.

"In the Central Provinces the Musalmans formed only 2·5 per cent. of the total population, but they were as fully alive to the importance of education as the rest of the community. In the higher schools, especially, their attendance was good, and orders had already been given that classes should be opened for the study of Arabic and Persian in all zilla schools in which there should be a sufficient demand. The Chief Commissioner did not think that any further measures were necessary. In Mysore the general state of Muhammadan education was very backward and unsatisfactory. The Chief Commissioner was of opinion that Hindustani schools should be established wherever a reasonably sufficient number of Muhammadan pupils were forthcoming to attend them; that Hindustani masters should be added to the existing schools of all descriptions wherever a class of pupils in that language could be formed; and that the subject of the provision of suitable school-books should be duly considered. The question of Muhammadan education had already engaged the anxious attention of the Chief Commissioner, who had repeatedly urged upon that community the necessity of taking further advantage of the facilities offered them, if they wished to keep pace with the progress made by other classes. The Muhammadans of Coorg were generally in very poor circumstances, and quite indifferent to the education of their children. The only measure which the Chief Commissioner thought practicable was to establish an efficient Hindustani class at Merkara, in connection with, or independent of, the central school, and the Director of Public Instruction had been instructed to make enquiries as to how this might best be done. The Musalmans of the Assigned Districts of Haiderabad were, it was stated, but few in number and depressed in social and intellectual condition relatively to the other classes of the people. It had always been one of the objects of the Local Administration to introduce into the ranks of the Commission a certain number of Musalmans. Measures had also been recently adopted for promoting the spread of education among that portion of the community, but it was too early to judge of their results." *

CHAPTER XXVIII.

CONCLUSIONS AND RECOMMENDATIONS OF THE EDUCATION COMMISSION OF 1882, ON THE SUBJECT OF MUHAMMADAN EDUCATION.—REPORTS OF THE LOCAL GOVERNMENTS THEREON.—VIEWS OF THE GOVERNMENT OF INDIA UPON THE SUBJECT.

Condition of English Education among Muhammadans in Colleges and Schools, as indicated by the statistics of 1881-82, in the Report of the Education Commission of 1882.

The account of the various measures adopted by the Local Governments, in consequence of the Resolutions of the Government of India on the subject of Muhammadan education, issued in 1871 and 1873, which has been given in the Report of the Education Commission of 1882, from which information has been incorporated in the preceding Chapter, was the basis of the conclusions arrived at by the Commission on that subject. And it was in view of those conclusions that the Commission proceeded to make certain definite recommendations for promotion of education among Muhammadans. Those conclusions and recommendations will be presently quoted; but in the meantime it is important to realize exactly the results of the progress of English education among Muhammadans as indicated by the various Statistical Tables, for the years 1881-82, which have been quoted in the preceding Chapter from the Report of the Commission. For the sake of clearness, and as bearing upon the main subject of this work, the following Tabular Statement has been prepared, by taking the figures given in the abovementioned tables and making calculations from them, so far as the attendance of Muhammadans, in Colleges and Schools teaching the English language, is concerned:—

* Report of the Education Commission of 1882, paras. 559–70, pp. 484–96.

Table showing the Attendance of Musalmans in the various Educational Institutions, Government, Aided, and Unaided as compared with the total attendance in 1881-82.

Provinces.	Class of Institution.	Total number of Students.	Musalmans.	Percentage.
Madras	Colleges, English ...	1,669	30	1·7
	High Schools, " ...	4,836	117	2·4
	Middle " " ...	18,553	723	3·8
	Total ...	25,058	870	3·4
Bombay	Colleges, English ...	475	7	1·4
	High Schools, " ...	5,731	118	2·0
	Middle " " ...	14,257	781	5·4
	Total ...	20,463	906	4·4
Bengal	Colleges, English ...	2,738	106	3·8
	High Schools, " ...	43,747	3,831	8·7
	Middle " " ...	37,959	5,032	13·2
	Total ...	84,444	8,969	10·6
N.-W. Provinces ...	Colleges, English ...	223	29	13·0
	High Schools, " ... / Middle " " ...	4,273	697	16·3
	Total ...	4,496	726	16·3
Oudh	Colleges, English ...	126	7	5·5
	High Schools, " ... / Middle " " ...	1,081	195	18·0
	Total ...	1,207	202	16·7
Punjab	Colleges, English ...	103	13	12·6
	High Schools, " ...	453	91	20·0
	Middle " " ...	2,671	703	26·3
	Total ...	3,227	807	25·0
All the above Provinces...	Colleges, *English*	5,334	192	3·6
	High and Middle Schools, *English*...	1,33,561	12,288	9·2
	Grand Total ...	1,38,895	12,480	8·9

Noticeable points in regard to the low percentage of Muhammadan students in English Colleges and Schools as compared with the percentage of Muhammadans in the population.

It will be observed in this Table that with the exception of the North-Western Provinces, the percentage of Muhammadans receiving English education is far below the percentage of Muhammadans in the total population in the various Provinces as will appear by comparing the percentages of the attendance of Muhammadan students with the percentages of Muhammadan population in the various Provinces given in the Table quoted from the Education Commission's Report at the outset of the preceding Chapter. Another important point to be noticed in the above Table is that the percentage of Muhammadans among the total number of students receiving English education diminishes as the class of education becomes of a higher standard; so much so that in Madras where the percentage of Muhammadan population is 6, the Muhammadans attending English Colleges form only 1·7 per cent. of the total number of students attending such Colleges; in Bombay where the percentage of the Muhammadan population is 15·4, the percentage of students in English Colleges is only 1·4; in Bengal where the percentage of the Muhammadans in the population is 32·3 the percentage of Muhammadan students in English Colleges is only 3·8, and, in the Punjab, while the percentage of the Muhammadans in the population is no less than 51·6, the percentage of Muhammadan students in the English Colleges is only 12·6. In making this comparison I have kept in view the Statistics of the percentages of the Muhammadans in the population as represented by the Report of the Education Commission; but the subject will be more fully discussed in the next Chapter of this work. Meanwhile it will be as well to point out that whilst in the Statistics of population given in the Table quoted at the outset of the preceding Chapter from the Education Commission's Report the percentage of Muhammadans in the population of the Provinces concerned is shown to be 22·8 per cent., the percentage of Muhammadan students in English Colleges as shown in the above table is only 3·6 per cent., and even if High and Middle schools teaching a lower standard of English the percentage of Muhammadan students is only 8·9 or nearly, 9 per cent. of the total number of students attending those institutions.

Upon the state of things as described in the preceding Chapter the Education Commission of 1882 summarized its conclusions and recommendations in the following terms:—

Conclusions of the Education Commission as to the condition of education among Muhammadans in 1882.

"In the foregoing pages, we have preferred to reproduce the statements made with regard to the condition of the Muhammadans in the several Provinces, rather than to attempt generalisations of our own. The wide differences in the circumstances of the Musalmans in the three Presidencies render such an attempt hazardous. But apart from the social and historical conditions of the Muhammadan Community in India, there are causes of a strictly educational character which heavily weight it in the race of life. The teaching of the mosque must precede the lessons of the school. The one object of a young Hindu is to obtain an education which will fit him for an official or a professional career. But before the young Muhammadan is allowed to turn his thoughts to secular instruction, he must commonly pass some years in going through a course of sacred learning. The Muhammadan boy, therefore, enters school later than the Hindu. In the second place, he very often leaves school at an earlier age. The Muhammadan parent belonging to the better classes is usually poorer than the Hindu parent in a corresponding social position. He cannot afford to give his son so complete an education. In the third place, irrespectively of his worldly means, the Muhammadan parent often chooses for his son while at school an education which will secure for him an honoured place among the learned of his own community rather than one which will command a success in the modern professions or in official life. The years which the young Hindu gives to English and Mathematics in a public school, the young Muhammadan devotes in a *Madrassa* to Arabic and the law and Theology of Islam. When such an education is completed, it is to the vocation of a man of learning, rather than to the more profitable professions that the thoughts of a promising Muhammadan youth naturally turn. The above are the three principal causes of an educational character which retard the prosperity of the Musalmans. It would be beyond the province of a strictly Educational Report to attempt generalisations based upon the social or historical conditions which affect the Muhammadan Community in India.

Recommendations of the Education Commission for promoting education among Muhammadans.

"The recommendations we proceed to make have been framed, we believe, not merely with a regard to justice, but with a leaning towards generosity. They are based not more upon the suggestions contained in the Provincial Reports than upon the evidence of witnesses and the representations of public bodies. They deal, we think, with every form of complaint that is grounded in fact, and they contemplate the various circumstances of various localities. Few of them, indeed, are of general application; many of them, we trust, will before long be rendered obsolete. Special encouragement to any class is in itself an evil; and it will be a sore reproach to the Musalmans if the pride they have shown in other matters does not stir them up to a course of honourable activity; to a determination that whatever their backwardness in the past, they will not suffer themselves to be outstripped in the future; to a conviction that self-help and self-sacrifice are at once nobler principles of conduct and surer paths to worldly success than sectarian reserve or the hope of exceptional indulgence.

"We have spoken of the causes; we here accept the fact that, at all events in many parts of the country, the Musalmans have fallen behind the rest of the population; we therefore recommend—

The recommendations formulated, with reasons in brief.

(1) *That the special encouragement of Muhammadan Education be regarded as a legitimate charge on Local, on Municipal, and on Provincial Funds.*

"The Muhammadan indigenous schools which are found in all parts of the country are established on a purely religious basis, and in most cases impart an education of the most elementary character. In order to encourage a wider utility, we recommend—

(2) *That indigenous Muhammadan Schools be liberally encouraged to add purely secular subjects to their course of instruction.*

"As the instruction given in Muhammadan Primary Schools differs considerably from that in the ordinary primary schools, we recommend—

(3) *That special standards for Muhammadan Primary Schools be prescribed.*

"In regard to the medium of instruction in Primary and Middle Schools, it appears that even in places where Hindustani is not the vernacular of the people, Muhammadans earnestly desire that their children should be educated in that language, and we therefore recommend—

(4) *That Hindustani be the principal medium for imparting instruction to Muhammadans in Primary and Middle Schools, except in localities where the Muhammadan Community desire that some other language be adopted.*

"In order that Muhammadans may be enabled to qualify for the lower grades of the public service, we recommend—

(5) *That the official vernacular, in places where it is not Hindustani, be added as a voluntary subject to the curriculum of Primary and Middle Schools for Muhammadans, maintained from public funds; and that arithmetic and accounts be taught through the medium of that vernacular.*

"To meet the complaint made in some parts of the country that due encouragement is not given to the language and literature of the Muhammadans, and that this circumstance has operated as one of the causes which have kept that community aloof from the Government system of education, we recommend—

(6) *That in localities where Muhammadans form a fair proportion of the population, provision be made in Middle and High Schools, maintained from public funds for imparting instruction in the Hindustani and Persian Languages.*

"It has been found that whilst Muhammadans in many places form a fair proportion of the students learning English, their number decreases as the standard of instruction rises; we therefore recommend—

(7) *That Higher English Education for Muhammadans, being the kind of education in which that community needs special help, be liberally encouraged.*

"It has been submitted, with much force, that the poverty of the Muhammadans is also one of the main reasons why education has not made satisfactory progress in that community; we therefore recommend—

(8) *That where necessary a graduated system of special scholarships for Muhammadans be established; to be awarded*

(*a*) *in Primary schools, and tenable in Middle Schools;*

(*b*) *in Middle Schools, and tenable in High Schools;*

(*c*) *on the results of the Matriculation and First Arts examinations, and tenable in colleges:* also

(9) *That in all classes of schools maintained from public funds, a certain proportion of free studentships be expressly reserved for Muhammadan students.*

"Complaints having been made that Muhammadan educational endowments have not always been applied to their proper uses, we recommend—

(10) *That in places where educational endowments for the benefit of Muhammadans exist, and are under the management of Government, the funds arising from such endowments be devoted to the advancement of education among Muhammadans exclusively.*

"And, further, in order that Muhammadan educational endowments may be utilised to the utmost, we recommend—

(11) *That where Muhammadan endowments exist, and are under the management of private individuals or bodies, inducements by liberal Grants-in-aid be offered to them to establish English-teaching schools or colleges on the Grants-in-aid System.*

"The employment of Muhammadans as teachers and inspecting officers among Muhammadans will, in our opinion, largely tend to popularise education among that community, and enable the Department to understand the special needs and wishes of the Muhammadans; we therefore recommend--

(12) *That where necessary, Normal Schools or classes for the training of Muhammadan teachers be established;*

(13) *That wherever instruction is given in Muhammadan schools, through the medium of Hindustani, endeavours be made to secure, as far as possible, Muhammadan teachers to give such instruction;* and—

(14) *That Muhammadan inspecting officers be employed more largely than hitherto for the inspection of Primary Schools for Muhammadans.*

"Another useful means of spreading knowledge among the Muhammadans will be the recognition and encouragement by the State of such associations as the *Anjuman-i-Islam* in Bombay, and the *Anjuman-i-Islamiya* in Lahore; we therefore recommend—

(15) *That Associations for the promotion of Muhammadan education be recognised and encouraged.*

"In order to secure the continuous attention of the Education Department to the subject of Muhammadan education, and to prevent the claims of the Muhammadans for special treatment from being overlooked, we recommend—

(16) *That in the Annual Reports on Public Instruction a special section be devoted to Muhammadan education.*

"In certain Provinces the backwardness of the Muhammadans in education has prevented them from obtaining any considerable share of appointments in the public service. But it has also been made a subject of complaint that, even in places where qualified Muhammadans are available, their services are not duly utilised by Government officers: we therefore recommend—

(17) *That the attention of Local Governments be invited to the question of the proportion in which patronage is distributed among educated Muhammadans and others.*"*

Government of India's Resolution, dated 23rd October, 1884, reserved subject of Muhammadan education for separate consideration.

Upon the Report of the Education Commission being submitted to the Government of India, that Government reviewed the Report, in its Resolution No. $\frac{10}{309}$, in the Home Department (Education), dated the 23rd October, 1884, but in regard to the above recommendations, only observed: "The Governor-General in Council has the subject of Muhammadan education at present under separate consideration; and will merely say here that, in view of the backward condition into which in some Provinces the members of that Community have fallen, he thinks it desirable to give them in some respects exceptional assistance."

Memorial of the National Muhammadan Association of Calcutta on Muhammadan education &c., in 1882.

Resolution of the Government of India dated 15th July, 1885, reviewing Muhammadan education and declaring policy of Government.

The "*separate consideration*" of the subject of Muhammadan education arose in the following manner. In February, 1882, a Memorial was addressed to His Excellency the Marquis of Ripon, by the National Muhammadan Association of Calcutta, calling attention to the decayed position of Muhammadans in India, to the causes which had in the opinion of the Memorialists led to this decadence, and to the circumstances which, in their belief, tended to perpetuate that condition. The Memorial was fully reported upon by the Local Governments, and was also discussed by the Education Commission of 1882. His Excellency was unable to deal with the question before his departure from India, but left on record an expression of his hope that it would receive full consideration at the hands of his successor, the Earl of Dufferin. Accordingly His Excellency in Council carefully considered the Memorial, together with the correspondence, reports and numerous pamphlets and papers on the subject, and on the 15th July, 1885, recorded a Resolution (No. $\frac{7}{215\cdot25}$, in the Home Department—Education) reviewing the history of the measures which had been adopted by Government since 1871, in the cause of Muhammadan education, and giving expression to the views of the Government on the subject, with special reference to the recommendations of the Education Commission. The Resolution possesses the greatest importance in the history of Muhammadan education in India, as it contains the latest declaration of the policy of the Government on the subject, and describes the main features of the points to which the attention of Government was directed in formulating that policy. The Resolution, after mentioning that the recommendations of the Education Commission had been considered by the Local Governments, gives a summary of their views, which may be incorporated here together with such observations as the Government of India made thereon in that Resolution.

The views of the Government of Madras were thus expressed in their letter No. 506, dated 22nd August, 1884.

* Report of the Education Commission, (1882), pp. 505–7.

"Special encouragement is already held out to Muhammadan education, and a further advance is contemplated in this direction, though not exactly on the lines suggested by the Commission. It is not thought desirable to dissociate this class so distinctly from the ordinary scheme of teaching, as, except, in a few localities, Muhammadans avail themselves freely of the advantages of the existing system. Thus neither special schools nor special Normal classes seem necessary; while the recommendations as to the Persian and Hindustani languages are hardly applicable to the peculiar linguistic conditions of the South, and ignore the extent to which the Muhammadans use its vernacular languages. At the same time the object of the recommendations meets with cordial approval."

Views of the Government of Madras on Muhammadan education, in 1884.

Upon these opinions the Government of India recorded the following observations on the abovementioned Resolution :—

Observations of the Government of India thereon.

"It has been shown...that the condition of the Muhammadans in Southern India is, from an educational point of view, by no means unsatisfactory. All funds, provincial, local, and municipal, are bound by the Grant-in-aid Code to give special encouragement to Muhammadan education. The experiment of separate schools has not been successful, and is not, the Director of Public Instruction thinks, necessary, except to some extent in Madras and one or two large Muhammadan centres, and for the Moplahs on the West Coast. Some increase of the subordinate inspecting agency for Muhammadan schools is, however, admittedly desirable. While the broad results for the whole Province leave perhaps little to desire, the Governor-General in Council thinks it would be well were the officers of the Educational Department directed to examine more particularly, in communication with district officers and the leading members of the Muhammadan community, the educational provision for the members of that community in each district, with a view to seeing whether, in special localities, more effect should not be given to some of the recommendations of the Commission. The backward state of the Moplahs seems especially to call for attention. The Governor-General in Council is disposed to agree with the Madras Government, that it is undesirable to accentuate the difference between Muhammadans and Hindus, by making Hindustani, in lieu of the current Vernacular, the medium of instruction, where the Muhammadans show themselves ready to attend the ordinary schools of the country. Where this is the case, the local Vernacular should be the ordinary medium, the special wants of Muhammadan youths being met by the formation of Hindustani classes and teaching them the Arabic character. There may, however, be tracts where Muhammadan feeling would prefer the establishment of special schools, and in such places the recommendations of the Commission should receive attention. In Secondary Schools of all kinds facilities for the study of Arabic or Persian should be offered wherever there is a real demand for this." *

The Government of Bombay, in their letter, No. 983, dated 6th June, 1884, after stating that "the special wants of Muhammadans have had attention," referred to the monthly grant of Rs. 500 towards the *Anjuman-i-Islam* School, since 1880, and added that "the Governor in Council is prepared to aid further in the extension of Muhammadan education should opportunity offer." Upon this brief statement of the matter the Government of India in the above Resolution observed :—

Views of the Government of Bombay on Muhammadan education, in 1884.

"Although here, as in Madras, the educational conditions of Muhammadan population, taken as a whole, is not altogether unsatisfactory, there can be no doubt that in certain localities, as in Sind, there is an urgent call for special measures; and the Governor-General in Council would wish to see the same further examination of local wants initiated that has been suggested for Madras. Some steps should certainly be taken to encourage Muhammadans to read up to the higher standards. At present here, as in other Provinces, they specially fail to pursue their studies beyond the lower stages." †

Observations of the Government of India thereon.

The Government of Bengal expressed their views in the following words, in their letter No. 2,285, dated 25th September, 1884:—

Views of the Government of Bengal on Muhammadan education, in 1884.

"The proposals for the support of special Muhammadan Schools, and for the special encouragement of Muhammadan education in ordinary schools, are worthy of liberal consideration. Many of them are already in force in this province; the chief innovation being that for the creation of a special class of scholarships for Muhammadan students. To this, no doubt, objection may be raised, just as objection has been, not without force, raised to the principle of this special proposal in Mr. Barbour's dissent. The Lieutenant-Governor, however, thinks that if it can be shown that in any locality the number of Muhammadans who gain scholarships is not in due proportion to their numbers and position, a fair case will have been made out for exceptional, though he will also add, temporary treatment. The other recommendations under this head are conceived in a liberal spirit, and may be accepted, except in so far as

* Resolution of the Government of India, in the Home Department (Education), No. $\frac{7}{215-25}$, dated 15th July, 1885.

† *Ib.*, para. 13.

they recognise the substitution of Hindustani for the Hindi Vernacular. If by Hindustani be meant that language which, written in the Hindi or Nagri character, is the common speech alike of Muhammadan and Hindu in Behar, the Lieutenant-Governor has no objection to offer. But if the recommendation means that the policy which has prevailed for some years, of conveying primary instruction to Muhammadans in Behar through Hindustani expressed in the Hindi character, is to be reversed, then the Lieutenant-Governor must very strongly dissent from the recommendation as being opposed to the true interests of the Muhammadans of Behar. Finally, the Lieutenant-Governor is not disposed to support the establishment of Normal Schools or classes for Muhammadan teachers exclusively. Little is gained by such separatism."*

These views were approved by the Government of India in the following terms:—

Approval thereof by the Government of India.

"The Governor-General in Council trusts that the Bengal Government will give effect to its views. There is no intention to reverse the decision of the Local Government in the matter of adoption of Hindi as the Court Language of Behar, and as the ordinary medium of instruction in the Primary Schools of that Province. Where the Muhammadan population is strong and likely to attach special importance to Oriental teaching of a Muhammadan type, care should be taken to meet this want, with a view to making the schools popular, and inducing the better classes to allow their children to push their studies eventually to a higher standard, especially in English. But equal care is necessary to prevent the absolute separation of the Muhammadan community from the rest of this population. It must also be borne in mind that it is only by an acquaintance with the current Vernacular that Muhammadans can hope to secure employment. It has already been shown in this Resolution that very much has been done by the Local Government to meet the requirements of the Muhammadans in Bengal, and it may fairly be said that they have now every opportunity offered them of securing a good education. If it is found that anything further is required in any part of the Province, or at any particular stage of the educational course, to advance the progress of the Muhammadan community, the Governor-General in Council feels sure that His Honour the Lieutenant-Governor will not stint the necessary outlay."†

Views of the Government of the N.-W. P. and Oudh on Muhammadan education, in 1884, and remarks of the Government of India thereon.

In the North-Western Provinces and Oudh, the Lieutenant-Governor, in a letter, dated 9th July, 1884, considered that no special measures on behalf of Muhammadans were required, as Mussalman education in those Provinces was by no means in a backward state, and it was said that the interests of the class would be duly attended to, and aid and encouragement on the part of State would not be wanting. Upon this state of the case the Government of India expressed the opinion that "it would seem to be sufficient if enquiry is made as to the necessity of special measures in any locality where the number of Muhammadans is unduly low in any grade of the educational course."‡

Views of the Punjab Government on Muhammadan education, in 1884.

The Government of the Punjab, in a letter, No. 916 of the 9th April, 1883, to the Government of India, in the Home Department, and, again in a letter to the Director of Public Instruction, No. 97, dated 20th March, 1884, expressed the opinion that no special measures were called for regarding the education of the Muhammadans as a class, and that they were not backward in taking advantage of the existing educational facilities.

Views of the Chief Commissioner of the Central Provinces on Muhammadan education, in 1884.

In the Central Provinces, the Chief Commissioner in a letter, dated 30th June, 1884, was opposed to the adoption of special measures in aid of the Muhammadans, and it was found that nothing was really required in those Provinces. The educational authorities were, however, directed to keep a watchful eye on any localities where the Muhammadan population was large and backward.

Views of the Administrations of Assam, Coorg, Berar, and British Burma, on Muhammadan education, in 1884.

In Assam it has been found that the Muhammadans are chiefly the agriculturists of Sylhet, who are not an impoverished class, and whose vernacular is Bengali, that sufficient provision is already made for Persian instruction in Secondary Schools where there was a demand for it. Similarly in Coorg it was found that sufficient provision was already made for the education of the few Muhammadans who live in that Province. Likewise in Berar, it was found that special provision had already been made for Muhammadans and the percentage of Mussalmans in the schools was larger, in proportion, than that of the Hindus. In British Burma, where there is hardly any indigenous Muhammadan population, where the resident Muhammadan population is but $4\frac{1}{2}$ per cent. of the whole, and where the great bulk of the people are Buddhists, the Chief Commissioner reported that the Mussalmans were on a fair equality with the other sections of the population.

* Resolution of the Government of India, in the Home Department (Education), No. $\frac{7}{215-25}$, dated 15th July 1885, para 13.

† *Ib.*, para. 13. ‡ *Ib.*, para, 13.

Upon the state of things, in the various provinces, as above described, the Government of India made the following observations:—

Views and suggestions of the Government of India as to encouragement of Muhammadan education in the various provinces in general.

"On the whole, the Governor-General in Council is satisfied that the attention which has once more been drawn to the subject of Muhammadan education will have the best results. His Excellency in Council attaches special importance to recommendation (16) of the Commission's Report, 'that in the Annual Reports of public instruction a special section be devoted to Muhammadan education.' These Reports should be precise and detailed, and discuss the position and advancement of the Muhammadan Community, not merely as a whole, but with reference to local variations, in order that the Government of India may be kept fully informed as to the state and progress of this important section of the community. For the attraction of Muhammadans to higher education, a liberal provision of scholarships is essential, and their wants must not be overlooked in the framing of any general scheme of scholarships for any Province, in pursuance of the orders of the Government of India on the Report of the Education Commission. Probably the appointment of special Muhammadan Inspecting Officers, to inspect not merely Primary Muhammadan Schools, but to enquire into Muhammadan education generally, would have a good effect in Bengal and other places where the Muhammadans are very backward. Such officers would bring the peculiar wants of their co-religionists more thoroughly to notice than can perhaps be expected from subordinate officers of a different faith. The action taken in those and other directions should be fully explained in the Annual Reports."*

Memorable passages in the Resolution of the Government of India, dated 15th July, 1885.

There are some other passages in the Resolution of the Government of India, from which the preceding quotations have been made, which deserve to be permanently preserved and remembered by the Muhammadan community. *Firstly*, as giving them a sound and statesmanly warning, and *secondly*, as conveying the sympathy which the Government of India has deigned to express towards the Muhammadans of India, respecting their future educational and other prospects and welfare. In regard to the recommendations of the Education Commission, for special encouragement of Muhammadan education, the Government of India made the following general observations, which must be taken to indicate the principles of its policy in respect of the matter:—

Muhammadans cannot advance without placing themselves in line with the Hindus in English education.

"It is only by frankly placing themselves in line with the Hindus, and taking full advantage of the Government system of high and especially of English education, that the Muhammadans can hope fairly to hold their own in respect of the better description of State appointments. This is clearly seen by the Memorialists themselves, and the Reports of Local Governments show, that in most Provinces a real advance has been made in this respect. The recommendations of the Commission are, as they themselves point out, not of universal application, and none of them need be taken to imply a leaning towards the maintenance of a distinctly Oriental training throughout the curriculum for Muhammadan pupils. The object of the Commission is to attract Muhammadan scholars by giving adequate prominence to those subjects to which their parents attach importance and to hold out special inducements to a backward class; but in applying the recommendations, due regard is everywhere to be paid to local circumstances, and care must be taken to avoid unnecessary widening of the line between Muhammadan and other classes of the community." †

Muhammadans cannot be exempted from qualifying tests for public service. Their interests in this respect should be duly watched.

"The Governor-General in Council does not consider it desirable or for the advantage of the Muhammadans themselves, that they should be exempted from those tests which are established to secure the admission of duly qualified candidates into the public service. Nor can special favour be shown them in open competitive examinations of any description. It is only by raising their own educational qualifications to the level already attained by other races, that the Muhammadans can hope to win appointments that are awarded as the result of examination. But there are a large number of appointments the gift of which lies in the hands of the Local Governments, the High Courts, or Local Officers. The Governor-General in Council desires that in those Provinces where Muhammadans do not receive their full share of State employment, the Local Governments and High Courts will endeavour to redress this inequality as opportunity offers, and will impress upon subordinate officers the importance of attending to this in their selection of candidates for appointments of the class last referred to. The subject of the extent to which Muhammadans are employed in offices under Government might usefully be noticed in the Annual Reports of Provincial Administrations." ‡

* Resolution of the Government of India, in the Home Department (Education), No. $\frac{7}{215-25}$, dated 15th July 1885, para. 14.

† *Ib.* para. 12. ‡ *Ib.* para. 22.

The Government is not neglectful of the efforts for educational improvement among Muhammadans.

Again, with reference to certain statements made in the Memorial of the National Muhammadan Association of Calcutta, the Resolution of the Government of India ends with the following paragraph :—

"The Governor-General in Council has felt it to be his duty in the preceding paragraphs to controvert various misconceptions which find place in the representations that have been laid before Government; but he will, as already stated, always take a lively interest in the advancement and well-being of the Muhammadan community; and he concurs in the remarks which not unfrequently occur in the local reports, that the very fact that a Memorial like that under notice has been presented, with the concurrence and approval of so many leading gentlemen in Bengal and elsewhere, indicates that the Muhammadans have themselves come to appreciate fully the necessity of moving with the times. They have now among them not a few highly educated and public spirited men who are keenly interested in the improvement and advancement of their co-religionists. The Local Governments are everywhere anxious to do all that they equitably can do to assist in this movement; and His Excellency in Council has little doubt that, within the next ten years, much greater progress will be made than has hitherto been recorded. It is the earnest desire of the Supreme Government to treat all classes of Her Majesty's subjects in India with absolute impartiality, and see all alike benefiting by the protection, the patronage, and the assistance of the State." *

Views of the Government of India, in its Resolution of 15th July 1885, on Muhammadan education, summarized.

The views of the Government of India, as indicated in the passages above quoted from its Resolution of the 15th July 1885, on Mahomedan education, may be summarized in the following clauses :—

(1.) The Muhammadans cannot hope fairly to hold their own in respect of the better description of State appointments, but by frankly placing themselves in line with the Hindus, and taking full advantage of the Government system of high and especially of English education.

(2) A special section should be devoted to Muhammadan education in the Annual Reports of Public Instruction, giving precise and detailed information, and discussing "the position and advancement of the Muhammadan community, not merely as a whole, but with reference to local variations, in order that the Government of India may be kept fully informed as to the state and progress of this important section of the community."

(3) For the attraction of Muhammadans to higher education, a liberal provision of Scholarships is essential and their wants must not be overlooked in the framing of any general scheme of scholarships for any Province.

(4) Special Muhammadan Inspecting Officers, to inspect and enquire into Muhammadan education generally, may be appointed in places where the Muhammadans are very backward.

(5) It is not desirable, or for the advantage of the Muhammadans themselves, that they should be exempted from those tests which are established to secure the admission of duly qualified candidates into the public service.

(6) Nor can special favour be shown them in open competitive examination of any description.

(7) It is the earnest desire of the Supreme Government to treat all classes of Her Majesty's subjects in India with absolute impartiality, and see all alike benefiting by the protection, patronage, and the assistance of the State.

CHAPTER XXIX.

PROGRESS OF ENGLISH EDUCATION AMONG MUHAMMADANS, 1881-82 TO 1891-92.—RESOLUTIONS OF THE GOVERNMENT OF INDIA ON THE SUBJECT, IN 1888 AND 1894.—DEFICIENCY OF HIGH ENGLISH EDUCATION AMONG MUHAMMADANS, 1882-92.

Statistics of Muhammadans receiving English Collegiate education in 1881-82.

In the Table showing the attendance in Arts Colleges for the year 1881-82, given in Chapter XIX. of this work (*vide* page 100 *ante*) the total number of students receiving University education in the various affiliated Colleges is shown to have amounted to 5,399. Of this number only 375 belonged to the minor miscellaneous sections of the

* Resolution of the Government of India, in the Home Department (Education), No. $\frac{7}{215-25}$, dated 15th July, 1885, para 25.

community* leaving 5,024 for the main bulk of the population, namely Hindus and Muhammadans. Their distribution in that year among the various classes of colleges, teaching English and affiliated to the Universities, appears from the following Table, which has been prepared from Table No. II at page 275 of the Report of the Indian Education Commission of 1882:—

CLASSIFICATION OF COLLEGE STUDENTS—HINDU AND MUHAMMADAN—FOR THE OFFICIAL YEAR 1881-82.

Provinces.		Departmental Colleges.		Aided Colleges.		Unaided Colleges.		Total.		Grand Total.
		Hindus.	Muhammadans.	Hindus.	Muhammadans.	Hindus.	Muhammadans.	Hindus.	Muhammadans.	
Madras ...	Number of pupils ...	704	12	688	18	110	...	1,502	30	1,532
	Percentage of pupils to the total number on the Rolls.	**94·88**	**1·62**	**85·68**	**2·24**	**88·71**	...	**89·99**	**1·80**	
Bombay ...	Number of pupils ...	249	6	75	1	25	...	349	7	356
	Percentage of pupils to the total number on the Rolls.	**80·06**	**1·93**	**53·95**	**·72**	**100**	...	**73·48**	**1·47**	
Bengal ...	Number of pupils ...	1,214	75	807	30	509	1	2,530	106	2,636
	Percentage of pupils to the total number on the Rolls.	**93·03**	**5·75**	**90·17**	**3·36**	**94·61**	**·19**	**92·41**	**3·87**	
N.-W. P. and Oudh ...	Number of pupils ...	155	14	133	21	15	1	303	36	339
	Percentage of pupils to the total number on the Rolls.	**90·12**	**8·14**	**84·71**	**13·38**	**75·**	**5·**	**86·82**	**10·32**	
Punjab ...	Number of pupils ...	84	13	...	...	...	...	84	13	97
	Percentage of pupils to the total number on the Rolls.	**81·55**	**12·63**	...	...	...	...	**81·55**	**12·63**	
Central Provinces ...	Number of pupils ...	59	5	...	...	...	...	59	5	64
	Percentage of pupils to the total number on the Rolls.	**90·77**	**7·69**	...	...	...	...	**90·77**	**7·69**	
Total for British India, excluding Ajmir and Burma ...		2,465	125	1,703	70	659	2	4,827	197	5,024
	Percentage of pupils to the total number on the Rolls.	**91·38**	**4·63**	**85·41**	**3·51**	**93·21**	**·28**	**89·41**	**3·65**	
	Proportion of each race or creed to total population...	**73·21**	**22·36**	**73·21**	**22·36**	**73·21**	**22·36**	**73·21**	**22·36**	

Backwardness of Muhammadans in English Collegiate education in 1882.

In the preceding Table it is to be noticed that in the total population of British India (excluding Ajmir and Burma) the percentage of Hindus to the total population is taken to be 73·21, and of the Muhammadans 22·36, whilst the percentage of Hindu students receiving University education in Colleges is shown to be 89·41, and of the Muhammadans only 3·65. The enormous disparity between the percentage of the Muhammadan population and the percentage of Muhammadan students receiving University education in Colleges is a lamentable fact, to which attention will be more fully invited in a later portion of this work. Meanwhile it may be said that, so far as higher English education is concerned, the Muhammadans were so seriously backward that, even in 1882, their proportion in the Colleges was less than *one-sixth* of what it should have been, considering their percentage in the total population.

* The minor sections of the community here mentioned are Sikhs, Parsis, Native Christians, Europeans, Eurasians and others. In regard to each of these races figures are given in separate columns, in Table No. II. of the Education Commission's Report of 1882, at page 275, and those figures, being added up yield a total of 375, as mentioned in the text.

Statistics of English education among Muhammadans during 1882-92.

A general view of the progress of English education among the Muhammadans, during the ten years following the Report of the Indian Education Commission of 1882, may be had from the following Table, which has been extracted from the Table given in paragraph 233, at page 322, of Mr. Nash's report, the column representing the percentage of Muhammadans to total population being taken from another table* in his Report, as representing the census of 1891.

CLASSIFICATION OF MUHAMMADAN PUPILS IN COLLEGES AND SCHOOLS, 1886-87 AND 1891-92.

Province.	Percentage of Muhammadans to total population (Census of 1891).	1886-87.						1891-92.					
		In Arts Colleges (English).		In Professional Colleges.		In Secondary Schools.		In Arts Colleges (English).		In Professional Colleges.		In Secondary Schools.	
		Muhammadans.	Percentage of Muhammadans.	Muhammadans.	Percentage of Muhammadans.	Muhammadans.	Percentage of Muhammadans.	Muhammadans.	Percentage of Muhammadans.	Muhammadans.	Percentage of Muhammadans.	Muhammadans.	Percentage of Muhammadans.
Madras	6·3	50	1·6	4	1·1	3,450	5·2	56	1·5	11	1·7	3,814	5·3
Bombay	16·3	25	2·6	10	1·4	1,657	4·4	35	2·6	9	1·8	2,117	4·9
Bengal	32·9	138	4·3	63	4·5	22,271	12·1	299	5·7	37	3·5	27,461	13·5
N.-W. P. and Oudh ...	13·5	63	13·2	34	13·5	14,367	21·6	249	19·0	140	17·7	11,782	21·9
Punjab	55·8	55	17·2	28	20·1	14,048	31·4	84	18·2	45	19·6	16,753	33·1
Central Provinces	2·4	7	7	...	...	471	11·2	13	5·6	4	4·9	2,217	9·3
Burma { Upper	1·4	...	...	...	...	...	...	...	...	...	...	26	3·6
Burma { Lower	4·5	...	...	...	...	422	4·9	...	...	...	...	543	5·3
Assam	27·1	...	...	...	...	1,640	15·5	...	...	...	...	1,550	15·0
Coorg	7·3	...	...	...	...	9	2·0	...	...	...	...	5	1·0
Hyderabad Assigned Districts (Berar)	7·2	...	...	...	...	309	6·6	...	...	...	...	384	8·3
Total ...	21·8	338	4·2	139	5·1	58,644	13·7	736	5·9	246	7·5	66,652	14·0

Deficiency in the progress of English Collegiate education among Muhammadans during 1882-92.

It will be observed that the percentage of Muhammadan pupils to the total number on the rolls in Arts Colleges was 3·65 in 1881-82, as shown in the Table given at the outset of this Chapter, whilst as shown in the preceding Table, the percentage rose to 4·2 in 1886-87, and to 5·9 in 1891-92, which may be taken as the latest available information upon the subject. Satisfactory as this progress may seem, it must not be forgotten that the percentage of Muhammadans to the total population is shown in the same Table as 21·8, so that it may be significantly said that, so far as English Collegiate education in Arts is concerned, the deficiency in the number of Muhammadan students in English Arts Colleges is nearly 16 per cent. with reference to the proportion of Muhammadans to the total population. In other words, the number of Muhammadan pupils in English Collegiate education is about one-fourth of what it should have been. It is, however, satisfactory to observe, with reference to the statistics given in the above Table, that between 1887 and 1892, in Arts Colleges, the number of Muhammadan students has increased from 338 to 736, and the percentage from 4·2 to 5·9; whilst in Professional Colleges their number has risen from 139 to 246, and the percentage also from 5·1 to 7·5. "The numerical increase is greatest in Law Colleges, from 99 to 172, but the students in Medical Colleges have increased in a greater ratio, from 16 to 39. In Engineering Colleges the increase is from 24 to 35, the latter number includes one student in the Madras Agricultural College, which in 1887 was classed as a School." †

Success of Muhammadans in University Examinations in 1887 and 1892.

The following Table ‡ shows the number of Muhammadans who passed the various University Examinations in 1886-87 and in 1891-92. The Bachelor of Science Degree of Bombay and the Bachelor of Oriental Learning of the Punjab University have both been included under the B.A. Examination, and all examinations intermediate between Matriculation and these degrees, have been included under the First Arts Examination.

* This Table is given at page 320 of Mr. Nash's Report, and the percentage of Muhammadans to total population in the various Provinces, according to the census of 1891, has been taken from the first column of that Table. The Table itself is omitted here as its figures deal indiscriminately with all classes of education, including Primary, Vernacular, and schools teaching the *Koran*, and it is impossible to extract separate information from it regarding the number of Muhammadans receiving English education.

† Progress of Education in India, 1887-88 to 1891-92. By A. M. Nash, Esquire, M. A. (1893), p. 323. ‡ Ib., p. 325.

STATEMENT SHOWING THE NUMBER OF MUHAMMADANS WHO PASSED THE VARIOUS UNIVERSITY EXAMINATIONS IN 1886-87 AND IN 1891-92.

1886-87.

Province.	Entrance. Total number passed.	Entrance. Total Muhammadans passed.	F.A. and Corresponding Examinations. Total number passed.	F.A. and Corresponding Examinations. Total Muhammadans passed.	B.A. including B.Sc. and B.O.L. Total number passed.	B.A. including B.Sc. and B.O.L. Total Muhammadans passed.	M.A. including M.O.L. Total number passed.	M.A. including M.O.L. Total Muhammadans passed.	B.L. Total number passed.	B.L. Total Muhammadans passed.	All Medical Examinations. Total number passed.	All Medical Examinations. Total Muhammadans passed.	All Engineering Examinations. Total number passed.	All Engineering Examinations. Total Muhammadans passed.
Madras	2,165	43	937	14	158	1	3	...	16	...	42	...	7	...
Bombay	527	5	289	6	81	3	8	...	18	...	119	1	20	...
Bengal	2,409	133	716	41	369	14	63	2	152	6	47	...	4	...
N.-W. P. and Oudh ...	477	82	96	13	66	9	6	...	...	...	...	...	...	..
Punjab	36	5	2	...	25	3	...	...	...	...	23	2	2	1
Central Provinces ...	132	10	27	1	13	1	1	...	...	...	...	...	...	...
Upper Burma... ...	...	...	...	..	..	...	...	...	...	...	...	...	...	...
Lower Burma... ...	39	...	6	...	1	...	...	..	...	...	...	...	...	...
Assam	97	3	...	...	...	...	...	.	..	...	...	...	...	...
Coorg	8	...	...	...	...	...	...	...	...	...	...	...	..	...
Hyderabad Assigned Districts (Berar) ...	11	...	...	...	...	...	...	...	...	..	...	..	...	...
Total ...	5,901	281	2,078	75	718	31	81	2	186	6	231	3	33	1

1891-92.

Province.	Entrance. Total number passed.	Entrance. Total Muhammadans passed.	F.A. and Corresponding Examinations. Total number passed.	F.A. and Corresponding Examinations. Total Muhammadans passed.	B.A. including B.Sc. and B.O.L. Total number passed.	B.A. including B.Sc. and B.O.L. Total Muhammadans passed.	M.A. including M.O.L. Total number passed.	M.A. including M.O.L. Total Muhammadans passed.	B.L. Total number passed.	B.L. Total Muhammadans passed.	All Medical Examinations. Total number passed.	All Medical Examinations. Total Muhammadans passed.	All Engineering Examinations. Total number passed.	All Engineering Examinations. Total Muhammadans passed.
Madras	2,374	33	970	10	316	...	6	...	48	1	32	...	6	...
Bombay	893	21	314	7	132	1	6	...	35	...	64	2	32	...
Bengal	1,695	85	1,011	47	273	14	46	1	48	4	135	1	9	..
N.-W. P. and Oudh ...	715	107	161	27	112	23	15	..	14	2	...	...	...	...
Punjab	619	157	160	26	49	18	8	1	...	...	33	5	...	...
Central Provinces ...	99	5	59	3	19	...	4	...	2	...	...	...	...	...
Upper Burma... ...	...	...	...	...	...	...	...	...	...	...	...	...	...	...
Lower Burma... ...	31	...	11	...	4	...	...	...	...	...	...	...	...	...
Assam	89	11	...	...	...	...	...	...	...	...	...	...	...	...
Coorg	7	...	...	...	...	...	..	...	...	...	...	...	...	...
Hyderabad Assigned Districts (Berar) ...	23	...	...	...	...	...	...	...	...	...	...	...	...	...
Total ...	6,545	419	2,695	120	905	51	80	2	147	7	264	8	47	...

Deficiency in the success of Muhammadans in Universities, compared with their percentage in the populaton, in 1891-92.

Perhaps the most convenient way, to show the general effect of this Table, as giving the latest available information regarding the progress of English education among Muhammadans, is to take the figures for 1891-92, given in that Table, as totals of successful candidates, with reference to the percentage of Muhammadan successful candidates in such totals, comparing such percentage with the percentage of Muhammadans in the total population of India. This comparison is shown in the following Table, in regard to the whole of British India:—

EXAMINATION.	Total number passed.	Total Muhammadans passed.	Percentage of Muhammadans passed.	Percentage of Muhammadans to total population.	Deficiency in the percentage of Muhammadans passed.
Entrance	6,545	419	6·3	21·8	15·5
F.A. and Corresponding Examinations ...	2,695	120	4·4	„	17·4
B.A., including B.Sc. and B.O.L. ...	905	51	5·7	„	16·1
M.A., including M.O.L.	80	2	2·5	„	19.3
B.L.	147	7	4·7	„	17·1
All Medical Examinations	264	8	3·4	„	18·4
All Engineering Examinations ...	47	...	0	„	21·8

The percentage of Muhammadans to the total population of India, adopted by Mr. Nash in his Report, is 21·8, and it is with reference to this percentage that the calculations in the last column of this Table have been made. It shows how, notwithstanding recent efforts, the Muhammadans are still backward in English education, specially in the higher classes—the deficiency in all the University Examinations being very prominent when the percentage of Muhammadans in the total population is borne in mind. Enormous efforts to promote English education among Muhammadans are still required to raise the percentage of their successful candidates in the University Examinations to the level of their percentage in the total population of India. Hitherto what has been achieved falls far short of what is required.

Views of the Government of India on Muhammadan education, in the Resolution dated 18th June 1888.

In regard to the condition of Muhammadan education in 1886-87, the following observations, to be found in the Resolution of the Government of India, in the Home Department (Education) No. 199, dated the 18th June, 1888, on Sir Alfred Croft's *Review of Education in India in 1886*, must be borne in mind, and may be quoted here:—

"Special recommendations for the education of Muhammadans were made by the Education Commission; and the Governor-General in Council, in Home Department Resolution, No. 7—215-25, of July 15th, 1885, reviewed the suggestions which had been made for the special treatment of this class. The Commission proposed a differential treatment of the Muhammadan community in respect to education, which the Government of India found itself unable to approve. In its Resolution just referred to, the Government of India pointed out that, if the Muhammadans desired to succeed in the competition of life with their Hindu fellow-subjects, the way lay in taking advantage, in the same manner as other classes do, of the high education provided by the Government. The Governor-General in Council is glad to think that the Muhammadans have themselves adopted this view of the subject. In 1881-82, there were 4,47,703 Muhammadan pupils; in 1885-86 they numbered 7,48,663, and in 1886-87, 7,52,441. The great increase in the first-mentioned period must not, however, be taken as showing that children not previously at school were brought under instruction. The increase is chiefly due to the extension of the State System of education, so as to include schools which were previously outside it. The percentage of Muhammadans to total pupils, which in 1881-82, was only 17·8, stood in 1886-87 at 22·5—practically a ratio identical with the proportion which the Muhammadan population (45 millions) bears to the total population (199 millions) of British India, according to the census of 1881. But if this steady and marked advance of the Muhammadan community in regard to education be a gratifying feature of the educational statistics for the past five years, a closer examination of the figures shews much room for improvement. Although the total number of Muhammadans under instruction compares favourably with the total number of Hindus, the number of the former receiving education of an advanced type is very small relatively to the number of Hindus under similar instruction. Out of a total of 23,03,812 Hindus attending all classes of schools, private and public, in 1886-87, 3,16,493 were in the secondary stage, while 9,634 were attending College. On the other hand, out of a total of 7,52,441 Muhammadans under instruction during the same year, only 58,222 were attending Secondary Schools, and only 587 attending College. Thus, while one out of every seven Hindu students was receiving the higher education, only one out of thirteen Muhammadan students had passed beyond the primary stage. To this condition of things, especially regarding collegiate education, His Excellency in Council would earnestly invite the attention of the Muhammadan community, and would impress on them the necessity of their taking advantage more largely of the educational facilities within their reach. The fact that the attendance of the Muhammadan students at Secondary Schools has since 1881-82 risen from 20,000 to over 58,000, shews, indeed, that progress is being made; but the progress might be more rapid."

Views of the Government of India on Muhammadan education, in the Resolution dated 7th September 1894.

Even later information in regard to the views of the Government of India on the subject of Muhammadan education in general, is contained in the Resolution * of the Government of India in the Home Department (Education), dated the 7th September 1894, of which paragraph 19 relates to the subject, and may be quoted here for convenient reference:—

"The subject of the education of Muhammadans has usually received separate comment. The total number of Muhammadan students enumerated in the returns, was 4,47,703 in 1881-82, and in 1886-87 it was 7,52,441 †; but this increase was partly the result of the extension of the State System, and covered schools previously excluded. It was remarked, in dealing with the figures of 1886-87, that a far larger proportion of Hindu than of Muhammadan students were receiving advanced instruction. Out of the 7,52,441 Muhammadan boys above mentioned, 58,222 only were attending Secondary Schools, and 587, only, were attending Colleges. In 1891-92 the total number of Muhammadan pupils at both public and private institutions was 8,87,236; and the percentage of Muhammadan pupils to total pupils was 23, the percentage of Muhammadans to total population in the area under consideration being, according to the census of 1891, 21·8. The number of pupils in 1892-93 was 8,94,241, or almost identical with the number attending school in 1891-92. Muhammadan children are, however, only 19·2 per cent. of the pupils in public institutions, and the great majority of the private schools attended by them are Koran Schools. Still there is an advance of nearly a hundred thousand in the number of Muhammadans attending public institutions, and the percentage of increase has been greater than in the case of Hindus. The number of Muhammadans attending Secondary Schools in 1891-92 was 66,652: 246 were in Professional Colleges and 736 in English Arts Colleges. The advance of this section of the population in respect of higher education has, therefore, not been rapid. It is noticed, however, that at all the University Examinations in Arts, except the M.A. Examination, the number of Muhammadan successful candidates has increased, both absolutely and relatively, to those of other religions: at the Matriculation Examination the increase is from 281 to 419. The employment in Madras and Bombay of a special Muhammadan Inspecting Staff has been followed by a large increase in the number of Primary Schools attended by Muhammadans. Muhammadan Assistant Inspectors have been appointed also for Eastern Bengal and Behar. In this and other Provinces there appears to be liberal pecuniary provision for Muhammadan education. Mr. Nash cites in paragraph 241 of his Review, a Resolution of the third Muhammadan Educational Congress held at Lahore in December 1888, and gives figures showing that, in the most recent years, the Muhammadans have made greater progress in the Punjab, than either Sikhs or Hindus, but they have still much ground to regain. In the Central Provinces the percentage of children at school is three times as high among Muhammadans as among Hindus, both for boys and for girls." ‡

Noticeable points in the above Resolution.

These remarks are no doubt satisfactory, on the whole, so far as Muhammadan education in general is concerned, and are a fit subject for congratulation to the Muhammadan community, but they must not forget (to use the words of the Government of India in the above quoted passage), that "the number of Muhammadans attending Secondary Schools in 1891-92 was 66,652: 246 were in Professional Colleges and 736 in English Arts Colleges. The advance of this section of the population in respect of higher education, has, therefore, not been rapid;" and again, "that in the most recent years the Muhammadans have made greater progress in the Punjab than either Sikhs or Hindus, but they have still much ground to regain."

* Reviewing Mr. Nash's Report on the Progress of Education in India, 1887-88 to 1891-92.

† The figures quoted in the Home Department Resolution, No. 199, dated 18th June 1888, are cited.

‡ Supplement to the *Gazette of India*, dated 8th September, 1894, page 1276.

Statistics of higher English education among Muhammadans considered, apart from other education in general.

But these are not the only points which deserve notice, in considering the question of the progress of English education among the Muhammadans, as represented by the latest statistics in Mr. Nash's Report. Much confusion upon this subject is liable to arise in the minds of Muhammadan educationists, by confounding the figures and statistics of all kinds and classes of education taken as a whole, in one lump. And since this work is concerned only with English education, especially of the higher or Collegiate type, imparted in institutions situate in large towns or cities, it is necessary to separate the statistics of higher English education from other kinds of education, and to give an approximate idea of the exact condition of that class of education among Muhammadans at the present time. The best way to make this matter clear is to take the figures given in Mr. Nash's Report as to the percentage of Muhammadans in the *Urban* population (at p. 321) and their percentage in English Arts and Professional Colleges, and Secondary Schools (at p. 322) during the official year 1891-92, and to indicate the results in the following Table :—

PROPORTION OF MUHAMMADANS IN THE URBAN POPULATION, AND IN ENGLISH COLLEGES AND SECONDARY SCHOOLS, IN 1891-92.

Province.	Percentage of Muhammadans in—			
	Arts Colleges.	Professional Colleges.	Secondary Schools.	Urban Population.
Madras	1·5	1·7	5·3	14·2
Bombay	2·6	1·8	4·9	17·8
Bengal	5·7	3·5	13·5	27·5
N.-W. Provinces and Oudh	19·0	17·7	21·9	33·9
Punjab	18·2	19·6	33·1	50·8
Central Provinces	5·6	4·9	9·3	16·0
Upper Burma	...	...	3·6	10·3
Lower Burma	...	...	5·3	
Assam	...	...	15·0	28·8
Coorg	...	...	1·0	23·3
Berar	...	...	8·3	20·7

Noticeable backwardness of Muhammadan Urban population in English Collegiate education.

In the above Table the percentages given in the columns of Arts Colleges and Urban population are most noticeable, nor are the percentages given in the column of Professional Colleges less important for comparison with the percentages shown in the column of the Urban population. Such a comparison will show that whilst in the matter of collegiate education the percentages of Muhammadans in the Colleges as compared with the percentages of the Muhammadans in the Urban population shows a disastrous state of backwardness, even in the matter of English education in Secondary Schools their backwardness is most lamentable. This state of things must be realized by every well-wisher of the progress of education among Muhammadans, and also by all who think calmly upon the broad general questions of the day, which require a careful consideration of the comparative progress of high English education among the various sections of the Indian population, for solution of vast problems of social, economical, and political import.

CHAPTER XXX.

GENERAL SURVEY OF THE STATISTICS OF HIGH ENGLISH EDUCATION AMONG MUHAMMADANS AS COMPARED WITH HINDUS, FROM THE ESTABLISHMENT OF THE INDIAN UNIVERSITIES TO THE PRESENT PERIOD—36 YEARS—1858 TO 1893.

Comparative statistics of Hindu and Muhammadan graduates of Indian Universities, 1857-93 proposed.

It is proposed in this chapter to take a general survey of the comparative progress of High English education among Hindus and Muhammadans, respectively, with reference to the statistics of success in the various examinations for degrees of the Indian Universities. The chapter concerns itself only with graduates; that is, with those who have succeeded in obtaining University Degrees, as distinguished from under-graduates who have either failed in obtaining degrees or have not pursued their studies up to that standard. A historical account of the establishment of the various Indian Universities, and the scope and character of the education recognised and controlled by them, has been given in Chapter XVIII of this work, and in this Chapter it is intended to describe with reference to statistics, the amount of success which they have achieved during thirty-six years, that is from the foundation of the Universities up to the present period (1893). It must be borne in mind that the Universities of Calcutta, Madras, and Bombay, were established in 1857, the Punjab University in 1882, and the Allahabad University in 1887, and the statistics of these various Universities must therefore be considered with reference to these various dates.

Multifariousness of the population of India.

The population of India consists of a vast conglomeration of races and creeds, and it is not an easy matter to offer any classification which would meet the approval of all ethnologists and politicians. A general view however of the population of India has been thus expressed by Sir William Hunter, in his work *The Indian Empire* (2nd ed. p. 52) :—

" According to the census of 1881, the comparatively pure descendants of the Aryan race (the Brahmins and Rajputs) still numbered 16 millions in British India; the mixed population, including lower caste Hindus, Aboriginal Tribes, and Christians, 138 millions; and the Muhammadans, 45 millions. These make up the 199 millions in British India in 1881. In the Feudatory States there appear to have been $5\frac{1}{4}$ millions of Brahmans and Rajputs; $46\frac{1}{4}$ millions of lower caste Hindus and Aboriginal Tribes; and 5 millions of Muhammadans,—making up the $56\frac{1}{2}$ millions in Feudatory India, in 1881. The Aboriginal element of the population was chiefly returned as low-caste Hindus. Only $4\frac{3}{4}$ millions were separately registered as non-Aryans, or Aborigines in British India; and $1\frac{3}{4}$ millions in the Feudatory States; making $6\frac{1}{2}$ millions for all India in 1881."

Population of British India in 1881.

To be more specific in regard to figures, the following Table has been compiled from the Tabular Statement Appendix X. given at page 703, of Sir William Hunter's work abovementioned :—

POPULATION OF BRITISH INDIA IN 1881.

Hindus	14,48,75,315
Muhammadans	4,51,27,033
Christians	11,68,589
Aboriginal Tribes	46,77,688
Miscellaneous	60,40,272
TOTAL ...	20,18,88,897

It will be seen from this Table that Hindus and Muhammadans, aggregating 19,00,02,348, form the main bulk of the population of India, leaving 1,18,86,549, of which no less than 46,77,688 belong to Aboriginal tribes in a very low state of civilisation, untouched by the Educational System. Under the heading "*Miscellaneous*" are included Buddhists (almost entirely in Burma), Jains, Parsis, Jews, etc., who in point of numbers, are too small to be separately dealt with in any statistical consideration of the general subject of the progress of University Education in India. Again, the social, political, and economical conditions of the European, Eurasian, and Native Christian population of India are so peculiar and different from the ordinary natives of India, that no conclusions of much significance can be arrived at by taking them into account for purposes of estimating the progress of high English education among the people of India in general.

Consideration of comparative statistics limited to Hindu and Muhammadan graduates, with reference to census of 1881, and University statistics, 1857-93.

This chapter is, therefore, limited to the consideration of the question how far High English education, as represented by the Indian University Degrees, has advanced among Hindus and Muhammadans, respectively, and since these two communities, not only numerically but also from social, political, and economical points of view, form the most important portion of the population, interesting and valuable conclusions may be drawn by forming an accurate estimate of the comparative progress which High English education has made among them. The figures of the census of 1881 have been adopted as the basis of calculations in this Chapter, because ordinarily a course of ten or twelve years' duration is necessary for a young native student to obtain a degree of the Indian Universities, and since the statistics of graduates in this chapter have been brought down to the year 1893, the census of the population in 1881 is a better basis of calculating progress of High English education, during the last ten or twelve years, than the latest census taken in 1891. Moreover, the two censuses have not altered the percentages of Hindus and Muhammadans in the total population, and therefore for purposes of comparison there can be no harm in preferring the census of 1881 to that of 1891, whilst it is obvious, that, since primary and secondary stages of education are not included within the scope of this chapter, which deals only with graduates of the Universities, the increase of population between 1881 and 1891 can have no great bearing upon the present condition of High English education in India.

Distribution of Hindu and Muhammadan population into castes, sects, &c., in 1881.

Dealing therefore only with Hindus and Muhammadans, whose aggregate population in 1881 amounted to 19,00,02,348, the following table * shows their distribution into castes, sects, and nationalities :—

HINDU AND MUHAMMADAN POPULATION OF BRITISH INDIA CLASSIFIED ACCORDING TO CASTE, SECT, AND NATIONALITY, IN 1881.

PROVINCES.	HINDUS.			MUHAMMADANS.			
	Brahmans.	Rajputs.	Other Castes.	Sunnis.	Shiahs.	Wahabis, Faraizis.	Unspecified.
Madras	11,22,070	2,07,465	2,71,68,143	17,58,375	44,378	1,102	1,29,706
Bombay	6,64,411	1,96,906	1,14,47,265	29,40,764	78,531	178	1,658
Bengal	27,54,100	14,09,354	4,12,89,352	2,09,64,657	2,62,293	2,144	4,75,630
Punjab	8,09,081	6,52,181	56,69,266	1,03,20,022	95,655	2,414	1,07,059
N.-W. P. and Oudh ...	46,55,204	30,27,400	3,03,70,790	57,52,056	1,70,547	28	255
Central Provinces ...	3,32,207	2,21,849	67,63,774	2,59,608	6,772	186	9,207
Assam	1,19,075	10,541	29,32,532	13,08,712	6,377	1,340	593
Berar	65,754	46,148	23,13,752	1,85,686	1,360	39	470
Ajmere	22,388	15,876	3,37,765	57,262	547	......	......
Coorg	2,445	480	1,59,564	12,540	1	......	......
British Burma	......	......	88,177	1,50,821	11,287	1,249	5,524
Total for British India ...	1,05,46,735	57,88,200	12,85,40,380	4,37,10,503	6,77,748	8,680	7,30,102

* Extracted from Appendix X., Hunter's *Indian Empire*; 2nd Ed., p. 703.

Distribution and percentages of the Hindu and Muhammadan population in the various Provinces, in 1881.

Taking the figures of this Table the following abstract Tabular Statement has been prepared, showing the totals of the various sub-divisions of Hindus and Muhammadans, respectively, and the percentage of each creed in the total Hindu and Muhammadan population, in the various Provinces of India, in 1881 :—

HINDU AND MUHAMMADAN POPULATIONS OF BRITISH INDIA, AS DISTRIBUTED AMONG THE VARIOUS PROVINCES, IN 1881.

PROVINCES.	Hindus.	Muhammadans.	Total.	PERCENTAGE.	
				Hindus.	Muhammadans.
Bengal	4,54,52,806	2,17,04,724	6,71,57,530	67·7	32·3
Assam	30,62,148	13,17,022	43,79,170	69·3	30·7
British Burma	88,177	1,68,881	2,57,058	34·3	65·7
Madras	2,84,97,678	19,33,561	3,04,31,239	93·7	6·3
Coorg	1,62,489	12,541	1,75,030	92·3	7·7
Bombay	2,23,08,582	30,21,131	1,53,29,713	80·3	19·7
Berar	24,25,654	1,87,555	26,13,209	92·8	7·2
Punjab	71,30,528	1,05,25,150	1,76,55,678	40·4	59·6
N.-W. P. and Oudh ...	3,80,53,394	59,22,886	4,39,76,280	86·6	13·4
Central Provinces ...	73,17,830	2,75,773	75,93,603	96·4	3·6
Ajmere	3,76,029	57,809	4,33,838	86·7	13·3
Total for British India ...	14,48,75,315	4,51,27,033	19,00,02,348	76·25	23·75

Hindu and Muhammadan population, classified according to jurisdiction of Indian Universities.

Upon the basis of the figures given in this Table an interesting calculation has been made, by classifying the various Provinces within the jurisdiction of each of the Indian Universities, and showing the totals of the Hindu and Muhammadan population under the jurisdiction of each University, and the distribution of the population into Hindus and Muhammadans, with the percentage of each community in the total Hindu and Muhammadan population. The results of the calculation are shown in the following Table :—

HINDU AND MUHAMMADAN POPULATION OF BRITISH INDIA UNDER THE JURISDICTION OF THE INDIAN UNIVERSITIES, ACCORDING TO THE CENSUS OF 1881.

UNIVERSITIES.	Provinces within the jurisdiction of the University.	Total Hindu and Muhammadan population.	DISTRIBUTION OF POPULATION INTO		PERCENTAGE.	
			Hindus.	Muhammadans.	Hindus.	Muhammadans.
Calcutta	Bengal, Assam, Burma ...	7,17,93,758	4,86,03,131	2,31,90,627	67·7	32·3
Madras	Madras, Coorg ...	3,06,06,269	2,86,60,167	19,46,102	93·6	6·4
Bombay	Bombay, Berar ...	1,79,42,922	1,47,34,236	32,08,686	82·1	17·9
Punjab	Punjab ...	1,76,55,678	71,30,528	1,05,25,150	40·4	59·6
Allahabad	N.-W. P. & Oudh, Central Provinces, Ajmere	5,20,03,721	4,57,47,253	62,56,468	88·0	12·0
Total		19,00,02,348	14,48,75,315	4,51,27,033	76·25	23·75

Percentages calculated with reference to the total Hindu and Muhammadan population only.

It must be borne in mind that the percentages given in this Table have not been calculated with reference to the total population of all sects and nationalities inhabiting India, but with reference only to the total Hindu and Muhammadan population, as it is with them only that this Chapter is concerned. The percentages are therefore naturally different from those usually given in the Government Census Reports, since the percentages of Hindus and Muhammadans are there calculated with reference to the entire population, including all creeds and nationalities. The scope of this Chapter is limited to a comparison of the progress of high English education among the Hindus on the one hand, and the Muhammadans on the other, and taking their aggregate population in British India, the calculations in the above Table show that whilst the percentage of Hindus is 76·25, the percentage of Muhammadans is 23·75. In other words the proportion of Muhammadans to Hindus in British India is $\frac{23{\cdot}75}{76{\cdot}25}$ or ·31, or $\frac{3}{10}$, that is, the Muhammadan population is more than one-fourth and less than one-third of the number of the Hindu population.

Comparative Statistics of Hindu and Muhammadan graduates, prepared from Calendars of Indian Universities, 1858-93, divided into periods of 6 years each.

Such being the proportion of Muhammadans to the Hindu population of British India, Statistics have been carefully prepared from the Calendars of the various Indian Universities, up to the year 1893, for describing the comparative progress which high English education has made among the two communities respectively. The following Table shows the successful results achieved by Hindus and Muhammadans, respectively, in the examinations for Degrees in the various Faculties of the Indian Universities during the 36 years, from 1858 to 1893, divided into periods of 6 years each :—

HINDU AND MUHAMMADAN GRADUATES IN THE VARIOUS FACULTIES OF THE INDIAN UNIVERSITIES DURING 36 YEARS, 1858 TO 1893, DIVIDED INTO PERIODS OF 6 YEARS EACH.

Period.	Arts.			Law.			Medicine and Surgery.			Engineering.			Total.		
	Number of graduates.		Percentage of Muhammadan graduates.	Number of graduates.		Percentage of Muhammadan graduates.	Number of graduates.		Percentage of Muhammadan graduates.	Number of graduates.		Percentage of Muhammadan graduates.	Number of graduates.		Percentage of Muhammadan graduates.
	Hindus.	Muhammadans.		Hindus.	Muhammadans.		Hindus.	Muhammadans.		Hindus.	Muhammadans.		Hindus.	Muhammadans.	
1858-63 ...	88	1	1·13	36	...	...	45	1	2·2	18	...	...	187	2	1·1
1864-69 ...	472	9	1·9	238	4	1·6	113	3	2·6	25	...	...	848	16	1·8
1870-75 ...	846	10	1·2	589	9	1·5	160	7	4·2	57	...	...	1,652	26	1·6
1876-81 ...	1,252	23	2·03	385	5	1·3	321	3	·93	128	...	...	2,086	31	1·5
1882-87 ...	2,978	110	3·6	827	37	4·3	292	6	2	130	2	1·5	4,227	155	3·6
1888-93 ...	4,079	246	5·7	1,462	55	3·6	308	14	4·3	232	1	·4	6,081	316	5·0
Total 1858-93 ...	9,715	399	3·9	3,537	110	3·02	1,239	34	2·7	590	3	·5	15,081	546	3·5
Average per year	269·9	11·1	...	98·2	3	...	34·4	·99	...	16·4	·1	...	418·9	15·1	...

Extreme paucity of Muhammadan graduates during the first four periods, 1858 to 1881.

It will be observed from this Table that during the first period of six years, only two Muhammadans succeeded in obtaining University Degrees, as against 187 Hindus; that in the second period their number was 16 as against 848 Hindus; that in the third period there were 26 Muhammadans as against 1,652 Hindus, and even in the fourth period their number was only 31, as against no less than 2,086 Hindu graduates. In other words, during the first 24 years following the establishment of the Indian Universities the total number of Muhammadan graduates was only 75; whilst even in the very first period of six years the number of Hindu graduates was as much as 187, and during the 24 years no less than 4,773, as against only 75 Muhammadans. During these 24 years the proportion of Muhammadan graduates in no period exceeded 1·8 or 1⅘ per cent. of the total Hindu and Muhammadan graduates; a state of things so unsatisfactory as to justify the observation that during a quarter of a century succeeding the establishment of the Indian Universities, the Muhammadans remained almost totally dormant and oblivious of their interests, so far as high English education was concerned.

Signs of progress among Muhammadan graduates, during the 5th and 6th periods, 1882-93.

The fifth period of six years (from 1882 to 1887), however, indicate some signs of progress, showing the number of Muhammadan graduates to have risen during that period to 155, as against 4,227 Hindus, yielding a proportion of 3·6 per cent. Similarly during the sixth period of six years (from 1888 to 1893) the number of Muhammadan graduates increased to 316, as against 6,081 Hindus, yielding a proportion of 5 per cent. during that period.

Statistics of graduates viewed in respect of the whole period, 1858-93.

These Statistics when viewed in respect of the whole period of 36 years show even more lamentable results, so far as the Muhammadans are concerned. The Table shows that during the whole period, 1858 to 1893, only 546 Muhammadans succeeded in obtaining University Degrees in the various branches of learning, as against no less than 15,081 Hindus, yielding a proportion of only 3·5, or 3½ per cent. in the total number of Hindu and Muhammadan graduates, and an yearly average of 15·1, as against 418·9 Hindus or a proportion of only $\frac{1}{28}$ of the average number of Hindu graduates per year. In the Tables given in this Chapter relating to the Hindu and Muhammadan population in British India it has been shown that whilst the percentage of Hindus is 76·25 that of the Muhammadans is 23·75, which should also have been the percentage of the Muhammadans in the total number of Hindu and Muhammadan graduates, if the Muhammadans had made as much progress in high English education as the Hindus. As the figures stand, the percentage of Muhammadan graduates being only 3·5 instead of 23·75, their deficiency is no less than 20·25 per cent.

Statistics of great disparity between Hindus and Muhammadans in high English education, 1858-93.

The great disparity between the progress of high English education among Hindus and Muhammadans may also be considered with reference to the various degrees of progress made in the various Provinces within the jurisdiction of the different Universities, during the 36 years from the establishment of the various Universities to the year 1893. For this purpose the following Table gives the necessary statistical information :—

HINDU AND MUHAMMADAN GRADUATES IN THE VARIOUS FACULTIES OF THE INDIAN UNIVERSITIES DURING 36 YEARS, 1858 TO 1893, CLASSIFIED ACCORDING TO THE VARIOUS UNIVERSITIES.

University.	Arts.			Law.			Medicine and Surgery.			Engineering.			Total.		
	Number of graduates.		Percentage of Muhammadan graduates.	Number of graduates.		Percentage of Muhammadan graduates.	Number of graduates.		Percentage of Muhammadan graduates.	Number of graduates.		Percentage of Muhammadan graduates.	Number of graduates.		Percentage of Muhammadan graduates.
	Hindus.	Muhammadans.		Hindus.	Muhammadans.		Hindus.	Muhammadans.		Hindus.	Muhammadans.		Hindus.	Muhammadans.	
Calcutta	4,981	203	3·9	2,588	76	2·8	694	10	1·4	177	1	·6	8,440	290	3·4
Madras	2,634	22	·9	465	5	1·1	59	2	3·3	78	...	...	3,236	29	·9
Bombay	1,424	26	1·8	345	3	·9	423	9	2·1	335	2	·6	2,527	30	1·2
Punjab	246	69	21·9	87	20	19·	63	13	17·1	...	...	...	396	102	25·8
Allahabad... ...	430	79	15·5	52	6	10·4	...	...	...	...	...	...	482	85	17·6
Total ...	9,715	399	3·9	3,537	110	3·02	1239	34	2·7	590	3	·5	15,081	546	3·5
Average per year	269·9	11·1	...	98·2	3	...	34·4	·99	...	16·4	·1	...	418·9	15·1	...

Backwardness of high English education among Muhammadans in the various Provinces, as shown by University Statistics, 1858–93.

It appears from this Table that the Muhammadans are most backward in the Madras Presidency, and that their condition is scarcely better in the Presidency of Bombay. It seems that, so far as high English education is concerned, the Muhammadans of Madras have remained almost entirely dormant during the last 36 years since the foundation of the University in that Presidency. The figures show that during that period, whilst no less than 3,236 Hindus obtained degrees in the various branches of learning, only 29 Muhammadans succeeded in obtaining degrees, not affording even a proportion of one to each 100 of Hindu graduates. Nearly as lamentable seems the condition of Muhammadans in the Presidency of Bombay, where only 30 Muhammadans obtained degrees, as against 2,527 Hindus, or a proportion of one to every 100 Hindu graduates. The Statistics of the University of Calcutta, no doubt, show better results. There 290 Muhammadans obtained degrees, as against 8,440 Hindus ; but even this number does not afford a large proportion of Muhammadans as it yields only about 3 Muhammadan graduates to every 100 Hindus, whilst the proportion of the Muhammadan to the Hindu population is 32·3 to 67·7 in the Provinces within the jurisdiction of the University of Calcutta. In the Punjab University, since its establishment, 102 Muhammadans have taken Degrees as against 396 Hindus, yielding a proportion of about 25 Muhammadans to every 100 Hindu graduates. But although this result may at first seem satisfactory in favour of the Muhammadans, in reality, quite the reverse is the case, since in that Province the proportion of the Muhammadan to the Hindu population is as 59·6 to 40·4—the Muhammadans being nearly 60 per cent. of the total Hindu and Muhammadan population. The only part of India where high English education may be said to have made satisfactory progress among the Muhammadans, are the Provinces within the jurisdiction of the Allahabad University. In that University, since its foundation in 1887 to the year 1893, no less than 85 Muhammadans obtained Degrees, as against 482 Hindus, yielding a proportion of 17 to every 100 Hindu graduates ; whilst the proportion of the Muhammadan to the Hindu population is as 12 to 88 in those Provinces. This satisfactory result is due entirely to the exceptional efforts which have been made in the North-Western Provinces to popularise and promote high English education for the Muhammadans, resulting in the foundation of the Muhammadan Anglo-Oriental College at Aligarh, which during the period concerned passed 25 out of the total 85 Muhammadan graduates of the Allahabad University abovementioned. Had such not been the case, the percentage of Muhammadan graduates in the Allahabad University also would have fallen below the percentage of the Muhammadans in the total Hindu and Muhammadan population of the North-Western Provinces and Oudh.

Number of graduates per 1,00,000 of the Hindu and Muhammadan population, respectively, 1858–93.

The Statistics of the relative progress of high English education among Hindus and Muhammadans respectively may be considered also from other points of view, to facilitate comparison. The following Table has been prepared to show the number of graduates per 100,000 of each population, and, conversely, the number of each population among whom one is a graduate. As in the preceding Tables in this Chapter, the number of population has been calculated according to the census of 1881, and the number of graduates has been obtained from the Calendars of the various Indian Universities, from their establishment up to the year 1893. The results are shown in the Table on the next page.

TABLE SHOWING THE NUMBER OF GRADUATES PER 100,000 OF EACH POPULATION, AND THE NUMBER OF EACH POPULATION AMONG WHOM ONE IS A GRADUATE, FROM THE ESTABLISHMENT OF THE VARIOUS INDIAN UNIVERSITIES TO THE YEAR 1893.

University.	Arts.				Law.				Medicine and Surgery.				Engineering.				Total.			
	Number of graduates per 100,000 of each population.		Number of each population among whom one is a graduate.		Number of graduates per 100,000 of each population.		Number of each population among whom one is a graduate.		Number of graduates per 100,000 of each population.		Number of each population among whom one is a graduate.		Number of graduates per 100,000 of each population.		Number of each population among whom one is a graduate.		Number of graduates per 100,000 of each population.		Number of each population among whom one is a graduate.	
	Hindus.	Muhammadans.	Hindus.	Muhammadans.	Hindus.	Muhammadans.	Hindus.	Muhammadans.	Hindus.	Muhammadans.	Hindus.	Muhammadans.	Hindus.	Muhammadans.	Hindus.	Muhammadans.	Hindus.	Muhammadans.	Hindus.	Muhammadans.
Calcutta	10·2	·8	9,757	1,14,288	5·3	·9	18,780	3,05,139	1·4	·04	70,177	23,19,062	·3	·004	2,74,537	2,31,90,627	17·3	1·2	5,611	79,967
Madras	9·2	1·2	10,888	88,459	1·6	·3	63,065	3,89,220	·2	·1	4,85,765	9,73,051	·2	...	3,67,488	...	11·2	1·5	8,856	67,106
Bombay	9·7	·81	10,340	1,23,103	2·3	·09	42,708	10,69,562	2·8	·2	34,832	3,56,521	2·2	·06	43,982	16,04,343	17·1	·9	5,830	1,06,956
Punjab	3·4	·65	28,985	1,52,538	1·2	·2	81,960	5,26,257	·9	·1	1,06,425	8,09,621	...	...	...	...	5·5	·6	18,006	1,03,187
Allahabad	·94	1·3	1,06,388	80,335	·1	·09	8,79,755	10,42,744	..	..	...	...	...	...	..	...	1·05	1·3	94,911	73,604
Total ...	6·7	·88	14,912	1,13,100	2·4	·24	40,959	4,10,245	·8	·07	1,16,929	13,27,265	·4	·006	2,45,551	1,50,42,344	10·4	1·2	9,606	82,650

In many respects this Table gives a clearer indication of the backwardness of the Muhammadans than any of the preceding Tables in this Chapter. The figures relating to the various Universities, and in the different branches of learning, are separately shown in the Table, and it is necessary only to invite attention to the columns of the totals. It will be observed that even in the Faculty of Arts, whilst the number of Hindu graduates is 6·7 per *lakh* of the Hindu population, the number of Muhammadan graduates is only ·88, that is less than even 1 per *lakh* of the Muhammadan population. To represent the same results in another way, as shown in the table, whilst there is one graduate among every 14,912 of the Hindu population, among Muhammadans there is one graduate among every 1,13,100 of the population of that creed. Deplorable as these results may seem, so far as Muhammadans are concerned, the Statistics of the Faculties of Law, Medicine and Engineering, show even worse results in a descending scale—a circumstance all the more lamentable as these subjects, being professional, lead to obtaining means of lucrative employment. The general results of the calculations in the Table are shown in the last main column, under the heading "*total.*" It shows that whilst there are 10·4 graduates among every *lakh* of the Hindu population, the figure of Muhammadan graduates is only 1·2 in every *lakh* of the population of that creed. Leaving the decimals out of account, it may be said that whilst there are 10 graduates among every *lakh* of Hindus, there is only 1 Muhammadan in every *lakh* of that population. In other words, high English education has made nearly ten-fold progress among Hindus, as compared with the progress among the Muhammadans. Putting the matter in a different form, as shown in the Table, whilst there is one graduate among every 9,606 Hindus, there is one graduate in every 82,650 of the Muhammadan population.

Progress of high English education among Hindus *ten* times as great as among Muhammadans, calculated per 1,00,000 of the population of each community, 1858–93.

These results are so obvious, as showing the backwardness of the Muhammadans in high English education, in comparison to the Hindus, that it is scarcely necessary to deal with the figures in other forms. But it is important from all points of view, for the future prosperity of India, that the disparity which exists between Hindus and Muhammadans in the matter of high English education should be fully realised, and accordingly, the following Table has been prepared with reference to the census of 1881, and the number of graduates obtained from the Calendars of the various Indian Universities from their beginning down to the year 1893 :—

Deficiency in the number of Muhammadan graduates, according to the ratio of the Muhammadan to the Hindu population, 1858–93.

TABLE SHOWING THE NUMBER OF MUHAMMADAN GRADUATES AS IT OUGHT TO BE ACCORDING TO THE RATIO OF THE MUHAMMADAN TO THE HINDU POPULATION, THE ACTUAL NUMBER OF MUHAMMADAN GRADUATES AND THE DEFICIENCY IN THEIR NUMBER, DURING 36 YEARS, 1858 TO 1893.

2	Arts.				Law.				Medicine and Surgery.				Engineering.				Total.			
	1	3	4	5	6	7	8	9	10	11	12	13	14	15	16	17	18	19	20	21
Universities.	Number of Muhammadan graduates as it ought to be, according to the ratio of the Muhammadan to the Hindu population.	Actual number of Muhammadan graduates.	Deficiency in the number of Muhammadan graduates.	Percentage of the actual number (column 3) of Muhammadan graduates in the number as it ought to be (column 2).	Number of Muhammadan graduates as it ought to be, according to the ratio of the Muhammadan to the Hindu population.	Actual number of Muhammadan graduates.	Deficiency in the number of Muhammadan graduates.	Percentage of the actual number (column 7) of Muhammadan graduates in the number as it ought to be (column 6).	Number of Muhammadan graduates as it ought to be, according to the ratio of the Muhammadan to the Hindu population.	Actual number of Muhammadan graduates.	Deficiency in the number of Muhammadan graduates.	Percentage of the actual number (column 11) of Muhammadan graduates in the number as it ought to be ((column 10).	Number of Muhammadan graduates as it ought to be, according to the ratio of the Muhammadan to the Hindu population.	Actual number of Muhammadan graduates.	Deficiency in the number of Muhammadan graduates.	Percentage of the actual number (column 14) of Muhammadan graduates in the number as it ought to be (column 13).	Number of Muhammadan graduates as it ought to be, according to the ratio of the Muhammadan to the Hindu population.	Actual number of Muhammadan graduates.	Deficiency in the number of Muhammadan graduates.	Percentage of the actual number (column 19) of Muhammadan graduates in the number as it ought to be (column 18).
Calcutta ...	2,376	203	2,173	8·6	1,234	76	1,158	6·2	331	10	321	3·02	84	1	83	1·2	4,025	290	3,725	7·2
Madras ...	178	22	156	12·3	31	5	26	16·1	4	2	2	50·0	5	0	5	0	218	29	189	13·3
Bombay ...	310	26	284	8·4	75	3	72	4·0	92	9	83	9·8	72	2	70	2·7	549	30	519	5·5
Punjab ...	363	69	294	19·0	128	20	108	15·6	92	13	79	14·1	...	...	...	...	583	102	481	17·5
Allahabad ...	59	79	—20*	133·9	7	6	1	85·7	...	...	...	...	...	...	...	...	66	85	—19*	128·7
Total ...	3,286	399	2,887	12·1	1,475	110	1,365	7·4	519	34	485	6·2	161	3	158	1·8	5,441	546	4,895	10·03

* Excess over the number required by the ratio.

Explanation of the preceding Table, as showing the extent of the deficiency of the Muhammadans in high English education, as compared with the Hindus, 1858-93.

In order to understand the calculations in this Table clearly, and if necessary to verify them, the figures of the Hindu and Muhammadan population, and the ratio of the one to the other, as shown in the preceding Tables* in this Chapter, must be borne in mind, and also the figures in the Tables† relating to the number and proportion of Hindu and Muhammadan graduates, respectively. With reference to these Statistics, the hypothesis is that the progress which high English education has made among the Hindus, may be taken to represent a satisfactory standard of intellectual progress, and the object of the comparison is to show how far the Muhammadans have fallen short of that standard, when the ratio of their population to the Hindu population is borne in mind—these proportions having been shown, with reference to the various Provinces‡ and Universities§ in the previous Tables in this Chapter. For example, taking the whole Hindu and Muhammadan population of British India, it has been shown in one of the previous Tables, that whilst the percentage of Hindus is 76·25, the percentage of Muhammadans is 23·75, and this represents the ratio of the one population to the other. Again, it has been shown in another Table, that whilst the total number of Hindu graduates in all the Universities, down to the year 1893, is 15,081, the number of Muhammadan graduates is only 546, yielding a percentage of only 3·5 in the total number of Hindu and Muhammadan graduates in British India. Bearing this in mind, each of the headings in the above Table has been sub-divided into four columns—the calculation in the first column of each heading having been made with reference to the ratio of the Muhammadan to the Hindu population. Thus when there are 15,081 Hindu graduates, the number of Muhammadan graduates should have been 5,441, instead of which, as a matter of fact, the actual number is only 546, leaving a deficiency of 4,895 graduates showing, as the last column under the heading "*total*" shows, that the success which the Muhammadans have actually achieved, ever since the foundation of the Indian Universities, is only 10·03 per cent., or $\frac{1}{10}$th of what it should have been. In other words, the backwardness of Muhammadans is nine times as great as their success, they having fallen 90 per cent. short of the standard which they should have achieved if progress of high English education among them had been proportionately as great as among the Hindus. To put the idea in a more concrete form, the condition of high English education among Muhammadans may be compared to a bank, of which the assets are 546 and the debts 4,895. To put the matter shortly, the Muhammadans of India may be said to be suffering from all the evils of bankruptcy in the matter of high English education.

Proportionate number of Muhammadan graduates, as it should have been, according to the ratio of the Muhammadan to the Hindu population, in 1858-93.

That this conclusion is justified, is shown by dealing with the Statistics from another point of view. Taking the figures of the total Hindu and Muhammadan graduates, the percentage of each race in such total number has been calculated, and taking the percentage of the Hindu graduates as a standard of satisfactory success, it is shown what the proportion of Muhammadans should have been if they had achieved as satisfactory progress as the Hindus in high English education. The following Table shows the results of such calculations, with reference to the various Faculties of Learning in the various Universities of India:—

* *Vide* pages 183, 184, *ante*. | † *Vide* page 185, *ante*. | ‡ *Vide* page 184, *ante*. | § *Vide* page 184, *ante*.

TABLE SHOWING THE NUMBER OF GRADUATES OF EACH RACE, PER 100 OF THE TOTAL HINDU AND MUHAMMADAN GRADUATES, AND THE PROPORTIONATE NUMBER OF MUHAMMADAN GRADUATES, AS IT SHOULD HAVE BEEN, ACCORDING TO THE RATIO OF THE MUHAMMADAN TO THE HINDU POPULATION.

Subject.	Calcutta.			Madras.			Bombay.			Punjab.			Allahabad.			Total.		
	Number of graduates, per 100 of the total Hindu and Muhammadan graduates.		Proportionate number of Muhammadan graduates, as it should have been, as compared with the number of Hindu graduates (in column 2), according to the ratio of the Muhammadan to the Hindu population.	Number of graduates per 100 of the total Hindu and Muhammadan graduates.		Proportionate number of Muhammadan graduates, as it should have been, as compared with the number of Hindu graduates (in column 5), according to the ratio of the Muhammadan to the Hindu population.	Number of graduates per 100 of the total Hindu and Muhammadan graduates.		Proportionate number of Muhammadan graduates, as it should have been, as compared with the number of Hindu graduates (in column 8), according to the ratio of the Muhammadan to the Hindu population.	Number of graduates per 100 of the total Hindu and Muhammadan graduates.		Proportionate number of Muhammadan graduates, as it should have been, as compared with the number of Hindu graduates (in column 11), according to the ratio of the Muhammadan to the Hindu population.	Number of graduates per 100 of the total Hindu and Muhammadan graduates.		Proportionate number of Muhammadan graduates, as it should have been, as compared with the number of Hindu graduates (in column 14), according to the ratio of the Muhammadan to the Hindu population.	Number of graduates per 100 of the total Hindu and Muhammadan graduates.		Proportionate number of Muhammadan graduates, as it should have been, as compared with the number of Hindu graduates (in column 17), according to the ratio of the Muhammadan to the Hindu population.
	Hindus.	Muhammadans.		Hindus	Muhammadans.		Hindus.	Muhammadans.		Hindus.	Muhammadans.		Hindus.	Muhammadans.		Hindus.	Muhammadans.	
1	2	3	4	5	6	7	8	9	10	11	12	13	14	15	16	17	18	19
Arts ... M.A. ...	96·94	3·06	46·1	98·0	2·0	6·7	99·1	·9	21·74	81·25	18·75	120·6	96·7	3·3	13·2	96·7	3·3	30·1
Arts ... B.A. ...	95·71	4·29	45·6	99·2	·8	6·8	98·1	1·9	21·5	77·7	22·3	115·0	82·8	17·2	11·3	95·85	4·15	29·8
Total, Arts	96·1	3·9	45·8	99·1	·9	6·7	98·2	1·8	21·5	78·1	21·9	115·2	84·5	15·5	11·5	96·1	3·9	29·9
Law	97·2	2·8	46·4	98·9	1·1	6·7	99·1	·9	21·7	81·0	19·0	119·5	89·6	10·4	12·4	96·98	3·02	30·2
Medicine	98·6	1·4	47·0	96·7	3·3	6·6	97·9	2·1	21·4	82·9	17·1	122·3	...	...	...	97·3	2·7	30·3
Engineering	99·4	·6	47·4	100	...	6·8	99·4	·6	21·8	...	...	..	...	...	...	99·5	·5	31·0
Grand Total ..	96·6	3·4	45·9	90·1	·9	6·8	98·8	1·2	21·5	74·2	25·8	109·2	82·4	17·6	11·2	96·5	3·5	30·0

(Opposite to page 193.)

DIAGRAM I.

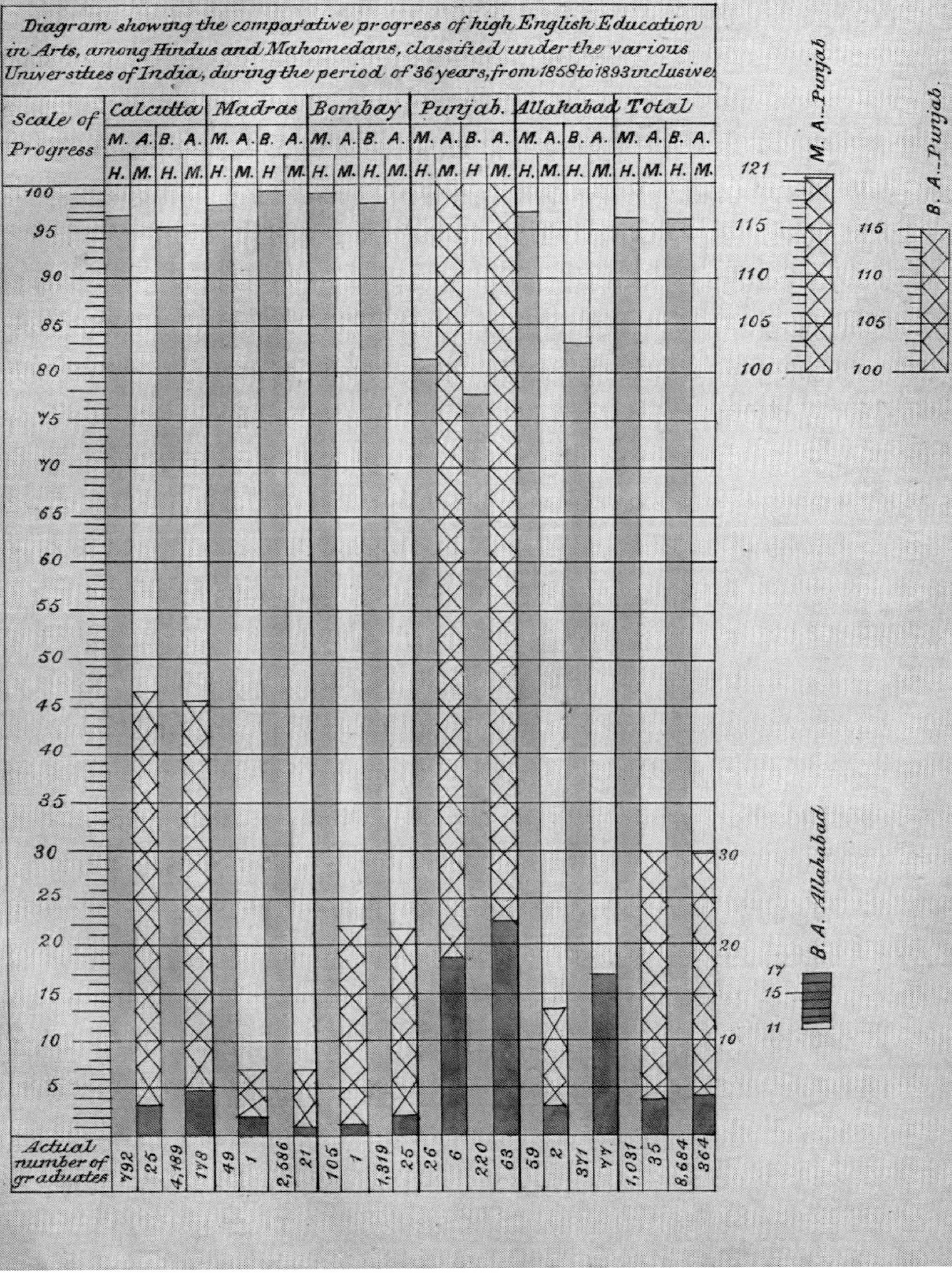

Calculations in the preceding Table explained.

The calculations contained in the last column of each of the subdivisions of this Table, namely, columns 4, 7, 10, 13, 16 and 19, require some explanation. The calculation has been made by taking the number of Hindu graduates, per 100 of the total Hindu and Muhammadan graduates (shown in columns 2, 5, 8, 11, 14 and 17), as the standard of satisfactory success, and upon that assumption, calculating, by the rule of three, what the proportionate number of Muhammadan graduates should have been, according to the ratio of the Muhammadan to the Hindu population, if the Muhammadans had achieved as much success in high English education as the Hindus—the success of the Hindus being in excess of what it should have been, in proportion to their number in the aggregate Hindu and Muhammadan population.

Diagram I, showing the comparative progress of high English education *in Arts* among Hindus and Muhammadans, 1858–93.

To illustrate the effect of the calculations contained in the preceding Table, so far as the Faculty of Arts is concerned, the accompanying diagram I. has been prepared on a uniform scale of 100 degrees, in columns placed in juxtaposition. The columns showing the progress of the Hindus are coloured pink, and those relating to the Muhammadans green, and the degrees up to which the columns have been coloured represent the actual progress of each, comparatively. The cross lines in the columns relating to the Muhammadans indicate the degrees of progress which the Muhammadans should have attained, if, with reference to the proportion of their population to the Hindu population, they had achieved as great a *rate* of success as the Hindus. In other words, the pink colours represent the calculations as to the M.A. and B.A. Degrees, in columns 2, 5, 8, 11, 14 and 17 of the above Table; the green colours represent the calculations contained in columns 3, 6, 9, 12, 15 and 18, and the cross lines in the columns relating to the Muhammadans represent the calculations contained in columns 4, 7, 10, 13, 16 and 19, in the above Table.

Figures necessary to understand the calculations in the Diagram I.

These explanations, when borne in mind, with reference to the calculations represented by the figures in the preceding Table, render the accompanying diagram easily intelligible, but for the sake of facilitating reference, the requisite figures for understanding the diagram are given in the following Table:—

UNIVERSITIES.	NUMBER PER 100 OF THE TOTAL HINDU AND MUHAMMADAN—						Proportionate number of Muhammadan graduates, as it should have been, as compared with the number of Hindu graduates, according to the ratio of the Muhammadan to the Hindu population.	
	POPULATION.		GRADUATES.					
			M.A.		B.A.			
	Hindus.	Muhammadans.	Hindus.	Muhammadans.	Hindus.	Muhammadans.	M.A.	B.A.
Calcutta ...	67·7	32·3	96·94	3·06	95·71	4·29	46·1	45·6
Madras ...	93·6	6·4	98·	2·	99·2	·8	6·7	6·8
Bombay ...	82·1	17·9	99·1	·9	98·1	1·9	21·74	21·5
Punjab ...	40·4	59·6	81·25	18·75	77·7	22·3	120·6	115·
Allahabad ...	88·	12·	96·7	3·3	82·8	17·2	13·2	11·3
Total for India ...	76·25	23·75	96·7	3·3	95·85	4·15	30·1	29·8

The accompanying Diagram (No. I.), showing the comparative progress of high English education *in Arts* among Hindus and Muhammadans, classified under the various Universities of India, during the period of 36 years, from 1858 to 1893, inclusive, is inserted here, and should be perused in the light of the statistics given in the preceding Table.

25

The foregoing Diagram explained.

To explain the foregoing diagram further—take the column relating to the M.A. Examination of the Calcutta University. The total number of M.A.'s during the 36 years, from 1858 to 1893 (both inclusive), was 817, of which 792 were Hindus, or 96·94 per cent. thus indicated in pink colour, up to nearly 97 degrees of the diagram, and the number of Muhammadans being only 25, or 3·06 per cent., the green colour accordingly covers a little more than 3 degrees of the diagram. But with reference to the population within the jurisdiction of the Calcutta University, the proportion of Hindus to Muhammadans is as 67·7 to 32·3, and if the Muhammadans had achieved the same rate of progress as the Hindus, the ratio of Muhammadan graduates would have been as 46·1 to 96·94 of the Hindus. The cross lines, therefore, in the column of the Muhammadan M.A.'s reach 46·1 degrees in the diagram, to denote the above calculation.

Again, in the columns of the diagram relating to the Punjab University the pink and green colours show the actual comparative progress of the Hindu and Muhammadan graduates, respectively, and the cross lines exceed the 100 degrees of the scale, reaching 120 degrees for the M.A.'s and 115 degrees for the B.A.'s, as represented on the margin of the diagram, which must be considered as a part of the diagram, under the heading of the Punjab University. The excessive deficiency thus indicated by the cross lines, in regard to the Punjab University is due to the fact that in that Province the proportion of the Hindu to the Muhammadan population is as 40·4 to 59·6, and the rate of progress achieved by the Hindu M.A.'s being 81·25 per cent., the proportionate number of Muhammadan M.A.'s, according to the ratio of the Muhammadan to the Hindu population, should have reached 120·6 degrees of the diagram, and the number of Hindu B.A.'s being 77·7 per cent. the number of Muhammadan graduates, with reference to the proportion of the Muhammadan to the Hindu population, should have reached 115 degrees, as represented on the margin of the diagram.

On the other hand, in the case of the B.A. degree of the Allahabad University, the green colour which represents the actual success of 77 Muhammadans, as against 371 Hindus (denoted by the pink colour), exceeds the proportion of the Muhammadan to the Hindu population, which is as 12 to 88 in the Provinces within the jurisdiction of that University. The excess is represented by 5·9 degrees coloured green on the margin of the diagram. This circumstance, as has once before been explained in this work, is due to the exceptionally strenuous efforts in behalf of English education which the Muhammadans, under the leadership of Sir Syed Ahmed, Khan Bahadur, K.C.S.I., have made by founding the Muhammadan Anglo-Oriental College at Aligarh, a brief history of which institution has been given in an earlier part of this work. (*Vide* pp. 163, 164 *ante*).

Abstract Tabular Statement, showing comparative progress of Hindus and Muhammadans in various branches of University Education, 1858–93.

To further elucidate the comparison between the progress made by Hindus and that made by Muhammadans, respectively, the following Table has been prepared showing an abstract of the comparative statistics of the various branches of learning recognized by the degrees of the various Indian Universities, from the time of their establishment up to the present, covering a period of 36 years, from 1858 to 1893, both inclusive:—

COMPARATIVE STATISTICS OF HIGH ENGLISH EDUCATION IN BRITISH INDIA AMONG HINDUS AND MUHAMMADANS, RESPECTIVELY, FOR THE 36 YEARS, FROM 1858 TO 1893.

Subjects.	Arts.		Law.		Medicine and Surgery.		Engineering.		Total.		Grand Total.
	Hindus.	Muhammadans.	Hindus.	Muhammadans.	Hindus.	Muhammadans.	Hindus.	Muhammadans.	Hindus.	Muhammadans.	
Number of graduates ...	9,715	399	3,537	110	1,239	34	590	3	15,081	546	15,627
Percentage of graduates ..	96·1	3·9	96·98	3·02	97·13	2·87	99·5	·5	96·5	3·5	......
Average number of graduates per year	269·9	11·1	98·2	3	34·4	·99	16·4	·1	418·9	15·1	434·08
Hindu and Muhammadan population of British India, according to the census of 1881	...	...	...	...	...	...	...	...	14,48,75,315	4,51,27,033	19,00,02,348

SUBJECTS.	ARTS.		LAW.		MEDICINE AND SURGERY.		ENGINEERING.		TOTAL.		GRAND TOTAL.
	Hindus.	Muhamma-dans.	Hindus.	Muhamma-dans.	Hindus.	Muhamma-dans.	Hindus.	Muhamma-dans.	Hindus.	Muhamma-dans.	
Percentage in the total Hindu and Muhammadan population of British India in 1881	...	...	...	...	...	...	...	...	76·25	23·75	......
Ratio of graduates, as it ought to be, according to the ratio of the Muhammadan to the Hindu population	96·1	29·9	96·98	30·2	97·13	30·3	99·5	31·0	96·5	30·	......
Number of Muhammadan graduates, as it ought to be, according to the ratio of the Muhammadan to the Hindu population ...	...	3,286	...	1,475	...	519	...	161	......	5,441	......
Actual number of Hindu and Muhammadan graduates	9,715	399	3,537	110	1,239	34	590	3	15,081	546	15,627
Deficiency in the number of Muhammadan graduates	...	2,887	...	1,365	...	485	...	158	......	4,895	......

Statistics of the backwardness of Muhammadans in all Departments of University Education, 1858–93.

The figures in this Table, when carefully considered are eloquent in themselves, as showing how enormously backward the Muhammadans are as compared with the Hindus. In all departments of learning recognised and controlled by the Indian Universities, Arts, Law, Medicine and Engineering, the Muhammadans have fallen far short of the standard of success which they should have achieved if the progress of high English education among them had been proportionate to their number in the population, as compared with the Hindus. Thus, in the Faculty of Arts, instead of 3,286 Muhammadan graduates, there are only 399, leaving a deficiency of no less than 2,887. Similarly, in the Faculty of Law, instead of 1,475 Muhammadan graduates, only 110 have succeeded, leaving a deficiency of no less than 1,365. In the Faculty of Medicine, instead of 519 there are only 34 Muhammadan graduates, showing a deficiency of 485; and in the Faculty of Engineering the number of Muhammadan graduates is only 3 instead of 161, leaving a deficiency of 158. The statistics, so far as the Muhammadans are concerned, appear more cogently lamentable when the figures in the columns of totals are considered. In the aggregate Hindu and Muhammadan population of British India the percentages are 76·25 Hindus and 23·75 Muhammadans; whilst the percentages in the aggregate number of Hindu and Muhammadan graduates are 96·5 Hindus and only 3·5 Muhammadans: the deficiency in the percentage being thus, 20·25.

Success of Muhammadans in University degrees only *one-tenth* of what it should have been in proportion to their population.

These statistics are equally lamentable for the Muhammadans, when considered in another manner. Ever since the establishment of the Indian Universities during a period of thirty-six years, from the year 1858 to 1893, the statistics calculated from the Calendars of the various Indian Universities, show (as in the above table) that 15,627 persons have taken degrees in the various branches of learning recognised and controlled by those Universities. Out of this 15,627 graduates no less than 15,081 were Hindus, whilst the Muhammadans were only 546. According to the ratio of the Muhammadans to the Hindus, in the aggregate Hindu and Muhammadan population, the number of Muhammadan graduates should have been no less than 5,441, instead of the actual figure 546, thus showing a deficiency of no less than 4,895. In other words, the Muhammadans have achieved only one-tenth of the success which they should have achieved, and their failure is nine times as much as their success; whilst as matters now stand, the number of Hindu graduates is more than 27 times as much as that of the Muhammadans instead of being a little over 3 times, according to the proportion existing between the Hindu and the Muhammadan populations. No rational well-wisher of India can grudge the satisfactory advance which the Hindus have made, but at the same time, he—whether as a politician or as a philanthropist—cannot help lamenting the fact that the Muhammadans have not made a commensurate progress in high English education in proportion to their number in the population.

Diagram II, showing the comparative progress of Hindus and Muhammadans in the Degrees of the Indian Universities, in various branches of learning, during 1858-93.

To render more easily intelligible the great disparity between Hindus and Muhammadans in high English education in the various branches of learning recognised by the degrees of the various Indian Universities, as shown in the preceding Table, the following diagram has been prepared on the same principles as the preceding diagram, and the figures given at the foot of the diagram, taken from the preceding Tables, will explain the degrees up to which the diagram has been coloured pink, as denoting the actual progress of the Hindus; and green, the actual progress of the Muhammadans, and the cross lines showing the point of progress which the Muhammadans should have achieved, if they had achieved the same *rate* of progress as the Hindus, with reference to the proportion of the Muhammadan to the Hindu population. The accompanying diagram showing the comparative progress of High English Education in various branches of knowledge among Hindus and Muhamamdans in the Universities of India during 36 years from 1858 to 1893, is inserted for perusal in the light of the preceding explanation.

The accompanying Diagram No. II is in itself eloquent in showing the deplorable backwardness of Muhammadans in all branches of high English education recognised by the Universities of India—a state of things which can never be lost sight of, in considering the various problems of moral, social, economical and political import, which need consideration during the present period of the history of the British rule in India. The Diagram might well suggest for its motto the following elegiac *Rubái* (رباعي), or Quartrain, of the celebrated living Muhammadan poet Maulvi Altaf Husain, *Hali*:—

رباعي مولانا حالي

پستي کا کوي حد سے گزرنا ديکھے • اسلام کا گر کر نہ اوبھرنا ديکھے

مانے نہ کبھي کہ مد ہی ہر جزر کے بعد • دريا کا ہمارے جو اوترنا ديکھے

Rate of progress of Muhammadan graduates in various Faculties of the Indian Universities, during 1858-93.

The statistics of high English education stated in this Chapter, have been, so far, considered with reference to the aggregate results of the working of the Indian Universities from their foundation up to the end of 1893—a period of 36 years. It is now important to consider the *rate* at which the Muhammadans have made progress in high English education during this long period. For this purpose, and for the sake of convenient reference, the following Table has been prepared as an extract from the Tabular Statement already given (*Vide* page 185, *ante*), showing the comparative statistics of Hindu and Muhammadan graduates in the various Faculties of the Indian Universities during 36 years, from 1858 to 1893, divided into periods of 6 years each:—

Period.	Percentage of Muhammadans in the total Hindu and Muhammadan graduates in the various Faculties of the Indian Universities, during 6 sexennial periods, from 1858 to 1893.						
	Arts.	Law.	Medicine and Surgery.	Engineering.	Total.	Percentage of Muhammadans in the total Hindu and Muhammadan population.	Deficiency in the percentage of Muhammadan graduates according to percentage of population.
1858–63	1·13	...	2·2	...	1·1	23·75	22·74
1864–69	1·9	1·6	2·6	...	1·8	„	21·95
1870–75	1·2	1·5	4·2	...	1·6	„	22·15
1876–81	2·03	1·3	0·93	...	1·5	„	22·25
1882–87	3·6	4·3	2·0	1·5	3·6	„	20·15
1888–93	5·7	3·6	4·3	0·4	5·0	„	18·75
Total, 1858 to 1893 ...	**3·9**	**3·02**	**2·7**	**·5**	**3·5**	**23·75**	**20·25**

(Opposite to page 196.)

DIAGRAM II.

Diagram showing the comparative progress of high English education in various branches of Knowledge among Hindus and Mahomedans in the Universities of India during 36 years from 1858 to 1893.

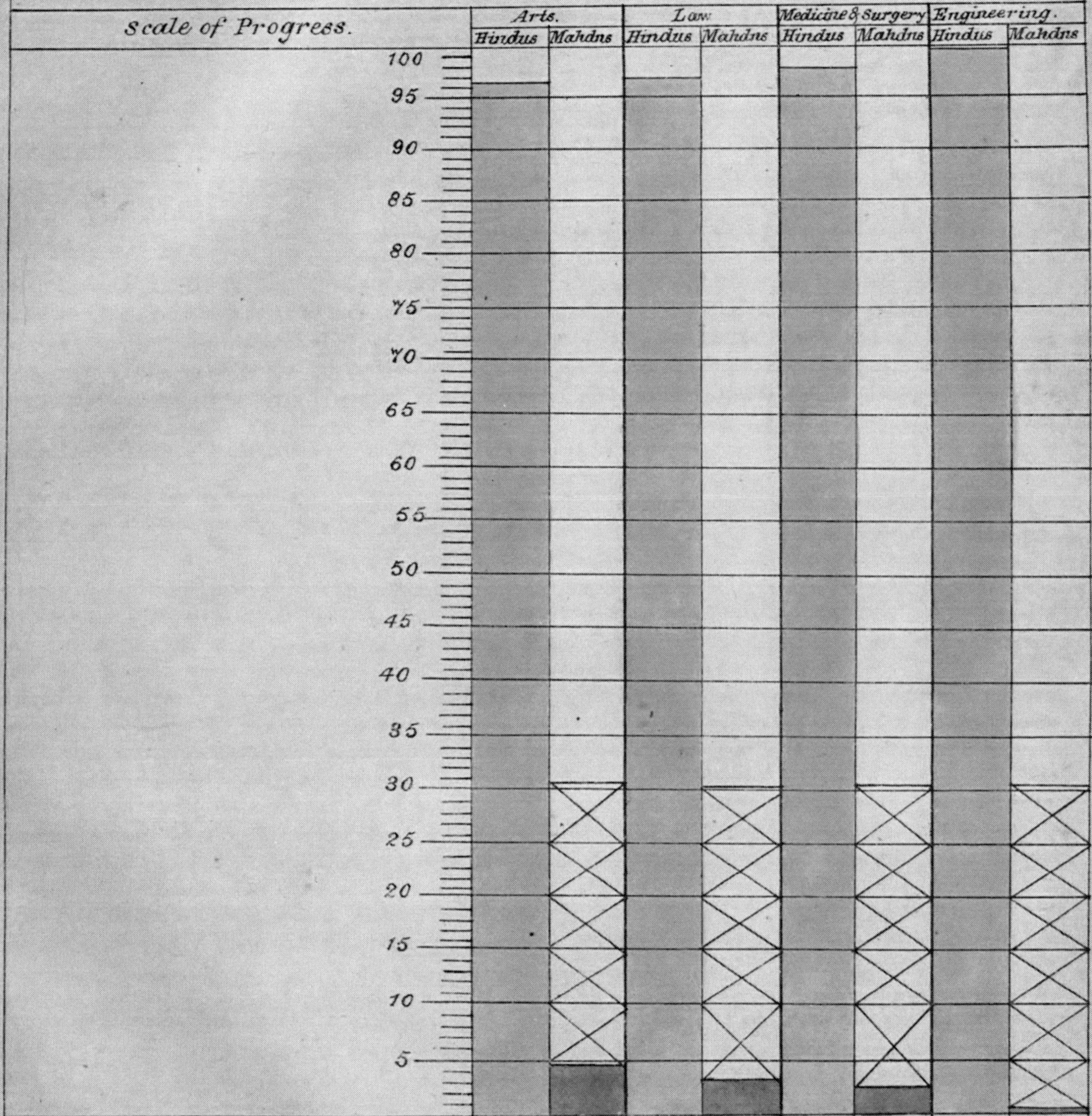

	Arts. Hindus	Arts. Mahdns	Law Hindus	Law Mahdns	Medicine & Surgery Hindus	Medicine & Surgery Mahdns	Engineering. Hindus	Engineering. Mahdns
Ratio of graduates as it ought to be according to the ratio of the Mahomedan to the Hindu population	96·1	29·9	96·98	30·2	97·13	30·3	99·5	31·0
Number of Mahomedan graduates as it ought to be according to the ratio of the Mahomedan to the Hindu population		3286		1475		519		161
Actual number of Hindu and Mahomedan graduates	9,715	399	3,537	110	1,239	34	590	3
Deficiency in the number of Mahomedan graduates.		2,887		1,365		485		158

Progress of Muhammadans in Indian Universities, up to 1875, inconsiderable.

It is evident from this Table that the progress of Muhammadans in high English education, as represented by the percentages of the various sexennial periods, has been very slow in all the various Faculties in which Degrees are granted in the Universities of India, and the last column of the Table shows the deficiency in the percentages during these various periods, with reference to the proportion of Muhammadans in the total Hindu and Muhammadan population. During the first three of these sexennial periods, namely, up to the end of the year 1875, the percentage of Muhammadans who succeeded in obtaining University Degrees was so inconsiderable that it can scarcely afford any estimate of the rate of progress made by the Muhammadans in this respect. The last three periods, however, deserve special consideration, and it is necessary to discuss the advance made by Muhammadans during those periods in the various branches of learning, and then to consider the statistics in respect of all the Faculties of the Indian Universities taken as a whole.

***Rate* of progress of Muhammadan graduates in the Faculty of Arts, 1881-93.**

In the *Faculty of Arts* the percentage of Muhammadans, in the total number of Hindu and Muhammadan graduates, was 2·03 during the sexennial period ending in the year 1881, and it increased to 3·6 during the next sexennial period ending in 1887, thus showing an advance of only 1·57 per cent. Again, during the last sexennial period, ending in 1893, the percentage of Muhammadans increased to 5·7, indicating an advance of 2·1, which is so far satisfactory; but the required percentage of Muhammadan graduates should have been 23·75, which is the percentage of Muhammadans in the total Hindu and Muhammadan population, and thus, the deficiency in the percentage still remaining is no less than 18·05, which, at the rate of progress indicated by 2·1, during the last sexennial period, would take more than 51 years to bring the percentage of Muhammadan graduates in the Faculty of Arts up to the percentage of the Muhammadans in the total Hindu and Muhammadan population.

***Rate* of progress of Muhammadan graduates in the Faculty of Law, 1881-93.**

In the *Faculty of Law* the percentage of Muhammadans in the total number of Hindu and Muhammadan graduates was 1·3 during the sexennial period ending in the year 1881. It increased to 4·3 during the next sexennial period ending in the year 1887, thus showing an advance of 3·0 per cent., which is, no doubt, considerable, and would have been satisfactory if it had not fallen during the last sexennial period, ending in 1893, when it fell to 3·6, thus showing a retrogression of ·7, leaving a deficiency of no less than 20·15, which is required to complete the percentage at 23·75, which is the percentage of the Muhammadans in the total Hindu and Muhammadan population. On account of this retrogression during the last sexennial period it is impossible to calculate at what period the Muhammadans may be expected to fill up the vacancy or deficiency in the number of graduates in the Faculty of Law; but some approximate calculation of the period required for this purpose may be made, perhaps, by comparing the percentage of the sexennial period ending in 1881 with the percentage of the sexennial period ending in 1887, when the highest rate of progress was achieved in an interval of 6 years. The percentage of Muhammadans in the total number of Hindu and Muhammadan graduates in the Faculty of Law during the sexennial period ending in 1881 was 1·3, and after the lapse of 6 years, namely, during the sexennial period ending in 1887, it rose to 4·3, thus showing an increase of 3·0 per cent. The deficiency in the percentage in 1893 was 20·15, which at the abovementioned rate of increase would require more than 40 years to bring the percentage of Muhammadan graduates in Law up to the percentage of the Muhammadans, *viz.*, 23·75, in the total Hindu and Muhammadan population.

***Rate* of progress of Muhammadan graduates in the Faculty of Medicine and Surgery, 1881-93.**

In the *Faculty of Medicine and Surgery* the percentage of Muhammadans in the total number of Hindu and Muhammadan graduates was only 0·93 per cent. during the sexennial period ending in 1881, and during the succeeding sexennial period ending in 1887, it rose to 2·0 per cent., thus showing an advance of 1·07 per cent. Again, during the next sexennial period ending in 1893, it rose from 2·0 to 4·3 per cent., showing an advance of 2·3 per cent., which may be said to be satisfactory. But the percentage of Muhammadans in the total Hindu and Muhammadan population being 23·75 per cent., the balance of percentage still requiring to be filled up is 19·45, which, at the last mentioned rate of increase during 6 years, would require more than 50 years.

***Rate* of progress of Muhammadan graduates in the Faculty of Engineering, 1881-93.**

In the *Faculty of Engineering* no Muhammadan succeeded in obtaining a Degree during the sexennial period ending in 1881, but in the next sexennial period ending in 1887, the percentage of Muhammadans in the total number of Hindu and Muhammadan graduates was 1·5, which would have been satisfactory, had it not fallen to 0·4 during the succeeding sexennial period ending in 1893; thus showing a retrogression of 1·1 per cent. Under these circumstances it is obvious that no prospective calculation can be made as to the period when the Muhammadans may be expected to fill up the deficiency of 23·35 still remaining to bring up the percentage to 23·75, which is the percentage of the Muhammadans in the total Hindu and Muhammadan population. However, if the highest rate of progress in the Faculty of Engineering, namely, 1·5 per cent., which was achieved by the Muhammadans during the sexennial period ending in 1887, be taken as an approximate measure of their future advance, even then, the deficiency in the percentage being no less than 23·35, it would take more than 93 years to bring up the percentage to 23·75, which is the percentage of the Muhammadans in the total Hindu and Muhammadan population.

Rate of progress of Muhammadan graduates in all the Faculties of the Indian Universities, from 1881 to 1893.

It is now important to consider the rate of progress of Muhammadan graduates in all the Faculties of the Indian Universities, taken as a whole. The statistics in the preceding Table being thus viewed, show that during the sexennial period ending in 1881, the percentage of Muhammadan graduates, in the total number of Hindu and Muhammadan graduates, in all the Faculties of the Indian Universities, was 1·5, and during the next sexennial period ending in 1887, it rose to 3·6, thus showing an advance of 2·1 per cent. Again, during the succeeding sexennial period ending in 1893, it rose to 5·0, showing an advance of 1·4 per cent. which may be taken as the latest, and, therefore, the approximate measure of future advance. But the percentage of Muhammadans in the total Hindu and Muhammadan population being 23·75, the balance of 18·75 per cent. would, at the abovementioned rate of advance (namely, 1·4 per cent. in 6 years), require more than 80 years to fill up the deficiency, and bring the percentage of Muhammadan graduates in all the University Faculties, taken as a whole, up to the percentage of the Muhammadans in the total Hindu and Muhammadan population, namely, 23·75 per cent. But even if the largest rate of advance made by Muhammadans, namely the advance made by them in the sexennial period ending in 1887, when their percentage rose from 1·5 to 3·6, namely, an advance of 2·1 in 6 years, be taken as the measure of approximate success in the future, the deficiency in the percentage being 18·75, would require more than 53 years to reach 23·75 per cent., which is the percentage of the Muhammadans in the total Hindu and Muhammadan population.

Future prospects of the Muhammadans in regard to University Degrees.

For the sake of conveniently comprehending the preceding calculations, as to the prospects of Muhammadan advance in the various Faculties of the Indian Universities in the future, the following Table has been prepared to show the results of the above calculations :—

FACULTIES.	Percentage of Muhammadans in 1888-93, among graduates.	Percentage of Muhammadans in the total Hindu and Muhammadan population.	Deficiency of Muhammadan percentage among graduates in 1888-93.	Highest rate of Muhammadan progress yet achieved in a sexennial period.	Approximate number of years required to raise the percentage of Muhammadan graduates to their percentage in total Hindu and Muhammadan population.
Arts	5·7	23·75	18·5	2·1	51
Law	3·6	„	20·15	3·0	40
Medicine and Surgery ...	4·3	„	19·45	2·3	50
Engineering	0·4	„	23·35	1·5	93
Total of all Faculties ...	5·0	23·75	18·75	2·1	53

This Table, which must be perused in the light of the calculations explained in the preceding paragraphs, leaves no doubt that, in respect of high English education, as represented by the University degrees, the Muhammadans are more than half a century behind their Hindu fellow-subjects, and that even the latest and the highest rate of progress yet made by the Muhammadans, falls far short of what is required to raise the percentage of Muhammadan graduates up to the level of the proportion of Muhammadans in the population of India.

Diagram III, showing the Rate of progress of Muhammadans in Indian Universities, from 1858 to 1893, explained.

To illustrate the effect of the preceding calculations, the accompanying Diagram III, has been prepared, showing the *Rate of progress* of high English education, in various branches of knowledge, among Muhammadans, in the Indian Universities, during 6 sexennial periods, from the year 1858 to 1893. The Diagram has been prepared on the same principles as the preceding Diagrams, with this difference, that, whilst in the preceding Diagrams all the 100 degrees of the scale were depicted, in the present Diagram only

DIAGRAM III.

(Opposite to page 198)

Diagram showing the Rate of progress of high English education in Various branches of knowledge among Mahomedans in the Indian Universities during 6 sexennial periods from 1858 to 1893 (inclusive.)

25 degrees, out of a scale of 100 degrees, are shown, since the percentage of Muhammadans in the total Hindu and Muhammadan population is only 23·75. The Diagram is, therefore, painted pink, up to 23·75 degrees, and the green colour represents the extent of the percentage of the Muhammadan graduates in the total number of Hindu and Muhammadan graduates during the various sexennial periods indicated at the foot of the Diagram. It will be observed that, although the progress made by the Muhammadans during the last two sexennial periods is noticeable, yet, as has been explained in the preceding observations, the rate of progress is far from being sufficient to enable them to attain their proper percentage within an approximate period. The pink colour in the Diagram, when compared with the green colour, shows the vast extent of the deficiency of the Muhammadans taking their percentage in the total Hindu and Muhammadan population as the reasonable standard of success at which they should aim. But it is not an uncommon opinion, entertained by some statesmen and political thinkers, that, although the past condition of Muhammadans, with respect to high English education was deplorable, the present condition of their progress is satisfactory, and leaves no room for further complaint or anxiety. It is, therefore, important to consider how far this opinion is justifiable, and the following Chapter will be devoted to the consideration of this subject.

CHAPTER XXXI.

POSITION OF MUHAMMADANS IN THE GENERAL POPULATION OF INDIA.—THE PRESENT *RATE* OF THE PROGRESS OF ENGLISH EDUCATION AMONG MUHAMMADANS IN COLLEGES AND SECONDARY SCHOOLS, AND ITS FUTURE PROSPECTS.

Position of the Muhammadans in the general population of India.

The preceding Chapter has been devoted to statistical calculations showing the backwardness of the Muhammadans in English education, with reference to their proportion in the Total Hindu and Muhammadan population of India, according to the Census of 1881, for reasons which have been already stated.* It seems advisable before closing this subject to give a general view of the position occupied by them in the general population of India, in various parts of the country. For this purpose the most trustworthy information available is contained in the *General Report* on the Census of India in 1891. After stating that the total Hindu or Brahmanic population of India in 1891 † amounted to 207,731,727, and that "the mean proportion of the Brahmanic to the total population is 72⅓ per cent." and that the Muhammadans amounted to 57,321,164, constituting 19·96 of the total Indian population, the Report describes the territorial distribution of the Brahmanists or Hindus, and then in regard to the Musalmans has the following observations :—

Territorial distribution of the Muhammadans in India.

"The next religion to come under review is that of Islam, which is taken here on account of its numerical importance. The Musalman population of the world has been roughly estimated at various amounts from 70 to 90 millions, so that whatever the real figure may be between those limits, the Indian Empire contains a large majority of the followers of the Prophet. No Province or large State, and probably few districts or other subdivisions in the plain country west of Burma, is without a certain number of Musalman inhabitants. We find them relatively most numerous, of course, in the North-West, where Sindh and Kashmir head the list, with 77 and 70 per cent. respectively. In the former there is a considerable foreign element, consisting of Balooch and Brahui from across the frontier, but the bulk of the population has been converted from a lax form of Brahmanism. For a short period in its history the province was under a Brahman regime, centered about Haiderabad. where it was disturbed and afterwards confirmed by Alexander the Great, but was overthrown not long afterwards by one of the numerous waves of Scythian origin that broke upon the west and north frontier of India before and shortly after the beginning of the Christian Era. According to the Chinese pilgrim Hiuen Tsang, Sindh was in the seventh century both barbarous and superstitious, and orthodoxy of any sort sat lightly upon its unscrupulous population, ‡ as it is said to do even now. In Kashmir, the present population, whether Skythic or Arya has been

* *Vide* page 183, *ante*.

† Census of India, 1891—*General Report*, by J. A. Baines, Esq., F. S. S., of the Indian Civil Service (1893), pp. 174, 175.

‡ The Cattle-breeders are of an unfeeling and hasty temper, given only to bloodshed. They have no masters, but shave their heads and adopt the mendicant's robes.

addicted within historic times to serpent worship, Buddhism and Brahmanism, by turns, before its conversion to Islam was undertaken by the Moghals during their summer visits to the valley. The Sikh rule succeeded, but left both Musalman peasant and Brahman professional alike untouched, except that the privileges of the latter were confirmed. In the North-West the tribes were probably converted from the side of Afghanistan, not from India, and their example was followed by the Mongoloid Thibetan races to the North along part of the Upper Indus. On the East, however, in Ladákh, the sparse population is still Buddhist, and along the South range intervening between the valley and the Panjab, there is a considerable Brahmanic element of comparatively pure Arya descent, but, on the whole, 70½ per cent. of the population of the State is Musalman. In the Panjab we have samples on the largest scale of both foreign immigration and local conversion. In the British portion of the province, 55¾ of the population professes Islam, the proportion rapidly rising towards the west and gradually falling as the Jamna is approached. On the States, the largest of which, with one exception, are under Sikh rule, Islam has made, of course, less impression, and it is returned by only 30 per cent. As has been said above, the outward observances of the faith are more or less strictly regarded where the religion is that of a large majority of the people, but left in abeyance where the conversion was effected by force or worldly pressure and without the example of foreign zealots to sustain devotion. The more martial races are converted to the extent of at least one-half, and the lowest class of the Brahmanic community favours alternatively Islam and Sikhism. Passing eastwards, we find the proportion of Musalmans high in the submontane tracts of the North-West Provinces, but below the average in the province as a whole. In Bengal, as we had occasion to note in connection with the density and migration of the population, there is a strong Musalman element, exceeding one-half the population, nearly all over the whole of the eastern division, and the same remark applies to the Surma Valley, now included in the Assam Province. It is in this part of the Country that the results of conversion are more marked in the circumstances of the population than anywhere else in India. We have seen that the growth of the population here has been more rapid than in any other division of the province, and the Provincial Census Superintendent attributes this in a great degree partly to conversion and partly to other ecclesiastical factors as they are understood in India. In the first place, there is the rise in *status*, then the range of diet is greater than amongst the Brahmanic classes. Thirdly, not only is marriage deferred till the bride is grown up, but there is no prohibition of widow-marriage, both of which are facts tending towards a longer life on the part of the women and a healthier offspring. In connection with this part of the country, we may mention the Musalman population of Lower Burma, which is largely indebted to Chittagong and its neighbourhood for its recruits, chiefly sea-faring people, supplemented by a certain influx of the trading Musalmans of Bombay and Madras, and the followers of the last Dehli princes, who were assigned a residence at Rangoon. The high proportion of Musalmans in the Bombay States and in Baroda, is, in its turn, partly due to the number of traders in Kachh and other Gujarath States, partly to that of the cultivators mentioned already—both foreign converts—who abound in that division of the Presidency. It must be remembered, too, that Gujarath was the seat of a considerable Musalman power in the days of Moghal rule in Upper India, and Cambay, Junagarh, Palarpur, Radhanpur, and Balasinur, testify to the extent and durability of its authority, as Sachin and Janjira do to the influence of the same religion amongst the foreign employes of the Maratha Chiefs. We can now turn to the parts of India where the proportion is the lowest. The Nadir of Islam, numerically speaking, is found in the Hill States under the Central Provinces, and, with the exception of Upper Burma, where there are now fewer immigrants of the Panthe class, in those provinces themselves. Next to these comes Mysore, in spite of its former period of Musalman rule. In fact, it nowhere appears that rulers of that faith, when detached from its centre in Upper India, surrounded themselves with large numbers of their co-religionists. Witness the case of Haiderabad, where, though the whole administration is in the hands of Musalmans, less than 10 per cent. of the population is of that faith, or only 2 per cent. more than in the neighbouring province of Bombay. The proportion in Madras would be very low, as it is in other parts of Southern India, were it not for the trading community of the Labbe on the East Coast, and the semi-trading, semi-agricultural Mappila of Malabar and its two adjacent States; for the local convert, in spite of the zeal of Tippoo, is not a considerable feature in the general population, though he is in sufficient force in the larger towns, as shown some years back at Salem, to present a strong front to infringement on what he considers his privileges by Brahmanical neighbours. The Musalman element in Central India is singularly low, seeing that it was the refuge for many years of wandering bands of marauders of considerable strength. But the strong hand of the two great Maratha powers and the exclusiveness of the Brahmanic Chiefs of comparatively pure race in the South-East of the Agency, tend to confine the foreign religion to the Musalman States, of which only one, Bhopal, is of considerable size. As regards the progress of the faith of Islam, little need be added to what has been already written above. It has been undoubtedly rapid in Eastern Bengal and has been perceptible, though on somewhat an uncertain basis, in the Panjab. Elsewhere, the increase seems to be mostly that due to normal growth. But so far as regards the large and heterogenous class of urban Musalmans found all over the country, it is possible that that growth may have been actually impeded by the difficulty found in getting a living under the new conditions of British rule. For the minimum of literary instruction required now as a passport to even the lower grades of middle class public employ is decidedly higher than it used to be, whilst the progress of learning amongst this class of Musalmans has not proportionately advanced, and with the comparatively small number of recruits for the army, police, and menial offices that is now found sufficient, few outlets remain available. It is possible that some such reason as this accounts for the fact that the general rate of increase outside the tracts abovementioned is a little below that found to prevail amongst the population as a whole." *

Rate of progress of English education among Muhammadans in Arts Colleges, 1882-92.

The last three sentences of the above extract are noticeable, as showing that one of the possible causes of the decadence of the Muhammadans may be attributed to "the difficulty found in getting a living, under the new conditions of British rule," and to the fact that "the progress of learning amongst this class of Musalmans has not proportionately advanced." It is, therefore, important to form some estimate as to the present condition of the progress of English education among Muhammadans in Colleges and Secondary Schools, and to ascertain the *rate* at which they have progressed during the last decade, of which statistics are available, namely, the years from 1882 to 1892. For this purpose, it will be necessary to refer back to some of the Tabular Statements already given in an earlier part of this work.† The best way to ascertain the *rate* of progress is to compare the percentages of the Muhammadan pupils in English Colleges and Schools at intervals of five years each, and the following Table has, accordingly, been prepared with reference to the statistics of the years 1882 and 1887, and 1892, and then, by taking the latest percentages of pupils, and deducting them from the percentages of the Muhammadan population in the various parts of India, according to the Census of 1891; the balance thus deduced representing the deficiency in the percentage of Muhammadan students‡ :—

Provinces.	Percentage of Muhammadans in the total number of students attending Arts Colleges (English) in—			Percentage of Muhammadans in total population. (Census of 1891).	Deficiency in the percentage of Muhammadan students, according to percentage of Muhammadans in total population.
	1882.	1887.	1892.		
Madras	1·7	1·6	1·5	6·3	4·8
Bombay	1·4	2·6	2·6	16·3	13·7
Bengal	3·8	4·3	5·7	32·9	27·2
North-West Provinces and Oudh ...	13·0	13·2	19·0	13·5	— 5·5
Punjab	12·6	17·2	18·2	55·8	37·6
Total ...	3·6	4·2	5·9	21 8	15·9

The statistics of this Table must be considered separately with regard to each Province, to form some approximate estimate of the future progress of English Collegiate Education among Muhammadans.

Rate of progress of Muhammadans in English Arts Colleges in Madras, 1882-92.

In *Madras*, the figures show that the percentage of Muhammadan pupils attending Arts Colleges was 1·7 in 1882, and decreased to 1·6 in 1887, and again fell to 1·5 in 1892, leaving a deficiency of no less than 4·8 per cent., with reference to percentage of the Muhammadans in the population of the Madras Presidency. This steady fall renders it impossible to estimate at what future period, if ever, the Muhammadans of Madras may be expected to make up the deficiency, which is more than *three* times as great as the percentage already achieved by them. Their case seems to be hopeless, unless, indeed, some exceptional measures are adopted in their behalf.

* Census of India, 1891— *General Report*, by J. A. Baines, Esq., F.S.S., of the Indian Civil Service (1893), pp. 174, 175.

† *Vide* Tables at pp. 168 and 177 *ante*.

‡ The percentages of Muhammadan students have been taken from the figures in the Table at page 168 *ante*; for the year 1882; and for the years 1887 and 1892, from the Table at page 177 *ante*; and the percentage of Muhammadans to the total population, from the Table given at page 320 of Mr. Nash's *Quinquennial Report on Education in India* (1893).

DIAGRAM IV.

(Opposite to page 203)

Diagram showing the Rate of progress of the percentage of Mahomedan pupils in English Arts Collages at 3 quinquennial periods, 1882 and 1887 and 1892 with reference to Census of 1891.

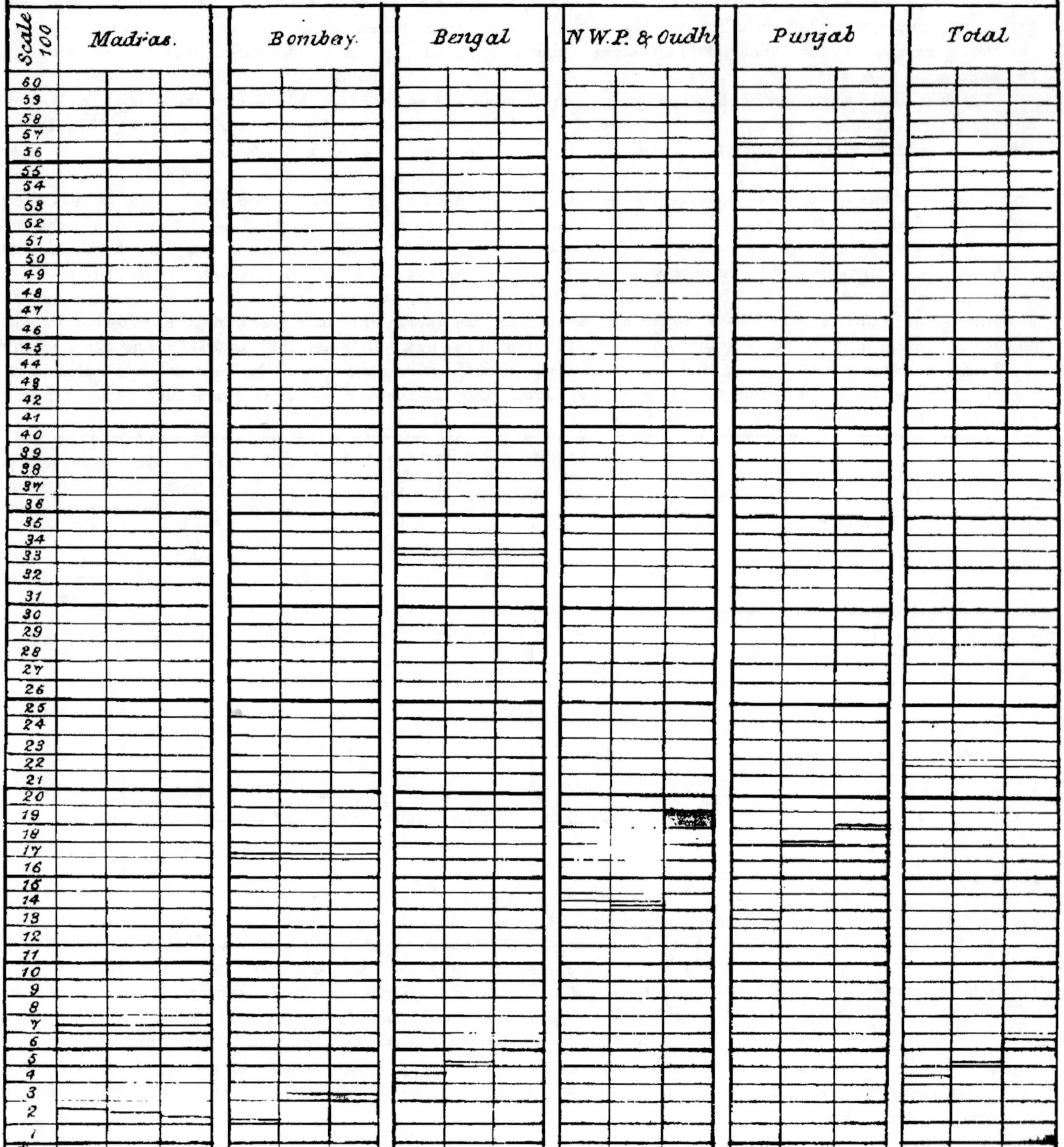

	Madras			Bombay			Bengal			N.W.P. & Oudh			Punjab			Total		
Period	1892	1887	1892	1882	1887	1892	1882	1887	1892	1882	1887	1892	1882	1887	1892	1882	1887	1892
Percent of pupils	1·[illegible]	1 6	1·5	1·4	2·6	2 [illegible]	3·8	4·5	5·[illegible]	13·[illegible]	13·[illegible]	19 [illegible]	12·6	17·2	18·2	3·[illegible]	4·2	5·9

DIAGRAM IV. (Opposite to page 203)

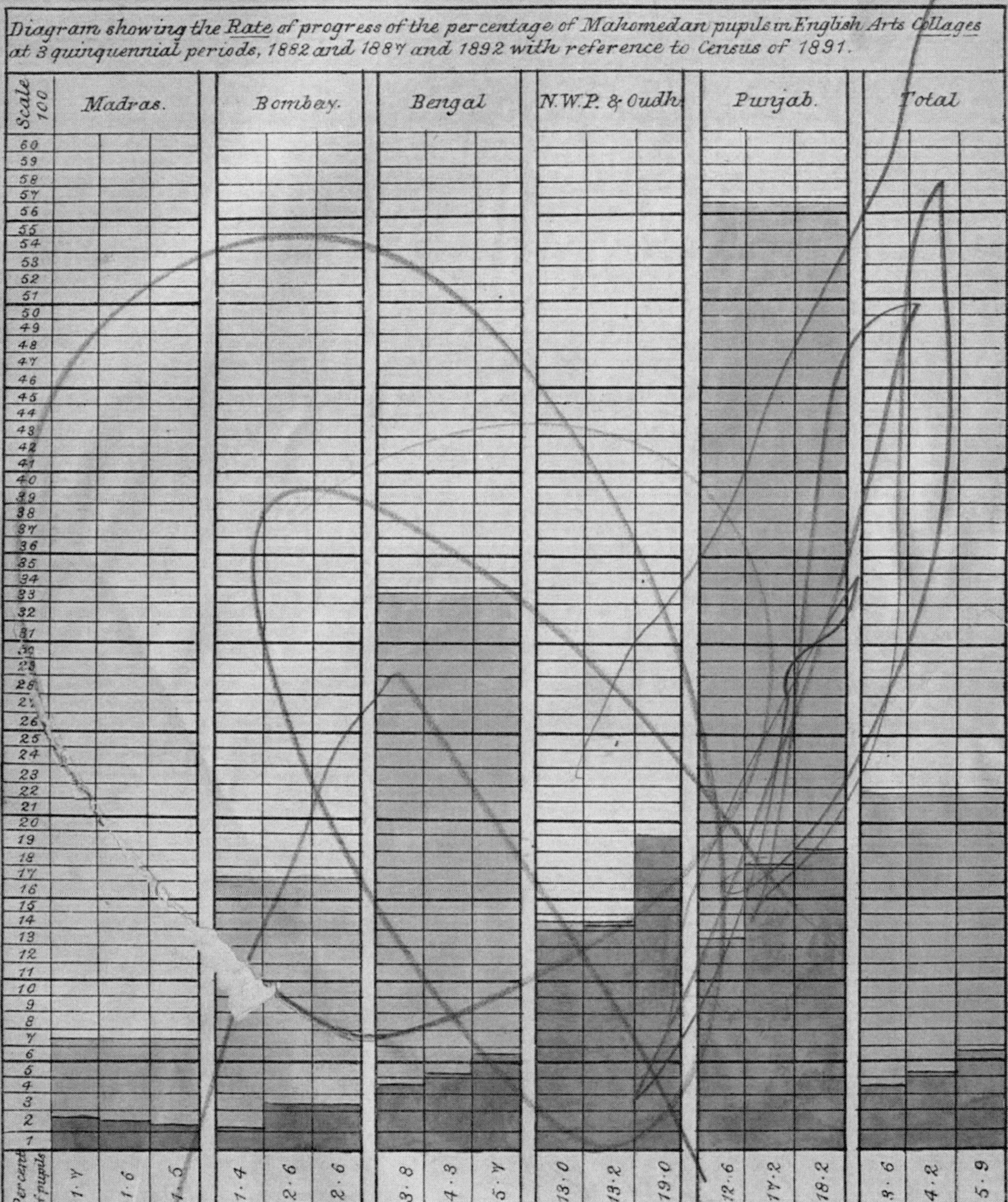

For the sake of convenient reference the following Table has been prepared indicating the results of the above calculations:—

Prospects of English education among Muhammadans in Arts Colleges.

Provinces.	Percentage of Muhammedans in English Arts Colleges in 1892.	Percentage of Muhammedans in the total population (Census of 1891).	Deficiency in the percentage of Muhammadans in English Arts Colleges in 1892.	Highest rate of Muhammadan progress yet achieved in 5 years.	Approximate number of years required to raise the percentage of Muhammadan students to the percentage of Muhammadans in total population.
Madras	1·5	6·3	4·8	...	...
Bombay	2·6	16·3	13·7	1·2	57
Bengal	5·7	32·9	27·2	1·4	61
N.-W. Provinces and Oudh ...	19·0	13·5	—5·5	...	...
Punjab	18·2	55·8	37·6	4·6	40
Total ...	5·9	21·8	15·9	1·7	45

It may therefore be said that on the whole the progress of English collegiate education among Muhammadans, even according to the latest statistics, has been far from being adequate to make up the deficiency, and that even at the highest rate of progress yet achieved during any quinquennial period, that community is nearly half a century behind their other compatriots.

Diagram IV. explained.

To make this calculation more easily comprehensible the accompanying Diagram IV., showing the *Rate* of progress in the percentage of Muhammadan pupils in English Arts Colleges at three quinquennial periods ending in the year 1882, and in 1887 and in 1892, respectively, has been prepared with reference to the census of 1891. The Diagram has been prepared on the same principles as the preceding Diagrams, taking only 60 degrees out of a scale of 100, as the percentage of Muhammadans does not exceed 55·8 in any Province. The pink colour represents the percentage of Muhammadans in the population of the various Provinces, and the green colour shows the percentage of the degrees of progress which they have achieved in point of attendance in English Arts Colleges at the various periods.

***Rate* of progress of English education among Muhammadans in Secondary Schools, 1882-92.**

It is now necessary to consider the statistics of Muhammadan students studying in English Secondary Schools and to ascertain the *rate* of progress at which they have advanced during the last decade of which statistics are available, namely the years 1882 to 1892. The following Table has been prepared with reference to the statistics of the years 1882 and 1887 and 1892, given in the Tabular Statements to be found in an earlier part of this work*:—

Provinces.	Percentage of Muhammadans in the total number of students attending High and Secondary Schools (English) in			Percentage of Muhammadans in total population. (Census of 1891.)	Deficiency in the percentage of Muhammadan students according to percentage of Muhammadans in total population.
	1882.	1887.	1892.		
Madras	2·4	5·2	5·3	6·3	1·0
Bombay	2·0	4·4	4·9	16·3	11·4
Bengal	8·7	12·1	13·5	32·9	19·4
N.-W. Provinces and Oudh ...	16·3	21·6	21·9	13·5	−8·4
Punjab	20·0	31·4	33·1	55·8	22·7
Total ...	9·2	13·7	14·0	21·8	7·8

The figures of this Table when compared with the statistics of the Table already given (*vide* p. 201 *ante*) in regard to the percentage of Muhammadan students in English Arts Colleges, shows that the percentage of Muhammadans in English Schools is higher than in Colleges, and this circumstance has led some persons to suppose that English education, however backward it may have been in the past, is now making a sufficiently rapid progress to enable them to attain their proper standard of progress in *high* English education within an approximate period. It is therefore necessary to discuss the statistics contained in the above Table with reference to each Province separately.

Rate of progress of Muhammadans in English Secondary Schools in Madras, 1882-92.

In *Madras* the attendance of students in High and Secondary Schools is not so backward as in Colleges. In 1882, the number of students in such Schools was 2·4 which rose to 5·2 in 1887, showing an advance of 2·8. But during the next quinquennial period ending in 1892, the percentage increased from 5·2 to 5·3 showing an advance of only 0·1 and leaving a deficiency of 1·0 to be made up to bring the percentage up to the level of the percentage of Muhammadans in the population of the Madras Presidency, *viz.*, 6·3. Therefore, if the rate of progress achieved during the latest quinquennial period ending in 1892, *viz.*, 0·1 per cent., during five years be taken as the standard of future progress, it would take another 50 years to make up the deficiency. On the other hand, if the rate of progress achieved during the quinquennial period ending in 1887, *viz.*, 2·8 per cent., be taken as the measure of advance, then the Muhammadans ought by this time to have attained their percentage in English Secondary Education equal to, if not superior to, their percentage in the population of the Madras Presidency in less than 2 years. But chances are that the abnormal rate of progress achieved by the Muhammadans in the quinquennial period ending in 1887, will not be repeated.

Rate of progress of Muhammadans in English Secondary Schools in Bombay, 1882-92.

In considering the figures of High and Secondary Schools in the *Bombay Presidency*, the percentage of Muhammadans in such Schools was 2·0 in 1882, and it made an abnormal advance of 2·4 in the next quinquennial period ending in 1887, but during the succeeding quinquennial period ending in 1892, it rose from 4·4 to 4·9 showing an advance of only 0·5 per cent., still leaving a deficiency of 11·4 which would take more than a century to fill up at the latest rate of progress. But even if the abnormal rate of progress achieved in the quinquennial period ending in 1887, *viz.*, 2·4 per cent. be taken as the measure of future progress, the deficiency still remaining cannot be expected to be filled up in less than 23 years.

Rate of progress of Muhammadans in English Secondary Schools in Bengal, 1882-92.

Taking the figures in *Bengal*, the percentage of Muhammdans in English High and Secondary Schools was 8·7 in 1882, and it made an abnormal progress in the next quinquennial period ending in 1887, when it reached 12·1 showing an advance of 3·4 per cent., but this rate of progress fell during the next quinquennial period ending in 1892, when the percentage rose from 12·1 to 13·5, showing an advance of only 1·4 per cent., in the five years, still leaving a deficiency of no less than 19·4 per cent., with reference to the percentage of Muhammadans in the population of Bengal, *viz.*, 32·9. At the rate of progress, *viz.*, 1·4 achieved during the latest quinquennial period ending in 1892, the deficiency could not be made up in less than 65 years. But even if the exceptional rate of progress, *viz.*, 3·4 per cent., achieved in the quinquennial period ending in 1887, be taken as the measure of future progress, it would take more than 28 years to make up the deficiency.

Rate of progress of Muhammadans in English Secondary Schools in the North-Western Provinces and Oudh, 1882-92.

In the *North-Western Provinces and Oudh*, the progress of the percentage of students in English High and Secondary Schools has been very satisfactory since 1882, and during the quinquennial period ending in 1892, it had reached 21·9 per cent., being 8·4 per cent. in advance of the percentage of Muhammadans in the population of those Provinces. The reason for this satisfactory circumstance will be explained later on in this Chapter.*

Rate of progress of Muhammadans in English Secondary Schools in the Punjab, 1882-92.

The figures in the *Punjab* relating to the percentage of Muhammadan students in English High and Secondary Schools are no doubt satisfactory, but not so much as they at first sight seem to be. In 1882, the percentage of Muhammadans in such schools was 20·0 and during the quinquennial period ending in 1887, it rose to 31·4 showing a very abnormal advance of 11·4 in the percentage. But this rate of advance, sudden as it was, fell equally suddenly during the next quinquennial period ending in 1892, when the percentage rose from 31·4 to 33·1 showing an advance of only 1·7, still leaving a deficiency of 22·7 with reference to the percentage of the Muhammadans in the population of the Punjab, *viz.*, 55·8. If the latest rate of advance, *viz.*, 1·7 per cent. achieved during the quinquennial period ending in 1892, be taken as the measure of future progress, it would take no less than 65 years to fill up the deficiency. On the other hand even if the abnormal rate of

* *Vide* page 206 *post*.

DIAGRAM V.

(Opposite to page 205.)

Diagram showing the Rate of progress of the percentage of Mahomedan pupils in English Schools at 3 quinquennial periods, 1882 and 1887 and 1892 with reference to Census of 1891.—

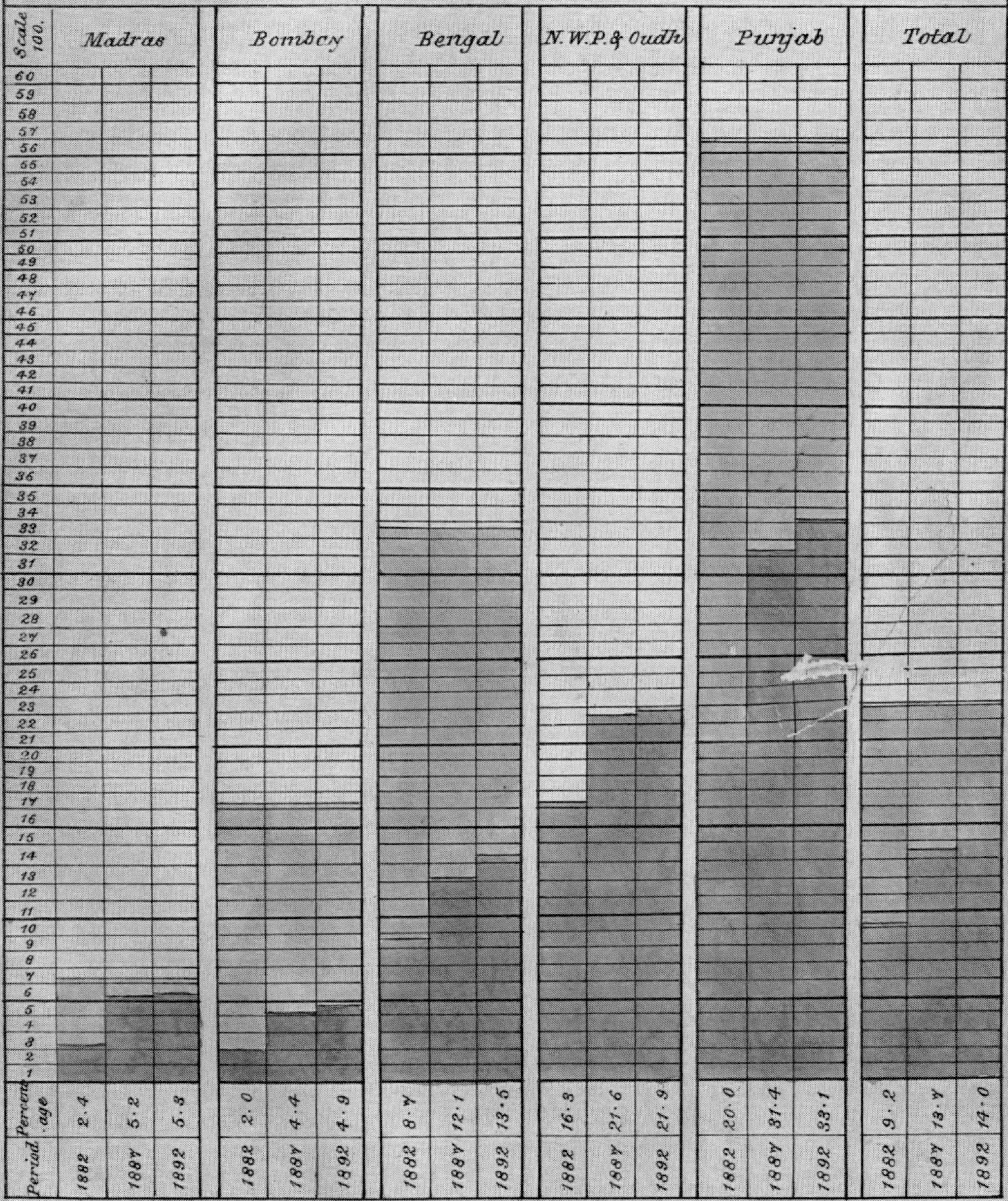

advance achieved during the quinquennial period ending in 1887, *viz.*, 11·4 be taken as the measure of future progress, about 10 years more are necessary to bring up the percentage of Muhammadan students in such schools to the level of the percentage of Muhammadans in the population of the Punjab. But there is no reasonable prospect of such a high rate of progress being repeated.

Total Rate of progress of Muhammadans in English Secondary Schools in India, 1882–92.

In considering the *total percentages* of all the abovementioned Provinces taken together, it will be observed that the percentage of Muhammadan students in High and Secondary Schools was 9·2 in 1882, and it made an abnormal advance during the next quinquennial period ending in 1887, when it rose to 13·7, showing an advance of 4·5 in the percentage. But this rate of progress fell suddenly during the next quinquennial period ending in 1892, when the percentage rose from 13·7 to 14·0 showing an advance of only 0·3 in the percentage, still leaving a deficiency of 7·8 with reference to the percentage of the Muhammadans in the total population of those Provinces, *viz.*, 21·8. If the latest rate of progress, *viz.*, 0·3 achieved during the last quinquennial period ending in 1892, be taken as the measure of future progress, it would require more than a century to fill up the deficiency. But even if the exceptional rate of progress achieved during the quinquennial period ending in 1887, *viz.*, 4·5 per cent., be taken as the standard of progress in the future, it would require nearly 10 years to bring up the percentage of Muhammadan students in English High and Secondary Schools to the level of the percentage of the Muhammadans in the population of all the above Provinces taken as a whole. But there is no expectation of the repetition of any such high rate of progress as was achieved in the quinquennial period ending in the year 1887, in the approximate future, unless indeed most exceptional measures are adopted in this behalf.

Prospects of English Education among Muhammadans in Secondary Schools.

As a summary of the preceding calculations and for the sake of convenient reference, the following Table has been prepared showing the results:—

PROVINCES.	Percentage of Muhammadans in High and Secondary Schools in 1892.	Percentage of Muhammadans in the total population (Census of 1891).	Deficiency in the percentage of Muhammadans in High and Secondary Schools in 1892.	Highest rate of Muhammadan progress yet achieved in 5 years.	Approximate number of years required to raise the percentage of Muhammadan students to the percentage of Muhammadans in total population.
Madras	5·3	6·3	1·0	2·8	2
Bombay	4·9	16·3	11·4	2·4	23
Bengal	13·5	32·9	19·4	3·4	28
N.-W. Provinces and Oudh ...	21·9	13·5	—8·4	...	...
Punjab	33·1	55·8	22·7	11·4	10
Total ...	14·0	21·8	7·8	4·5	10

It will thus be observed that even according to the most favourable calculations based upon the highest rate of advance ever achieved during a quinquennial period, the number of Muhammadans in English High and Secondary Schools is below their percentage in the population, and that most strenuous efforts are still required to promote English education among them, the more so, as the rate of progress during the last quinquennial period ending in 1892, is far less in nearly all the Provinces than it was in the quinquennial period ending in 1887 when, principally owing to the recommendations of the Education Commission of 1882, exceptional measures were adopted to promote English Education among Muhammadans.

Diagram V. explained.

For the sake of easily comprehending the preceding observations and calculations, the accompanying Diagram V., showing the *Rate* of progress in the percentage of Muhammadan pupils in English High and Secondary Schools at three quinquennial periods ending in the year 1882, and in 1887 and 1892, respectively, has been prepared with reference to the Census of 1891, on the same principles as the preceding Diagram—the pink colour representing the percentage of Muhammadans in the population of various Provinces, and the green colour representing the percentage of Muhammadans in such schools at various periods.

Apparent increase of English Education among Muhammadans in the N.-W. Provinces and Oudh explained.

Such being the condition of the percentage of Muhammadan students, it will be observed from the preceding Tables,* as well as the Diagrams IV. and V. that, in all Provinces except the North-Western Provinces and Oudh, the percentage of Muhammadan students in English Colleges and Schools falls short of the percentage of the Muhammadans in the total population of the various Provinces. There are two reasons for this circumstance. The principal reason is the independent efforts made by the Muhammadans of this part of the country, under the leadership of Sir Syed Ahmed Khan Bahadur, K.C.S.I., to advance English Education among their co-religionists—a movement† of which the effects have been perceptible also in the neighbouring Province of the Punjab where the founder of the movement has a large number of followers and fellow-workers. Another reason, to use the words of Mr. A. M. Nash in his Quinquennial Review of the *Progress of Education in India*, 1887–92 (at page 323), is that, "in the North-Western Provinces the percentage of Muhammadans among the urban population is higher than in any other Province except the Punjab; this probably is sufficient to account for the fact that Muhammadans form a larger proportion of the pupils in secondary than in primary schools, the former being usually opened only in towns, and the latter chiefly in rural districts; but the large percentage in Colleges of all kinds seems to indicate a greater appreciation of the value of higher education than is met with among members of this community in other provinces. This is a natural consequence of their superior social status, being to a great extent the decendants of a former ruling race, while in Bengal, for example, a large proportion of the Muhammadans are the descendants of converts from the aboriginal tribes, and the lower classes of Hindus.......... In the Punjab there has been a considerable increase in all classes of institutions, and the percentages are much higher than elsewhere; but it must be remembered that Muhammadans form the majority of the population, so that all the percentages are lower than they should be." ‡

Urban population of India, considered for educational questions.

The fact is that by far the greatest portion of the population of India consists of agriculturists and other rural communities which are not touched by the system of English education. In the census of India taken in 1891, "we find, then, out of the 717,549 places returned at the census, only 2,035 classed as towns, and the rest under the head of villages. The urban population is in the proportion of 9·48 per cent. to 90·52 of rural. In British territory, the proportion falls to 9·22, and in Feudatory States it rises to 10·38 per cent.§ Again, "the stage of social aggregation at which a community ceases to be rural, and passes into the category of urban, can nowhere be sharply defined. In no two countries is the line drawn on the same principle, so that comparison of the respective classes has to be confined to the places the population of which is assumed to be universally a guarantee of their urban character, and the respective proportions of urban and rural, as a whole, have been voted to be beyond the scope of international statistics. As regards the smaller aggregates, the population standard is liable to be as delusive as the constitutional test, for their size depends very much on the density of the country and the physical resources which determine the bent of the occupation of its inhabitants. The title of town again, is conventional in most countries, and applied in consideration of varying constitutional distinctions, such as those of city and borough, in England. In India the difficulty of classifying these small places is peculiarly felt in the present day, when the rapid extension of railways and other means of communication brings with it a very considerable amount of shifting of the trading and mechanical communities from place to place. It becomes necessary, therefore, to adopt three general tests with reference to the smaller units of population. *First*, that of constitution, that is, has the place been established as a municipality, or brought under some similar regulation for police and sanitary purposes? *Secondly*, if neither of these methods of local government has been applied, is the proportion of the trading and industrial population to the total equal to, or greater than, that of the agricultural? In the latter case the general numerical standard of 5,000 inhabitants was prescribed, as experience shows that taking the whole country together, this represents about the limit of urban preponderance." ||

Proportion of Muhammadans in *Urban* population best test of progress of English education among them. Diagram VI. explained.

The proportion of the Muhammadans in the urban population is the best test of their progress in English education, as English Colleges and Schools are all situate in towns of larger size than even the definition of urban population as above stated would comprehend, and that definition excludes agriculturists and other rural population to whom English education does not apply. It is, therefore, important to consider the progress of English education among *urban* Muhammadans, and for

* *Vide* pp. 201 and 203 *ante*.

† An account of this movement for English education among Muhammadans has already been given at pp 162–64 *ante*.

‡ *Progress of Education in India*, 1887–92. By A. M. Nash, Esq., M.A. (1893), p. 323.

§ *General Report on Census of India*, 1891. By J. A. Baines, Esq. (1893), p. 42.

|| *Ib.* p. 42.

DIAGRAM VI. (Opposite to page 206)

Diagram showing proportion of Mahamedans in the Urban population and in English Colleges and Secondary Schools in 1891–92.

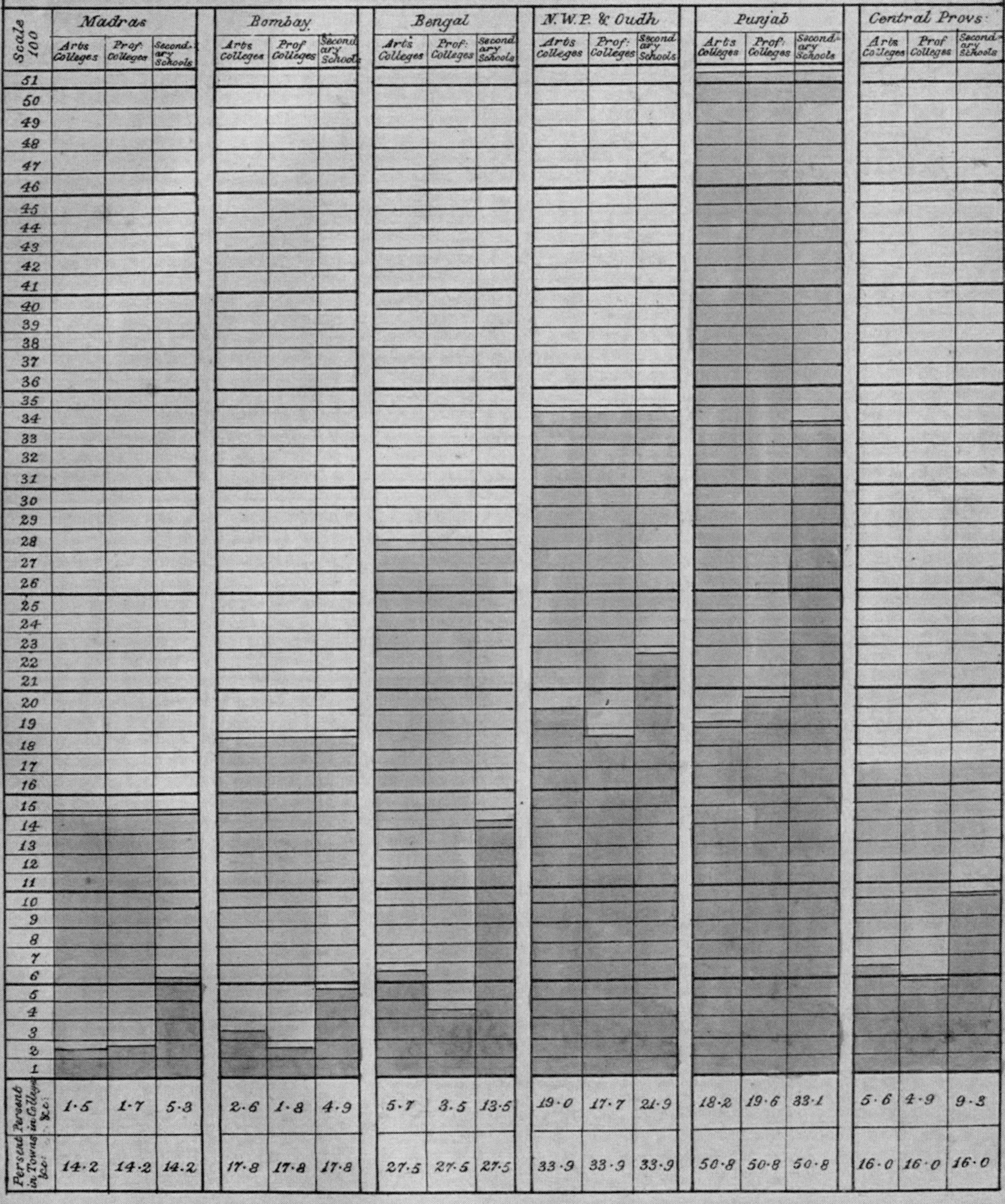

DIAGRAM VII

(Opposite to page 207)

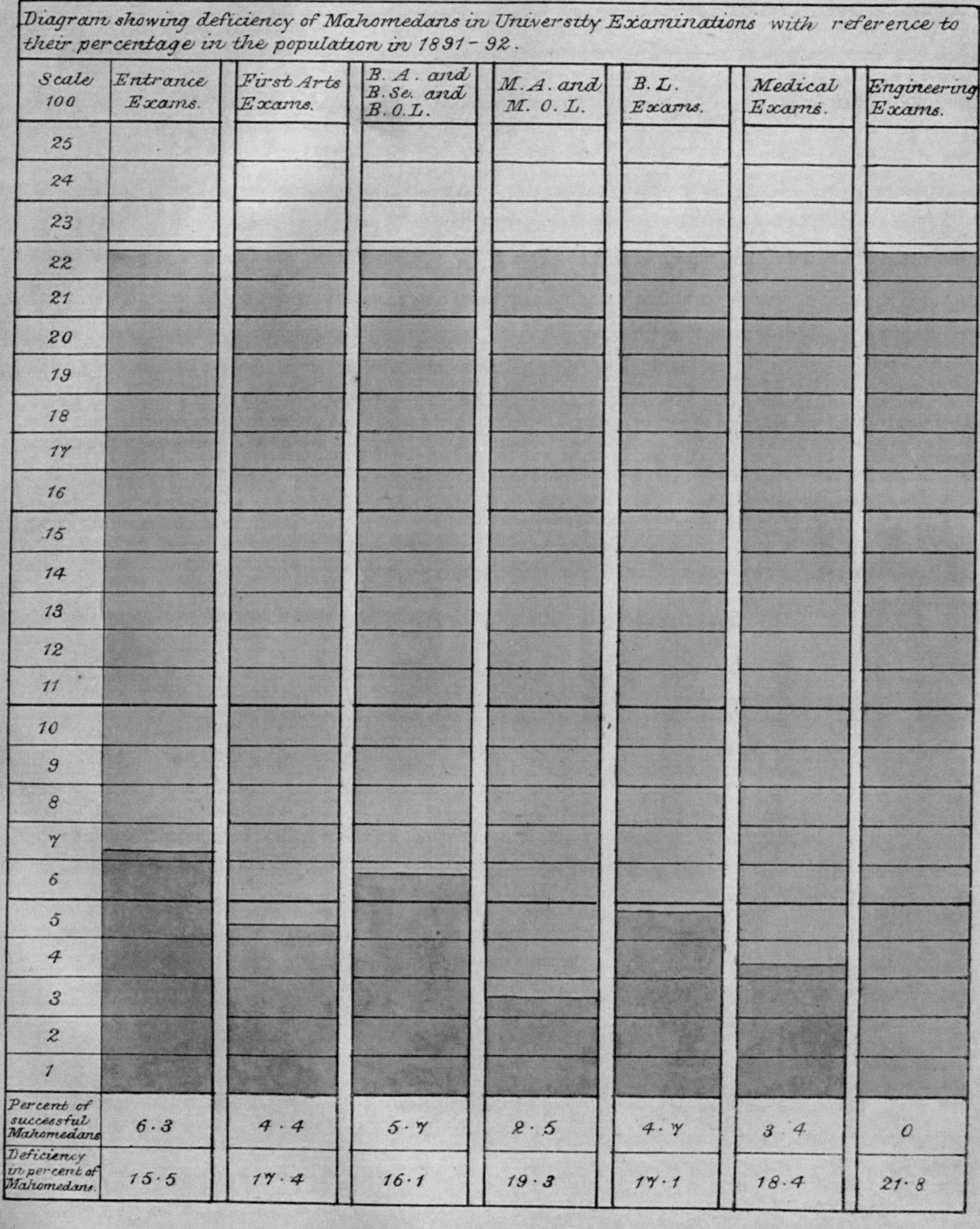

this purpose it is necessary to refer back to the statistics contained in the Table already given (at page 181 *ante*) showing the proportion of Muhammadans in the urban population and in English Colleges and Secondary Schools in various Provinces in 1891-92. From the figures contained in that Table, the following Diagram VI. has been prepared on the same principles as the preceding Diagram, the pink colour representing the percentage of the urban population, and the green colour the percentage of Muhammadan students in such institutions. In other words the pink colour represents the extent of the deficiency in the percentage of Muhammadan students with reference to the percentage of the Muhammadans in the urban population. It will thus be seen that according to this test even in the North-Western Provinces and Oudh, there is a vast deficiency in the percentage of Muhammadan students in every class of English education, and strenuous efforts are still necessary to bring up the percentage of Muhammadan students in English Colleges and Schools to the level of the percentage of Muhammadans in the urban population of the North-Western Provinces and Oudh.

Percentage of Muhamedans in the *Urban* population of the N.-W. Provinces and Oudh.

In regard to the progress of English education among Muhammadans in the North-Western Provinces and Oudh, and the extent of employment in the Public Service to which such education entitles them, much misapprehension is liable to arise by taking the percentage of Muhammadans in the general population of this part of the country, *viz.*, 13·5, and ignoring their percentage in the urban population which is no less than 33·9 or nearly 34 per cent. Upon this subject the views expressed by an eminent statesman, Sir Auckland Colvin, formerly Financial Member of the Supreme Council of the Viceroy of India and more recently Lieutenant-Governor of the North-Western Provinces and Oudh, deserve to be remembered. In the course of a reply to an Address presented to him by the Trustees of the Muhammadan Anglo-Oriental College at Aligrah, on the 23rd October 1892, he said:—

Sir Auckland Colvin's views as to the proportionate claims of Muhammadans in education and public service in the N.-W. P. and Oudh.

"And now, before concluding, I have a word to add of a somewhat more personal nature. Among other criticisms to which the administration of the last five years has been subjected, has, I have observed, been the criticism that it has given an undue preference to Muhammadans. That I have a very strong feeling of regard towards the Muhammadan community, and many friends I hope amongst them, I gladly admit. Were it otherwise, I should be indifferent to claims of which the force may not be apparent to some who lead the reproach I refer to, but which I should be very sorry for a moment to ignore—the claims of gratitude. I have on a comparatively recent occasion expressed the obligation under which I find myself to all those Muhammadans among whom I worked in Egypt, from the head of the State to the humble functionary; from those who were opposed to me no less than from those with whose sentiment I was in accord. From very many Muhammadans in this country, too, I have throughout my life received, and am indebted for the greatest aid and the most useful advice; though so far as this country is concerned, I may say the same of my friends among the Hindu community. Nor should I have taken this occasion to say anything on the subject, had the criticism been a purely personal one. But it implies an abuse of public patronage, and a misuse of the means of preferment which are placed in my hands by higher authority, because there is possibly no better test of preference shown to one or the other section of the community than the exercise of the power of patronage vested in the head of the administration. A few figures will throw some light on the question, so far as this particular criticism is concerned............ It may be said that as the Hindus in these Provinces are more numerous than the Muhammadans, preferment or distinction should be granted in numerical proportion. But if we leave out of sight the vast masses of the agricultural population, and take into consideration only the classes to whom, in such matters, consideration is limited, the disproportion almost wholly disappears. I have referred to this criticism because, as I have said, it is concerned with the discharge of my public duties."*

Diagram VII. explained.

To give a general view of the present condition of English education in British India, it is necessary to revert to the statistics contained in the Table (at page 179 *ante*) already given, showing the deficiency in the success of Muhammadans in all the various University Examinations in British India in 1891-92, as compared with the percentage of Muhammadans in the general population, *viz.*, 21·8. With this object the accompanying Diagram VII. has been prepared upon the same principles as the preceding Diagrams, and with reference to the statistics of the abovementioned Table—the pink colour up to 21·8 representing the percentage of the Muhammadans in the total population, and the green colour the extent of percentage which the Muhammadans achieved by their success in the various University Examinations in 1891-92. In other words the pink colour shows the vast extent of the deficiency of Muhammadans in all the various University Examinations in British India in 1891-92; and it will be observed that in the Engineering Examinations not even one Muhammadan was successful.

* *The Aligarh Institute Gazette* of 8th November, 1892, pp. 1174 and 1175.

CHAPTER XXXII.

GENERAL SPREAD OF ENGLISH EDUCATION IN INDIA, ACCORDING TO THE CENSUS OF 1891.

Statistics of the general spread of English Education in 1891.

The object of this Chapter is to furnish the best available Statistical information regarding the general spread of English education among the various sections of the population of India at the present time, to enable those who are interested in the religious, moral, social, and political regeneration of India, to form an approximate estimate of the effect which their plans and schemes are likely to have, so far as they depend upon a knowledge of the English language for their success or failure. "Where the task of public instruction is undertaken by the State, to the extent that it is in India, the function of a census of Literacy is to supplement the current record of progress in regard to this important matter." And accordingly the *General Report* of the Census of India in 1891, contains various Statistical Tabular Statements, which supply the requisite information, and from them the following Table* has been prepared :—

TABLE SHOWING LITERACY AND KNOWLEDGE OF THE ENGLISH LANGUAGE AMONG THE VARIOUS CLASSES OF THE POPULATION OF INDIA, ACCORDING TO THE CENSUS OF 1891.

Class.	Caste Group.	Population returning Literacy.			Percentage of the English-knowing in each group on—	
		Total.	Literates.	Knowing English.	Total English-knowing Literates (of all Groups).	Total Literates of the (particular) Group.
A.—Agricultural & Pastoral.	I.—Military—Agricultural ...	24,815,250	978,226	15,163	2·82	1·55
	II.—Agricultural	45,860,061	1,314,452	31,364	5·83	2·39
	III.—Cattle Breeders and Graziers.	11,006,956	131,015	3,468	0·65	2·65
	IV.—Field Labourers... ...	8,162,851	151,502	2,346	0·44	1·55
	V.—Forest Tribes	13,217,795	53,400	1,071	0·20	2·01
	Total ...	**103,062,913**	**2,628,595**	**53,412**	**9·94**	**2·03**
B.—Professional.	VI.—Priests	12,860,386	2,029,870	109,105	20·29	5·37
	VII.—Ascetics and Devotees ...	2,231,334	120.809	1,671	0·31	1·38
	VIII.—Temple Servants ...	285,940	29,500	384	0·07	1·30
	IX.—Genealogists	419,306	23,942	240	0·04	1·00
	X.—Writers	2,450.824	572,708	49,133	9·13	8·58
	XI.—Astrologers, &c.... ...	264,748	46,532	5,247	0·97	11·28
	XII.—Ballad Reciters and Musicians	521,641	7,113	38	0·01	0·53
	XIII.—Singers and Dancers ...	124.845	8,263	98	0·02	1·19
	XIV.—Mimes	27,428	1,061	2	...	0·19
	Total ...	**19,186,452**	**2,839,798**	**165,918**	**30·84**	**5·84**
C.—Commercial.	XV.—Traders	10.785,525	1,658,905	35,484	6·60	2·14
	XVI.—Pedlers	119.732	1,703	11	...	0·65
	XVII.—Carriers by Pack Animals ...	897,208	7,265	61	0·01	0·84
	Total ...	**11,802,465**	**1,667,873**	**35,556**	**6·61**	**2·13**

* The *first* column of the Table showing the classification, has been taken from page 188, and the last *two* columns showing the percentages of the English-knowing, from page 220 of the Report, and the figures from page 54–56 of the *General Tables*, Vol. II.

Class.	Caste Group.	Population returning Literacy.			Percentage of the English-knowing in each Group on—	
		Total.	Literates.	Knowing English.	Total English-knowing Literates (of all Groups).	Total Literates of the (particular) Group.
D.—Artisans and Village Menials.	XVIII.—Goldsmiths, &c.... ...	1,497,218	145,228	1,402	0·26	0·97
	XIX.—Barbers	3,366,345	84,539	1,809	0·33	2·14
	XX.—Blacksmiths	2,416,747	61,180	1,147	0·21	1·87
	XXI.—Carpenters and Masons ...	2,951,000	117,378	1,295	0·24	1·10
	XXII.—Brass and Copper Smelters...	287,701	24,253	452	0·08	1·86
	XXIII.—Tailors	612,572	28,430	776	0·14	2·73
	XXIV.—Grain Parchers, &c. ...	1,394,944	45,845	905	0·17	1·97
	XXV.—Betel-leaf, &c., Sellers ...	236,854	16,102	664	0·12	4·12
	XXVI.—Weavers and Dyers ...	8,290,809	251,021	4,841	0·90	1·93
	XXVII.—Washermen	2,669,231	28,836	664	0·12	2·30
	XXVIII.—Cotton Cleaners... ...	789,527	5,038	39	0·01	0·77
	XXIX.—Shepherds and Blanket Weavers	4,679,388	47,831	1,090	0·20	2·28
	XXX.—Oil Pressers	4,367,089	140,469	3,043	0·57	2·17
	XXXI.—Potters and Brickmakers ...	2,999,262	41,239	1,395	0·26	3·38
	XXXII.—Glass and Lac Workers ...	141,091	3,618	217	0·04	5·10
	XXXIII.—Salt and Lime Workers ...	1,407,879	18,211	139	0·03	0·76
	XXXIV.—Goldsmiths' Refuse Cleaners .	5,278	100	...	...	...
	XXXV.—Iron Smelters and Gold Washers	24,893	175	1	...	0·57
	XXXVI.—Fishermen, &c.	8,311,672	93,657	1,921	0·36	2·05
	XXXVII.—Rice Pounders and Servants. .	178,360	2,550	29	0·01	1·14
	XXXVIII.—Distillers and Toddy Drawers	4,826,294	294,670	3,906	0·74	1·33
	XXXIX.—Butchers	519,688	3,292	54	0·01	1·64
	XL.—Leather Workers ...	12,032,920	64,126	722	0·13	1·13
	XLI.—Village Watchmen and Menials	12,279,544	76,260	2,354	0·44	3·09
	XLII.—Scavengers	3,450,913	20,438	665	0·12	3·25
	Total ...	**79,737,174**	**1,614,486**	**29,530**	**5·49**	**1·83**

Class.	Caste Group.	Population returning Literacy.			Percentage of the English-knowing in each Group on—	
		Total.	Literates.	Knowing English.	Total English-knowing Literates (of all Groups).	Total Literates of the (particular) Group.
E.—Vagrants.	XLIII.—Itinerant Grindstone Makers .	16,427	84	...	...	...
	XLIV.— Ditto Earth Workers and Stone Dressers ...	1,090,836	3,558	64	0·01	1·80
	XLV.—Itinerant Knife and Sword Grinders	12,486	152	3	...	1·97
	XLVI.—Itinerant Mat and Cane Makers	584,127	3,551	28	0·01	0·79
	XLVII.—Hunters and Fowlers ...	730,662	5,752	90	0·02	1·56
	XLVIII.—Miscellaneous Vagrants ...	326,973	3,881	51	0·01	1·31
	XLIX.—Acrobats, Jugglers, and Snake Charmers	255,681	3,310	143	0·03	4·32
	Total ...	**3,017,192**	**20,288**	**379**	**0·08**	**1·87**
F.—Races and Indefinite Titles.	L.—Musalmans bearing Foreign Titles *	32,834,755	1,141,912	33,282	6·19	2·91
	LI.—Thibetan and Nipali Races ...	214,021	12,077	373	0·07	3·09
	LII.—Burmese, Chinese, and Malay Races	7,316,377	1,512,800	3,100	0·58	0·20
	LIII.—Western Asiatic Races ...	106,610	48,510	16,049	2·98	33·08
	LIV.—Mixed Asiatic Races ...	19,821	1,583	26	...	1·64
	LV.—Indefinite Indian Titles ...	2,845,461	169,037	6,677	1·24	3·95
	LVI.—Europeans, Americans, &c. ...	161,414	118,222	113,247	21·06	95·79
	LVII.—Eurasians	80,900	42,217	38,532	7·16	91·27
	LVIII.—Indian Christians ...	1,896,698	248,486	40,449	7·38	16·28
	LIX.—Goanese and Portuguese ...	28,366	4,783	1,252	0·37	26·18
	LX.—Africans	18,292	582	29	0·01	4·98
	Total ...	**45,522,715**	**3,300,209**	**253,016**	**47·04**	**7·67**
	Grand Total ...	**262,328,956 †**	**12,071,249**	**537,811**		

Concentration of Literacy, especially English, in certain classes of the population.

The diffusion of instruction through the community is appreciated more accurately when we have before us the relative extent to which it pervades each of the groups of castes or races under which the population has been classified in the above Table, according to the *General Report* of the Census of 1891 (*vide* page 188); but for the sake of convenient reference it will be advisable to quote here the remarks contained in that Report (pages 222 and 223), so far as the percentage of the English-knowing section of the population is concerned :—

* This class is explained at page 207 of the *General Report* of the Census of 1891 to include persons denominating themselves *Shaikh*, *Pathan*, *Moghal*, *Saiad*, *Balooch*, *Turk*, and *Arab*, and it is stated that they form nearly 12 per cent. of the population. Other Muhammadans not falling under the above titles are not therefore included in the figure given in the Table.

† This figure is given as the Grand Total in the Report of the Census of India, 1891, *General Tables*, Volume II, page 56. The totals for each class have been calculated for this work, and their Grand Total, according to calculation, yields 262,328,911, making a difference of only 45, which is inconsiderable.

Proportion of the English-knowing Literates.

"Amongst the literates are 5·83 per cent. of the total body of English-knowers, and these, in turn, form 2·39 per cent. of the literates in the group, so that in every 10,000, six know that language, or one in 1,667. With this explanation, the figures may be left to speak for themselves, so far as the details are concerned, and it is worth-while to bring to notice here only the more prominent features in this curious return. For instance, if both sexes be taken together, as in the first section of the Table, it will be seen that in 11 groups only, are the literate as high as 10 per cent. on the included population. The marginal extract reproduces the information regarding these 11. They comprise just under 14 per cent. of the population, just over half the literate population, and more than three-fourths of those who can read and write English. If the collection be re-grouped into more minute sections, it will be seen that the Brahmans, Writers, Traders' Native Christians, Temple Servants and Herbalists, &c., who constitute the strictly native portion of the whole, contain 11 per cent. of the population, 38 of the literate, and 45 of the English-knowers. The Burmese and Parsis, with the few Armenians and Jews, come next, with 2·8 per cent. of the population, nearly 13 of the literate, and just above 3½ per cent. of those who know English. Finally, we have the European and Eurasian element, which accounts for just under one in a thousand of the population, 13 in the same number of the literate, and 283 of the English-knowing part of the community. Outside this circle is found about 23 per cent. of the latter population, or about the same proportion as is contributed by the Europeans and Parsis, &c., taken together. It will also be noticed that the Brahmans, Writers, and Europeans monopolise more than half of this class of the literate, and the Traders, Eurasians, and Native Christians, a fifth more. As regards the introduction of the Herbalist and Astrologer, it should be explained that the former is apparently one of the best-instructed classes in Eastern Bengal, to which part of the country he is, as a separate caste, confined. The Temple Servant group, again, owes its position to the Sátáni of Madras and Mysore, where this class is most prevalent.

Caste Group, or Race.	Percentage on totals of— Population.	Literates.	English-knowing Literates.
1. Priests	4·90	16·81	20·29
2. Temple Servants	0·11	0·26	0 07
3. Writers	0·94	4·74	9·13
4. Herbalists, &c.	0·10	0·39	0·97
5 Traders	4·11	13·74	6·60
6. Burmese	2·79	12·53	0·58
7. Parsis, &c.	0·04	0·42	2·98
8. Europeans	0·06	0·98	21·06
9. Eurasians	0·03	0·35	7·16
10. Native Christians ...	0·72	2·05	7·38
11. Goanese Christians ...	0·01	0·05	0·37
Total ...	**13·81**	**52·31**	**76·59**

Literacy, especially English, among the males.

"We may now turn from the general section of the Table to that which treats of males only. Here we find that no less than 20 of the 60 groups returns 10 per cent., and over, of literates in its community. The additions to the former list are the Devotees, Genealogists, Goldsmiths, Brass-smiths, Betel-leaf Sellers, Distillers, Nepali and Thibetan tribes, and the mixed races of Burma, with the group that had to be set apart for indefinite entries, containing a good number of the writing castes serving at a distance from their native province, and thus entered under some misconstructed title. These additions enlarge the scope of the collection considerably. Instead of 14 per cent. of the population we get over 18 of the males, with 58½ per cent. of the literate of that sex, and 79½ per cent. of those who know English. The groups in which female instruction is more prevalent take, of course, a lower place in this Statement than the last. This remark applies to the Writers, Temple Servants, Herbalists, &c., Parsis, &c., Burmese, Europeans, Eurasians, Native Christians and Goanese, to all of the former sections in fact, except to Traders and Brahmans. In the case of the former, there is no doubt that some of the difference is attributable to the number of literate men who come from Rajputana, &c., to the centres of commerce in British Territory without their families, but more to the general cause, namely, apathy, as in the case of Brahmans." *

Caste Group, &c.	Percentage on totals of— Males.	Literate Males.	English-knowing Literate Males.
1. Priests	4·96	16·98	20·29
2. Devotees	0·87	1·01	0·31
3. Temple Servants	0·11	0·23	0·07
4. Genealogists	0·16	0·20	0·04
5. Writers	0·92	4·66	9·13
6. Herbalists, &c.	0·10	0·34	0·97
7. Traders	4·15	14·09	6·60
8. Goldsmiths	0·57	1·24	0·26
9. Brass-smiths	0·11	0·21	0·08
10. Betel-leaf Sellers	0·09	0·14	0·12
11. Distillers, &c.	1·80	2·47	0·74
12. Thibetans	0·09	0·10	0·07
13. Burmese	2·72	12·46	0·58
14. Burmese, Mixed	0·01	0·01	—
15. Parsis, &c.	0·04	0·26	2·98
16 Indefinite Indians	1·11	1·37	1·24
17. Europeans	0·09	0·81	21·06
18. Eurasians	0·03	0·19	7·16
19. Native Christians	0·72	1·67	7·38
20. Goanese Christians	0 01	0·04	0·37
Total ...	**18·66**	**58·48**	**79·45**

* *General Report* of the Census of India, 1891, by J. A. Baines, Esq., pages 222 and 223.

Abstract of Statistics of English Literates.

As an abstract of the preceding Table, showing Literacy and knowledge of the English language among the various classes of the population of India, the following Table has been prepared for convenient reference :—

Class of Groups.	Population returning Literacy.			Percentage of the English-knowing in each Group on—	
	Total.	Literates.	Knowing English.	Total English-knowing Literates (of all Groups).	Total Literates (of the particular Group.
A.—Agricultural and Pastoral	103,062,913	2,628,595	53,412	9·94	2·03
B.—Professional	19,186,452	2,839,798	165,918	30·84	5·84
C.—Commercial	11,802,465	1,667,873	35,556	6·61	2·13
D.—Artizans and Village Menials	79,737,174	1,614,486	29,530	5·49	1·83
E.—Vagrants	3,017,192	20,288	379	0·08	1·87
F.—Races and Indefinite Titles	45,522,715	3,300,209	253,016	47·04	7·67
Total ...	**262,328,911**	**12,071,249**	**537,811**		

Remarks on the Statistics of English-knowing Literates.

In regard to the figures relating to English-knowing Literates, as shown in the preceding Tables, the following observations occur in the *General Report* of the Census of India of 1891, by Mr. J. A. Baines, of the Indian Civil Service, at page 224 :—

"The return of those who know English shows a ratio of 4·4 per cent. on the total literates. We must subtract, however, the Europeans and Eurasians from the account, which then amounts to 3·2 only, or 1·4 in every thousand of the community. From the detailed Table it will be seen that, excluding the Europeans, Eurasians, Nipalis, Africans, and Parsis, the latter proportion to the literates of the group is achieved only in the case of the Brahmans, Writers, and Herbalists, with the group of the indefinite castes. There are, it is true, four or five other groups that show a percentage slightly in excess of this, but they are all chiefly recruited from Bengal, where this part of the enumeration seems to have been unsatisfactory, since nowhere else do we find the Scavenger, Potter, and Acrobat in such exalted company. The entire number returned, as knowing English, including Europeans and Eurasians, was 537,811, or 386,032, if the foreign element be excluded. This, too, includes a certain proportion of those who are not yet emancipated from their studies, as has been already remarked in the beginning of the Chapter. Some of the Superintendents, on the other hand, seem to think that the return includes, from excess of caution, only those who habitually use English in their daily life, and not the numerous class that learn a certain amount of that language at school, but carry the use of it no further than the last examination before their escape from that stage, and cease to be able to read and write it after the lapse of a few years. The census return seems to compare but poorly with the Departmental Record in this respect, for the latter gives an average number of pupils studying English of 290,741 per annum during the last decade, beginning with 187,420, and ending with 353,515. The average period of study is not accurately known, but one would have expected to find at least 700,000 or 800,000 of the above number amongst the English-knowing literates. But apparently the study of English ends in a very rudimentary stage ; for with an average annual attendance of nearly 337,000, studying in that language for the last five years, only 15,200 presented themselves for the Matriculation Examination at the Universities, or 76,000 during the whole period. As English is the language of instruction at the colleges affiliated to the latter institutions, it is presumably an important subject at the Matriculation test, if not the most important. But we find from the same returns from which the above quotations are made, that the ratio of the successful for the five years in question was 47·74 in Calcutta, 26·87 in Madras, and 25·41 in Bombay. The other Universities need not be counted, as they are, comparatively speaking, in their infancy. But at any rate the out-turn of 25,680 in five years of youths up to Matriculation standard, even with the possible successes under the sixth standard elsewhere, are scarcely results that need make the census returns blush on comparison."*

This Chapter may be appropriately closed with the following extracts from the *General Report* of the Census of India of 1891 :—

General extent of Literacy.

" The final computation made above brings us to the fact that in India, as a whole, the very moderate average of 46 literate persons in a thousand, is not attained by 81·35 per cent. of the population, but is the result of greater prevalance of instruction amongst the remaining 18·65. In the case of the males alone, the standard rises to 87 per 1,000, but it is not reached by more than 18·89 per cent. of the sex, leaving 81·11 below it."†

Condition of Literature.

" In the Chapter on occupation, it was shown how small a fraction lived by literature, and though the annual returns show an imposing array of publications, the review of the literary activity of the year, by the Official Reporter, is rather discouraging reading. According to this authority, a few works on Sanskrit texts, with an occasional drama on a historical occurrence or a subject of the day, are all that are likely to survive the year of their birth. A good deal of this infant mortality, so to speak, seems to be attributable to the very high proportion of the publications which deal with the text-books prescribed for University or school examinations, or other ephemeral works designed for the same market. The most striking characteristic of the out-turn seems to be the absence of originality in scientific or imaginative works. The list does not want variety, as will be seen from the marginal statement of subjects, with, of course, the qualification that rather over a third are translations or re-publications. The language in which the works are issued, also, is a matter not devoid of interest, and it appears that in English 660 were published, with 955 in polyglot, 2,157 in a Vernacular tongue, and 424 in the three Oriental classical languages. But a more favourite out-let for budding talent is found in journalism, of which we find 490 exponents in the list. The largest circulation is stated to be 20,000, in the case of one paper in Bengal ; about 6,000 is the maximum in Bombay, and 5,000 in Madras. Elsewhere, it seems to rarely reach a thousand. This does not represent, of course, nearly the number of readers, for the economical practice of private circulation, or of perusal at cheap libraries, is far more extended in India than in many other countries. But lithography and disregard for typographical appearance enables an enterprising publicist to start a local broadsheet at a very small cost, and what with the restrictions of career imposed upon themselves by a solely literary caste or two, no country, probably, has more representatives than India of the hero of the Romaic ballad :—

PROVINCE.	Books published in 1890-91.
Madras	1,022
Bombay	2,044
Bengal	1,225
N.-W. Provinces	1,107
Burma	149
Assam	22
Berar	13
Central Provinces	13
Total ...	5,595

SUBJECT.	No. of Publications.
Art	80
Biography	58
Drama	185
Fiction	262
History and Geography	128
Languages	612
Law	71
Mathematics	158
Medicine	127
Philosophy	149
Poetry	672
Politics	13
Religion	770
Science	119
Travels	5
Unclassed	2,116
Total ...	5,595

Θερμὸς ἔιμαι πατριώτης, καὶ κουκ κουλια 'γω δὲν βάφω,
Ἢ ὕπαυργημα με δίδεις ἤ εφημερίδ γράφω.

" This digression from the results of the Census has been unduly lengthened, but when so much is heard, as at present, of the literate classes of India, it is just as well to define the limitations of that term. It may thus be judged how far the φῶς ἀφεγγὴς of the handful of people, to whom, under the most liberal interpretation, the term can be said to apply, is to be held capable of illuminating the thoughts and conditions of the vast mass from whom the very education, apart from the traditions, of that close corporation, inclines them to stand aloof." ‡

* *General Report of the Census of India in* 1891, by J. A. Baines, Esquire, p. 224.

† *Ib.* | ‡ *Ib.*, p. 226.

CHAPTER XXXIII.

EXPECTATIONS AND VIEWS OF EMINENT STATESMEN REGARDING THE POLITICAL, SOCIAL, MORAL, AND RELIGIOUS EFFECTS OF ENGLISH EDUCATION AMONG THE PEOPLE OF INDIA.—OPINIONS OF THE EDUCATION COMMISSION OF 1882 ON THE SUBJECT.

Comprehensive aspects of the effects of English Education in India.

The preceding chapters of this work have been devoted to delineation of the facts and figures connected with the progress of English education in India from its earliest commencement down to the present period. What the effects of such education have been, in their various aspects, remains to be considered. "In every difficulty that meets us in the consideration or treatment of measures designed to further the cause of commercial progress or of political security in India, we involuntarily recur to the one solution of every problem—*education.* Is it the obstacle in the way of an extended circulation of a paper currency that puzzles the financier? The remedy is *education.* Are we hampered by a necessary restriction of expenditure in the matter of public works of general utility, by reason of the enormous drain upon the resources of the country for a military establishment without which it is vain to hope that disaffection can be suppressed and political excitement subdued? The remedy is *education.* Are we dismayed at the slow pace with which liberal ideas make good their advance against the obstruction of ignorance, bigotry, and superstition? The remedy is *education.* Are we puzzled at the strange anomaly presented by a whole race, or races, preferring the arbitrary and capricious despotism of native governments to the organized administration of British rule? We know that it is to the schoolmaster chiefly we must look to aid in removing from the mental vision of the people the veil that shuts out the light. Do we ask how we shall raise the agricultural population of India to the status of a free community? The answer is *education.* Do we ask how to secure permanent and lasting peace, apart, of course, from the distant danger of foreign invasion? The answer is *education.* Do we ask how we shall break the fetters of caste that bind millions of our fellow-subjects in social bondage? The answer is *education.* Do we wonder how it is that, after a century and a half of intercourse, the people of India are still as far separated from us as if there were scarce the bond of a common nature to unite us to each other? The answer is to be found in the slender efforts and the slow progress of *education.*" *

Effects of English Education classified.

Such being the comprehensive character of the subject of English education in India its effects upon the people must necessarily be multifarious. Their various aspects may be classified under the following heads :—

(1) Effect on *Religious belief: (a)* among Hindus, *(b)* among Muhammadans.

(2) Effect on *Moral opinions and conduct.*

(3) Effect on *Social manners and customs.*

(4) Effect on *Economical condition.*

(5) Effect on *Political thought and action.*

Discussion of effects of English Education liable to controversy; but views of eminent Statesmen important.

Whilst these various aspects of English education in India are extremely interesting and of supreme importance to the present and future welfare of the people of India under the British rule, it cannot be denied that a proper discussion of them is fraught with vast and numerous difficulties. In the absence of statistical information upon these various heads of enquiry any treatment of the subjects can scarcely escape becoming controversial, and sentiments and tendencies of the controversialists are liable to take the place of unvarnished facts and accurate figures. In truth, accurate information upon these various aspects of English education in India is not available for purposes of a historical narrative such as the present work is intended to be, and the best course seems to be to leave these subjects to essayists to discuss whether the religious, social, moral, economical and political effects of English education in India have been baneful or beneficial. For the purposes of this work, however, it seems sufficient to collect here the various opinions of eminent Statesmen, expressed at different times, upon the general tendency and effects of English education on the people of India. Such opinions are not only valuable for their intrinsic merits, but

* *The Administration of India.* By Iltudus Thomas Prichard, Vol. II, pp. 75 and 76.

much historical worth and importance is to be attached to them as representing the views of distinguished Statesmen who have actually taken important part in the administration of India during various periods of its history. And, in order to secure their views from the risk of being unconsciously misrepresented or inadequately expressed, the best course seems to be to quote them in their own words. Some of those opinions were written at a period when the policy of spreading English education among the people of India had not yet been affirmed, some were expressed at the very outset of the adoption of the policy of English education, whilst others were expressed at various stages and periods of the last half century as the effects of English education became noticeable among the people. The chronological order is therefore most suitable for presenting those opinions for the perusal of the reader, in preference to the order in which the various aspects of the effects of English education have been classified in the preceding paragraph.

Anticipations of the Rt. Hon'ble Charles Grant as to political effects of English Education: a forecast, 1792-97.

First and foremost, therefore, are the anticipatory views of the Right Hon'ble Mr. Charles Grant, an eminent Director of the East India Company, and a distinguished Member of Parliament who flourished during the latter part of the last and the beginning of the present century and of whom an account has already been given in this work * as the author of a philanthropic treatise on the moral and intellectual condition of the Natives of India, and the means of improving it. He wrote the treatise between the years 1792 and 1797, and in dealing with various objections which had been urged against his scheme of spreading English education in India, he went on to deal with the forecast of its political aspects in the following words :—†

Political objection to the spread of English Education formulated.

"Another objection still remains to be stated, one of an opposite nature to some of those which have been discussed, and in appearance more formidable than any of them. Its constituent idea is *the danger which might result from the adoption of the proposed plan.* Put in its strongest and amplest terms, it may be thus expressed : '*If the English language, if English opinions, and improvements, are introduced in our Asiatic possessions, into Bengal for instance ; if Christianity, specially, is established in that quarter ; and if, together with these changes, many Englishmen colonize there, will not the people learn to desire English liberty and the English form of Government, a share in the legislation of their own country, and commissions in the army maintained in that country ? Will not the army thence become, in time, wholly provincial, officered by natives of India, without attachment to the sovereign state ? Will not the people at length come to think it a hardship to be subject, and to pay tribute, to a foreign country : and finally, will they not cast off that subjection, and assert their independence ?*'

"Before we proceed to offer a reply to this objection, it is fair to remark, that whoever seriously entertains it, cannot also entertain those which may be advanced against the practicability of the plan, or the possibility of its succeeding. And in like manner, he who thinks success hopeless, can feel no real alarm for the danger which another might conceive success to be capable of producing. Hence, though every man is unquestionably entitled to follow the best decision of his own judgment, yet in this case, an opposition, increased in numbers by contradictory principles, would therefore be diminished in argumentative strength, since objections incompatible with each other could not both be valid.

Colonization of Europeans in India is a separate question from Education.

"It will be proper likewise, previously to separate and exclude from this complex objection some parts of it, which can, with no justice, be reckoned among the imaginable consequences of any estimated improvement in the state of our Indian subjects. Such are the free colonization of Europeans in that country, and the gradual transfer of Military appointments and Military power into the hands of provincials. These are things which do not depend on the admission of any particular religion into our territories, or its exclusion ; nor upon the will of the people inhabiting them ; but upon the Government of this country. They are wholly unnecessary ; they would, in our humble apprehension, be most unwise ; and that light which we now possess regarding our Eastern affairs, that sound policy in the management of them, of which late years have furnished so many proofs, forbid the admission of suppositions so superfluous and extravagant.

Presence of a certain number of Europeans for Public Service and Commerce, &c., necessary in India, but unlicensed adventurers should be excluded.

"With respect to colonization, the nature of our connection with that country, renders the residence there of a certain number of Europeans, for the various lines of public service, necessary. The admission of a further number as merchants, navigators, artists, and professional men, is useful and important ; but beyond such a fair proportion as may be requisite for these different lines of employment, and the prosecution of useful improvements and enterprizes, in which the energy and skill of Europeans are essential, their ingress into that country ought not to

* *Vide page 3, ante.* † *Printed Parliamentary Papers relating to the Affairs of India ; General,* Appendix I (1832), pp. 72–84.

be permitted, for otherwise a new race might spring up, with larger pretensions, and more untractable than the Hindus. Those also admitted should be laid under particular restrictions; the more considerable settlements should be confined to the sea coasts; and the laws against the entrance of unlicensed adventurers be strictly enforced; for these adventurers may be of nations hostile to our interests, they will be less known, less to be depended on by us, more liable to fail of success in their own views, and from necessity be more likely to colonize. But in all the decent and liberal classes of Europeans, there is ever an ardent desire to return at length to their native country; and hardly an instance can be found of any person, capable from his circumstances of following this course, who has deliberately chosen to make India his ultimate home. The state of native society there, may, no doubt, contribute to form this disposition; but the Indian climate is not congenial to the European constitution, and the strong endearing attachments of early days, with the rational judgment of maturer years, powerfully impel the natives of this happy island to their original seat.*

Employment of Natives to Military Command unnecessary.

"The other idea, which makes our Indian power to depend at length on provincial officers and soldiers, proceeds upon the supposition of previous unrestrained colonization, which has just been shown to be needless and inadmissible, and upon other imagined changes, into the probability of which we need not now examine. For upon any hypothesis compatible with our retention of the country, it is not conceivable how we should ever be exposed to the danger here alleged. Is it not among the first prerogatives of government to select its military servants? What inducement could possibly arise to transfer the delicate and important trust of Military command from the natives of this country to those less connected with it? Do we act thus with our American Colonies, peopled by subjects of the British race? As we now ultimately depend not only on British officers, but

* The following remarks, added as a postscript to the first copy of this tract, and intended to apply to the subject of the Company's Charter, then about to be renewed, it may still not be improper to insert here.

"Lest the scope of these observations should be misunderstood, the writer begs leave to declare, that he is no advocate for any system of intercourse between this country and our Eastern territories, which shall give Europeans an unlimited freedom of entrance there; but would most earnestly deprecate all schemes, of which such unlimited freedom should be the professed basis, or the actual, though unavowed consequence. There is a question concerned here, of far greater importance than the merely commercial one of an open or a restricted trade to India; it is a question that involves in it the welfare, both of Great Britain and of our Asiatic possessions.

"If the subjects of this country are permitted, at their pleasure, to visit those possessions as they may our American colonies though professedly but for the purposes of traffic, great numbers of them will settle; for mercantile transactions must entail residence, because it will be impossible for a Government to say, that all such transactions shall be closed, and the parties be gone within a certain time, or to take cognizance in this manner of the conduct of every individual; and if such a measure were at first attempted, it would not continue any time. All the lines of trade and manufactures would soon be overstocked, and then men would seek to fasten themselves on the soil. Colonization would therefore very soon commence in India, especially in Bengal; those whom uncontrolled enterprizes in commerce would carry thither, would see a rich soil apprehend great scope for exertions and regard the natives as a subjected people, feeble, timid and contemptible; all things would tempt them, and many, both agents and seamen, would remain. But the increase of Europeans there would not be regulated by the gradual progress of colonial industry. Multitudes of the needy and the idle allured by the fame of that country, and eager to seize novel privileges, would flock thither at once. Britain would, in a short space, be thinned of inhabitants, and those Eastern provinces filled with a new race of adventurers, many of them low and licentious. Being there, they must subsist; they would spread themselves throughout the country, would run into the Inland trade, fix themselves wherever they could on the lands, domineer over the natives, harass, extrude, exasperate them, and at length provoke them to plots and insurrections; they would be bold and assuming towards our own Government there; its present form calculated chiefly for the natives would not be sufficiently coercive in such a new state of things, and hardly any Government which we could maintain in that quarter, would control swarms of Europeans, thus let loose, and animated by the spirit of adventure and acquisition. Nor would the emigrations be confined to our countrymen only. If we tolerate the practice of free colonization in India, people from all the nations in Europe would resort thither, mix with other subjects, and aggravate the mischiefs of such an invading system. In a certain degree, we should have that lawless destructive scene acted over again which the Spaniards exhibited when they first poured into America. It was thus that the Portuguese power in the East declined. The intolerable license of the roving adventurers of that nation rendered them odious to the natives and armed the coasts and islands of India against them, so that weakened before, they fell an easy prey to the Dutch. And thus too, we should ourselves be exposed, perhaps at no distant period, to the danger of general convulsion and revolt in those possessions which, prudently guarded and cultivated, may, under the favour of Providence, to conciliate which should be our first care, be preserved for ages, to our great advantage, and the happiness of their native inhabitants.

"The question now, therefore, with respect to these possessions, is not whether all British subjects shall have a right to trade thither in their own persons, but whether the natives shall be protected from being overrun and oppressed by foreigners. A different cause recommends that the intercourse with these provinces be still carried on by one national organ, like the India Company. At first, such a collective body was preferred, as a better defence against the arbitrary and rapacious temper of the native governments. Now that the countries are our own, such a limited channel is also preferable, to save this nation, and our Asiatic subjects, from the evils which might accrue from too great a transfusion of the people of Europe among the Hindus."

on British troops, so, in the opinion of most competent judges, an opinion which appears to be indisputably solid and important, *ought we to do in all time to come.**

Disaffection to foreign dominion and taxation.

Among the articles unreasonably crowded into the objection now to be examined, are those which state the people as becoming, in consequence of some future supposed events and combinations, dissatisfied at the payment of a foreign tribute, and with subjection to a foreign country. Is it to be thought, that such ideas are then only to have existence, or that the people have in any past time been contented under the dominion of strangers? Surely not. The only point for consideration here is, their comparative acquiescence in this condition under their present circumstances, and under those which it is assumed may hereafter arise.

Political objection to English Education is a purely hypothetical conjecture opposed to Christian principles.

"We shall now enter upon the consideration of the objection itself; and the first things which attract our attention here, are the *foundation* on which the whole of this objection rests, and the *principle* upon which it proceeds. The *foundation* is *pure hypothesis*, or conjecture; and hypothesis supported by no real experience of any case similar to the one assumed to happen, nor by any just analogy. Some general apprehension, prepossession, or unexamined suspicion, suggests the possibility of certain events; and to this suggestion, without any satisfaction concerning the premises on which it is advanced, or the conclusion deduced from it, without regard to all the other relations of the subject in question, we are required to give our assent. The *principle* of the objection, at least equally remarkable, is plainly no other than this, that to prevent the remotest chance of such consequences as the proposed improvements might produce, our Asiatic subjects must be for ever held in the same state of ignorance and error in which they now are. 'Give them not,' says the unstrained sense of this objection, 'the light of true religion, teach them not a better system of morals, provide no stated means for their public or private instruction, impart not to them our knowledge of Nature, be not liberal to them, even in communicating the principles of our arts; afford them, in a word, no benefit whatever of light and improvement, lest our interest should in some future period suffer; keep them blind and wretched for all generations, lest our authority should be shaken, or our supremacy over them incur the slightest possible risk.' Surely those who may have inconsiderately lent themselves to this objection will not, upon a clear deliberate view of its principles seek to justify or to contend for it. A Christian nation cannot possibly maintain or countenance such a principle. To do so would be virtually to trample upon every sentiment which we profess in religion or in morals. It would be to make ourselves parties in all the impositions of the Brahminical system, and in effect to hold with its priests, the doctrine of Demetrius,† 'by this craft, *we* have our wealth.' To enlarge upon so very obvious an argument must be unnecessary.

Tendency of Christian teaching favours submission and good order among the people.

"Besides the series of effects which the objection professedly supposes, certain other positions are tacitly comprehended in it, which next claim our notice. It implies, that the establishment of Christianity in a country may, on the whole, prove unfavourable, or less favourable, than some other religious institution, to good Government; that its efficacy, may, on the whole, be inferior in securing the subordination, obedience, and attachment of the people, and the authority of the sovereign. Since, reason, experience, and general consent, have fully decided against this position, it would be superfluous and unbecoming to enter into any refutation of it. It is certainly one of the grossest misconceptions of the nature and tendency of the religion of the Gospel, which is known to afford precepts, motives, and encouragements to lawful submission and good order, infinitely more powerful and efficacious than those of any other system. Its real genius is so contrary to licentiousness and anarchy that as we have seen in a late memorable instance, their triumph can be raised only upon its extinction. If we would read the judgment of enlightened Europe upon this subject in a single sentence, the celebrated author already quoted, who spent a long life in profound and certainly unbigotted investigations into the nature of different systems of religion and law, may supply it. 'True Christians,' says he 'must be citizens thoroughly enlightened respecting their duties, with the greatest zeal for fulfilling them; the more they feel the obligations of religion, the more must they be sensible of what they owe to their country. The principles of Christianity well engraven on the heart, must be infinitely stronger than the false honour of Monarchies, the human virtues of republics, and the servile fear of despotic states.'‡

* If, upon premises very opposite to those on which the objections we are now answering are grounded, a doubt should be started of the propriety of keeping any people perpetually under foreign rule, this would be to agitate a question involving the right of conquest, and the nature of government; but it might perhaps be sufficient to reply, that we can foresee no period in which we may not govern our Asiatic subjects, more happily for them than they can be governed by themselves or any other power; and doing this we should not expose them to needless danger from without and from within, by giving the military power into their hands.

† Acts Chap. 19—Page 64.

‡ L'Esprit des Loix, Liv. XXIV. Chapter 6.

"The objection implies also, that rather than expose ourselves to the possibility of suffering future evils, which it is assumed Christianity might ultimately introduce, we should forego great advantages which are confessedly within our reach. The probability of effecting considerable improvements is not denied; it is, on the contrary, supposed; and this supposition constitutes the very ground of resistance. 'Though the field be spacious and much might be done, attempt not to benefit either your subjects or yourselves, lest success should, at some very distant day, be abused. Let us not do moral good, that political evil may not come.' Such is the language of the objection; an acquiescence in the propriety of which, since the duty of aiming at those salutary meliorations has been sufficiently established, would imply this further notion, 'that the way of duty is not, on the whole, the way of prosperity.' It is enough to have pointed out these exceptionable positions.

Advantages of Christianity do not forbode any possible political evils.

"But another still remains to be mentioned, which goes to the essence of the present subject. The objection silently assumes, 'that in a system opposite to the one proposed in this essay, must consist our future safety and stability in India.' The high importance of this proposition, not surely one of such intuitive evidence as to command instant assent, entitles it to particular consideration; but that consideration will be more conveniently bestowed, after we have viewed the direct matter of the objection, to which we now proceed.

"It alleges then, the probability of the utmost possible success from the adoption of a system of improvement, and the greatest possible abuse of that success. We have no design to exaggerate the effects or events which are necessary to justify these large conjectures; but we apprehend, that upon any reasonable estimate of them, they will be found to form a long series of stages, not only in the advancing, but also in the descending scale of human society; for no partial change in the people, either with respect to opinions or to numbers, seems adequate to the production of them. Let us endeavour therefore, to trace the career which is thus imagined, and to expand to the view, the various gradations of that ample progression by which we are to be conducted through greatness to decline. First, the diffusion of a foreign language, of foreign opinions and arts, of a spirit and religion the most dissimilar to those of the natives, who are a people exceedingly numerous, and from remote antiquity peculiarly attached to their own customs and notions; next a large increase of Agriculture, Manufactures, Commerce; with new wants, tastes, and luxuries; a great demand for English productions and fashions; and a gradual separation from neighbouring nations, in whom these changes, probably misrepresented to them, would beget disgust and aversion to the converted Hindus. The objection must imply moreover, not only the rise of just notions of civil liberty, but that they have become deeply rooted in a country where despotism seems to have been in all ages and to be still, the natural and only idea of Government;* it must imply vigour and unanimity to assert this liberty; then (before it can be abused) the possession and enjoyment of it; after this, a progress to licentiousness; and lastly, the violent dissolution of their connection with their sole protector, in the midst of nations become hostile to them, without a rational prospect of improving their situation, if they threw themselves upon the support of other European or Native powers, or of maintaining independence if they stood alone.

Possible political danger from diffusion of English literature science and religion too remote for practical consideration.

"To what distant age, may we not now ask, does this immense process lead us? If we even contract it to any space which an objector could urge as at all commensurate to the assumed consequences, should we still, in reasoning upon such conjectural delineations, stand upon any solid foundation? Would we act in serious and great concerns, even of private individual import, upon such precarious remote contingencies? Do they not set us afloat upon the ocean of possibilities, where the prospect, extended so far as to become wholly indistinct, confounds sea and sky, and in interspersed clouds of many shapes gives fancy easily to discover formidable promontories and rocks?

"But if we look to known realities to some of the many and great obstacles which will stand in the way of any such political revolution as is imagined, we shall be at a loss to give any sober satisfactory account of the manner in which they are to be removed. We insist not on the difficulty of disseminating, only by just and rational means, a new religion opposed by inveterate habits and prejudices. The friends of that scheme, indeed, dare not speak of success, with the confidence which the language of the objection seems to favour; yet they are not without hope; and they are animated by a conviction, that even a partial diffusion of Christianity, would improve the whole mass of society. But if we inquire, for instance, into the probable period of the general abolition of Castes, which allowing it ever to happen,

Abolition of caste prejudices and improvement of religious and social feelings will be so gradual that no violent revolution need be apprehended.

* The government of the Seikhs, though it have more of an aristocratic or republican form, seems no real exception to this observation, still less the aristocratic connection of the Mahratta chiefs.

must be conceived, in the natural order of things to precede some other supposed changes, what place shall we assign to it? Some point we may venture to say, not within our ken; and beyond which, it seems vain to stretch our political solicitude in so changeable a world as this, wherein political prediction is so often baffled; perhaps indeed, because it is so seldom connected with present duty. Supposing however, the tendency of events to be towards such an abolition, we may conclude, that the progress to it will be gradual. With the institution of Castes are blended not only religious doctrines and legal privileges, but the whole system of Hindu manners. Deep rooted prejudices, combined with strong interests and immemorial habits, cannot reasonably be expected to give way to sudden impressions. The entire manners and usages of a people do not change at once. The institution therefore, will not be deprived of its power by any violent rupture or convulsion. And even after the doctrine of Castes shall have lost its religious authority, and its tyrannical influence in Society, (still arguing on the supposition that these things may happen), the manners which it contributed to form, will, in a considerable degree, and for a certain time, remain. Among the Malabar converts to Christianity, distinctions of caste have not lost all their force; the habit of separation, the repulsive feelings, the secluding reserves, which spring from that source, though abated, still exist in some degree perhaps analagous to the ceremonial prejudices of the first Christian Jews. As long as a principle of this nature remains in Society, preventive as it will be of an inter-communion in marriages and professions, no formidable political association is likely to arise. Hence as the decline of the institution of Castes will be slow and imperceptible, so the moment of its expiration will be unperceived; subsequent observation only will discover that it is past: therefore neither can this change be a signal for new events.

Spread of the Gospel and European civilization not conducive to desiring a popular form of Government or assertion of independence.

"The grand danger with which the objection alarms us, is that the communication of the Gospel and of European light, may probably be introductive of a popular form of government and the assertion of independence. Upon what grounds is it inferred, that these effects must follow in any case, especially in the most unlikely case of the Hindus? The establishment of Christianity in a country, does not necessarily bring after it a free political Constitution. The early Christians made no attempts to change forms of government; the spirit of the Gospel does not encourage even any disposition which might lead to such attempts. Christianity has been long the religion of many parts of Europe, and of various protestant states, where the form of government is not popular. It is its peculiar excellence, and an argument of its intended universality, that it may subsist under different forms of government, and in all render men happy, and even societies flourishing; whereas the Muhammadan and Hindu Systems are built upon the foundation of political despotism, and adapted, in various instances, only to the climates that gave them birth. Christianity seeks moral good, and general happiness. It does not, in the pursuit of these objects, erect a peculiar political system; it views politics through the safe medium of morals, and subjects them to the laws of universal rectitude.

Christianity cannot supersede the debilitating effects of Eastern climate.

"Nor are we to expect, that Christianity is entirely to supersede the effects of physical causes. The debilitating nature of the climate of our Eastern territories, and its unfavourable influence upon the human constitution, have been already mentioned,* and by others represented in strong colours: 'Notwithstanding' says the celebrated historian of the British Transactions in Hindustan, 'the general effeminacy of character which is visible in all the Indians throughout the empire, the natives of Bengal are still of weaker frame, and more enervated disposition than those of any other province; bodily strength, courage, and fortitude, are unknown; even the labour of the common people is totally void of energy; and they are of a stupidity, which neither wishes, nor seems to be capable of extending its operations into any variety of mechanical dexterity. All those of the better castes, who are not fixed to the loom are bred to the details of traffic and money, in which their patience and perseverance are as great as their detestation of danger, and aversion to bodily fatigue.'† From this striking description ought to be excepted the Military tribes, to whom it will not properly apply, and the general features, we must take the liberty to say, are overcharged: but having made due allowances on these accounts, the picture will certainly possess no faint resemblance of the original.

"Indolence, pusillanimity, insensibility, as they proceed not wholly from physical sources, would be at least partially corrected by moral improvement; but the influences of a tropical sun would still be oppressive. The

* Chap. III, pp. 39, &c.

† Part II, Page 5th of the History of Military Transactions, &c., by Mr. Orme, an author well entitled to the high rank he holds in public estimation, by his generally just and comprehensive views of the subjects which he treats, the clearness, accuracy, vigour and dignity of his narration; but not appealed to in the former part of this Tract in the account there given of the state of Society among the Hindus, from an idea that he had not any large opportunities of intimately observing the conduct and manners of the middling and lower classes who live remote from European intercourse.

slight structure of the human body, with its ordinary concomitants, still forming the taste to a vegetable diet, would ill second ardent designs, even if the mind were vigorous enough to conceive them. In the early formation of the relations and habits of domestic life, which modify, in no inconsiderable degree, the Hindu character, there would be no material innovation. The nature of the country adds to the effects of the climate. It is unfavourable for long journeys; and the Hindus, in general a remotely inland people, have a strong aversion to the sea; even the air of it is offensive to them. They are thus deprived of all the advantages which the intercourses of navigation and an acquaintance with the world at large, would procure to them. Nor is there the least probability, that they will ever become maritime; and as little likely are they to become in other respects, an enterprising people. More calculated for passive suffering than for arduous attempts, they little love such exertions as freedom demands, and wish rather to be protected, than to have the trouble of protecting themselves.

Vegetable diet and absence of maritime taste among the Hindus will check ardent designs of independence.

"Where then is the rational ground for apprehending, that such a race will ever become turbulent for English liberty? A spirit of English liberty is not to be caught from a written description of it, by distant and feeble Asiatics especially. It was not originally conceived nor conveyed by a theoretical scheme. It has grown in the succession of ages from the active exertions of the human powers; and perhaps can be relished only by a people thus prepared. Example is more likely to inspire a taste for it than report; but the nations of Europe have seen that liberty and its great effects, without being led to the imitation of it; for the French revolution proceeds not upon its principles; it is an eruption of atheism and anarchy.

Natives of India will not become turbulent for English liberty.

"The English inhabiting our settlements in India, have no share in the British Government there. Some are employed as servants of the Public, but no one possesses any legislative right. Why then should we give to the Natives, even if they aspired to it, as it is unlikely that they will thus aspire, what we properly refuse to our own people? The British inhabitants would be extremely averse to such a participation. Our Government, as it is now constituted, interests Europeans in its support, without the danger which colonization might ultimately incur, their views of establishment and of final comfort centering in the mother country.

Absence of representative rights for the English inhabitants in India will prevent Natives from claiming such rights.

"The conduct of the British American colonies has raised in some minds, confused surmisings and apprehensions of the possibility of similar proceedings on the part of our Indian provinces. These alarms are easily caught by such persons, as shrink from the idea of whatever might have a remote tendency to advance our Asiatic subjects in the scale of human beings; conceiving (with what political truth may perhaps hereafter appear) that the more entirely they continue in their present ignorance, superstition, and degradation, the more secure is our dominion over them.* But never surely were apprehensions more destitute of

Conduct of British American colonies furnishes no example for India owing to dissimilarity of physical, intellectual and moral conditions. Natives will prefer British protection to independence.

* From the mischief which has recently been done in this country, by the dissemination of pernicious publications among the lower people, some persons seem inclined to think, that it would be better for the national security and tranquility, if that class of the community received no education. As this opinion touches very nearly the main argument which is maintained in the present Tract, the writer, though conscious that neither his ability, nor the limited space of a note, can do justice to the subject, hopes he shall be pardoned in throwing out a few observations upon it.

Springing probably from much better motives than the old exploded maxim, that "ignorance is the mother of devotion," it nevertheless seems to go upon a principle of a similar kind, it seems to imply, that "ignorance is the surest source of obedience." But it is presumed, that neither history nor reason will justify such a position in any sound sense, or indeed in any sense at all, unless a Government could be supposed to confine all the knowledge of a country to itself. *Knowledge* has been said, with apparent truth, *to be a species of power.* The *knowing* have power over the *ignorant;* even the *pretence of knowledge,* where *ignorance only* is opposed to it, has a similar advantage; and *knowledge,* like other kinds of power, the more exclusively it is possessed, the more it may be made an instrument of abuse. In the dark ages, when the stock of learning and information was comparatively little, and that little was shared only among a few, the abuses of knowledge and of pretended knowledge, and the ill consequences of those abuses, were greater than they have been in more enlightened times. In our own country, what numerous and gross evils prevailed in society from these causes? Corrupt churchmen and ambitious nobles, (who had the credit of superior intelligence as well as the honour of superior rank), led the common people within their respective spheres, as they pleased. The common people indeed, had then a spirit of implicit obedience, but it subjected them continually to the impositions of those who assumed the direction of them, and generally to the detriment of the nation at large. Hence the history of this island, prior to the Reformation, exhibits a frequent succession of internal convulsions. That grand event introduced new light, and it was diffused among the lower orders whose instruction became thenceforth an object of particular care. The consequences were, greater internal order, peace and stability; thence sprung enlarged industry, adventurous enterprises, and all the long succession of prosperity which this country has enjoyed.

solid foundation. There is, and there ever must be, an essential dissimilarity between the two cases. The Americans were, in fact, Englishmen, (with some infusion of foreign Europeans which may have contributed to alienate the colonies from this country), they possessed all the energy of the European character, all the lights of Europe; they were born in a temperate climate, nursed in the largest principles of freedom; nay the seeds of

We have advanced to a high degree of improvement in sciences and arts, in all the conveniences and enjoyments of civil life. Vast commerce has brought vast wealth; and wealth has been followed by its too inseparable attendant, corruption of manners. Our old solid principles, which were the foundation of our greatness have been gradually falling into disregard and neglect. They might have been well enough in our humbler beginnings, or in a less liberal age; but increased lights, greater elevation, and a fulness of all means of gratification, have seemed to many to plead first for relaxation, and then for the admission of other principles allowing a suitable enlargement in indulgences without fear. This spirit has spread through the whole mass of society. Writings and representations have helped the diffusion of it. Its effects have been visible on morals, and on the happiness of private life. Reverence for religion and for government has decayed. Both have been insidiously attacked from time to time; and at length, as the more mature produce of this spirit, some disdaining the measured advances hitherto made in unprincipling men, and encouraged by the fatal consummation of a like career in a neighbouring country, have openly and furiously attempted the subversion of all legitimate authority, human and divine. The incendiary torch and the secret mine, have been industriously employed to destroy the venerable fabrics of our religion and our constitution. Seditious and atheistical writings, superlative in the impudence of their falsehood, have been particularly adapted to the vulgar taste; and obviously, because the ignorance of the vulgar exposes them to easier imposition, as the too general example which they had long seen around them, pre-disposed them to progressive boldness in licentiousness. Then it is, that some men seeing the foundations of our political existence thus attacked, begin to argue from the abuse of a thing against its use, and to think it would be better for the community, that the lower people should not be instructed even to read, as by such privation they would, it is conceived, be inaccessible to infection from the press. But in fact, the evils of which we complain, originate in no small degree from the ignorance that has naturally followed the dereliction of right principles. The symptoms indicate a method of cure contrary to that which is proposed. The habit is diseased; the disorder, too deep to be reached externally, requires that the application be directed to its source. A return to ignorance may hasten the destruction of a society become corrupt through refinement, but can hardly contribute to restore it to soundness. At our advanced stage of improvement, it must be vain to imagine, that any retrograde movement we could effect in knowledge, would avail to secure the common mind from agitations and commotions. If any scheme of that kind even succeeded so far as to confine knowledge again among a smaller number, it could not reach to such characters as are now zealous to loosen and root out all received opinions in religion and Government; but they would, on the contrary, be able to do more mischief than they effect now, because the more profound were the ignorance of the multitude, the more scope would there be, as in the dark ages, for the arts and activity of wicked men to work upon their credulity. Of this France has furnished a recent instance, too memorable to be ever forgotten.

The want of knowledge and principle among the lower classes, left them a prey to Jacobinical impostures and delusions, by which they were hurried at once into the atrocities of anarchy and atheism.

It is not then by exposing our common people, unarmed and defenceless, to the daring blasphemies and sophistries of the preachers of impiety and sedition, that we can hope to keep them quiet. Our security lies, and lies only, in diffusing good instruction and right principles among them. In this too, the French revolutionists have afforded a lesson, which may suggest something useful to us. They endeavour that the minds of the people may not remain in that unfurnished state, of which they made advantage; but that the young especially, may be imbued with the tenets and prejudices favourable to their cause.

It is perhaps a mistake to suppose, that the common people among us, who have been most prone to tumult and disorder, are such as can read and write, or that the tendencies to commotion which have appeared, are to be ascribed to any degree of education possessed by that class. Besides that one reader in a circle or in a village would be sufficient to disseminate what was level to the vulgar understanding and acceptable to vulgar prejudices, and that the lower ranks are more affected by what they see or hear, than by what they read; those tendencies have chiefly manifested themselves in large towns, abounding with manufacturers, or idle vagabonds destitute of character or qualities sufficient to procure an honest livelihood, and it is therefore fair to presume, the least instructed part of the community. The manufacturers, generally put to work when yet children, often receive no education. When grown up, they are, not unfrequently congregated in large numbers, sometimes without due attention to decorum; they encourage each other in vice; and the gains of their labour enable them to pass the time of relaxation, in which they commonly include what ought to be allowed to sacred purposes, in dissolute indulgence. Among people of this character, there is combustible matter already prepared for the designs of those who seek to kindle discontent and disturbance. But the writer of these observations had occasion, not long ago, to see a contrast to this description, in a populous country parish. In that district there were very few persons of sufficient age, who could not read. The people were in general sober, decent, regular in their attendance on public worship; and in the course of twenty preceeding years, one instance of the commission of a capital crime among them had not occurred. The doctrines of Paine found little to work upon in such a community; the Bible was reverenced there, and every man kept steadily within his own place.

But we are not left in this case to smaller instances of individual observation. An experiment has been going on upon a large scale for a long series of years, in the sight of the whole nation, in the two countries of Ireland and Scotland. The common classes of the former country have unhappily been too generally kept in ignorance to the present day; and are not the consequences most obvious and most serious? How lamentably are the lower people there distinguished by vicious, turbulent, and lawless proceedings? In what division of the British dominions has there appeared so great a propensity to embrace democratic, disorganizing principles? And it is observable, that these principles, and the barbarities of which we hear so much, have prevailed chiefly in remoter, less enlightened parts of the kingdom, whilst the vicinities of Dublin, Cork, and other considerable places more civilised by knowledge, have been more orderly and quiet. Scotland, on the contrary, has been remarkable for attention to the instruction of the lower classes of its inhabi-

republicanism were sown in the first formation of the leading colonies. They had already a popular government. They were inured to arms, to hardships, and toils. The spirit of improvement animated them in a thousand different lines. They were expert seamen; their country abounded in excellent harbours; and in their geographical situation, they were (with the exception of one or two of our detached, more recently settled colonies) the sole civilized people in a great tract of continent, which seemed to offer to them the tempting prospect of becoming there the only political power. With all this, they were near enough to our insidious enemies to be constantly instigated to resistance by their arts, and effectually aided by their arms and resources. To what one of these many particulars, shall we discover a parallel among our Hindu subjects? To none, as they now are; and in various important points, no resemblance is ever to be expected. The origin, the physical character and condition, the intellectual, moral, and political state of the Hindus, have already appeared, in the course of this essay, to be totally different. On their local circumstances only, it remains to say, in addition to what was before intimated, a few words. If they were ever 'to exalt the spear of enmity' against their ancient masters, they would do so almost environed by Hindus, whose faith they had renounced, and to whom their apostacy would have rendered them odious. Could they trust such neighbours as allies, or resist them as enemies? What their interest would obviously require them to avoid, surely we have no right to assume that they would be so unwise as to commit. And if they called in the assistance of an European power, would they thus obtain independence, or only change one master for another? On all the coast of Hindustan there are but three or four good ports, and these at great distances from each other; though the shore is in many places accessible to an invading force, and there are some tolerable harbours in the islands of the Bay of Bengal of which an enemy could take great advantage. Now, if the Hindus could be renovated in every other particular, no assignable period can be imagined for their acquiring and practising the art of navigation; and therefore, those of them now subject to Great Britain must, in their supposed new circumstances, not only continue to need the supply of many wants from that country, but always be exposed to the hostile approaches of the navies of Europe. By a people so circumstanced, it does not appear how independence is attainable. They must, in effect, be at the mercy of the strongest maritime power. Whilst therefore, we continue to be that power, it is rather to be expected that their own interest, and the preference which their imitation of our manners will have given us over other European nations, will jointly induce them to remain safe under our protection; as these motives, on their part, will strengthen us in India against European

tants, and they have, in general been distinguished for near two centuries past by a spirit of sobriety and order. In the more remote inaccessible parts of that country, whither, obstructed by particular causes, light penetrated more slowly, regularity and good order were also of later establishment; but the natives of those divisions misguided into excess on some occasions now long past, have since been as eminent for a quiet and peaceable demeanour at home, as for standing numerously in the foremost ranks of those who have bled for the interests and the honour of this country in every quarter of the globe; and at the present critical juncture have come conspicuously forward, in many bands for the support of our constitution and our religion, against all enemies, foreign and domestic.

Indeed, if we were even to set aside the consideration of religion, and the good principles it inculcates, and to regard knowledge merely as power, or as an instrument of civilization, we might safely rest the present question upon this ground.

The diffusion of knowledge would, in the end render, a nation more disposed to check the admission of disorganizing principles. Doctrines it is admitted, while new, might make, as they often do, an irregular impression; but at length these irregularities would be corrected by good sense and reflection; and surely literature, even in its lowest stages, must be allowed to be more favourable to the production of good sense and reflection than ignorance.

But when we take into the question the influence of religion and all its salutary principles, certainly no one who considers their force and tendency can hesitate how to decide. Christianity was given to be "*a light to the world;*" ignorance is declared in the inspired writings to be one of the leading causes of the ruin of the Jewish nation, and of the vices of the Heathens. The ancient Pharisees were condemned by the Author of our religion for taking away the key of knowledge, that is, the use of the Scriptures from the people; which also has been eminently the sin of the Romish Church. It is, on the contrary, a stated prayer of the Church of England, that the people may so *read* the Word of God as duly to profit by it; and as that word "*thoroughly furnishes*" those who submit to it "*for all good works*" so where else shall we find such pointed authoritative precepts for the due regulation, order, and peace of society? "*Put the people in mind to be subject to principalities and powers, and to obey Magistrates, not only for fear of human punishment, but for conscience sake; to submit to every ordinance of man for the Lord's sake, whether it be to the King as supreme, or to Governors as sent by him, for so is the will of God. Prayers, are to be made for Kings and all in authority, that we may lead a quiet and peaceable life, in all godliness and honesty.* Christians are commanded "*to study to be quiet and to mind their own business, to fear God and the King, and not to meddle with those who are given to change.*"

Those therefore, we would, by withholding the knowledge of letters from the vulgar, abridge the use of the Scriptures, would in fact aid the views of such as wish to overthrow our Christian faith and our civil establishment. If there be any who misuse the doctrines of the Gospel, by teaching a wild and shallow religion, which may indeed too easily connect with political error and disorder, the remedy must assuredly be, in this or in any similar case, not to leave the field entirely to mistaken guides, but more strenuously to oppose error by truth; and if the same zeal, the same *personal interest,* with which the emissaries of sedition have laboured, were universally employed on the other side, rationally and solidly to inculcate right principles and wholesome instructions, we might comfortably hope, that the attempts of domestic and foreign enemies to excite internal troubles among us would end in their disappointment and disgrace.

invaders, and so contribute to maintain our naval superiority at home; which superiority, in the present state of our Hindu subjects, is still more necessary for the preservation of our Eastern possessions, than it would be on the supposed approximation of that people to the British character.

Difference between the American Revolution and possibilities in India.

"It may now be fair to inquire into the propriety with which that species of doubt or apprehension, which has just been considered, insinuates, as it does, some moral relation between the American Revolution, and such principles as are proposed to be introduced among our Indian subjects. Is it to be supposed, that if the Americans, being in their physical character, their local and political circumstances, the same, had professed Muhammadanism, or any pagan religion, they would not have been at least, equally prone to a revolution? If we had maintained in America, the same kind of despotic government which has prevailed in the East, where the sovereign, when despatching a viceroy to a distant province, could seldom know that he should not soon have to send an army to reduce him to obedience, will it be asserted that our authority would have been better or equally secured? But after all that is said of the separation of the American colonies from Great Britain, it is now a fact well known, that it did not spring from the general disposition, or the previous design of the people: in the possession of all the advantages which have been enumerated, they had not become impatient for independence; and among the reasons to be assigned for the attachment which then still remained among them for this country, may certainly be reckoned their possession of the same language and religion.

Comparison between the American Colonists and Natives of India.

"If it be urged, that a comparison between the American Colonists, and the natives of our Eastern territories, can be justly instituted only in considering the latter, not as they are at present, but as they would be after all the proposed improvements were diffused among them, it may be answered, that our previous statement of the effects of these improvements, affords matter for this comparison, so far as things contingent and unknown, can be compared with things established and known; and that, it is fair, for a double reason, to state the present disparity between the two races of people, first to show the immense career which the Hindus have yet to run, even in the prosecution of such improvments as are attainable, and secondly to demonstrate, that in the character, situation and circumstances of the Americans, at the æra of their revolution, there were radical important distinctions, which no improvement, on the part of the Hindus, could annihilate; or in other words, that they could never be expected to arrive at the point at which the Americans then stood.

Political liberty cannot flourish among the timid submissive people of India

"Indeed, those who know the country of Hindustan will probably think that political liberty is the last thing likely to flourish there. Though that country has been, from causes of a different nature which will be hereafter noticed, always subject to revolutions and convulsions; a revolution, the idea and act of the popular mind, upon the principles, or rather from an abuse of the principles of civil liberty, would be as great a political phenomenon as the world has exhibited, and one of which Asia has given no example. To bring a timid submissive people, whom the Tartars called '*worshippers of power*' up to the manliness of the European character, to elevate the feeblest of them, the Bengalese, to so high a point of energy, that like the American descendants of the British themselves, they should plan the daring project of an independent empire, seems to be something beyond what has yet been seen, or is reasonably to be expected from the effects of institutions, civil or religious, upon nations.

Spread of English civilization will promote prosperity, reciprocal commerce, and wealth in India.

"Having thus considered the adverse consequences held forth by the objection, it may now be proper to notice more particularly, the favourable suppositions which it contains. The dangers it fears, are the dangers of prosperity. If then, this prosperity were realized, and the produce, the manufactures, and the riches of the country were greatly increased, as according to the objection, English manners, tastes and wants, must also have become common, would not exports thither, and the reciprocal commerce arising from the change (not to reckon the imposts which merchandise, now hardly taxed at all, would then easily bear) be proportionably augmented? For what series of years, and with what multiplying powers, may we then conceive this augmentation to be progressive? Large as the assertion may seem, perhaps the shortest term we could assign to it would produce an accumulation of commercial profits and advantages, more than tantamount to a very high valuation of the fee-simple of our provinces, if we could suppose a sale of them to be now made. And it is fair also to admit, that if the country were finally lost, our commerce might still be necessary to it, and possibly even continue to increase. Such then, would be the conclusion afforded by this formidable objection, if for the sake of argument we were to allow the process described in it to go on without resistance to its exceptionable parts. But we trust, we have already shewn, that it is not entitled to this concession, and that whilst it holds forth evils, only as distant and hypothetical, it is obliged, as the sole ground of its apprehension, to admit advantages to be certain and proximate.

Importance of the question: "What are the best means of perpetuating the British Empire in India?"

"It remains now to examine one important position, already mentioned to be tacitly contained in the objection, 'that in a system, opposite to the one here proposed, must consist our future safety and stability in India.' Unwilling as the writer is, to enter on so delicate a subject, and, indeed, inadequate to the due treatment of it, he feels himself called by his argument, to make some circumspect observations upon it. Certainly in a political view the great question which this country has to determine respecting India is, 'What are the best means of perpetuating our empire there?'* Not what set of measures or line of policy may suit with the aspects of the day, or keep up the motion of the machine of Government; but upon what general principles may we best hope to make our connection with that country permanent, and, as far as we can, indissoluble? Towards the determination of this question, perhaps, it will be well to revert to the past history of our Indian Provinces (or let us say to those of Bengal in particular, the chief seat of our dominion) and to the character of the Natives of them. The English, it is true, were at first guided in their Eastern Administration, rather by nascent events, than by abstract principles or recorded experience; but, however natural this may be, in the progress to establishment, a more extended survey of the course of past affairs in the acquired country, with their causes and consequences, may well befit the new possessors, when firmly settled in their power. It is not perhaps enough to exempt them from this review, that they follow a system of Government widely different from the system of their predecessors, and are themselves a very different people. Among their Asiatic subjects, certain general properties which belong to human nature, and certain peculiar qualities resulting from a peculiar composition of society, may be expected to have a steady operation, where not controlled by stronger influences. If we look back then to the history of Bengal for five centuries, we shall find, that except in the period when the Moghal Empire was in its vigour, and the component parts of it thereby kept in peace with each other, that country has been the scene of frequent revolutions; and we cannot fail to discover that as the despotism of Eastern Government may be reckoned the first and remote principle of such changes, so they have immediately proceeded from two causes, the lawless spirit of ambitious adventure common among all the military tribes of Hindustan, and the nature of the general mass of the people inhabiting that region.

Muhammadan conquest of India made by soldiers of fortune.

"The Persians and Tartars, who have poured into it from early ages, have generally been soldiers of fortune, who brought little with them but their swords. With these they have not unfrequently carved their way to dignity and empire. Power has been, and is their darling object; nothing was scrupled by them to obtain it; the history of Muhammadan rule in Hindustan is full of treasons, assassinations, fratricides, even parricide is not unknown to it. These Northern adventurers by their spirit and pursuits, became in fact an accession, of more active and stronger qualities indeed, to the military division of the people of Hindustan. The Hindus, though held to be less prone to the shedding of blood, have not however, carried their nicety far, when the prize of sovereignty or authority has been in question; but among them, sanguinary ambition has been usually confined to the Brahmins and the military caste; to the latter more.

Military Hindus and Muhammadans form a great standing army of mercenaries, ready to be hired for any species of warfare, with an eye to plunder.

"The military class of the Hindus, which in its institution has some of the features of a militia, forms in reality a great standing army of mercenaries, ready to be hired on all occasions, though usually not obliged to enter into actual service. Thus the sovereign of a country cannot always command their assistance, whilst the existence of such a body may often render a domestic competitor, or a foreign enemy, formidable to him. From this copious source, any man of enterprise, whatever were his views or pretensions, could always find partisans, if he had funds to entertain them; the treasure of the prince has been often used by his servants, to hire men to despoil him also of his throne. No character has been so bad, no cause so unjust, as not to find an army to support it if there were money to pay them. The members of the military caste, conceiving themselves destined by their creation to fight, often take up arms with the same indifference and indiscrimination as a labourer takes up a spade; insomuch that it has not been unusual to see a defeated army join the standard of the victor, upon the same principle which carries the labourer from one employer, with whom business runs low, to another whose service and means he deems more sure. The military Muhammadans (for many of the descendants of the Tartars who settled in Hindostan fell into the lines of civil life) are equally ready as the military Hindus to engage themselves in commotions, quarrels, and any species of warfare, both having always in times of confusion, an eye to plunder.

* Some will be ready to answer: "By securing to the people their religion and laws;" and in the just sense of the words, namely that no violent change in either, contrary to the sense of the people, is to be enforced. We agree to the proposition; but what if the religion should be less favourable to our dominion than another system, and the people were induced voluntarily to make that other their religion; would not the change be for our interest?

"From this institution of a military class, the wisdom of which is surely impeached by the general effects it has produced, the military spirit came at length to reside almost wholly in one portion of the people. And hence may, in part at least, have followed the abjectness of the inferior tribes, composing the main body of the nation, and their want of public spirit. However much they may, on different accounts, have preferred a Hindu to a Muhammadan Government, no instance is recollected of their rising to support any Native Prince, or keep out any invader. The whole history of the Muhammadan Empires in Hindustan, as well as the traces we have of the anterior government of the Hindus, and what we see in modern days, all concur to prove the slavish disposition of that people, and their want of attachment to their rulers.

Military dominancy in India, both Hindu and Muhammadan has generated slavish disposition of the population in general.

"From these several causes, the despotic genius of Eastern Government, the exclusive hereditary allotment of the military profession to one class, and the abject character of the people, have proceeded the great encouragement of individuals to the violent assumption of power, and the frequency of insurrections, convulsions, and revolutions in that country. And the same causes though their operation may, by various circumstances, be occasionally suspended, will as long as they exist, have a tendency to produce the same effects. Hindustan has alternately been united under one great head, or partitioned into many states. New conquerors have, in different ages, appeared on that Continent, who increasing as they went on, have at length, by the vast number of their followers, overwhelmed every thing that opposed them. We now, indeed, see the empire of the Moghals prostrate, and may be apt to think, that, arranged as the politics and powers of Hindustan are, the same order of things is not likely to return; but it was upon the subversion of the Patan Empire that the Moghals rose, and may not a new adventurer, and a new horde from Tartary, establish yet another dynasty? It was perfectly in the option of Nadirshah, when he entered Delhi as a conqueror, in 1739, to have done this.* And if one of those scourges of mankind who have so frequently desolated India, should again arise, sending his fame, and the idea of his 'happy destiny' before him, might not the multitudes collected in his progress, poured out at length into the remote quarter of Bengal, endanger our existence there? Whether we suppose him to advance in the first flush of conquest, or after he had given a central consolidation to his power, he would be backed by the resources of a vast inland region, by large armies of horse, and myriads of infantry. If we now figure to ourselves the progress of his operations, it will not bring them nearer; it will be in order that we may be better guarded against them. The Tartars, unaccustomed to cope with our steady military gallantry and skill, might be repeatedly repulsed. Still fresh swarms of assailants might be brought forward, and season after season, invasion be renewed. We could bring few cavalry into the field; the numerous squadrons of the enemy might waste and exhaust the country; the landholders, from whom the revenues are derived, would, as is usual in Hindustan, upon the appearance of commotion, withhold the payment of their rents; the produce of the districts which the enemy might occupy, they would immediately appropriate; and the credit of our Government, as indeed we even now experience in times of exigency, would not procure us any adequate supplies. We should thus be straitened and embarrassed in our resources; suspicions of our stability might arise in the minds of our subjects, and among them would be a great number of the military caste, unemployed by us, and ready to make their own use of any promising occasion. Many of those subjects, won by the splendour of new power, and the proud display of an imperial standard, or desirous of securing an early interest, perhaps indulging new hopes from a revolution, would fall away from us: others would wish for a cessation of predatory vexations, at the expense of our expulsion.

Frequent conquests of India by foreigners. Possible dangers to British Rule from similar swarms of barbarous assailants.

"The Sepoys, whose attachment to us has appeared surprising, though the causes of it seem neither inexplicable nor immutable, supplied tardily and perhaps only partially with the pay, of which the regular advance had before so conciliated them to our service; and instead of being animated by the career of victory, cooped up in a dubious defensive warfare, might also be tempted to listen to the large offers of a dazzling leader, in whom their ready notions of fatalism might easily present to them a new *king of the world*. In such an arduous crisis, we trust that everything to be expected from bravery, fortitude and military science, would be performed on our part; but must not our lasting dependence be chiefly on British troops, on our maritime power, and on supplies by sea? With all these, it is very easy to see how oppressive, how threatening, a long struggle, maintained under such circumstances, possibly by aids derived from the mother-

Loyalty of the Sepoys though surprising, neither inexplicable nor immutable, may be endangered by a dazzling leader. Loyalty of the people important and achievable by spreading English enlightenment.

* If he had, we might probably have still been mere merchants in India.

country, must be to us; how much also it must shake our interests and our stability in the rest of India. Now in any such state of things, in any case of the same nature, less extreme, what would be of more importance to us, what could so effectually fortify our cause, as to have the people of our territories sincerely attached to our government; to have established in their minds such an affectionate participation in our lot, such an union with our interests, as should counteract the defection, defalcations, and treachery, to be otherwise apprehended from the ordinary bent and practice of the Asiatic character? We should thus have the service of all the resources which our rich Provinces contained; we should have the steady adherence and coöperation of the people, and in this way, might certainly confound and baffle even the powerful preparations of an imperial despot, to whose affairs long and spirited resistance might prove highly detrimental, by encouraging distant Provinces which he had before overrun, to throw off the yoke. And how are our subjects to be formed to a disposition thus favourable to us, to be changed thus in their character, but by new principles, sentiments, and tastes, leading to new views, conduct, and manners; all which would, by one and the same effect, identify their cause with ours, and proportionably separate them from opposite interests? It is not, we may venture to affirm, from such a change, but in continuing as we are, that we stand most exposed to the dangers of political revolution.

Assimilation and a common bond of union between the English and the Natives necessary for permanence of British dominion in India.

"The objection which conceives remote evils to result from a plan of improvement, does not advert to others which may, in the meantime, arise from causes of a different kind. We join with it in the desire of securing in permanence, the fair possession this country has obtained (more, it may be concluded, by the over-ruling dispensation of Providence, than by any scheme of man), but differ as to the means. To us it appears, that nothing promises so fair for the end proposed, as engaging the attachment and regard of the people, and removing those causes which have hitherto made them so acquiescent in every change. It was this passive temper, joined to the expectations which many might entertain from the deposition of the reigning Nabob, that contributed to our easy acquisition of the country; but the same temper would render our hold of it less sure in any arduous contest. At present, we are every way different from the people whom we hold in subjection; different in country, in language, in manners, in customs, in sentiments, and in religion; their interest also, for the reasons mentioned in the early part of this memoir, they must conceive to be different from ours. What then can be a healing principle with regard to all these points, but a principle of *assimilation, a common bond*, which shall give to both parties the reality and the conviction of mutual benefit from the connexion? Without an uniting principle, a conjoining tie of this nature, we can suppose the country to be, in fact, retained only by mere power; but in the same degree that an identity of sentiments and principles would be established, we should exhibit a sight new in the region of Hindustan, a people actively attached, cordially affected to their Government, and thus augmenting its strength. In this laudable way we should become more formidable to the other powers of that Continent, we should be best secured against foreign enemies, insurrections and the dangers of an hereditary military body; we should have more support from the mass of the people, and in a word, be most effectually guarded against a revolution.

Policy of Alexander the Great in assimilating Asiatic subjects to the Grecian system, and winning their loyalty, should be followed by the English in India.

"It is remarkable, that the radical principle of the conclusion thus made, a conclusion to which an acquaintance with the Indian character, and the experience that progressive time has afforded of the effects of knowledge, particularly the divine knowledge of Christianity, may now easily lead an ordinary mind, directed, according to the judicious historian of *The Ancient European Intercourse with India*, the policy of the Grecian conqueror of that country, in securing his Eastern acquisitions. However different, in other respects, the circumstances of that celebrated personage may be from ours, in this we agree with him, that we have an Asiatic Empire to maintain. And Dr. Robertson, who in acknowledging the eccentricities of that extraordinary man, gives him also the credit of profound political views, observes, 'He early perceived, *that to render his authority secure and permanent, it must be established in the affection of the nations he had subdued, and maintained by their arms;* and that in order to acquire this advantage, all distinctions between the victors and the vanquished must be abolished, and his European and Asiatic subjects be incorporated, and become one people, *by obeying the same laws, and by adopting the same manners, institutions, and discipline.*' It is the leading idea only of this policy, that is meant to be applied here; and that leading idea is plainly the principle of *assimilation.* It would neither suit us, nor our subjects, to act upon it universally, as Alexander proposed. We ought not to wish, that the distinctions between the two races should be lost, or to aim at introducing into Asia laws framed for this country; but to attach our subjects by affection, by interest, by winning them to our religion and our sentiments,—this would be at once to add to their happiness, and to arrive at the same object which the great conqueror had in view, that of rendering our authority 'permanent and secure.'

New principles of attachment, activity and industry among the people of India will be conducive to their loyalty to the British rule.

"This policy is recommended by some other considerations, which shall be briefly noticed. It is sufficiently understood, that since our first appearance on the theatre of Indian war and politics, the Native powers have improved in military discipline, and that we now find it necessary to bring into the field, armies proportionably larger than those that served to achieve our early victories. Having so interesting an evidence of the capability of the Natives to improve, there appears no good reason to conclude, that their advancement in military skill may not be further progressive. It is extemely probable, that the beneficial effects of our civil policy will also in time force themselves upon their attention, and from the cogent motive of self-interest, produce at least some imitations. All the advances they make in the arts of war or of peace, will serve to lessen that superiority in both, by which, under the disadvantages attaching to us as foreigners, and with forces comparatively small, we have acquired an ascendency among the powers of Hindustan. The nearer we approach to an equality, the more these disadvantages will be felt. Our business seems to be, therefore, by new resources in policy still to preserve the relative rank in which we have hitherto stood; and what can more directly conduce to this end, than to infuse new principles of attachment, of activity, and industry, among the people we govern, thus strengthening their character, and drawing additional support from them.

Revolutions in Europe, such as the French, affect Indian politics.

"The European nations have an undisputed possession of the Indian seas, and are now so much connected with the Continent of India, that every material change which takes place in them, may be expected, in some shape or other, to extend its influence thither. It cannot be irrational, therefore, to suppose, that the astonishing events which have lately convulsed Europe, and are likely to produce consequences durable and momentous, may have their bearings upon our Asiatic interests. That exorbitant ambitious power which seeks our destruction, may aim, by different channels and instruments, to excite troubles and disorders in our possessions, or to embroil us with our Indian neighbours. The Cape of Good Hope, the head of a vast country, in a fine climate, and singular in the felicity of its position for a great emporium, whether it remain with us or fall under French influence, will probably, by a change already begun in its internal policy, swarm, at no distant period, with a numerous race, of European character and descent, planted at the entrance into the Indian seas and within two months' sail of the Indian coasts. Another great colony of the same race, in a climate equally favourable to the human constitution, is springing up on the Eastern side of the Indian Ocean. The appearance of many adventurers of these descriptions on the shores of Hindustan, as one day they may be expected to appear (a day perhaps nearer than it is possible to bring other apprehended improvements), can hardly fail to have some effect upon the political affairs of that country, those of the native princes, as well as our own. In all these, or any other supposable cases then, the more closely we bind the people under our rule to ourselves, the more firmly shall we be prepared, in that quarter, against adverse events and combinations.

Knowledge of English character and manners will conciliate the Natives.

"It may be urged by some, in opposition to the systematical improvement here proposed, that the influence of the British Government and character, especially where the intermixture of Europeans is large, will of itself gradually produce a change in the sentiments of our Eastern subjects. Let this position be, to a certain degree, admitted; it is one interesting enough to merit some attention. The English, in their obscure commercial state, were little known or regarded by the people whom they now govern. Their elevation to power, brought into public display all the particulars of their character, with their manners and customs. These, in various instances, at first shocked the prejudices of the Hindus, who thought, with a kind of horror, of the new masters to whom they bowed. But by degrees they perceived, that usages the most repugnant to their ideas, were free of that turpitude which they had associated with them. They found these foreigners superior to them in general powers and knowledge, in personal honour and humanity; and at length saw the British Government assume a character of equity and patriotism, unknown in their preceding administrations. These qualities, it shall be granted, have a tendency to conciliate in some measure, the natives *who are near enough to observe them.* Among those who live in our settlements or are much connected with Europeans, long habits of intercourse have softened down repugnancies, or blunted the sensations which our manners at first inspired; and there is in such, an apparent, perhaps a real abatement of jealousy and solicitude respecting their own notions and punctilios.

Indifference of Englishmen to religion will render Natives indifferent to every system of religion.

"But in all these varying aspects of the European character, something essential to those disposed to fall into an imitation of it has been absent. Men that meet together in this country for the purposes of business, seldom enter into communication respecting the foundations of their faith and practice; any serious discussion of this nature occurs still more rarely there. The indifference for religion which Mr. Hume ascribes to the English in general of the present age (he calls it profound indifference,) may there pass for liberal toleration, or complaisant forbearance towards inferiors of another faith. Discovering in their intercourse with us little of the nature of the religion we profess, they will not, of course, be apt to refer the good qualities of which the English appear possessed, to that source; nor will they know that the national standard of morals formed from it, has an influence, even upon the conduct of those who pay no particular regard to a religious system. If then any of the Hindus should, in time, feel some tendency to imitate that freedom in manners, sentiments, and intercourse, that latitude as to religious opinions and observances, which they see in their European masters, what would be the consequence but evidently this, that they *would be loosened from their own religious prejudices*, not by the previous reception of another system in their stead, but by becoming indifferent to *every system*. For a transition from one error to another is, it must be acknowledged, more readily made, than a transition from error to truth.

"Error is more easily imbibed, more hardly eradicated; truth more slowly received, more easily resigned.

Anarchical principles liable to take the place of superstitious religion.

And in this way it is, that if we conceive the *anarchal* principles which have burst forth in Europe ever to spread to India, they will be most likely to have their entrance. Indeed, so wonderfully contagious do they appear to be, so congenial to the worst qualities of human nature, that it may be difficult to point out a place where they can find nothing to fasten upon. Societies in which much corruption and much superstition prevail, seem in general more liable to them, than those in which true religion and morals are still strongly rooted. The French, it will readily be allowed, fell into them more readily than they would have embraced any scheme of personal reformation, or a more pure and strictly practical religious system. The abuses of civil and religious institutions lead to them, and furnish the most plausible pretences for them. False principles, and the fooleries of a false religion, even when used to support things good in themselves, as government and subordination, would ill stand before such arts and abilities as have lately assailed the truth. Truth only is invincible. To teach it therefore, is to take the surest means of excluding the infection of licentious disorganizing sophistries. A change from false religion to the true, is a movement from an exposed place to a strong fortress; and every advance made in the system of moral and religious instruction here recommended, so far from opening the way to those loose latitudinarian notions which tend to a rejection of all authority, would establish rights, human and divine, upon their proper basis, and bind the conscience to the observance of them.

"To these considerations, which on the whole may certainly be deemed not unworthy of attention, two other reflections may serve to give additional weight.

Increase of low class Europeans in India liable to contaminate the Natives, and increasing prosperity of landlords tends to strengthen pride and disorderly propensities for which English religion and morals provide a remedy.

First, it is to be feared that the number of the lower Europeans will go on to increase in our territories; they mix most with the Natives, and by them the worst part of our manners will be exhibited. *Secondly*,— By the security which we have with great wisdom given to the land tenures of Bengal, the value of property there, and the consideration arising from the possession of it, will naturally be enhanced, so that in process of time, the owners of large estates, hitherto little productive to them, may become of consequence by their wealth and possessions. We know also, that increasing prosperity tends to strengthen pride and disorderly propensities. Here again, therefore, we find motives for the introduction of our principles; for if some at least, both of the higher and lower orders, may be led, by European manners, to adopt new ideas of relaxation, at the same time that new powers are put into the hands of the former, we ought, in good policy and reason, to communicate to them a system which, divested of all burthensome unnecessary ceremonies, and all superstitious folly, is yet calculated to produce a purer and higher influence than their own, upon the general moral conduct, and all the relative duties of life. As then we have already been gradually led, by good sense and expediency, to introduce regulations derived from our national ideas and principles into the Government and management of our possessions, their advantage and our safety may dispose us also to wish that our religion and moral principles might obtain a fair establishment there; for if we can suppose that through the increasing relations between Europe and India, the common lights and manners of Europeans adventuring thither, should ever make a strong impression, unaccompanied by the knowledge of those principles, which do not propagate themselves spontaneously, and are not to be implanted without culture and care, that change might not be favourable to our interests; since the present circumstances of Europe seem emphatically to point out, that nothing but such principles can be depended upon, for keeping subjects in obedience and subordination." *

To these observations, the Right Honourable Mr. Charles Grant, author of the Treatise from which the

Mr. Charles Grant's Note to his Treatise.

preceding quotation has been given, added a *Note* which contains interesting information and may be quoted here:—

* Printed Parliamentary Papers relating to the Affairs of India; *General*, Appendix I; Public (1832), pp. 72–84.

"These several objections and the answers to them, excepting the sixth and seventh, were, as to their substance and scope, committed to writing in the latter end of the year 1792, though not then in any shape brought into notice. In April 1793, a discussion took place in a General Court of Proprietors of East India Stock, in which almost all the same objections were advanced, by persons with whom the writer never had any communication on such subjects. This was an occasion of two resolutions which the House of Commons, very honourably for itself, had voted in the view of introducing the purport of them into the Act of Parliament then about to be passed, for renewing the Charter of the East India Company. The Resolutions were these—

Resolutions passed by the House of Commons on the subject of educating India in 1793.

"'RESOLVED, That it is the opinion of this House, that it is the peculiar and bounden duty of the legislature, to promote, by *all just* and *prudent means* the interests and happiness of the inhabitants of the British dominions in India; and that for these ends, such measures ought to be adopted as may *gradually* tend to their advancement in *useful knowledge*, and to *their religious and moral improvement.*

"'RESOLVED, That sufficient means of religious worship and instruction be provided for all persons of the Protestant communion in the service, or under the protection of the East India Company in Asia, proper ministers being from time to time sent out from Great Britain for those purposes; and that a chaplain be maintained on board every ship of 500 tons burthen, and upwards, in the East India Company's employ; and that morever, no such ministers or chaplains shall be sent out, or appointed until they first shall have been approved of, by the Archbishop of Canterbury, or the Bishop of London, for the time being.'

"Several Proprietors of East India Stock made a violent attack upon these resolutions, and the following is an abstract of all the arguments or objections urged against them, as they are reported by Mr. Woodfall. It is with reluctance that any reference is made here to the opinions there given because they stand connected with particular names, and it is far from being the wish of the writer to introduce any thing that may seem to have even a remote tendency to personality; but as opinions delivered in a public assembly, and afterwards made more public by the press, are fairly open to animadversion, so justice to the present subject, renders some notice of those now in question, indispensable.

Discussion of the subject in the Court of Proprietors of East India Stock in 1793.

"OBJECTIONS STATED GENERALLY. 'That sending Missionaries into our Eastern territories, is the most wild, extravagant, expensive, unjustifiable project, that ever was suggested by the most visionary speculator. That the principle is obnoxious, impolitic, unnecessary, full of mischief, dangerous, useless, unlimited.'

Objections urged in the discussion.

"SPECIFIC ARGUMENTS, *First Class.* 'The plan would be dangerous and impolitic; it would affect the peace and ultimate security of our possessions. It tends to endanger and injure our affairs there most fatally, it would either produce disturbances, or bring the Christian religion into contempt. Holding one faith or religion, is the most strong common cause with mankind, and the moment that took place in India there would be an end of British supremacy.

Arguments employed in the controversy.

'That the principle of proselyting was *impolitic,* and was, or ought to be exploded, in so enlightened a period as the eighteenth century.'

'That it would be a most serious and fatal disaster, if natives of character,* even a hundred thousand of them, were converted to Christianity.'

'That the establishment of seminaries and colleges in America, was one of the most efficient causes of the loss of that country. That suffering young clergymen (who are usually of pleasurable habits), to overrun the interior of India would be dangerous, and prove ultimately destructive to the Company's interest.'

* It will be remembered, that these are chiefly *Idolaters,* something of whose character and worship we have already seen. With whatever indifference idolatry may be viewed, and however venial it may be accounted in these times, even by persons born in Christian countries, it is a crime against which the displeasure of the holy and true God, the sovereign and unerring judge of the qualities of actions, is expressed with peculiar indignation, contempt, and abhorrence throughout that revelation which He hath vouchsafed to us; and it is therein shewn to have often brought on, by its nature and effects, the misery and ruin of individuals and of nations.

Even the wiser men of ancient Pagan Europe, between the superstition of which, and the idolatry of the Hindus an identity has been proved (by Sir William Jones, in the Asiatic Transactions, Vol. I), saw and complained of the evils of their popular system of religion. Cicero brings in an Epicurean philosopher arraigning that system in severe terms. "The most absurd things," observes he "are said by the poets, things which are noxious even by the agreeable style in which they are conveyed; for they have introduced Gods mad with anger, inflamed with lust and have presented to our view their wars, battles, fightings, wounds; their hatred, differences, strivings; their births, deaths, complaints, lamentations, their lusts, exceeding in every kind of intemperance; their adulteries, fetters their lying with mankind, and mortals begotten of immortal gods." (De Nat. Deor. Lib. I. § 16). And again, in the person of a Stoic he thus reprobates the same system. "The introduction of feigned gods, has begotten false opinions, and turbulent errors and superstitions, no better than old wives' fables for the figures of the gods, their ages, dress and ornaments are set forth, their alliances, marriages,

"*Second Class.* 'The scheme would be unsuccessful. It is extravagant to hope for the conversion of the natives. They are invincibly attached to their own castes; their prejudices, manners and habits are all against a change.'

'It is vain to attempt to overcome prejudices fixed by the practice of ages far exceeding the time in which Britons had any idea of religion at all. The attempt is, in these views, idle, absurd and impracticable.'

'Only the dregs of the people can be converted; they will pretend conversion, and disgrace Christianity.'

'The higher and more respectable natives are people of the purest morality, and strictest virtue' (this was said only by one speaker who knew little of India).

'The services of religion are devoutly performed in the Company's settlements and ships, either by clergymen or laymen, and their ecclesiastical establishments are sufficient.'

"*Third Class.* 'The *scheme would be expensive.* The expense would be enormous, intolerable; one, two, or three hundred thousand pounds.'

"*Fourth Class.* 'The scheme would be unlimited in respect of the numbers and qualifications of the missionaries.'

"All these objections will be found already answered in the text. A few brief remarks upon them may however be proper, and will be sufficient here.

The objections and arguments answered.

"1*st*.—The objections urged in general terms are merely declamatory. They are accompanied by no reasonings or elucidations. But *the principle* which they censure as the most wild, extravagant, unjustifiable, mischievous, dangerous, useless, impolitic that ever was suggested by the most visionary speculator, *is the principle of the Gospel itself.*

"The Gospel was propagated by missionaries; missionaries planted it in the different countries of Europe, almost all those countries have, in imitation of the same practice, sent missionaries into infidel parts, and how is it possible for men to communicate it otherwise? In this kingdom, two Societies are established by royal charter for propagating the Gospel in Heathen lands, and there is a third Society of long standing, employed in the same object which enrolls among its members, many of the most eminent persons of the nation. So much for the antiquity, authority, and general acknowledgment of *this principle* which is treated as if nothing like it had ever been heard of before.

"2*nd*.—It is obvious, that the first and second classes of specific objections, militate against each other. Since the scheme proposes only a pacific exposition of Christian truths, it cannot be both dangerous and unsuccessful. The danger is avowedly founded mainly, if not wholly, on the supposition of success. If success therefore is not to be hoped for, where is the danger? And again if the scheme really threatens so much danger what becomes of the argument against success?

"These contradictory objections cannot both be just. The same speaker, however, who is reported to have 'thanked God' that the conversion of the natives would be a matter of *impracticability*, strenuously opposed the scheme on this ground, that the moment they and we came to hold one faith there would be an end of our supremacy in the East; but if he thought it *impracticable* to convert them to our faith, with what reason could he urge the *danger* which would follow from such conversion as a serious and alarming objection? When the *cause* does not *exist*, neither can that which can only flow from it as its effect.

"3rd.—The *principle of not communicating to the Hindus the Christian religion, lest this should in the end destroy our Government over them*, is however here fairly acknowledged and argued upon. The establishment of seminaries and colleges in our American Colonies, is in the same spirit adverted to in a way of warning, as if Christianity had produced the revolution there, when in fact they were men of infidel opinions who planned both the American and French Revolutions.

"The reason assigned in justification of this precautionary principle also deserves attention, 'because holding one religion is the most strong common cause with mankind.' If the proposal had been that the English should become converts to Hinduism, this argument might have been well placed; but applied to the present scheme, it can only operate in favour of it.

"4th.—It is curious to find it alleged, among the arguments against the proposed clauses, that some of the Hindus were too good, and others too bad to be converted.

affinities and all are reduced to the similitude of human imbecility. They are brought in as men disturbed by passion; we hear of their lusts, sickness, anger; yea as fables tell us the gods have not wanted wars and battles............ These things are said and *believed* most sottishly and are full of extreme vanity and futility." (Ibid. Lib. II. § 28).

To these base gods, however, temples were erected, and divine honours paid. They had their costly trains of priests, services, sacrifices, festivals and games. Some of their rites were atrociously cruel, others infamous for debauchery, prostitution and the most unbridled excesses. Hence corruption was diffused among the people, the moral system, even of the philosophers, was very defective and their allowed practices, in some respects abominable.

Mr. Swartz's Vindication of Missionary effort.

"This was advanced by only one gentleman, little acquainted with India, whose speech happening by a common newspaper to reach the Rev. Mr. Swartz, already noticed as long a Missionary of distinguished reputation in the Tanjore and Trichinopoly districts, produced from him a vindication of the conduct and effects of the Mission in which he is concerned. A vindication framed indeed in modest and simple terms, suitable to the character of the writer, but highly honourable to the cause of Missions, and though he intended it not to his own. This piece, too good to be concealed, has been printed in the Transactions of the English Society for Promoting Christian Knowledge, and a copy of it is given in the Appendix.

Novelty of the assertion that the higher Natives have pure morality and strict virtue.

"The assertion of the same speaker, that the higher natives of India are people of the purest morality and strictest virtue, is altogether new, and in palpable opposition to testimony and experience. Upon the Gospel scheme no man is too good or too bad for the benefits it proposes; and there is a very large class between the best and the worst, of whom the speaker took no notice. His other assertion, that the ceremonies of religion, or the service of the Common-prayer Book, were with great decency and devotion regularly performed by laymen on board the Company's ships, and on land, in places where there happened to be no clergyman, is a topic for ridicule, if the subject were not of so serious a kind; the reverse of this assertion being so notorious. And is there no use for a minister of religion, but to perform a ceremony, or to read a form of prayer once a week?

Objection as to expensiveness of the scheme of Education unwarranted.

"5th.—The objections urged on the ground of the *unlimited* expense of the scheme, the *unlimited* numbers of the clergy that would be sent, their *improper* character, and *their roving through the country*, all go upon assumptions not only unwarranted but contradicted by the tenor of the clauses themselves, and in opposition to the dictates of common sense. The Directors of the Company were themselves to be entrusted with the execution of the scheme; they were to judge of the number of Missionaries sufficient; they were to regulate the expense. Was it conceivable that they would have gone in either article to a length burthensome or dangerous to the Company? Was it conceivable that they would have suffered Missionaries to ramble, at their pleasure, through the country, if the Missionaries sent should have been men so disposed? But can it be imagined, that the friends of the scheme and the respectable authorities whose testimonials were to render the Missionaries receivable by the Company (not to force them into their employ), would have had so little regard to the success of their own object, as to select persons the least likely to promote it? In fact, the danger was of another kind; so much was left in the discretion of the Directors that if they should have had the disposition, they might also have possessed the power very materially to thwart the prosecution of the scheme. And as to the real number and expense of Missionaries at first, the former, if proper persons should have been found, would perhaps have been thirty, and the annual charge of their establishment, including dwellings, probably about fourteen thousand pounds.

Opposition to Christianizing India unjustifiable.

"*6th.*—Upon the whole of this discussion it appears to have been undertaken with a vehement determination against the principle of introducing Christianity among our Asiatic subjects; but without much previous consideration or a large acquaintance with its bearings and relations, still less with a dispassionate temper of mind for arguments subversive of each other assertions palpably erroneous, assumptions clearly unwarrantable, were pressed into the opposition; the question was argued chiefly upon a partial view of supposed political expediency and the supreme importance, authority, and command, of Christianity, were left out of sight.

"It ought to be remarked, upon the second of the two resolutions passed in the House of Commons, that the maintenance of a Chaplain on board every ship of considerable size, employed in the long navigation to and from India, was the early spontaneous practice of the Company, and enjoined to them in the Charters of King William and Queen Anne, the clauses of which, respecting this point, the said resolution did no more than revive."*

Sir Charles Trevelyan's views on the education of the people of India, 1838.

Such then was the state of public opinion in England upon the subject of introducing English Education in India towards the end of the last century. Next in point of time and importance are the views expressed by Sir Charles Trevelyan† in a Treatise which he wrote "*On the Education of the People of India,*" in 1838, and from it the following extracts may be quoted:—

* Printed Parliamentary Papers relating to the Affairs of India; *General*, Appendix I, *Public* (1832), pp. 84–86, *Note*.

† A distinguished Member of the Indian Civil Service who after having served as Assistant Resident at Delhi, held an important office in the Secretariat of the Government of India, and married a sister of Lord Macaulay. He subsequently held an important office in England and afterwards became a Member of the Supreme Council in India, and finally was for some time Governor of the Presidency of Madras. He lived to a good old age in retirement, and died not many years ago, leaving a son, Sir George Trevelyan, a distinguished Member of Parliament.

Opportuneness of introducing English Education in India 1838.

"Many circumstances indicate that the time has arrived for taking up the question of Indian National instruction in a way in which it has never yet been taken up. Obstacles, which formerly prevented the Government from taking decisive steps, have disappeared: unexpected facilities have come to light. The mind of India has taken a new spring. Substitutes are required to fill up the void created by the passing away of antiquated systems. The people want instruction: the Government wants well-educated servants to fill the responsible situations which have been opened to the natives. Every thing concurs to prove that this important subject ought no longer to be regarded only as an amusement for the leisure hours of benevolent persons. It must now be taken up as a great public question, with that seriousness and resolution to make the necessary sacrifices which the interests at stake require."*

Natives ready to co-operate with Government in English Education.

Then after stating various reasons, tending to show the necessity for spreading English Education in India, he goes on to say:—"The† most decisive proof that the time has arrived for taking up the subject of national education is, that all classes of the community are now ready to co-operate with the Government. A few years ago the education of the natives was regarded by the Europeans either with aversion or contempt, as they happened to consider it as a dangerous interference with native prejudice, or as a chimerical undertaking unworthy of a man of sense. Now there are few stations at which there are not one or more European officers, who would be glad of an opportunity of aiding the Committee in the prosecution of its plans. The discussions which took place between the advocates of the rival systems, by strongly drawing attention to the question, and, in a manner, forcing people to an examination of it, greatly contributed to this result. All are now more or less interested and well informed on the subject; and what is of still more importance, all are of one mind about it, and have a settled and well understood plan to pursue. Whatever differences of opinion may linger among retired Indians in England, there are none now in India; or, at least, the adherents of the old system form such an exceedingly small minority, that it is unnecessary to mention them when speaking of the general sense of the European community.

Efforts of the Missionaries to spread English Education.

"The missionaries, taking advantage of the prevailing feeling, have established numerous excellent seminaries, at which many thousand native youth are receiving a sound, and in some cases, a liberal English Education. English, Scotch, Americans, and Germans, concur in availing themselves of the English language as a powerful instrument of native improvement. English priests, lately sent from Rome to take charge of the Roman Catholic Christians of Portuguese and native descent, have had recourse to the same means for enlightening their numerous and degraded flocks. The Portuguese language (another instance of the confusion of tongues which has so long distracted and dissipated the mind of India) has been discarded from the churches and schools: and the English Liturgy has been introduced, and large English seminaries have been established. There are also institutions at which the youth of English and of mixed English and native descent receive as good a scientific and literary education as is consistent with the early period at which they enter into active life. Most of our school-masters have been drawn from this class; and, as they possess the trustworthiness and a great degree of the energy of the European character, combined with an intimate acquaintance with the native habits and language, they are no mean auxiliaries in the cause of native education.‡

Real desire of Natives to obtain English Education.

"This harmony of effort, however, would be of little avail if it were not founded on a real desire on the part of the natives themselves to obtain the benefit of European instruction. The curiosity of the people is thoroughly roused, and the passion for English knowledge has penetrated the most obscure, and extended to the most remote parts of India. The steam boats, passing up and down the Ganges, are boarded by native boys, begging not for money, but for books.§ The

* Trevelyan, *On the Education of the People of India* (1838); pp. 143, 144.

† *Ib.*, pp. 164–69.

‡ The institutions which have rendered most service in this way are, the Verulam Academy, the Parental Academic Institution, the High School, and the Military Orphan Asylum. Similar assistance may now be expected from the noble foundation of General Martin, and a large Proprietory School which has lately been established in the Himalaya Mountains.

§ Some gentlemen coming to Calcutta were astonished at the eagerness with which they were pressed for books by a troop of boys, who boarded the steamer from an obscure place, called Comercally. A Plato was lying on the table, and one of the party asked a boy whether that would serve his purpose. 'Oh! yes,' he exclaimed, 'give me any book; all I want is a book.' The gentleman at last hit upon the expedient of cutting up an old *Quarterly Review*, and distributing the articles among them. In the evening, when some of the party went ashore, the boys of the town flocked round them, expressing their regret that there was no English School in the place, and saying that they hoped that the Governor-General, to whom they had made an application on the subject, when he passed on his way up the country, would establish one.

chiefs of the Punjab, a country which has never been subdued by the British arms, made so many applications to the Political Agent on the frontier to procure an English Education for their children, that the Government has found it necessary to attach a schoolmaster to his establishment. The tide of literature is even rolling back from India to Persia, and the Supreme Government lately sent a large supply of English books for the use of the King of Persia's military seminary, the students of which were reported to be actuated by a strong zeal for European learning. The extent to which the Pasha of Egypt is engaged in enlightening his subjects, through the medium of English and the other European languages, is too well known to need any detail. The time has certainly arrived when the ancient debt of civilization which Europe owes to Asia* is about to be repaid; and the sciences, cradled in the East and brought to maturity in the West, are now by a final effort about to overspread the world."†

Political tendency of English Education in India.

Having thus described the opportuneness of extending English education in India, Sir Charles Trevelyan proceeded to consider the political tendencies of the different systems of education in use in India at that time (1838), and expressed his views in the following words:—

Undoubted duty of England to educate India.

"There can be no dispute as to what our duty as the rulers of India requires us to do. But it has been said, and may be said again, that whatever our duty may be, it is not our policy to enlighten the natives of India; that the sooner they grow to man's estates, the sooner they will be able to do without us; and that by giving them knowledge, we are giving them power, of which they will make the first use against ourselves.

Feeling of honest Englishmen to administer India for the benefit of its people.

"If our interest and our duty were really opposed to each other, every good man, every honest Englishman, would know which to prefer. Our national experience has given us too deep a sense of the true ends of Government, to allow us to think of carrying on the administration of India except for the benefit of the people of India. A nation which made so great a sacrifice to redeem a few hundred thousand negroes from slavery, would shudder at the idea of keeping a hundred millions of Indians in the bondage of ignorance, with all its frightful consequences, by means of a political system supported by the revenue taken from the Indians themselves. Whether we govern India ten or a thousand years, we will do our duty by it: we will look, not to the probable duration of our trust, but to the satisfactory discharge of it, so long as it shall please God to continue it to us. Happily, however, we are not on this occasion called upon to make any effort of disinterested magnanimity. Interest and duty are never really separated in the affairs of nations, any more than they are in those of individuals; and in this case they are indissolubly united, as a very slight examination will suffice to show.

The Muhammadan and Hindu systems of Government criticised.

"The Arabian or Muhammadan system is based on the exercise of power and the indulgence of passion. Pride, ambition, the love of rule, and of sensual enjoyment, are called in to the aid of religion. The earth is the inheritance of the faithful: all besides are infidel usurpers, with whom no measures are to be kept, except what

* The early civilization of Greece by settlers from Phœnicia and Egypt, the philosophical systems of Pythagoras and Plato; the knowledge of chemistry, medicine, and mathematics, which emanated in a later age from the Arabian Schools of Cordova and Salerno, attest the obligations we are under to the Eastern world. The greatest boon of all, our admirable system of arithmetical notation, which has facilitated in an incalculable degree the improvement of the sciences and the transaction of every kind of business for which the use of numbers is requisite, is distinctly traceable through the Arabs to the Hindus: we call it the Arabian, the Arabs call it the Hindu system, and the Hindus attribute the invention of it to their gods. It has been practised in India from a period which precedes all written and traditionary memorials.

† It may be as well to mention some of the probable causes of the existing stage of native feeling on this subject. The *First* is the same which gave rise to the revival of learning, and the cultivation of the Vernacular languages in Europe, or the increase in the number and importance of the middle class of society. External peace, internal security of property, arising from a regular administration of justice, increased facilities to trade, the permanent settlement of the land revenue of the Lower, and a long settlement of that of the Upper Provinces, have all contributed to raise up a class between the Nawab and the ryot, which derives its consequence from the exercise of industry and enterprise, which is possessed of the leisure necessary for literary pursuits, and which, being a creation of our own, is naturally inclined to imitate us, and to adopt our views. *Secondly,*—The people feeling themselves safe in their persons and property, and being relieved from the harassing anxieties which daily attend those who live under a barbarous arbitrary government, enjoy that peace of mind, without which it is impossible that Letters can be successfully cultivated. *Thirdly,*—The natives cannot fail to be struck by our moral and intellectual superiority; and they are led, by the combined influence of curiosity and emulation, to search for the causes of it in our literature. This motive has led the Russians and Turks, and other entirely independent nations, to cultivate foreign literature; and it cannot, therefore, excite wonder that the Hindus, who stand in such a close relation to us, should have been influenced by it. *Fourthly,*—A liberal English Education is the surest road to promotion. It is by far the best education the natives can get; and the Government must always select the best instructed persons, that are to be had, for the public service. *Lastly,*—The Hindus have always been a literary people; but as the body of the nation were shut out by the Brahmins from all participation in their own learning, they eagerly avail themselves of what is now offered by us to their acceptance, recommended as it is by so many attractions.

policy may require. Universal dominion belongs to the Muhammadans by divine right. Their religion obliges them to establish their predominance by the sword; and those who refuse to conform are to be kept in a state of slavish subjection. The Hindu system, although less fierce and aggressive than the Muhammadan, is still more exclusive: all who are not Hindus are impure outcasts, fit only for the most degraded employments; and, of course, utterly disqualified for the duties of Government, which are reserved for the Military, under the guidance of the priestly caste. Such is the political tendency of the Arabic and Sanskrit systems of learning. Happily for us, these principles exist in their full force only in books written in difficult languages, and in the minds of a few learned men; and they are very faintly reflected in the feelings and opinions of the body of the people. But what will be thought of that plan of national education which would revive them and make them popular; would be perpetually reminding the Muhammadans that we are infidel usurpers of some of the fairest realms of the Faithful; and the Hindus, that we are unclean beasts, with whom it is a sin and a shame to have any friendly intercourse. Our bitterest enemies could not desire more than that we should propagate systems of learning which excite the strongest feelings of human nature against ourselves.

Effect of English literature favourable to maintenance of British rule.

"The spirit of English literature, on the other hand, cannot but be favorable to the English connection. Familiarly acquainted with us by means of our literature, the Indian youth almost cease to regard us as foreigners. They speak of our great men with the same enthusiasm as we do. Educated in the same way, interested in the same objects, engaged in the same pursuits with ourselves, they become more English than Hindus, just as the Roman provincials became more Romans than Gauls or Italians. What is it that makes us what we are, except living and conversing with English people, and imbibing English thoughts and habits of mind? They do so too: they daily converse with the best and wisest Englishmen through the medium of their works; and form, perhaps, a higher idea of our nation than if their intercourse with it were of a more personal kind. Admitted behind the scenes, they become acquainted with the principles which guide our proceedings; they see how sincerely we study the benefit of India in the measures of our administration; and from violent opponents, or sullen conformists, they are converted into zealous and intelligent co-operators with us. They learn to make a proper use of the freedom of discussion which exists under our Government, by observing how we use it ourselves; and they cease to think of violent remedies, because they are convinced that there is no indisposition on our part to satisfy every real want of the country. Dishonest and bad rulers alone derive any advantage from the ignorance of their subjects. As long as we study the benefit of India in our measures, the confidence and affection of the people will increase in proportion to their knowledge of us.

Infusion of European ideas will render Natives dependent on English protection.

"But this is not all. There is a principle in human nature which impels all mankind to aim at improving their condition: every individual has his plan of happiness: every community has its ideas of securing the national honour and prosperity. This powerful and universal principle, in some shape or other, is in a state of constant activity; and if it be not enlisted on our side, it must be arrayed against us. As long as the natives are left to brood over their former independence, their sole specific for improving their condition is, the immediate and total expulsion of the English. A native patriot of the old school has no notion of anything beyond this: his attention has never been called to any other mode of restoring the dignity and prosperity of his country. It is only by the infusion of European ideas, that a new direction can be given to the national views. The young men brought up at our seminaries, turn with contempt from the barbarous despotisms under which their ancestors groaned, to the prospect of improving their national institutions on the English model. Instead of regarding us with dislike, they court our society, and look upon us as their natural protectors and benefactors: the summit of their ambition is, to resemble us; and, under our auspices, they hope to elevate the character of their countrymen, and to prepare them by gradual steps for the enjoyment of a well-regulated and therefore a secure and a happy independence. So far from having the idea of driving the English into the sea uppermost in their minds, they have no notion of any improvement, but such as rivets their connection with the English, and makes them dependent on English protection and instruction. In the re-establishment of the old native governments, they see only the destruction of their most cherished hopes, and a state of great personal insecurity for themselves.

Connection of England with India cannot be permanent.

"The existing connection between two such distant countries as England and India, cannot, in the nature of things, be permanent: no effort of policy can prevent the natives from ultimately regaining their independence. But there are two ways of arriving at this point. One of these is, through the medium of revolution; the other, through that of reform. In one, the forward movement is sudden and violent; in the other, it is gradual and peaceable. One must end in a complete alienation of mind and separation of interests between ourselves and the natives; the other in a permanent alliance, founded on mutual benefit and good-will.

"The only means at our disposal for preventing the one and securing the other class of results is, to set the natives on a process of European improvement, to which they are already sufficiently inclined. They will then cease to desire and aim at independence on the old Indian footing. A sudden change will then be impossible; and a long continuance of our present connection with India will even be assured to us. A Mahratta or Muhammadan despotism might be re-established in a month; but a century would scarcely suffice to prepare the people for self-government on the European model. The political education of a nation must be a work of time, and while it is in progress, we shall be as safe as it will be possible for us to be. The natives will not rise against us, because we shall stoop to raise them: there will be no reaction, because there will be no pressure: the national activity will be fully and harmlessly employed in acquiring and diffusing European knowledge, and in naturalising European institutions. The educated classes, knowing that the elevation of their country on these principles can only be worked out under our protection, will naturally cling to us. They even now do so. There is no class of our subjects to whom we are so thoroughly necessary as those whose opinions have been cast in the English mould: they are spoiled for a purely native regime; they have everything to fear from the premature establishment of a native Government; their education would mark them out for persecution; the feelings of independence, the literary and scientific pursuits, the plans of improvement in which they indulged under our Government, must be exchanged for the servility and prostration of mind which characterise an Asiatic Court. This class is at present a small minority, but it is continually receiving accessions from the youth who are brought up at the different English seminaries. It will in time become the majority; and it will then be necessary to modify the political institutions to suit the increased intelligence of the people, and their capacity for self-government.

Natives educated in English will mould their prospects under British protection.

"The change will thus be peaceably and gradually effected: there will be no struggle, no mutual exasperation; the natives will have independence, after first learning how to make a good use of it: we shall exchange profitable subjects for still more profitable allies. The present administrative connection benefits families, but a strict commercial union between the first manufacturing and the first producing country in the world, would be a solid foundation of strength and prosperity to our whole nation. If this course be adopted, there will, properly speaking, be no separation. A precarious and temporary relation will almost imperceptibly pass into another far more durable and beneficial. Trained by us to happiness and independence, and endowed with our learning and our political institutions, India will remain the proudest monument of British benevolence; and we shall long continue to reap, in the affectionate attachment of the people, and in a great commercial intercourse with their splendid country,* the fruit of that liberal and enlightened policy which suggested to us this line of conduct.

Gradual independence of India will be friendly to British commercial intercourse.

"In following this course we should be trying no new experiment. The Romans at once civilised the nations of Europe, and attached them to their rule by Romanising them; or, in other words, by educating them in the Roman Literature and Arts, and teaching them to emulate their conquerors instead of opposing them. Acquisitions made by superiority in war, were consolidated by superiority in the arts of peace; and the remembrance of the original violence was lost in that of the benefits which resulted from it. The provincials of Italy, Spain, Africa, and Gaul, having no ambition except to imitate the Romans, and to share their privileges with them, remained to the last faithful subjects of the empire; and the union was at last dissolved, not by internal revolt, but by the shock of external violence, which involved conquerors and conquered in one common overthrow. The Indians will, I hope, soon stand in the same position towards us in which we once stood towards the Romans. Tacitus informs us, that it was the policy of Julius Agricola to instruct the sons of the leading men among the Britons in the literature and science of Rome, and to give them a taste for the refinements of Roman civilization.† We all know how well this plan answered. From being obstinate enemies, the Britons soon became attached and confiding friends; and they made more strenuous efforts to retain the Romans, than their ancestors had done to resist their invasion. It will be a shame to us if, with our greatly superior advantages,

The example of Romans in civilizing Europe and creating independent friendly nationalities must be followed.

* The present trade with India can give no idea of what it is capable of becoming: the productive powers of the country are immense: the population of British India alone, without including the Native States, is more than three times that of all the rest of the British Empire. By governing well, and promoting to the utmost of our power the growth of wealth, intelligence, and enterprise in its vast population, we shall be able to make India a source of wealth and strength to our nation in time to come, with which nothing in our past history furnishes any parallel.

† The words of Tacitus are: "Jam vero principum filios liberalibus artibus erudire, et ingenia Britannorum studiis Gallorum anteferre, ut qui modo linguam Romanam abnuebant, eloquentiam concupiscerent. Inde etiam habitus nostri honour et frequens toga. Paulatimque discessum ad delinimenta vitiorum, porticus et balnea et conviviorum elegantiam; idque apud imperitos humanitas vocabatur cum pars servitutis esset."

we also do not make our premature departure be dreaded as a calamity. It must not be said in after ages, that 'the groans of the Britons' were elicited by the breaking up of the Roman Empire; and the groans of the Indians by the continued existence of the British.

"We may also take a lesson from the Muhammadans whose conquests have been so extensive and so permanent.

Policy of the Emperor Akbar to be adopted.

From the Indian Archipelago to Portugal, Arabic was established as the language of religion, of literature and of law, the vernacular tongues were saturated with it; and the youth of the conquered countries soon began to vie with their first instructors in every branch of Muhammadan learning. A polite education was understood to mean a Muhammadan Education; and the most cultivated and active minds were everywhere engaged on the side of the Muhammadan system. The Emperor Akbar followed up this policy in India. Arabicised Persian was adopted as the language of his dynasty; and the direction thereby given to the national sympathies and ideas greatly contributed to produce that feeling of veneration for the family which has long survived the loss of its power. This feeling, which in Europe would be called loyalty, is common to those who have been brought up in the old learning, but is very rarely found in connection with an English Education. The policy of our predecessors, although seldom worthy of imitation, was both very sound and very successful in this respect. If we adopt the same policy, it will be more beneficial to the natives in proportion as English contains a greater fund of true knowledge than Arabic and Persian: and it will be more beneficial to us in proportion as the natives will study English more zealously and extensively than they did Arabic and Persian, and will be more completely changed by it in feeling and opinion.

"These views were not worked out by reflection, but were forced on me by actual observation and experience.

Ambition of English-educated Natives for a national representative assembly gradually terminating the English Rule.

I passed some years in parts of India, where, owing to the comparative novelty of our rule and to the absence of any attempt to alter the current of native feeling, the national habits of thinking remained unchanged. There, high and low, rich and poor, had only one idea of improving their political condition. The upper classes lived upon the prospect of regaining their former pre-eminence; and the lower, upon that of having the avenues to wealth and distinction reopened to them by the re-establishment of a Native Government. Even sensible and comparatively well affected natives had no notion that there was any remedy for the existing depressed state of their nation except the sudden and absolute expulsion of the English. After that, I resided for some years in Bengal, and there I found quite another set of ideas prevalent among the educated natives. Instead of thinking of cutting the throats of the English, they were aspiring to sit with them on the grand jury, or on the bench of Magistrates. Instead of speculating on Punjab or Nepaulese politics, they were discussing the advantages of printing and free discussion, in oratorical English speeches, at debating societies which they had established among themselves. The most sanguine dimly look forward in the distant future to the establishment of a national representative assembly as the consummation of their hopes—all of them being fully sensible that these plans of improvement could only be worked out with the aid and protection of the British Government by the gradual improvement of their countrymen in knowledge and morality; and that the re-establishment of a Muhammadan or any other native regime would at once render all such views impracticable and ridiculous. No doubt, both these schemes of national improvement suppose the termination of the English rule; but while that event is the beginning of one, it is only the conclusion of the other. In one, the sudden and violent overthrow of our government is a necessary preliminary, in the other, a long continuance of our administration, and the gradual withdrawal of it as the people become fit to govern themselves, are equally indispensable.

"Our Native Army is justly regarded as the pillar of our Indian empire; and no plan of benefiting either the

Popular education will secure loyalty of Native Army.

natives or ourselves can be worth anything which does not rest on the supposition that this pillar will remain unbroken. It is therefore of importance to inquire how this essential element of power is likely to be affected by the course of policy which has been described. The Indian Army is made up of two entirely distinct parts; the English officers, and the Native officers and men. The former will, under any circumstances, stand firm to their national interests: the latter will be animated by the feelings of the class of society from which they are drawn, except so far as those feelings may be modified by professional interests and habits. The native officers rise from the ranks; and the ranks are recruited from the labouring class, which is the last that will be affected by any system of national education. Not one in five hundred of the boys who are instructed in the Zillah Seminaries, will enlist in the army. If the Sepoys are educated anywhere, it must be in the village schools; and the organisation of those schools will be the concluding measure of the series. The instruction given to the labouring class can never be more than merely elementary. They have not leisure for more. But, such as it is, they will be indebted for it to us; and as it will form part of a system established and superintended by ourselves, we shall take care that it is of a kind calculated to inspire feelings of attachment to the British connection. After this, the young men who enlist in the army will become imbued with the military spirit, and moulded by the habits of military obedience. I leave to others to judge whether this training is calculated to make better and more attached, or worse and more disaffected, soldiers than the state of entire neglect, as regards their moral and intellectual improvement, in which the whole class are at present left. I never heard that the education given in the national schools unfitted the common people of England for the ranks of the army, although the inducements to honourable and faithful service, which are open to them after they enter the army, are much inferior to those which are held out to our Sepoys.

Notwithstanding religious neutrality of the State, English education will defeat superstitious priest-craft of Hindus and mollify the Muhammadans.

"Religious instruction forms no part of the object of the Government seminaries. It would be impossible for the State to interfere at all with native education on any other condition; and this is now so well understood, that religious jealousy offers no obstruction to our success. The general favour with which English education is regarded, and the multitudes who flock to our schools, prove this to be the case. The Brahmans, it is true, ruled supreme over the old system. It was moulded for the express purpose of enabling them to hold the minds of men in thraldom; and ages had fixed the stamp of solidity upon it. Upon this ground they were unassailable. But popular education, through the medium of the English language, is an entirely new element, with which they are incapable of dealing. It did not enter into the calculation of the founders of their system; and they have no machinery to oppose to it. Although they have been priest-ridden for ages, the people of India are, for all purposes of improvement, a new, and more than a new, people. Their appetite for knowledge has been whetted by their long-compelled fast; and aware of the superiority of the new learning, they devour it more greedily than they ever would have done Sanskrit lore, even if that lore had not been withheld from them; they bring to the task, vacant minds and excited curiosity, absence of prejudice, and an inextinguishable thirst for information. They cannot return under the dominion of the Brahmans. The spell has been for ever broken. Hinduism is not a religion which will bear examination. It is so entirely destitute of any thing like evidence, and is identified with so many gross immoralities and physical absurdities, that it gives way at once before the light of European science. Muhammadanism is made of tougher materials; yet, even a Muhammadan youth who has received an English education, is a very different person from one who has been taught according to the perfect manner of the law of his fathers. As this change advances, India will become quite another country: nothing more will be heard of excitable religious feelings; priest-craft will no longer be able to work by ignorance; knowledge and power will pass from a dominant caste to the people themselves; the whole nation will co-operate with us in reforming institutions, the possibility of altering which could never have been contemplated if events had taken any other course; and many causes will concur to introduce a more wholesome state of morals, which, of all the changes that can take place, is the one in which the public welfare is most concerned.

Question of education in India could be solved by spending the interest of only £1,000,000 annually, and secure attachment of Natives to British Rule.

"There has been a time at which each of the other branches of the public service has particularly commanded attention. The Commercial, the Political, the Judicial, the Revenue Departments, have in turn been the subject of special consideration; and decisive steps have been taken to put them on a satisfactory footing. My object will be sufficiently attained, if I succeed in producing a conviction that the time has arrived for taking up the question of public instruction in the same spirit, and with the same determination to employ whatever means may be requisite for accomplishing the object in view. The absence of any sensible proof that increased taxation is attended with any proportionate benefit to India, has long been extremely disheartening both to the natives and to the European public officers serving in that country.* The entire abolition of the transit duties, and the establishment of an adequate system of public instruction, would furnish this proof, and would excite the warmest gratitude of every body who from any cause feels interested in the welfare of India. The interest of a single million sterling,† in addition to what is already expended, would be sufficient to answer every present purpose as far as education is concerned. Even on the narrowest view of national interest, a million could not be better invested. It would ensure the moral and intellectual emancipation of the people of India, and would render them at once attached to our rule and worthy of our alliance."‡

* A large proportion of the land in the Bengal and Agra Presidencies is held tax-free; but, although nothing can be more unreasonable than that persons who benefit by the protection of the Government should contribute nothing to its support, and throw the whole burden on the rest, it is impossible at present to induce the natives to view the subject in this light. Their invariable answer is, that while it is certain that some will be worse off, they see no reason to suppose that they will themselves be better off if the exempted lands are brought under contribution.

† The Parliamentary assignment of ten thousand pounds a year still remains to be accounted for to the Committee of Public Instruction, from July 1813 to May 1821, with compound interest up to the date of payment.

‡ Trevelyan, *On the Education of the People of India*, pp. 187–205.

The above-quoted views were written by Sir Charles Trevelyan so long ago as 1838, and it will be interesting to see how far his anticipations as to the effect of English education in breaking down Hindu superstition and priest-craft were justified during the thirty years that followed. For this purpose the testimony of a contemporary historian, Mr. Iltudus Thomas Prichard, is available. In his work on the "*Administration of India, from* 1859 *to* 1868," he devotes a whole Chapter to the subject of social progress in India, and the following passages may be quoted from his work :—

Sir Charles Trevelyan's forecast of English education how far realized.

"No one who has passed twenty consecutive years in India can fail to have observed the great change which attended the transfer of the country to the direct dominion of the Crown. The year of the rebellion, 1857-58, was an epoch in the modern history of India from which future writers will date the commencement of an era of reform. And it is certain that if the administration between 1859 and 1869 has been successful, we ought to be able to trace its results in a general improvement in the condition of the people. * * * * * * * * * * *

Religious and social effect of English education up to the decade ending in 1868.

"Among the classes of the native population which come into contact with European civilization, in cosequence of their being located in the Presidency cities and on the great lines of railway, the change during the last ten years has been very marked. Much of the prejudice and ignorant confidence of Orientals in their own superiority, which has always formed so prominent a feature in their character, has yielded to liberal ideas developed by education, combined with commercial intercourse with European nations. Even the strongholds of Hindu susperstition, so long intact, have been unable to withstand the progress of thought and the new sect of Brahmos is daily increasing in influence, and gathering converts in all the large cities on the Bengal side. The tenet of this new sect are a sort of compromise between Hindusim and common sense. Brahmoism more nearly approaches the deism of Europe in the earlier part of the present century than any of the systems of philosophy promulgated in the East. Finding that the fables of the Hindu Mythology (which formed no part of the Hindu religion as inculcated by the earlier sages) were unable to stand the test of reason, and were rapidly losing their hold upon the minds of the people, and unwilling at the same time to embrace Christianity—which came to them recommended indeed by the preaching of Missionaries, but not by the practice of the bulk of the English with whom they came in contact,—the founders of this school endeavoured to enunciate a philosophic and religious system grounded on those ideas of natural religion which commend themselves to the reason and instincts of mankind. The Brahmos are, in fact, deists, but they inculcate the strictest observance of the moral law. As such, it is difficult to perceive, as some writers do, in the present movement any indication of a tendency towards Christianity. On the contrary, it would seem as if the system of State Education preserving the strictest neutrality in religious questions is producing exactly the results which might have been anticipated. A Hindu educated in our schools and colleges finds it impossible to believe, for instance, that the world rests on the back of a tortoise or the horns of a bull. Uninstructed in the Christian faith, he is well acquainted with the history of modern discovery, and more or less proficient in natural science, having at the same time an innate tendency towards metaphysical speculations. He therefore gladly takes refuge in a system which in its observance of the moral law satisfies the higher aspirations of his mind, and in its speculative tenets on the existence of a Divine Creator and Ruler of the Universe is sufficient to fill the void caused by a rejection of the mythological fables which amused him as a child. Practically, for many years, the few thoughtful men among the Hindus have, I believe, abandoned the superstitions of the *Purans*, but fettered by the bonds of caste, and detered by the bad example of Englishmen from embracing a religion whose followers seemed to ignore the connexion between precept and practice, and unable to find a refuge anywhere, they were content to live and die in the faith of their forefathers, believing as much as they could bring their minds not to reject, and leaving the great riddle to be solved hereafter.

Rise of Brahmoism superseding Hindu prejudices and superstitions.

"In intellectual acquirements and natural capacity, the various classes of natives differ very materially. Christianity has very little present prospect of success among the Hindus and Muhammadans of our older Provinces; but wherever it has been preached among the ruder tribes of the interior, it has generally been received with some enthusiasm. It is of course only natural that the simple minds of the barbarous descendants of the aborigines who are to be met with in mountainous tracts in various parts of the Continent of Central India, and in one portion of Rajpootana, in Bengal Proper, and in Burmah, should be more easily impressed with the truths of Christianity than the Hindu wedded to a system of Philosophy and long inured to the slavery of caste, or than the fanatical Muhammadan; to either, a system of religion whose great principle is that of self-sacrifice is so utterly foreign that we may cease to wonder at the little effect as yet produced by the teaching of our Missionaries.

Little effect of Christianity in the more advanced provinces.

Caste prejudices gradually yielding.

"Caste prejudices, however, are gradually yielding, natives are beginning to understand the value of co-operation, and to see that an irksome system which has been imposed by general consent may by general consent be shaken off. Quite recently a reformer, whose name deserves to be recorded, Pearee Lall, has by persevering agitation succeeded in getting up meetings at all the large cities in the Upper Provinces, and in inducing a large and influential sect of Brahmins to discontinue the old-established custom of expensive marriages which has involved so many families in debt and ruin.

Native Societies and Associations.

"In many parts of India the natives now have their societies and associations, which meet at stated periods and discuss questions of social science. At these congresses all the forms used among ourselves at public meetings are strictly observed; the members address the chairman, and the proceedings are duly recorded and published at the expense of the association under the auspices of the Secretary. In Oude, the Talookdars' Association has a little more of a political character as they not unfrequently discuss questions having reference to their rights and privileges.

Surprise of European travellers at the absence of social intercourse between the English and the Natives.

"India is occasionally visited by travellers from the Continent of Europe—Frenchmen, Germans, Italians—who in the pursuit of business or pleasure spend a few months rambling over the Continent. These observers are always struck most forcibly with what is beyond a doubt one of the strangest features in our position in the country, *viz.*, the utter absence of anything like social intercourse between the races. Englishmen meet Natives in business, and there their connexion ceases. After being upwards of a century in the country, we have never penetrated the barrier of reserve in which the native shelters himself from social intercourse with the Englishman. In Bombay the attempt at amalgamation has been occasionally made, with very indifferent success. It seems as if there was on both sides a deep rooted antipathy to meeting on an equality in social position which no efforts can overcome.

Absence of commensality between the English and the Natives precludes real intimacy.

"One reason of this is the existence of habits and customs which preclude Englishmen and Natives from eating and drinking together. It is a theory, not grounded on a very exalted view of human life, but it seems as if it were one of the laws of Nature, and one of the demarcations between man and the lower order of animals, that social intercourse among the former should be best developed by the process of consuming food in company. Two men dine together, and become friends: two dogs eat out of the same dish, and the chances are that they fight over their food. The Englishman and the Oriental cannot amalgamate socially, because their habits and prejudices entail on them the necessity of taking their meals apart. Community of interest is a weaker bond than similarity of taste and manner. This is a truism, but it is a truism aptly illustrated in the conditions of life in India, where the Englishman and the Native, subjects of one sovereign, originally of one race, with common sympathies and unity of interests, may meet one another many times daily, week after week, year after year, in their ordinary avocations, and yet never advance one step towards real intimacy or friendship."*

These observations do not go to show that the expectations of Sir Charles Trevelyan had been realized within thirty years from the time when he wrote (1838), for the remarks of Mr. Prichard describe the state of things as they were in 1868. In chronological order, therefore, come the views of the Indian Education Commission of 1882, and the following passages may be quoted from their Report:—

The Education Commission's opinion as to the effect of English Collegiate instruction upon the enlightenment of the people,—1882.

"An estimate of the effect which collegiate instruction has had upon the general education and enlightenment of the people must in fairness be accompanied by a reference to the objects which it sets before itself. The reformers of 1835, to whom the system is due, claimed that only by an education in English, and after European methods, could we hope to raise the moral and intellectual tone of Indian Society and supply the administration with a competent body of public servants. To what degree, then, have these objects been attained? Our answer is in the testimony of witnesses before this Commission, in the thoughtful opinions delivered from time to time by men whose position has given them ample opportunities of judging, and in the facts obvious to all eyes throughout the country. And that answer is conclusive: if not that collegiate education has fulfilled all the expectations entertained of it, at least that it has not disappointed the hopes of a sober judgment. Many mistakes in the methods employed have been pointed out and corrected by maturer experience. Much done has had to be undone. Not a little yet remains for gradual re-consideration. So, too, of the recipients of our college education it is by no means pretended that they are the very crown and flower of Indian humanity. Many unlovely defects of character still

* *Administration of India*, by Iltudus Thomas Prichard, Vol. II., pp. 96–100.

give occasion of scorn to those who are nothing if not critical. Of superficial learning, and of pretentious self-assertion manifested in a variety of ways, there has no doubt been plenty. It would be strange if it were otherwise. For in no country under any circumstance has there been equal or similar encouragement to the development of such and other faults. The surroundings of the Indian student are not always favourable to the development of a high type of character. Neither in the labour nor in the recreations of those about him does he find much that sorts with his intellectual pursuits. Living in an atmosphere of ignorance his sense of superiority is in danger of becoming conceit. Reverence for the current forms of the religion of his country seem difficult to him, when face to face with dogmas which science has exploded, and a disposition to scoff does not beautify his nature. Nor is it possible, at least in Government Colleges, to appeal in a large and systematic manner to that religious teaching which has been found to be the most universal basis of morality. Again, his intercourse with the ruling race is not wholly without its drawbacks. Unwise enthusiasts flatter him with hopes and prophecies. The advantages he enjoys give him a distorted idea of claims to be urged upon a Government that has done so much for him. His self-reliance weakens with encouragement, or he is irritated and rebuked by the chilly courtesies of English reserve. The narrow circle of his life; the absence of facilities for travel, whereby his sympathies and experience might be enlarged; the strong temptation to lay aside his studies so soon as employment supplies his moderate necessities; the scanty inducement to fit himself for higher duties,—all help to dwarf the moral and intellectual growth and to foster those faults against which satirists, good humoured or bitter, have directed so many shafts. All the greater therefore is the credit due to him when he rises above the influences by which he is surrounded; and, whatever his weaknesses, it may be safely said that they who best know the educated native have the most to urge in his favour. It may also be safely said that many of the faults charged against the earlier generation of college students are disappearing as an English education is less regarded in the light of a rare distinction. Some of those faults were born of the time and the circumstances; some had root in a system of instruction now every where becoming more thorough and more scientific.

The professions which the majority of English-educated Natives adopt.

"Of the professions to which a student takes on leaving college, the most favourite are Government Service and the Law. In the latter will generally be found those whose talents are brightest, and in whom self-reliance is most strong; in the former, those who, from narrowness of circumstances or from a doubt of their own powers, have been glad to accept employment, sometimes of a very humble kind. As a Government Servant, the ex-student is found everywhere and in all branches of the Administration; as a clerk, as a subordinate Judicial, and Revenue, or Police Officer; as a Professor in a College, or Teacher in a School; in various capacities in the Department of Public Works, the Forest Department, the Telegraph, the Railway, the Medical Service. In all he holds appointments involving considerable trust and exercising zeal, energy, activity. And in some Provinces he has attained his present position despite strenuous antagonism on the part of his countrymen brought up in the old school, who were naturally anxious to keep in their families posts regarded, from length of tenure, as hereditary possessions. That this antagonism was for so long so efficient resulted, in a considerable measure, from an unwillingness on the part of Civil Officers to employ a class of men with whom they had but slight acquaintance, and who were without the necessary apprenticeship to official life; such unwillingness is now becoming a thing of the past. Throughout the country Civil Officers have begun to discover and readily to acknowledge, that in integrity, capacity for work, intelligence, industry, the subordinate trained in college excels his fellow brought up according to the traditions of the past. At the Bar, a profession which in many ways is eminently suited to the bent of the native mind, the ex-students of our colleges have made their way with honourable success. Even in the Presidency towns, though pitted against distinguished English lawyers, they carry off a large share of the practice, acquitting themselves with especial credit in civil cases. If their legal acumen has, for its very subtlety, sometimes been the subject of doubtful compliment, many of their number are conspicuous for grasp of subject, and breadth of view. Though pleading in a foreign tongue, they not seldom display an eloquence and power of debate which would command admiration before any English tribunal. Some of the ablest of them have attained to the Bench of the Calcutta High Court; and last year during the absence of the Chief Justice, his high post was filled by Mr. Justice Romesh Chunder Mittra. Madras and Bombay tell the same tale, and though in the more backward Provinces the number of distinguished advocates is not large, a Musalman gentleman, once a student of the Benares College, was recently called to fill a vacancy in the Allahabad High Court. In the District Courts, where of old chicanery and many questionable devices so largely prevailed, the influence of the educated native pleader has generally been of a healthy kind. And when this is the case it is especially creditable to him. For, away from the eye of those whose disapproval would mean loss of professional caste, and exposed to influences and temptations such as perhaps advocacy in no other country confronts, he has need of a strong moral rectitude and much earnestness of purpose. But with the support of the wholesome pride which the members of his profession feel in so honourable a career, it every day becomes easier to him to emulate the dignity and self-respect which are so pre-eminently characteristic of the English Bar. Government service and the Law, as we have said, engage the attention of the majority of our graduates and undergraduates. A smaller number betake themselves to private service as clerks, assistants, or managers. Some engage in trade. They are, however, comparatively few in number for commerce needs capital, and hereditary aptitude for business, neither of which is usually possessed in any sufficient degree by those educated in our Colleges. Where, indeed, a commercial career is chosen by them, the general testimony is of the same purport as that borne to the credit with which they fill other positions in life. Such testimony coming from various quarters, and having reference to a variety of occupations, we might easily quote at great length.

Favourable opinions of Sir M. R. Westropp, Sir W. Wedderburn, and Sir Charles Turner.

"It may be enough to cite the opinions of a few gentlemen of high position and varied experience. In such a list no one perhaps has a better right to a foremost place than Sir M. R. Westropp, who, first as a Puisne Judge of the High Court and afterwards, for nearly twenty years, as Chief Justice of Bombay, had daily opportunity of gauging the capacity and character of men trained in the Colleges of the Presidency. In reply to an address presented to him last year on his retirement from the Bench, his Lordship remarked: 'In tone, in learning, in every thing that was important for professional men, the Pleaders of the High Court were pre-eminent, and they were now, whatever their predecessors in the Sadar Adalat might have been in a by-gone generation, a highly honourable body. This had been proved by their own acts; and, what was more, they had proved themselves liberal and generous, as circumstances which he had had the opportunity of noticing, would show. It had been a great pleasure to him to see so much of them and to notice their daily conduct for so many years, and the feeling of satisfaction which he experienced was shared by all the Judges. The educational institutions now in existence in Bombay contributed greatly to the class of men who succeeded in passing the examination for the career of High Court Pleaders and Subordinate Judges. He trusted the improvement in education might go on. It had penetrated to a considerable extent among the Pleaders in the mofussil also; but the soldiers of the old garrison were too firmly in possession to be dislodged speedily. In the mofussil the old practitioner had a stronghold, but his place was being gradually filled by the alumni of the Elphinstone High School and of the University of Bombay. That they might go on and prosper was the earnest desire of himself and brethren.' Of similar tenour was the evidence given before the Commission by Sir William Wedderburn. In Madras, Chief Justice Sir Charles Turner, whose many years acquaintance with the North-Western Provinces has varied his experience, remarked in his Convocation address delivered in 1881, before the University of Madras:—'Modern India has proved by examples that are known to, and honoured by, all in this assembly that her sons can qualify themselves to hold their own with the best of European talent in the Council Chamber, on the Bench, at the Bar, and in the mart. The time cannot be far distant when she will produce her philosopher, her moralist, her reformer.'

Morality of ex-students of English Colleges and their efforts to advance enlightenment.

"Of the morality of our ex-students question has sometimes been made; not so much perhaps because experience justified an accusation, as because it was pre-supposed that those who received no definite religious instruction must necessarily have but little reverence for a moral law to which were attached no divine sanctions. There is, however, no reason whatever why a scientific education should lower the standard of conduct. It is true that such an education tends to weaken and destroy primitive beliefs, but morality is independent of those beliefs, and a young man's studies at college are certainly not calculated to weaken his appreciation of moral truths. Nor in estimating the effect which collegiate education has had upon religious belief ought we to forget the large extent to which students have joined the Brahmo Samaj and other theistic associations of the same character, or the constant prominence given in their public writings and discussions to the subject of a reformed faith. In the restricted sense of integrity, the higher level that prevails is certified by the evidence of words. It is not merely the Government officer who now feels himself able to place reliance upon the uprightness of his subordinate. The same is the case with commercial men, with managers of banks, with Railway Companies. Dishonest servants are, of course, sometimes found among highly educated natives of India, as they are sometimes found among highly educated natives of England. And equally, of course, the most has been made of such instances to discredit an education novel in kind and therefore disliked by many. If again, under the term morality, we include those qualities which tend to the general welfare of a people, then in a larger sense has the highly-educated native vindicated his claim to our respect. For it is he whose enterprise and enthusiasm have done much to rouse self-effort in education, and whose munificence has not seldom made that effort possible. It is he who has created the native press in its most intelligent form. His are the various societies, literary and scientific, societies for religious and for social reform. To his activity it is due that vernacular literature is so rapidly multiplying its utility. From his number have come men who have guided the policy of Native States at critical times, and filled with dignity important offices under the British Government.

Deficiency of English-educated Natives in loftiness of motives, courtesy and good manners, explained.

"Still, desirous as we are fully to acknowledge the good effects of collegiate education, we do not shut our eyes to certain deficiencies of result and certain positive evils ascribed to various defects of system. We cannot affirm that in education has been found a sufficient cure for the comparative absence of lofty motive and of a sense of public duty which for long centuries has been an admitted drawback on so much that is attractive in the character of Natives of India. We cannot deny that though the standard of morality is higher than it was, it is still a morality based to a large extent upon considerations of a prudent self-interest, rather than upon any higher principles of action. Moral strength of purpose under circumstances in which such strength has nothing but itself to rely upon is too often conspicuous for its absence; and great intellectual attainments are by no means always accompanied by great elevation of character. On the other hand, however, it must not be forgotten, that improvement in this matter, especially under the conditions imposed by the past history of the country, must be the work of several generations. In the minor matter of courtesy and good manners, it is also objected that there has been a distinct deterioration; that in their desire to cast off the reproach of subservience, educated natives have mistaken rudeness of behaviour for dignified independence. This charge within certain limits admits of no dispute. Still, it is a result at which we cannot greatly wonder when we take into account the ugly faults and unpleasant symptoms that accompany a period of transition. Again, those who most fully recognise the general improvement, ascribe it to influences of which education is but one, and by no means the most prominent one; though to this it may perhaps be replied that it is education which has brought about a state of mind upon which alone those other influences could work. There is another respect, of a different, and more special character, in which collegiate education has as yet certainly failed. With a few brilliant exceptions, no eminent scholars are to be found in the long list of University Graduates. Two reasons, however, go a great way to account for this fact. One is to be found in the character of the academic system in its earlier days. That system aimed rather at giving a general education than at encouraging special knowledge. The more recent reforms all tend towards the substitution of a small number of subjects for the multifarious requirements which experience has condemned. A second reason is the poverty of the Indian student. To one out of five hundred, perhaps, it is a matter of indifference whether, when he goes out into the world, he can at once earn his livelihood. With the rest, employment in some shape or other is a necessity; and that employment rarely leaves him leisure or inclination to carry on studies of which he has but come to the threshold. Private liberality has done much for education in many directions. But the endowment of research is not one of these directions. A life of learned ease is almost unknown to the Indian student; his success must be success of a practical character; his ambition waits upon his daily wants.

English Collegiate Education on the whole beneficial.

"In judging of the results already attained, many allowances have to be made; above all the allowances of time. Even in the most advanced Province of India, collegiate education of the present type is barely fifty years old, in some parts of the country its life measures less than half that span; in some it has not yet begun. It must be remembered, too, that that education is of exotic growth, or, rather, that it has been imposed upon the country by an alien power. If the advent of the philosopher, the moralist, the reformer, of which Sir Charles Turner is so hopeful, be still 'a far-off adorable dream,' it is but a sober estimate which declares that, directly or indirectly, collegiate education has been beneficial in a variety of ways to an extensive portion of a vast empire." *

Importance of the Views of eminent Indian Statesmen as to the general effects of English Education.

Such being the collective views of the Indian Education Commission of 1882, it is interesting as well as instructive, to compare them with the opinions of various eminent Indian Statesmen, such as Sir Richard Temple, a distinguished member of the Indian Civil Service, who, after a long and varied experience in holding high administrative posts in various parts of India, became Finance Minister of India, and subsequently Lieutenant-Governor of Bengal, and finally Governor of Bombay, from which important office he retired and is now a Member of the House of Commons. As to the effects of English education he observes as follows:—

Sir Richard Temple's views as to early effects of English Education.

"Among the educated Natives, the first-fruit of the new education was an improved standard of rectitude and integrity. The men themselves saw that this was the case, and attributed it unhesitatingly to educational influences. Much, happily, was due to this cause, much also was assignable to other causes, such as the improvement of official and professional prospects for those who had character as well as ability. The change for the better was percept-

* Report of the Indian Education Commission (1882); pp. 300–304.

able with the utmost distinctness in the upper classes of the Native officials, especially in the Judicial Department. When I had first known Calcutta, more than twenty years ago, honesty among these men was, according to common repute, the exception; now by the same repute, dishonesty was the exception and honesty the rule. Indeed I scarcely then expected to live to see the change for the better in these respects which I now saw.

Enlightenment of the Brahmo sect. Desire of educated Natives of ruling the Country while the Europeans were to defend it.

"There was, on the whole, an upheaval of the Native mind in Bengal consequent on the spread of secular education, although the influence of Christian Missions, however great elsewhere, was not much felt in Calcutta. The principal factor was the Brahmo sect, of which the adherents gathered largely at the capital and were scattered throughout the country. In religion they followed the precepts of the Bible without acknowledging the divinity of Christ; but they accepted in addition many doctrines of the Hindu sacred writings. There had been a Hindu Synod named the '*Dharma Sabha*,' instituted to counteract these innovations by recalling the thoughts of the faithful to the ancient ways; many organs of opinion also spoke as if the old belief survived. But it was doubtful whether any resistance, passive or active, would long withstand the advance of new opinions. The existing tendencies were rendering educated Hindus less submissive in tone and language than formerly, more erect in mental and moral stature in the presence of Europeans, even jealous of the superior positions held by Europeans in the country, not altogether disposed to acquiesce in their present status, but rather inclined to criticise the conduct and policy of the Government and to demand increased privileges. Without going so far as to ask for representative institutions, they aspired to have a greater share than previously in governing themselves, though they had not formed exact ideas as to how that share was to be secured. They perhaps desired in effect to have the satisfaction of ruling the country while the Europeans had the labour of defending it. They had an overweening notion of their own intellectual ability, believing themselves to be in this respect equal to any nation and superior to most races. They cherished the notion that wherever brainwork might be absolutely required in India they would rise like oil to the surface of water.

Uneasiness and restlessness of the Native Press.

"This uneasiness and restlessness—all the more irksome as arising from no definable cause, and not being susceptible of any specific remedy—found vent in the Vernacular Press. Of these utterances some were certainly disloyal or even worse, while others were merely captious, peevish, fractious, petulant. On the other hand, there was frank outspoken criticism of men, measures or policy, which was not to be confounded with disloyalty, and which did good every way, as exercising the faculties of the critics and pointing a moral to those criticized. There was also much, which if rightly interpreted, was tantamount to real loyalty such as freemen owe to their liege.

Some critics deprecated high education.

"It was probably the contemplation of these faults which induced many observers to deprecate the high or superior education which was being given. Some critics recommended that Government should withdraw from taking part in high education, leaving it to private enterprise, and devote to the promotion of primary education all the resources which could be afforded by the State. So far from coinciding in that view, however, we strove to foster alike both kinds of education, higher and lower. We diffused superior instruction by the establishment of additional colleges in the interior of the country, at the same time developing the village schools and adding tens of thousands every month to the number of children under primary instruction. The policy was to refrain from supporting any branch of education entirely by the State resources, but to induce the people themselves to contribute at least half. This proportion was maintained for the whole educational expenditure, and also for the education of each sort, upper or lower.

Undue and disproportionate attention to literature and philosophy to the sacrifice of scientific and practical instruction.

"The real fault in the high education was the undue and disproportionate attention devoted to literature and philosophy, as compared with physical science and the cognate branches of practical instruction. This caused the legal, judicial and administrative professions to be overcrowded, while the scientific and practical professions relating to civil and mechanical engineering, to chemistry, botany, agriculture, and the like, were starved and neglected. It was impossible at that time to remedy this fault without the co-operation of the Calcutta University. But this institution relating to other provinces besides Bengal, and being under the Government of India, was not amenable to the Government of Bengal. Meanwhile the difficulty which very many highly educated men, even graduates of the University, found in obtaining suitable employment, was producing discontent."*

Important questions enunciated by Sir Richard Temple as to the effect of British Rule upon the Indian people.

In the concluding Chapter of the same work Sir Richard Temple has enunciated certain important questions relating to the effect of the British Rule upon the people of India. After dealing with the first question, *viz.*, "What is the economic and financial effect of British rule upon the masses of the people; that is to say, are they growing poorer or richer, irrespective of the question whether India as an

* *Men and Events of my Time in India.* By Sir Richard Temple, *Bart.*, G.C.S.I., C.I.E., D.C.L.; pp. 430–33.

empire is increasing or decreasing in wealth and prosperity ?"—at some length, he goes on to say :—

Has English Education elevated Native character ?

"The *second* question stands thus : has the English or Western education elevated the character of the cultivated classes of the Natives ? Has this elevation been obtained at the cost of originality in the Natives, and has it lessened the chance of their self-development on natural and therefore Asiatic lines ? Ought the education to be in English or in the Indian vernaculars ?

English Education has taught integrity and removed superstition, and improved morality and intellectual capacity.

"Now, the English or Western education has greatly elevated the character of the Natives who have come within its influence. It has taught them truthfulness and honour both morally and intellectually. It has made them regard with aversion that which is false and dishonest. It has imbued them with a love of abstract truth and a desire to exercise the reason with fearless impartiality, to insist upon knowing the why and the wherefore for the faith they may be required to accept. They will no longer tolerate superstitions or any absurdity whatsoever. This improvement is conspicuously manifest in their public conduct, and in all those relations of life which may be called external in contradistinction to domestic. It must doubtless affect benefically their home-life also, but regarding that an European has but little means of judging. In one essential part of domestic conduct they are exemplary, and that comprises the efforts put forth by them to impart the new education to their sons. The sacrifices they make, and the self-denial they undergo, for this object, will hardly be surpassed in the most advanced nations. How far the education of itself has endowed them with amiability, with charitable sentiments and other gentle virtues, may be doubtful ; for it will probably be held that they possessed these virtues before. They take hopeful views of the life to come after the death of this body, and respecting the eternal destiny of man. They form positive conceptions regarding the human soul and its expansive capacities under other conditions of existence. They acknowledge their responsibility to God for their thoughts, words and deeds. Some few of them have been charged with yielding to intemperance, a vice which is not confined to the West, but has always existed in the East also. But this fault has never been enough to detract from the repute of the education and the educated. As a rule, the young men are temperate, steady, and capable of mental effort long sustained.

Ethical and scientific instruction, combined with good example of the British Rule, have important educational effects.

"The education is imparted directly or indirectly in two ways. The primary way consists of definite instruction in ethics or the science of human duty, of the inferences derivable from Western history and literature, of the mental training from logic and mathematics, and (most important of all) from daily contact and conversation wth European Professors. The secondary way consists in the contemplation of the example set by the British Government in India in its wise legislation, its dispensation of justice between man and man, its humane administration, its scientific and mechanical achievements, its conscientious efforts for the good of the people. The educational effect of these things upon the population at large may be greater than is, perhaps, imagined by those who are engaged in the thick of affairs.

Moral and spiritual effect of English literature beneficial, and creates enthusiasm of humanity.

"The effect of this education, direct and indirect, undoubtedly was, in the first instance, to suppress the natural originality of the educated. Formerly, they oft-times, indeed, kept their minds at a fairly high level, observing a right standard. But oft-times they descended to the depths of moral and mental degradation ; from such slough they have been extricated by education, and now breathe a purer air. For a time, bewildered by the superiority of the new civilization, they sought nothing beyond it. They crammed their memories with bare facts ; they learnt the noblest prose or poetry by rote and repeated it mechanically. But this tendency, militating against their originality, operates less and less forcibly with every decade, and its disappearance after one or two generations may be anticipated. They no longer accept a doctrine, secular or religious, merely because it is a result of Western civilization. They search for new standards of their own, outside Europe and its ways. For that purpose they go far afield, reverting to the remotest periods of Asiatic Philosophy, and in spirit crossing the Atlantic to grope for light in the New World. Their antiquarian research is frequently (though perhaps not always) conducted after a method quite their own. Despite their Western preoccupations, it is towards their own traditions that their loving gaze is turned. Their study of Shakespeare, Milton, Bacon, Locke, does not in the least diminish their reverent allegiance to the Asiatic heroes, poets, saints and law-givers of old. Morally, almost spiritually, they approach Christianity, verging actually towards its very borders. But though they venerate its efficacy, they decline to profess it as a religion. Their interpretation of the poetry in Nature differs from ours ; while learning our notion of 'the unseen universe,' they do not adopt it unreservedly. They will study the writings of philosophers and economists as Bentham or Malthus, and criticize the conclusions therein set forth. Their ideas regarding the theory of punishment and several branches of civil and criminal law, differ essentially from those which we strive to impress upon them by our legislation. They frequently controvert the economic conclusions which we assert regarding the material condition of their country. In such arguments they often apply the established doctrines of political economy to complex statistics in a manner which, if not just, is really original. The 'enthusiasm of humanity' is one of the principles which Christianity introduced into the world; and they have caught some of its sacred fire. But, once touched by this hallowed sentiment, they have followed its dictates with an earnestness all their own. Numberless instances of their farsighted munificence might be cited in illustration.

Indian Art.

"In former ages there was little of philosophizing in respect to Indian art, but much of real art existed. In later times there has been much philosophizing but less of actual art. At one moment there was danger lest the very life of Indian art should be stifled by European influence. The European instructors, however, awoke to the danger in time, and now full play is allowed to the fine originality of the Native genius.

Distinguished administrators of Native States.

"The British system, in which the Native administrators are now trained, does at first suppress their natural originality. On the other hand, it may be argued that some of the salient features in our system have their prototypes among the Indians — for instance, the settlement of the land under Todar Mall, the Minister of Akbar the Great, is in several respects a model for British arrangements. The Native States, indeed, copy much that belongs to the British Government, and curiously appreciate English official designations for every department, civil or military. Yet they retain in their management very much which, being their own, must be regarded as original, and which is thought by some, rightly or wrongly, to be better suited to the Natives than our own method. Of living statesmen among the Natives, Salar Jang of Hyderabad, perhaps, has become Europeanized in his method of administration. But Dinkar Rao of Gwalior, was quite original, so was Kirpa Ram of Jammu, and more especially Jang Bahadur of Nepal, who governed after his own fashion with hardly any tincture of European notions. Madhava Rao of Baroda, too, though Anglicized to some extent, is quite Asiatic *au fond*, and, if left to his own resources entirely, would evince striking originality.

The Mahratta Brahmins profit by English Education.

"The Mahratta Brahmans, again, some of the very ablest among the *élèves* of the modern education, keep their minds riveted upon national models, and would strenuously repudiate the notion of their inner thoughts being transformed by what they have been learning. They must-perforce admire much of all the moral and intellectual novelties to which they have been introduced. On the other hand, it is to be feared that nothing can shake many of the prepossessions, favourable to their own ideas and adverse to ours, which have gained strength from father to son through many centuries. They will learn much from us, and may even acquire new faculties, for all that, as a race they will retain their individuality. Their Association, named the *Sarva Janik Sabha*, may be hypercritical, but is certainly original.

Native Authors.

"In authorship the educated Natives are prolific even in English, and in the Vernacular the mass of current literature is known to few Europeans, save those who, like Garcin de Tassy, make it their special study. Native authors have produced some works of original merit, but not so many as might have been expected.

Progress of physical science among Natives.

"Respecting physical science, they are already apt in verifying its teachings by experiment. Whether they will become discoverers cannot be predicted, for as yet our State Education, though now improving fast, has been quite deficient in all branches of this science, except the medical where it has always been excellent. Nor can any forecast be hazarded as to whether they will be inventors, for as yet their natural ingenuity has been but little developed by mechanical instruction. But the constant spectacle of wonder-working mechanism, under British management, must stimulate their thoughts.

New religious sects due to English Education.

"The new religious sects which have arisen or are arising — the Brahmos of the east and north of India, the similar communities in the west — are essentially original, notwithstanding that they owe their origin to the new education. There is a philosophic mysticism, a transcendentalism, about them which, so far from being derived from the Western teaching given them, is positively opposed to it. They gather all they can from European instructors in Christianity, and then apply the instruction after a manner of their own.

English Education will not impair the originality of the Natives.

"Taking all these considerations together, we may trust that the English or Western Education will not impair the originality of the educated, nor lessen the chance of their self development. It would be sad if these men were confined to springs of thought belonging not to themselves but to their masters; in that case their mental growth would be sickly and stunted. We can never desire that they should be intellectually prostrate before us in servile imitation. But there is no probability of this happening; on the contrary, while abandoning some things of their own, and adopting others from us, they are likely to cherish the essence of nearly all that is indigenous. Already this development of theirs is moving in what must be called Asiatic lines—as the lines are not exactly European—and will probably diverge still more in an Oriental direction. So far from lessening this chance for them, our instruction has been the main factor in producing it. The education has furnished them mentally with wings; and though fledgelings as yet, they are essaying flight, and none can now foresee how high they will soar. Without it, no such possibility has been opened out for them. For they had lost all power of self-improvement when British rule dawned upon their horizon. By reason of the invasions from without, the disturbances from within, the disruption of ancient systems, the submergence of learning by floods of violence, they had long lost all means of recovering themselves.

Female education in need of benevolent effort.

"Female education offers the greatest field now open to benevolent effort; in no other respect socially is there so much which needs doing, and which might practically be done. Doubtless some great result will ere long be attained, and that will affect mightily the coming generation. It is not likely that the Western education will at all extinguish the originality of mind which Indian women often have, notwithstanding the repressive influences of centuries. The flashes of ability and the sparks of character which have emanated from them—despite disadvantages which to European women would seem incredible—afford indications of what they may become hereafter, when their minds shall be freed.

Indian Vernacular literature encouraged.

"As to whether the superior education generally ought to be in English or in the Indian Vernaculars—it may be said that while English is, and must be, the medium of imparting much of the best and highest education—the various vernaculars, eighteen in number, will probably continue as at present to be the media for instructing the masses. The cultivation of the vernaculars does certainly strengthen originality among the Natives. Despite their thirst for Western literature, the educated classes in common with the rest of their countrymen, venerate their own languages, whether classical or spoken. As the old vernacular literature is both scanty and obsolete, the necessity of providing food for the mind of the rising generation is evoking, and will yet further evoke, the original talent of native authors. The Government has responded to the popular sentiment by promoting the culture of the vernaculars to a degree unknown even among the best of the preceding Native Governments. Indeed, the successful vigour with which this is done by the British in India, is a fact probably unique in the history of conquering races.

What effect has English education on existing religions.

"The *third* question is stated thus: is the Western education subverting the several existing religions, and if so, is Christianity advancing sufficiently to take their place? How far is the system of caste shaken?

Christianity has not affected Muhammadanism; but the educated classes of Hindus adopt Theism, and Christianity is rapidly advancing among the masses, but not among the educated classes.

"The Western education has not affected the Muhammadan faith. It has subverted the Hindu faith, or the Brahmanical religion, among the educated classes of Hindus, but not among the masses. The educated people on abandoning what may be termed the religion of mediæval Hinduism, do not become irreligious, but revert to the primitive Hindu faith, or else adopt some form of Theism. Christianity is not advancing sufficiently to take the place of the heathen religions whenever they are renounced. It is growing, however, absolutely fast, though it still covers but a small part of the ground, relatively to the vastness of the population. But the number of the Native Christians has increased at the rate of fifty per cent. in every decade for the last thirty years, or one generation, and with the existing Missionary agencies, some considerable ratio of increase will probably be maintained. Whether any decided expansion shall occur, must depend upon the efforts of the Christian Churches. It may occur largely if the Missionary zeal and the resources of the Churches shall increase. Meanwhile, the results, as compared with the agency employed, are quite satisfactory to all concerned. Christianity has made no rapid way among the educated classes by reason of their education. Some of them become Christians, some also among the humbler classes; the proportion of high-caste and humble-caste men among the Native Christians probably does not differ from the proportion of the same castes in the population generally. On the other hand, the Missions may, if their means be adequate, effect decisive progress among the aboriginal races and others who are outside caste, numbering in all 27 millions. The conduct of the Native Christian Communities, now reckoning nearly half a million of souls, is good, and worthy of the faith they profess. With judicious guidance and encouragement from Europeans, there is every chance of a Native Christian Church being organised with native clergy and deacons, sustained by the congregations. Such a Church may have liberty to grow in an Indian or Asiatic manner suitable to the circumstances of the East.

Caste is shaken among educated classes, but not among the masses.

"Respecting caste, it is shaken somewhat among the educated classes, and inroads in various directions have been made into its well-guarded pale. Many tendencies of the age, too, militate against its prevalence. Nevertheless, it is as yet quite unshaken among the masses, and it possesses social as well as religious force.

Are educated Natives discontented?

"The *fourth* question is in this wise: are the educated Natives likely to become discontented with their existing status, socially and politically, and to ask for privileges which the British Government can hardly consent to grant?

Discontent of educated Natives in British Territories as distinguished from Native States.

"In the Native States, which comprise statistically one-fifth of our empire, and should be estimated morally at a higher proportion, the educated Natives are not at all likely to become discontented with their status socially and politically. On the contrary they are there finding already, and will find still more as time rolls on, a scope and a sphere for their ambition and their energies. But in the British territories they are now feeling this discontent, and may perhaps feel it in an increasing degree. It has sprung up within twenty years and has grown somewhat during the last decade. British rule being what it is, the presence of Europeans in all, or almost all, the important posts is absolutely essential, and must necessarily bar a career of the best sort for the educated Natives, who, seeing this, must sooner or later become dissatisfied. This disadvantage under our Government is being, and may yet further be, mitigated, but cannot be wholly avoided. Nor does this fact, *per se*, prove any superiority on behalf of the Native States over British rule. For it is the British paramount power that enables the Native States to be what they are; without the ægis of England, they would relapse into the barbarism whereby education is stamped out under the iron heel of violence, and careers are closed to all save the stalwart.

Discontent of educated Natives owing to exclusion from European society in India.

"Socially the educated Natives probably are discontented at not being admitted more than they are to European society in India; but they will doubtless secure this admission, more and more, as they become qualified for it. On the other hand, Europeans have been in a still stricter degree debarred from Native society. But as the dominion of caste recedes, and as Native ladies become educated, there may possibly be a social union between Europeans and Indians such as no previous era has witnessed.

Demand by educated Natives for improved status and emoluments.

"The educated Natives will ask for much that the Government can concede, such as improved status and emoluments in the public service, besides opportunities of influential usefulness by serving in honorary capacities for the welfare of the community as gentlemen serve in England. The progress, which the Government has secured for them in these directions within the last generation, is an earnest of similar benefits to come. It is to be hoped that they will entreat the Government to give a more practical turn to several branches of the higher education, and to impart scientific instruction more largely and efficiently than heretofore, so that they may acquire the knowledge necessary for carving out new careers.

Importance of educating non-official Natives to feel public spirit.

"Our object should be to educate the character as well as the intellect, teaching the non-official Natives to feel public spirit, and the official Natives to bear responsibility. Hitherto we have succeeded most in training Natives to rise to high posts in the Judicial Service. Our ambition should be, however, to train them for the executive posts, demanding the sterner qualities on which Englishmen justly pride themselves. Most of these posts must needs continue to be held by Europeans; it would be dangerous to place such duties in the hands of Natives. Still there are many posts of a responsible character, which Natives might occupy, if only they were endowed with the more robust qualities. It should be the aim of the Government to endow them with such qualities, by means of education direct and indirect.

Natives will desire representative institutions.

"They will also ask for some privileges which the British Government cannot concede in full, inasmuch as they will express a desire for representative institutions in the English sense of the term. They seldom formulate such requests very specifically, for although they themselves understand the meaning of 'representation,' they remember that the vast majority of their countrymen do not. They perhaps would like an Oligarchical Council to be formed from among themselves by some State procedure, or else that the power of electing should rest with the educated only, who form but a very small minority of the people; but they have never, probably, thought out such schemes. They certainly wish to have the power of the purse, which power would dominate the internal administration, while they are quite content to leave to the Government the duty of external defence.

"Now the Government, believing that the elective franchise had a good moral effect upon those who are reasonably qualified to exercise it, has already entrusted, subject to an ultimate control by the State, the municipal administration of the capital cities of Calcutta and Bombay to corporations elected by the rate-payers, and has extended, or is likely to extend, the principle to the largest municipalities in the interior of the country. Further, the Government seems disposed to entrust some share of power respecting local and provincial finances to elected representatives; but here it cannot relinquish its controlling authority. The native members of the Legislative Councils are at present appointed by the Governor-General. Possibly they might be elected, if only any constituency for such a purpose could be devised; it would indeed be difficult to devise such. At all events, however, the Government could not allow them to have anything approaching a majority or equality in the Council. That source of power it must retain in its own hands.

Elective franchise already allowed in municipalities of Indian Capital Cities may be extended even for Legislative Councils.

"Some observers may hold that if high education tends to political discontent, the Government should prudently refrain from imparting it. But such a view could not be maintained in the nineteenth century. Surely it is our bounden duty to give to the Natives the benefit of all that we know ourselves. If we admit that there are cases in which plain dictates of duty must be followed and reliance placed on Providence for the result, then here is an example of the strongest kind. Politically we are so secure that we can afford to be generous in imparting knowledge, even though, in some respects, disaffection were to spring up in consequence; but in fact true loyalty and contentment in other and more important respects will thereby be produced or confirmed. At all events this is an occasion for putting into practice the maxim, 'Be just, and fear not.'" *

High education should not be abandoned owing to political discontent.

In another of his works on India the same eminent statesman, Sir Richard Temple, makes the following observations in regard to the effects of English education in India:—

"The educated class is drawn from the several sections of society which have been already mentioned. The education of this class is for the most part derived from the national instruction introduced by the British Government. There are, indeed, some educated men, whose instruction has been obtained purely from indigenous sources, independently of aid from their foreign rulers, has been kept strictly within the ancient grooves, has been conducted in rustic cloisters, monastic establishments, or the shade of sacred groves, and is directed chiefly to religious objects. These men, though still numerous, must be decreasing gradually throughout the country. Men of business are still to be seen, who have been educated only in the old style, and whose practical talent and acuteness have not been developed by modern instruction. They are, however, becoming more and more rare, and will soon pass away without successors of the same type, for their sons are all educated in the new style. Thus, the only educated class that need now be observed consists of men brought up under British supervision, for whose mental and moral condition the British Government is responsible. These men follow other professions, besides the public service, such as the bar and other legal pursuits, private practice in medicine, commerce and banking, Civil Engineering, mechanical industries and the like. But many of them enter the public service in its various grades from the humblest to the highest. They thus become members of one homogeneous profession, which equals, probably in magnitude and certainly in importance, all the other professions taken together. It is this dominant and leading profession which most readily admits of specific observation, and in which the results of the national education can be best tested.

The educated classes in India brought up under British supervision follow various professions.

"That the natural intelligence of the educated men is sharpened by rigid method, and that their mental stamina are strengthened by discipline, will be surely assumed. That their minds are open to the reception of new influences, expanded into a large growth, drawn towards wider spheres, raised into higher regions of thought, and fixed in grooves of stricter accuracy, may be reasonably expected. That they are steadier officers, cleverer men of business, abler administrators, better workers and apter learners, from being thus educated, is easily conceivable. The harder questions relate to the effect of the education on the conduct of these men, on their trustworthiness and integrity, their loyalty to the British Sovereign, their gratitude to their foreign instructors, their attachment to Western civilization, and their sentiments in regard to the existing order of things. The answers to such questions, if thoughtfully rendered, will be found quite as satisfactory as could be fairly anticipated.

Intelligence, integrity, and loyalty of educated Natives satisfactory on the whole.

"In the first place, a due and proper standard of rectitude among the Native officials of the Upper and Middle Grades has been obtained. Such men are now regarded as gentlemen in the best sense of the term, that is, as men of honour. Their character is not impugned, their rectitude is trusted by public opinion, corruption on their part is not suspected. In this description, as in all general descriptions, there

Rectitude of Native officials of the Upper and Middle Grades traceable to influences of English education.

* *Men and Events of my Time in India.* By Sir Richard Temple, *Bart.*, G.C.S.I., C.I.E., D.C.L., pp. 494–504.

must be reservations and exceptions, but such is the tone pervading these bright parts of the picture. Of the numerous changes which have of late years arisen in India, this particular change is among the most noteworthy. For many authorities, still surviving, can remember the time when such Native officials were not regarded as men of honour, when their uprightness and integrity were constantly impugned, when their conduct was frequently distrusted, when imputations of corruption were bruited abroad. One cause of the moral improvement, now perceptible, springs from the better organization of the public service. The men are, by the concession of adequate salaries, placed in a position superior to temptation. They are embodied in regular departments, which have grades ascending like the steps of a ladder, offer scope for ambition and open out prospects of promotion to be seen through the vista of coming years. Thus they are so situated that they shall have everything to gain by fidelity, and everything to lose by misconduct. Another and a higher cause of the improvement is traceable to the influences of Western education, the moral teaching imparted by European culture, the practical ideas of duty thereby infused, the virtuous principles thus instilled, the companionship of English instructors and the association with them in the daily life at school or college. It is to these two main causes that the Natives themselves attribute the amelioration which is happily seen.

Misconduct of educated Natives of lower grade.

"In the lower grades of educated Natives, however, misconduct is still common, and, but too frequent even in the middle grades. Still it will be found to exist almost exactly in proportion as the advantages, moral and material, allowed to these grades fall short of those beneficiently granted to the upper grades.

Advance and improvement of the legal profession among Natives.

"Together with the public service, the profession of the law has advanced *paripassu*. This great profession is for the most part a product of British rule, and is divided, as in England, into two branches, like those of Barristers and Solicitors. Admission to the Native Bar is regulated by tests and examinations, which ensure the profession of high qualifications by those who apply for it. An almost equal improvement is visible in the Native Barristers as in the Native Judges, and a standard of professional etiquette prevails, formed on the English model. The standard was much lower in former days, when advocates but too often connived at or participated in malpractices and even in frauds. Any remnants of these evils, which may still linger in the profession, will ere long be eliminated. As now constituted, the Native Bar is fast becoming a power in the country; its independence of demeanour, freedom of speech and sympathy with the people, are raising it daily in public estimation. Its conduct fosters the salutary belief, which is settling down in the minds of the Natives, to the effect that the British system of civil justice constitutes a real palladium of their liberties and privileges. Its loyalty will be true towards the Government which is its foster-father. Improvements, similar in kind but much less in degree, are taking place in the profession of the Law, which branch includes Attorneys, Solicitors, and all other legal practitioners. These Native practitioners formerly had a very evil repute for stimulating wrongful litigation, promoting fraud and poisoning the moral atmosphere around the precincts of the Courts. Of this mischief, much has been removed by the improvements in the Native Bench and Bar, and by the operation of public opinion; but much, unfortunately, remains.

Expansion of the Post-Office an instance of the mental and moral progress of the Natives.

"As an instance of the mental and moral progress of the Natives, the expansion of the Post-Office may be mentioned. The Government has adopted the principle of all the reforms which have proved so successful in England. By amalgamating under one administration the imperial and local Post-Offices in the various provinces of the empire, postal facilities have been placed within reach of every large village throughout the country. The increase of letter-writing and of postal business has been remarkable. Within the last fifteen years, the number of Post-Offices has increased from 2,200 to 5,500, the length of postal lines from 48,000 to 58,000 miles. The amount of receipts in cash from the public has risen from £401,000 to £660,000 per annum, exclusive of official postage; and the number of covers delivered from 59 millions to 131 millions annually. A portion of the increase in correspondence is due to the Government and its servants, also to the non-Official Europeans; but the mass of it is due to the Natives, under the influences of education.

Importance of the effects of English Education among the Natives with reference to the British Rule being a Foreign Government.

"The foreign Government in India must be prepared to realize the fact that the hearts of educated Natives are deeply stirred by the Western education, and that an active process of mental fermentation is setting in. These men are from their youth instructed in matters concerning the rise, progress, zenith, decline and fall of empires; the relative dimensions, population and resources of the several great Powers of the world; the constitution, legislature and privileges of States monarchical, constitutional, despotic, republican; the territorial arrangements consequent on modern warfare; the various nationalities of which kingdoms are composed. It follows that they will observe current events whether peaceful or warlike with an appreciative insight, and will speculate on the effect which such events may produce on the fortunes of England. A competent knowledge of the recent history of their own country will show them how often the commerce and the fortunes of India herself have been affected by events occurring in distant regions. For example, by the civil contest in America, by the wars in the Crimea, China and Turkey. An extensive Vernacular Press is growing up, which offers brief summaries of the political affairs and occurrences of the world. The English Press in India presents daily, full extracts of all the best news and opinions of the press in England, together with comments suited to the currents of public thought in India, and is read by the English-speaking Natives with as much attention as by the English themselves. Native trading firms have their head-quarters or their branches in the United Kingdom or on the Continent of Europe, and will ere long have them even on the other side of the Atlantic. For these reasons, England must, whenever she engages in affairs of world-wide importance, be prepared to reckon with a mass of Native opinion instructed to a degree heretofore unknown. The lights are various in which Natives regard alternatives of peace or war. If in any conjuncture it should appear that, on a fair consideration of her own interest and honour, England ought to fight and yet holds back from fighting, then the Natives would be quicker than ever to draw the gravest inferences. If after anxious suspense, the English standard, ever to Eastern eyes the symbol of victory in the end, is unfurled, it is followed by the hopes and prayers of the majority of the Natives. More than once of late, when the inevitable moment seemed near, utterances of loyalty and god-speed arose from the organs of Native opinion in all parts of the country. Still, as a rule, the Natives raise their voice decidedly for peace, not at any price, but at some sacrifice, rather than for incurring the risks of war, with the certainty of special taxation in the present and the probability of the public burdens being augmented in the future. They certainly are adverse to an aggressive, and favorable to a pacific policy.

Aspirations of educated Natives for self-government and political power.

"The educated Natives are also moved by aspirations for self-government, for political power, and even for representative institutions, the concession of which does not at present fall within the range of practical politics. Such ideas have been mooted in former times, but have never been so fully defined, nor so openly declared, as they are at present. The reports of Parliamentary debates, concerning India and the East proximately or remotely, are scanned by the Natives with anxious interest. The utterances of English orators or statesmen vindicating the character, conduct, status and interests, fiscal and financial, of the people of India, are welcomed by the Natives with a gratitude as deeply felt as it is fervently expressed. The name of any member of either house of Parliament, who by word or deed espouses the cause of the Natives, soon becomes a household word among them. Although benevolence is admitted by them to be a prominent feature of British rule, still after having been for so many centuries the sport of despots, the prey of conquerors and the victims of revolution, they have an ineradicable fear that the English nation may prove to be not wholly an exception to the rule of selfishness and harshness which has so often prevailed with foreign and absolute rulers. They seem always glad to be reassured by responsible and influential persons regarding the kind and good intentions of England, and such assurances cannot be too often repeated. There has been of late a tendency with some Natives to rely for sympathy and support specially on particular parties or sections of parties among the politicians of England. But this tendency is deprecated by the best organs of Native opinion, on the manifest grounds that the Natives are the very last persons who should encourage the notion of India ever becoming a battle-field for party-strife in England, and that all political parties ought to be urged to co-operate for the object of benefiting their Indian fellow-subjects.

Part taken by the Natives in local self-government.

"Thoughtful Englishmen may remember that self-government among the Natives is one of the goals to which many of the administrative arrangements of India are tending. Natives are appointed members of the Legislative Council of the Governor-General for all India, of and the local legislatures of Madras, Bombay and Bengal. They are Honorary Magistrates in the interior of the districts; they serve as jurymen, as assessors to aid the Judges in criminal trials, as members of arbitration tribunals and of conciliation courts in civil causes. They take part in the administration of the funds raised by the road cess and other local cesses, in the management of schools, hospitals, dispensaries and other institutions. They furnish the great majority of the Commissioners in the Municipalities, which exist in the capital cities, and are scattered over the length and breadth of the empire. They thus become the responsible trustees, administrators or controllers of the rates for levying the local taxes. In Calcutta and Bombay specially, and in some other central places, they enjoy as rate-payers the electoral franchise for the election of members of the Municipal Corporations. The system whereby, in so many parts of the country, village communities are constituted, or village headmen are vested with petty powers in police matters, is the very embodiment of the principle of self-government in the rural districts.

Native Associations for representing wishes or grievances to the Government.

"Native Associations are formed for the avowed purpose of representing their views, wishes or grievances to the authorities Several of these bodies, such as the 'British Indian Association' of Calcutta, the 'Amjuman' of Lahore, the 'Sarva Janik Sabha' of Bombay, can make their voice heard, not only in India, but even as far as England. Such societies are regarded by the Government, as affording the means for legitimately and temperately representing or vindicating the opinions of the Natives. Their memorials and addresses, though sometimes transgressing the limits of propriety, are, as a rule, fully reasoned and moderately expressed.

Personal kindness a loveable characteristic of the Natives.

"Personal kindness and charity have always been among the most loveable characteristics of the Natives. These sentiments have induced men to support not only their female relatives and their aged or helpless connexions, which is well, but also their able-bodied and idle male relatives, which is not well. Many a rising man is weighted in his career by listless persons who hang about him, instead of shifting for themselves. This tendency, which has been heretofore excessive, is diminished by the influences of education. Virtuous and most commendable sacrifices are often made by Natives, who stint and pinch themselves in order to afford a good education to their young relations. The youths thus educated generally recompense their friends for these sacrifices, by evincing a resolute spirit of self-help.

Charitable benevolence of the Natives.

"The sympathy of Natives, also spreads beyond the circle of relations, friends or dependents. It extends to the miserable wherever met with, to the living community at large, and to the needs of posterity yet unborn. The charity of Natives is, indeed, often misdirected, but is generously profuse. Every Native, who makes a fortune, immediately gives away a part of it to works of public usefulness or charity. Every city in the empire is improved, endowed or beautified, by the benevolence or munificence of individual citizens. In prosperous years the sums, thus nobly dispensed, are enormous; and even in the worst years, the source of this bounty never runs dry. In the interior of the country, works of public utility, on the roadsides and in many other spots, attest the spirit of philanthropy which prevails among wealthy Natives. In many provinces the Government wisely publishes a list of the works of public utility constructed by individuals; these publications redound to the credit of those concerned.

Recognition by Government of charitable endowments by Natives.

"The Government always delights to honour the Natives who thus devote a portion of their substance to the welfare of their countrymen. Patents of Native nobility are discriminately granted to meritorious persons. Successive Viceroys of India have studied the unwritten rules which govern the constitution of Native nobility, and have granted Native titles judiciously and considerately to persons recommended for their good deeds by the several Local Governments; a moral force of some potency is thus exercised. British decorations of the 'Star of India' are bestowed upon Natives; knighthood not unfrequently has been granted to them, and in rare instances a Baronetcy has been conferred: the new Order of 'The Indian Empire' has many Native members: The effect of these measures upon Native sentiments is to encourage loyalty and public spirit.

Education in India defective in respect of physical and natural sciences.

"Sound as the national education may have been in respect of history, literature, practical morality and political philosophy, it has been, and still is, defective in respect of the physical and natural sciences. Yet, scientific study, the value of which is now recognized in all countries, has in India a special importance. It qualifies the Native youth for professions in which they have hitherto had but little place. It diverts from the elder professions, namely, the law and the public service, some of the students who would otherwise overcrowd those professions. It displays before the Natives fresh ranges of thought and new modes of thinking. It tends to correct some of the faults which are admitted to exist in the Native mind, while educing and developing many of its best qualities and faculties. In two of the most immediately important among the scientific professions, namely, medicine and civil engineering, the Government has done for the Natives everything that could reasonably be expected. Hundreds of Native engineers, architects, physicians and surgeons have been, and are being, sent forth into the world. In respect of other sciences also, something has been effected, but the greater part of what is needed still remains to be accomplished. The important step which the Universities in India have recently taken, by granting degrees in science will essentially affect the standards and aims of the national education.

Muhammadanism not shaken by English Education, but educated Hindus become sceptics.

"Reflection upon all these things will lead thoughtful persons to inquire—'What are the religious tendencies of the Natives?' In the first place, the faith of the Muhammadans does not seem to have received any shock from Western education and civilization. Nor has the Hindu faith been shaken with the mass of the Hindus, who follow the ancestral idolatry with the same simplicity as of yore. The faith is dubious with Hindus who have some tincture of education, and who probably regard their national religion with half doubt and half belief, much as the Greeks and Romans regarded the gods of their fathers. But among highly educated Hindus, the faith is dead or dying. With some it has been shattered well-nigh to the very base, while from the minds of others it has already vanished like the fabric of a vision.

Educated Natives discard Hindu Mythology without becoming Atheists or Materialists. The Brahmos, or Theists, likely to expand.

"Many educated Natives have long cast away the last shreds of their belief in the mythology, the sacred story and the future world of Hinduism. But they do not become irreligious men, nor atheists, nor materialists. They believe in the immortality of the human soul, in the existence of abstract principles of right and wrong, in the omnipresence of a Supreme Being, who is the creator and preserver of all things, who is absolutely just and good, to whom all men are accountable after death for deeds done in this life. They adopt a morality resembling that inculcated by Christianity, and sometimes expressly derived from the Christian Scriptures. Occasionally they listen to sermons preached from texts in the New Testament. By some they would be called Deists or Theists. They call themselves *Brahmos* or *Adhi-Brahmos*, members of the *Brahmo-Samaj* or of the *Prarthana-Samaj*, and quite recently they have sometimes adopted the name of Theosophists. The spread of the *Brahmo* sect, first in Bengal and then in other provinces, is one of the phenomena of the time in India. Keshab Chandar Sen, a man of high qualities and gifts, is among the best known of its leaders. Its nomenclature signifies 'The believers in the One Creator of all men and things.' Its growth is understood to have been recently checked by some internal dissensions, but is probably destined to expand further. Its marriage rites have formed a subject of special legislation. The divine origin of certain castes is discarded by it, and caste is regarded merely as a human institution, like the social grades of civilized countries.

Educated Hindus investigate the ethics and primeval religion of their pre-historic ancestors, contained in the *Vedas*.

"But, with all these changes, it is remarkable that educated Hindus are bestowing more attention than has ever yet been bestowed in modern times on the ideas, ethics, and primeval religion which prevailed in the pre-historic period of their ancestry. They cast a reverential retrospect towards the dawn of Hindu time, when the day-spring of genius visited their race, before mists arose to obscure the truth, or fables were invented to mar the simplicity of natural religion, or errors grew up to mislead the conscience and to sully the intuitive perceptions of right and wrong. The writings thus studied are comprehended in the name of Vedic Literature, which name has now, to educated Hindus, the same sacred significance that 'Scripture' has to Christians. Thus, as a result of Western education, the later and more elaborate writings of the Hindu priesthood are disregarded, while the earliest literature of Hinduism is studied with renewed veneration.

The unsatisfied condition of educated Natives liable to find vent in disloyalty of Native newspapers.

"There is frequent discussion in India regarding the operation of these influences, moral and mental, upon the loyalty of the educated Natives towards the British Government and nation. Fears have been expressed lest unsatisfied ambition, want of suitable employment, and habits of criticizing unreservedly the existing order of things, should gradually undermine the loyalty and gratitude which these men ought to feel. Such fears, though not fully justified by the facts, have been aroused by divers symptoms deserving attention, and have been aggravated by the conduct of at least a portion of the Native Vernacular Press, consisting of newspapers published in the various languages of the country. Of the Native newspapers published in the English Language, as yet few in number, some are distinguished by loyalty and good sense as well as by cultivated ability, and are creditable products of the new education; as, for instance, the *Hindu Patriot* of Calcutta. Others are notable for a latitude of criticism which, though extreme, does not transgress the limits ordinarily claimed for journalism."*

Later on, in discussing the same subject, he makes the following observations:—

Danger of discontent among educated Natives for want of suitable employment.

"There is danger of discontent being engendered in the minds of educated Natives if adequate and suitable employment does not offer itself to them in various directions. As all the arts and sciences which have helped to make England what she is, are offered for, even pressed on, the acceptance of the Natives, it must be expected that those who do accept these advantages will be animated by hopes and stirred by emotions, to which they were previously strangers. They will evince an increasing jealousy of any monopoly of advantage in any respect being maintained in favour of Europeans. They are already raising a cry, louder and louder, the purport of which is 'India for the Indians.' They discern, or think they discern, undue liberality in some, and unwise parsimony in other branches of the public expenditure, in reference to Native interests.

* *India in* 1880. By Sir Richard Temple, *Bart.*, G.C.S.I., C.I.E., D.C.L., pp. 121–32.

Government unable to provide careers for all educated Natives; but there is room for practical professions, such as Civil Engineering, Scientific Agriculture, &c.

"The fulfilment of these ideas is only in part within the power of the Government, being dependent on the progress of affairs in the country at large. In so far as its means permit, the Government is bound to attend, indeed, has attended, and is constantly attending, to this subject, which is so essential to the mental and moral progress of the Natives. The most effective means at the present time consists of advancement in the Public Service. It is towards this that the ambition of educated Natives is, too exclusively directed, and regarding this that complaints are too frequently preferred. No well-wisher of the Natives considers that the Government has yet succeeded in doing nearly all that needs to be done in this cardinal respect. Still, every candid observer must admit that the story of the measures taken by the Government for gradually improving the pay, promotion, privileges, pensions and official prospects of the Natives in all grades of its service, forms one of the brightest pages in the annals of British India. Natives have been raised to some of the highest spheres in the country, such as the Legislative Councils and the High Courts of Judicature. The regulations have been improved, and the facilities enlarged, for their admission to that Covenanted Civil Service, which is mainly filled by the highest class of European officials in the country. The improvement of the emoluments of Native officials must be gradual, and the fact of its being so gradual may diminish the sense of its real magnitude. Some of it is due to the necessity which the Government felt of remunerating its servants more highly when the money value of everything rose, and when the remuneration of all sorts of private employment increased. There remains much, however, that is attributable to the well-meaning desire of the Government to do its duty by the educated Natives. The Government is not able to provide careers for all the Natives who become educated. There is danger lest the youths from schools and colleges should resort too exclusively to overstocked professions, such as the Law and Public Service. Graduates of a University may be seen applying for lowly-paid appointments, wandering from office to office, or struggling for the practice of a petty practitioner. It were better far that such men should make careers for themselves not only in trade, business, or private employ, but also in other professions which spring from the applied sciences. Such professions are in India fast expanding in connexion with civil engineering, mechanical industries, medicine, practical chemistry, botany, arboriculture, horticulture, scientific agriculture, geology, art principles applied to manufactures, and the like. But for the successful pursuit of careers, in some of these departments, more educational facilities are needed than any which as yet exist. It is in the gradual supplying of such needs that the Government can best co-operate with the enterprise of individuals or with the collective efforts of the Native community.

Good done by benevolent Societies, such as the National Indian Association in England.

"All tendencies towards good are assisted by the private Societies, such as the National Indian Association, which shew the Natives that they are cared for, and thought of, by benevolent people, ladies and gentlemen, in England. Lasting friendships are formed in English circles by Natives who visit England, and these men communicate to their countrymen happy impressions regarding society in the centres of English life. It is especially desirable that Natives should be encouraged to finish their education in England, and for such an education the ancient Universities afford the best and highest opportunities. It was for this purpose that the Indian Institute has been recently established at Oxford through the kindly solicitude and the unremitting exertions of Professor Monier Williams.

English education tends to heartfelt allegiance of the Natives towards the English nation.

"Of late certain symptoms of disloyalty manifested by some limited sections of certain educated classes, have caused reflections to be made against the effects of education upon Native loyalty. But that disloyalty was traceable to social and traditional circumstances quite apart from educational causes, and was checked, not fostered or encouraged, by education. There doubtless will be found disloyal individuals among the educated classes, as there are among all classes in a country subjected to foreign rule. Nevertheless, a well-founded assurance may be entertained that those Natives who have learned to think through the medium of the language, and are imbued with the literature and the philosophy of England, will bear towards the English nation that heartfelt allegiance which men may feel without at all relinquishing their own nationality. The Natives certainly are anxious to be considered loyal. Nothing wounds and irritates more than imputations of disloyalty; and nothing gratifies them more than a frank and cordial acknowledgment of their loyalty.

Promising prospect of the mental and moral progress of the Natives.

"This view of the mental and moral progress of the Natives shews many gleams of sunshine, as it were, in the national prospect. The peasantry retain the moral robustness for which they were famed in troublous times, have new virtues which are developed in an era of peace and security, and are, at least passively, loyal to the British Government. Some of the humblest classes are beginning to feel sentiments of independence unknown before. The trading and banking classes, though not always free from the charge of grasping usuriousness, are full of enterprising energy, and are actively loyal to the political system under which they thrive. Though, in some provinces, the upper classes are unavoidably depressed, grieving over the decay of their territorial influence and fretting under the restraints of a civilized administration, they yet form in other provinces a wealthy and lettered class, whose interests are founded absolutely on the stability of British rule. The moral effects of the national education are clearly perceptible. The educated classes are happily advancing in rectitude and integrity, and are striving for self-improvement. Though the field for their employment has not yet been widened so much as they may have expected, and though the existing professions are becoming over-crowded, still their status and prospects have been greatly improved, and new professions are arising in many directions. Many of these men have divorced themselves from the superstitions by which their race had been so long enthralled; and though their religious state is far from that which is to be desired, still they have not inclined towards infidelity or materialism. They are indeed moved by political aspirations, but still feel thankful for the many improvements already effected in their condition, and hopeful of future benefits. Though intelligently alive to the import of passing events among the great powers of the world, they yet trust in the might of England to preserve her empire. Though there are occasionally symptoms of discontent and disloyalty here and there, still there is every assurance that the great majority of the men whose minds are formed by the language, literature, and science of England, will remain faithful to the British Sovereign and nation."*

Sir Richard Temple's views as to moral instruction.

There is one more passage from Sir Richard Temple's work which may with advantage be quoted here, as giving expression to his views on the much-vexed question of moral instruction in English colleges and schools. His opinions are expressed in the following words:—

"Above and beyond all the sorts of instruction, which have yet been indicated, is the instruction in ethics, or the science of human duty. While the Native youths are taught human duty, comprising the relations of man to man, they are necessarily taught something of their duty towards God, although the teachers are precluded from adverting to religion. One of the effects of good teaching in history or literature must be to inculcate, always incidentally and often directly, much of the general duty of man. Thus, happily, much is effected in this most important direction. The instruction might, however, be better systematized than it now is; sometimes text-books are prescribed for it, and sometimes not; in some institutions it is as an obligatory subject, in others it is optional. These variations in practice are found only in the Government institutions; the subject is obligatory in the Missionary institutions. It were well if the several Universities should see fit to take up the matter in an uniform manner. Their action determines the teaching in the colleges and high schools, the example of these superior institutions is sure to be followed by the middle class institutions, and ultimately by the primary schools, until a system of national instruction in ethics is established. The Natives will certainly be the willing subjects of such teaching. Many of them, while thankfully acknowledging all that has been done in this direction, do yet lament that a more systematic effort is not made to unfold before the minds of the young those eternal principles of right and wrong, which serve as beacons for the due conduct of life, and which ought especially to be included in an educational system that unavoidably excludes religious teaching."†

Sir John Strachey's Lectures on India before the University of Cambridge in 1884.

It is now important to quote the views of another eminent statesman, Sir John Strachey, who after having held various important offices in the Indian Civil Service rose to the membership of the Supreme Council of India and became Lieutenant-Governor of the North-Western Provinces, and again Finance Minister of India, from which office he retired and was appointed a member of the Council of the Secretary of State for India. In 1884, on the invitation of the Historical Board, he gave a course of lectures on India before the University of Cambridge, and from that work the following quotations are borrowed:—

His estimate of the expenditure on education in 1885-86, and the extent of literacy in India.

"In 1885-86 the total expenditure of the State on education was £2,420,000, of which about £1,290,000 was contributed from imperial, provincial, and municipal funds, and the rest was derived from fees, endowments, and other sources. In every province a considerable sum is raised by rates on the land for local purposes, and in almost every instance a share of it is devoted to education. Some, but not many, of the towns contribute liberally from municipal resources. It will be understood from the account which I have given, that although progress has been made during the last thirty years, a very small proportion of the population of India has received even elementary instruction. The information given by the census of 1881 is incomplete; but out of about 116,500,000 males, for whom returns are furnished, only 10,500,000, including those under instruction, were recorded as being able to read and write, and 106,000,000 as illiterate. At the same time, out of a

* *India in 1880.* By Sir Richard Temple, *Bart.*, G.C.S.I., C.I.E., D.C.L., pp. 133–37.

† *Ib.*, pp. 154, 155.

female population of 111,800,000, no less than 111,400,000, were illiterate; only about 400,000 could read and write, or were being instructed.

Number of highly educated Natives extremely small; graduates being below 5,000 during 20 years ending with 1883.

"If we turn to higher education, I am afraid that the numerical results are not much better. The number of Natives of India who can be called highly educated, according to a European standard, is extremely small. I have already mentioned that in ten years only 365 graduates passed the M.A. Examination in all the Indian Universities. Sir Henry Maine tells us that in the twenty years ending with 1883 not more than 5,000 M.A. and B.A. Degrees were given altogether. 'I will assume,' he says 'that every man who has taken a Bachelor of Arts Degree is sufficiently educated to have valuable ideas on politics; and for the purpose of including all who, in any sense, can be called educated men, I will multiply the total by five. That gives 25,000 Indian gentlemen of an education and age to take an interest, or a part, in politics. But the population of all India—of British India and of the dependent States—is rather over 250,000,000 souls. Thus the proportion of the educated element to the rest of the population is as 25,000—which is probably much above the mark—is to 250,000,000, which is below the true total.'*

Sir Henry Maine's estimate of 25,000 well educated Indian gentlemen is much above the actual number.

"I have no doubt that Sir Henry Maine was right in his belief that 25,000 is much above the actual number of Indian gentlemen who can be called educated, and among the 123,000,000, of Hindu and Muhammadan women in India, there are probably not 500 to whom that term could properly be applied. Sir M. E. Grant Duff has estimated that in Madras—probably, as he says, the most educated and Anglicised part of India—the proportion of graduates to the population is thirty-eight to a million. It will be understood that I am now speaking of those only who have received an English education. The number of Brahmans who are more or less learned in ancient Sanskrit literature is considerable, although there are not many great scholars; but, with rare exceptions, they have no acquaintance with any branches of Western knowlege.

English-knowing Natives fit for ordinary clerical work numerous, and some rise to higher ranks in the services and professions.

"The Natives of India who have learned enough English for ordinary clerical work, and for many employments in which a knowledge of our language is required, are numerous. They hold almost all the minor appointments in the Government offices; they are a highly useful, efficient and unassuming class, but they have, as a rule, no pretensions to be called educated men. The great majority of the young men at our higher schools and colleges go there because it is a certain way of getting on in life. It is a very successful way, both for themselves and their employers, but they are as a rule content with the minimum amount of English education which enables them to perform their work. A certain number of them continue their studies and are more ambitious. They often obtain employment in the Executive Service, and in some provinces they supply a large proportion of the Native Judges. I have already said how high a character these officers have earned for their attainments and integrity. Some of them have reached, as judges of the High Courts, the highest judicial rank which anyone, whether he be Native or English, can attain in India. Many practice at the Bar with as great success as Englishmen; others are professors and masters in the colleges and schools, or are in charge of the numerous hospitals and dispensaries. Out of 1,696 graduates of the Calcutta University, between 1871 and 1882, 1,155 are known to have entered the Public Service, or to have become lawyers, or doctors, or civil engineers. In 1882, out of 971 graduates at Madras, 796 were holding remunerative employment in various professions. In 1887, in Bengal, among 623 native officers holding the principal posts in the Executive and Judicial Services, 542 had either passed the Entrance or First Arts Examination, or had taken degrees. In Madras and Bombay more than 50 per cent. of posts of the same class were filled by men with similar qualifications. In Northern India English education has made less progress and the proportion is smaller.

Enormous mass of Indian ignorance is a great danger to the British Rule.

"The facts that I have given show how small an impression has hitherto been made on the enormous mass of Indian ignorance. Among all the dangers to which our dominion in India is exposed, this ignorance is the greatest. So long as it continues, no one can say what unreasoning panic may not spread like wildfire through the country, or what may be its consequences. No one now doubts that the mutiny of the Bengal Army, whatever it may subsequently have become, had its real and sole origin in a panic of this kind, in the general and honest belief of the soldiers that our Government intended to destroy their caste, which involved everything that was most valuable to them in this world and in the next. It is hardly less true now than it was in 1857, that we are liable at all times

* *The Reign of Queen Victoria.—'India,'* vol. I., p. 526. It is shown by the Report of the Public Service Commission, 1886-87, Appendix M, that the actual number of M.A. and B.A. Degrees given in the twenty years ending with 1883, was 4,526, or less than Sir Henry Maine's estimate.

to such dangers as this. Ignorance is their foundation, and there is no safeguard against them except the increased knowledge of the people. We must not undervalue, however, the progress that has been made; nor, when we remember how short a time has elapsed since our own country, under far less difficult circumstances, began to recognise the necessity of elementary education, ought we hastily to blame the Government in India for not having accomplished more. Four years before the Queen's accession no public money was granted in England for elementary schools. In 1885 the grants by Parliament and from rates had risen to £4,000,000. In the whole of India, excepting the North-Western Provinces, when the Government was transferred to the Crown, there were only some 2,000 Government and aided elementary schools, with less than 200,000 scholars. When we consider that in 1886 there were more than 70,000 of these schools, and more than 2,500,000 scholars, we must admit that things are better than they were.

Sufficient encouragement not yet given to science and industrial arts. Native Surgeons and Native Judges best results of English education.

"I have spoken of the controversy of 1835, which under Lord Macaulay's influence, ended with the decision that English literature and science must be the basis of higher education in India. Very little science was taught in those days even in England, and still less in India; and it was the study, not of English science, but of English classical literature, that was practically encouraged. As Sir Henry Maine has often pointed out, the strict and sober tests of truth which modern science can alone supply, were exactly the element that was wanting in the education of Orientals, and especially of Hindus. 'Native thought and literature' as he says, 'is elaborately inaccurate; it is supremely and deliberately careless of all precision in magnitude, number, and time.' 'The Indian intellect stood in need, beyond everything else, of stricter criteria of truth. It required a treatment to harden and brace it, and scientific teaching was exactly the tonic which its infirmities called for.' Even at the present time, although matters in this respect are somewhat better than they were, science holds a very secondary place in the Indian Universities; the progress of literary education has been considerable, but no sufficient encouragement has been given to the study of science and its application to the industrial arts. We may find an illustration of the truth of Sir Henry Maine's remarks in the remarkable success achieved by Natives of India whose professions have a more or less scientific, exact, and practical basis. This is especially the case with those who have devoted themselves to the study and practice of European Surgery and medicine, and to that of Anglo-Indian Law, the character of which is eminently accurate and precise. The best results of English education in India are seen in the Native Surgeons and in the Native Judges; the worst results are seen in those whose education has been merely literary. Natives have not been successful as Engineers. As a rule, they dislike physical exertions that can be avoided. A good Engineer must be himself a master of mechanical arts, always ready in case of necessity to make use of his own hands, and this is usually not agreeable to the educated Native, especially in Bengal and Southern India.

Study of English rightly encouraged for Western knowledge, but Oriental literature unduly ignored.

"No one will doubt that it was right to encourage the study of the English language. For a Native of India there is plainly no other key by which he can unlock the stores of Western knowledge, and without it he cannot hope to take any prominent part in the higher branches of the public administration. Whether it was right, apart from the higher claims of science, to assign to the classical literature of England the almost exclusive position which it has held in the Indian educational system, and almost to ignore the existence of the literature of the East, is another matter. I think that the views of Warren Hastings and Sir William Jones were nearer the truth than those of Lord Macaulay. If they could have taken part in the discussions of 1835, they would have said that while the study of English classical literature would be most valuable to Hindus and Muhammadans, it was not less desirable that they should study the literature of their own people and kinsmen. A Hindu would often reap more advantage from the *Mahabharata* and the plays of *Kalidasa*, than from *Paradise Lost* and *Hamlet*, and *Othello*. A Muhammadan youth would appreciate the noble poetry of Arabia more than that of England, the *Sháhnámeh* would be more profitable to him than translations of *Homer*, and he would probably learn more wisdom from *Omar Khayyam* than from European philosophers. No one will now sympathise with the contempt with which Lord Macaulay treated the ancient literature of the East. Whatever may be its value, in comparison with our own, it abounds in works which rank among the remarkable achievements of human genius."*

Further passages quoted from Sir John Strachey's work on India.

Sir John Strachey's work on India contains some more passages which deserve consideration in considering the effects of English education in India, and they are so important that they are quoted here :—

* *India.* By Sir John Strachey, G.C.S.I., pp. 186–92.

English-speaking Bengalis support the zemindars, to the detriment of the ryots, and misrepresent motives of the Government in newspapers.

"English education has unfortunately hardly begun to penetrate to the cultivating classes in Bengal, and until lately, they have found few champions among their own countrymen. The sympathies and the support of that section of the English-speaking Bengalis, which has been able, or desirous, to make its voice heard, have been for the most part enlisted on the side of the zemindars, and to the detriment of the ryots. The time will come when this will cease to be true—already, I hope, things are better than they were—but hitherto the ryots have had mainly to look to their English rulers for the defence of their interests. Every measure of political importance is discussed by the organs of the educated classes in Bengal. Not long ago there could be no doubt as to what would be the reception of any measure that seemed to threaten the interests of the zemindars. No taxation affecting them could be imposed without the cry being raised that the solemn pledges of the Permanent Settlement were being violated by an unscrupulous Government. Every measure which has had for its object the more just distribution of the public burdens has, as a rule, met with nothing but opposition. We were told that to reduce the salt-tax was folly; let it be increased if the Government wants more money. The abolition of customs duties on cotton goods was solely prompted by the desire to benefit the manufacturers of Manchester, and by the base political purpose of gaining votes in Lancashire. Educated Bengalis were not to be deceived by the profession that we desired to give to the people of India cheaper salt and cheaper clothing.

Absence of sympathy among English-speaking Natives of Bengal towards their less instructed countrymen.

"Thus, through the influence of the Associations and the newspapers of Bengalis taught in our schools and colleges, English education in Bengal has given frequent aid to the perpetuation of past injustice and to the prevention of reform. I am happy to believe that this is now less true than it was; for I am told that the ryots of Bengal are beginning to find earnest and capable friends among their own people. Still, I fear, there can be no doubt that, for a long time to come, it will be only to their English rulers that they will be able to look for protection and justice. I said in a former lecture,* that an unfortunate result of our system of higher education in India has been the want of sympathy which many of the English-speaking Natives, especially in Bengal, show towards the poorer and less instructed classes of their countrymen. The shallow and imperfect education, which is all that they usually obtain, is derived entirely from English sources. They learn enough of English habits of thought to enable them to imitate us, sometimes in things that are good, but sometimes in things that it would have been better to avoid. They learn almost nothing about their own country, and seem frequently to care little for their own people. I need hardly say that there are very many honourable exceptions to be made to general statements of this kind. Some of the most benevolent and most enlightened men that I have known in India have been educated Natives of Bengal.

Native English newspapers of Bengal often disloyal, foolish, and shamefully scurrilous.

"It is a serious misfortune that discredit should so often be thrown on the results of English education by the foolish talk and disloyal writing of a section of the English-speaking Bengalis. Many of them are gifted with a very remarkable faculty of fluent speech and writing. I have heard of no men in any country enamoured of their own verbosity in so extraordinary a degree. Although to our taste, their English is often ridiculously magniloquent, few foreigners master so completely the difficulties of our language. Their newspapers, published in English, are sometimes, so far as their style is concerned, extremely well written, but, with honourable exceptions, they are disloyal, foolish, and sometimes shamefully scurrilous.

Uncivilized customs and horrid and cruel practices still prevalent in India, and not reprobated by educated Hindus.

"There is no province in India without customs which we think must be repugnant to all civilised men, but which are almost universally respected because they are believed to have been Divinely ordained, or to have come down from a remote antiquity. There is hardly a province in which horrid and cruel practices would not instantly spring into vigorous life if our watchfulness were relaxed. The prohibition of the burning of widows was, and is still, utterly disapproved by all but a small minority of Hindus. I do not believe that the majority even of the most highly educated classes approve it. I gave you, in a previous lecture, an account of the wholesale murder of female children, which has gone on for centuries, a custom against which no Hindu, however enlightened, raises his voice, and which, with all our efforts, we have not yet succeeded in eradicating. But for us, even in the provinces where education has made its greatest progress, *Kali* would still claim her human victims. Not many years ago, in a time of drought, near a railway station twenty-five miles from Calcutta, a human head was found before her idol, decked with flowers; and in another temple in Bengal a boy was savagely murdered and offered to the goddess.† While this book was passing through the Press, a ghastly story came from the Central Provinces of the sacrifice of a young man to the local gods,

* Lecture VII., p. 196.

† *Imperial Gazetteer of India*, Art. 'India.'

in obedience to a widely prevalent belief and ancient practice that this is a sure means of obtaining a plentiful harvest. Horrors such as these receive no general condemnation in India, nor does the determination of our Government that they shall be suppressed gain for us any approval even from the educated classes.

Child marriages among Hindus lead to early degraded widowhood, yet educated Hindus do not reprobate the custom, or help Government to suppress it.

"There are in India many questions of another order which it is far more difficult to solve, because we cannot deal with them by the strong hand of the law. I will mention one only as an illustration, the custom of child-marriage. It would be difficult to imagine anything more abominable than its frequent consequences, by which multitudes of girls of ten or twelve, or less, are given over to outrage, or are doomed to lives of miserable and degraded widowhood. Some of the most holy Brahmans of Bengal make a living by being husbands. A child of twelve is given, as perhaps the fortieth or fiftieth wife of some old man; sometimes two sisters are given to the same man, and sometimes to one who has not long to live. Though it may be certain that the girl must soon be a widow, even this is considered preferable to allowing her to remain unmarried. Every one has heard of the wretched fate which widowhood in India involves.* What could be more valuable and interesting than to learn the opinions and receive the advice of highly educated Natives of India on such subjects as these, and to know that they were striving, by the example of their own lives, to teach their less-instructed countrymen to abondon these abominations? What greater encouragement could be given to those who desire to see educated Natives admitted to a larger share in the administration than the certainty that they were anxious to help us towards ampler knowledge of the wants and failings of the people, and to make us better able to deal with problems that now seem too hard to solve? You would be much mistaken if you supposed that in regard to any of these great social questions the Government has ever received advice or assistance from the much-talking section of the Bengalis. I must class with them a considerable number of the Maratha Brahmans of Bombay, and of the English-speaking Hindus of Madras. You might search the proceedings of their Societies, you might examine the files of their newspapers, and the reports of their speeches at their public Meetings, and you would not find one word of reprobation of the atrocious practices which, under the cover of immemorial custom, are followed throughout India, or one word of a desire to help our Government to suppress them.

Educated Natives, whilst asking for political franchisement, have no real desire for reform in social and religious usages.

"It is not difficult to understand why these terrible questions are avoided. Some of these Native gentlemen are silent, because they dare not, by speaking of them, bring themselves into collision with the cherished beliefs and prejudices of their countrymen; others, and I have no doubt the majority, are silent because, in regard to these matters, they are at heart as intensely conservative as the mass of the population, and have no desire for changes in social and religious usages which have come down from a venerable antiquity. It is much safer to talk about 'political enfranchisement,' and it is easy, in this way, to obtain the applause of Englishmen who know nothing of the facts and the difficulties with which the true friends of Indian progress have to deal, but who have an undoubting faith that so-called popular institutions are good for all men, under all circumstances.

The Indian National Congress, whilst putting forth political aspirations, excludes all social reforms, and is chiefly composed of men of small education, who do not represent the people of India.

"I have now before me the report of a great political gathering, the 'so-called Indian National Congress, This, we are informed by the report, was a political body met together to represent to our rulers our political aspirations,' and we are expressly told 'that it had nothing to do with social questions. The object aimed at was the political enfranchisement of the country,' by the introduction of representative institutions. I do not propose to refer at any length to the declared objects of these political agitators who have lately been making themselves more and more prominent in India. If you look at their voluminous speeches and proceedings, you will not discern the smallest recognition of the terrible problems of which I have given some illustrations, but you will find no lack of sedition and hatred of the British Government, thinly veiled under frequent and fulsome expressions of devotion and loyalty. I am far from believing that the majority of these gentlemen are really disloyal. They are, for the most part, well-meaning men of small education, but with a good knowledge of our language, who have learnt to pour forth the commonplaces of English politics, and who listen with delight to their own eloquence, which they half believe to be inspired by feelings akin to those which they have read about in Burke and Macaulay. They easily obtain a hearing from sentimental philanthropists, and from those Englishmen who see nothing good in any political institution, except those of their own peculiar type, and assume that certain abstract principles are always applicable to the Government of all sorts and conditions of men. Many Englishmen who read these harangues, honestly believe that they are listening to the genuine expression of the just expectations of the great 'People of India,' which has no existence, but the non-existence of which, I am afraid, they are not likely to learn.

* *Modern Hinduism.* By W. J. Wilkins, p. 347.

Legitimate claims of the Natives of India to hold important public offices should be satisfied.

"Men of a very different stamp, who well deserve the respect of their countrymen and of their rulers, have not unfrequently been drawn into apparent and partial argreement with these political agitators, by the legitimate feeling that Natives of India do not obtain their just share in the public administration. This is a feeling which has my sympathy. There are political aspirations which loyal Natives may with complete propriety express, and which it is right that we should endeavour to satisfy ; but let us take care that we satisfy them wisely. I said, in a previous lecture* that I should return to the subject of the admission of the Natives of India to the more important public offices. I showed that the greater part of the civil administration is already in their hands, that the Native Civil Service performs its duties, as a whole, with high efficiency, but at the same time I stated my opinion that much remains to be done in throwing open to Natives posts now reserved for Englishmen.

Appointments should be given to the Natives of India of approved merit and ability, but the same tests of selection which apply to Englishmen are not applicable to the Natives of India.

"Subject to certain conditions, the true principles on which we ought to treat this question of the wider employment of Natives in posts of importance was laid down in the Act of Parliament passed in 1870 to which I have already referred, but I cannot think that it has hitherto been properly applied. That principle is that almost all offices in India shall be open to Natives, but to those only 'of proved merit and ability.' In the case of Englishmen, whether in India or at home, it is safe to say that appointments to offices in the higher branches of the public service shall ordinarily be filled by those who, in competitive examinations in their boyhood, are successful in satisfying certain literary and other tests ; but to think of applying such a system to the Natives of India is nothing less than absurd. Not the least important part of the competitive examination of the young Englishman was passed for him by his forefathers, who, as we have a right to assume, have transmitted to him not only their physical courage, but the powers of independent judgment, the decision of character, the habits of thought, and generally those qualities that are necessary for the Government of men and the discharge of the various duties of civilised life, and which have given us our empire. The stock-in-trade with which Englishmen start in life is not that of Bengalis ; but I must not say this of Englishmen only, for it is equally true of the nobler races of India, although their time has not come for competitive examinations.

The greater executive powers of Government cannot be entrusted to Natives, owing to the exigencies of the British dominion.

"Few would go further than I would go in opening the public service in India to Natives 'of proved merit and ability,' but it is well to avoid 'political hypocrisy.' 'Is there,' Lord Salisbury asked, 'any man who will have the hardihood to tell me, that it is within the range of possibility, that a man in India should be appointed Lieutenant-Governor of a province, or Chief Commissioner, or Commander-in-Chief of the Army, or Viceroy, without any regard whatever to his race ?' Some will answer even this question in the affirmative. There will always be people ready to accept with composure any political folly, provided that it involves some triumph of sentiment over sense, and some appearance of national humiliation. When we say that we cannot always. in our government of India, ignore differences of race, this is only another way of saying that the English in India, are a handful of foreigners governing 250 millions of people. I have said that we are not foreigners in India in the sense in which we are foreigners in Paris, and that the people of one Indian province are often as much foreigners to the people of another province, as we are ourselves ; still, we are foreigners, and although I suppose that no foreign Government was ever accepted with less repugnance than that with which the British Government is accepted in India, the fact remains that there never was a country, and never will be, in which the Government of foreigners is really popular. It will be the beginning of the end of our empire when we forget this elementary fact, and entrust the greater executive powers to the hands of Natives, on the assumption that they will always be faithful and strong supporters of our Government. In this there is nothing offensive or disparaging to the Natives of India. It simply means that we are foreigners, and that, not only in our own interests, but because it is our highest duty towards India itself, we intend to maintain our dominion. We cannot foresee the time in which the cessation of our rule would not be the signal for universal anarchy and ruin, and it is clear that the only hope for India is the long continuance of the benevolent but strong government of Englishmen. Let us give to the Natives the largest possible share in the administration. In some branches of the service there is almost no limit to the share of public employment which they may properly receive. This is especially true of the judicial service, for which Natives have shown themselves eminently qualified, and in which the higher offices are equal in importance and dignity, and emolument, to almost any of the great offices of the State. I would grudge them no such offices. But let there be no hypocrisy about our intention to keep in the hands of our own people those executive posts—and there are not very many of them—on which and on our political and military power, our actual hold of the country depends. Our Governors of

* Lecture X., pp. 261, 262.

Provinces, the chief officers of our army, our magistrates of districts and their principal executive subordinates, ought to be Englishmen, under all circumstances that we can now foresee.

Legitimate claims of Englishmen, and the feelings of the Muhammadans, in connection with the administration of India, should not be ignored.

"It is not only in regard to the employment in India of our own countrymen that we ought never to forget differences of race. It is quite, as essential to remember them in connection with the employment of Natives. I have, in these lectures, repeatedly insisted on the fact that there is really no such country as India; that such terms, as 'People of India' and 'Natives of India,' are meaningless, in the sense in which they are frequently used; that no countries and no people in Europe differ from each other so profoundly as countries and peoples differ in India; that it would be as reasonable to suppose that English, French, Spaniards, Greeks and Germans will ultimately become one nation, as to suppose such a thing of Bengalis, Sikhs, Marathas, Rajputs and Pathans. No good administration or permanent political security is possible unless facts of this kind are remembered. It ought never to be forgotten that you can never assume that, because a man is a 'Native of India,' he has any natural claim, different in kind from that of an Englishman, to be employed in the public service in every part of India. Often, indeed, you may go much further. I used no terms of exaggeration when I said that a Native of Calcutta is more of a foreigner to the hardy races on the frontiers of Northern India than an Englishman can be. To suppose that the manlier races of India could ever be governed through feeble and effeminate foreigners of another Indian country, however intellectually acute those foreigners may be—that Sikhs and Pathans, for instance, should submit to be ruled by Bengalis—is to suppose an absurdity. The Muhammadan gentleman who remembers the position which his ancestors once held, accepts with natural regret, but with no humiliation, the government of Englishmen. Although he may not love them, he admits that they must be respected. But the thought of being subject to the orders of a Bengali fills him with indignation and contempt. The educated Bengali, although his reasons might be very different, would feel equal disgust at the thought of having his affairs administered by Sikhs and by Pathans. To allow Natives 'of proved merit and ability' to take a larger part in the administration of their own country is right and politic; to affirm that they have any similar claims in countries where they are foreigners is foolish.

Natives of Northern India unwilling to be governed by Bengali district officers.

"I remember a conversation which I once had with a Native of Northern India, a man of great sagacity, whose position, wealth, and influence made him one of the most important personages in his province. Discussions were going on respecting the propriety of making it easier for Natives of India to enter the Covenanted Civil Service, and on the suggestion that, with that object, competitive examinations should be held in India as well as in England. I asked him what he thought about this proposal, and his first answer, given in a manner which showed that he took little interest in the subject, was to the effect that he supposed it was a good one. 'I am afraid,' I said, 'that for a long time to come there would be no candidates from this part of India; it is only in Bengal that young men could be found who would have any chance of success in such an examination as that required. The result would be that you would some day have a Bengali as your chief district officer.' I shall not forget the scorn with which he drew himself up and replied to me, 'And does any one think that we, the men of this country, would stand that? Do you suppose that you could govern us with Bengalis? Never!'

Speeches of Sir Syed Ahmed Khan on the political nostrums of the so-called National Congresses.

"This book was almost ready for the press when the reports reached England of some remarkable speeches made by Sir Syed Ahmad Khan at two great meetings of Muhammadans in Northern India. I referred in a previous lecture to Sir Syed Ahmad Khan, and to the work to which his life has been devoted.* I mention these speeches because they illustrate, with greater authority than that of any Englishman, the practical importance of the fact on which I have repeatedly insisted, with which I began these lectures, and with which I wish to end them, that the most essential of all things to be learnt about India is that India is a continent filled with the most diverse elements. The special aim of Sir Syed Ahmad Khan was to protest on behalf of his Muhammadan fellow-countrymen against the notion that they—'men of the blood of those who made not only Arabia but Asia and Europe to tremble, who for seven hundred years in India had imperial sway'—could be treated as belonging to the same nation as Bengalis, and to express his contempt for the political nostrums which the so-called 'National Congresses' propose to apply throughout India. If these were adopted, the result, he says, would be that 'there would be no part of the country in which we should see at the tables of justice and authority any faces except those of Bengalis. I am delighted to see the Bengalis making progress, but what would be the result on the public administration? Do you think that the Rajput and the fiery Pathan would remain in peace under Bengalis.' These are illustrations of the opinions of a man universally honoured, who is entitled to speak on behalf of all that is best and most enlightened among the Muhammadans of

* Lecture VII., pp. 175–79.

Northern India. 'It is better,' says Machiavelli, 'to follow the real truth of things than an imaginary view of them. For many republics and princedoms have been imagined which were never seen or known to exist in reality.' If intelligent people in England would make themselves acquainted with 'the real truth of things,' they would appreciate at their true value the utterances of those agitators who, with some success in this country, pose as the representatives of an imaginary Indian Nation, 'never seen or known to exist in reality.'

The *Pax Britannica* the greatest blessing to India.

"I must now bring these lectures to a close. I have endeavoured to give to you some general idea of what India is, and of the results which she has obtained from the establishment of our power. No reasonable man can doubt the answer that we must give to the question whether the 200 millions of our Indian subjects have benefited by our Government. The first great and obvious fact, overshadowing all other facts in significance, is this, that in place of a condition of society given up, as it was immediately before our time, to anarchy and to the liability to every conceivable form of violence and oppression, you have now absolute peace. Let not this unspeakable blessing of the *Pax Britannica* be forgotten. There are not many European countries where protection to life and property is so complete. Excepting England and her colonies, and the United States of America, there is hardly a country in the world where there is so little needless interference, on the part of the Government, with personal liberty, or such freedom in the public expression of opinion in matters of politics and religion. Except when sometimes for a moment the fanaticism and intolerance of rival sects of Muhammadans and Hindus burst into violent conflict, and show what would instantly follow if the stong hand of our Government were withdrawn, unbroken tranquillity prevails. Justice is administered under laws of unequalled excellence and simplicity. There is no country possessing a civilised administration where taxation is so light or commerce is more free. Mr. J. S. Mill, declared his belief that the British Government in India was 'not only one of the purest in intention, but one of the most beneficent in act, ever known among mankind.' I do not doubt that this is still truer now. Whether all this makes our Government really popular is another question.

Lord Lawrence's saying as to prosperity of India under British Rule.

"When Lord Lawrence was Viceroy, in 1867, many of the most experienced officers in India were invited to give their opinion whether our Government was more generally popular than that in the Native States. As might have been anticipated, nearly all the answers were affirmative; but I shall only refer to that of Lord Lawrence himself. His conclusion was given in these words. 'The masses of the people are incontestably more prosperous, and—*sua si bona norint*—far more happy in British territory than they are under Native rulers.' No Englishman knew India better than Lord Lawrence. That the people had been made more prosperous by our administration was, in his opinion, beyond controversy, but when it came to the question of their happiness and of our popularity, well—yes; at any rate they *ought* to be more happy. The proviso is significant, '*sua si bona norint.*'

Enlightened Government not likely to be popular in India.

"The truth is that, in a country in the condition of India, the more actively enlightened our Government becomes, the less likely it is to be popular. Our Government is highly respected; the confidence of the people in our justice is unlimited. That accomplished traveller, Baron von Hübner, says in his excellent book, '*Through the British Empire*,' that if proof were needed to show how deeply rooted among the people is this trust in English justice, he would quote the fact that throughout India the Native prefers, in Civil and still more in Criminal Cases, to go before an English Judge. 'I think,' he says, 'it would be impossible to render a more flattering testimony to British rule.' The duty was once imposed upon me of transferring a number of villages which had long been included in a British district to one of the best-governed of the Native States. I shall not forget the loud and universal protests of the people against the cruel injustice with which they considered they were being treated. Every one who has had experience of similar cases tells the same story. Nevertheless, I cannot say that our Government is loved; it is too good for that.

Imperfect sympathy between the Natives and their English rulers.

"The sympathies between the people and their English rulers can hardly be anything but imperfect. The system of caste and the differences in all our habits make social intimacy difficult. The stories that are sometimes told about the frequent insolence and brutality of Englishmen are false, but it cannot be denied that the ordinary Englishman is too rough and vigorous and straightforward to be a very agreeable person to the majority of the Natives of India. These, however, are not reasons which seriously effect the popularity of our Government. I repeat that, because it is good it can hardly be popular.

Conservatism of the Indian population prevents appreciation of enlightened improvements.

"I never heard of a great measure of improvement that was popular in India, even among the classes that have received the largest share of education. The people are intensely conservative and intensely ignorant, wedded, to an extent difficult for Europeans to understand, to every ancient custom, and between their customs and religion no line of distinction can be drawn. We often deceive ourselves in regard to the changes that are taking place. We believe that our Western knowledge, our railways, and our telegraphs must be breaking up the whole fabric of Hinduism, but these things have touched in reality only the merest fringe of the ideas and beliefs of the population of India. The vast masses of the people remain in a different world from ours. They hate everything new, and they especially hate almost everything that we look upon as progress.

India should be governed on sound principles of political prudence, regardless of the prejudices and superstitions of the people.

"It would thus be an error to suppose that the British Government is administered in a manner that altogether commends itself to the majority of the Indian population. This we cannot help. Considerations of political prudence compel us to tolerate much that we should wish to alter, but, subject to this condition our duty is plain. It is to use the power which we possess for no other purpose than to govern India on the principles which our superior knowledge tells us are right, although they may often be unpopular, and may offend the prejudices and superstitions of the people. I will quote to you Sir James Stephen's summmary of the principles which would be really popular in India, and of those which we enforce, and with it I may fitly close these lectures :—

Sir James Stephen's view of the political situation of the British administration in India, quoted.

"The English in India are the representatives of a belligerent civilisation. The phrase is epigramatic, but it is strictly true. The English in India are the representatives of peace compelled by force. The Muhammadans would like to tyranise over Hindus in particular, and in general to propose to every one the alternative between the Koran, the tribute, and the sword. The Hindus would like to rule—over Hindus at least—according to the principles of the Brahmanical religion. They would like to be able to condemn to social infamy every one, who, being born a Hindu, did not observe their rites. They would like to see *suttee* practised, to prevent the re-marriage of widows who were not burnt, to do away with the laws which prevent a change of religion from producing civil disabilties, to prevent a low-caste man from trying or even testifying against a Brahman; and Muhammadans, and Hindus, and Sikhs would all alike wish to settle their old accounts and see who is master. The belligerent civilisation of which I spoke consists in the suppression by force of all these pretensions, and in compelling by force all sorts and conditions of men in British India to tolerate each other. Should the British Government abdicate its functions, it would soon turn order into chaos. No country in the world is more orderly, more quiet, or more peaceful than British India as it is; but if the vigour of the Government should ever be relaxed, if it should lose its essential unity of purpose, and fall into hands either weak or unfaithful, chaos would come again like a flood." *

Sir Alfred Lyall's views on the influence of Europe on India and her prospects.

These quotations may be continued with the opinions of a philosophic thinker and Indian Statesman, Sir Alfred Lyall, who, after having filled many important political offices, was for some years Lieutenant-Governor of the North-Western Provinces and Oudh, from which high office he retired not long ago to become a member of the Council of the Secretary of State for India. The following passages are taken from his *Asiatic Studies* :—

Analogy between the Roman conquests in Europe and the English Empire in India, and the religious future of the people.

"If we may draw a broad analogy between the social and political changes worked upon the Western world by the Roman conquests, and that which is being worked upon the great continent of India by English dominion, then it may not be rash to prolong the parallel, and to speculate on the probability of some consequences following, in the latter case, not unlike those which ensued in the former. We are changing the whole atmosphere in which fantastic superstitions grow and flourish. We may expect that these old forms of supernaturalism will suddenly thaw and subside without any outward stroke upon them, and without long premonitory sypmtoms of internal dissolution; like icebergs that have at last floated into a warmer sea, which topple over at the invisible melting of their submarine base. At this moment Hindusim still overshadows the land; the intricate jungle of creeds and worships appears thick and strong as ever; yet one may conjecture that its roots are being effectually cut away. Uncertainty and insecurity prolonged what ignorance and stagnation had produced; but the old order has now changed, giving place to new. The last stand made against the new system of peace and law by the warlike and unruly elements of the population was from 1846 to 1858. Never perhaps in all the history of India has more decisive fighting been compressed into twelve years; the English scattered two formidable disciplined armies, the Sikh army and their own sepoys, and dissolved two incipient kingdoms that might have hardened into nationalities: they prevailed over the momentary fanaticism of the Hindu and the enthusiasm of the Muhammadan; they employed these two forces, to each counteract and repress the other; they disarmed India, and closed for the present its military era. We have now established reasonable personal security and free communications; we are giving to the Indians leisure and education, the scientific method and the critical spirit; we are opening to them the flood-gates behind which

* *India.* By Sir John Strachey, G.C.S.I.; pp. 351–68.

Western knowledge is piled in far greater volume than the stream of Grecian philosophy which the Romans distributed over their empire, when they made the source accessible and its outflow easy. It is not easy to conceive any more interesting subject for historical speculation than the probable effect upon India, and consequently upon the civilization of all Asia, of the English dominion, for though it would be most presumptuous to attempt any kind of prediction as to the nature or bent of India's religious future, yet we may look forward to a wide and rapid transformation in two or three generations, if England's rule only be as durable as it has every appearance of being. It seems possible that the old Gods of Hinduism will die in these new elements of intellectual light and air, as quickly as a netful of fish lifted up out of the water; that the alteration in the religious needs of such an intellectual people as the Hindus, which will have been caused by a change in their circumstances, will make it impossible for them to find in their new world a place for their ancient deities. Their primitive forms will fade and disappear silently, as witchcraft vanished from Europe, and as all such delusions become gradually extinguished. In the movement itself there is nothing new, but in India it promises to go on with speed and intensity unprecedented; for she has been taken in tow by Europe, where we are now going forward with steam at high pressure; and herein seems to lie the peculiar interest, perhaps the danger, of the Indian situation. At certain epochs the progressive nations of the world find it necessary to readjust the intellectual equilibrium, that is to say, to establish afresh a certain harmony between what they believe and what they know. One of the earliest symptoms that knowledge and belief are falling out of balance is perceptible in what has been called the *malaise religieux*, which was seen in the Roman Empire before Christianity cured it, and which one may fancy to be visible in India already. It may possibly be that very 'spirit of unrest,' which Dr. W. W. Hunter has detected among Indian Muhammadans, as it is probably at the bottom of the Muhammadan revival, which Mr. W. G. Palgrave believes to be taking place throughout all Islam. It seems certainly indicated by numerous sectarian advances among the Hindus towards a more spiritual kind of creed; toward mystical interpretations, at least, of substantial polytheism, and toward such an abstract dogma as that upon which is founded the profession of the Brahmo Somâj. In the north it is fermenting among various sects, and in the south it appears in the demand recently made to Government by educated Hindus for the reform of their religious endowments, a demand that will carry us and them far if we attempt to comply with it; for any serious attempt to purify the abuses of polytheism and to establish the external worship upon a decent and rational system, can hardly fail to let in views and principles that may disintegrate the very foundations of the whole edifice.

Solid universal peace established by the British Rule in India will accelerate Indian progress and intellectual expansion; but the cement of some binding idea necessary.

"Thus there may be grounds for anticipating that a solid universal peace and the impetus given by Europe must together cause such rapid intellectual expansion that India will now be carried swiftly through phases which have occupied long stages in the lifetime of all other nations. The Hindu now makes in two days a journey that occupied a month ten years ago, because the English have laid down their railways before the Indians had invented the paved road; and his mental development may advance by similar overleaping of intermediate improvements. And whereas hitherto new religious ideas have constantly sprung up in India, and have as constantly withered or been dissipated for want of protection and undisturbed culture, any such ideas that may hereafter arise will be fostered and may spread uninterruptedly, if they have the principle of persistent growth. Some great movement is likely to come about in India, if only the peace lasts; but what may be the complexion of that movement, and whither its gravitation, is a question which time only can answer. Orderly Christian rule has given to Islam in India an opportunity for becoming regenerate, and for reuniting its strength, which it owes entirely to us. We have restored its communications by sea and by land; we have already felt some of the consequences of pulling down the barriers which Ranjit Singh and his Sikhs set upon our North-western Frontier, between the Muhammadans of India and the rest of Western Asia. Muhammadanism may yet occupy a larger space in the history of Indian rationalism; but it must make haste, or the country may drift beyond it. Some may think that Christianity will, a second time in the world's history, step into the vacancy created by a great territorial empire, and occupy the tracts laid open by the upheaval of a whole continent to a new intellectual and moral level. But the state of thought in Western Europe hardly encourages conjecture that India will receive from that quarter any such decisive impulse as that which overturned the decaying paganism of Greece and Rome just at the time when the *Pax Romana* had at last brought local beliefs into jarring collision one with another, and into contact with the profound spiritualism of Asia. The influence of Europe on India is essentially industrial and scientific; England's business in particular is to construct there some firm political system under which all other social relations may be reared and directed; but here comes in the difficulty of founding and keeping steady any such edifice without the cement of some binding idea. It is in the religious life that Asiatic communities still find the reason of their existence, and the repose of it. When the Indian has gained his intellectual freedom, there remains to be seen what he will do with it; and the solution of this problem is of incalculable importance to our successful management of the empire. The general tendencies of modern thought are towards doubt and negation; the sum total of what we call civilization is to such a society as that in India a dissolving force; it is the pouring of new wines into old skins; the cutting away of anchors instead of hauling them up, so that in the next emergency there are none to throw out. Conquest and civilization together must sweep away the old convictions and prejudices; and unless some great enthusiasm rushes in to fill the vacancy thus created, we may find ourselves called to preside over some sort of spiritual interregnum.

Unwisdom of demolishing old-world fabrics suddenly must be obviated in India.

"Such transitional periods are apt to be troublesome to Governments. In India the English difficulty is that, whatever the religious movement may be, we cannot expect to take part in or guide it, because we are in many ways so far ahead of, or at least, too far removed from, the mass of the people whom we have to manage, that our superiority begets want of sympathy, and in our desire to lead them we lose patience and discrimination. On the other hand, there is already springing up among the Natives of India an advanced party, of those who are easily inoculated with the Voltairean spirit, with contempt for irrational beliefs, and for institutions that seem absurd on the face of them. But all our European experiments in social science have taught us the unwisdom of demolishing old-world fabrics which no one is yet prepared to replace by anything else. Caste, for instance, looks unnecessary and burdensome; it is wildly abused by Europeans,* to whom the Brahmanic rules of behaviour seem unmeaning and unpractical; but these things will tumble quite fast enough without our knocking out their key-stones by premature legislation. It is hardly our interest to bring them down with a crash. We have ourselves to overcome the rather superficial contempt which an European naturally conceives for societies and habits of thought different from those within the range of his own ordinary experience; and also to avoid instilling too much of the destructive spirit into the mind of Young India: remembering that for English and Natives the paramount object is now to preserve social continuity. M. Pierre Lafitte, in his 'Considérations Générales sur l'ensemble de la Civilization Chinoise,' quotes from a book,† in which an English Protestant Missionary describes China as undergoing a succession of moral earthquakes, and congratulates Europe on the total ruin of 'fossil prejudices,' bigotry, and superstition, which these 'terrible convulsions' are causing. Storms and hurricanes, Mr. Mylne, had observed, purify the air. But M. Lafitte remarks that this is to welcome a state of violent agitation ending in complete anarchy; and that to talk of convulsions as the conditions of progress has a dangerous resemblance to revolutionary jargon, though the writer may not mean it. Hurricanes clear the earth as well as the air, and earthquakes are not very discriminating in their operations. It is certain, at any rate, that moral earthquakes and cyclones in the Indian climate will severely test the stability of our rule, and we are by no means concerned to encourage them. M. Lafitte, in the lecture just mentioned, points out the vague notions of progress and civilization upon which people rely who desire to pull down a society which they do not comprehend, or whose real aim is sometimes no more than the exploitation of the East by the West. He protests, for example, against the English raising a jubilee over the re-marriage of Hindu widows, and he thinks we had no business whatever to make war on the old custom by legalising breaches of it. It is possible that M. Lafitte himself may have been verging on the error of judging the East by the West, and may not have recollected that in India very many girls become widows at an age when they would still be in an European nursery. Here is good cause for interference, and there are other cases in which the action of our own law courts, in stereotyping and inforcing, invariably, customs that were naturally very elastic and varying, tended to check the natural modifications according to circumstances, the sloughing off of decayed forms, so that special legislation became necessary. Yet, withal, there is something to be said against our passing any laws to abolish social rules which do not concern us personally, and which do not openly violate morality; and there is everything to be said against being impatient with people who, belonging to a different social formation, are reluctant to give up hastily, the very principles on which their society has been moulded. Such impatience is akin to the injustice with which, as has been often remarked, we are too much accustomed to treat the past, forgetting that written records tell us very little indeed of what really went on, and can still less explain how and why people felt and acted a few centuries ago. This is, indeed, the reason why an opportunity of studying closely the condition and progress of such a country as India is most valuable, because we can there look round at things which we can hardly realise by looking behind us on them. We are turning back, as it were, along the broad path of history, and by seeing with our own eyes the scenes we have often tried to look at through old books, blurred with ignorance and prejudice, we get at more clear notions of, and sympathy with, those bygone

* "Caste is the devil's yoke ... ... Hindu widowhood is Satan's masterpiece. ... ... Jagunnath was invented by devils." See "A Plea for Indian Missions," by Alexander Forbes, 1865; a pamphlet which is not only unfair to Satan, but which betrays a curious tendency toward that very same superstitious polytheism (the belief in a multitude of evil spirits) which the writer is denouncing.

† *La Vie réelle en Chine*, par le Révérend C. Mylne, 1858.

times, when men from whom we are descended—who were of like passions with ourselves, nor inferior in intellect—yet firmly held beliefs which their posterity rejects with contempt, and conscientiously did deeds which we now read of with horror and amazement.

Duty of the English to mount guard over India during the transitional period.

"All that the English need do, is to keep the peace and clear the way. Our vocation just now is to mount guard over India during the transitional period, which may be expected to follow, much as we used to station a company of soldiers to keep order at Jagannâth's festival in the days of the East India Company. Jagannâth himself may be safely left exposed to the rising tide of that intellectual advancement which the people must certainly work out for themselves if they only keep pace and have patience. No doubt this negative attitude, this standing aloof, is an imperfect and not altogether well-secured position, for a political system founded mainly upon considerations of material interests and well-being has been declared by high philosophic authority to be unstable. We have not yet sailed out of the region of religious storms in India; and though spiritual enthusiasm may be gradually subsiding in fervour, yet it may also tend to combine and organise its forces, as polytheism melts down and concentrates. Against such impulses, among men who will still die for a rule of faith, as our forefathers did so often, material considerations must occasionally avail little. But there is, at any rate, one gospel which the English can preach and practise in India, the gospel of high political morality, which, because it is a complete novelty and new light among Asiatic rulers, should for that reason be the characteristic note of our administration; and to maintain it we may risk much misunderstanding of motive. We must even endure temporary loss of that reputation for high-handed consistency, whatever it may be worth, which is to be maintained by upholding a blunder once committed, and by stooping to the untrained public opinion which would applaud it. We cannot undertake in any way the spiritual direction of Hindus; but neither are we prepared to take lessons from them upon questions of public morality. A certain line of conduct may be congenial to the notions of Native Princes or people; but our Governors and chief rulers go to India, not to be taught, but to teach, the duties of rulership, and to instruct the consciences of half-barbarous communities.

Educated Natives should realize that quarrels with the English Government upon administrative details are ruinously premature.

"Finally, we may hope, that all reflecting and far-sighted Natives of that class which we are rapidly training up in large towns to political knowledge and social freedom, will perceive that England's prime function in India is at present this, to superintend the tranquil elevation of the whole moral and intellectual standard. Those who are interested in such a change in the ethics of their country, in broadening the realms of the known and the true, must see, how ruinously premature it is to quarrel with the English Government upon details of administration, or even upon what are called constitutional questions. The peculiar crisis and conjuncture of Indian affairs at the end of the last century brought out one supremely strong Government by the same pressure of circumstances which has struck out the type of all empires. A modern empire means the maintenance of order by the undisputed predominance of one all-powerful member of a federation; and where representative assemblies, in the English sense of the term, are impossible, it is the best machine for collecting public opinion over a wide area among dissociated communities. It is the most efficient instrument of comprehensive reforms in law and Government, and the most powerful engine whereby one confessedly superior race can control and lead other races left without nationality or a working social organization. It breaks up the antipathies, narrowness, and exclusive antagonism which always check the growth of earlier civilizations, and which have hitherto lain like rusty fetters on India. If ever the imperial system was necessary and fitted to a time and country, it is to India as we now see it." *

Sir Monier Williams' views on Government education in India.

To these extracts may be added the views of Sir Monier Williams, the distinguished Professor of Sanskrit at the University of Oxford, who from his position and previous studies, had special advantages for forming an intelligent judgment on the subject of English education in India during his visit to this country not many years ago. His general impressions are thus expressed:—

Educational responsibility of the English in India.

"If our whole educational responsibility is bounded by the instruction of the upper classes of the people in European knowledge, we may, perhaps, take credit to ourselves for a fairly respectable fulfilment of our obligations. But if our mission be to educate as well as instruct, to draw out as well as put in, to form the mind as well as inform it, to teach our pupils how to become their future self-teachers, to develop symmetrically their physical as well as mental, moral, and religious faculties, then I fear we have left undone much that we ought to have done, and acquitted ourselves imperfectly of the duties our position in India imposes upon us. Let me first glance at our so-called higher education.

* *Asiatic Studies.* By Sir Alfred C. Lyall, K.C.B., C.I.E.; pp. 298-306.

"In traversing India from North to South, from East to West, I visited many High Schools, examined many classes, conversed with many young Indians under education at our Colleges, and was brought into contact with a large number who had passed the University matriculation examination, as well as with a few who had taken their degrees, and earned distinction for high proficiency. I certainly met some really well-educated men—like Rao Bahadur Gopal Hari Deshmukh, lately appointed a joint judge—who, by their character and acquirements, were fitted to fill any office or shine in any society. But in plain truth, I was not always favourably impressed with the general results of our higher educational efforts. I came across a few well-informed men, many half-informed men, and a great many ill-informed and ill-formed men—men, I mean, without true strength of character and with ill-balanced minds. Such men may have read a great deal, but if they think at all, think loosely. Many are great talkers. They may be said to suffer from attacks of verbal diarrhœa, and generally talk plausibly, but write inaccurately. They are not given to much sustained exertion. Or if such men act at all, they act as if guided by no settled principles, and as if wholly irresponsible for their spoken and written words. They know nothing of the motive power, restraining force, or comforting efficacy of steadfast faith in any religious system whatever, whether false or true. They neglect their own languages, disregard their own literatures, abjure their own religions, despise their own philosophies, break their own caste-rules, and deride their own time-honoured customs, without becoming good English scholars, honest sceptics, wise thinkers, earnest Christians, or loyal subjects of the British Empire.

Unsatisfactory general results of higher English education.

"Yet it cannot be said that we make higher education consist in the mere imparting of information, and nothing more. We really effect a mighty transformation in the character of our pupils. We teach a Native to believe in himself. We deprecate his not desiring to be better than his fathers. We bid him beware of merging his personality in his caste. We imbue him with an intense consciousness of individual existence. We puff him up with an overweening opinion of his own sufficiency. We inflate him with a sublime sense of his own importance as a distinct unit in the body politic. We reveal to him the meaning of 'I am,' 'I can,' 'I will,' 'I shall,' and 'I know,' without inculcating any lesson of 'I ought,' and 'I ought not,' without implanting any sense of responsibility to, and dependence on, an Eternal, Almighty, and All-wise Being for life, for strength, and for knowledge—without, in short, imparting real self-knowledge, or teaching true self-mastery, or instilling high principles and high motives. Such a system carries with it its own nemesis. After much labour we rulers of India turn out what we call an educated Native. Whereupon he turns round upon us, and, instead of thanking us for the trouble we have taken in his behalf, revenges himself upon us for the injury we have inflicted on his character by applying the imperfect education he has received to the injury of his teachers. The spitefully seditious writing which our Government has lately found it necessary to repress by summary measures is due to this cause.

Tendencies of English education.

"And how have we discharged the debt we owe to the lower classes? Let the truth here also be told with all plainness. In their case we have not yet matured any effective scheme—not even for the proper informing of their minds, much less for the proper forming of their characters ... A good beginning has been made in some parts of India. But I fear we have as yet barely stirred the outer surface of the vast inert mass of popular ignorance and superstition." *

Absence of effective scheme for educating the lower classes.

These extracts may be fitly closed with a hopeful passage from an Address delivered by Sir Alexander J. Arbuthnot, K.C.S.I., formerly a Member of the Supreme Council of India, as Vice-Chancellor at the Convocation of the Calcutta University, on 13th March, 1880:—

Sir Alexander Arbuthnot's views as to prospects of English education.

"Gentlemen, this is the last occasion on which I shall ever address a public assembly in India. For the last five and twenty years a great part of my official life has been employed in dealing with questions bearing upon the education of the people of this land, and I am glad that my last prominent official act should be connected with that important object. It may be said in one sense as regards education in India, that it is still the day of small things; but it cannot be denied that if we look back to the time when the Indian Universities were first established, little more than three and twenty years ago,—still more so, if we look back to a period ten or twenty years earlier—the advance which has been since accomplished, has been very great and very real. The measures which have conferred so great a benefit upon you, the graduates and undergraduates of this University, were not carried out without much discussion and much conflict of opinion. The question was fought over in its every phase. There was first the famous controversy between those whom, for brevity, I may call the Orientalists and the

* *Modern India and the Indians.* By Professor Monier Williams; 3rd ed., pp. 302–305.

Europeans; between those who advocated the exclusive application of the educational funds to instruction in Oriental learning and in ancient but obsolete and fantastic science, and those who contended for the diffusion of European literature and of modern science, principally through the medium of the English language. There was then the battle between those who urged that the instruction should be entirely secular and those who contended that instruction without religion was of no value at all—a battle which was perhaps more keenly fought in my old Presidency of Madras than in any other part of India. These particular controversies have long been appeased. The teachers and pupils in the purely secular Government Colleges and Schools, and the teachers and pupils in the Missionary institutions, now meet together upon common ground, and compete in a generous rivalry for the degrees and honours of the Indian Universities. The great question of primary education, the importance of which is admitted in all quarters, is making a sure and certain advance. But as regards that higher education, for the encouragement of which our universities exist, we must not imagine that the contest has altogether died out. The opposition has now assumed a different phase, and it is now often alleged that the high education which is imparted in our Colleges and Schools fosters political discontent, and that the seditious writing which defaced the pages of some of the Vernacular Newspapers a few years ago, was the outcome of our Collegiate and University system. Gentlemen, I need hardly tell you that I should not be filling the position which I have the honour to hold in this University, if I shared this opinion. My conviction is, that the more thorough and the more complete the education is which we impart to the people of India, the better fitted they will be to appreciate the blessings of British rule, and the more they will deprecate any material change in the existing order of things. The British Government in India need not fear the light. It need not dread fair and legitimate criticism. But the charge to which I have alluded, emanating as it sometimes does from men in high and responsible positions, is not a charge which ought to be entirely ignored. Unjust and unfounded as it may be,—and as I for one believe it to be,—it is a charge which ought to be borne in mind by those who have a real interest in Native progress, by those who feel, as I and my colleagues in this Senate feel, that the happiness and prosperity, and I will add the good Government, of this country, the purity and efficiency of the administration, both judicial and executive, are closely connected with the character of the education imparted in our colleges and schools; and the knowledge that such charges are made, ought to lead all who have an influence in determining the character of the instruction which is tested by this University, to make it as sound and as deep and as practical as they can, and to do what in them lies to check any superficial semblance of learning which may bring our educational system into disrepute."

CHAPTER XXXIV.

RECAPITULATION AND PROSPECTS OF ENGLISH EDUCATION IN INDIA.

Various stages of the policy of English education recapitulated.

In Chapter IX of this work a summary has been given of the various stages of the policy of education in India from the earliest beginning of the British rule to the year 1830. The whole of that time has been divided into six distinct periods, or stages, according to the nature of the policy and measures adopted by the Government for the education of the Natives of India. In the next, Chapter X, it has been shown how the five years between 1830 and 1835 form the most important period in the history of English education in India, how the views of Lord Macaulay in favour of English education, contained in his celebrated minute, dated the 2nd February 1835, and adopted by Lord William Bentinck in the Government Resolution dated the 7th March 1835, terminated the cantroversy between the Orientalists and the supporters of English education in favour of the latter, marking a distinct epoch in the annals of the British administration in India. It has also been shown that, whatever the views of individual statesmen may have been, the policy of religious neutrality in matters of education was declared by Lord William Bentinck even at the outset of English education in India, how it was repeatedly approved by the Court of Directors and strongly re-affirmed in their Despatch of 13th April 1858, and has never since been departed from, notwithstanding the opposition of Missionaries. The policy of English education which was inaugurated in 1835, may, in connection with the *six* stages of educational policy described in Chapter IX of this work, be regarded as the *seventh* stage, and it continued with more or less success till the year 1854. The *eighth* stage of the policy of education begins with the comprehensive Despatch of the Court of Directors, dated 19th July, 1854, of which an account has been given in Chapter XVII of this work, and under which two important events took place—*first*, the formation of the Educational Department, and, *secondly*, the establishment of the Indian Universities in 1857 to 1882, of which an account has been given in Chapter XVIII of this work. In the same sequence and chronological order the *ninth* stage of the policy of education may be said to have been inaugurated by the Indian Education Commission of 1882, of which an account has been given in Chapters XIX to XXII of this work. Shortly stated, in the words of Sir W. W. Hunter, who was President of the Commission, "the Commission's Recommendations strongly affirmed the principle of self-help in the extension of High Schools and Colleges, and laid particular stress on the duty of assisting primary education from Provincial and Municipal funds. They endeavoured to provide for certain sections of the people, particularly the Muhammadans, who for various causes had found themselves unable to avail themselves fully of the State System of public instruction, or in regard to whom that system had proved defective. The general effect of the Commission's labours, and of the Government Resolution based thereon is to give a more liberal recognition to private effort of every kind, and to schools and colleges conducted on the system of grants-in-aid."*

Present policy of English education, based upon the approved recommendations of the Education Commission of 1882.

The policy thus inaugurated has undergone no change, and ample account and statistics of the progress of English education under it, have been given in the main body of this work. And in the last preceding Chapter the views of eminent statesmen in regard to the policy of English education in India, and the social, moral, and political effects which it has produced upon the people of India in general have been extensively quoted to enable the reader to form his own opinion upon the best and most authoritative information available respecting these interesting topics. The present writer's object being to supply a narrative of events and statistical information, he has closely adhered to the narrative and refrained from setting forth opinions of his own on various controversial questions more suited to an essay than to a history. There are some passages, however, in the writings of others on the subject of the past, present, and future of English education in India which deserve attention and may be suitably quoted in this Chapter.

Professor Seeley's views on the mutual influence of England and India.

In his celebrated Lectures on the *Expansion of England* the distinguished Professor J. R. Seeley of the University of Cambridge, devotes a whole Lecture to the subject of the mutual influence of England and India, and, in the following passages, deals with the broader aspects of education:—

Policy of non-interference with Indian life and thought abandoned in 1813.

"England had broken the toils that threatened to imprison her. But how far was she who had so stoutly refused to be influenced by India, entitled to influence India in her turn. We could not fail to see the enormous difference between our civilisation and that of India, we could not fail on the whole, greatly to prefer our own. But had we any right to impose our views upon the Natives? We had our own Christianity, our own views of philosophy, of history and science; but were we not bound by a sort of tacit contract with the Natives to hold all these things officially in abeyance? This was the view which was taken at first. It was not admitted that England was to play the part of Rome to her empire; no; she was to put her civilisation on one side and govern according to Indian ideas. This view was the more winning as the new and mysterious world of Sanscrit learning was revealing itself to those first generations of Anglo-Indians. They were under the charm of a remote philosophy and a fantastic history. They were, as it was said, Brahminised and would not hear of admitting into their enchanted Oriental enclosure either the Christianity or any of the learning of the West. I have not space left in this lecture to do more than indicate how we were gradually led to give up this view and to stand out boldly as teachers and civilisers. The change began in 1813, when on the renewal of the Company's charter, a sum was directed to be appropriated to the revival of learning and the introduction of useful arts and sciences. Over this enactment an Education Committee wrangled for twenty years. Were we to use our own judgments, or were we to understand learning and science in the Oriental sense? Were we to teach Sanskrit and Arabic, or English?

Policy of giving English education settled in 1835, and improved in 1854.

"Never on this earth was a more momentous question discussed. Under Lord William Bentinck in 1835, the discussion came to a head, and by a remarkable coincidence a famous man was on the spot to give lustre to, and take lustre from, a memorable controversy. It was Macaulay's Minute that decided the question in favor of English. In that Minute or in Sir C. Trevelyan's volume on '*Education in India*,' you can study it. Only remark a strange oversight that was made. The question was discussed as if the choice lay between teaching Sanskrit and Arabic on the one hand, or English on the other. All these languages alike are to the mass of the population utterly strange. Arabic and English are foreign, and Sanskrit is to the Hindus what Latin is to the Natives of Europe. It is the original language out of which the principal spoken languages have been formed, but it is dead. It has been dead a far longer time than Latin, for it had ceased to be a spoken language in the third

* *The Indian Empire.* By Sir W. W. Hunter, 2nd Ed., p. 429.

century before Christ. By far the greater part of the famous Sanskrit poems and writings, philosophical or theological, were written artificially and by a learned effort, like the Latin poems of Vida and Sannazaro. Now over Sanskrit Macaulay had an easy victory, for he had only to show that English had poetry at least as good—and philosophy, history and science a great deal better. But why should there be no choice but between dead languages? Could Macaulay really fancy it possible to teach two hundred and fifty millions of Asiatics English? Probably not, probably he thought only of creating a small learned class. I imagine too, that his own classical training had implanted in his mind a fixed assumption that a dead language is necessary to education. But if India is really to be enlightened, evidently it must be through the medium neither of Sanscrit nor of English, but of the vernaculars, that is Hindustani, Hindi, Bengali, &c. These under some vague impression that they were too rude to be made the vehicles of science or philosophy, Macaulay almost refuses to consider, but against these his arguments in favour of English would have been powerless. But though this great oversight was made—it has since been remarked and since the education despatch of Sir Charles Wood in 1854, in some measure repaired—the decision to which Macaulay's Minute led remains the great landmark in the history of our Empire considered as an institute of civilisation. It marks the moment when we deliberately recognised that a function had devolved on us in Asia similar to that which Rome fulfilled in Europe, the greatest function which any Government can ever be called upon to discharge." *

Another author, Mr. F. W. Thomas, in an Essay on the "*History and Prospects of British Education in India*" (which won the LeBas Prize in 1890), has also expressed certain opinions which may be incorporated here in his own words as follows:—

Mr. F. W. Thomas' Essay on British Education in India, 1890

"The sum of what we have to say is this. It is unlikely that English will ever become the general language either of literature or of every-day life in India. For primary education it is unnecessary at present, and for high education necessary. The amount of English desirable in middle schools is a local question. But it is necessary that, at any rate, some fair relation be established between the amount of funds devoted to the three branches. This proportion is liable to change: possibly in a few years there will be a considerable extension of the middle classes in India. The proportion, therefore, of funds devoted to the various kinds of education ought to be fixed for short periods, and to be open to revision. Probably a literary education has up to the present been too much fostered at the expense of a practical one. This is a matter for further consideration. The essential thing is that the Department, as long as it manages the schools, should not ignorantly interfere, or divert the education of the Hindus into unnatural and specified channels. It should keep in touch with the development actually proceeding, and only interpose with authoritative directions where social, political and educational science give a clear verdict as to what is right and what is wrong. Perhaps the system of grants-in-aid will supply the best solution of this as of other questions.

Summary of Mr. Thomas' views.

"What has been said so far, concerning religion and the English language, from the nature of the case refers chiefly to the higher education and to the upper classes of the educated population. Primary education is nearly the same the world over, and it is in connection with the secondary training and the classes who receive it that difficulties oftenest arise. It is among these classes that are found those who are destined to guide the future of the people, and hence it is on this ground that questions of principle are oftenest discussed. Nevertheless, primary education is of infinitely greater moment, and in India its importance is even higher than elsewhere. India is remarkable for the numerical insignificance of the middle and upper classes. The dumb masses, proportionally more numerous, are more ignorant than in other civilised countries. Caring only for their caste and local interests, they seldom raise their voice in questions feverishly debated in the ranks above, and even under the greatest extremities of oppression they commonly make no stir. Thus they are not seldom forgotten amid the clamours of the small but noisy classes with whom the English chiefly come in contact, who are but, as it were, the foam on the surface of the ocean. Millions of Hindus live and die without seeing an English face. To them the sole representatives of intellect and culture are the Brahmans, and to this day these wield, in the interior, an unlimited and terrible authority. On the day on which I write, in countless villages in India, the Hindu women have sought as an honour the permission to drink the water in which a Brahman has washed his feet. It is then a fatal error to lose sight either of the influence of Brahmanism, which is said to make more converts every year than do all the other religions in India, and which is in the main hostile to and contemptuous of foreign knowledge, or of the ignorant millions who are its willing slaves. The shock of English influence has fallen as yet chiefly on the middle classes, who are becoming against their will more and more affected by it. It is they who fill the Government Schools and Colleges. For them the native newspapers are written. The masses still lead the same, simple, monotonous, and idyllic life which the Greek invaders beheld with such amazement.

Importance of primary education in India.

* *The Expansion of England.* By J. R. Seeley, M.A., pp. 251–253.

English education has done very little for the masses of the people.

"What has English education done for this portion of the people? It is to be feared, very little. Accepting the ordinary calculation, the $2\frac{1}{2}$ millions of boys in primary schools will correspond to a population of $33\frac{1}{3}$ millions out of a total of 250 millions. Do we need to be told that, when only $3\frac{1}{2}$ out of $37\frac{1}{2}$ millions of children are receiving any instruction at all, these belong to only a very small extent, to the lower classes? Until 1882 what are known as the 'low castes' were practically excluded from Government Schools; and the Commission, in recommending that the regulation dealing with the question which was proposed in the despatch of 1854, should be re-affirmed as a principle, was obliged to advise caution in its application, and even to suggest the provision of special schools. The 'low castes' it is true, number only about 18 millions; but it is evident that the main body of the mixed castes is receiving no benefit from the State. It is obvious that with the present funds to be devoted to education there is little hope of, at any rate, soon making any considerable advance. Of any immediate increase in the funds there seems no prospect, English and Hindu agreeing that further taxation is not at present possible. The day when compulsory education may be feasible is evidently very far distant. The only way in which at present any great extension is possible is by aided and unaided schools taking the place of those maintained by the department. But we are told that primary schools have no tendency to increase spontaneously in this manner. It is only by increasing the general taxable wealth of the country—a topic to which we shall have to recur—that general education can ever be effected.

Elementary education should be safe-guarded.

"For the present it is of the greatest importance that elementary education should not suffer by neglect. It needs special attention, if only from the fact that it has many enemies. To pass by the tendency of local bodies to encourage superior in preference to inferior schools, we find the principle still openly proclaimed and defended, that it is the business of the English to create a highly educated class, who will then transmit their culture to lower strata in society. Primary education is or was already provided for by the Natives themselves. It is useless for Government to waste its funds on doing expensively what the Natives themselves can do as well and much more cheaply."†

* * * * * * * * * * * * * * * * * * * *

The filtering-down theory of education is fallacious.

"In the 'filtering-down' theory no trust can be put. The larger features of the character of nations do not change. The intensely sacerdotal spirit of the chief Indian caste, the one which benefits most largely by English education, is not dead. The rules of caste are as rigid as ever. The exclusiveness, which has reigned for three thousand years, is as rampant as before. Of any thing like public feeling and mutual confidence and help there is no hope for many a year. It is not conceivable that knowledge should under these circumstances filter down. There is no evidence that it has filtered down. As we said above, elementary education has no tendency to advance spontaneously, and it has to be carefully protected even from the bodies who administer it. In the work above alluded to, Sir Roper Lethbridge supplies the best refutation of his own views. The necessity of first creating an educated class, he says, is recognized by the Native public opinion. Every statesman who has been suspected of intending to divert any sums from high to elementary teaching has evoked a storm of unpopularity. The case of Sir George Campbell is quoted, whose services to primary education in Bengal we have commemorated. Are these facts in favour of the 'filtering-down' theory, rejected in 1854 and rejected in 1882? The newspapers, it is well known, are in the hands of the class which fills the High Schools and Colleges. Does their vituperation of Sir George Campbell testify to a strong desire to benefit the poorer classes, or to benefit any one but themselves?

A highly educated literary class not needed for social requirements of India, and produces discontented sedition.

"Lastly the necessity of having a 'highly educated' class is altogether denied, if we are to take the phrase, in the accepted sense. There is an education which sharpens the critical, but destroys the inventive faculty, an education which produces politicians, newspaper writers, and men of general capacity and culture. While largely literary it is not wholly so, but often embraces the general principles of many sciences. It is the chief means of producing a refined and cultured society. In a backward society such an education is an anomaly, is unnatural, and out of place. This is the case in India. The education given in the Schools and Colleges there is of the kind we have indicated. We suspect, and this adds force to our argument, that it is often second-rate in its kind. Of the population of India, nearly seven-tenths directly, and nine-tenths altogether, are supported by agriculture. A great manufacturing and trading class is not yet created. Commissions in the Army are not open to the natives. Beside a few writers, the Bench, the Bar, and the Government service may be said to represent the whole of the small middle class. The highest class in point of wealth, the Native princes and landlords, is largely illiterate. The Brahmans possess

† *The History and Prospects of British Education in India* being the *LeBas Prize Essay for* 1890. By F. W. Thomas, Scholar of Trinity College, Cambridge (1891); pp. 134, 137.

all degrees of wealth: the most important of them are the representatives of the orthodox party which is opposed to English culture. Under these circumstances what room is there for a cultured and leisured society such as the current education is calculated to produce? There is none. Such a society is an expensive luxury which only highly developed nations can afford to maintain. How, then, can a poor country like India support such a society in addition to the existing aristocracies of wealth and religion? The eighty thousand students in High Schools and Colleges are more than are at present needed. The professions suitable for educated men are notoriously glutted, and a large and discontented surplus is left, whose disappointment vents itself in perpetually carping at the Government, vilifying the officials, blackmailing, and spreading sedition. Beaten out of the professions by the competition of better men, and often suspected by the orthodox or even excommunicated from caste, these men have no trades or other occupations to which they can turn, even were it not too late. They are lucky if they have not entirely unfitted themselves for, and can obtain, some wretchedly paid clerkship under merchants and tradesmen.

Technical and professional education needed for material prosperity of India and good feeling among its population.

"Meanwhile technical education is still 'under consideration.' The medical profession is not popular, and civil engineering is shunned by the educated Hindu, who scorns anything practical or involving bodily labour. The wealth of the country in coal, in iron and other metals, lies almost entirely neglected. The people are still clothed in cottons from Manchester. The plough which the *rayat* uses is the same that he used three thousand years ago. The country has been denuded of forests; and that which should be used to enrich the land is burned for fuel. Sanitation and emigration are equally unpopular. The works of art, which at European exhibitions have been applauded as marvels of taste and delicate skill, are produced with the rudest instruments and the greatest expenditure of labour and time. The patterns of which they are copies are of venerable antiquity. Originality in design and execution has been dead for many centuries, and the rule of the English can only testify to 'a general decay of the native arts.' Every commercial or manufacturing enterprise which has sprung up during the last century, including even the cultivation of tea, has been introduced and managed by Englishmen. Under these circumstances, need it be said that what is most desiderated, is new knowledge, applied to every kind of production? Need we instance the great advance recently made in English skilled work, owing to the extension of practically applied science, and of a knowledge of the principles of art? The spread of technical education and practical science is a matter scarcely second in importance to the spread of primary education itself. It is from this source chiefly that we must look for the vast increase in material wealth for which the country supplies such great natural advantages. Such an increase is not only desirable: it is imperative. Of the previous checks on population in India, wars and famines, the former have ceased to operate, and the latter have been provided against by the most careful precautions. The mass of the people is growing at a rate which will double it in the course of a century, and already farms which previously maintained only one family have to provide for two or three. The increase in the extent of land under cultivation which has been going on for the last century cannot proceed indefinitely. The only method left of providing for the growing population is to improve the existing methods of production to introduce new methods by which the land may be induced to yield more, and to create a surplus wealth which will enable India to purchase from other countries. To this end a great extension of practical scientific, and of technical education is not only one means, it is far the greatest means. By model farms and manufactories, by suggesting the introduction of new staples of production, the Public Works Department can do something. But it is only by creating an interest in the practical applications of science, by making it understood that a high education is not merely a literary and *quasi*-scientific or mathematical training, but embraces every kind of knowledge which is considerable in extent, well-ordered, and clearly grasped. We are led, then, to this conclusion. It is not high education that India needs; it is practical scientific education. It is not by a highly educated society that modern knowledge is to be introduced. The attempt would result—as it has already resulted—in fostering an unpopular party, which, though it has its merits and numbers not a few able and upright men, has up to the present been characterized by want of originality, and to some extent by a proclivity to imitate the English, and abuse them. Let knowledge be introduced in such a way as to give a practical test of its value by improving arts and manufactures, and increasing men's actual power over nature for the production of wealth. We are far from neglecting the desirability of general culture. But this has a spontaneous tendency to grow up where it is needed. On no ground does it appear to be the great desideratum for India at this moment. It is to the spread of practical knowledge, the influence of which can be impaired by no sophistries, religious or otherwise, that we have chiefly to look not only for the advance in material prosperity which is so greatly needed, but also for the breaking down of prejudice and the encouragement of fellow-feeling between men. Under these circumstances too much stress cannot be laid on the desirability of technical education now so long promised, and of a great extension in High Schools and Colleges of the study of the physical sciences. It is not to be expected that the Government can often create new industries by itself, but by turning a stream of science on the existing arts, and by causing it to be understood that a knowledge of material nature is as worthy an object as is a wide acquaintance with metaphysics or the capacity to write flowery English, it may not only produce immediate results, but lay the foundations for future prosperity."* * * * * * *

Upper classes of India backward in education.

"The upper classes on whom much depends, still require considerable attention. It is extremely desirable that the natural leaders of the people, whether they be spiritual authorities as the Brahmans, or dependent on wealth and position for their importance, should not remain apart from the general drift of education. As a body the orthodox Brahmans are well affected towards the English, whose treatment of them contrasts vividly with the oppression which they suffered under their previous rulers; and now that the Punjab University has been created especially for oriental studies, and that Sanskrit is once more held in honour in the land of the Veda, it seems that they have, as a body, little to complain of. Their undoubted intellectual superiority, and the unlimited authority which they wield over two hundred millions of Hindus, make their loyalty a matter of peculiar moment. The nobles and rich classes are of considerable, if less, importance. But, as special schools have been provided for them, where every precaution is taken against the intrusion of their inferiors, this class, in the absence of any opposing cause, cannot long remain apart. It is obvious how much the conferring of honorary distinctions, employment in important posts under Government, and other political measures, can contribute to produce this extremely desirable result. In no stage of society is it anything but dangerous that those who possess leisure, high spirit, and heriditary capacity for ruling, should remain discontented, disaffected, and unemployed."† * * * * * * * * * * * * *

The future prospects of English education.

"The future of British education in India, conditioned as it must be by various influences, may be variously construed. It is obvious how greatly the whole future of the empire would be effected, should some part of it be found colonizable by the English race, or on the other hand should the British power sustain a serious reverse. Nor must we overlook the possibility of a reaction against European knowledge, or of a religious revival. So far as can be judged, however, none of these events are at all probable. Education must for many a year be directed by an English Government, and on the same lines as at present. Of the higher instruction the English language must long remain the chief medium, as well as one of the most important subjects. But we must repeat once more how desirable it is that physical science, the truths of which can be everywhere tested, should receive a larger share of attention than hitherto. In a country where twenty thousand men and women die yearly from the bite of the cobra alone, medicine, at any rate, would seem to be worth studying. Again, the attention of educated Hindus might well be turned to a greater extent on India itself. In what region do animals and plants afford a more interesting study? Where is there more scope for geology and meteorology? In what part of the world is the action of water of greater theoretical and practical moment? Nowhere do ethnological and linguistic problems attain to a higher degree of complexity and importance. Nowhere does a larger mass of material lie ready to the hand of the student of archæology, custom, law and usage, or, finally of the science of religion. In short, both the land and the people offer a vast field for research of every kind, which should be least of all neglected by those who have the right to lay claim to both as in a special sense their own.

No great improvements can be expected till the richer classes are attracted to English education.

"But we cannot expect to hear of any great improvements or scientific discoveries until research is more largely endowed, and until the rich have been attracted to the new learning. At present scarcely any one studies except with a view to a profession, and almost the only real students are the representatives of a dead society and religion. If the educated Brahmans could, without losing their present position, be attracted to the movement, their superior gifts might give a great impulse to the civilization of India. Now are they entirely obdurate. Even from their short intercourse with the Greeks, they learnt something which they have gratefully recorded. Many of the best students are Brahmans, and now that an English education confers such great advantages, there is hope that interest ‡ will induce the learned class to anticipate the decay of their authority.

Importance of English education to the emancipation of the lower classes.

"For the lower classes English education has something of the character of an emancipation. The uneducated Hindu is enslaved in three ways. He is the slave of custom and caste, of Brahmanism, and of superstition. A great number of the *rayats* are, in addition, enslaved to the money-lenders. From all of these it is desirable that they should be set free. Here lies the great importance of the extension of primary education. Among the

* *The History and Prospects of British Education in India* being the *LeBas Prize Essay for* 1890. By F. W. Thomas, Scholar of Trinity College, Cambridge (1891); pp. 138–42.

† *Ib.*, pp. 143, 144.

‡ I am informed that a Pandit who knows English can easily earn Rs. 100 a month, while if ignorant of English, he cannot often expect more than Rs. 10.

subjects now taught in elementary schools at least two are calculated to free the children from errors engrained in their parents, I mean history and geography. To learn that the world was not made for the Brahmanical Indians, that the earth does not consist of concentric rings with India at the centre, nor does it rest on the back of a tortoise, cannot but have the secondary result of shaking belief in many other childish fables. Where a little elementary science is taught, if it do nothing else, it may make it plain that, whatever be the power of the Brahman, he cannot make water boil at any other temperature than that at which it naturally boils, and that even a million repetitions of Rama's name will not create a good crop without manure, or keep fever away from unsanitary homes. Arithmetic, if properly taught, may reveal at what a fearful disadvantage money is borrowed when interest is at twelve per cent., and thus encourage prudence by adding to it the power of calculation. But it is not from mere teaching that the desired results can be expected to flow. To attend a school, conducted by non-Brahmanical authorities, in which the high caste boy is treated exactly as the low caste boy, and where facts are taught independently of religious interpretation, must tend to rub the edges off many ancient prejudices. It is here that the great importance of the provision of Normal Schools and trained teachers comes in : it is obvious how much good can be done by a single able and well-disposed teacher, and how much harm by one ill-disposed. What is to be expected from Primary Schools is not that the children should pick up very much information — a few plain facts will suffice — but that they should learn that there are things which are everywhere and at all times immovably true, and should experience the futility of many prejudices which their parents are not likely to be able to shake off; that it should be as widely as possible known that in the eyes of the Government, at any rate, there is no difference between Brahman, Sudra, and outcast, but individuals of every class must rank by individual merits alone.

Brief retrospect of the history of English education.

" We will now add a brief retrospect. The English found in India a widespread system of elementary and higher education, of which the former was mainly practical, the latter mainly literary, philosophical, and religious. The first period of British effort, which ended in 1823, was occupied with petty and isolated endeavours, in most cases of a charitable nature and conducted by Missionaries. During the next period, extending to the year 1854, the Government began steadily to devote attention to the cause of higher education. This period is more interesting than either that which preceded or that which followed, because during it the most important questions of principle, the position of the English language and of elementary education, were discussed and settled. In 1854, the despatch of Sir Charles Wood set forth at length the lines on which operations have since been conducted. Hence the period from 1854, may be described as one of administration. The chief innovation was the introduction of local rates devoted in part to the support of chiefly primary instruction. From 1870 to 1881, the mistaken policy became general of encouraging departmental as opposed to aided, and higher as opposed to elementary, education. Since the important Commission of 1882-83 this policy has been discontinued. In point of numbers, aided schools now hold the first place: the department comes next; then unaided but inspected; lastly, entirely private enterprise. The indigenous schools have been either absorbed or replaced, and few any longer remain. The Missionaries have acquired considerable control over secondary education, but have not neglected primary. About 200,000 children are at present under their instruction. In the future, elementary schools should still be the chief care, but a proper proportion of institutions of a higher class ought to be maintained. In the latter the training should be less literary, and to a greater extent scientific, than it has hitherto been. Provision is being made for the education of the Native Nobles. Endowment for research is a great desideratum. The education of women still presents practical difficulties, and needs unremitting attention. Religious and moral instruction should not be generally attempted, but the Bible might, should the Natives desire it, be with caution locally introduced. On the subject of the use of the English language no dogmatic position can be adopted : the question must be permitted to settle itself in the natural way by general convenience, which alone possesses the *arbitrium ac norma loquendi.* The system of local control is one of great promise, but will for some time need careful watching. Compulsory attendance at school is a still distant goal. For the present the best policy is to foster private effort, which spreads the expenditure over a wide area, and provides a solution for some difficult questions. As regards the sums to be expended, there is little prospect of considerable immediate increase. This will have to await the advance of general prosperity, which depends on many causes, but can be greatly fostered by the encouragement of practical and scientific training. On the whole, what has been done bears numerically but a small proportion to what remains to be effected.

Conclusion.

" Dull as it may have seemed in the telling, the history of British Education in India is not uninteresting. The reaction of the West on the East, and the revival of peoples everywhere visible, in Japan, in China, in India, is a phenomenon as remarkable as any in history. In India, a country where a social order in theory not unlike the ideal Republic of Plato, has been based for two thousand years on a deep philosophy in some respects similar to his, the study of this revival cannot be without attraction for educated men. A primitive society has suddenly awoke to find itself face to face with an enemy it is powerless to resist. The system of caste, excellent in many respects * and of unrivalled tenacity, is neither habile nor productive enough for the requirements of the modern world-wide competition, from which it would be idle to expect that India can stand aside. Caste, it is truly held, must either pass away or suffer modification, and herewith the foundations of Hindu society must be reconstructed. The modern world, where it does not absorb, cannot but corrupt and destroy. Of its emissaries, the teacher and the missionary, the repeating rifle and the rum bottle, one or other is sure to find an entrance. It was fortunate for India that the missionary and the teacher arrived first, though the rum-bottle has of late years made alarming progress. In the East British Education is an agent at once destructive and constructive. Its negative influence, which has been sometimes only too apparent, is active even where least perceived: its positive influence has latterly given many signs of its working. There, for the present, the matter rests. But, whatever may be the future of the English connection with India, it is at any rate certain that, apart from improbabilities, 'by planting our language, our knowledge, and our opinions, in our Asiatic territories we have put a great work beyond the reach of contingencies.' The ideas which have been introduced cannot be ineffective or forgotten among a people so interested in intellectual questions as are the Hindus. They cannot but germinate, and finally change the whole face of Native society. To many the destruction of the old idyllic life, with its sacred and immemorial customs, even perhaps with its enormities, may give cause for regret. The present is, if strong, yet also prosaic. The future must share many of its characteristics. But we may perhaps here apply the words of a great English poet :—

> Haply, the river of Time—
> As it grows, as the towns on its marge
> Fling their wavering lights
> On a wider, statelier stream—
> May acquire, if not the calm
> Of its early mountainous shore,
> Yet a solemn peace of its own." †

* On this subject, Prof. Monier Williams has some remarks in his *Brahmanism and Hinduism ; Vide* Chap. XVIII, and esp. p. 461.

† *The History and Progress of British Education in India* being the *Le Bas Prize Essay* for 1890. By F. W. Thomas, Scholar of Trinity College, Cambridge (1891); pp. 145–150.